Lecture Notes in Computer Science 13928

Founding Editors

The series Lecture Notes in Computer Science (LNCS), including its subseries Lecture Notes in Artificial Intelligence (LNAI) and Lecture Notes in Bioinformatics (LNBI), has established itself as a medium for the publication of new developments in computer science and information technology research, teaching, and education.

LNCS enjoys close cooperation with the computer science R & D community, the series counts many renowned academics among its volume editors and paper authors, and collaborates with prestigious societies. Its mission is to serve this international community by providing an invaluable service, mainly focused on the publication of conference and workshop proceedings and postproceedings. LNCS commenced publication in 1973.

Thais Batista · Tomáš Bureš · Claudia Raibulet ·
Henry Muccini
Editors

Software Architecture

ECSA 2022 Tracks
and Workshops

Prague, Czech Republic, September 19–23, 2022
Revised Selected Papers

 Springer

Editors
Thais Batista ⓘ
Federal University of Rio Grande do Norte
Natal, Brazil

Tomáš Bureš ⓘ
Charles University
Prague, Czech Republic

Claudia Raibulet ⓘ
Vrije Universiteit Amsterdam
Amsterdam, The Netherlands

Henry Muccini ⓘ
University of L'Aquila
L'Aquila, Italy

ISSN 0302-9743   ISSN 1611-3349 (electronic)
Lecture Notes in Computer Science
ISBN 978-3-031-36888-2   ISBN 978-3-031-36889-9 (eBook)
https://doi.org/10.1007/978-3-031-36889-9

Preface

The European Conference on Software Architecture (ECSA) is the premier European conference aimed at bringing together leading researchers and practitioners to present and discuss the most recent, innovative, and significant findings and experiences in the field of software architecture research and practice. ECSA 2022 was held in Prague, Czech Republic, in a hybrid mode, during September 19–23, 2022, with attendees from all over the world. Accepted contributions for the main research track are included in the conference proceedings, published in this Springer Lecture Notes in Computer Science volume.

In addition to the main research track, ECSA 2022 included an industry track, a Diversity, Equity and Inclusion track (DE&I), a doctoral symposium, a tools and demonstrations track, and a tutorials track. ECSA 2022 also offered nine workshops on diverse topics related to the software architecture discipline:

- The 6th International Workshop on Formal Approaches for Advanced Computing Systems (FAACS)
- The 9th Workshop on Software Architecture Erosion and Architectural Consistency (SAEroCon)
- The 2nd International Workshop on Mining Software Repositories for Software Architecture (MSR4SA)
- The 3rd Workshop on Systems, Architectures, and Solutions for Industry 4.0 (SASI4)
- The 5th Context-aware, Autonomous and Smart Architecture International Workshop (CASA)
- The 8th International Workshop on Automotive System/Software Architectures (WASA)
- The 2nd International Workshop on Software Architecture and Machine Learning (SAML)
- The 1st International Workshop on Digital Twin Architecture (TwinArch)
- The 2nd International Workshop on Designing and Measuring Security in Software Architectures (DeMeSSA)

This volume contains a selection of revised and extended contributions from all these satellite events of ECSA 2022. We received 61 submissions for the tracks and doctoral symposium. From this list, after selection by the Program Committee, 32 papers are included in the post-proceedings. Each submission was reviewed by at least three referees. We used the EasyChair conference system to manage the submission and review process.

We thank the Program Committee members of all the tracks and the additional reviewers that reviewed the revised and extended versions of papers.

We acknowledge the prompt and professional support from Springer, who published these proceedings as part of the Lecture Notes in Computer Science series. Finally, we would like to thank the authors of all these submissions for their contributions.

June 2022

Thais Batista
Tomas Bures
Claudia Raibulet
Henry Muccini

Organization

General Co-chairs

Thais Batista   Federal University of Rio Grande do Norte, Brazil
Tomas Bures   Charles University, Czech Republic

Workshop and Tutorial Co-chairs

Claudia Raibulet   Vrije Universiteit Amsterdam, The Netherlands
Henry Muccini   University of L'Aquila, Italy

Program Committee

Aldeida Aleti	Monash University, Australia
Paolo Arcaini	National Institute of Informatics, Japan
Thais Batista	Federal University of Rio Grande do Norte, Brazil
Christian Berger	University of Gothenburg, Sweden
Justus Bogner	University of Stuttgart, Germany
Silvia Bonfanti	University of Bergamo, Italy
Barbora Buhnova	Masaryk University, Czech Republic
Tomas Bures	Charles University in Prague, Czech Republic
Matteo Camilli	Politecnico di Milano, Italy
Rafael Capilla	Universidad Rey Juan Carlos, Spain
Federico Ciccozzi	Mälardalen University, Sweden
Javier Camara	University of Malaga, Spain
Yanja Dajsuren	Eindhoven University of Technology, The Netherlands
Remco de Boer	ArchiXL, The Netherlands
Martina De Sanctis	Gran Sasso Science Institute, Italy
Jamal El Hachem	Université de Bretagne Sud (UBS), France
Christoph Elsner	Siemens AG, Germany
Neil Ernst	University of Victoria, Canada
Robert Heinrich	Karlsruhe Institute of Technology, Germany
Sebastian Herold	Karlstad University, Sweden
Helena Holmstrom Olsson	University of Malmo, Sweden
Jasmin Jahic	University of Cambridge, UK

Michael Keeling	Kiavi, USA
Kisub Kim	Singapore Management University, Singapore
Tsutomu Kobayashi	Japan Aerospace Exploration Agency, Japan
Stefan Kugele	Technische Hochschule Ingolstadt, Germany
Thomas Kuhn	Fraunhofer IESE, Germany
Axel Legay	UCLouvain, Belgium
Henry Muccini	University of L'Aquila, Italy
Pablo Oliveira Antonino	Fraunhofer IESE, Germany
Flavio Oquendo	Université de Bretagne Sud (UBS), France
Diego Perez-Palacin	Linnaeus University, Sweden
Pasqualina Potena	Research Institutes of Sweden, Sweden
Claudia Raibulet	University of Milano-Bicocca, Italy
Elvinia Riccobene	University of Milan, Italy
Genaina Rodrigues	University of Brasilia, Brazil
Patrizia Scandurra	University of Bergamo, Italy
Marjan Sirjani	Mälardalen University, Sweden
Mohamed Soliman	University of Groningen, The Netherlands
Miroslaw Staron	University of Gothenburg, Sweden
Catia Trubiani	Gran Sasso Science Institute, Italy
Katja Tuma	Vrije Universiteit Amsterdam, The Netherlands
Karthik Vaidhyanathan	University of L'Aquila, Italy
André van Hoorn	University of Hamburg, Germany
Roberto Verdecchia	Vrije Universiteit Amsterdam, The Netherlands
Mirko Viroli	University of Bologna, Italy
Martijn Werf	Utrecht University, The Netherlands
Marion Wiese	Universität Hamburg, Germany
Jørn Ølmheim	Statoil ASA, Norway

Contents

Industry Track

Blockchain-Based Architecture of Immutable Document Repository

Szymon Kijas(⊠) 🆔 and Andrzej Zalewski 🆔

Warsaw University of Technology, Warsaw, Poland
{szymon.kijas,andrzej.zalewski}@pw.edu.pl

Abstract. The paper presents architecture of blockchain-based immutable document repository, called Durable Media. The system was designed to ensure long-term document storage while enabling access to the documents by various users and verification of document's authenticity. The system is used by banks, e-commerce companies and thousands of their clients in Poland.

Keywords: blockchain · durable media · distributed architecture

1 Introduction

Blockchain [3] is perceived as a foundation of many future developments in distributed software systems engineering. Here, we present how it has been employed as a foundation of an architecture for immutable document repository. The concept of such repository (called Durable Media) was introduced about two decades ago by the EU directives: MIFiD [1] and PSD2 [2]. Its purpose is to enable access to the stored documents, while guaranteeing that their contents has remained unchanged since upload. It also supports verification if a given document is identical with the corresponding document stored on Durable Media system.

2 Showcase of Durable Media System

2.1 Business Context and the Purpose of the System

The Durable Media was developed for the storage of documents such as loan or bank account agreement, installments schedules etc. Once saved by a bank they can be retrieved by customers and their consistency with the original can also be confirmed. The key requirements for the system are:

1) Publishing documents by banks and other institutions from financial sector or eCommerce (referred to as *participants* of the Durable Media system). Publication of a document in Durable Media system should replace traditional means of document delivery (emails, post).

© The Author(s), under exclusive license to Springer Nature Switzerland AG 2023
T. Batista et al. (Eds.): ECSA 2022, LNCS 13928, pp. 3–10, 2023.
https://doi.org/10.1007/978-3-031-36889-9_1

2) Publishing private documents (available after user authentication). Documents, such as loan agreements, must not be publicly accessible, therefore the system must allow for various methods of user authentication.
3) Avoiding disputes about the original content of a document by ensuring documents' immutability.
4) Enabling end-users (e.g., banks' clients) to access documents and verify at any time whether their documents are consistent with those stored in the repository (authenticity).
5) It is particularly important that the data is physically secured, but it is equally important to build up confidence of the end-users.
6) Banks require that documents are physically stored on a secure WORM (Write Once Read Many) matrix. This results from the legal regulations in Poland. Other participants may also accept using ECMS (Enterprise Content Management System) for document storage.

2.2 Key Architectural Decisions

The key architectural decisions [6] are presented below:

Architectural problem No. 1: It must not be possible to remove or change the stored documents before the statutory deadline.
Solution: WORM matrix used as a physical storage.
Rationale: The WORM matrix provides temporary and main data storage space. If a document is moved from the temporary to the main space, it can no longer be removed. The document will be erased from the matrix after a predetermined retention period.

The initial version of the Durable Media system was used only to publish public documents. ECMS was used for their storage. Later on, banks have been legally obliged to use the WORM matrix in order to publish private documents in the Durable Media. The only alternative solution approved by the regulator was to store documents entirely on the blockchain network. However, if many millions of documents were physically stored in a blockchain-based system, such a solution would turn out to be inefficient in terms of performance and storage utilization.

Architectural Problem No. 2: This is the key and the most complex issue, in which many business factors cross. It includes the following subproblems:

a) Documents must be physically stored in a system belonging to a trusted organization.
b) It should be ensured that documents cannot be altered without a trace.
c) Sharing the control of the integrity of the document metadata repository among the system's participants (banks, regulator, trusted institution).
d) If a participant connected to the system has its own data repository, its data must be identical with the corresponding data in the repository of a trusted organization.
e) The trusted organization is responsible for managing such a distributed document repository.
f) Document metadata of the participants has to be separated from the access of other participants.

g) Moreover, the number of blockchain nodes in data center of a trusted organization have to be minimized in order to reduce network traffic between blockchain nodes (ensuring better maintainability).

h) Possibility to connect another institution that could control the repository - another trusted organization (e.g., financial regulator).

Solution: Actually, each of the above problems could be analyzed separately, however, the only solution that resolves all of them simultaneously turned out to be **blockchain network based on Hyperledger Fabric protocol** [7].

It is an open-source protocol that enables to create an efficient private blockchain network that allows the business logic of the participants to be separated from others using independent channels (see Fig. 1). The channels provided for each participant (Durable Media customer), are stretched between the client's nodes and the node of the trusted organization.

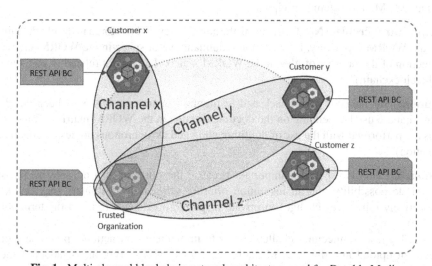

Fig. 1. Multi-channel blockchain network architecture used for Durable Media.

Rationale: The decentralization of the document metadata database enables to share control over data integrity among participants of the system (blockchain network node owners), while ensuring immutability of the stored documents indicates blockchain architecture.

However, as metadata of the documents cannot be dispersed over many unfamiliar places on the Internet, the open blockchain networks such as Ethereum [4] or Bitcoin [5] cannot be applied. A tool to create a private blockchain network is needed.

Another requirement was to configure the blockchain network so that only trusted organization node could manage the transactions hosting so called ordering service.

Blockchain implemented in Hyperledger Fabric inherently meet the above requirements.

Independent channels provided by the Hyperledger Fabric provide the following advantages:

- limitation of internet traffic.
- limitation of internal databases of blockchain nodes.
- facilitating the onboarding of new clients because the deployment is limited to creating a blockchain node for a new client (in their data center) and implementing the appropriate business logic to the node in a trusted organization.
- simplified debugging.

As an alternative to the blockchain-based architecture, we considered a solution, in which blockchain would be replaced by a network of WORM matrix nodes. In such case, replicas of all documents would be stored in both the client's and the trusted organization's replicated nodes of the WORM matrix cluster. This seemed to be the simplest of all the considered architectural options, though, it would be too expensive for Durable Media system participants.

Architectural Problem No. 3: Ensuring the consistency of data stored in the blockchain and the WORM repository. Limiting the redundant use of space in the WORM matrix (reduction of the number of files in the WORM matrix that are not related to metadata in the blockchain).

Solution: Mechanisms of rollback and resumption of transactions have been developed (that are used depending on the document status in the WORM matrix). Transactions are performed with the use of multithreading and asynchronous processes queuing (isolation).

Rationale: This is especially important because the purpose of a durable media is to exclude possibility that an institution offering services to customers (e.g., bank) retroactively introduces changes to private or public documents (e.g., in the terms of service).

The biggest architectural challenge was to implement transactional processing of document upload into the WORM matrix combined with storing its metadata in the blockchain network. A transaction was split into two operations:

- Document upload – verification of completeness and registration of the document with metadata in the WORM in temporary space.
- Publication of the document – saving the document in the WORM matrix and in case of success saving the remaining data in the blockchain.

In case of failure there are two possible scenarios:

- Rollback to the state before the start of the transaction, if it is still possible, as the data written to the WORM matrix is impossible to remove.

- Repeating the operation – an attempt to complete the entire transaction in the case of successful writing to the WORM matrix and an error occurrence while storing the metadata in the blockchain.

The alternative solution was to leave garbage documents in both repositories. However, it would have been particularly inefficient in terms of WORM matrix utilization and the cost of system's operation. Leaving an unused block in a blockchain (documents are actually stored in a WORM matrix) is a minor issue because it utilizes just a few kilobytes of memory, which cost is marginal. A bigger problem would be to leave superfluous files in the WORM array, especially documents moved from the temporary space to the main space, from which the data cannot be removed for a pre-assumed retention period (in our case, usually a minimum of five years). In the business model we use, the WORM matrix is hosted by a cloud operator and we pay for each document stored in this matrix.

Architectural Problem No. 4: Enabling access to documents after the termination of the client's relationship with the bank (or other institution), for example, bank's client should be able to access his loan agreement even after paying off the debt.

Solution: Creation of two independent portals with access to the document repository. Creating a replication mechanism of user identification data.

Rationale: The requirement of providing a mechanism enabling the verification and download of the published document both from the level of trusted organization and the system stakeholders was met by:

- Creating two independent portals, namely, hosted by Durable Media client (e.g., bank) and by a trusted organization.
- Creating a mechanism for transferring information about the customers who have terminated the relationships with bank (or other institution), in order to open local accounts for them in the portal of a trusted organization.

It would be possible to use only a single portal implemented by the trusted organization. This would result in the necessity of downloading and verifying documents by a large number of clients of other system's participants from trusted organization. Our purpose was to develop a solution, in which only customers whose relationship with a financial institution (e.g. bank) was terminated, could download and verify documents through the portal of the trusted organization.

2.3 Architecture Presentation

Finally, an architecture presented in the Fig. 2 was developed. The architecture is presented as a component diagram that presents the distribution of system components among participants of different types.

The diagram in Fig. 2 shows:

- the components installed on premises in the data center of a trusted organization,

- components installed in the cloud that belong to a trusted organization and the infrastructure of an exemplary client.

The blockchain network has been stretched among a trusted institution and its customers. The node on the side of the trusted organization is more complex because it oversees the entire network and the data of all system customers (the node on the client side stores only the data of this client).

Only hashes from documents and their metadata are stored in the blockchain network. Documents are stored in WORM (Write Once Read Many) matrix in the cloud or in ECMS (Enterprise Content Management System) that is installed on premises.

Components of portal for document management (e.g., document publication component, document sharing component, API component – that are presented as a single component on the diagram) are hosted in containers as a set of microservices. All the components of the portal are automatically scalable, which means that their instances can be automatically created as load soars.

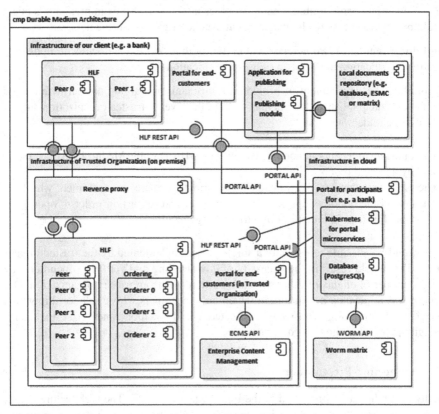

Fig. 2. Blockchain-based system architecture including local and cloud components as well as sample customer infrastructure.

Additionally, there is a second front-end of the portal that is installed on premises (this is an access interface for end-customers who have closed their relationship with the clients of trusted organization).

The alternative architecture that was considered where the distributed document repository that would be based on WORM matrices is presented in Fig. 3. From the perspective of the number of components, this architecture is much simpler in comparison to the architecture presented in Fig. 2. However, purchasing and maintaining a WORM array is far more costly than deploying and maintaining a blockchain node based on a free technology like Hyperledger Fabric. WORM-based architecture is characterized by a lower scalability and flexibility than blockchain-based architecture. The ability to disperse a cluster of WORM matrixes is very limited because by default, there can be two matrixes in a cluster which would result in either a custom configuration making us dependent on the matrixes vendor or the need for the trusted organization to have

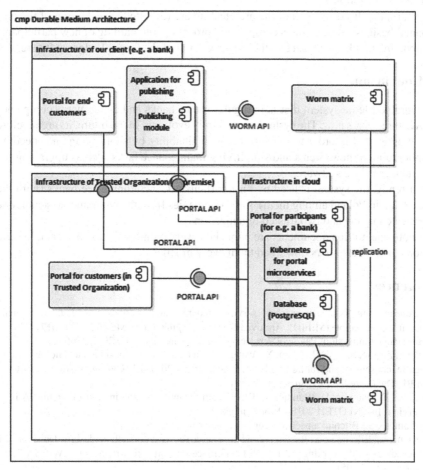

Fig. 3. WORM-based system architecture including local and cloud components as well as sample customer infrastructure.

a separate matrix for each bank or other institution. It would also be difficult to connect a second trusted organization because in such a situation there would have to be a minimum of three WORM matrixes in the cluster. In such a WORM-based architecture the documents would have to be transferred via Internet in order to replicate them between repositories. This turned out to be hugely resource-consuming in the case of configuration with several trusted organizations.

2.4 Pros and Cons of the Architecture

The major advantage of the presented architecture is its scalability and flexibility. It is possible to store documents in the system in two ways (safer but more expensive using the WORM matrix and cheaper for less demanding participants using the ECMS).

The second important advantage is separation of business logic of each participant (the participant's document metadata is stored only in its blockchain node and node of a trusted organization).

In turn, the disadvantages of the architecture are (despite the separation of the participants' business logic) quite a complicated process of onboarding of new participants and updating blockchain nodes to the newer version of the Hyper Ledger software.

3   Conclusion

The Durable Media system that is in regular use of banks and e-commerce companies for over three years now. The system is constantly evolving. In the future, its architecture will be optimized in order to improve its maintainability by simplifying and speeding up onboarding of new clients and simplifying maintenance tasks such as upgrading the Hyperledger Fabric software.

Currently, the system is used by nine participants, including three banks (with the largest bank in Poland among them), three companies from the e-commerce sector, one insurance company and two trusted organizations.

About one million documents are published every month in Durable Media. Several millions of end customers download them every month.

References

1. European Commission: Investment services and regulated markets - Markets in financial instruments directive (MiFID), Archived from the original on 23 March 2017 (2017)
2. European Commission: Payment services (PSD 2) - Directive (EU) 2015/2366 (2015)
3. Zheng, Z., Xie, S., Dai, H., Chen, X., Wang, H.: An overview of blockchain technology: architecture, consensus, and future trends. In: Proceedings - 2017 IEEE 6th International Congress on Big Data, Big Data Congress 2017 (2017)
4. Vujičić, D., Jagodić, D., Randić, S.: Blockchain technology, bitcoin, and Ethereum: A brief overview. In: INFOTEH 2018 - Proceedings (2018)
5. Nakamoto, S.: Bitcoin: a peer-to-peer electronic cash system (2008)
6. Jansen, A., Bosch, J.: Software architecture as a set of architectural design decisions. In: Proceedings - 5th Working IEEE/IFIP Conference on Software Architecture, WICSA 2005, pp. 109–120 (2005)
7. Androulaki, E., et al.: Hyperledger fabric: a distributed operating system for permissioned blockchains. In: Proceedings of the 13th EuroSys Conference, EuroSys 2018 (2018)

An Overview About Terravis Architecture Large-Scale Business Process Integration for Swiss Land Register Processes

Daniel Lübke[✉] [iD]

Digital Solution Architecture GmbH, Hannover, Germany
daniel.luebke@digital-solution-architecture.com
https://www.digital-solution-architecture.com

Abstract. This paper presents the process integration platform Terravis as a Software Architecture Showcase. We will describe the current architecture as well as challenges and lessons learned, which we encountered.

Keywords: Software Architecture · Industry Case Description · Business Process Automation

1 Introduction and History of Terravis

Terravis is a Swiss large-scale process integration platform that integrates land registries, notaries, banks, surveyors, and other parties participating in land registry transactions [2]. Both the legal and system landscape in this domain is very distributed and federated in Switzerland: While there is Swiss law governing land registry aspects, the more concrete regulation and laws are cantonal (a canton corresponds to a state in the US). Also, different notary systems, four official languages, different software systems, and cantonal fee models are adding to the complexity of the system. Consequently, offering digitized end-to-end business processes is both a technical and a political task to integrate more than 1000 different parties.

Terravis is a project of the SIX Group AG, which is a back-office service provider in Switzerland owned by the Swiss banks. After the definition of a Swiss-wide XML-based land register data model called GBDBS [1], the implementation was moved to SIX Group in 2009 as part of a public-private partnership. SIX Group was regarded as a neutral player between the Swiss federation and Swiss cantons and its relationships to banks were deemed to help to roll out this system.

Terravis is a central platform, which eases both technical integration (by integrating to Terravis instead of creating thousands of point-to-point integrations) and regulatory integration (e.g., Terravis knows which forms to choose for a certain business case in a certain canton). This paper will present the underlying architecture and lessons learned of this project, which is one of its kind.

T. Batista et al. (Eds.): ECSA 2022, LNCS 13928, pp. 11–18, 2023.
https://doi.org/10.1007/978-3-031-36889-9_2

2 Desired Quality Attributes

This section will shortly summarize a subset of some desired quality attributes of Terravis. An architecture can only be judged against the required quality attributes. As such, this is the foundation for the decisions outlined later.

Auditability & Fees (Q1): Access to land register and Nominee data must be fully audited and fees for transactions must be credited and debited to the correct partners.

Digitally, legally binding documents: According to Swiss law certain regulations, including legally-binding digital signatures are only possible as signed PDF documents (no XML).

Archival (Q2): All process-related documents must be archived for regulatory purposes.

Partners can use all features (Q3): If Terravis rolls out a new feature or process variant and exposing the new API versions, other partners might not necessarily have integrated their systems yet. This, Terravis is required to additionally offer a Web portal that can be used in parallel to the integration. This, in turn, resulted in multi-channel capabilities of the platform.

No Storage of Land Register Data (Q4): Due to regulatory requirements land register data must not be stored centrally, which also prohibits caching.

Short time-to-market (Q5): Terravis' success is rooted in the ability to release desired features quickly.

Sustainable development speed (Q6): Terravis must be extendable, and its lifecycle decoupled as much as possible from integrating systems.

3 Architecture Description

Terravis is developed using Java (starting from 1.5 and now using 11). Web applications are developed using an in-house – but in the meantime discontinued – framework. Its use was mandated by enterprise architecture when the project was started. Backend components are developed using Spring, Spring-WS, Hibernate and others. Java applications are deployed in Apache Tomcat which in the meantime is packaged in Docker containers. Data is stored in MS SQL Server databases.

Processes are deployed as single deployment units. Also, functional components are designed as their own deployable services (e.g., document generation or adapters to external systems).

Figure 1 shows the high-level structure of Terravis: Its main components are Query for land register data access, Process Automation for all business processes, and Nominee for functions related to trustee management. In addition, two services for managing master data and centralized audit & fee complement the overall structure. Alongside those functional components is a portal, which consists of user interfaces as a drop-in replacement for partner systems, where partners are not yet (fully) integrated. Thus, the service cut is not vertical,

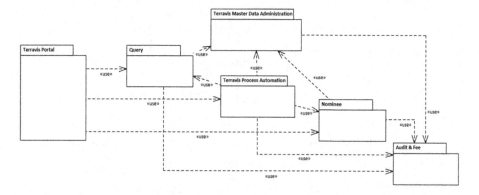

Fig. 1. High-Level Component Structure of Terravis

because the UI can be either an external system or the portal. The only exception is the master data administration which contains UI, business and persistence logic. Instead, Terravis mostly consists of backend services, without user interface.

Within this paper we focus on the Process Automation component. Its components are shown in Fig. 2.

It was decided to use a Business Process Management System (BPMS) for process automation. By using the BPMS' event log, many parts of process auditing (Q1) are already solved. Additionally, all completed process instances of a day are collected by a nightly job and stored in a fee database, thereby using BPMS process persistence to provide trusted data for fees and consequent invoicing (Q1).

The BPMS is sandwiched between two logical Enterprise Service Bus (ESB) components: the Auth and Routing Services. These two services implement the Claim-Check pattern [3], which routes the contents of PDF documents around the processes and thus the BPMS to remove unnecessary load. This is done by archiving documents in messages and replacing them with their archive ID. Thereby, document archival requirements are satisfied and incoming documents are guaranteed on an infrastructure level to be stored in the digital archive (Q2).

The requirement of adding Web portals for accessing the functionality led to an important architectural principle: Web portals must not have a home advantage! They are only allowed to use the same APIs which are offered to partners. Consequently, the portal serves as a reference implementation and validates the API design.

Originally, Terravis was designed as a pure backend integration platform. However, it became quickly evident that partners were not able to integrate with Terravis as quickly as hoped and to keep up with new process capabilities and variants. Thus, a Web portal has been created as a drop-in replacement for a partner system (Q3). This required multi-channel capabilities, which are also realized in the aforementioned ESB components: Each request contains the

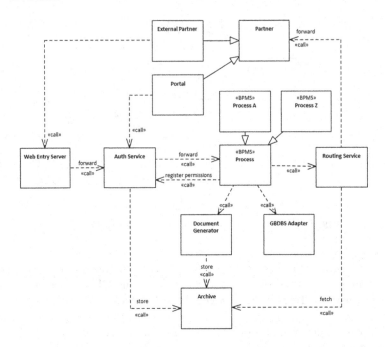

Fig. 2. Structure of the Process Automation component

system from which it originated (portal or external), which is set by the Auth Service and processes, and is evaluated by the Routing Service to send requests to their correct endpoints.

Not being able to neither cache nor store land register data means that data have to be fetched on every request from the land register system (Q4). Because it is unknown for any ID to which land register it belongs to, certain optimizations have been made and implemented in the GBDBS Adapter: Known IDs are stored in a lookup table with the owning land register and thus for known IDs only one land register system needs to be contacted. If a process knows the owning land register it will pass this to the GBDBS Adapter. If a process knows the canton then the canton is passed to the GBDBS Adapter which will then contact this canton's land registers only. If none of the above applies, the GBDBS Adapter will query all Swiss land registers. Because this is a very expensive operation, such requests are throttled to avoid blocking too many resources and creating overload on land register systems.

4   API Design Principles

Because Terravis' main purpose is to enable cross-partner – and thus cross-system – business process integration, the success of the platform to a large part depends on the quality of its APIs. This especially includes developer-

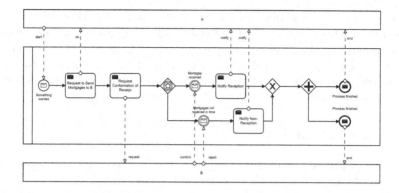

Fig. 3. Operation Naming Conventions of APIs in a Process Context

friendliness, reliability, and evolvability. Terravis decided on the following principles and guidelines for its APIs:

- The protocol to be used is SOAP over HTTPS with client certificate authentication. Client certificates were required by regulation.
- All request messages contain a header implementing the Context Representation pattern [8], which includes a unique request ID as well as business process IDs, and user authentication information. This allows moving much functionality, e.g., multi-channel (Q3), to the infrastructure, and improves analysis of problems and logging.
- Operations have a clear naming schema (see Fig. 3), especially the verb in the operation name, e.g., get (fetch data), start (starting a process), request (request an asynchronous operation), confirm/reject (response to a request), do (request an action without acknowledgement), notify (notification without response), and end (signal end of a process).
- Pagination Pattern is to be used if the requester is a UI component (portal context only) and if the number of returned values is unknown or possibly too large.
- The Request Bundle pattern [8] to batch multiple, independent requests of the same type is to be used if at least one use case is known to profit from it. For example getParcelsByIds can fetch details for 1 to 10 parcels with a single request. This reduces the number of requests, which are especially costly in this context due the inability to cache data and fetch data from remote land register systems.

To balance API stability requirements and the need to further develop and improve existing business processes, Terravis uses a combination of the Two In Production and Limited Lifetime Guarantee patterns [6]: Terravis offers the latest two API versions in parallel. If a third version is released, the oldest active version is deprecated and will be decommissioned after 18 months. These rather generous timespans reflect the requirements and development lead times encountered with many partners and their respective software vendors.

Terravis uses the Semantic Versioning scheme [6] for its APIs: In our interpretation the first number represents incompatible changes, the second number represents changes that are either compatible, can be transformed to be compatible or create a new process (which can be configured on a business partner level to remain compatible), and the third number contain fixes which are guaranteed to be inplace, compatible changes.

5   Lessons Learned

As with every project there were decisions that worked well and those from which we could learn. Things that worked well include:

- Architect for future needs (e.g., version transformations for the APIs) but choose a simple implementation: Draft but do not implement components that are not yet required.
- Portal as a reference implementation without home advantage: This principle enabled us to detect gaps in newly designed APIs because the portal consumes all publicly offered APIs.
- Use a workflow engine for processes: This decision dramatically increased development speed and offers audit and support functionality out of the box.
- Contract-First: Terravis has greatly benefited from contract-first development, which was enabled by using WSDL and XML Schema. At the beginning of the project, no viable REST/HTTP alternative was available. This has changed since the introduction of first Swagger and now OpenAPI. Contract-First also allowed for much better testing of components in unit [5] and regression tests [4].
- Context Representation: By defining a standardized data structure for passing on request metadata, authentication and logging logic could be moved into infrastructure components relieving developers of repetitive tasks and reducing the likelihood of severe errors in these areas.

What we changed along the way:

- Initially, APIs were organized by partner type, e.g., there was an API that covered all interactions for any bank, there was another one for notaries etc. This led to unnecessary coupling and thus constraints on the evolution of APIs; especially, when developing and show casing new processes, e.g., when using Experimental Previews [6]. Thus, we decided to have a single API for each partner type in each process, e.g., Px-Bank and Px-Notary for a process X, in which notaries and banks interact. This approach follows the Interface Segregation Principle [7] better and reduced coupling between processes noticeably.
- Check-Claim pattern for documents: Initially we routed documents through the BPMS. With increasing load this quickly led to an incredible use of resources. To address this, the Check-Claim pattern was added, which we should have done from the beginning and later enabled an easy adoption of a digital archive.

What did not work well:

- The mandated Land Registry API is very generic and there are many possible syntax variants for achieving the same semantics. It is hard to develop against this API and testing is difficult as well. API coverage metrics are next to meaningless, when using such generic APIs.
- Certificate Management with partners: Two-Way-SSL was required by regulation and generally works well. However, certificate rotations usually fails because partners let their certificates expire or fail to configure new Terravis certificates in time.
- Direct calls to partner systems: Because no queuing system was available at SIX Group at that time, we chose to call partners directly. Having all technical connections from partners to us would increase stability and reduce support effort.
- Build coupling of APIs/WSDLs: APIs can be designed and cut well. If a build unnecessarily couples them by packaging them in shared projects, these advantages quickly vanish. Developers like to do this because it seems to be more convenient. There needs to be more governance to avoid this.
- API operations should have a clear designation and parties should know the context in which they Using out-of-band messages (e.g., a NotifyDepotBooking message could indicate a booking within an existing process instance or could be the signal that a new process was started.)

6   Conclusions and Outlook

Within this paper we shared the general principles and decisions behind the Terravis platform successfully connecting land registries, notaries, banks and others to conduct thousands of processes a month. We shared what went well and what we would do otherwise if we could travel back in time. We hope that this helps others to avoid the same mistakes and gives some insights into our decision making.

References

1. GBDBS XML Schema. https://share.ech.ch/xmlns/eCH-0173/index.html. Accessed 15 July 2022
2. Berli, W., Lübke, D., Möckli, W.: Terravis - large scale business process integration between public and private partners. In: Plödereder, E., Grunske, L., Schneider, E., Ull, D. (eds.) Proceedings INFORMATIK 2014. Lecture Notes in Informatics (LNI), vol. P-232, pp. 1075–1090. Gesellschaft für Informatik e.V., Gesellschaft für Informatik e.V. (2014)
3. Hohpe, G., Woolf, B.: Enterprise Integration Patterns: Designing, Building, and Deploying Messaging Solutions. Addison-Wesley Professional, Boston (2004)
4. Lübke, D.: Selecting and prioritizing regression test suites by production usage risk in time-constrained environments. In: Winkler, D., Biffl, S., Mendez, D., Bergsmann, J. (eds.) SWQD 2020. LNBIP, vol. 371, pp. 31–50. Springer, Cham (2020). https://doi.org/10.1007/978-3-030-35510-4_3

5. Lübke, D., Greenyer, J., Vatlin, D.: Effectiveness of combinatorial test design with executable business processes. In: Lübke, D., Pautasso, C. (eds.) Empirical Studies on the Development of Executable Business Processes, pp. 199–223. Springer, Cham (2019). https://doi.org/10.1007/978-3-030-17666-2_9
6. Lübke, D., Zimmermann, O., Pautasso, C., Zdun, U., Stocker, M.: Interface evolution patterns: balancing compatibility and extensibility across service life cycles. In: Proceedings of the 24th European Conference on Pattern Languages of Programs, pp. 1–24 (2019)
7. Martin, R.C., Newkirk, J., Koss, R.S.: Agile Software Development: Principles, Patterns, and Practices, vol. 2. Prentice Hall, Upper Saddle River (2003)
8. Zimmermann, O., Stocker, M., Lübke, D., Zdun, U., Pautasso, C.: Patterns for API design-simplifying integration with loosely coupled message exchanges (2022)

Architectural Revision
of the E-Assessment System JACK

Michael Striewe[✉]

University of Duisburg-Essen, Essen, Germany
`michael.striewe@paluno.uni-due.de`

Abstract. The paper presents an architectural show case of the web-based e-assessment system JACK. After 12 years of service, the basic architecture of the system has been revised in recent years to overcome several shortcomings of the old architecture. In particular, the original design was too inflexible for further extensions by new grading modules, caused unnecessary restrictions with respect to synchronous and asynchronous grading, and was too generic with respect to exercise specific configuration. The architectural revision achieved to overcome these shortcomings by introducing a message queue as an additional subsystem and moving the border between generic and specific pieces of code. The new architecture is in productive use, includes some legacy components that will be migrated later, shows positive effects for developers and end-users, and allows for further improvements.

Keywords: E-Assessment System · Distributed System Architecture · Asynchronous Tasks · Message Queue

1 Introduction

The e-assessment system JACK allows to automate the process of grading and feedback generation for homework exercises and exams in higher education in various domains. The basic design of the architecture (see Fig. 1 for an overview) is unchanged from its origins more than 12 years ago [1], while the actual implementation has been updated [2]. The general design has proven to be suitable for productive work and several extensions [3,4].

JACK supports complex exercises like programming assignments, that require long-running grading processes (i. e. grading a single submission may take several minutes) but also simple exercises like multiple choice questions that can be graded instantly. It also offers some features for content generation, e. g. for mathematical exercises. In fact, it includes all typical frontend and educational components of an e-assessment system [5] except for a pedagogical module. Together with the general handling of exercises and submissions, grading and content generation form the "business logic" of the e-assessment system. The business logic uses external, specialized services when necessary, e. g. for user authentication with a central university authentication system, or for domain-specific features like computer-algebra-systems for mathematics.

© The Author(s), under exclusive license to Springer Nature Switzerland AG 2023
T. Batista et al. (Eds.): ECSA 2022, LNCS 13928, pp. 19–26, 2023.
https://doi.org/10.1007/978-3-031-36889-9_3

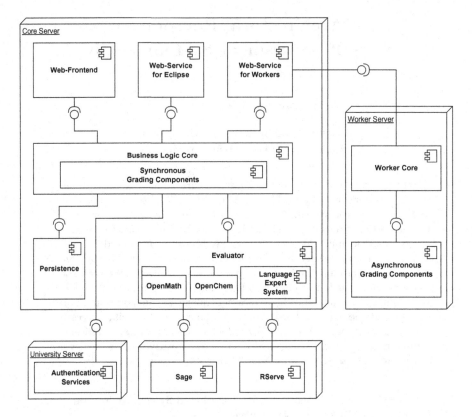

Fig. 1. Original JACK architecture that includes synchronous and asynchronous grading components as well as additional sub-systems for domain specific evaluation.

Across all use cases in different domains the system must be able to cope with several hundred concurrent users. To fulfill the related requirements regarding high availability and low response times, it is designed as a distributed system: A "server" part providing the user interface and managing data storage is realized as a JEE application, while a "worker" part performing most of the long-running grading processes is realized as a set of independent worker components processing their jobs asynchronously. The architecture assures scalability, since an arbitrary number of workers can serve an arbitrary number of JACK servers. Nevertheless, the long-term experience revealed specific issues with respect to the maintainability and extensibility of the system and caused a major architectural revision in recent years.

The current paper reports on the results of the problem analysis for the given architecture in Sect. 2. It presents the revised architecture that is supposed to solve the problems in Sect. 3. Section 4 provides an initial and preliminary assessment on whether the solution is indeed an improvement of the situation.

2   Problem Analysis

The problem analysis for the existing architecture identified three main problems that will be discussed in the following paragraphs.

Due to the requirements for the very first version of JACK, the design puts an emphasis on asynchronous grading processes that are executed on the worker part of the architecture. Later on, simpler exercise types like multiple choice or fill-in-the-gaps exercises were introduced that did not require long-running grading processes. To avoid unnecessary network communication and delays by queing short-running processes, additional components for synchronous grading processes were introduced in the server part of the architecture. One design decision at that time was to have a uniform interface for all grading components, while the actual implementation may be either synchronous in the server part or asynchronous in the worker part. However, it turned out that the handling of tasks for synchronous and asynchronous grading processes is quite different and that there are no processes for which both variants of implementations were required. Consequently, *the uniform interface for all grading components caused unnecessary restrictions without providing additional value* (problem 1).

The worker part of the architecture has been implemented using the "evaluator as facade" pattern [6], with a "worker core" acting as facade and several grading components acting as plug-ins that do the actual processing. On the one hand, that turned out to be very beneficial. New grading components could be implemented very quickly, since the facade handles all standard duties for communication with the server part, so that each grading component can focus solely on its actual duties. On the other hand, it turned out to cause unnecessary maintenance effort. The facade and its counterpart in the server part basically handle the exchange of a generic message format (because all specific handling is deferred to the grading components) and the queing of pending grading tasks. There is no need to use and maintain custom components for such duties, since there are re-usable components available for that purpose. Moreover, the facade is written in Java based on the OSGi framework and hence each grading component must also be written in Java, which is not necessarily appropriate for grading components that are supposed to grade exercises in programming languages like C++ or .NET. Some grading components actually created workarounds for that with a stub in Java and an actual grading server in some other language (e.g. [7,8]). Finally, each worker core must be configured with a list of servers it should connect to. This requires detailed documentation to keep an overview on which worker communicates with which server to make sure that there will be no heavily overloaded servers while some workers are idle all the time. Consequently, *the implementation of the worker part of the architecture was too inflexible and provided more significant drawbacks than benefits* (problem 2).

The use of the generic message format mentioned above was also motivated by the idea that the design should allow to attach any grading component to any exercise type, e.g. to use the same grading component for static code analysis on different types of programming exercises. Consequently, the server must provide a user interface that allows users to make a proper selection and map the specific exercise artifacts to the inputs required by the individual grading component. However, it turned out that this option was never used in practice. Instead, there is a fixed set of grading components that are used with each particular exercise type. Moreover, the possibility to connect every grading component with every exercise type frequently caused misconfigurations that required additional error handling. Consequently, *the configuration options per exercise type turned out as too generic, causing unnecessary and confusing flexibility* (problem 3).

3   Solution Architecture

Fig. 2 shows the revised architecture. It makes two significant changes to the architecture to address the problems. The revision did not follow a formal design or decision process. Instead, developers discussed the results of the problem analysis and shared their experience with alternative designs from other systems or from literature. Based on these discussions, promising ideas where selected, implemented in small prototypes, discussed again, and finally selected to be included in the architectural revision.

The first key idea is to use a uniform interface not for single grading components but for the business logic of each exercise type. The interface defines a

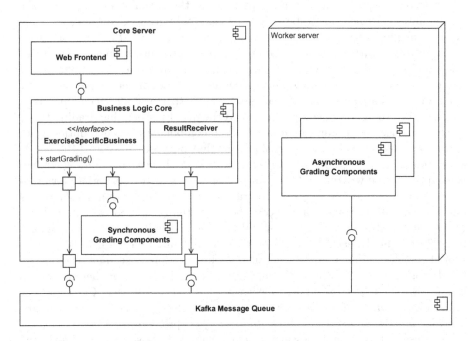

Fig. 2. New JACK architecture for grading components. For the sake of simplicity, actual exercise specific components implementing the interface are not shown in the diagram and original components that remained unchanged (web-service for Eclipse, Persistence, Evaluator) are also ignored.

uniform set of methods for handling grading (method `startGrading()` in Fig. 2), content generation, and similar processing steps for all exercise types. This was supposed to tackle problem 1 and partially problem 3. While the original architecture allowed exercise authors to connect any grading component to any exercise types, its now up to the system developers to define meaningful connections when implementing the method `startGrading()` of the interface. The implementation of that method can be completely different for each exercise type, so that one type may decide to make a synchronous call to some grading component within the server part, while another type may use an asynchronous grading component. It is even possible that an exercise type does not call any additional grading component, but realizes grading directly with a few lines of code within the business logic. It is also possible that an exercise type uses both synchronous and asynchronous grading tasks. Notably, it is still possible that an exercise type implements several different ways of grading and exercise authors may thus still choose which of those they would like to use in a particular exercise.

The second key idea is to introduce a Kafka message queue[1] as an additional sub-system and to define specific message types for each connection between an exercise type and an asynchronous grading component using Google Protocol Buffers[2] for serialization. This was supposed to tackle problem 2 and also help with problem 3. On the side of the grading components there is no longer the need to conform to the facade. Instead, they only need access to the message queue and must be able to read and write three message formats: One format is specific for the connection between a particular exercise type and the particular grading component. Designers of new grading components or exercise types are free in defining that format. The only requirement is that it includes a message in a second, generic format that contains some essential meta-information about the single grading task. The third format is also generic and must be used by all grading components to report their results. The abolishment of the facade also implies that grading components can be written in different programming languages, as long as the proper access to the Kafka message queue as well as using Protocol Buffers is possible in that language.

4   Initial Solution Assessment

At the time of writing this paper, the new architecture is implemented and in productive use. Three previously existing grading components for asynchronous grading have been migrated to services connecting to the message queue as standalone Spring Boot[3] applications. One new grading component has also been created based on that framework. The old facade has been extended with the capability to read from the new message queue as well, so that old grading components can also be used in the new architecture without migration. The

---

[1] https://kafka.apache.org/.

[2] https://developers.google.com/protocol-buffers.

[3] https://spring.io/projects/spring-boot.

new architecture thus allows for a smooth transition and step-wise migration of legacy components. So far, no grading components in other programming languages have been created in the context of JACK. However, the same architectural solution is also used in another project [9], re-using one of the grading components from JACK and adding several others also in other programming languages.

Due to the fact that the message queue has been introduced as an explicit component, *scaling and distribution has become easier* for asynchronous grading processes. It is no longer necessary to configure individual associations between workers and servers. Instead, all servers write to the same message queue into designated channels for each grading component. All instances of grading components listen to their respective channel, process their tasks and write results to the same queue into designated channels for each server. Hence, manual assignment of workers to servers is no longer needed. With proper configuration of the messaging services, response times are also lower than in the old architecture and come close to local method calls, as long as the queue is not overloaded.

Synchronous grading components have been re-implemented for the server part, as there is no longer the need to conform to a specific interface. This *improved the readability of the code and makes maintenance easier.*

The *user interface has become cleaner and more intuitive to use,* since each exercise type now only offers specific configuration options for its grading components. At the same time, it has become *easier for developers to add new features to grading components,* that require additional configuration options. As a downside, the business logic code for each exercise type gets more specific, making it harder for developers who are not familiar with a specific exercise type to make changes to that code. Consequently, similar problems might be solved differently in different exercise types. The respective message formats may also contain different fields for the same kind of information. Notably, this is no step back behind the quality of the old architecture. Instead, the same kind of duplications could also exist in the configuration files used in the old architecture.

The use of a generic message format for returning the grading results has been discussed quite a lot among the developers, since it restricts the way in which grades and feedback can be reported. The main argument for accepting the restriction was the fact that the user interface should use a somewhat uniform presentation of feedback anyway and hence the grading components are only supposed to create raw, but structured feedback data. Nevertheless, the architecture is still open to include additional, specific message elements in the result message format, if that turns out to be necessary. At the time of writing this paper, no such requirement came up so far. Moreover, Protocol Buffers themselves support backward compatibility, so that additional fields can be added to the format, without an urgent need to update all grading components immediately.

An actual drawback of the new architecture is the need to write additional code for proper monitoring of message delivery. In the old architecture, the workers connected directly to servers, so that each call could be logged. Moreover, the queue of waiting grading tasks was maintained directly within the server part. Consequently, any server could raise warnings when the queue got overloaded or if a worker picked up a task, but did not report results. In the new architecture, there is no longer a direct connection and hence additional code is necessary to monitor the amount of waiting grading tasks inside the message queue. Moreover, grading components must send additional notices when they pick up a grading task if these should be monitored. Since there is no longer a facade for all grading components, there is no single place where such additional messaging can be implemented. Instead, it must be implemented in each grading component. At the time of writing this paper, monitoring is not yet up to the level it was with the old architecture, requiring more frequent manual inspection of all components to ensure proper productive operation.

5   Future Work and Lessons Learned

The architectural revision of the e-assessment system JACK has created a significant improvement of the system architecture. That improvement in turn created benefits both for developers and for end-users. At the same time, it allowed for a smooth transition in which some legacy components are still in productive use. These components will be re-implemented in the future. Since messaging turned out to be quite fast, there is also the idea of skipping synchronous grading components at all. Instead, all grading components could be connected via the message queue, which makes the architecture even cleaner, more scalable and robust.

Although an e-assessment system is a quite special type of system, at least some of the aspects discussed in this paper apply to a broader range of systems:

- It is not generally beneficial to make the design as generic as possible. The original design used uniform interfaces for grading components, leaving it up to the end-user to define actual component connections. This mixes domain knowledge about exercise types with technical knowledge about system components. The new design moves the interface to a more appropriate place that separates the decisions made by end-users (i.e. which exercise type to use) from the decisions made by developers (i.e. which component connections are meaningful).
- Using a facade is mixed blessing. The old architecture used a facade to implement asynchronous grading components and thus implied restrictions on how to implement these components. The new architecture overcomes these restrictions but at the same time looses the possibility to implement common monitoring capabilities within the facade. The gain of flexibility was more beneficial in our case, but it might be different in others.
- Ready-to-use sub-components can be introduced with a smooth transition for legacy components. While the new message queue allowed to attach new grading components once it was in place, there was no need to rework existing components immediately. Instead, a minor change to the existing facade was enough to keep everything working. Developers could thus focus on getting

one side of the queue right (in our case reworking the business logic of the server part of JACK), avoiding to work on both sides at the same time.

References

1. Striewe, M., Balz, M., Goedicke, M.: A flexible and modular software architecture for computer aided assessments and automated marking. In: Proceedings of the First International Conference on Computer Supported Education (CSEDU), 23–26 March 2009, Lisboa, Portugal, vol. 2. INSTICC, pp. 54–61 (2009)
2. Striewe, M., Zurmaar, B., Goedicke, M.: Evolution of the e-assessment framework jack. In: Gemeinsamer Tagungsband der Workshops der Tagung Software Engineering 2015, Dresden, Germany, 17.-18. März 2015, pp. 118–120 (2015). https://ceur-ws.org/Vol-1337/paper20.pdf
3. Striewe, M.: An architecture for modular grading and feedback generation for complex exercises. Sci. Comput. Program. **129**, 35–47 (2016). https://www.sciencedirect.com/science/article/pii/S0167642316300260
4. Pobel, S., Striewe, M.: Domain-specific extensions for an e-assessment system. In: Herzog, M.A., Kubincová, Z., Han, P., Temperini, M. (eds.) ICWL 2019. LNCS, vol. 11841, pp. 327–331. Springer, Cham (2019). https://doi.org/10.1007/978-3-030-35758-0_32
5. Striewe, M.: Components and design alternatives in e-assessment systems. In: Bures, T., Duchien, L., Inverardi, P. (eds.) ECSA 2019. LNCS, vol. 11681, pp. 220–228. Springer, Cham (2019). https://doi.org/10.1007/978-3-030-29983-5_15
6. Striewe, M.: Design patterns for submission evaluation within e-assessment systems. In: 26th European Conference on Pattern Languages of Programs, ser. EuroPLoP 2021, pp. 32:1–32:10 (2021)
7. Hesse, T., Wagner, A., Paech, B.: Automated assessment of C++ programming exercises with unit tests. In: Proceedings of the First Workshop Automatische Bewertung von Programmieraufgaben (ABP 2013) (2013). https://ceur-ws.org/Vol-1067/abp2013_submission_7.pdf
8. D'Amico, M.: Konzeption universeller.NET-Prüfkomponenten für das E-assessment-system jack. In: Proceedings of the Second Workshop "Automatische Bewertung von Programmieraufgaben (2015). https://ceur-ws.org/Vol-1496/paper1.pdf
9. Ullrich, M., et al.: Platform architecture for the diagram assessment domain. In: Proceedings of the Software Engineering 2021 Satellite Events, Braunschweig/Virtual, Germany, 22–26 February 2021 (2021). https://ceur-ws.org/Vol-2814/paper-A6-4.pdf

Tools and Demonstrations Track

ExpressO: From Express.js Implementation Code to OpenAPI Interface Descriptions

Souhaila Serbout[✉][iD], Alessandro Romanelli, and Cesare Pautasso[iD]

Software Institute (USI), Lugano, Switzerland
{souhaila.serbout,alessandro.romanelli,cesare.pautasso}@usi.ch

Abstract. The current paper presents a novel Command Line Interface (CLI) tool called ExpressO. This tool is specifically developed for developers who seek to analyze Web APIs implemented using the Express.js framework. ExpressO can automatically extract a specification written in OpenAPI, which is a widely used interface description language. The extracted specification consists of all the implemented endpoints, response status codes, and path and query parameters. Additionally, apart from facilitating automatic documentation generation for the API, ExpressO can also automatically verify the conformity of the Web API interface to its implementation, based on the Express.js framework.

The tool has been released on the npm component registry as 'expresso-api', and can be globally installed using the command:
`npm install -g expresso-api`.

Keywords: OpenAPI Specification · REST API · Express.js · Documentation generation

1 Introduction

In Continuous Software Development (CSD), the usage of modern software architecture tooling [18] and executable documentation is highly recommended [28, 30]. Ensuring that documentation is continuously consistent with the implementation throughout the software development cycle is required in order to avoid informal communication and tacit knowledge sharing between the software development team members [21]. Web APIs are a particular type of software for which producing up-to-date documentation is a must because it is a crucial artifact to support the API's learnability by developers [24]. Documenting small systems may be trivial, however when scaling up the size of the backend, producing and maintaining the desired documentation can prove challenging and quite resource-intensive.

As an attempt to solve this problem, ExpressO is a tool that helps Express.js [29] developers to generate documentation for their APIs taking nothing as input other than the backend code they already wrote. The obtained documentation is compliant with the OpenAPI specification [1]. While the automatically generated artifacts can be manually augmented with natural language

T. Batista et al. (Eds.): ECSA 2022, LNCS 13928, pp. 29–44, 2023.
https://doi.org/10.1007/978-3-031-36889-9_4

descriptions, easing the rapid generation of API documentation, ExpressO can also check the consistency of the interface extracted from the implementation with the existing documentation, thus highlighting gaps between the interface documentation and the corresponding implementation code.

We target the Express.js framework due to its wide adoption and the lack of tools that can extract the OpenAPI description only based on the implementation code itself. Existing tools such as Express OpenAPI [27] or swagger-autogen [2] require additional code annotations or time-consuming configuration steps to produce similar results.

2   Background: OpenAPI

APIs can be described using natural language, informal models, or general-purpose modeling languages. There exist also machine-readable Domain Specific Languages [14] for describing them, such as RAML [3], WADL [17], WSDL [11], I/O Docs [4], and OpenAPI [1], which gained more importance in the five last years by being selected as a standard language for APIs description.

For what concerns our tool, OpenAPI describes an API as a set of endpoints $\mathcal{E}$, which may receive zero or more parameters $\mathcal{P}$ and produce one or more expected responses for each endpoint $\mathcal{R}$.

$$APIComponents = \{c, c \in \mathcal{E} \cup \mathcal{P} \cup \mathcal{R}\}$$

From now on we call the endpoints, the parameters and the responses: 'API Components'.

OpenAPI descriptions comprehend also metadata about the API and description fields with values written in natural language. They also contain detailed descriptions of operations' request and response bodies, which can be specified using JSON Schema when exchanging JSON message payloads.

There is a broad set of emerging tools and approaches centered around the OpenAPI standard [5]: test cases generation [12,22], API analytics tools [13,26], as well as implementation code for client skeletons and server stubs (e.g. [23]). ExpressO focuses on the opposite problem: generating interface descriptions starting from the implementation code.

In our study, we utilize OpenAPI [20] as the standard target language for documenting the extracted Web API. To generate a valid OpenAPI specification, it is essential to extract all the necessary information from the backend code to populate the required fields in the OpenAPI metamodel. An example of such a specification, produced by the OpenAPI Initiative [19], is presented in Listing 1.1. We have highlighted the API Components that are essential for a valid specification in green. The fields that are not mandatory but can enhance the specification's detail are marked in orange. The optional fields that are typically written in natural language to provide additional insights about the API Components are shaded in gray.

Listing 1.1. Example of OAS3.0. Properties highlighting: green → must-have, orange → nice-to-have, gray → out of scope / user defined.

```
1   {
2       "openapi": "3.0.0",
3       "info": {
4         "version": "1.0.0",
5         "title": "Swagger Petstore",
6         "license": {
7           "name": "MIT"
8         }
9       },
10      "servers": [
11        {
12          "url": "http://petstore.swagger.io/v1"
13        }
14      ],
15      "paths": {
16        "/pets": {
17          "get": {
18            "summary": "List all pets",
19            "operationId": "listPets",
20            "tags": [
21              "pets"
22            ],
23            "parameters": [
24              {
25                "name": "limit",
26                "in": "query",
27                "description": "How many items to return at one time (max 100)",
28                "required": false,
29                "schema": {
30                  "type": "integer",
31                  "format": "int32"
32                }
33              }
34            ],
35            "responses": {
36              "200": {
37                "description": "A paged array of pets",
38                "headers": {
39                  "x-next": {
40                    "description": "A link to the next page of responses",
41                    "schema": {
42                      "type": "string"
43                    }
44                  }
45                },
46                "content": {
47                  "application/json": {
48                    "schema": {
49                      "$ref": "#/components/schemas/Pets"
50                    }
51                  }
52                }
53              }
54            }
55          }
56        }
57  }
```

Omitting the human-readable fields, such as description, summary, and tags, which may require user input, our proposed approach discussed in Sect. 5 can generate a rudimentary specification that covers all the essential fields, describing an endpoint in terms of its **path**, **HTTP methods**, and **response**

codes. Additionally, by conducting a static analysis of the routes, ExpressO can obtain the relevant **parameter** details.

3   Related Work

While other methods have attempted to extract structured REST API documentation from unstructured sources [10], our work focuses on generating documentation directly from the source code, assuming that the API has been implemented using the Express.js framework.

Unlike Express OpenAPI [27], which requires the user to provide an OpenAPI description containing the API's metadata as input and explicitly annotate each Express.js route with the corresponding OpenAPI metadata, ExpressO does not necessitate any input beyond the Express.js backend code. In the former case, the developer can add human-readable descriptions to be included in the resulting API, but the interface and implementation specifications are mixed in the same source code. Developers must rewrite the information already present in the previously written endpoint code. Express OpenAPI then combines the pieces to produce a coherent document that is served statically.

On the other hand, swagger-autogen [2] can be run with the backend to generate documentation each time the backend is executed. These modules are independent of any backend framework and assume that the backend implements routes following the conventions of Express.js.

Table 1 provides an overview of the input requirements for ExpressO, Express OpenAPI, and swagger-autogen. The comparison results of the ExpressO's Comparator are more granular and detailed than the ones produced by similar tools. **OAS Diff** [15] only provides a count of the modified or added API Components. Instead, **OpenAPI Diff by Microsoft Azure** [16] has as main goal to detect breaking changes as it outputs a report that classifies the changes affecting each API Component. An in comparison with other JSON/YAML diff tools ExpressO's Comparator provides a more domain specific reports grouping the detected differences by API components: endpoints, parameters, and responses.

4   Use Cases

In the design of the tool we envisioned the following use cases:

Table 1. Inputs required by different OpenAPI generation tools

	Code annotations	Basic description	Config file	Backend code
Express OpenAPI 2015	Yes	Yes	No	Yes
Swagger-autogen 2020	No	No	Yes	Yes
ExpressO 2022	No	No	No	Yes

1. Helping developers to keep both the implementation code and the interface documentation continuously synchronized; For that, the user can use the `'expresso generate'` CLI command to generate the new specification corresponding to the current version of the implementation.
2. Helping API designers to verify whether the implementation matches the structure they modeled and track the progress of an API development project; This corresponds to the CLI command `'expresso compare'` which compares two given input specifications, or the `'expresso test'` which generates an OpenAPI specification for the backend then compares it to an input reference specification. The tool will generate both a human-readable and a machine-readable report about what has been matched and what is missing for each specification.
3. Making it easier for developers to detect breaking changes by using ExpressO to compare the OpenAPI description of the current version of the API with a previously generated specification, also using the `'expresso compare'`. The comparison report can be used as ground truth to perform Regression Testing on the new changes;
4. Supporting researchers who want to perform empirical studies on real-world APIs. Using ExpressO they can automatically extract well-formatted knowledge from the Express.js source code of a large set of projects, by simply running the `'expresso generate'` for each of the projects.

5   ExpressO

5.1   Approach

ExpressO is a command-line interface (CLI) tool designed to extract the essential components from the source code of an Express.js project and produce a valid OpenAPI specification that describes the REST API. The tool uses a combination of static and dynamic analyses. The dynamic analysis involves injecting a Proxy component, which replaces the `express` npm package in the input project. This Proxy is used to intercept calls that configure the API routing table and extract the code of the corresponding function handlers. The Analyzer then performs static analysis on this code to extract information about the request parameters and response status codes.

The only input that the system requires to generate a specification for a REST API is the original source code. ExpressO first identifies the application entry point file and creates an abstract syntax tree that is scanned for all usages of the Express app that listens on a port. Once all the source files have been analyzed, a data structure holds the properties of the respective endpoints, routers, and applications.

To avoid altering the source code, ExpressO replaces the express.js NPM package with an instrumented version of the same, called the Proxy. The Proxy acts as an intermediary between the system and the original express functionality, allowing access to the latter whilst keeping track of calls being made by the 'Express.Application' object. By intercepting every call made to the Express

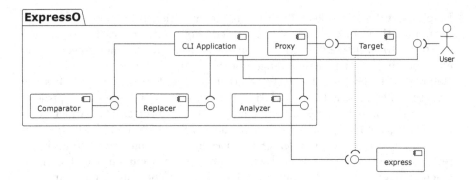

Fig. 1. Logical view of ExpressO

framework, the Proxy collects data in a data structure that is able to store all the information needed to reconstruct the API description. Specifically, the Proxy builds the API routing table by linking each endpoint path and method combination with the corresponding handler function. Then, by running a static analysis on the handler code, ExpressO retrieves the response codes and parameters of a given endpoint.

The hybrid approach employed by ExpressO, which combines both static and dynamic analysis techniques, enables the tool to extract the endpoints of deeply modular backends without having to statically analyze their entire code. While static analysis alone requires navigation through the imports and exports of several files, which can be a slow process when traversing large code-bases, the dynamic analysis component of ExpressO allows for more efficient extraction of endpoint information. By intercepting every call made to the Express framework, the Proxy component of ExpressO collects the data needed to reconstruct the API description without the need for time-consuming static analysis of all the backend code.

5.2   Architecture

We depict an overview of the logical view of the architecture of ExpressO in Fig. 1. In the rest of this section, we explain in detail the different software components part of the ExpressO tool, which will be separately demonstrated.

CLI Application. ExpressO utilizes the CLI Application interface to provide access to its functionalities. The available command lines are illustrated in Fig. 2. In the simplest case, where developers want to generate a specification without any customization, they can run the tool with the command `expresso generate`, as most parameters have default values. Additionally, other available commands are presented in Fig. 2.

Replacer. The Replacer module is responsible for generating a functioning copy of an Express.js backend that can be initiated by the CLI Application module as a Child Process. This module performs an additional task of substituting the original express package inside the `node_modules` directory with the Proxy component. This replacement enables the working copy to utilize our Proxy module in the same way as the original express module, without requiring any modification to the input code. Moreover, the ExpressO module is retrieved from the `node_modules` of the npm global packages, which must be present to utilize the CLI Application. This approach eliminates the need to install `expresso-api` both locally and globally, reducing the burden on users to maintain both installations up-to-date.

```
[[~] expresso --help                                                       11:42:37  ]

Usage: expresso [expresso-options] [command] [command-options]

Available options:
 -H  --help      Prints to console command line commands and options
 -V  --version   Prints to console the current version of expresso

Available commands:
 generate   Generates OpenAPI specification for the Express.js project in the current directory
 test       Generates OpenAPI specification and compares it with a user-provided ground truth
 compare    Compares two OpenAPI specifications regardless of version or format

All commands can be further inspected with: expresso [command] [-H | --help]
```

Fig. 2. ExpressO Command Line Help

Proxy. The Proxy module plays a crucial role in intercepting all calls made to the Express framework and storing relevant information about the routes and corresponding request handler code. This information is then used to extract the API components necessary to generate a valid OpenAPI specification. It is important to note that the Proxy intercepts only the route configuration setup calls on the express framework itself and not the calls made to actual API endpoints by test clients. In other words, the Proxy operates at the backend start-up phase and captures the necessary information about the routes and handlers without actually executing them. While the command used to start the backend can be customized, the default command used in the experiments was `npm start` with no additional inputs.

Child Process. Upon invoking the Replacer and creating a working copy, the CLI Application generates a Child Process that executes the modified version of the project with the replaced module, including the Proxy. Our approach involves terminating the Child Process upon the first write-out to the intermediate model representation file.

Analyser. The analyzer module is responsible for parsing the intermediate model representation, which is stored as a JSON file, back into a working data structure. This allows the representation to be statically analyzed using the npm package abstract-syntax-tree [6].

Regarding parameters, for the first release of ExpressO, we limit the definition of parameters to two types: **Path** and **Query** parameters. Other parameter types, such as Cookies and Headers, are not supported in the furrent version of the tool.

When an endpoint is retrieved, the parameters used within that endpoint are detected by statically analyzing the route.

Comparator. The comparator module is designed to read and compare two OpenAPI descriptions (API_{source} and API_{target}), which can be written in either YAML or JSON format and may be in similar or different versions of OpenAPI. The comparison is done based on the criteria described in the rest of this section.

5.3   API Comparison and Coverage Report

While comparing the two API descriptions, the comparator computes and reports the following:

– **Matched**: the set of API Components present in both descriptions.

$$M = API_{source} \cap API_{target}$$

– **Partially matched**: when some API path parameters are present in both specifications, but their names do not exactly match.

$$PM = \{c, c \in API_{target} \land \exists c' \in API_{source} | c \approx c'\}$$

The partial matching feature is implemented to address discrepancies in the naming of path parameters between the Express.js routes in the code and the corresponding paths in the target OpenAPI description being compared. This is because some developers may use different names for the same path parameter in the code and the OpenAPI description, even though they are semantically equivalent or referring to the same parameter. This can create issues during the comparison process.

To address this, when performing the match, parameter names are not required since path parameters are positional and their name serves only to identify them as they are referenced from the code. Therefore, the names used in the target specifications are usually human-comprehensible, while the names generated from the implementation code are more direct.

For example, consider a path p_i : `/users/userId` for an endpoint E_i in API_{source}, and a path p'_j : `/users/username` for an endpoint $E'j$ in API_{target}. Although the parameter names are different, these paths represent the same endpoint template with a fixed `/users/` segment followed by one parametric segment. Hence, they should be matched: $p_i \approx p'_j$. Consequently, we consider that the endpoints are partially matching: $E_i \approx E'_j$, irrespective of the path parameter names.

```
(base) → backend-viajes git:(master) × expresso compare expresso-openapi.json:swagger.yaml
Results for OpenAPI specification comparison between the following files:
 - expresso-openapi.json
 - swagger.yaml

Endpoints coverage ───────────────────────── 83.33% (5/6 Endpoints)
███████████████████████████████████████░░░░░░░░░░░░░░░░░░
Strict coverage (no partials) ───────────── 50.00% (3/6 Endpoints)
[███████████████████████████░░░░░░░░░░░░░░░░░░░░░░░░░░░░░░

Missing (1):
 GET  /

No extra entities detected

Matched (3):
 GET    /api/v1/travels
 POST   /api/v1/travels
 GET    /api/v1/travels/find

Partially matched (2):
 DELETE  /api/v1/travels/{id|_id}
 PATCH   /api/v1/travels/{id|_id}

Responses coverage ───────────────────────── 20.00% (3/15 Responses)
██████████░░░░░░░░░░░░░░░░░░░░░░░░░░░░░░░░░░░░░░░░░░░░░░░░
Strict coverage (no partials) ───────────── 20.00% (3/15 Responses)
██████████░░░░░░░░░░░░░░░░░░░░░░░░░░░░░░░░░░░░░░░░░░░░░░░░

Missing (12):
 200  GET    /
 403  GET    /api/v1/travels
 500  GET    /api/v1/travels
 500  POST   /api/v1/travels
 404  GET    /api/v1/travels/find
 500  GET    /api/v1/travels/find
 204  DELETE /api/v1/travels/{id}
 404  DELETE /api/v1/travels/{id}
 500  DELETE /api/v1/travels/{id}
 201  PATCH  /api/v1/travels/{id}
 404  PATCH  /api/v1/travels/{id}
 500  PATCH  /api/v1/travels/{id}

Extra (7):
 400  GET    /api/v1/travels
 400  POST   /api/v1/travels
 400  GET    /api/v1/travels/find
 200  DELETE /api/v1/travels/{_id}
 400  DELETE /api/v1/travels/{_id}
 200  PATCH  /api/v1/travels/{_id}
 400  PATCH  /api/v1/travels/{_id}

Matched (3):
 200  GET    /api/v1/travels
 201  POST   /api/v1/travels
 200  GET    /api/v1/travels/find

No partially matched entities detected

Parameters coverage ──────────────────────── 100.00% (2/2 Parameters)
████████████████████████████████████████████████████████
Strict coverage (no partials) ───────────── 0.00% (0/2 Parameters)
░░░░░░░░░░░░░░░░░░░░░░░░░░░░░░░░░░░░░░░░░░░░░░░░░░░░░░░░░░

No missing entities detected

Extra (3):
 x-user      GET  /api/v1/travels
 id_cliente  GET  /api/v1/travels/find
 estado      GET  /api/v1/travels/find

No matched entities detected

Partially matched (2):
 id|_id  DELETE  /api/v1/travels/{id|_id}
 id|_id  PATCH   /api/v1/travels/{id|_id}
```

Fig. 3. Snapshot of a human-readable coverage report example generated by ExpressO for an Express.js project found on GitHub [7]

- **Missing**: elements that are only present in the target specification;

$$MISS = \{c, c \in API_{target} \land c \notin API_{source}\}$$

- **Additional**: elements that are only present in the compared specification;

$$ADD = \{c, c \in API_{source} \land c \notin API_{target}\}$$

Although the comparator module can be utilized to compare any two HTTP APIs described using OpenAPI, its primary purpose is to assess the level of coverage achieved when comparing the generated description with a ground truth description. To achieve this, we have established two metrics to evaluate the coverage level of each API component:

- **Strict Coverage**: how many matched API Components over the total number of API_{source} Components;

$$C_{\text{strict}} = \frac{\text{size}(M)}{\text{size}(API_{source})}$$

- **Broad Coverage**: how many matched and partially matched API Components over the total number of API_{source} Components;

$$C_{\text{broad}} = \frac{\text{size}(M) + \text{size}(PM)}{\text{size}(API_{source})}$$

The objective of these metrics is to accurately quantify the degree to which generated documentation matches the ground truth (the specification found in the software repository). While manually-created documentation can be more exhaustive, our primary focus is on ensuring that we can accurately identify all endpoints along with their associated responses and parameters.

In addiction to printing the coverage metrics in machine-readable JSON file format, this module also serves as a reporting tool that outputs the comparison data in a human-readable format, producing a report in the terminal (as shown in Fig. 3).

6   Evaluation

In [25], we presented an extensive evaluation of ExpressO using a dataset of 91 Express.js projects collected from GitHub. These projects have been selected because they include the OpenAPI description of the corresponding API that we used to compute the coverage metrics, using the original specification shared in the software repository as a ground truth.

Web first selected projects that can be directly run with an `npm install && npm start` command, then filtered the ones containing an OpenAPI description file. We then remove from the dataset the projects that take more than 10s to start with an `npm start`. In Fig. 4 we show in details the dataset filtering decision tree, and in Table 2 we show the APIs size distribution computed from the OpenAPI descriptions found in each of the 91 remaining projects.

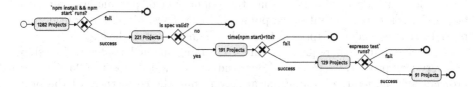

Fig. 4. The decision tree followed to filter the Express.js projects used in the evaluation of ExpressO

Table 2. Distribution of number of paths and operations metrics

	μ	σ	Min	25%	50%	75%	Max
#Paths	4.42	4.18	1	2	3	5	30
#Operations	6.38	6.92	1	2	5	7	53

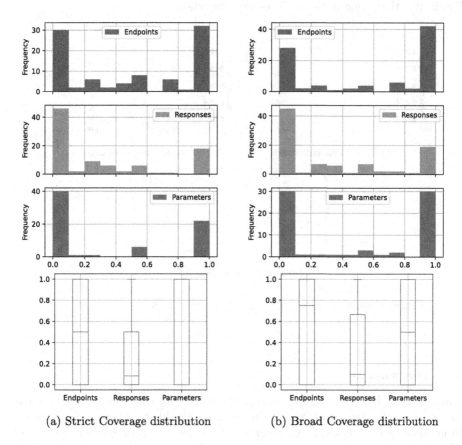

(a) Strict Coverage distribution   (b) Broad Coverage distribution

Fig. 5. C_{strict} and C_{broad} computed values distribution in 91 projects

In Fig. 5 it can be observed that the population of parameters seems to be smaller compared to that of endpoints and responses. Moreover, considering partial matches enables ExpressO to reach a higher coverage level.

As swagger-autogen requires a time-consuming manual configuration step for every new project, we restricted our study to a smaller subset of 23 working projects for comparative evaluation, after verifying the correctness of the produced output. Although ExpressO could generate valid specs for all 91 projects, it took us 33 attempts on different repositories to generate 23 usable specifications. In 30% of cases, swagger-autogen failed to produce valid documentation.

6.1   API Components Coverage

Fig. 6 depicts the computation of the C_{strict} metric by comparing the specifications generated by ExpressO and swagger-autogen against the specifications found in the projects which are considered a ground truth. A values of 1 indicates that all the features in the original specification were matched, while a value of 0 indicates that none of the features were matched.

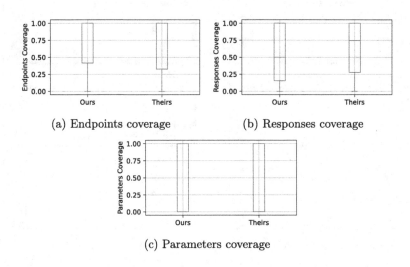

(a) Endpoints coverage   (b) Responses coverage

(c) Parameters coverage

Fig. 6. Computed values of C_{strict} of ExpressO's vs. swagger-autogen

6.2   Performance

Time Taken by ExpressO. Because we are able to profile our system, when we ran it on the dataset of 20 repositories we were able to differentiate between time taken by the Replacer, Analyzer and Child Process components separately. This gives us the median execution time breakdown visualized in Fig. 7: Child Process 2017 ms; Analyzer 123 ms;

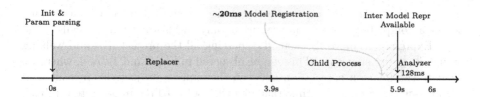

Fig. 7. Timeline of `expresso generate` command at the component level

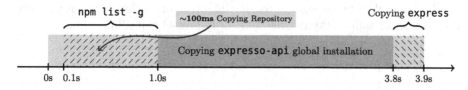

Fig. 8. Timeline of `Replacer` component

As we can see from Fig. 8, the repository size has a very minor effect on the overall time.

ExpressO vs. Swagger-Autogen. While in the case of ExpressO, the time that matters is the one it takes to analyze code, and generate the specification, in the case of swagger-autogen to produce a specification it is needed to keep in mind that it involves manual configuration. We distinguish: (1) Time To Start (TTS): the time elapsed from when a project is cloned and installed, to the moment that we are able to run our analysis; (2) Time To Run (TTR): the time taken to analyze the backend and produce the specification.

In the following results, our main focus was on TTR, particularly in comparing the performance of Analyzer with swagger-autogen. To evaluate the TTR of swagger-autogen accurately, we need to consider the time required to set up the swagger.js file by configuring it correctly. This is a manual activity that varies in duration depending on the user's experience with swagger-autogen and familiarity with the backend. In the initial run, we consider our system to have superior performance if a user cannot complete the necessary steps to use swagger-autogen within 5.8 s (Table 3). In subsequent runs, this manual step is no longer necessary to be fair.

Table 3. Performance Comparison (Average Execution Time)

	TTS	TTR	Total
swagger-autogen	>0	265 ms	>265 ms
expresso	5917 ms	123 ms	6040 ms

ExpressO is not affected by the total size of the input code in the same way as a completely static analysis, as it only needs to listen for calls made to the Express.js framework, instead of parsing all the project files and walking through its entire structure. This can be observed in Fig. 9 and Table 4, where we calculate the Pearson correlation between the express project size measured in lines of code (LOC) and the time taken by the tools (TTR), in order to establish if there is a statistical correlation between these two variables. The first row of the table shows that there is a strong correlation between the LOC of a project and the time taken by swagger-autogen, while the correlation between the API size (number of endpoints) and the TTR of ExpressO is medium.

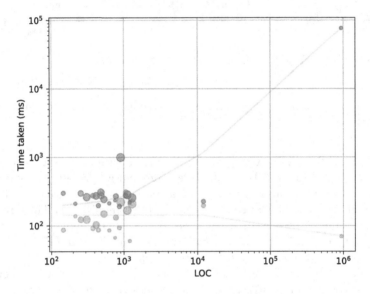

Fig. 9. Logarithmic scatter plot comparison between **Analyzer** (orange) and `swagger-autogen` (green) timings, with linear trendlines. The size of a datapoint relates to the number of declared endpoints

Table 4. Corr. of Time To Run (TTR) against implementation size (LOC) and output API size (Endpoints)

		Correlation	p-value
LOC	swagger-autogen	0.9999	0.000
LOC	expresso	−0.2292	0.3310
Endpoints	expresso	0.4841	0.030
Endpoints	swagger-autogen	−0.220	0.3501

7   Conclusion

In this paper, we introduce ExpressO, a tool that automatically extracts a skeleton of OpenAPI descriptionsfrom the corresponding JavaScript implementation based on the Express.js framework. Unlike existing automatic generation tools such as swagger-autogen, ExpressO does not require any time-consuming manual configuration and can be immediately used on any Express.js compliant project. While most existing tools for extracting interfaces from implementation support a code-first approach to API development, where the implementation is manually annotated with metadata that should be extracted and published as part of the OpenAPI description, ExpressO supports an API-first approach [9]. It can compare the API description extracted from the code with a given OpenAPI description to verify that the paths, operations, response codes, and parameters are implemented as advertised. ExpressO instead supports an API-first approach [9], as it can compare the API description extracted from the code with a given OpenAPI description to check whether the paths, operations, response codes, and parameters are indeed implemented as advertised.

Although currently, the tool only supports Express.js backends, its hybrid approach combining static and dynamic analysis can be applied to other back-end frameworks whose route configuration settings can be instrumented and intercepted similarly. We aim to extend the tool to support a broader range of inputs (APIs whose backend is implemented using other frameworks and other programming languages) and outputs (API descriptions conforming to other specifications, e.g. RAML). ExpressO is freely available on the npm registry under the "expresso-api" name [8].

Acknowledgements. This work was partially supported by the SNF with the API-ACE project number 184692.

References

1. OpenAPI Initiative. https://www.openapis.org/
2. https://github.com/davibaltar/swagger-autogen
3. RAML. https://raml.org/
4. I/O Docs. https://support.mashery.com/docs/read/IO_Docs
5. OpenAPI.Tools. https://openapi.tools/
6. https://www.npmjs.com/package/abstract-syntax-tree
7. https://github.com/FIS-Proyecto-Equipo1/backend-viajes
8. https://www.npmjs.com/package/expresso-api
9. Beaulieu, N., Dascalu, S.M., Hand, E.: API-first design: a survey of the state of academia and industry. In: Latifi, S. (ed.) 19th International Conference on Information Technology-New Generations, ITNG 2022. AISC, vol. 1421, pp. 73–79. Springer, Cham (2022). https://doi.org/10.1007/978-3-030-97652-1_10
10. Cao, H., Falleri, J.-R., Blanc, X.: Automated generation of REST API specification from plain HTML documentation. In: Maximilien, M., Vallecillo, A., Wang, J., Oriol, M. (eds.) ICSOC 2017. LNCS, vol. 10601, pp. 453–461. Springer, Cham (2017). https://doi.org/10.1007/978-3-319-69035-3_32

11. Christensen, E.: Web services description language (wsdl) 1.1. https://www.w3.org/TR/2001/NOTE-wsdl-20010315 (2001)
12. Corradini, D., Zampieri, A., Pasqua, M., Ceccato, M.: Restats: a test coverage tool for restful APIS. In: 2021 IEEE International Conference on Software Maintenance and Evolution (ICSME), pp. 594–598. IEEE (2021)
13. Di Lauro, F., Serbout, S., Pautasso, C.: Towards large-scale empirical assessment of web APIs evolution. In: Brambilla, M., Chbeir, R., Frasincar, F., Manolescu, I. (eds.) ICWE 2021. LNCS, vol. 12706, pp. 124–138. Springer, Cham (2021). https://doi.org/10.1007/978-3-030-74296-6_10
14. Fowler, M.: Domain-Specific Languages. Pearson Education, London (2010)
15. GitHub-Repository: Openapi diff. https://github.com/tufin/oasdiff
16. GitHub-repository: Openapi diff by microsoft azure. https://github.com/Azure/openapi-diff
17. Hadley, M.J.: Web application description language (wadl). Technical Report, USA (2006)
18. Hasselbring, W.: Software Architecture: Past, Present, Future. In: The Essence of Software Engineering, pp. 169–184. Springer, Cham (2018). https://doi.org/10.1007/978-3-319-73897-0_10
19. Initiative, O.: Oas v3.0 petstore example. https://github.com/OAI/OpenAPI-Specification/blob/main/examples/v3.0/petstore.json
20. Initiative, O.: Openapi v3.1.0 specification. https://spec.openapis.org/oas/v3.1.0
21. Jongeling, R., Fredriksson, J., Ciccozzi, F., Cicchetti, A., Carlson, J.: Towards consistency checking between a system model and its implementation. In: Babur, Ö., Denil, J., Vogel-Heuser, B. (eds.) ICSMM 2020. CCIS, vol. 1262, pp. 30–39. Springer, Cham (2020). https://doi.org/10.1007/978-3-030-58167-1_3
22. Karlsson, S., Čaušević, A., Sundmark, D.: Quickrest: property-based test generation of openapi-described restful APIS. In: 2020 IEEE 13th International Conference on Software Testing, Validation and Verification (ICST), pp. 131–141. IEEE (2020)
23. Koren, I., Klamma, R.: The exploitation of OpenAPI documentation for the generation of web frontends. In: Companion of the The Web Conference 2018 on The Web Conference 2018 - WWW 2018, pp. 781–787 (2018)
24. Robillard, M.P.: What makes APIS hard to learn? answers from developers. IEEE Softw. **26**(6), 27–34 (2009)
25. Romanelli, A.: ExpressO. Master's thesis, Faculty of Informatics, University of Lugano (2022). https://thesis.bul.sbu.usi.ch/theses/2035-2122Romanelli/pdf?1674133800
26. Serbout, S., Di Lauro, F., Pautasso, C.: Web APIS structures and data models analysis. In: 2022 IEEE 19th International Conference on Software Architecture Companion (ICSA-C), pp. 84–91. IEEE (2022)
27. Spencer, J.: Express openapi. https://github.com/kogosoftwarellc/open-api
28. Theunissen, T., van Heesch, U., Avgeriou, P.: A mapping study on documentation in continuous software development. Inf. Softw. Technol. **142**, 106733 (2022)
29. TJ Holowaychuk, S., et al.: Express.js documentation. https://expressjs.com/en/5x/api.html
30. Van Heesch, U., Theunissen, T., Zimmermann, O., Zdun, U.: Software specification and documentation in continuous software development: a focus group report. In: Proceedings of the 22nd European Conference on Pattern Languages of Programs, pp. 1–13 (2017)

Tool-Based Attack Graph Estimation and Scenario Analysis for Software Architectures

Maximilian Walter[✉][ID] and Ralf Reussner[ID]

KASTEL – Institute of Information Security and Dependability, Karlsruhe Institute
of Technology (KIT), Karlsruhe, Germany
{maximilian.walter,ralf.reussner}@kit.edu

Abstract. With the increase of connected systems and the ongoing digitalization of various aspects of our life, the security demands for software increase. Software architects should design a secure and resistant system. One solution can be the identification of attack paths or the usage of an access control policy analysis. However, due to the system complexity identifying an attack path or analyzing access control policies is hard. Current attack path calculation approaches, often only focus on the network topology and do not consider the more fine-grained information a software architecture can provide, such as the components or deployment. In addition, the impact of access control policies for a given scenario is unclear. We developed an open-source attack propagation tool, which can calculate an attack graph based on the software architecture. This tool could help software architects to identify potential critical attack paths. Additionally, we extended the used access control metamodel to support a scenario-based access control analysis.

Keywords: Attack Propagation · Software Architecture · Security

1 Introduction

Through the digitalization of our lives, more and more systems are connected with each other. This connection enables us to build smart systems and exchange data between different services. These connected systems should be resilient against cyber-attacks. One possibility to achieve this is by analyzing potential attack paths or access control policies.

However, estimating attack paths or analyzing access control policies is complicated. In advanced persistent threat (APT) [6], attackers often combine multiple security issues, such as vulnerabilities and access control properties, into one

This work was supported by the German Research Foundation (DFG) under project number 432576552, HE8596/1-1 (FluidTrust), as well as by funding from the topic Engineering Secure Systems of the Helmholtz Association (HGF) and by KASTEL Security Research Labs.

T. Batista et al. (Eds.): ECSA 2022, LNCS 13928, pp. 45–61, 2023.
https://doi.org/10.1007/978-3-031-36889-9_5

complex attack path. For instance, attackers often start with a phishing attack to get credentials and access to an element and then use this as a starting point to further attack the system [17]. This behavior can be reduced to first getting access to a subsystem and then propagating further by exploiting different vulnerabilities. This pattern can also be seen in other incidents, such as in [34].

Existing attack path propagation approaches such as [9,44] often only consider a network topology or a very reduced access control model. In contrast, other approaches with more fine-grained access control, such as Bloodhound [5] are very specific to the application domain for instance the Active Directory.

In addition, if an access control policy changes, it is often unclear what the impact for a specific scenario might be. A small policy change might lead to a too restrictive policy and blocks a legitimate and essential usage scenario, such as access to a machine in a production process. A policy change could potentially also have the opposite effect and be too open. This in turn enables malicious users to access data they should not be able to. Also, changes in the scenario are unclear. For instance, if the context of a user scenario changes, such as the access from a different location, it is unclear whether the user can still perform the scenario.

For solving these security issues, we developed an attack propagation analysis [40,41] which uses a software architecture together with a fine-grained access control model to estimate potential attack paths. Software architects annotate vulnerabilities and access control policies to architectural elements and specify an attacker. The attacker contains the initial starting point, the capabilities (the attacks they can perform), and the knowledge (known credentials) of an attacker. Based on the provided information, our analysis calculates an attack graph. Software architects can use this attack graph to identify and evaluate potential attack paths. In addition, we extended the developed access control metamodel to support a scenario-based access control analysis. It enables architects to analyze certain intended usage scenarios against the software architecture together with access control policies and decide whether the scenarios are possible or not.

We will present our open-source Eclipse plugins[1] for the attack propagation and our short demonstration video[2]. We introduce our running example in Sect. 2. In Sect. 3, we describe the features of our original tool and in Sect. 3.3 describe the results of our tool. Afterward, we introduce our newly added scenario analysis in Sect. 4 and Sect. 5. The evaluation for our extension can be found in Sect. 6. Related work is described in Sect. 7. Section 8 concludes the paper and describes our future work.

2 Running Example

Figure 1 illustrates our running example. It is based on a scenario from a previous research project with industrial partners [2] that we extended in previous work [40] by adding vulnerabilities and access control information. It is settled in an Industry 4.0 environment.

---

[1] https://fluidtrust.github.io/attack-propagation-doc/.
[2] https://youtu.be/wiefWdTO9lo.

In the scenario, a manufacturer (M) has a `Machine`. The `Machine` stores its data at the `ProductionDataStorage` which is deployed on the `StorageServer`. The `Machine` can be accessed by a `Terminal`, deployed on the `TerminalServer`. The `Terminal` is used by a technician from the service contractor (S). Because the machine data might contain sensitive data, S can only access the terminal during an incident such as a broken machine. Besides the machine part, there is the `ProductStorage`, which contains sensitive data about the product, such as blueprints. Therefore, S should have no access to this data. The `LocalNetwork` connects the different devices. A user with the attribute `Admin` has access to the `StorageServer` and `TerminalServer`. The `TerminalServer` is vulnerable to CVE-2021-28374 [29]. As stated in the vulnerability's description, CVE-2021-28374 can leak credentials.

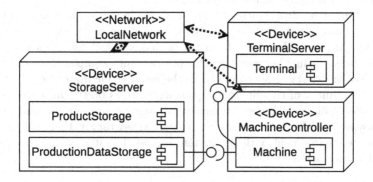

Fig. 1. Simplified architecture overview running example based on [40]

3   Attack Propagation Tool

Our attack propagation tool consists of three features, the software architecture modeling, an extension to model vulnerabilities and access control properties, and the attack propagation analysis.

3.1   Modeling Software Architecture

Our tooling is based on the existing Palladio-Bench, which extends the Eclipse Modelling Edition with Palladio Component Model (PCM) [31] specific editors and analyses. The Palladio-Bench is open-source and freely available. We also provide our extensions and the analysis freely as an open-source project. PCM is an Architecture Description Language (ADL) for the component-based development process. The modeled software architectures can be analyzed in various quality analyses such as performance [31] or confidentiality [33].

In PCM, software architects model the different aspects of the architecture in different models. In the **repository** model, a software architect can specify the components and their required and provided interfaces. The interfaces specify services with parameters and return values. Components can implement these services or delegate them to other services. These implemented services are called ServiceEffectSpecification (SEFF). The repository also contains datatype specifications necessary for the services. For our running example, we would specify the interfaces and the components there. For instance, for the `Machine`, we would specify a component *Machine* which provides the services for the `Terminal` and requires the services provided by `ProductionDataStorage`.

These specified components are then combined in the `system` model. Here, the different components are instantiated and wired together. The instantiated components are called *AssemblyContext*. For instance, in our running example, we instantiate the components and wire them together, e.g., the instantiated `Machine` is connected with the instantiated `Terminal`.

The different hardware elements are modeled in the `resourceenvironment` model. It contains *ResourceContainers* for processing nodes such as servers or notebooks and *LinkingResources* for network elements such as switches or routers. It also contains the link between them. In our running example, all elements with `<<Device>>` or `<<Network>>` would be in the resource environment.

The deployment of the different *AssemblyContexts* on the *ResourceContainers* is modeled in the `allocation` model, for instance, in our running example, the deployment of the `Terminal` on the `TerminalServer`. It, therefore, connects the resource environment with the system model. The usage model models the aggregated user behavior.

3.2 Attack Propagation Modeling

Our attack propagation extension [40] extends the existing PCM model by allowing to specify vulnerabilities and access control policies for certain architectural elements. In our case, these elements are *BasicComponents* as components in PCM, *AssemblyContexts*, *ServiceSpecifications*, *ResourceContainers*, and *LinkingResources*. In our tool, the access control properties are modeled in the `context` model. The access control specification is based on the eXtensible Access Control Markup Language (XACML) [43] standard for access control policy specification. We extended some elements such as the matching and attribute selection for easier modeling in PCM (see Fig. 4). Software architects can specify with our extension access control policies and the attributes used in the access control decision. This allows us to support Attribute-based Access Control (ABAC) [15] for our access control policies. Reusing parts of XACML is beneficial since software architects or security experts might already be familiar with the standard and can therefore reuse their knowledge.

The vulnerability and attack specification is modeled in the `attacker` model. The vulnerability specification is based on the commonly used vulnerability classifications Common Weakness Enumeration (CWE) [26], Common Vulnerabilities and Exposure (CVE) [25], and Common Vulnerability Scoring System (CVSS) [8]. These classifications are often used by vendors or vulnerability databases such as the US. National Vulnerability Database (NVD) [30]. This allows software

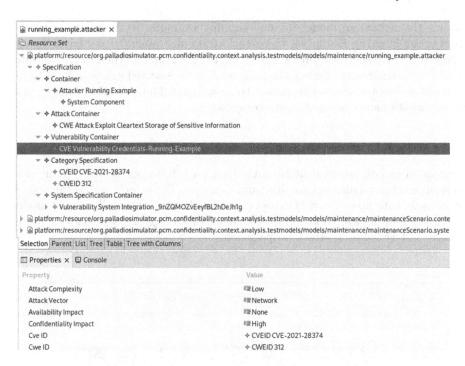

Fig. 2. Overview of the attacker model editor

architects to reuse the existing knowledge about vulnerabilities. For instance, our running example contains the vulnerability CVE-2021-28374 [29]. Based on the description in the NVD, the software architects can know that credentials could be leaked and that the vulnerability can be exploited remotely. This information can then be added to our model (see also Fig. 2) and is considered in the attack propagation.

Besides specifying the software architecture, access control policies and vulnerabilities, our analysis also needs the attacker as input. For the attacker, we specify the starting point in the software architecture, the capabilities and the knowledge about access properties. The starting point in the architecture can be an *Assembly Context*, *LinkingResource* or *ResourceContainer*. The capabilities are the type of attacks an attacker can perform, i.e., the vulnerabilities they can exploit. Here, we also reused the CVE and CWE concept. For instance, the vulnerability in our running example can be exploited by CWE-312 [27] since CVE-2021-28374 is part of CWE-312. Therefore, an attacker with the capability CWE-312 can exploit this vulnerability. The attributes used in the access control specification are knowledge about access properties. For instance, if an attacker in our running example has the Admin attribute, they could access the StorageServer and TerminalServer.

All these models can be edited with editors integrated into Eclipse. Figure 2 shows an overview of the attacker model editor. An overview of the new model elements can be found in our previous publication [40]. This model

shows the `attacker` model for our running example. It shows the attacker
(`Attacker Running Example`), the attack, the vulnerability (selected element),
the CWE/CVE specification `Category Specification` and the integration into
PCM (`System Specification Container`). For the selected vulnerability (blue),
the editor shows additional properties (bottom part). These are properties for the
vulnerabilities such as a `Low` attack complexity.

3.3 Attack Propagation Analysis and Tool Results

Our analysis [40] then calculates an attack path from one starting point and
returns a list of all affected architectural elements. The attack path is calculated
iteratively until no new element can be affected. It works internally similar as the
KAMP [14] approach. However, they focussed on change propagation for maintenance, and we focus on attack propagation.

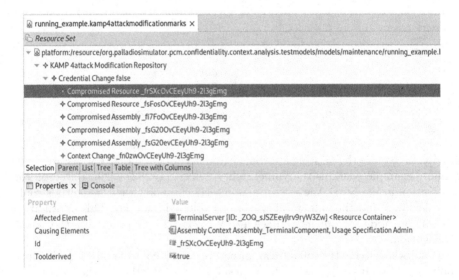

Fig. 3. Overview analysis output

The results of our attack propagation analysis are stored in the `kamp4attack-`
`modificationmarks` model. An excerpt is shown in Fig. 3. In our case, it contains
the attack path from the `Terminal` to the `StorageSever` by exploiting the vulnerability of the `TerminalServer` and getting the `Admin` credential. For instance, the
selected element is the `TerminalServer`. In the properties view (bottom part) the
software architect can see the `Affected Element` (here `TerminalServer`) and the
reason (`Causing Effect`). Additionally, it contains an ID and the `Toolderived`
property. The last property indicates that the analysis decided that the element
is affected and that it was not one of the initial elements. Besides this detailed list

overview, our tooling can create a graph overview, where the connection between different elements is easier to recognize.

These analysis results can now be used by software architects. They have a list of affected elements and the reason. They can use this information to break potential attack paths. This could be done, for instance, by introducing mitigation approaches such as changing the credentials or updating the system. Afterward, they could remove the vulnerability from the attacker model and reanalyze the system to find out whether this mitigation approach solves the problem. However, the analysis could also be used to make trade-off decisions. For instance, a mitigation approach could be very costly either in system performance or monetary value. Here, architects could analyze different models with and without the mitigation and decide whether the risk is acceptable or whether they should choose the more secure system regardless of the cost. While our analysis cannot derive the other quality metrics, PCM already has support for various quality aspects like performance or cost [31] and the modeled system could be reused.

4   Modeling Architectural Access Control

As described in Sect. 3.2, our attack propagation tool uses an access control model based on XACML. So far, we have not investigated a scenario-based analysis for usage and misusage scenarios. In contrast to the attack propagation, we focus on verifying whether modelled usage scenarios are possible with the given software architecture and access control policies. This is especially important in evolutionary settings, where policies or scenarios change and system architects want to identify, whether the intended scenario is possible with the given architecture and access control policies.

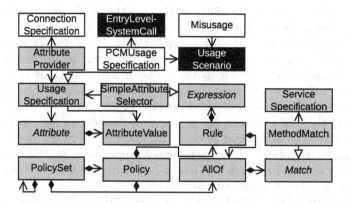

Fig. 4. Simplified access control policy metamodel with PCM integration

The access control metamodel (see Fig. 4) contains mostly reused elements (gray) from our attack propagation tool. However, we needed to add some new elements (white) to annotate the PCM usage scenario description with context attributes. The black elements (`UsageScenario`, `EntryLevelSystemCall`) are original PCM elements. We first describe how a policy is specified and afterwards how we can assign attributes to a usage scenario.

All access control policies are contained in a `PolicySet`. It can consist of multiple `PolicySets` and `Policy` elements. A `Policy` can have multiple `Rule` elements. A `Rule` contains the actual access condition (as the `Expression`) and the result such as Permit or Deny. The `AllOf` specifies the target for which architectural elements the `Rule` or `Expression` should be applied. Because the target definition allows multiple `Rule` elements for one architectural element, there could exist multiple different access decisions. Therefore, the `PolicySet` and `Policy` have combination algorithms to reduce the decisions to one (see [43]). For a `Rule` or a `Policy` also multiple `AllOf` elements can be assigned. These multiple elements build a logical disjunction. Each `AllOf` element has multiple `Match` elements building a logical conjunction. The `Match` consists of boolean operations. For the `Match` we extended the XACML with custom match elements to better support the integration into PCM. `MethodMatch` is used to identify instantiated services with the `ServiceSpecification` element. PCM currently does not support the differentiation of instantiated services natively, therefore we added the `ServiceSpecification` element. It is a mapping between a service and the instantiated component. The `Expression` models the condition. The `SimpleAttributeSelector` wraps a simple attribute comparison. This eases the specification of a simple attribute condition. `UsageSpecification` is a tuple of `Attribute` and its concrete value as `AttributeValue`. For instance, in our running example, the role is a `Attribute` and the concrete role "technician" is a `AttributeValue`. `Attribute` elements can have references to certain architectural elements. This reference is later important for the model transformation to select the correct origin of an attribute.

For our running example, a policy could be as described in Listing 1.1. For simplicity reason, we only use one `Rule` and left out the PCM integration part. The combination algorithm is `Deny_Unless_Permit`, which states that every request is denied, unless there is a rule with a permit result. The `Rule` "Technician with Machine failure" has an expression that states that the requestor needs the role technician. In addition, other attributes can be added. The `AllOf` states that it targets a method. In the commented part, the correct element is selected.

Besides modeling the access control policy, we also need to model the user behavior and the user's context. In our previous publication [40], we only modeled the attacker and not normal users. Additionally, the behavior of the attacker was only modeled implicitly through the attack propagation, and the context was automatically derived from attacks. Here, we explicitly model the intended usage and the system context during a scenario.

The usage scenario in PCM describes the usage of the system during a specified scenario and it contains the `EntryLevelSystemCall` elements, which describe the called services by a user. In our approach, we enrich the `UsageScenario` with context information. The context is in our case the attributes used in the access control decision. The attributes are defined by the `PCMUsageSpecification`. Besides

```
1    PolicySet {
2      combining:Deny_Unless_Permit
3      Policy{
4        combining:Deny_Unless_Permit
5        Rule{
6          name:"Technician with Machine failure"
7          decision:permit
8          Expression{
9            And{
10             SimpleAttributeSelector{
11               UsageSpecification{
12                 attribute:role
13                 value:technician
14               }}/* further attribute conditions*/
15           }}
16           AllOf{
17             MethodMatch{ /* integration into pcm */ }}}}}
```

Listing 1.1. Simplified textual representation of technican policy for services

setting the context for the whole scenario, we also allow architects to specify the context for each `EntryLevelSystemCall`. This allows architects to specify context changes within a scenario. The context of an `EntryLevelSystemCall` overwrites the context of the `UsageScenario`.

Additionally, architects can specify context changes within a service. This is useful for internal access control. For instance, in our running example, the `Machine` retrieves the log data from the `ProductionDataStorage`. This action can happen on the user level, such as that the requestor is forwarded (here technician), or it can be done on the system level. In the last case the `Machine` would be the requestor at `ProductionDataStorage`. For modeling this context change, we added the `ConnectionSpecification` together with the `AttributProvider`. The `AttributProvider` is used in our attack propagation analysis for modeling that architectural elements can provide attributes. Here, we extended it with the `ConnectionSpecification`. This enables architects to specify that the context changes for certain connectors between services.

Besides modeling the intended usage with the usage scenario, we also enable the modeling of misusage scenarios. Misusage scenarios are based on misuscases [36] and mal-activity diagrams [35]. The idea is that architects can model scenarios that should not be possible. For instance, a possible misusage scenario for our running example could be that the technician gets access to the terminal without the machine in the failure state. In our case, architects can model this scenario by reusing the concepts of the normal usage scenario. However, in addition to modeling the scenario, they can create a `Misusage` element and assign an `UsageScenario`. In this case the `UsageScenario` is considered as a misusage scenario.

5   Analyzing Access Control Policies

After specifying the misusage and usage scenarios, and the access control policies, we can analyze each scenario for access control violations. Software architects can use these violations to change the access control policies or adapt the scenario to remove the violations. Our analysis consists of two steps. The first step is transforming our architectural access control model into a valid XACML file. We define valid, here, as valid according the XSD schema definition for the XACML 3.0 standard [43]. We can reuse the transformation from the attack propagation.

The second part is the scenario analysis. The scenario analysis first determines the context for each `UsageScenario`. Then it identifies the context for each `EntryLevelSystemCall` of a scenario. This context is either derived from the scenario when the call does not specify its own context or uses the specified context for the `EntryLevelSystemCall`. Then the analysis follows the call hierarchy of the services for each system call. There, it uses the `ExternalCall` from the SEFF to first identify the service type and then use the system model to determine the instantiated service. For identifying the instantiated service, we use the `AssemblyConnectors` of PCM. The analysis compares them together with the service type to the `ConnectionSpecification` elements of the `AttributeProvider` elements. If there exists at least one matching, it replaces the context, with the context for the `ConnectionSpecification`.

We then generate a valid XACML request out of the context for each instantiated service call and query a Policy Decision Point (PDP). The PDP evaluates the request based on the loaded policies and returns the access decision. This decision is then saved together with the instantiated service. During the request generation, we assign the `UsageSpecification` from the context to the three categories (subject, environment, resource) XACML uses and assign if necessary from which entity they come from. In XACML, this is called issuer.

After evaluating all access decisions for each scenario, the analysis decides whether a scenario is marked in the output as passed or not. For normal scenarios, the analysis marks a scenario as passed if every service call in it is permitted. For misusage scenarios, the analysis marks a scenario as passed if at least one service called is denied.

6   Evaluation

The evaluation of our attack propagation tool can be found in Walter et al. [40]. For the new scenario analysis, we describe the evaluation here. We follow the goal question metric approach [3]. Our evaluation goal is the *functional correctness* of our analysis. The analysis results should be correctly derived from the input model. Our evaluation questions are: **Q1** *Can the analysis determine the correct access decision for service calls?* **Q2** *Can the analysis determine the correct decision from usage scenarios or misusage scenarios?*

Question **Q1** focuses on the access decision for a service call. Here, we want to investigate whether every access decision for every service call is correct. This question is important since we later use the results of the access decision to determine whether a scenario is passed. **Q2** investigates whether, based on the access decisions, the correct result for a scenario or misusage scenario is determined. This is important since these are the actual output results. For **Q1** and **Q2**, we use the Jaccard Coefficient (JC) [23] defined as $JC(A, B) = \frac{|A \cap B|}{|A \cup B|}$. It is used to compare the two sets A and B for equalness. The value range is from 1.0 for two equal sets to 0.0 for no intersection. The metric is used also in other design-time approaches in the PCM context such as [13]. The JC does not consider the order of elements. However, in our case we do not need the order (see Sect. 6.1).

6.1   Evaluation Design

In our evaluation, we use four case studies since case studies might provide better insights, show applicability, and increase the comparability between different approaches. We first describe the design for the different evaluation questions and introduce our used case studies afterwards.

For answering **Q1** and **Q2**, we manually create reference outputs for each case study. Afterwards, we compared the reference outputs against the results of the analysis. For **Q1** we see the access control decision as a set of tuples consisting of the access decision, the scenario, the connector, the intended service, the origin service and the involved instantiated component. These tuples are independent of each other, describe the access decisions and their order is irrelevant.

The scenario decision can also be seen as a tuple consisting of the scenario and the decision whether it is passed. The actual order of the scenarios is also not important for this tuple. Therefore, we can apply the JC and answer **Q2**. For the scenario analysis, we made sure that we had at least one normal scenario and one misusage scenario based on the description of the case study.

The first case study is the confidentiality case study TravelPlanner [20]. It is used in different confidentiality analyses, such as [22,40]. We base our model on the model from [22]. The TravelPlanner describes the process of booking a flight from a mobile application. The main goal is that the credit card used for booking data must be explicitly declassified before the other entities can use it. In our scenario, we modelled this by adding an attribute for the classification.

Our second case study is based on the education example from Margrave [11]. We created, based on their description, a simple architecture model and created usage and misusage scenarios. The access control policies are also based on their description and their dataset. We need to adapt them since their policies are written for an older XACML version and do not contain the PCM references.

The third case study is based on the ABAC Banking case from [33]. It describes a simple banking system with branches in different regions. For each region, only the manager is allowed to handle celebrity customers. Regular customers are handled by a clerk. For our evaluation, we slightly adapted the access control model from a dataflow-based definition to a service-based definition since our approach only works on the service level. Additionally, we investigated the scenarios for the clerk and manager handling customers in the US branch and a misusage scenario where the clerk tries to handle a celebrity customer.

Our fourth case study is our running example. We investigate the scenario described in Sect. 2, scenarios regarding the saving of log data, accessing the product storage component. As a misusage scenario we investigated, that the technician tries to access the data without a machine failure.

6.2 Results and Discussion

For **Q1** and **Q2**, we achieve a JC from 1.0 for every case study. These are perfect results. These results are perfect since the case studies are small, and we only consider the decision (either access or pass). This simplifies the result. These results mean that for every scenario, our expected reference set is equally comparable to the result of the analysis. This indicates that our analysis works correctly. Based on this, architects could use our approach for analyzing the access control decisions for different scenarios. This enables them to analyze different alternative scenarios with various access control policies and see possible results. This analysis could help to harden the system by defining stricter access control policies and evaluating whether these stricter policies would still enable the use of the system in a certain scenario. Additionally, it can help in policy changes to not forget malicious scenarios by explicitly modelling them as misusage scenarios and analyzing them. This can help to prohibit malicious usage through policy changes, because the misusage scenario can automatically check for violations after a policy change.

6.3 Threats to Validity

Based on the guidelines for case study validity from Runeson et al. [32], we categorize our threats to validity into four categories.

Internal Validity: This discusses that only the expected factors influence the results. Because of the different input models and that we evaluate only the result, our evaluation highly depends on the used models. Even more, we manually created the output models. We try to lower the risk by using mostly external case studies and deriving the expected results based on their descriptions. Another threat is the size of the models since the models are quite small. However, they already cover our approach's important functionality, such as the context derivation, transformation of the access control model, access control decisions, and misusage and scenario analysis. Therefore, adding more architectural elements might increase the number of result objects but would not gain more insights. Hence, we assume the risk to be low.

External Validity: This is how useful the results are for other researchers and, therefore, how generalizable the results are. Using a case study based evaluation, we might increase the insights into the problem, but the case study might be not representative. Therefore, we choose mostly external case studies, which are used in various approaches such as [20, 22, 40]. Additionally, the maintenance case study (the running example) is based on a scenario from our industrial partners in a previous research project [2]. These external case studies and the industrial one lower the risk of the representativeness. However, the results so far only indicate the functional correctness of the analyses and not the correctness of the approach in general. Therefore, we plan to address this in the future and investigate further case studies and scenarios.

Construct Validity: In our case, this is whether the metrics are appropriate for the intended goal. For **Q1** and **Q2**, we use the JC. It is also used in similar approaches, such as [13]. Its main restriction is that it cannot differentiate the order between elements. However, in our cases, as discussed in Section Sect. 6.1, the order is not relevant. Additionally, for **Q1** and **Q2**, we consider correctness as that the analysis output is equal to the reference output and this is the intended goal for the metric. Therefore, we consider the risk for the metrics to be low.

Reliability: This describes whether other researchers can reproduce the results later. By using statistical metrics we avoid subjective interpretation and therefore can increase reproducibility. Additionally, our dataset [42] allows other researchers to verify the results.

6.4   Limitations

For our approach, we need an architectural model to annotate the system policies. While this is not always true, there exist reengineering approaches, such as Kirschner et al. [21], which help to create one from existing software.

Regarding the dynamic changes of context attributes, we specify that they are at least foreseeable during design time so that they can be expressed in the policies. This is similar to our definition of dynamic changes [39]. Context attributes or scenarios which are not considered during runtime cannot be analyzed.

7   Related Work

We list related approaches regarding our attack propagation in Walter et al. [40]. Here, we focussed on approaches regarding the scenario analysis. We categorized the related work in access control models, access control policy analyses and model-driven confidentiality analyses.

Access Control Models: Role-based access control (RBAC) [10] considers the role for the access decision. However, usually, the role is the only context that is considered. Organisation-based access control (OrBAC) [19] was developed for complex access control policies within an organization and supports multiple different contexts [7]. However, the industrial application is currently very limited. ABAC [15] also considers the context for access decision. ABAC is often described as a dynamic access control approach. XACML [43] is an implementation of ABAC.

Access Control Policy Analyses: Jabal et al. [16] analyze various policy analysis approaches. Margrave [11] is a XACML based verification and change-impact analysis. It uses binary decision trees to decide whether a user can perform certain operations or determine the impact of a policy change. In contrast to our approach, they do not consider the software architecture or misusage scenarios. Alberti et al. [1] analyze a modified RBAC model with additional properties, which can be seen as context properties. One analysis aspect from them is the delegation of RBAC policies. Our approach does not consider the delegation, but we support different scenarios and misusage based on the software architecture. Another XACML based analysis is developed by Turkmen et al. [38]. They internally use satisfiability modulo theories (SMT) to analyze different access control properties such as a change impact and attribute hiding [38]. Overall, there exists different policy analyses approach. However, so far they do not support the scenario-based analysis based on the software architecture. Nevertheless, the XACML based approaches can be used in combination with our access control analysis since XACML files could be used as a universal exchange format.

Model-driven Confidentiality Analyses. Various approaches for model-driven confidentiality analyses exist [28]. We focus here on the most relevant for us. UMLsec [18] is a security extension for UML. It can analyze various security properties such as secure exchange and secure communication. However, they do so far not consider a fine-grained access control model as it is necessary for our running example. Another security extension for UML is SecureUML [24]. It uses an RBAC policy model that can be extended by OCL statements to support context properties. Additionally, it also supports an automatic policy analysis [4]. In contrast, we can consider misusage scenarios in our analysis, and our modeling closely follows an industrial standard which eases the modeling. Data-centric Palladio [33] is a dataflow-based security analysis for the Palladio approach [31]. It provides different analyses such as information flow or access control. However, our extension is defined on the service declaration and not on data objects, and they do not support misusage scenarios. Another dataflow information flow analysis is SecDFD [37]. In contrast, we support misusage scenarios and work on the software architecture. Turkmen et al. [12] present a confidentiality analysis based on timed automatons to analyze the real-time properties of a system. The iFlow approach [20] is a confidentiality analysis for information flow by using UML profiles. In contrast to both previous mentioned ones, we focus more on access control and misusage scenarios.

8 Conclusion and Future Development

In this paper, we first presented our tool for an attack propagation [40]. The tool can help software architects to build more secure systems by providing potential attack paths, which can be broken by introducing mitigation strategies. Secondly, we introduced our approach for a scenario-based access control analysis based on the software architecture. It extends, the access control metamodel from our attack propagation tool and enables software architects to analyze the intended usage and misusage scenarios against the modeled software architecture and the specified software architecture. Our evaluation indicates, that we can detect access violations for system calls and deduce whether scenarios are possible based on the access control decision.

In the future, we want to extend our attack propagation approach by considering advanced mitigation strategies. Additionally, we plan to develop a new security analysis using our metamodel, such as an attack surface analysis and apply both our existing analyses in more case studies. Besides adding new functionality, we also plan to improve the documentation and usability. Here, our focus is on better editor support and error handling. Another open point is the scalability of our analyses. We want to investigate whether we can improve the runtime behavior for more extensive systems.

References

1. Alberti, F., Armando, A., Ranise, S.: Efficient symbolic automated analysis of administrative attribute-based RBAC-policies. In: ASIACCS, p. 165 (2011). ISBN 978-1-4503-0564-8. https://doi.org/10.1145/1966913.1966935, https://portal.acm.org/citation.cfm?doid=1966913.1966935
2. Al-Ali, R., Heinrich, R., Hnetynka, P., Juan-Verdejo, A., Seifermann, S., Walter, M.: Modeling of dynamic trust contracts for industry 4.0 systems. In: ECSA-C, ACM (2018). https://doi.org/10.1145/3241403.3241450
3. Caldiera, V.R.B.G., Rombach, H.D.: The goal question metric approach. Encyclopedia Softw. Eng. 528–532 (1994)
4. Basin, D., et al.: Automated analysis of security-design models. Inf. Softw. Technol. **51**(5), 815–831 (2009)
5. BloodHound Enterprise. https://bloodhoundenterprise.io/. Assessed 05 Oct 2021
6. Cole, E.: Advanced persistent threat: understanding the danger and how to protect your organization. Newnes (2012). ISBN 978-1597499491
7. Cuppens, F., Miège, A.: Modelling contexts in the or-bac model. In: ACSAC, pp. 416–425 (2003)
8. CVSS SIG. https://www.first.org/cvss/. Assessed 25 Oct 2021
9. Deloglos, C., Elks, C., Tantawy, A.: An attacker modeling framework for the assessment of cyber-physical systems security. In: Casimiro, A., Ortmeier, F., Bitsch, F., Ferreira, P. (eds.) SAFECOMP 2020. LNCS, vol. 12234, pp. 150–163. Springer, Cham (2020). https://doi.org/10.1007/978-3-030-54549-9_10
10. Ferraiolo, D., Cugini, J., Kuhn, D.R.: Role-based access control (RBAC): features and motivations. In: ACSAC, pp. 241–248 (1995)
11. Fisler, K., Krishnamurthi, S., Meyerovich, L.A., Tschantz, M.C.: Verification and change-impact analysis of access-control policies. In: ICSE, p. 196 (2005). https://doi.org/10.1145/1062455.1062502
12. Gerking, C., Schubert, D.: In: ICSA, pp. 61–70, 03. ISBN 978-1-7281-0528-4. https://doi.org/10.1109/ICSA.2019.00015
13. Heinrich, R.: Architectural runtime models for integrating runtime observations and component-based models. JSS **169**, 110722 (2020)
14. Heinrich, R., Koch, S., Cha, S., Busch, K., Reussner, R., Vogel-Heuser, B.: Architecture-based change impact analysis in cross-disciplinary automated production systems. JSS **146**, 167–185 (2018). ISSN 0164-1212. https://doi.org/10.1016/j.jss.2018.08.058, https://www.sciencedirect.com/science/article/pii/S0164121218301717
15. Hu, V., et al.: Attribute-based access control. Computer **48**(2), 85–88 (2015). ISSN 0018-9162. https://doi.org/10.1109/MC.2015.33

16. Jabal, A.A., et al.: Methods and tools for policy analysis. ACM Comput. Surv. **51**(6), 1–35 (2019.) ISSN 03600300. https://doi.org/10.1145/3295749

17. Johns, E.: Cyber security breaches survey 2021: Statistical release. Media & Sport, UK and Ipsos Mori, Technical report, Department for Digital, Culture (2021)

18. Jürjens, J.: UMLsec: extending UML for secure systems development. In: Jézéquel, J.-M., Hussmann, H., Cook, S. (eds.) UML 2002. LNCS, vol. 2460, pp. 412–425. Springer, Heidelberg (2002). https://doi.org/10.1007/3-540-45800-X_32

19. Kalam, A., et al.: In: POLICY 2003, 06. https://doi.org/10.1109/POLICY.2003.1206966

20. Katkalov, K., Stenzel, K., Borek, M., Reif, W.: Model-driven development of information flow-secure systems with iflow. In: SOCIALCOM 2013, pp. 51–56. https://doi.org/10.1109/SocialCom.2013.14

21. Kirschner, Y.R., et al.: Automatic derivation of vulnerability models for software architectures. In: ICSA-C (accepted, to appear) (2023)

22. Kramer, M.E., Hecker, M., Greiner, S., Bao, K., Yurchenko, K.: Model-driven specification and analysis of confidentiality in component-based systems. Technical Report 12, KIT-Department of Informatics (2017)

23. Levandowsky, M., Winter, D.: Distance between sets. Nature **234**(5323), 34–35 (1971)

24. Lodderstedt, T., Basin, D., Doser, J.: SecureUML: a UML-based modeling language for model-driven security. In: Jézéquel, J.-M., Hussmann, H., Cook, S. (eds.) UML 2002. LNCS, vol. 2460, pp. 426–441. Springer, Heidelberg (2002). https://doi.org/10.1007/3-540-45800-X_33

25. MITRE: CVE. https://cve.mitre.org/. Assessed 25 Oct 2021

26. MITRE: CWE. https://cwe.mitre.org/. Assessed 25 Oct 2021

27. MITRE: CWE-312. https://cwe.mitre.org/data/definitions/312.html. Assessed 25 Oct 10 2021

28. Nguyen, P.H., Kramer, M., Klein, J., Le Traon, Y.: An extensive systematic review on the model-driven development of secure systems. Inf. Softw. Technol. **68**, 62–81 (2015). ISSN 09505849. https://doi.org/10.1016/j.infsof.2015.08.006

29. NIST. Cve-2021-28374. https://nvd.nist.gov/vuln/detail/CVE-2021-28374

30. NVD. https://nvd.nist.gov/vuln. Assessed 25 Oct 2021

31. Reussner, R., et al.: Modeling and Simulating Software Architectures - The Palladio Approach. MIT Press, Cambridge, MA, October 2016. ISBN 9780262034760. https://mitpress.mit.edu/books/modeling-and-simulating-software-architectures

32. Runeson, P., Höst, M.: Guidelines for conducting and reporting case study research in software engineering **14**(2), 131 (2009). ISSN 1573–7616. https://doi.org/10.1007/s10664-008-9102-8

33. Seifermann, S., Heinrich, R., Werle, D., Reussner, R.: Detecting violations of access control and information flow policies in data flow diagrams. JSS **184**, 1873–1228 (2021). ISSN 0164–1212

34. Xiaokui, S., Ke, T., Andrew, C., Danfeng, Y.: Breaking the target: an analysis of target data breach and lessons learned (2017). https://arxiv.org/abs/1701.04940

35. Sindre, G.: Mal-activity diagrams for capturing attacks on business processes. In: Sawyer, P., Paech, B., Heymans, P. (eds.) REFSQ 2007. LNCS, vol. 4542, pp. 355–366. Springer, Heidelberg (2007). https://doi.org/10.1007/978-3-540-73031-6_27

36. Sindre, G., Opdahl, A.L.: Eliciting security requirements with misuse cases. Requirements Eng. **10**(1), 34–44 (2005). ISSN 0947–3602, 1432–010X. https://doi.org/10.1007/s00766-004-0194-4

37. Tuma, K., Scandariato, R., Balliu, M.: Flaws in flows: unveiling design flaws via information flow analysis. In: ICSA, pp. 191–200 (2019). https://doi.org/10.1109/ICSA.2019.00028
38. Turkmen, F., den Hartog, J., Ranise, S., Zannone, N.: Analysis of XACML policies with SMT. In: Focardi, R., Myers, A. (eds.) POST 2015. LNCS, vol. 9036, pp. 115–134. Springer, Heidelberg (2015). https://doi.org/10.1007/978-3-662-46666-7_7
39. Walter, M., Seifermann, S., Heinrich, R.: A taxonomy of dynamic changes affecting confidentiality. In: 11th Workshop Design For Future - Langlebige Softwaresysteme (2020)
40. Walter, M., Heinrich, R., Reussner, R.: Architectural attack propagation analysis for identifying confidentiality issues. In: IEEE ICSA, pp. 1–12 (2022). https://doi.org/10.1109/ICSA53651.2022.00009
41. Walter, M., et al.: Architectural attack propagation in industry 4.0. at - Automatisierungstechnik (accepted, to appear) (2023)
42. Walter, M., et al.: Dataset: palladio context-based scenario analysis (2022). https://doi.org/10.5281/zenodo.7431562
43. XACML. https://docs.oasis-open.org/xacml/3.0/xacml-3.0-core-spec-osen.html. Accessed 25 Oct 2021
44. Yuan, B., et al.: An attack path generation methods based on graph database. In: ITNEC, pp. 1905–1910 (2020)

Apache Kafka as a Middleware to Support the PLC-Service Bus Architecture with IEC 61499

Virendra Ashiwal[1]($\boxtimes$), Antonio M. Gutierrez[2], Konstantin Aschbacher[3], and Alois Zoitl[2]

[1] LIT CPS Lab, Johannes Kepler University, 4040 Linz, Austria
virendra.ashiwal@jku.at
[2] CDL VaSiCS, LIT CPS Lab, Johannes Kepler University, 4040 Linz, Austria
[3] Johannes Kepler University, 4040 Linz, Austria

Abstract. Flexible, loosely coupled, and adaptable PLC software is required to meet the current market demand for customization, improved product quality, and variability in manufacturing systems. The PLC-Service bus is an architecture that improves flexibility and adaptability and provides loosely coupled PLC software. This paper integrates Apache Kafka as a network layer into Eclipse 4diac™ (open source IEC 61499 implementation) to use state-of-the-art messaging functionality and implement the PLC-Service bus architecture. With this tool, we can easily configure and orchestrate PLC software based on events. Also, the number of monitor tools for Apache Kafka allows us to avoid ad-hoc developments and use existing out-of-the-box solutions to monitor and analyze the message traffic.
Video: https://www.youtube.com/watch?v=j3Gbk1BhMzE.

Keywords: IEC 61499 · PLC software · PLC-Service Bus · Factory automation · Middleware technology · Apache Kafka

1 Introduction

Programmable logic controllers (PLCs) are an essential component of production systems for automating and controlling machines and their processes. IEC 61131 [6] and IEC 61499 [22] are two available standards providing guidelines for a PLC software architecture and programming in the industrial automation domain. Vendors and consumers of automation technology have largely adopted the IEC-61131 [6] standard for PLC programming. According to [6], PLC software comprises many program organization units (POUs), the smallest units of software components. These POUs can be a function, a function block, or a program. This paper uses the term "software components" for POUs. In practice, global variables are heavily used to establish interaction between these software components [18,28], resulting in tight coupling, less flexibility, less adaptability, and high cost for maintenance [11]. The PLC-Service Bus architectural concept

T. Batista et al. (Eds.): ECSA 2022, LNCS 13928, pp. 62–74, 2023.
https://doi.org/10.1007/978-3-031-36889-9_6

was proposed in [11] to address these identified issues. The architecture was inspired by enterprise service bus [14] to introduce loose coupling in PLC software using a middleware. IEC 61499 is a visual programming language for PLC software. We identified the suitability of IEC 61499 for the PLC-Service Bus architecture in our previous work [8]. IEC 61499 provides infrastructure support to integrate middleware technology for the PLC-Service Bus, but there is no tool that provides middleware as a network protocol.

This paper validates the software architecture concept in the industrial domain, because one-to-one direct mapping of architectural concepts is not possible due to domain-specific constraints. This paper provides a way to integrate middleware in an IEC 61499-based tool for PLC application engineers so they can design their PLC software without putting affords for networking and communication. Apache Kafka is considered as middleware in this paper. The background of the PLC-Service Bus and its message interaction patterns are described in the next section. An existing ad-hoc implementation with its limitation are presented in Sect. 3. The integration of Apache Kafka is described in Sect. 4. A running example and the implementation to integrate Apache Kafka as a network layer for IEC 61499 are described in Sect. 5. Related work is reviewed in Sect. 6. Section 7 discusses the benefits and limitations of Kafka as a middleware technology for the PLC software. Finally, Sect. 8 concludes with future work.

2   Background

This section describes the background of the architecture and provides an introduction to IEC 61499.

2.1   Architectural Background

PLC-Service Bus: The PLC-Service Bus is an architectural concept [11] for the PLC software to improve its flexibility, adaptability, and enable loose coupling between its software components. A software component is the smallest independent unit in the architecture, and it is where each machine's functions are programmed. Therefore, each software component is independent and can be updated separately to meet future needs. In order to provide overall machine functionality, software components at the PLC-Service Bus use middleware to interact; thus, they are all loosely coupled. In our previous work [11], we identified requirements for the architecture to fulfill the domain constraint of industrial automation. We have also identified a catalog of message interaction patterns (MIPs), which empower software components to interact with each other.

Message Interaction Patterns (MIPs): Interaction patterns are best practices, good designs, and ways of capturing experiences in a way that allows others to reuse them. They are well established in mainstream enterprise software domain [21]. Very few of them have been utilized in PLC software. We analyzed the applicability of these patterns for the PLC-Service Bus architecture with its requirements; as a result, a catalog of MIPs was identified [10]. MIPs for the PLC-Service Bus are grouped as follows: (i) Message Construction, (ii) Message Channels, (iii) Message Endpoints, (iv) Message Routing, and (v) Message Translation. These identified MIPs are essential for software components within the architecture to communicate with each other to provide certain machine functionality. The applicability of these MIPs to a production system depends on its process and product workflow. Ashiwal et al. (2012, implementing) describe a method for identifying these MIPs for a manufacturing system.

2.2 IEC 61499

With the increasing share of software being used in the industrial automation domain, a demand for distributed control systems has emerged. IEC 61499 describes a domain-specific modeling language that can be used to build distributed control systems that are portable, interoperable, configurable, distributable, and re-configurable [5]. Individual pieces of the distributed system have intelligence and can interact with one another. An application in IEC 61499 consists of one or more function blocks (FBs). These FBs are programmed with IEC 61131–3 programming languages, which are specific for PLCs. IEC 61499 provide three kinds of FBs: (i) Basic FBs (BFB) provide a state machine functionality, (ii) Composite FBs (CFB) simply provide networked IEC 61499 FBs, and (iii) Service interface FBs (SIFB) provide access to specific parts of a hardware and can be also used to integrate any communication with third parties.

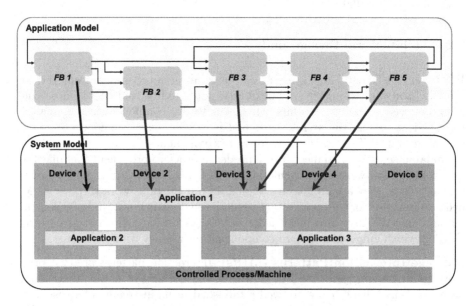

Fig. 1. IEC 61499 based application [5]

Once the application has been developed, it can be distributed among the respective control devices, as shown in Fig. 1. In this paper, we are using the Eclipse 4diac project to implement the PLC-Service Bus architecture. The Eclipse 4diac project's goal is to provide an open, IEC 61499-compliant framework for reference implementation. It provides two main parts: (i) **4diac IDE** and (ii) **4diac FORTE**. 4diac IDE provides an engineering environment to design and model distributed control applications. We will use 4diac IDE to implement software components as its encapsulated function blocks. The 4diac IDE already provides some library types, but it is also possible to create custom types as required. The 4diac IDE already supports some of the MIPs identified in our previous work [8], nevertheless, there is also the possibility to implement other MIPs as FBs. And 4diac FORTE provides an IEC 61499 runtime environment that supports execution of IEC 61499-based control applications on embedded devices. It is a small, portable C++-based implementation. 4diac FORTE supports multi-threading, and it runs on top of a real-time operating system [4].

3   PLC-Service Bus with IEC 61499

This section discusses the current status of implementing a production system based on the PLC-Service Bus with IEC 61499 and its current limitations.

3.1   Ad-hoc Implementation

With the available list of requirements [11], and catalog of MIPs [10], in [9], the authors have provided an approach to implement the PLC software of a production system based on the PLC-Service Bus architecture with IEC 61499. IEC 61499 is a graphical programming language based on function blocks which uses event-based execution for interaction between its software components and does not support global variables. Therefore, IEC 61499 supports reusability without any hidden dependencies and strong support of encapsulation by the standard.

As a first step, MIPs from the production system were identified and then cross-checked to see if the relevant supporting MIPs were available in IEC 61499. We used event-driven process chain (EPC) [24] to identify existing MIPs in a given production system. With EPC, an automation engineer can easily see the interaction between software components, which would help him understand the overall process of implementing PLC software. Any MIP which is not supported by IEC 61499 needs to be implemented by an automation engineer. Once software components of relevant production systems (FBs in IEC 61499) were available, event messages and events with data messages from IEC 61499 were used as the message creation pattern of the MIPs. These messages were transported via publish-subscribe function blocks to their receiver-side software components. These publish-subscribe function blocks support the publish-subscribe pattern by the message channel group from the MIPs of the PLC-Service Bus architecture.

3.2   Limitations

Although IEC 61499 supports some requirements for the PLC-Service Bus, it does not have all the equivalent MIPs of the PLC-Service Bus by default. Engineers can implement the missing MIPs from scratch with FB, but it is time-consuming [8]. As we know, MIPs of the PLC-Service Bus architecture were identified from the enterprise domain with the applicability of the architecture and its requirements [10]. Therefore, MIPs, which are not feasible to implement in IEC 61499, can be integrated using suitable state-of-the-art middleware technology from the enterprise domain as a message channel. IEC 61499 was initially designed to support distributed architecture rather than middleware architecture. However, middleware technology can be integrated using IEC 61499's communication network infrastructure available for the distribution architecture.

4   Apache Kafka with IEC 61499

In this part, we will first discuss Apache Kafka's suitability as middleware for the PLC-Service Bus architecture and then demonstrate its integration as a network layer with the Eclipse 4diac project.

4.1   Suitability of Apache Kafka as a Middleware

Authors in [9] provide a two stage approach to identify suitable middleware technology for the PLC-Service Bus architecture. In the first stage, suitable middlewares for IEC 61499 were shortlisted. Then, these shortlisted middleware technologies were compared based on the requirements [11] of the PLC-Service Bus architecture which are essential for the handling and interaction aspects of the software components. Apache Kafka and Data Distribution Service (DDS) were identified as suitable middleware technologies for the PLC-Service Bus architecture in IEC 61499. This paper focuses on integrating Apache Kafka with 4diac FORTE.

In today's data-driven, connected production system, it's really important to have an ecosystem like Apache Kafka that provides an open, scalable, and reliable infrastructure for integrating and processing data. Apache Kafka supports event streaming, making it possible to process huge amounts of data in real time. It also opens a door to the integration of advanced data processing pipelines, such as AI/ML integration, down to the PLC level.

4.2   Integration of Apache Kafka

This paper uses Eclipse 4diac [4], an open source project based on IEC 61499 for implementation. Section 2 provide background information for Eclipse 4diac. The Eclipse 4diac project contains 4diac IDE [2] as a development environment and 4diac FORTE [1] as a runtime environment. 4diac FORTE contains communication network infrastructure (SIFB FBs) to support integration of Apache Kafka.

4diac FORTE implements a layer design pattern to have a flexible network interface and to support any future adaptation of a protocol in 4diac FORTE. An overview of the network layer is shown in Fig. 2. A generic interface as defined

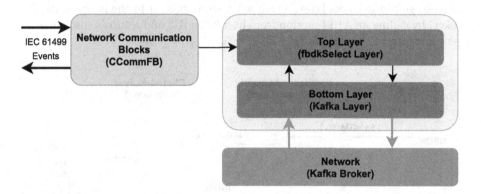

Fig. 2. Overview of the Network Layer

in Eclipse 4diac documentation [3] is available for integrating a new protocol. This interface defines functions for each of these layers, such as

- (I) openConnection: called by FB to open a connection and has to be implemented by every layer and by the network stack,
- (II) closeConnection: called by the FB to close a connection, has to be implemented by every layer and by the network stack,
- (III) sendData: called by the function block to send a message over the network, has to be implemented by every layer and by the network stack,
- (IV) recvData: called when new messages are received from the network, has to be implemented by every layer.
- (V) processInterrupt: called from the network stack when a layer needs to process data.

CCommFB is a class of network communication FBs, i.e. *PUBLISH* and *SUBSCRIBE*. These FBs are available at 4diac IDE for an application engineer to use as an interface to a network where they can publish or subscribe to specific messages. With the ad-hoc implementation, there was the limitation of using *SUBSCRIBE* FB and *PUBLISH* FB only with the same amount of data pins. With our *fbdkSelect layer* as shown in Fig. 2, we addressed this issue. The *fbdkSelect layer* communicates with these FBs for publishing and subscribing messages. And finally, we have developed a *Kafka layer*[1], that uses *librdkafka* [16], an Apache Kafka C++ client library at 4diac FORTE. The *Kafka layer* receives the data from the *fbdkSelect layer* in the case of publishing, and in the case of subscribing, it provides the messages from the Apache Kafka broker. The *Kafka layer* uses ASN.1 encoding and TCP connection as a transport layer.

---

[1] https://github.com/KonstiBPC/4diac-kafka.

A sequence diagram for publishing a message is shown in Fig. 3. The basic functionality of the layer design pattern is to get the data from the above layer, pack it and pass it to the layer beneath. The fbdkSelect layer gets the message from *PUBLISH* FB when *REQ+* is triggered. It will call *:sendData(..)* and pass the message to the Kafka layer, which will then publish it to the network (Kafka broker) by calling an API function from librdkafka [16] and return a confirmation event message to the *PUBLISH* FB.

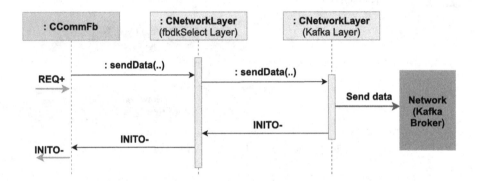

Fig. 3. Send data from 4diac application to Kafka Broker

A sequence diagram for receiving a message via *SUBSCRIBE* FB is shown in Fig. 4. Here, the working of the fbdkSelect layer is similar to that previously described. With polling, a new message from the network (Kafka broker) can be received at the Kafka layer. Here, 4diac FORTE implements an External Handler, responsible for processing external interrupts and starting new event chain execution threads. The Kafka layer invokes the FB thread by calling *:interruptCommFB(..)*. Once the external event is received, *SUBSCRIBE* FB will call *:processInterrupt(..)*. Following that *:recvData(..)* will be called from the Kafka layer to the fbdkSelect layer until *SUBSCRIBE* FB receives the message and triggers the CNF+/IND+ event.

5   Using Apache Kafka as Middleware for the PLC-Service Bus

With Apache Kafka as network layer in 4diac FORTE, it brings middleware support. This section implements running example based on the PLC-Service Bus architecture using Apache Kafka as middleware in IEC 61499.

5.1   Running Example

As a running example, we considered station 3 from the VDMA R+A OPC UA Demonstrator[2] [31]. This station is responsible for placing two caps on each side

---

[2] https://www.youtube.com/watch?v=pUtSA8g9owY&ab_channel=fortiss.

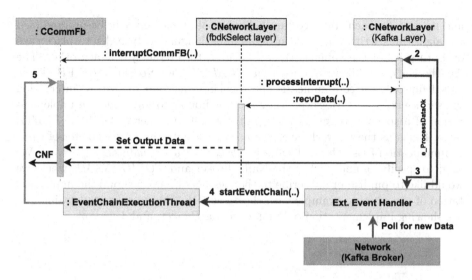

Fig. 4. Receiving data from 4diac application to Kafka Broker

of the spinner. There are seven main mechatronics components in the station: (i) a *Bunker* which provides the caps (without a precise position), (ii) a *Vibrator* to enforce that desired cap is in a reachable position with the proper orientation, (iii) a *Camera* to evaluates if at least one available caps at the *Vibrator* matches the required color by the spinner and is reachable by the *Axis*, (iv) a *Vacuum Gripper* which grabs and presses the caps on the spinner, (v) an *Axis* which moves a cap from *Vibrator* to the spinner, (vi) a *Gripper* to hold the spinner while it is capped and to rotate it with 180° so that the same process of placing cap can be performed on the other side of the spinner, (vii) a *Lifter* for vertically ascending and descending the spinner to the position of the *Gripper*.

In [8], we proposed a design based on independent components for each element of the station that communicate through events. However, in the paper, the implementation of the PLC-Service Bus was developed using IEC 61499, which is subject to certain limitations, identified in the Sect. 3.

5.2 Implementation

With Apache Kafka as middleware integrated with 4diac FORTE, we implement our running example with the PLC-Service Bus architecture in IEC 61499. Using EPC, MIPs from the running example were identified with the approach described in [8]. The identified MIPs are event message, document message, content filter, and publish-subscribe pattern. A detailed explanation is already available in [8]. Each element of station 3 is programmed as a basic FB in IEC 61499 in an encapsulated way. The basic FB [22] contains events and data as the interface to the outside world and a state machine called Event Execution Control (ECC) to show the element's behavior. ECC changes its state based on input events and its data. In each state, certain behaviors of an element can be programmed via algorithms written in PLC programming languages. In order to place caps on both sides of the spinner, these FBs need to interact with each other. The Apache Kafka middleware is used via *PUBLISH* and *SUBSCRIBE* FB. These FBs define only the communication protocol interface and an abstract interaction via service sequence. However, they are not bound to any concrete implementation of a specific communication protocol [20]. In order to let 4diac FORTE select Kafka as the network layer, we need to specify the ID parameter of these communication FBs. The ID format is *"fbdk[ ].kafka[<ipaddress>:<port>]"*. We need to specify *ip* and *port* of the Kafka broker and *TOPIC_NAME* where we would like to publish or subscribe to the message. Figure 5 shows the implementation of our running example with the 4diac IDE. Due to space constraints, we are showing implementation only for *Camera, Bunker,* and *Vibrator.*

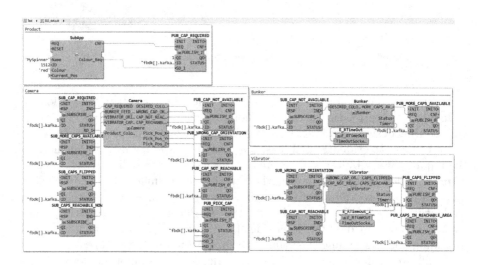

Fig. 5. PLC software based on PLC-Service bus architecture with IEC 61499

6   Related Work

The middleware concept is already been explored in the embedded and robotics domains. The Common Object Request Broker Architecture (CORBA) was released in 1991 by the Object Management Group (OMG) as middleware for distributed object computing [7]. In 2004 D.C. Schmidt et al. [25] discussed the importance of middleware for distributed real-time and embedded system.

In the field of industrial automation, however, it has been only in recent years, that there has been an increase amount of literature on middleware solutions [12,19,23,27,30]. All of them are focused on the shop floor and how different devices and applications can share data to make Industry 4.0 scenarios possible. Authors in [17, 26, 29] compare various well-known middlewares. In [13] proposes a platform to address data collection from machinery on the shop floor using Apache Kafka. Apache Kafka is used for data acquisition for predictive maintenance in [15]. However, the use of middleware for PLC software had never been discussed before the PLC-Service Bus architecture was proposed in [11].

7   Discussion

The developed *Kafka layer* enables a PLC-service Bus based on Apache Kafka middleware with support for a catalog of MIPs. The integration mechanism relies on the network layer, so additional implementation can be considered to support more middleware technologies (e.g., DDS, RabbitMQ, and ActiveMQ). In order to connect a new 4diac application (e.g., Camera) as a component in our system, we only need to configure the config ID at *PUBLISH/SUBSCRIBE* FBs with middleware endpoint. The events are mapped to topics in Apache Kafka, and each publication or subscription interface could be independently configured to a different middleware.

Because of its performance and low latency, Apache Kafka is widely used in the industry. It also provides federation mechanisms that can be adapted to performance or deployment requirements in a way that is transparent to the software components. Also, Apache Kafka provides the infrastructure to monitor and log events, and there are several out-of-the-box solutions to analyze and monitor Apache Kafka's execution. For example, we have configured a Grafana platform to monitor our example scenario. In Fig. 6, we depict a simulated execution trace where each time a *CAP REQUIRED* event is triggered (which is the starting event for the station 3), a *WRONG CAP ORIENTATION* event is produced. This behavior results from a simulation, but it should be considered a potential malfunction in a real scenario. Such tools can track events, monitor performance, or predict possible errors.

Fig. 6. Monitoring of Apache Kafka Topics using Grafana

In the current implementation and running scenario, there are still some MIPs not supported (e.g. Message Routing) that remains as future work.

8   Conclusion and Future Work

In this work, we have initially discussed the current status and limitations of the PLC-Service Bus with IEC 61499. Later, we presented how to integrate Apache Kafka as middleware technology for the architecture implementation in IEC 61499. A running example shows how to use Apache Kafka in IEC 61499 as PLC-service Bus to orchestrate the different machines in a capping station.

As future work, in addition to implementing additional MIPs, we consider the evaluation of the architecture should be the main focus.

Acknowledgements. The financial support by the Austrian Federal Ministry for Digital and Economic Affairs, the National Foundation for Research, Technology and Development, and the Christian Doppler Research Association is gratefully acknowledged.

References

1. 4diac FORTE. https://www.eclipse.org/4diac/en_rte.php
2. 4diac IDE. https://www.eclipse.org/4diac/en_ide.php
3. Communication architecture. https://www.eclipse.org/4diac/en_help.php?helppage=html/development/forte_communicationArchitecture.html
4. Eclipse 4diac - Open source PLC framework for industrial automation & control. https://www.eclipse.org/4diac/index.php
5. Eclipse 4diac documentation. https://www.eclipse.org/4diac/en_help.php?helppage=html/before4DIAC/iec61499.html. Accessed 29 Dec 2022
6. Programmable controllers-part 3: programming languages. Standard IEC 61131–3:2013, International Electrotechnical Commission
7. Common object request broker architecture. https://www.omg.org/spec/CORBA/1.0. August 1991. Accessed 04 Jan 2023
8. Ashiwal, V., Gutierrez, A.M., Zoitl, A.: Implementing a PLC-service bus with IEC 61499. In: 2022 IEEE 5th International Conference on Industrial Cyber-Physical Systems (ICPS), pp. 01–07 (2022). https://doi.org/10.1109/ICPS51978.2022.9816929
9. Ashiwal, V., Majumder, M., Zoitl, A.: Evaluation of middleware technologies for the plc-service bus in IEC 61499. In: 2022 IEEE 27th International Conference on Emerging Technologies and Factory Automation (ETFA), pp. 1–4 (2022). https://doi.org/10.1109/ETFA52439.2022.9921536
10. Ashiwal, V., Zoitl, A.: Messaging interaction patterns for a service bus concept of PLC-software. In: 2021 26th IEEE International Conference on Emerging Technologies and Factory Automation (ETFA), pp. 1–8 (2021). https://doi.org/10.1109/ETFA45728.2021.9613638
11. Ashiwal, V., Zoitl, A., Konnerth, M.: A service bus concept for modular and adaptable PLC-software. In: 2020 25th IEEE International Conference on Emerging Technologies and Factory Automation (ETFA), vol. 1, pp. 22–29 (2020). https://doi.org/10.1109/ETFA46521.2020.9211908
12. Balador, A., Ericsson, N., Bakhshi, Z.: Communication middleware technologies for industrial distributed control systems: a literature review. In: 2017 22nd IEEE International Conference on Emerging Technologies and Factory Automation (ETFA), pp. 1–6 (2017). https://doi.org/10.1109/ETFA.2017.8247730

13. Bosi, F., et al.: Cloud-enabled smart data collection in shop floor environments for industry 4.0. In: 2019 15th IEEE International Workshop on Factory Communication Systems (WFCS), pp. 1–8 (2019). https://doi.org/10.1109/WFCS.2019.8757952

14. Breest, M., Schulte, R.: An introduction to the enterprise service bus (2006)

15. Canizo, M., Onieva, E., Conde, A., Charramendieta, S., Trujillo, S.: Real-time predictive maintenance for wind turbines using big data frameworks. In: 2017 IEEE International Conference on Prognostics and Health Management (ICPHM), pp. 70–77 (2017). https://doi.org/10.1109/ICPHM.2017.7998308

16. Edenhill, M.: librdkafka - the apache kafka c/c++ client library, June 2022. https://github.com/edenhill/librdkafka

17. Fu, G., Zhang, Y., Yu, G.: A fair comparison of message queuing systems. IEEE Access **9**, 421–432 (2021). https://doi.org/10.1109/ACCESS.2020.3046503

18. Fuchs, J., Feldmann, S., Legat, C., Vogel-Heuser, B.: Identification of design patterns for IEC 61131-3 in machine and plant manufacturing. IFAC Proc. Volumes **47**(3), 6092–6097 (2014) https://doi.org/10.3182/20140824-6-ZA-1003.01595, https://www.sciencedirect.com/science/article/pii/S1474667016425668, 19th IFAC World Congress

19. Gosewehr, F., Wermann, J., Borsych, W., Colombo, A.W.: Apache camel based implementation of an industrial middleware solution. In: 2018 IEEE Industrial Cyber-Physical Systems (ICPS), pp. 523–528 (2018). https://doi.org/10.1109/ICPHYS.2018.8390760

20. Hofmann, M., Rooker, M., Zoitl, A.: Improved communication model for an IEC 61499 runtime environment. In: ETFA2011, pp. 1–7 (2011). https://doi.org/10.1109/ETFA.2011.6059121

21. Hohpe, G., Woolf, B.: Enterprise Integration Patterns: Designing, Building, and Deploying Messaging Solutions. Addison-Wesley Longman Publishing Co., Inc, USA (2003)

22. IEC TC65/WG6: IEC 61499-1, function blocks - part 1: architecture v2.0: Edition 2.0 https://www.iec.ch

23. Neves, D.T., Santos, M., Pinto, M.: Reactor: a middleware as a service to interact with objects remotely. In: 2015 IEEE International Conference on Industrial Technology (ICIT), pp. 2433–2439 (2015). https://doi.org/10.1109/ICIT.2015.7125456

24. Scheer, A.W., Thomas, O., Adam, O.: Process modeling using event-driven process chains, chap. 6, pp. 119–145. John Wiley & Sons, Ltd (2005). https://doi.org/10.1002/0471741442.ch6,https://onlinelibrary.wiley.com/doi/abs/10.1002/0471741442.ch6

25. Schmidt, D.C., Gokhale, A., Schantz, R.E., Loyall, J.P.: Middleware r&d challenges for distributed real-time and embedded systems. SIGBED Rev. **1**(1), 6–12 (2004). https://doi.org/10.1145/1121554.1121556

26. Sommer, P., Schellroth, F., Fischer, M., Schlechtendahl, J.: Message-oriented middleware for industrial production systems. In: 2018 IEEE 14th International Conference on Automation Science and Engineering (CASE), pp. 1217–1223 (2018). https://doi.org/10.1109/COASE.2018.8560493

27. Strljic, M.M., Vollmann, C., Riedel, O.: Shop-floor service connector - a message-oriented middleware focused on the usability and infrastructure requirements of SMEs developing smart services. In: 2020 3rd IEEE International Conference on Knowledge Innovation and Invention (ICKII), pp. 37–40 (2020). https://doi.org/10.1109/ICKII50300.2020.9318831

28. Wenger, M., Hametner, R., Zoitl, A.: Iec 61131–3 control applications vs. control applications transformed in IEC 61499. IFAC Proc. Volumes **43**(4), 30–35 (2010). https://doi.org/10.3182/20100701-2-PT-4011.00007, https://www. sciencedirect.com/science/article/pii/S1474667015301130, 10th IFAC Workshop on Intelligent Manufacturing Systems

29. Yongguo, J., Qiang, L., Changshuai, Q., Jian, S., Qianqian, L.: Message-oriented middleware: a review. 2019 5th International Conference on Big Data Computing and Communications (BIGCOM), pp. 88–97 (2019)

30. Zarte, M., Pechmann, A., Wermann, J., Gosewehr, F., Colombo, A.W.: Building an industry 4.0-compliant lab environment to demonstrate connectivity between shop floor and it levels of an enterprise. In: IECON 2016–42nd Annual Conference of the IEEE Industrial Electronics Society, pp. 6590–6595 (2016). https://doi.org/ 10.1109/IECON.2016.7792956

31. Zimmermann, P., Axmann, E., Brandenbourger, B., Dorofeev, K., Mankowski, A., Zanini, P.: Skill-based engineering and control on field-device-level with OPC UA. In: 2019 24th IEEE International Conference on Emerging Technologies and Factory Automation (ETFA), pp. 1101–1108 (2019). https://doi.org/10.1109/ETFA. 2019.8869473

A Toolchain for Simulation Component Specification and Identification

Sandro Koch$^{(\boxtimes)}$ and Frederik Reiche

KASTEL – Institute of Information Security and Dependability, Karlsruhe Institute
of Technology (KIT), Karlsruhe, Germany
{sandro.koch,frederik.reiche}@kit.edu

Abstract. Reusing a simulation or parts of it is difficult, because simulations are tightly coupled to a specific domain or even to the analysed system. In a set of simulation components, either publicly available or from internal repositories, it is difficult for simulation developers to find simulation components that can be reused in a new context. They have to understand the structure and the behaviour of a component to determine, whether it fits for the new context. To address this problem, we introduce our toolchain that allows simulation developers to specify the structure and behaviour of a simulation component. We utilise a state-of-the-art graph database and an SMT theorem prover to compare a simulation components. This allows simulation developers to compare and search for simulation components that can be reused instead of being redeveloped.

Keywords: simulation reuse · component compare · simulation
specification · domain-specific modelling language

1 Introduction

The specification of a software architecture, e.g. UML class models, is an abstraction of the actual code of the software system. The software architecture covers the structure of the software system; for the behaviour of a system, a different type of model is necessary. In the context of a simulation, the behaviour of the simulation and the behaviour of the system are very similar. For a software system's performance simulation, the developer must understand how to implement the simulation and how a performance simulation functions. To reduce the complexity and the effort of implementing a simulation, especially reimplementing already existing parts of a simulation, we proposed our approach to specify the structure and behaviour simulation components [10]. We use the specification of simulation components to identify other components with similar structures

This work was funded by the Deutsche Forschungsgemeinschaft (DFG, German Research Foundation) – Project number 499241390 (FeCoMASS) and by the Federal Ministry of Education and Research (BMBF) under the funding number 01IS18067D (RESPOND).

T. Batista et al. (Eds.): ECSA 2022, LNCS 13928, pp. 75–89, 2023.
https://doi.org/10.1007/978-3-031-36889-9_7

and behaviour. Our approach allows the simulation developer to compare and find simulation components they can reuse in subsequent simulation projects. We decompose a simulation into individual features that allow the simulation developer to manage and reuse them individually. A *simulation feature* is an abstraction of a system's property that the simulation can analyse, for example, the property *throughput* to simulate the performance of a system. We focus on implementing a simulation feature, the *simulation component*. A simulation component comprises packages, classes, and simulation algorithms.

The toolchain we present in this paper allows simulation developers to specify the structure and behaviour of a simulation component by using model-based editors. We use the specification to compare simulation components to find simulation components that the simulation developer can reuse in a different context. To compare simulation components, we use two approaches. First, our tool uses the specification to compare the structure of the simulation components to identify whether the compared simulation components are structurally identical. However, an identical structure is insufficient to determine a reusable simulation feature [18]. Therefore, we also implemented the second step, comparing a simulation component based on the behaviour.

This paper is structured as follows: In Sect. 2 we present approaches related to this work. In Sect. 3 we introduce our toolchain: First, we present the specification part in Sect. 3.1, and then we present the identification part in Sect. 3.2. Finally, in Sect. 4 we conclude the paper, and in Sect. 5 we present the next steps we planned for the toolchain.

2   Related Work

For source code comparison we found the tool JPlag which can find similarities in Java, C#, C, and C++ source code [14]. JPlag is used to detect software plagiarism. Gitchel et al. [7] developed the tool SIM, which compares source code written in C, Java, Pascal, and Lisp. Its approach is similar to JPlag, both use a tokeniser approach for comparing the source code. SIM is also able to take the correctness, style and uniqueness of the code into account. Measure Of Software Similarity (MOOS) is another tool that can compare source code [17]. In contrast to JPlag and SIM does MOOS support 26 different programming languages [1]. These tools focus on similarities regarding the structure of the source code, in contrast to our work is the behaviour is not part of their analyses.

Another approach, FOCUS, by Ringert et al. [16] provides a mathematical semantics for the specification of structure and behaviour of software systems. FOCUS can also specify quality and domain-specific properties of a software system [11]. Graphical approaches such as UML-based Activity Diagrams, Flow Diagrams or Activity Cycle Diagrams can be used to describe the structure of a simulation and specify the flow of events [2]. FOCUS and UML are too broad, they can model any kind of software system; therefore, they require additional training for non-domain experts to model *Discrete-Event Simulation* (DES).

The refinement of relations and various forms of simulation dependencies are investigated by Milner [12]. Clarke et al. [4] investigate the satisfaction of temporal logic formulas by automata, and Richters et al. [15] check the consistency of object structures regarding data structures. The *Discrete Event System Specification* (DEVS) formalism [22] is a formal approach to describing and analysing discrete event systems. Other approaches, like Condition Specification Language (CSL) [13] or the OMNeT++ framework [20], combine simulation specifications with a description language. These approaches use general-purpose languages like C or Java for their specification, comparing these specifications would require to compare the structure and behaviour on the source-code level. Our approach allows the straightforward transformation of declarative expressions to *Satisfiability Modulo Theories* (SMT)-instances and their comparison with an SMT-solver.

For the specification of an architecture for distributed simulations that allow the interoperability and reuse [9] of simulations, the *High-Level Architecture* (HLA) was developed by the Modelling and Simulation Coordination Office of the US Department of Defence. Another specification approach, the *Functional Mock-up Interface* (FMI) [3] standard, helps to define an interface for exchanging information and coupling between heterogeneous software systems used for Model Exchange and Co-Simulation. Both approaches, the HLA and the FMI, can be combined to facilitate the reuse of simulation models in complex engineered systems [6]. However, in contrast to our work, these approaches lack the ability to compare and identify simulation components.

3 The Toolchain for Simulation Specification and Simulation Component Identification

We separated our toolchain to specify and identify simulation components into two parts. Figure 1 depicts the third-party tools we used and the tools we developed to realise the specification and identification of simulation components.

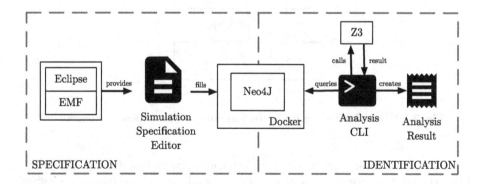

Fig. 1. Specification and Analysis Toolchain

Our contributions are the *Simulation Specification Editor*, the *Analysis Command Line Interface (CLI)*, and the *Analysis Results*; they are depicted in black. This section details how we implemented the toolchain and how it is used. First, in Sect. 3.1, we present how one can specify simulation components with our tooling. Second, in Sect. 3.2, we present how one can use our tooling to identify similar simulation components.

3.1   Specification of Simulation Components

The Simulation Specification Editor is based on our metamodels from our previous work [10]. Events, entities, and attributes are the three elements that make up what we refer to as the structure of a simulation. According to this viewpoint on the structure of a simulation, an event is nothing more than a different object devoid of any behavioural characteristics. The structure of a discrete event simulation can be modelled using the metamodel that is shown in Fig. 2. A *Simulation* is made of a collection of *Entities* and *Events*, and each *Entity* is made of a collection of typed *Attributes*. In addition, *Events* can read *Attributes* of *Entities*. This dependency indicates which attributes are affected by an event. Because performing a read operation on an attribute has no impact on the simulation world, this relationship is considered to be a component of the structural metamodel.

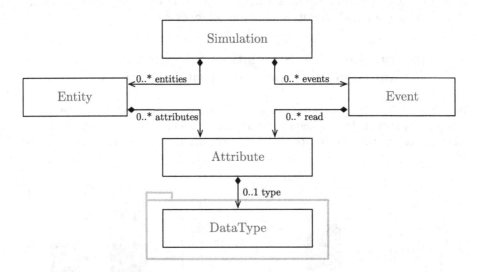

Fig. 2. Metamodel for Specifying the Structure of Simulation Components

The metamodel used to describe the behavioural aspects is displayed in Fig. 3. Even though the term behaviour can have several distinct meanings, we define the behaviour of a simulation to be the impacts of events on the state of the simulation world, i.e., changes to attributes that are triggered through events.

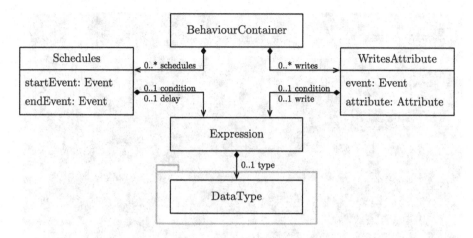

Fig. 3. Metamodel for Specifying the Behaviour of Simulation Components

When attempting to specify the behaviour of a simulation, in addition to the structure of the simulation, two additional notions are required. (i) During its execution, a simulation will modify the simulation world. The metamodel must be able to specify modified attributes in order for it to express changes to the simulation world. Furthermore, the metamodel must be able to provide to model the modification of attributes in order for it to express changes to the simulation world. These changes are included as part of the simulation's specification. (ii) In DES, attribute changes can only take place during events. Furthermore, an event can occur at any time, which signifies a change in the simulation world. The order in which events are scheduled and the times at which they occur indirectly will influence the simulation world's status. Events will cause other events to be delayed in their scheduling.

In order to specify a simulation, we implemented the metamodels in the *Eclipse Modelling Framework* (EMF)[1]. EMF is an extension of the Integrated Development Environment (IDE) Eclipse. EMF provides graphical editors to create metamodels, and it also provides developers with code generators to create code stubs of the metamodel classes and tree-editors for the metamodels.

As shown in Fig. 1, EMF provides the editor to create the simulation specification. We utilised the tree-based editors so that the simulation developer could model a simulation component graphically. The simulation developer can model the structure and behaviour of a simulation component in the tree editor. It is necessary to model both: the structure and the behaviour of a simulation component to compare and identify identical components [10]. Figure 4 shows the tree editor in Eclipse to specify simulation components.

Each simulation component is stored in a `*.structure` file. The developer can edit these files with the *structure tree-editor*. Each node in the editor is created with a unique *ID* and *name* property. The *root node* represents the

---

[1] https://www.eclipse.org/modeling/emf/.

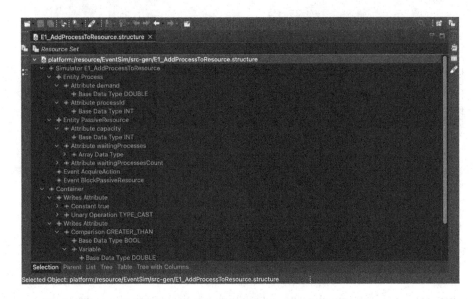

Fig. 4. Simulation Specification Editor

simulation component; the developer can add a description in addition to the ID and name. The root node contains *entities* and *events*. All entities have *attributes* that are either *base datatypes* like integers or booleans, or *arrays* or *enums*. Each event can reference any number of attributes to indicate a *reads* relationship.

In order to separate the structure from the behaviour, the behaviour is modelled in a separate section, but it is stored in the same file. The metamodels of structure and behaviour are modelled according to the reference architecture for domain-specific modelling languages [8]. The modular structure of the metamodels allows us to maintain and extend the metamodels separately and use an editor that references both metamodels. The behaviour consists of *writes attribute* and *schedules* relationships. According to our metamodel, each writes attribute is linked to one event. When the event is fired, the writes attribute contains a condition; if this condition is true, the referenced attribute gets changed. How an attribute is changed is also modelled in the writes attribute.

Events are also able to schedule other events. To model the scheduling of events, developers can add the *schedules* node to the tree editor. A schedules node references the causing event and the event to schedule. In order to determine whether the simulation component schedules an event, the node also contains the condition and a reference to the attributes that are evaluated.

For the specification to be used for comparison, we transform the specification into a graph (cf. Koch et al. [10]). In Fig. 5, we show an example of the structural information stored in the graph. The stored simulation component represents the simulation of a traffic light. The graph contains one *entity*, two *attributes* and two *events*. The entity *TrafficLight* represents the simulated traffic light. The *TrafficLight* contains the two attributes *colourTraffic* and *waitingPedes.* The attribute *colourTraffic* represents the colour of the traffic light (red or green), and the attribute *waitingPedes.* represents the number of pedestrians that wait at the traffic light. Besides the entity and the two attributes, the graph also contains the events *PedestrianRed* and *PedestrianGreen*. The event *PedestrianGreen* can change the colour of the traffic light, as it has a writes relation on the attribute *colourTraffic*. The event *PedestrianGreen* also reads the number of waiting pedestrians. How we represent the structure and behaviour of simulation components differs from how we differentiate structure and behaviour when we compare them. The behaviour information is part of the graph (i.e., schedules- and writes relations), and the expressions are annotated on these relations. However, when our tool compares the structure of the simulation components, the annotated information about the behaviour is discarded; thus, Fig. 5 only contains the structural information (i.e., nodes and edges). The usage of expressions in schedules- and writes-relationships, which reflects a paradigm orthogonal to the graph notation, is why the behaviour specification of the simulation component cannot be compared using a graph-based method (cf. [10]). The behaviour is stored as annotations on the schedules- and writes-relations; thus, the graph-isomorphism approach cannot determine the behaviour's similarity. The expressions representing the simulation component's behaviour are first-order logic statements. We transform these statements into SMT statements (as introduced in [10]).

Fig. 5. Graph-representation of Structural Elements

The specification in its graph form is stored in the graph database Neo4J[2] as shown in Fig. 1. Our tool provides an interface to save the specification in the database. For convenience, we recommend running the Neo4J database in a Docker container.

Although the database is used to store the transformed specifications and to perform the analysis to compare the specifications structurally, the user can visualise each stored graph via the Neo4J UI. Figure 6 shows the graphs of six simulation components of various sizes. The blue nodes represent a simulation component. The yellow nodes represent the entities of a simulation component. The red nodes represent the events of a simulation component. The grey nodes represent

---

[2] https://neo4j.com/.

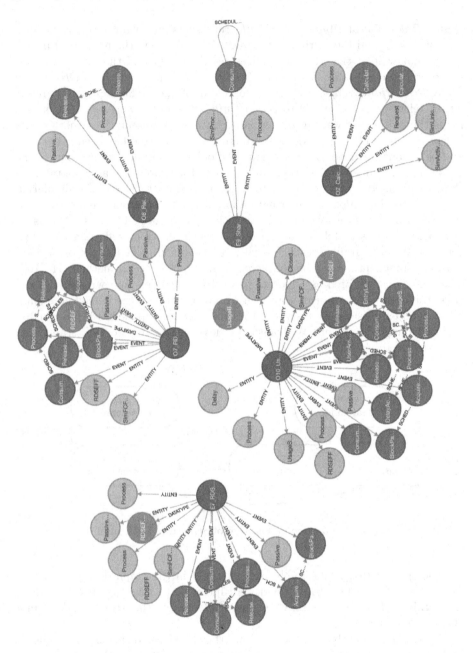

Fig. 6. Simulation Specification Graph Visualisation (Color figure online)

the datatypes of the simulation component. Reads- and writes-relationships are represented by arrows between events and datatypes. Arrows between events also represent schedules-relationships. Although it is possible to modify the graphs in the Neo4J user interface, the editor does not automatically update the specification in the tree editor based on the changed graph. Therefore, we recommend using only the tree-based editor to modify the specifications.

3.2   Identification of Simulation Components

The specification of structure and behaviour of simulation components can serve as documentation for the simulation. The analysis developers can use these specifications to understand the software better, and if necessary, they can compare these specifications manually. However, besides the specification of simulation components, our toolchain can also compare these specifications regarding their structure and behaviour. To extend the specification's purpose and allow the identification of similar simulation components, we present a second tool. Our second tool, the Analysis CLI, utilises the graphs derived from the simulation specifications. Therefore, it accesses the Neo4J database to identify identical simulation components based on their specification. Comparing two simulation components is separated into two steps. First, the Analysis CLI performs a graph-isomorphism analysis [19] in the Neo4J database. This analysis checks whether the nodes and edges of a graph A can be mapped onto another graph B, i.e. whether the structure is identical. The graph B that is searched can have the same number of nodes and edges or a higher number of nodes and edges. We use the graph-isomorphism implementation by Cordio [5], which is available as plugin for the Neo4J database, for the subgraph analysis. Second, if the graph-isomorphism identifies a structural match, the Analysis CLI proceeds with the behaviour analysis. The behaviour information stored in the behaviour meta-model is transformed into SMT statements based on the SMT-LIB standard[3]. These statements are then analysed by an SMT-Solver. For our toolchain, we use the *Z3 Theorem Prover* by Microsoft [21].

Tool Setup: The user of our tool can access the functionality of our tooling via a CLI. We developed the CLI to enable the user to compare the specifications of simulation components regarding their structure and behaviour. The CLI acts as an interface so that the user does not have to invoke the graph-isomorphism and behaviour analysis manually. Before the user can compare the specifications, they must install the Z3 Theorem Prover and provide the path to it. They can either extend the systems `PATH` variable manually or they use the following command of the CLI:

```
sim-compare z3 <PATH TO libz3.dylib>
sim-compare z3java <PATH TO libz3java.dylib
```

Listing 1.1. Z3 Theorem Prover Setup

Whether the user must manually modify the `PATH` variable or invoke the commands of our CLI depends on the used operating system. In the context of

---

[3] https://smtlib.cs.uiowa.edu/.

the Analysis CLI, we tested the prerequisite commands for the operating system MacOS. For more information and further instructions, please visit the official Z3 website[4] or the GitHub page[5].

Furthermore, the user must have access to a running Neo4J instance with the installed graph-isomorphism plugin. The default setting is that the tool assumes that a standard Neo4J instance is running locally with the default user and password. If the user wants to use a different configuration of the Neo4J database, they can use the following commands:

```
sim - compare  neoip  <IP>
sim - compare  neopw  <PASSWORD>
```

Listing 1.2. Neo4J Setup

With the command `neoip`, the user sets the IP according to their Neo4J installation. If they use another password, with the command `neopw` the user can change the password corresponding to their Neo4J installation.

Analysis: Before the user can compare two specifications, they need to know which simulation specifications are available for the analyses. Therefore, we provide the command `list`, which prints all simulation components that are stored in the Neo4J Database. The print shows the names of the simulation components.

```
sim - compare  list
```

Listing 1.3. List all Simulation Components

The user can compare two simulation components at a time with the information on which simulation components are available. The command `compare <SIM_A> <SIM_B>` allows the user to compare two simulation components:

```
sim - compare  compare  <SIM_A>  <SIM_B>
```

Listing 1.4. Compare Simulation Components Command

The two parameters, `<SIM_A>` and `<SIM_B>`, represent the names of the specifications of the two simulation components the user wants to compare. Although the user can modify the entries in the database, i.e. change the structural and behavioural specifications; we recommend avoiding using the Neo4J interface to modify the entries. The changes are not part of the specification model; therefore, the changes will get lost when the database gets updated. The `compare` command first invokes the structural comparison of the graphs by using the graph-isomorphism plugin. If the graph-isomorphism analysis yields a positive

---

[4] https://www.microsoft.com/en-us/research/project/z3-3/.
[5] https://github.com/Z3Prover/z3.

result, the schedules- and writes-relationships are transformed into SMT statements. Based on these SMT statements, the Z3 performs a satisfiable analysis, i.e., a behavioural comparison.

Results: The results depend on whether the structural and behavioural analysis is successful. After invoking the `sim-compare compare <SIM_A> <SIM_B>` command, the analysis result can have four outcomes. Figure 7 depicts the sequencing of the analysis and the possible results. In the remainder of this section, we go through the sequence, and we present the different results, depending on the structural and behavioural analysis.

After the user starts the analysis, the two specifications are first compared regarding their structure. The first result specifies whether the graph-isomorphism analysis yields a negative result, i.e. they do not match structurally. Listing 1.5 shows the result, when the simulation component `SIM_A` is compared to `SIM_B` and the graph-isomorphism yields no result.

```
Compare SIM_A and SIM_B
No isomorphism between simulator graphs!
```

Listing 1.5. No Subgraph Found

The second result can be that the graph-isomorphism yields a positive result. Listing 1.6 shows an excerpt of the result of the successful graph-isomorphism analysis. Instead of the output `No isomorphism between simulator graphs!` the analysis proceeds and starts the behavioural analysis by transforming the schedules- and writes-relationships into SMT statements. The graph-isomorphism analysis can have multiple mappings of nodes and edges; thus, each mapping needs to be analysed. The currently analysed mapping is indicated by the placeholder n, and the total number of mappings is indicated by the placeholder m.

```
Compare SIM_A and SIM_B
...
Testing mapping n out of m:
```

Listing 1.6. Successful Subgraph Analysis

After the graph-isomorphism analysis, each mapping is analysed regarding the matching behaviour. As graph-isomorphism can yield more than one result, each result will be compared. The analysis proceeds until the SMT-Solver finds a solution or the behaviour is not identical. Listing 1.7 shows the results for a mapping that is not identical (`SMT status: UNSATISFIABLE`).

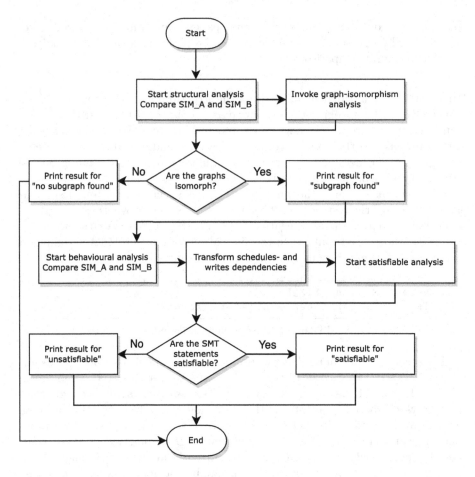

Fig. 7. Sequencing of the Analysis

```
Compare SIM_A and SIM_B
...
Testing mapping n out of m:
Comparing 'XYZ writes demand' with 'ABC writes demand'
SMT status: UNSATISFIABLE
```

Listing 1.7. Behaviour does not match

If the graph-isomorphism analysis was successful and the behaviour is identical, the results show a mapping of the events and entities that yielded the result. Listing 1.8 shows the result of a successful graph-isomorphism and behaviour analysis.

```
. . .
Testing mapping n out of m:
Comparing 'XYZ writes demand' with 'ABC writes demand'
Behaviour identical with mapping:
[Event] EventA = EventC
. . .
[Entity] EntityA = EntityZ
. . .
```

Listing 1.8. Matching Behaviour

4 Conclusion

In this paper, we present a toolchain for specifying and comparing components of discrete event simulations. The specification allows the developer to model the simulation components' structure and behaviour. During the development phase, our toolchain helps the developers find already implemented components of a simulation by comparing the desired specification to the specifications of already existing simulation components. Thus, the developers can avoid reimplementing simulation components that already exist. Also, before the implementation phase or during maintenance, our toolchain can be used; it can help the software architect to find simulation components with different designs that have the required structure and behaviour of the project at hand. Thus, they can analyse the found simulation components regarding their design to determine which design has already been done and is already used. In order to compare the specifications, the models are transformed into a graph notation and then stored in a graph database. We run a graph-isomorphism analysis based on the graph notation to find similar structures of specified simulation components. Suppose the structural analysis yields a positive result, i. e. the compared graph is isomorph; the toolchain starts the behaviour comparison. The behaviour comparison converts the specifications of the simulation components into SMT-notation, which we utilised to analyse the specifications regarding similar behaviour. Finding related simulation components allows software architects to reuse existing simulation components while reducing the effort required to create new simulation components. Thus, they can reuse simulation components that they otherwise would implement again.

5 Future Development

The evaluation of our approach in [10] showed that it is possible to specify and compare simulation components based on their structure and behaviour. To extend our evaluation, we have to model more components of simulations of different domains. Our tree editor is cumbersome when modelling many simulation components. Thus, we have to improve the usability of the editor to be able to model more than a hand full of entities and events. It is hard to track complex writes- and schedules-relationships of events, which makes the modelling process prone to errors. Therefore, we plan to implement a graphical or textual language to specify simulation components more quickly. Furthermore, our similarity analysis needs to identify specifications that match less than 100%. Thus, we plan to extend our approach so that we can identify simulation specifications that do not match perfectly. This would enable us to help the software architects in the system design to explore more alternative designs.

References

1. Ahadi, A., Mathieson, L.: A comparison of three popular source code similarity tools for detecting student plagiarism. In: ACM International Conference Proceeding Series, pp. 112–117. Association for Computing Machinery (2019). https://doi.org/10.1145/3286960.3286974
2. Balsamo, S., Marzolla, M.: Simulation modeling of UML software architectures. In: 17th European Simulation Mulitconference, vol. 3, pp. 562–567. Society for Modelling and Simulation International, SCS European Publishing House (2003)
3. Blockwitz, T., et al.: Functional mockup interface 2.0: the standard for tool independent exchange of simulation models. In: Proceedings of the 9th International MODELICA Conference, 3–5 September 2012, Munich, Germany, vol. 76, pp. 173–184 (2012). https://doi.org/10.3384/ecp12076173
4. Clarke, E.M., Emerson, E.A., Sistla, A.P.: Automatic verification of finite-state concurrent systems using temporal logic specifications. ACM Trans. Program. Lang. Syst. **8**, 244–263 (1983)
5. Cordio, S.: csb/neo4j-plugins/subgraph-isomorphism at master · msstate-dasi/csb. https://github.com/msstate-dasi/csb/tree/master/neo4j-plugins/subgraph-isomorphism. Accessed 01 July 2022
6. Falcone, A., Garro, A.: Distributed co-simulation of complex engineered systems by combining the high level architecture and functional mock-up interface. Simul. Model. Pract. Theory **97**, 101967 (2019). https://doi.org/10.1016/j.simpat.2019.101967. https://www.sciencedirect.com/science/article/pii/S1569190X19301005
7. Gitchell, D., Tran, N.: Sim: a utility for detecting similarity in computer programs. SIGCSE Bull. **31**(1), 266–270 (1999). https://doi.org/10.1145/384266.299783
8. Heinrich, R., Strittmatter, M., Reussner, R.: A layered reference architecture for metamodels to tailor quality modeling and analysis. IEEE Trans. Softw. Eng. **47**, 26 (2019)
9. IEEE: 1516-2010 - IEEE Standard for Modeling and Simulation High Level Architecture (HLA). Technical report (2010). https://doi.org/10.1109/IEEESTD.2010.5553440
10. Koch, S., Hamann, E., Heinrich, R., Reussner, R.: Feature-based investigation of simulation structure and behaviour. In: Gerostathopoulos, I., Lewis, G., Batista, T., Bureš, T. (eds.) European Conference on Software Architecture, pp. 178–185. Springer, Cham (2022). https://doi.org/10.1007/978-3-031-16697-6_13
11. Maoz, S., et al.: OCL framework to verify extra-functional properties in component and connector models. In: 3rd International Workshop on Executable Modeling, Austin, p. 7. CEUR, RWTH Aachen (2017)
12. Milner, R.: Communication and Concurrency. PHI Series in Computer Science. Prentice Hall (1989)

13. Overstreet, C., Nance, R.: A specification language to assist in analysis of discrete event simulation models. Commun. ACM **28**, 190–201 (1985). https://doi.org/10.1145/2786.2792

14. Prechelt, L., Malpohl, G., Philippsen, M.: Finding plagiarisms among a set of programs with JPlag. J. Univ. Comput. Sci. **8**(11), 1016–1038 (2002)

15. Richters, M., Gogolla, M.: Validating UML models and OCL constraints. In: Evans, A., Kent, S., Selic, B. (eds.) UML 2000. LNCS, vol. 1939, pp. 265–277. Springer, Heidelberg (2000). https://doi.org/10.1007/3-540-40011-7_19

16. Ringert, J.O., Rumpe, B.: A little synopsis on streams, stream processing functions, and state-based stream processing. Int. J. Softw. Inform. **5**, 29–53 (2011)

17. Schleimer, S., Wilkerson, D.S., Aiken, A.: Winnowing: local algorithms for document fingerprinting. In: Proceedings of the ACM SIGMOD International Conference on Management of Data, pp. 76–85 (2003)

18. Talcott, C., et al.: Composition of languages, models, and analyses. In: Heinrich, R., Durán, F., Talcott, C., Zschaler, S. (eds.) Composing Model-Based Analysis Tools, pp. 45–70. Springer, Cham (2021). https://doi.org/10.1007/978-3-030-81915-6_4

19. Ullmann, J.R.: An Algorithm for Subgraph Isomorphism. Technical report 1 (1976). https://doi.org/10.1145/321921.321925

20. Varga, A.: Omnet++. In: Wehrle, K., Güneş, M., Gross, J. (eds.) Modeling and Tools for Network Simulation, pp. 35–59. Springer, Heidelberg (2010). https://doi.org/10.1007/978-3-642-12331-3_3

21. Z3Prover: z3: The Z3 Theorem Prover (2019). https://github.com/Z3Prover/z3

22. Zeigler, B.P., Prähofer, H., Kim, T.G.: Theory of Modeling and Simulation: Integrating Discrete Event and Continuous Complex Dynamic Systems, 2 edn. Academic Press, San Diego (2000). http://www.gbv.de/dms/goettingen/302567488.pdf

DAT: Data Architecture Modeling Tool for Data-Driven Applications

Moamin Abughazala[1]([⊠]) [iD], Henry Muccini[1] [iD], and Mohammad Sharaf[2]

[1] University of L'Aquila, L'Aquila, Italy
`moamin.abughazala@graduate.univaq.it, henry.muccini@univaq.it`
[2] An Najah N. University, Nablus, Palestine
`sharaf@najah.edu`

Abstract. Data is the key to success for any Data-Driven Organization, and managing it is considered the most challenging task. Data Architecture (DA) focuses on describing, collecting, storing, processing, and analyzing the data to meet business needs. In this tool demo paper, we present the DAT, a model-driven engineering tool enabling data architects, data engineers, and other stakeholders to describe how data flows through the system and provides a blueprint for managing data that saves time and effort dedicated to Data Architectures for IoT applications. We evaluated this work by modeling five case studies, receiving expressiveness and ease of use feedback from two companies, more than six researchers, and eighteen undergraduate students from the software architecture course.

Keywords: Data Architecture Modeling Tool · Data-Driven · Data Architecture

1 Introduction

The International Data Corporation (IDC) [4] expects that by 2025 there will be more than 175 zettabytes of valuable data for a compounded annual growth rate of 61%. Ninety zettabytes of data will be from IoT devices, and 30% of the data generated will be consumed in real-time. A *data architecture* is an integrated set of specification artifacts used to define data requirements, guide integration, control data assets, and align data investments with business strategy. It also includes an integrated collection of master blueprints at different levels of abstraction [11].

This tool demo paper presents the *Data Architecture Modeling Tool (DAT)*, an architecture modeling tool for the model-driven engineering of data architecture for data-driven applications.

DAT (Data Architecture Modeling Tool) is a data architecture modeling tool for IoT applications that shows how data flows through the system and provides a blueprint for it. It allows the stakeholders to describe two levels of data architecture: high-level Architecture (HLA) and Low-Level Architecture (LLA). It focuses on representing the data from source to destination and shows formats, processing types, storage, analysis types, and how to consume it.

T. Batista et al. (Eds.): ECSA 2022, LNCS 13928, pp. 90–101, 2023.
https://doi.org/10.1007/978-3-031-36889-9_8

The rest of this tool demo paper is organized as follows. The methodology is presented in Sect. 2. The application of DAT to a real case study is described in Sect. 3. The DAT evaluation is presented in Sect. 4. Related work is discussed in Sect. 5, while conclusions are drawn in Sect. 6.

2   Background

The main focus of this paper is to describe the data architecture of IoT applications through the *Data Modeling Language (DAML)*. Section 2.1 shows ISO/IEC/IEEE 42010:2011 standard. CAPS Framework in Sect. 2.2. Section 2.4 shows DAML and reports on the technologies used to implement the DAT.

2.1   IEEE/ISO/IEC 42010 Architecture Description

Our work is built on the conceptual foundations of the ISO/IEC/IEEE 42010:2011, *Systems and software engineering — Architecture description* [12] standard, to investigate the essential elements of data architecture description for IoT applications. The standard handles architecture description (AD), the practices of recording software, system, and enterprise architectures so that architectures can be understood, documented, analyzed, and realized. Architecture descriptions can take many forms, from informal to carefully specified models.

The content model for an architecture description is illustrated in Fig. 1. The *Architecture viewpoint* is a fundamental building block representing common ways of expressing recurring architectural concerns reusable across projects and organizations. It encapsulates *model kinds* framing particular *concerns* for a specific audience of system *stakeholders*. The concerns determine what the model kinds must be able to express: e.g., security, reliability, cost, etc. A model determines the notations, conventions, methods, and techniques. Viewpoints, defining the contents of each architecture *view*, are built up from one or more model kinds and *correspondence rules*, linking them together to maintain consistency.

2.2   The CAPS Modeling Framework

CAPS [13] is an environment where Situational Aware Cyber-Physical Systems (SiA-CPS) can be described through software, hardware, and physical space models. The CAPS found three main architectural viewpoints of extreme importance when describing a SiA-CPS: the software architecture structural and behavioral view (SAML), the hardware view (HWML), and the physical space view (SPML).

This environment is composed of the CAPS modeling framework[1] and the CAPS code generation framework [16,17] that aim to support the architecture description, reasoning, design decision process, and evaluation of the CAPS architecture in terms of data traffic load, battery level and energy consumption of its nodes.

---

[1] CAPS: http://caps.disim.univaq.it/.

2.3 The Important of Data Architecture

Data architecture is important because it helps organizations manage and use their data effectively. Some specific reasons why data architecture is important to include:

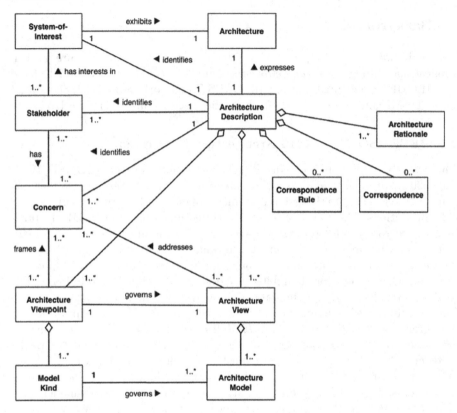

Fig. 1. Content model of an architecture description (ISO/IEC/IEEE 42010)

1. Data quality: it helps to collect, store, and use data consistently and accurately. This is important for maintaining data integrity and reliability and avoiding errors or inconsistencies impacting business operations.
2. Data security: it helps to protect data from unauthorized access or modification and ensure that it is used compliantly and ethically. This is particularly important in industries with strict regulations, such as healthcare or finance.
3. Organizational efficiency: it helps organizations better understand and manage their data, increasing efficiency and productivity. By defining the structures, policies, and standards that govern data within an organization, data architecture can help streamline processes and improve decision-making.
4. Business intelligence and analytics: it is essential for organizations to collect, store, and analyze large amounts of data. This can support better decision-making, improve customer relationships, and drive business growth.

5. Scalability and flexibility: A well-designed data architecture can support the growth and evolution of an organization. It allows organizations to easily add new data sources, incorporate new technologies, and adapt to changing business needs.

2.4 The DAT Tool

The DAT modeling framework[2,3] gives data architects the ability to define a *data view* for data-driven IoT Applications through the DAML modeling language [1].

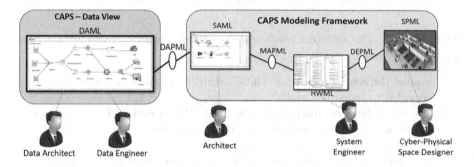

Fig. 2. The Data View of CAPS

Technologies. Our tool is based on MDE. For that, we use Eclipse Modeling Framework (EMF) [6] for building tools and applications based on the structure data model, which consists of three main parts, EMF Core, includes a meta-model for describing the models. EMF Editors contains generic reusable classes for building editors for EMF models. Eclipse Epsilon [5] is a Java-based scripting language for model-based software engineering tasks (e.g., model-to-model transformation and model validation) which strongly support EMF and works with UML, XML, Simulink, etc. To create graphical editors and views for the EMF models, we used Eugenia [7]. It is a tool to create a graphical model editor by generating the .gmfgraph, .gmftool, and .gmfmap models that the GMF editor from a single annotated Ecore meta-model needs.

DAT implements the DAML meta-model to be considered a fourth view (data view) for the CAPS, as shown in Fig. 2. How the DAT supports the modeling of data views and its application to actual use cases will be presented in Sect. 3.

Methodology. DAT is built based on a meta-model containing a data architecture as a top root meta-class. Any **data architecture** of IoT can contain a set of **DataNodes** (components) and **connections**. A Component is considered a

---

[2] DAT Tool Source Code can be found at https://github.com/moamina/DAT.
[3] DAT Tool video demo: https://youtu.be/Du0VDg1CLlQ.

computational unit with an internal state and a known interface [3]. Data nodes can interact by passing data through **data ports**. A component's internal state is denoted by the current behavior of data representation and its values. Data representation includes *data formats, storage technologies, location, and processing type*. Every Node Behavior has a set of behavioral elements denoted by actions and events that depict the data flow within the component. This element can be executed when a previous action in the behavioral data flow has been achieved or triggered by an event like **ReceiveData**. Other main actions are **Generation, Ingestion, Process, Store, Analyze,** and **Consume**. An **event** is triggered in response to the external stimulus of the component. To show the data flow and connection between the events and actions, we use **links**.

Steps to Use. The architect needs to follow the following steps to use the tool to model any case:

1. Download the source code from The GitHub[4] and follow the steps in the tool demo video to lunch the tool[5].
2. Define which level of abstraction you need (High-Level or Low-Level). You could use a single Data Node at the High-Level, whereas you need to define the structure and behavior at the low level.
3. Define the main data nodes and the connection between them to determine the order of each node, such as the data source is the first data node. Ingestion comes the second one, and the connection shows the data flow from the source to the ingestion data node.
4. At the internal behavior, you could use data elements (low-level elements), such as data formats (JSON, XML, Video, ...), and sub-operation, such as (classification, data reduction, cleaning, validation, filter, classification, ...).

3   Real Use Cases

This section introduces the existing data architecture description used by three companies contributing to the DAT tool. We have chosen three cases from five cases to present our tool in the tool paper.

3.1   Operational Data Warehouse

The data warehouse (DW) depends on data from different sources within the operational company system. These data sources can be data from RDS (MySQL Relational-DB), documents-based data in DynamoDB, and real-time data streams. The DW has data batching mechanisms that perform (complete data Extract, Transform, and Load (ETL)) processes on these data sources to load into the final DW tables and data models for reporting purposes. The ETL

---

[4] DAT Tool Source Code can be found at https://github.com/moamina/DAT.
[5] DAT Tool video demo: https://youtu.be/Du0VDg1CLlQ.

process is built through data batches using large-scale data processing and a file system (e.g., AWS S3). Batches run in an hourly-based fashion. The final DW data model is saved in Column-oriented format using AWS S3.

Data from RDS will wait a specific time to be extracted, transformed, and saved in the column-oriented format on file system technology (AWS S3). For the data that comes from DynamoDB streams or real-time data streams, financial details will be added to part of this data for reporting purposes. Then this data is sent to the ingestion stage, extracted, transformed into a column-oriented format, and stored on file system technology (AWS S3) that will be consumed later by the batches to be processed and saved in the final tables.

The ETL batches will check for the new files on the staging tables; whenever a new file is found, the batch will extract the data, transform it, and save the related final tables on the final DW. Once the data is ready in the final tables, it will be ready to be queried for reporting and data export purposes.

Data-consuming micro-services use a query engine (Presto) to query the data in the DW. DW consumers could be reports, dashboards, or others. Report generator micro-services provide all the reports and dashboards with data. The warehouse exporter is responsible for creating data CSV exported files based on specific data templates and sending them to external customer endpoints such as(SFTP, FTP, S3, and emails). Reporting management, the purpose of this service is to manage and maintain the end user's custom configurations and settings of their preference in the dashboards and reports layouts. Tagging management, this service is built for a specific custom report (Operational Flash Dash) that gives the end user ability to decide on and design his report hierarchy and data drill down from the manager position perspective.

3.2 Hydre

This case Fig. 3 from Lambda+ paper's author [10], is from a (Cocktail) research project which aims to study the discourses in two domains in health and food, as well as to identify weak signals in real-time using social network data. The data come from Twitter, compute real-time insights and store data for exploratory analysis.

The case contains other components. The master dataset is implemented with file system technology (Hadoop HDFS). Raw data (tweets) are stored as lines of files, and data re-processing can be done by reading and sending each line as is in another Kafka topic. The streaming ETL uses Kafka consumers to insert data in the micro-batch. The streaming ETL applies transformations and then stores tweets in the storage component. That includes relational, graph, and time series DBMSs. These databases are used for exploratory analyzes, mainly performed with Jupyter notebooks. Alongside, the real-time insights component extracts and aggregates several information about the harvesting, such as popular hashtags or users, using Kafka Streams. It stores the results in the time series database. Although this insertion is a side-effect of the stream processing, it is an idempotent action because the count of the elements will always yield the same result with an effective once guarantee. This result is stored for each element, replacing the old value if it already exists.

3.3 Errors Data Pipeline

This case shows the data pipeline for data errors from different printers. The error data text files come from other printers in JSON format. The data represent the error that happened in different printers, and the data could be the version of the printer, location, ink type, software version, time, etc. the data will be sent to AWS S3 and saved in the same format. The customer could see the raw error data using a query engine. The data will be processed and transferred into helpful information after a specific time, then converted to parquet format (Column-oriented). After that, the data will be transformed to CSV format and then to relation database format to be ready for query from the customer.

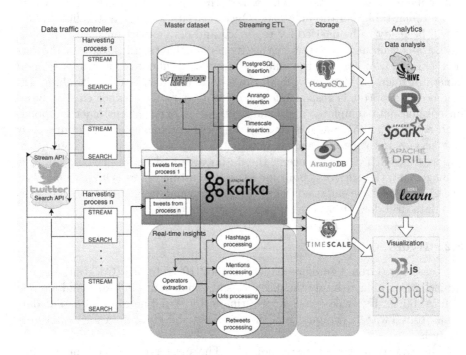

Fig. 3. The Hydre architecture

4 Evaluation

The DAT cases were evaluated through interviews with seven industry professionals from two companies of different domains and different maturity levels and one external researcher; Table 1 shows more about the roles of the evaluators. The evaluation section will be structured in terms of agreements and suggestions for improvement.

Table 1. Outline of use cases and roles of the evaluators

Company	Use cases	Experts Roles
Company A	Operational Data Warehouse	Big Data Team Lead
		Big Data Architect
	Analytical Data Warehouse	Big Data Engineer
		Big Data Architect
Company B	Data Pipeline	Big Data Team Lead
		Big Data Architect
		Big Data Engineer
Researchers	Data Architectures (Lambda, Kappa)	Researcher
Locally	NdR Data Architecture	Students

4.1 Errors Data Pipeline

Figure 5 shows the Errors Data Pipeline using DAT. The first author presented the models and collected the practitioners' feedback.

Agreements: The model described the data flow from generation to destination. The model was easy to understand for new data engineers. The tool has the flexibility to change and add new nodes.

Suggestion: It is good to include the data quality metrics that could apply to the data at each stage.

4.2 Hydre

Figure 4 shows the Hydre model using DAT. The first author presented the models and collected feedback from Lambda+'s author.

Agreements: The model represents very well the Hydre case. The indications of when data are stored on disk are helpful, especially when working on a big data architecture with people who don't know each technology's details. The real-time and batch elements are useful as well.

Suggestion: the first suggestion is similar to the first case related to data interaction patterns. The second suggestion was a starting point for us to provide two levels of architecture, High-level architecture (HLA) and Low-Level architecture (LLA).

4.3 Operational Data Warehouse

Figure 6 shows the ODW model using DAT. The first author presented the models and collected the practitioners' feedback.

Agreements: The model was able to describe the details of the case and was easy to share and understand by different teams in other parts of the world.

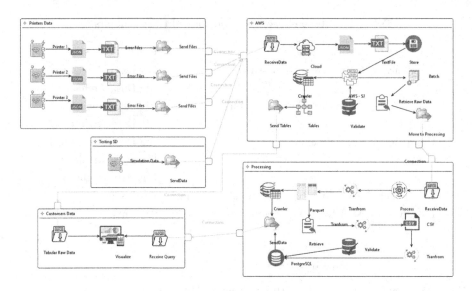

Fig. 4. Errors Data Pipeline

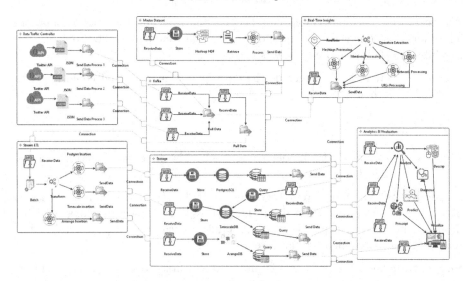

Fig. 5. Hydre (Lambda+ Example)

The model was a good communication language between team members, which means easy to avoid misinterpretations.

Suggestion: In the current version of the DAT, the only way to show how different components interact with each other is to send/receive data. The suggestion was to include all data interaction patterns (request/response, publish/subscribe, pull/push, and others).

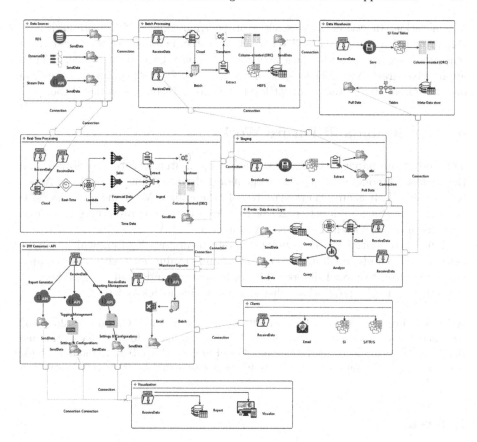

Fig. 6. Operational Data Warehouse

5 Related Work

This section reviews relevant studies that are related to exploiting the most related research to data-driven IoT. Raj and Bosch [15] proposed a conceptual model for a data pipeline, which contains two main components (nodes and connectors); the node represents the main abstract data node, and the connection represents the way to carry and transmit the data between nodes. The DAT provided two levels of architecture, HLA (High-Level Architecture) and LLA (Low-Level Architecture), which is a more details architecture that gives the ability to model the behavior of each node by describing sub-action, data formats, location, processing type, etc. Borelli [2] proposed a classification for main software components and their relationships to model a software architecture for particular IoT applications. These components represent the abstract components. DAT can describe all of the mentioned components and their behavior too. Erraissi [8,9] proposed a meta-model for data sources, ingestion layers, and Big Data visualization layer. DAT can describe the data in each layer (source or generation, Ingestion, Processing, storing, Analyzing, and Consuming). Nesi [14] provided a solution based on a set of instruments to collect the data in real-time, store, and audit data flow for IoT smart City architecture. DAT is an architecture-driven tool to show how data flow from the source to the final destination at an abstract concept level; it is not a technologies-based tool.

6   Conclusion and Future Work

This tool demo paper has presented the DAT, an architecture description, and the associated modeling platform for the model-driven engineering of Data Architecture for IoT. It is implemented on top of f the Eclipse Modeling Framework. It can allow the stack-holders to describe two levels of data architectures, high-level Architecture (HLA) and Low-Level Architecture (LLA).

This is an initial starting point for our future work plan, which can be extended to include finishing the current running evaluations with other companies and trying to model different big data patterns and architectures. Second, try to integrate the DAT with other existing technologies and tools.

Acknowledgment. The authors would like to thank Prof. Giovanni Stilo, Prof. Annabelle Gillet (Lambda+), Prof. Karthik Vaidhyanathan, Mostafa Shaer, Itay, and Roi from HP Team, Mustafa Tamim and Anas Eid from Harri Team, Mudassir Malik, Apurvanand Sahay, and Arsene Indamutsa as a researcher for their contributions in the evaluation.

References

1. Abughazala, M., Muccini, H.: Modeling data analytics architecture for IoT applications using dat. In: 2023 IEEE 20th International Conference on Software Architecture Companion (ICSA-C), pp. 284–291 (2023). https://doi.org/10.1109/ICSA-C57050.2023.00066
2. Borelli, F., Biondi, G., Horita, F., Kamienski, C.: Architectural software patterns for the development of IoT smart applications. arXiv preprint arXiv:2003.04781 (2020)
3. Szyperski, C.: Component Software. Beyond Object Oriented Programming. Addison Wesley, Boston (1998)
4. International Data Corporation: How IDC's industry cloudpath & SaaSPath surveys can inform your cloud/SaaS strategy (2019). https://blogs.idc.com/2019/09/04/how-idcs-industry-cloudpath-saaspath-surveys-can-inform-your-cloud-saas-strategy/
5. Eclipse Foundation: Eclipse epsilon (2009). https://www.eclipse.org/epsilon/
6. Eclipse Foundation: Eclipse modeling framework (2009). https://www.eclipse.org/modeling/emf/
7. Eclipse Foundation: Graphical model editor development with Eugenia/GMF (2009). https://www.eclipse.org/epsilon/doc/eugenia/
8. Erraissi, A., Belangour, A.: Data sources and ingestion big data layers: meta-modeling of key concepts and features. Int. J. Eng. Technol. **7**(4), 3607–3612 (2018)

9. Erraissi, A., Mouad, B., Belangour, A.: A big data visualization layer meta-model proposition. In: 2019 8th International Conference on Modeling Simulation and Applied Optimization (ICMSAO), pp. 1–5. IEEE (2019)

10. Gillet, A., Leclercq, É., Cullot, N.: Lambda+, the renewal of the lambda architecture: category theory to the rescue. In: La Rosa, M., Sadiq, S., Teniente, E. (eds.) CAiSE 2021. LNCS, vol. 12751, pp. 381–396. Springer, Cham (2021). https://doi.org/10.1007/978-3-030-79382-1_23

11. DAMA International: DAMA-DMBOK: Data Management Body of Knowledge, 2nd edn. Technics Publications, LLC, Denville (2017)

12. ISO/IEC/IEEE: ISO/IEC/IEEE 42010:2011 Systems and software engineering - Architecture description (2011)

13. Muccini, H., Sharaf, M.: Caps: architecture description of situational aware cyber physical systems. In: 2017 IEEE International Conference on Software Architecture (ICSA), pp. 211–220. IEEE (2017)

14. Nesi, P., Pantaleo, G., Paolucci, M., Zaza, I.: Auditing and assessment of data traffic flows in an IoT architecture. In: 2018 IEEE 4th International Conference on Collaboration and Internet Computing (CIC), pp. 388–391. IEEE (2018)

15. Raj, A., Bosch, J., Olsson, H.H., Wang, T.J.: Modelling data pipelines. In: 2020 46th Euromicro Conference on Software Engineering and Advanced Applications (SEAA), pp. 13–20. IEEE (2020)

16. Sharaf, M., Abughazala, M., Muccini, H.: Arduino realization of caps IoT architecture descriptions. In: Proceedings of the 12th European Conference on Software Architecture: Companion Proceedings, pp. 1–4 (2018)

17. Sharaf, M., Abughazala, M., Muccini, H., Abusair, M.: An architecture framework for modelling and simulation of situational-aware cyber-physical systems. In: Lopes, A., de Lemos, R. (eds.) ECSA 2017. LNCS, vol. 10475, pp. 95–111. Springer, Cham (2017). https://doi.org/10.1007/978-3-319-65831-5_7

Doctoral Symposium

Controlling Automatic Experiment-Driven Systems Using Statistics and Machine Learning

Milad Abdullah[(✉)] [iD]

Charles University, Prague, Czech Republic
`abdullah@d3s.mff.cuni.cz`

Abstract. Experiments are used in many modern systems to optimize their operation. Such experiment-driven systems are used in various fields, such as web-based systems, smart-* systems, and various self-adaptive systems. There is a class of these systems that derive their data from running simulations or another type of computation, such as in digital twins, online planning using probabilistic model-checking, or performance benchmarking. To obtain statistically significant results, these systems must repeat the experiments multiple times. As a result, they consume extensive computation resources. The GraalVM benchmarking project detects performance changes in the GraalVM compiler. However, the benchmarking project has an extensive usage of computational resources and time. The doctoral research project proposed in this paper focuses on controlling the experiments with the goal of reducing computation costs. The plan is to use statistical and machine learning approaches to predict the outcomes of experiments and select the experiments yielding more useful information. As an evaluation, we are applying these methods to the GraalVM benchmarking project; the initial results confirm that these methods have the potential to significantly reduce computation costs.

Keywords: Experiment-Driven Systems · Statistics · Machine Learning

1 Introduction

Modern systems often optimise themselves using experimentation. This ranges from simple semi-automated A/B testing to systems that experiment continuously and automatically. For example, a system may experiment with its different architecture configurations and measure the QoS property of interest (for instance, performance, latency, availability, power consumption, etc.).

Experiment-driven systems can perform self-experiments by running some computations such as simulations or benchmarks. Often, the outcomes of these experiments are probabilistic or noisy (such as simulations of partially unknown

T. Batista et al. (Eds.): ECSA 2022, LNCS 13928, pp. 105–119, 2023.
https://doi.org/10.1007/978-3-031-36889-9_9

environments or measurements of different QoS properties). Repeating experimentation is a common approach to obtaining accurate results from simulations or benchmarks. However, this approach has a high computational resource consumption. According to [29], experiment-driven systems perform more efficiently when they are controlled with data-driven methods, such as Machine Learning, which can closely predict the results of an experiment. Machine-learning applications rely heavily on data availability and work well when the data volume is large enough. Historical data helps build more accurate machine-learning models for experiment-driven systems that have been used for a while.

Controlling experimentation is a trending subject in major industrial companies such as Google, Microsoft, Amazon, etc. [16]. These experiments evaluate software updates' functionality, performance measurements, and long-term usability effects. A prominent representative of self-experimentation is performance benchmarking. Performance has become vital to many software projects (e.g. MongoDB[1] or GraalVM[2]) that some have even integrated automated performance testing into their development process to track performance continually and to detect performance changes between individual releases.

A modern approach to control an experiment-driven system is by using data-driven models. To suggest a suitable data-driven model, it is crucial to understand the physical system, the simulation, and the expected data format [17]. In modern data-driven approaches such as machine learning, the understanding of the provided data and features is reached with the model itself. However, according to [25], there exists no standard approach for integrating machine learning models at software architecture loops. Moreover, it is essential to know about controlling the experimentation online.

This PhD project plans to develop data-driven models and methods for controlling experimentation to reduce computation costs.

The general goals of this project are:

1. Analyse data extracted from experiment-driven systems and investigate patterns using data-driven methods, leading to early result predictions.
2. Provide a systematic way to control an experiment-driven system to minimise computation costs.
3. Implement and evaluate the framework in which an experiment-driven system is controlled.

The running example for this project will be the GraalVM benchmarking project, in which its data is available[3] for the public. The project evaluates the GraalVM compiler commits and reports performance changes; however, it suffers from high computation costs. For an overview of the example, please refer to Sect. 3. Two main reasons push us to select the GRaalVM benchmarking project as the running example: (1) it is a vast benchmarking project with hundreds of benchmark executions per day, and (2) it has been implemented and maintained at the department of the principal researcher.

---

[1] www.mongodb.com.

[2] www.graalvm.org.

[3] https://graal.d3s.mff.cuni.cz.

The rest of this project proposal is prepared as follows: for a background on the experiment-driven systems and the related works around them, refer to Sects. 2 and 8. The motivation behind this project can be found in Sect. 4. The methodology is located in Sect. 5, and evaluation strategy and research questions can be read in Sect. 6. The early results are reported in Sect. 7.

2   Background

This section gives a brief background on Experiment-driven systems and controlling them.

2.1   What is an Experiment-Driven System?

Software companies are shifting towards (semi)-automated software releases, so it is essential to test these updates and changes to detect potential problems. These problems could be related to a software project's functionality or performance. The necessity of regular and systematic evaluation of the software after each (or a group of) updates pushes developers to use an experiment-driven system. An experiment-driven system tests the new software changes in an environment that covers all possible configurations and settings in which the software may be used. Many experimentation environments consider various hardware and operating system configurations to detect performance bugs.

For developers, it is crucial to have the experiment results before the release reaches the clients. Occasionally, clients can be involved in providing feedback on the product's performance. However, there are a few issues with this approach: First, a client may only notice a performance change when it is significant enough for them. Second, a client may be already affected by the performance change: let's say the damage is already done. Last but not least, a client may not regularly use all software features to note a performance change in them.

On the other hand, an experiment-driven system will evaluate all software components with any change, given different configurations and possible environments. Considering this as the systematic approach to detect performance regressions, we should also consider the computation costs behind testing all possible configurations.

2.2   A Use-Case of an Experiment-Driven System

Detection of software performance changes is a valuable service for developers, which helps them locate performance bugs. Even relatively small changes in the source code of the software projects affect their performance [27]. Performance is such a critical property of modern software projects that they have embedded experiment-driven systems alongside their primary implementation, for instance: HotSpot, MongoDB, GraalVM, etc.

Unlike functionality testing, a limited set of test cases may not detect performance regressions. To confidently report a performance change, the software needs to be tested by one or more suites of benchmarks for various sizes of workloads [10]. Furthermore, the operating system configuration, hardware setup and other factors may influence performance testing results.

Experiment-driven systems usually prepare numerous experiments for various hardware types, operating system configurations, version branches (e.g. community or enterprise editions, git branches, releases, etc.), and other variations. Often, the outcomes of these experiments are probabilistic or noisy [2]. It is a common approach to repeat experimentation to obtain accurate results from simulations or benchmarks [6]. However, this approach has a high computational resource consumption.

2.3   Reducing Experiment Driven Systems Computation Costs

Perhaps a mainstream approach to reduce costs is made by selecting test cases which are probable to find performance changes and omitting ones which will not. However, this raises the question: on what bases could we select tests?

Another way to reduce the computation costs is to run the benchmark suite infrequently (e.g. before each release, weekly twice, ... etc.). However, executing the benchmark suite infrequently will not precisely find the commit responsible for the performance change. Furthermore, the developers may not be aware that some commits improve performance while others degrade it because the performance effects of different commits may cancel each other out.

Usually, the high computation cost is caused due to numerous benchmark (harness) runs. Reducing the number of runs could lead to noisy and probabilistic results because each run is biased by the hardware and software configurations. After each run, the usual approach is to restart the machine and re-execute the benchmark suites. The methods proposed in this work favour gathering more information on the existing benchmark results rather than gathering new data. We consider that gathering new benchmark runs is more costly than repeating computations on the already available results.

2.4   Controlling Experiment-Driven Systems

Automation approaches such as AI and data-driven methods are being used to reduce human interaction and costs in experiment-driven systems. For instance, machine learning methods could be used to learn from historical data and learn vital features that will lead to automation. An example of automatically controlling experimentation is learning from the extracted data or meta-data. Learned models could alter experimentation parameters online and affect how the system reacts. A more straightforward application of AI in experiment-driven systems could be feature engineering in white-box analysis, leading to performance changes. Some developers use genetic algorithms to generate many test cases in an experiment-driven system and choose those more likely to contain regression results.

In this PhD project, we investigate methods to reduce the computation costs of such projects. We do so by early stopping an experiment if we predict that the experiment will not find any performance regressions. Our work is based on [1], in which we use statistical methods to determine the probability of an experiment detecting performance regression with fewer benchmark executions.

3   Running Example

An example to validate our approaches is the GraalVM benchmarking project [8], which has been developed and maintained by the same department where this doctoral research proposal is conducted. The GraalVM benchmarks are intended to detect significant performance changes between different versions of the GraalVM compiler. To obtain accurate results to determine a change with confidence, benchmarking should repeat the experiments multiple times. The GraalVM benchmarking project consists of the following configurations:

- 2 Machine Types.
- 12 Compiler Configurations.
- More than 16 different version types (i.e., JDK-11 Community Edition, JDK-17 Enterprise Edition ...).
- 5 different benchmark suites.
- More than 100 Benchmarks.

The benchmarking project executes every combination of <*Machine Type, Configuration, Benchmark*> for each new commit in each version where the change is made. Each benchmark is executed multiple *iterations*, and often, the first few iterations are omitted because they are considered warm-up iterations. Literature on warm-up and warm-up detection could be found in [5,28]. After several benchmark executions, the machine is restarted, and the same benchmark is re-executed (again, multiple iterations). From this point on, the repetition is called a *run*, and its purpose is to ensure that the machine setup is not affecting the benchmark results. In most cases, there are 33 runs, which consists of 50–300 benchmark execution. The results from benchmark execution consist of data regarding execution time, instruction counts, memory usage, etc.

In a performance measurement environment that runs thousands of tests on a software project with multiple commits per day, dedicating minutes to hours per experiment on all tests to gather data for all commits, is challenging in terms of execution costs. This increases in the case of the GraalVM benchmarking project, which runs nearly a hundred different benchmarks per commit of the compiler.

Currently, the GraalVM benchmarking project is constantly running on 36 machines (16×8 and 20×4 cores in total). Executing all benchmarks on one commit with one virtual machine configuration will take about 12 days of computation. The benchmarking is usually run by two or more virtual machine configurations, which stretches things further. Considering there are approximately 2–10 commits per day, it can be argued that the benchmarking is three orders of magnitude slower than required.

This PhD project aims to reduce the computation costs by selecting which experiments need to be run and how often. That includes the question of whether we can stop an experiment early by predicting that it is not likely to provide data that would point to a significant performance change. One of the goals of this project is to be embedded along with the implementation of benchmarking project so that it works as a controller of such experiment-driven systems.

4   Motivation

Developers of modern software projects are interested to know if and to what extent the new updates affect the performance of the software. The evaluation of such systems is done by benchmarking projects and they are often computationally costly. These costs are the result of numerous experiments required for detecting performance changes. Moreover, the results of performance evaluation are urgent, and cannot be delayed. This is because of (1) the frequency of updates and (2) developers immediately need to know if their latest changes had any impact on the software performance.

An example of a performance benchmarking project can be seen in GraalVM and MongoDB. This work takes the GraalVM project as the running example. The central issue in the GraalVM benchmarking project is the time needed to run all test cases. Performance changes in environments with just-in-time (JIT) compilation (such as GraalVM), are only detectable once the system is warm [6]. A testing environment is warm when the system is under full load (e.g. all hardware and software cashes are warm), with the warm-up time ranging from seconds to minutes [5]. These factors further expand for experiment-driven systems which evaluate compilers, because the input size is nondeterministic.

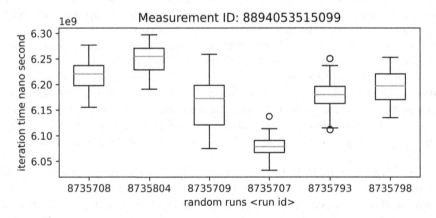

Fig. 1. Distribution of time measurements of 6 executions of the same benchmark under the same settings. It is shown that the results of the benchmark executions are noisy and a decision on accurate results requires more runs.

In such environments, multiple test executions are needed to collect a representative set of samples [13]. In (Fig. 1), it is shown that within the same configuration, same setting and the same benchmark, multiple runs yield different results. These factors combined, for each commit 3–4 h of benchmark execution is required.

Our analysis of the GraalVM benchmarking data shows that 75–78% of the benchmark executions do not yield any performance changes, but still, they are needed to be run. Furthermore, we are not entirely sure which features of gathered data could be used to early determine outcomes. We also do not have a clear view of the methods that could help us detect unnecessary benchmark executions. The solution suggested in this work is two-fold:

1. Investigate methods that could provide early prediction of a benchmark execution if it yields performance changes or not.
2. Finding features that are critical in finding the usefulness of benchmark execution and help us decide to continue or stop them.

5   Research Goals and Methodology

The research goals of the proposed project are:

1. Management and reduction of resource consumption in automated experimentation, in particular being evaluated on the GraalVM benchmarking using data-driven methods such as machine learning or statistical approaches.
2. Developing a framework featuring statistical and machine learning-based approaches to control experiment-driven systems. The framework should be general to handle other cases (in addition to GraalVM) such as [28].
3. Formulate a systematic approach to be taken for different experiment-driven systems, using the methods that have been developed in this project.

The steps to arrive at all goals are listed below:

1. Collect and review the related publications regarding experimentation controlling methods thoroughly, in the first year. Share an example of the methods and gather preliminary results, in a related workshop or conference.
2. Analysis of the modes of the distribution of measured data in the GraalVM benchmarking project using Machine Learning in the second year. The goal is to find patterns that will contribute to a better prediction of changes in the performance of the GraalVM compiler. Provide an example of ML-based white-box analysis of the GraalVM benchmarking and show how it can be useful.
3. Develop a framework for formulating the pipelines of the work in the third year of the study. In this step, we intend to present the results to GraalVM developers (i.e. Oracle) - to get feedback from them. The aim is to develop a framework which facilities controlling any experiment-driven system, using statistics and machine learning methods.

4. Evaluate the framework with two examples, (1) the GraalVM benchmarks, and (2) a different experiment-driven system that will be selected during the study. The evaluation step will be carried out in the fourth year of the study. The final evaluation of the project reflects how an experiment-driven method will be systematically formed.

6 Evaluation Strategy

In this section, the strategy to evaluate our work is provided. In this project proposal, we provide preliminary results for RQ1. Then we provide strategies to answer other research questions:

6.1 Preliminary Evaluation

RQ1 To what extent can we expect to reduce the cost of computation in an experiment-driven system?

The aim of *RQ1* is to find areas where the computation costs could be minimized, but the accuracy of performance detection does not drop. Since we would keep the number of benchmark, configuration and machine types intact, one of the only places where we could control is the number of benchmark executions (runs).

For the *RQ1*, we use a method in which we will look at various sizes of benchmark executions. Originally, the benchmarking would repeat the experiments multiple times to obtain accurate measurement results. The difference between versions is computed using a statistical test (namely the z-test [26]). In the preliminary results, we have shown that it is possible to use data from past experiments to compute a threshold for the p-value (of the z-test). We control the experiments based on the p-value computed by the z-test over a few of the initial measurements collected in the experiment. If the p-value is below a threshold, we assume that it is unlikely to detect a statistically significant difference even if more runs of the benchmark are executed. Therefore, in this case, the execution of the experiment is stopped. If the p-value is above (or equal to) the threshold, we continue the experiment because it has the potential to show the difference. Setting the p-value threshold allows us to control the probability that a benchmark is stopped incorrectly.

As per our running example, for each combination, there usually exist 33 runs. We are interested to see if, with fewer runs, we can arrive at similar conclusions. First, we compute differences between two versions of the same category using all runs. Then we establish a threshold, where we identify where we consider a performance change. Using this threshold, we then recompute the differences this time with fewer runs, i.e. 10 runs Fig. 2. We will repeat this experiment for different run sizes, for example, 15 runs of the old version vs 20 runs of the newer version Fig. 3. In both experiments, shown in Fig. 2 and Fig. 3, we distribute the re-computed versions with and without performance changes to see if, with fewer runs, we can achieve similar results.

Having such experiments indicates that it is possible to stop some experiments with fewer runs; however, we also pay with having some incorrect benchmark stops, which eventually would find performance regressions. Finally, we need to decide on the type of error we could face; (1) stop experiments where they may eventually find performance changes; (2) continue experiments where they would not find any performance changes. To arrive at an answer for *RQ1*, we require to evaluate the entire benchmark suites of GraalVM and later apply similar methods for a different data set.

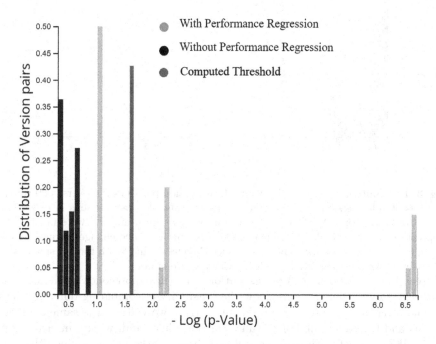

Fig. 2. Distribution of generated p-values from version pairs (10 runs versus 10 runs). 10 Runs of older versions were compared with 10 runs of newer versions in instruction counts. Correctly stopped 73% of the benchmark executions, and 13% were incorrectly stopped. The versions where we label them with performance changes should lie on the right side, and those without performance changes should lie on the left side of the yellow line (*computedthreshold* = 1.6). (Color figure online)

6.2   Evaluation Strategy

We ask the following research questions, and for them, we provide a plan for addressing them in future works:

RQ2 What are the key elements that can affect controlling an experiment-driven system?

As for *RQ2*, we will look at different metrics yielded by the benchmark executions. For example, the results of Fig. 2 are a comparison of instruction counts,

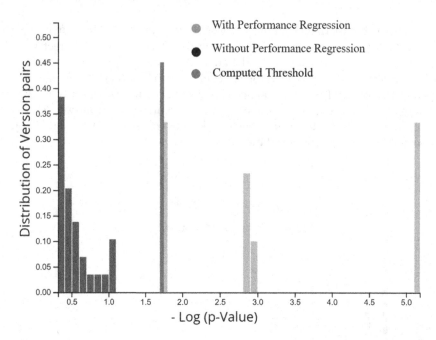

Fig. 3. Distribution of generated p-values from version pairs (15 runs versus 20 runs). 15 Runs of older versions were compared with 20 runs of newer versions in execution time. Correctly stopped 90% of the benchmark executions, and 2% were incorrectly stopped. The versions where we label them with performance changes should lie on the right side, and those without performance changes should lie on the left side of the yellow line (*computedthreshold* = 1.7). (Color figure online)

whereas the results of Fig. 3 are execution time (in nanoseconds) comparisons. With this experiment, we only show the possibility of comparing different metrics; however, as a strategy, for different metrics, we will use the same configurations and the same number of runs. On the other hand, we are interested to see if different configurations and different benchmarks behave differently in a controlled environment. We are looking at the significance of various factors in experiment-driven systems.

RQ3 What are the ways to use data-driven models to control and automate experiment-driven systems?

RQ4 In what concept are we limited by the black-box analysis, and are we required to check the inner side of experimentation?

The goal of *RQ3* is to investigate methods that we can use AI or data-driven models to aid in controlling experiment-driven systems. A strategy that looks for places where for example, Machine learning could be useful has two main tasks: (1) find behaviours that could be learned and predicted, (2) survey machine learning methods and identify the best model for controlling experiment-driven systems such as work of [3]. For both tasks, we have to understand the expected results of both black-box and white-box analysis. In cases where we no more can arrive at meaningful models for black-box data, we then intend to answer

RQ4. It is important to understand what can be done in terms of controlling experimenting without looking at the source codes. This is where we require to have a boundary and identify points where black-box analysis is no more answering the cause. Therefore, to answer *RQ4*, we need to ensure that no further improvements are possible without going deep into the code level.

By answering the targeted research questions, we could arrive at a level of understanding of what concept and how an experiment-driven system can be automated. The general goal of the evaluation is to have a systematic method to manage experimentation in favour of reducing costs. This work starts by looking at different ways where the computation costs can be reduced while keeping the quality of service, such as performance regression testing, intact.

7   Preliminary Results

The first results in this line of work have been shared with the community in our recent position paper [1]. In this work, we highlighted an example of controlling the GraalVM benchmarking project with a statistical method. The work selects one of the benchmarks and illustrates that with a data-driven model, we can predict performance changes in the GraalVM compiler.

The indicative results show that when we aim at 10% of benchmarks stopped incorrectly, we can save about 30% of the computation time. Though the 10% may sound like a high number, it is necessary to keep in mind that the performance change does not go away and is likely to be discovered in an experiment over the next commit of the software. This means for instance that there is only 0.1% chance that an experiment that could discover a performance change would be wrongly stopped throughout three subsequent commits.

This promising result indicates that the benchmark outcomes can be foreseen with the available data, and if further data is required the benchmarking can continue. The initial results also provide information regarding the metrics we extract from benchmark execution. For example, we started to focus on *iteration time ns*, but we then provide similar results on *instruction counts*. Indicating that the results available in the benchmark execution map our approach and that we are not limited by the type of extracted data.

8   Related Works

The approaches with the focus on industrial benefits of controlling the experiment-driven systems are seen in research works by major software companies [11,16]. Researchers from Microsoft, Google, Facebook, Amazon, etc. [16] have agreed that one of the challenges facing online controlled experiments, is the quality of data and if it is possible to deal with it using Machine Learning. In a contrasting study [11], it is pointed out that occasionally early automatic stops of experiment-driven systems could be harmful. In the proposed Ph.D. project with the focus on GraalVM, we are facing a similar situation where a trade-off needs to be done in the number of experiments being executed and stopped early and the error rates of falsely reporting a change and missing a true performance change.

There have been attempts to reduce the test size of benchmarking such as multi-variate testing (MVT) or the approach in the study by Grano et al. [15]. Although existing techniques can help reduce the total test volume, the reduction is not enough to avoid skipping tested commits. In a similar study [18] authors introduced a statistic method namely *Always Valid p-Value*, for continuous monitoring of A/B tests. Although reducing benchmarking volume is promising, expert knowledge is required to decide on the appropriate test size. In this PhD project, we plan to reduce computing costs without skipping test cases.

Some research groups have been looking at prioritizing test cases and running first those which are predicted to find performance regressions based on [24]. For example, Altiero et al. [4] use genetic algorithms to populate test cases and those with a higher probability of finding performance regressions will survive and are executed first. In a similar approach [21], the entire process of populating and selecting test cases, is automated. However, these approaches require prior knowledge of how to formulate test cases where a change can be detected.

There are recent frameworks that use data-driven methods such as Artificial Intelligence (AI), for controlling experiment-driven systems are trending; for example, (DACBench) [12], (SEAByTE) [22] and (SaFReL) [20]. In DACBench [12], authors aim to dynamically control the target algorithm's hyperparameters to improve its performance using AI. SEAByTE Artifact [22] aims at improving the automation of an experimentation pipeline of a micro-service system. However, both approaches are specific to an experimentation schema, and they do not provide an approach in which AI models could control experiment-driven systems. SaFReL [20] is an autonomous performance evaluation framework using self-adaptive fuzzy reinforcement learning, which generates the target performance test cases for various programs. The focus of SaFRel is on how to learn to generate test cases rather than increasing the efficiency of performance testing. By looking at the static code, Labeer et al. [19] have the tools to predict if a performance testing environment eventually becomes stable. They utilize machine learning models to predict whether a benchmark will be stable or not ahead of execution.

The closest study to our approach is found [3,14,23]. The authors of [3] use Decision Forest with Random Over Sampling to provide more significant performance regression detection for code changes. This approach reduces the cost of testing by 50% using a classifier, but it requires white-box analysis. Similarly, in both studies [14,23], they control experiment-driven systems online using data-driven methods, but their work is built on optimization strategies and white-box analysis. On the other hand, according to Costa et al. [9] which show practices that will not work well with Java's Microbenchmark Harness (JMH), developers must be careful integrating automation in their approaches.

This study is based on previous research work [7] which is developed in the department of the principal researcher. The project proposed in this paper aims to extend the current existing work and provide a formal approach to applying machine learning and statistics in experiment-driven systems.

9   Conclusion

The doctoral research project described in this paper outlines the research objectives and methodology designated for controlling experiment-driven systems using machine learning and statistical algorithms. The experiment-driven systems such as benchmarking and simulation projects are computationally costly. Studies suggest controlling these experiment-driven systems with data-driven methods such as Machine Learning, promises less computational costs.

Thus, we propose controlling the experiment-driven systems with machine learning and statistical methods. As the running example, we focus on the GraalVM benchmarking project. We illustrated that with a statistical approach, it is possible to reduce the computation costs up to 30% for some benchmarks, by stopping the experiments whose results are predictable.

Acknowledgment. This work has been partially supported by the EU project ExtremeXP grant agreement 101093164, partially by Charles University institutional funding SVV 260698/2023, and partially by the Charles University Grant Agency project 408622.

References

1. Abdullah, M., Bulej, L., Bures, T., Hnetynka, P., Horky, V., Tuma, P.: Reducing experiment costs in automated software performance regression detection. In: 2022 48th Euromicro Conference on Software Engineering and Advanced Applications (SEAA), Gran Canaria, Spain, pp. 56–59. IEEE (2022). https://doi.org/10.1109/SEAA56994.2022.00017
2. Ali, S., Hafeez, Y., Hussain, S., Yang, S.: Enhanced regression testing technique for agile software development and continuous integration strategies. Software Qual. J. **28**(2), 397–423 (2019). https://doi.org/10.1007/s11219-019-09463-4
3. ALShoaibi, D., Gupta, H., Mendelson, M., Jenhani, I., Mrad, A.B., Mkaouer, M.W.: Learning to characterize performance regression introducing code changes. In: Proceedings of the 37th ACM/SIGAPP Symposium on Applied Computing, Virtual Event, pp. 1590–1597. ACM (2022). https://doi.org/10.1145/3477314.3507150
4. Altiero, F., Colella, G., Corazza, A., Di Martino, S., Peron, A., Starace, L.L.L.: Change-aware regression test prioritization using genetic algorithms. In: 2022 48th Euromicro Conference on Software Engineering and Advanced Applications (SEAA), Gran Canaria, Spain, pp. 125–132. IEEE (2022). https://doi.org/10.1109/SEAA56994.2022.00028
5. Barrett, E., Bolz-Tereick, C.F., Killick, R., Mount, S., Tratt, L.: Virtual machine warmup blows hot and cold. Proc. ACM Program. Lang. **1**(OOPSLA), 1–27 (2017). https://doi.org/10.1145/3133876
6. Bukh, P.N.D.: Review of the art of computer systems performance analysis, techniques for experimental design, measurement, simulation and modeling. Interfaces **22**(4), 113–115 (1992)
7. Bulej, L., et al.: Unit testing performance with stochastic performance logic. Autom. Softw. Eng. **24**(1), 139–187 (2016). https://doi.org/10.1007/s10515-015-0188-0

8. Bulej, L., Horký, V., Tůma, P.: Tracking Performance of Graal on Public Benchmarks, p. 7258108 Bytes (2021). https://doi.org/10.6084/M9.FIGSHARE. 14447148. Artwork Size: 7258108 Bytes Publisher: figshare

9. Costa, D., Bezemer, C.P., Leitner, P., Andrzejak, A.: What's wrong with my benchmark results? Studying bad practices in JMH benchmarks. IEEE Trans. Softw. Eng. **47**(7), 1452–1467 (2021). https://doi.org/10.1109/TSE.2019.2925345

10. De Oliveira, A.B., Fischmeister, S., Diwan, A., Hauswirth, M., Sweeney, P.F.: Perphecy: performance regression test selection made simple but effective. In: 2017 IEEE International Conference on Software Testing, Verification and Validation (ICST), Tokyo, pp. 103–113. IEEE (2017). https://doi.org/10.1109/ICST.2017.17

11. Deng, A., Lu, J., Chen, S.: Continuous monitoring of A/B tests without pain: optional stopping in Bayesian testing. In: 2016 IEEE International Conference on Data Science and Advanced Analytics (DSAA), Montreal, QC, Canada, pp. 243–252. IEEE (2016). https://doi.org/10.1109/DSAA.2016.33

12. Eimer, T., Biedenkapp, A., Reimer, M., Adriansen, S., Hutter, F., Lindauer, M.: DACBench: a benchmark library for dynamic algorithm configuration. In: Proceedings of the Thirtieth International Joint Conference on Artificial Intelligence, pp. 1668–1674. International Joint Conferences on Artificial Intelligence Organization, Montreal, Canada (2021). https://doi.org/10.24963/ijcai.2021/230

13. Georges, A., Eeckhout, L., Buytaert, D.: Java performance evaluation through rigorous replay compilation. In: Proceedings of the 23rd ACM SIGPLAN Conference on Object-Oriented Programming Systems Languages and Applications, Nashville, TN, USA, pp. 367–384. ACM (2008). https://doi.org/10.1145/1449764.1449794

14. Gerostathopoulos, I., Plasil, F., Prehofer, C., Thomas, J., Bischl, B.: Automated online experiment-driven adaptation-mechanics and cost aspects. IEEE Access **9**, 58079–58087 (2021). https://doi.org/10.1109/ACCESS.2021.3071809

15. Grano, G., Laaber, C., Panichella, A., Panichella, S.: Testing with fewer resources: an adaptive approach to performance-aware test case generation. IEEE Trans. Software Eng. **47**(11), 2332–2347 (2021). https://doi.org/10.1109/TSE.2019.2946773

16. Gupta, S., et al.: Top challenges from the first practical online controlled experiments summit. ACM SIGKDD Explor. Newsl. **21**(1), 20–35 (2019). https://doi.org/10.1145/3331651.3331655

17. Habib, M.K., Ayankoso, S.A., Nagata, F.: Data-driven modeling: concept, techniques, challenges and a case study. In: 2021 IEEE International Conference on Mechatronics and Automation (ICMA), Takamatsu, Japan, pp. 1000–1007. IEEE (2021). https://doi.org/10.1109/ICMA52036.2021.9512658

18. Johari, R., Koomen, P., Pekelis, L., Walsh, D.: Always valid inference: continuous monitoring of A/B tests. Oper. Res. **70**(3), 1806–1821 (2022). https://doi.org/10.1287/opre.2021.2135

19. Laaber, C., Basmaci, M., Salza, P.: Predicting unstable software benchmarks using static source code features. Empir. Softw. Eng. **26**(6), 1–53 (2021). https://doi.org/10.1007/s10664-021-09996-y

20. Moghadam, M.H., Saadatmand, M., Borg, M., Bohlin, M., Lisper, B.: An autonomous performance testing framework using self-adaptive fuzzy reinforcement learning. Softw. Qual. J. (6), 1–33 (2021). https://doi.org/10.1007/s11219-020-09532-z

21. Pecorelli, F., Grano, G., Palomba, F., Gall, H.C., De Lucia, A.: Toward Granular Automatic Unit Test Case Generation (2022). https://doi.org/10.48550/ARXIV.2204.05561

22. Quin, F., Weyns, D.: SEAByTE: a self-adaptive micro-service system artifact for automating A/B testing. In: Proceedings of the 17th Symposium on Software Engineering for Adaptive and Self-Managing Systems, Pittsburgh, Pennsylvania, pp. 77–83. ACM (2022). https://doi.org/10.1145/3524844.3528081

23. Reichelt, D.G., Kuhne, S., Hasselbring, W.: PeASS: a tool for identifying performance changes at code level. In: 2019 34th IEEE/ACM International Conference on Automated Software Engineering (ASE), San Diego, CA, USA, pp. 1146–1149. IEEE (2019). https://doi.org/10.1109/ASE.2019.00123

24. Rothermel, G., Untch, R., Chu, C., Harrold, M.: Prioritizing test cases for regression testing. IEEE Trans. Software Eng. **27**(10), 929–948 (2001). https://doi.org/10.1109/32.962562

25. Saputri, T.R.D., Lee, S.W.: The application of machine learning in self-adaptive systems: a systematic literature review. IEEE Access **8**, 205948–205967 (2020). https://doi.org/10.1109/ACCESS.2020.3036037

26. Sheskin, D.J.: Handbook of Parametric and Nonparametric Statistical Procedures, 5 edn. Chapman and Hall/CRC, Boca Raton (2011). https://doi.org/10.1201/9780429186196

27. Smith, C.U.: Software performance antipatterns in cyber-physical systems. In: Proceedings of the ACM/SPEC International Conference on Performance Engineering, Edmonton, AB, Canada, pp. 173–180. ACM (2020). https://doi.org/10.1145/3358960.3379138

28. Traini, L., Cortellessa, V., Di Pompeo, D., Tucci, M.: Towards effective assessment of steady state performance in Java software: are we there yet? Empir. Softw. Eng. **28**(1), 13 (2023). https://doi.org/10.1007/s10664-022-10247-x

29. Vemulapati, J., Khastgir, A.S., Savalgi, C.: AI based performance benchmarking & analysis of big data and cloud powered applications: an in depth view. In: Proceedings of the 2019 ACM/SPEC International Conference on Performance Engineering, Mumbai, India, pp. 103–109. ACM (2019). https://doi.org/10.1145/3297663.3309676

Tutorials

Trust Management in the Internet of Everything

Barbora Buhnova[✉]

Faculty of Informatics, Masaryk University, Brno, Czech Republic
buhnova@mail.muni.cz

Abstract. Digitalization is leading us towards a future where people, processes, data and things are not only interacting with each other, but might start forming societies on their own. In these dynamic systems enhanced by artificial intelligence, trust management on the level of human-to-machine as well as machine-to-machine interaction becomes an essential ingredient in supervising safe and secure progress of our digitalized future. This tutorial paper discusses the essential elements of trust management in complex digital ecosystems, guiding the reader through the definitions and core concepts of trust management. Furthermore, it explains how trust-building can be leveraged to support people in safe interaction with other (possibly autonomous) digital agents, as trust governance may allow the ecosystem to trigger an auto-immune response towards untrusted digital agents, protecting human safety.

Keywords: Trust Management · Internet of Everything · Autonomous Ecosystems · Software Architecture

1 Introduction

The Internet of Everything (IoE), which is constructed by networking people, processes, data and things (e.g., devices, appliances, vehicles) [8], is reshaping the vision of how humans and autonomous systems could engage in common collaborative goals. While this advanced digitalization opens up numerous opportunities for our sustainable future, it also imposes new safety concerns regarding the undesirable behavior of autonomous digital actors in these ecosystems (e.g., a driverless car intentionally causing dangerous road consequences).

Trustworthiness does not guarantee trust. Although approaches exist to ensure trustworthiness of the individual ecosystem components, via improving their security, reliability, availability, etc., trust is difficult to get addressed via such solutions due to the fact that trust is conceptually a belief about a system that is out of our control. Therefore, although the system might declare its trustworthiness, this does not give us any guarantee that it can be trusted. This is an effect of the fact that malicious agents can enter the ecosystem with the intention to disrupt the basic functionality of a network for malicious purposes while keeping their malicious intentions hidden behind announced collaborative goals [7,28].

T. Batista et al. (Eds.): ECSA 2022, LNCS 13928, pp. 123–137, 2023.
https://doi.org/10.1007/978-3-031-36889-9_10

Immune-response capabilities of trust-based ecosystems. One promising strategy in supporting the safe progress of human-machine partnership in the presence of malicious entities within IoE is based on involving the intelligence inside the individual ecosystem agents, which could be directed towards real-time detection of trust-breaking behaviour in other agents [15] so that problematic agents are detected and isolated before they can engage in harmful behaviour. An effective trust-management system is, therefore, imperative for detecting and dealing with misbehaving agents before they jeopardize the ecosystem functionality [28].

Scope of this paper. This paper serves as supporting material for a tutorial that gives an introduction to the main elements of trust management in complex digital ecosystems. We discuss the understanding of trust in traditional domains, such as psychology, sociology or economics, leading us to the emerging debates on how trust can be understood in the context of the Internet of Everything. We go through the individual components of trust management, including trust evaluation and its influencing factors (e.g., feeling vulnerable), trust propagation (e.g., via reputation), and trust updates (e.g., via dynamic certification schemes). We give an overview of the current open discussions about the centralized/global vs decentralized/local trust management strategies and discuss their risks and related trust attacks (e.g., self-promotion or whitewashing).

As the topic of trust governance in the context of dynamic autonomous ecosystems involving human-machine interplay is very recent, the paper also presents some insights from the interactive part of the tutorial, which was organized as a working session around the most pressing research questions on the topic, touching e.g. the topics of higher values in digital ecosystems (such as ethics or fairness), privacy concerns and human-inherent subjectivity of trust.

2 Understanding Trust

While the research on trust in the context of Internet of Everything is quite recent, substantial body of knowledge exists in various research areas, namely discussing the definition of trust and approaches to building and managing trust. The main concepts relevant in the area of the Internet of Everything are outlined in this section.

2.1 Definitions of Trust

Trust is a complex phenomenon that has been studied in different contexts. This section outlines the definitions of trust in different domains.

- *Trust in Sociology:* Subjective probability that another party will perform an action that will not hurt my interest under uncertainty or ignorance [9].

- *Trust in Philosophy:* Risky action deriving from personal, moral relationships between two entities [21].

- *Trust in Economics:* Expectation upon a risky action under uncertainty and ignorance based on the calculated incentives for the action [17].

- *Trust in Psychology:* Cognitive learning process obtained from social experiences based on the consequences of trusting behaviors [27].

- *Trust in International Relations:* Belief that the other party is trustworthy with the willingness to reciprocate cooperation [20].

- *Trust in Automation:* Attitude or belief that an agent will help achieve another agent's goal in a situation characterized by uncertainty and vulnerability [22].

In what follows, i.e. in IoE ecosystems, we adopt the definition inspired from the context of automation, extending the understanding of the agents to intelligent systems as well as humans and things, i.e. understanding trust as *"the attitude or belief of an agent (trustor) to achieve a specific goal in interaction with another agent (trustee) under uncertainty and vulnerability"* (Fig. 1).

2.2 Characteristics of Trust

Trust in general is characterized by the following three characteristics [10,28]:

- *Subjective:* Trust is viewed using the centrality of an agent, wherein the trust is computed based on trustor's observation (i.e., direct trust) as well as the opinion (i.e., feedback or indirect trust) of the other agents.

- *Asymmetric:* Trust is an asymmetric property, i.e., if an agent A trusts another agent B, it does not guarantee that B also trusts A.

- *Transitive:* System agent A is more likely to develop trust towards an agent B if A trust agent C that trusts agent B.

2.3 Scope of Trust Evaluation

When evaluating trust, the scope of the considered context makes a difference. The scope that is typically considered is [10,28]:

- *Local:* It represents the trust based on an agent-agent relationship, wherein an agent evaluates the trustworthiness of another agent using local information such as its current observation and past experience.

- *Global:* In comparison to the local trust, the global trust is considered as the reputation of an agent within the ecosystem, wherein the reputation each agent might be influenced by the local trust score of each of the other agents in the ecosystem.

- *Context-specific:* Trust of an agent towards another agent varies with context. A trust relation between the agents is usually dynamic and depends on multiple factors such as temporal factors or location.

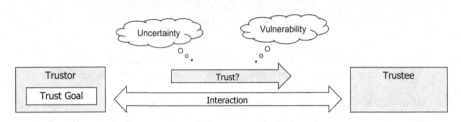

Fig. 1. Trust Definition for the Context of Internet of Everything (inspired from [22]).

2.4   Trust Components

Trust of one agent (trustor) in another (trustee) is being built via combining the mechanisms of direct trust (based on local and highly context-specific experience with the other agent) and indirect trust (possibly global reputation of the agent) [29]. The two are later combined via the component of trust decision (see Fig. 2).

– *Direct Trust* represents an individual judgment by the trustor from its direct interaction with the trustee. Specifically, it is being based on a combination of present and past experience (direct observation) of the trustor with the trustee. In this regard, mechanisms need to be in place to evaluate the experience during runtime interaction of the trustor with the trustee (possibly mimicking human cognitive processes) without exposing its vulnerabilities.

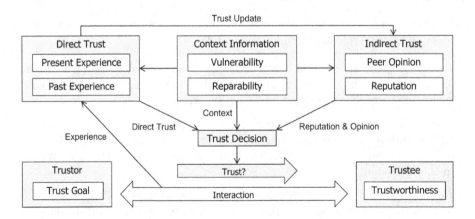

Fig. 2. Trust Management Components.

- *Indirect Trust* is being inferred based on propagated opinions from different trust paths to judge the reputation of a trustee. The primary sources are thus the trusted peers of the trustor (their opinions and recommendation) and an authority overseeing the reputation of the trustee within the ecosystem. In this regard, mechanisms need to be in place to update the reputation and propagate it through the ecosystem.

- *Context Information* influences the trust decision to reflect on the current situation of the trustor in which the trust decision is being made (e.g. how vulnerable it feels in interaction with the trustee, what risks it takes, whether the trustee will be held accountable in case of malicious behaviour, whether the possible harm is reversible or would be compensated, i.e. reparability is ensured). Besides, broader contextual information also influences the direct and indirect trust computation.

3   Trust Management Activities

The individual trust management activities are connected to the evaluation of the direct trust, management of the indirect trust, and the combination of the two in a trust decision [28].

3.1   Direct-Trust Evaluation

The assessment of direct trust involves the computation of trust metrics characterizing the present/past experience together with aggregating the results into a trust score via trust formation.

Trust Metrics refer to the features that are chosen and combined in trust computation. These features can refer to:

- *QoS Metrics*, which represent the confidence that an agent is able to offer high quality of the delivered service, e.g. in terms of reliability, availability, security or accuracy [30].

- *Social Metrics*, which represent the social relationships among ecosystem agents, which can include integrity, benevolence, honesty, friendship, openness, altruism, or unselfishness [16,26].

Trust Formation forms the trust based on one of the following strategies [28]:

- *Single aspect*, e.g., in terms of a positive or negative threshold for a specific trust metric.

- *Multiple aspects*, i.e., more sophisticated trust model that includes various trust metrics [3].

- *Aspect aggregation*, i.e. multiple aspects aggregated in a single trust score, for instance via a Weighted Sum, Belief Theory, Bayesian System, Fuzzy Logic, Regression Analysis, or Machine Learning [28].

3.2 Indirect-Trust Management

The management of the indirect trust involves trust updates and trust propagation to ensure up-to-date opinion and reputation information that can feed trust decisions.

Trust Update. At the end of a transaction or at any specified time interval, trust reputation of a trustee needs to be updated, which typically happens in one of the following ways:

- *Event-driven:* trust is updated after each transaction or once an event has occurred [4], which however increases the traffic overhead in the network.
- *Time-driven:* trust is collected and updated periodically after a given interval of time [25].
- *Hybrid:* trust is updated periodically and/or in case of an event (after an interaction) [30].

Trust Propagation. Trust propagation facilitates the understanding of how the trust propagates in the ecosystem and is generally categorized in [28]:

- *Centralized schemes* rely on a centralized entity that is primarily responsible for (a) gathering trust-related information for the purpose of trust computation and (b) propagating it in the ecosystem [26]. Centralized controlled frameworks are vulnerable to a single point of failure, which can cause the entire ecosystem trust to collapse.
- *Distributed schemes* rely on the individual agents being responsible for both trust computation and propagation within the ecosystem without any central authority [4]. This scheme faces other inherent challenges, like honest trust computation, managing computational capabilities and unbiased trust propagation within the ecosystem.
- *Hybrid schemes* are aimed at mitigating the challenges of the two earlier schemes, dividing the propagation into two categories, i.e., (1) locally distributed and globally centralized, and (2) locally centralized and globally distributed [26].

3.3 Trust Decision

After computing the direct-trust score of a trustee and understanding its indirect-trust reputation (from the peers and/or central authority), the main purpose of a trust management system is to identify whether the trustee is to be considered trustworthy or untrustworthy by means of [28]:

- *Threshold-based decision:* where the decision is taken on the basis of either a rank-based function or a (possibly dynamically changing) threshold value.
- *Policy-based decision:* where more complex policies are used to identify and decide whether an agent is classified as trustworthy or not by using contextual information, e.g. in terms of location or temporal factors.

Table 1. Social Values in terms of Ethical Principles [18]

1	Transparency	Transparency, explainability, explicability, understandability, interpretability, communication, disclosure, showing
2	Justice and fairness	Justice, fairness, consistency, inclusion, equality, equity, (non-)bias, (non-)discrimination, diversity, plurality, accessibility, reversibility, remedy, redress, challenge, access and distribution
3	Non-maleficence	Non-maleficence, security, safety, harm, protection, precaution, prevention, integrity (bodily or mental), non-subversion
4	Responsibility	Responsibility, accountability, liability, acting with integrity
5	Privacy	Privacy, personal or private information
6	Beneficence	Benefits, beneficence, well-being, peace, social good, common good
7	Freedom and autonomy	Freedom, autonomy, consent, choice, self-determination, liberty, empowerment
8	Trust	Trust
9	Sustainability	Sustainability, environment (nature), energy, resources (energy)
10	Dignity	Dignity
11	Solidarity	Solidarity, social security, cohesion

4 Trust-Based Mechanisms for Ecosystem Wellbeing

Once we have a way to assess the trustworthiness of the individual ecosystem members, we can employ the information in the actual support of the wellbeing of the ecosystem, e.g. in terms of its safety, fairness, solidarity, or other values (see Table 1) [12,18]. Some examples of wellbeing-promoting mechanisms follow.

Incentives in Terms of Reward and Punishment. One of the essential mechanisms for promoting ecosystem wellbeing is the ability of the ecosystem to incentivize behaviours that contribute to promoting the agreed values in the ecosystem. This is being done via the mechanisms of reward and punishment, which can be based e.g. on the actual trust score of the agent, or on the relative change (recent increase/decrease) of the trust score [13,14].

Evidence Collection for Justification and Reparation. To ensure fairness in the ecosystem, mechanisms need to be in place that not only help us see there might be discrimination or unfairness happening in the system (e.g. newly joining agents having a hard time gaining sufficient trust needed to be allowed to participate fully in the ecosystem), but also help us justify decisions that might be opposed by certain ecosystem agents, or to correct trust misjudgment [13].

Besides, evidence collection is a promising tool to detect trust attacks (discussed in Sect. 5) and hidden malicious intentions of ecosystem agents before they get fully revealed (discussed in Sect. 7).

Safety Assurance in the Face of Untrusted Agents. One of the essential ingredients of the *immune-response capabilities of trust-based ecosystems* envisioned in Sect. 1 is the ability to isolate the misbehaving agents to protect the safety of the ecosystem. While this might be easy to do in the scenarios where trust navigates spreading of information or services (the trustor simply avoids using the knowledge and services by untrustworthy agents), it becomes challenging when trust shall navigate physical safety (e.g. to avoid collision with a malicious vehicle). In the latter case, an action by the authority overseeing agents' reputation might be needed, e.g., imposing restrictions of the agent function in effect of the reputation falling below certain threshold. In such cases, it is crucial to apply the mechanisms of adaptive function restriction to mitigate the risk of misjudging the trustworthiness of an agent [11].

5 Trust Attacks

Given the fact that trust is largely influenced by the belief and perception of the individual ecosystem agents, there is a high risk of trust attacks, which can take different forms (see Fig. 3), summarized below.

Individual Attacks: refer to the attacks launched by an individual agent, which can take form of [2,28]:

- *Self-Promoting Attacks:* In this type of attack, an agent promotes its significance by providing good recommendation for itself so as to be selected as a service provider, and then acts maliciously.
- *Whitewashing Attacks:* In this attack, an agent exits and re-joins the ecosystem to recover its reputation and to wash-away its own bad reputation.
- *Discriminatory Attacks:* In this type of attack, an agent explicitly attacks other agents that do not have common friends with it, i.e. it performs well for a particular service/agent and badly for some other services/agents.
- *Opportunistic Service Attacks:* In this type of attack, an agent might offer a great service to improve its reputation when its reputation falls too low.
- *On-Off Attacks:* In this type of attack, an agent provides good and bad services on and off (randomly) to avoid being labeled as a low-reputed agent.

Collusion-based Attacks: represent the attacks launched by a group of agents to either provide a high rating or low rating to a particular agent, such as [24]:

- *Bad-Mouthing Attacks:* In this type of attack, a group of agents diminishes the reputation of a trustworthy agent within the ecosystem by providing bad recommendations about it.

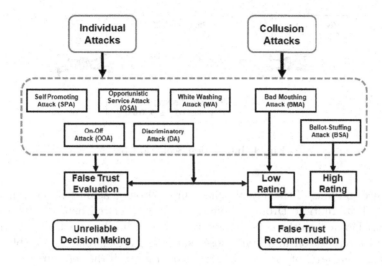

Fig. 3. Trust Attacks [28].

- *Ballot-Stuffing Attacks:* In this type of attack, a group of agents boosts the reputation of bad agents within the ecosystem by providing good recommendations for them.

6   Scenarios

This section discusses examples of trust-management scenarios in the context of vehicular ecosystems, where trust management is crucial to avoid safety consequences of misbehaviour of individual smart agents.

6.1   Collision Avoidance with Misbehaving Vehicle

Consider a situation of a vehicle (trustor) getting in the proximity of another vehicle (trustee), which could possibly be misbehaving (either due to a fault or being intentionally malicious) with an increased risk of causing a collision. In such a scenario, the possibility to collect present experience influencing the direct-trust evaluation is limited due to the risk of collision in case of very close interaction. A way to support the experience building in such a case, which we have explored in [15], is illustrated in Fig. 4 on an example of two drones. Consider Drone 1 (trustor) evaluating its direct trust in Drone 2 (trustee). The present-experience evaluation supporting the trust building in this scenario is formed in the following steps: First, Drone 1 asks Drone 2 to declare its intended behaviour in form of a Digital Twin (declared behaviour) that can be used by Drone 1 within the direct-trust evaluation process. In response, Drone 2 shares its Digital Twin (DT), which is checked by Drone 1 for its trustworthiness (absence of malicious actions) and then (if harmless), Drone 1 employs the DT in runtime

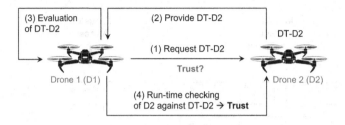

Fig. 4. Interaction Scenario [15].

compliance checking of the actual behaviour of Drone 2 against its Digital Twin (D2-DT). If at runtime Drone 2 deviates from its declared behaviour, Drone 1 can report Drone 2 to the ecosystem governance authority, which can internally decrease its reputation and start closer surveillance of Drone 2, possibly even employing some level of safeguarding of its operation (if the reputation falls too low or the associated threat gets too high).

6.2   Trust in Run-time Update Downloaded to a Vehicle

The evolution in smart driving functions is pushing for frequent runtime updates being downloaded to the vehicles to improve their functionality, quality (e.g. vulnerability correction) or A/B test future software evolution. While numerous procedures are in place to ensure the trustworthiness of the software updates being downloaded to the vehicle, the risk is still there that these updates can contain vulnerabilities or hidden intended faults manifesting into malicious behavior [6]. This can be caused even intentionally, with the help of an insider attacker engaged in the software update development. In this scenario, the vehicle shall have mechanisms in place to gradually build trust in the new software update before it allows it to control its critical driving functions, where both direct-trust evaluation and indirect-trust management can be integrated into the trust-building process. In [6], we have explored the potential of the Digital Twin of the update also in this scenario, to facilitate the experience gaining via predictive simulation of the update with the help of the Digital Twin.

6.3   Trust-based Vehicle Admission in a Platoon

In the future automotive ecosystems, the formation of vehicle platoons is envisioned to support the traffic flow and reduced fuel consumption for more sustainable smart mobility. Consider a scenario where at the entry point of a highway, a vehicle can download a software solution that would assist it in platooning coordination [1]. When driving in a platoon, vehicles benefit from reduced fuel consumption due to reduced air friction, but the complex dynamics of collaborative and competitive forces could raise trust concerns about the safety of riding in such close proximity to other vehicles [7]. In this scenario, a vehicle in the platoon ecosystem can suddenly accelerate or decelerate and cause multiple car crashes within the platoon. Such a behavior can be caused by a fault or malicious intentions of the individual vehicle, or by a logic bomb in the downloaded software solution responsible for the platooning coordination, caused by a vulnerability inserted e.g. by a malicious insider working for the software provider. In this way, the solution can combine the two approaches outlined in the previous two scenarios.

6.4 Human-to-Vehicle Trust Building in Autonomous Driving

The future automotive systems will be subject to a gradual process towards fully autonomous driving. During the process, human responsibilities will be gradually replaced by autonomous driving functions, at a speed governed by the level of trust of the humans in the autonomous driving capabilities of the vehicles. The acceptance of any new level of autonomy shall be built up gradually and governed by trust-management mechanisms, to ensure acceptance by both drivers and pedestrians. In [5], we envision the incremental development of autonomy on the road as a win-win situation for instrumenting the building of trust on both sides. In order to build a trusting relationship, the driver and the system shall in our view evolve together in a process that creates sustainable trust and supports the interchange between the human trustor with a smart software trustee.

6.5 Information Exchange in Coordinated Ecosystem Moves

An interesting scenario that came up in the tutorial discussion is linked to the high reliance on information exchange in coordinated ecosystem moves, e.g. when one vehicle is overtaking another one (whether driver-less or with a driver, possibly a cyclist) and needs to know its planned speed, when an emergency vehicle needs to be given priority when passing through a crossing, or when a human needs to be let to cross the street. Trust in this case needs to be built not only in the other agent in the ecosystem, but also in the actual information being exchanged, which could be influenced e.g. by a faulty sensor. In this regard, an interesting trust scenario is also between a vehicle and its own sensor, which might be faulty. And a great comment was given also about the individual pieces of information (e.g. that there is ice on the road in a particular location), which could act as the first-class IoE ecosystem entities with their own trust score governed by indirect trust management.

7 Challenges of Trust Management in IoE

Besides the trust attacks, which bring a considerable challenge in designing robust trust management systems, numerous other challenges of trust management in IoE have been discussed with the tutorial participants, and also outlined in literature [28]. We summarize the key challenges below.

Situational Scope of Trust. There is high context-dependence of trust, namely in terms of the location and time in their broader understanding [19]. Besides, the peer network can change depending on the context of trust evaluation, similarly to the human context, where a person who can be trusted in the context of their own expertise, might be still untrustworthy in a field of knowledge where the person relies on the opinion of peers influenced by misinformation. This is also a reason why reputation shall be contextualized, as the reputation of an agent might be influenced by various dimensions of the context in which the trustworthiness is judged.

Subjectivity of Trust. Trust is a highly subjective concept, being influenced not only by the context of the trustor, but also the individual trust goal of the trustor (the reason for which the trust is being established) and the factors inherent to the individual trustor (e.g. the willingness to take risk and trust despite the uncertainty, or willingness to rely on the peers recommendation). Furthermore, the peer network that influences the trust decision might itself be subjective or biased, which causes the propagation of subjectivity and bias in the ecosystem.

Default Trust Score of New Agents. The current trust management solutions presume the initial trust score of a newly joined agent to be within the range $< 0; 0.5 >$ [28]. Choosing the initial trust score (so-called cold start problem) is challenging on both sides of the interval. When the initial trust score is close to 0.5 (i.e. neutral, neither trustworthy nor untrustworthy) [3], this might lead to a malicious agent abusing its trust level to cause harm before it identifies as untrustworthy, or to white-wash its reputation by leaving and re-joining the ecosystem under new identity. On the other hand, when the initial trust score is close to 0, the new agent might never get the chance to engage with the rest of the ecosystem (i.e., not being trusted).

Trust Erosion. Besides the fact that the trust score of any agent in the IoE ecosystem varies with time, its trust score (or reputation) is also subject to decay if there are no or too few interactions the agent is involved in [29]. It is therefore important to consider the trust values lifespan where the trust score of inactive agents shall be subject to decay after a particular duration of time [28].

Detection of Hidden Malicious Intentions. As the overview of trust attacks above has shown, the malicious intentions of the IoE ecosystem agents can be very well hidden and hard to detect. Furthermore, when we employ very sensitive methods of detection, e.g. the discussed runtime compliance checking of the declared and actual trustee behaviour [15], we run into the risk of misjudging the trustworthiness of the agent, possibly reporting it as suspicious due to a slight deviation in the declared-actual behaviour although it might be well-behaving (with a deviation related to the accuracy of the declared behaviour). In that regard, it is crucial to have mechanisms in place for long-term evidence collection that can support richer reasoning on the behavioral patterns of the agents in the ecosystem, indicating e.g. the patterns resembling trust attacks or hiding the attempts of misbehaviour.

Building Trust in the Trustworthy. Although much of the text has been centered around trust management directed towards detecting untrustworthy agents, it is equally important to explore methods supporting trust building in the trustworthy agents. Indeed, the fact that an agent is trustworthy does not guarantee it will be trusted by others, especially in face of trust attacks or biased peer opinion that might be directed against it. One of the promising techniques in promoting trust in this context is based on the ability of an agent to give evidence of its trustworthiness. In the context of AI-enhanced agents, for instance, this might be based on the explanation of agents' actions, which is shown to have positive influence on human participation and willingness to engage with the digital agents [23].

High Degree of Dynamism and Uncertainty in IoE. As illustrated by different examples in this section, the dynamism and uncertainty inherent to the Internet of Everything is enormous. Agents can join and leave the ecosystem anytime, and they have very limited information about each other, facing high unpredictability of other agents and their environment. In such conditions, crucial information that is needed to make a trust decision might be missing, pushing trust models to include built-in mechanisms to deal with uncertainty and bias in the decisions.

8   Conclusion

In the context of Internet of Everything (IoE), human and digital agents form coalitions for achieving collaborative or individual goals. In a constant risk of malicious attacks, ecosystem participants ask for strong guarantees of their collaborators' trustworthiness, which can be achieved via the mechanisms of trust management. In this paper, we have presented the emerging research field of trust management in the context of IoE, discussing the definitions, concepts, examples of scenarios and research challenges relevant to the community of software architecture, which undergoes the transition from rather stable systems of systems towards dynamic autonomous ecosystems [1].

Acknowledgement. The work was supported by ERDF "CyberSecurity, Cyber-Crime and Critical Information Infrastructures Center of Excellence" (No. CZ.02.1.01/0.0/0.0/16_019/ 0000822).

References

1. Capilla, R., Cioroaica, E., Buhnova, B., Bosch, J.: On autonomous dynamic software ecosystems. IEEE Trans. Eng. Manage. **69**(6), 3633–3647 (2022)
2. Chahal, R.K., Kumar, N., Batra, S.: Trust management in social internet of things: a taxonomy, open issues, and challenges. Comput. Commun. **150**, 13–46 (2020)
3. Chen, R., Bao, F., Guo, J.: Trust-based service management for social internet of things systems. IEEE Trans. Dependable Secure Comput. **13**(6), 684–696 (2015)
4. Chen, R., Guo, J., Bao, F.: Trust management for SOA-based IoT and its application to service composition. IEEE Trans. Serv. Comput. **9**(3), 482–495 (2014)

5. Cioroaica, E., Buhnova, B., Kuhn, T., Schneider, D.: Building trust in the untrustable. In: 2020 IEEE/ACM 42nd International Conference on Software Engineering: Software Engineering in Society (ICSE-SEIS), pp. 21–24. IEEE (2020)
6. Cioroaica, E., Kuhn, T., Buhnova, B.: (Do not) trust in ecosystems. In: 2019 IEEE/ACM 41st International Conference on Software Engineering: New Ideas and Emerging Results (ICSE-NIER), pp. 9–12. IEEE (2019)
7. Cioroaica, E., Purohit, A., Buhnova, B., Schneider, D.: Goals within trust-based digital ecosystems. In: 2021 IEEE/ACM Joint 9th International Workshop on Software Engineering for Systems-of-Systems and 15th Workshop on Distributed Software Development, Software Ecosystems and Systems-of-Systems (SESoS/WDES), pp. 1–7. IEEE (2021)
8. Farias da Costa, V.C., Oliveira, L., de Souza, J.: Internet of everything (IoE) taxonomies: a survey and a novel knowledge-based taxonomy. Sensors. **21**(2), 568 (2021)
9. Gambetta, D., et al.: Can we trust trust. Trust: Making Breaking Cooper. Relat. **13**, 213–237 (2000)
10. Ghafari, S.M., et al.: A survey on trust prediction in online social networks. IEEE Access **8**, 144292–144309 (2020)
11. Halasz, D., Buhnova, B.: Rethinking safety in autonomous ecosystems. In: 2022 17th Conference on Computer Science and Intelligence Systems (FedCSIS). IEEE (2022)
12. Bangui, H., Buhnova, B., Ge, M.: Social internet of things: ethical AI principles in trust management. In: 14th International Conference on Ambient Systems, Networks and Technologies (ANT-2023). Procedia Computer Science (2023)
13. Bangui, H., Ge, M., Buhnova, B.: Deep-learning based reputation model for indirect trust management. In: 14th International Conference on Ambient Systems, Networks and Technologies (ANT-2023). Procedia Computer Science (2023)
14. Bangui, H., Cioroaica, E., Ge, M., Buhnova, B.: Deep-learning based trust management with self-adaptation in the internet of behavior. In: Proceedings of the 38th Annual ACM Symposium on Applied Computing. ACM (2023)
15. Iqbal, D., Buhnova, B.: Model-based approach for building trust in autonomous drones through digital twins. In: 2022 IEEE International Conference on Systems, Man, and Cybernetics (SMC), pp. 656–662. IEEE (2022)
16. Iqbal, D., Buhnova, B., Cioroaica, E.: Digital twins for trust building in autonomous drones through dynamic safety evaluation. In: Proceedings of the 18th International Conference on Evaluation of Novel Approaches to Software Engineering (ENASE). Scitepress (2023)
17. James, H.S., Jr.: The trust paradox: a survey of economic inquiries into the nature of trust and trustworthiness. J. Econ. Behav. Organ. **47**(3), 291–307 (2002)
18. Jobin, A., Ienca, M., Vayena, E.: The global landscape of AI ethics guidelines. Nat. Mach. Intell. **1**(9), 389–399 (2019)
19. Khan, W.Z., Hakak, S., Khan, M.K., et al.: Trust management in social internet of things: architectures, recent advancements, and future challenges. IEEE Internet Things J. **8**(10), 7768–7788 (2020)
20. Kydd, A.H.: Trust and mistrust in international relations. Princeton University Press (2007)
21. Lagerspetz, O.: Trust: The tacit demand. Kluwer Academic Publishers (1998)
22. Lee, J.D., See, K.A.: Trust in automation: designing for appropriate reliance. Hum. Factors **46**(1), 50–80 (2004)

23. Li, N., Cámara, J., Garlan, D., Schmerl, B.: Reasoning about when to provide explanation for human-involved self-adaptive systems. In: 2020 IEEE International Conference on Autonomic Computing and Self-Organizing Systems (ACSOS), pp. 195–204. IEEE (2020)

24. Marche, C., Nitti, M.: Trust-related attacks and their detection: a trust management model for the social IoT. IEEE Trans. Netw. Serv. Manage. 18(3), 3297–3308 (2020)

25. Namal, S., Gamaarachchi, H., MyoungLee, G., Um, T.W.: Autonomic trust management in cloud-based and highly dynamic IoT applications. In: 2015 ITU Kaleidoscope: Trust in the Information Society (K-2015), pp. 1–8. IEEE (2015)

26. Nitti, M., Girau, R., Atzori, L.: Trustworthiness management in the social internet of things. IEEE Trans. Knowl. Data Eng. 26(5), 1253–1266 (2013)

27. Rotter, J.B.: Interpersonal trust, trustworthiness, and gullibility. Am. Psychol. 35(1), 1 (1980)

28. Sagar, S., Mahmood, A., Sheng, Q.Z., Pabani, J.K., Zhang, W.E.: Understanding the trustworthiness management in the social internet of things: A survey. arXiv preprint arXiv:2202.03624 (2022)

29. Truong, N.B., Um, T.W., Zhou, B., Lee, G.M.: From personal experience to global reputation for trust evaluation in the social internet of things. In: GLOBECOM 2017–2017 IEEE Global Communications Conference, pp. 1–7. IEEE (2017)

30. Xiao, H., Sidhu, N., Christianson, B.: Guarantor and reputation based trust model for social internet of things. In: 2015 International Wireless Communications and Mobile Computing Conference (IWCMC), pp. 600–605. IEEE (2015)

Continuous Dependability Assessment of Microservice Systems

Alberto Avritzer[1]([✉]), Matteo Camilli[2], Andrea Janes[3], Barbara Russo[4],
Catia Trubiani[5], and André van Hoorn[6]

[1] eSulab Solutions, Princeton, NJ, USA
beto@esulabsolutions.com
[2] Politecnico di Milano, Milan, Italy
matteo.camilli@polimi.it
[3] FHV Vorarlberg University of Applied Sciences, Dornbirn, Austria
andrea.janes@fhv.at
[4] Free University of Bozen-Bolzano, Bolzano, Italy
barbara.russo@unibz.it
[5] Gran Sasso Science Institute, L'Aquila, Italy
catia.trubiani@gssi.it
[6] University of Hamburg, Hamburg, Germany
andre.van.hoorn@uni-hamburg.de

Abstract. In this paper, we overview the tutorial presented at the 16th European Conference on Software Architecture. The tutorial's goal was to summarize the challenges and approaches for verification and validation in microservices systems. We introduced the PPTAM approach for dependability assessment. PPTAM employs a variety of architectural artifacts and steps, including the use of operational data obtained from production-level application performance management (APM) tools, the automated assessment of load tests based on defined scalability requirements, and the development of computationally efficient algorithms for software performance anti-pattern (SPA) detection that could be implemented in CI/CD pipelines.

Keywords: Microservices · scalability testing · software performance anti-patterns

1 Introduction

Performance assessment and improvement of microservices systems are challenging tasks as they require systematic and continuous analysis of complex dynamic ecosystems [17] by engineers and operators having expertise in performance engineering practices. Indeed, systematic assessment must be performed continuously during both development (e.g., testing) and operations (e.g., monitoring) to ensure microservices meet their required level of performance. Thus,

T. Batista et al. (Eds.): ECSA 2022, LNCS 13928, pp. 138–147, 2023.
https://doi.org/10.1007/978-3-031-36889-9_11

performance engineers need proper tools that support automated and continuous performance monitoring and assessment of microservices systems running on highly configurable and dynamic environments.

We recently developed an approach and tooling support for performance monitoring and analysis that automatically detects performance problems (e.g., scalability bottlenecks, problematic configurations) and software performance anti-patterns (e.g., application hiccups, expensive DB calls).

The major contributions of our approach are as follows:

1. Definition of the domain-based scalability metric to quantify the supported scale of operation of microservices systems according to the system, its configuration, and target operational profiles [5,6].
2. Introduction and extensive evaluation of the domain-based approach for scalability assessment of microservices using load tests [5,6].
3. Implementation of the open source PPTAM tooling infrastructure [4,5,7].
4. Definition of a multi-variate approach for efficient software performance anti-pattern detection and characterization [2,3].

We derived our empirical results from the application to three different systems, two web applications for e-commerce that are well-known in the research community, Sock Shop [6,13] and Train Ticket [12], a real telecommunication system developed by Ericsson [2,9], and a large digital transformation system [15]. The approach has been also validated through a simulation model based on Palladio that enabled SPA injection into the Ericsson telecom system and the collection of accuracy measures. Our approach has also been applied to a traffic system to evaluate alternative deployment architectures for microservices against the monolithic one [10,11].

Our tutorial at the 16th European Conference on Software Architecture (ECSA 2022) presented an overview of our approach and tooling infrastructure. In addition, we presented (i) a demo of PPTAM including the automated approach for the evaluation of domain-based scalability that is based on the microservice architecture's ability to satisfy the performance requirement under varying workload; (ii) empirical results derived from a benchmark microservice architecture; and (iii) an illustration of the multivariate approach for detecting scalability bottlenecks and SPAs.

This paper summarizes the approach and refers the interested reader to the relevant publications that include comprehensive discussions and further details. The rest of the paper is organized as follows. In Sect. 2 we introduce the notion of Domain-based Metric and how to exploit it for scalability assessment of microservices systems. In Sect. 3 we give an overview of the PPTAM tooling infrastructure. In Sect. 4 we describe the multivariate SPA detection approach and we conclude the paper in Sect. 5.

2 Domain-based Metric and Scalability Assessment

In [5,6], we introduced a quantitative approach for the performance assessment of microservice architecture deployment alternatives. The approach uses automated performance testing results to quantitatively assess each architecture deployment configuration in terms of a domain-based metric. For performance testing, we focus on load tests based on operational workload situations. We define workload situation as an abstract concept to represent the output of operational data analysis per application domain, e.g., the number of concurrent users in e-commerce systems or arrival/transaction rate in the banking domain.

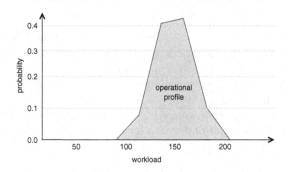

Fig. 1. Operational profile describing the probability of occurrence of each workload situation in production (adapted from [15]).

We combine analysis of operational profile data with load testing results to generate a domain metric dashboard. The dashboard illustrates system scalability with respect to the operational profile distribution in production, i.e., the empirical distribution of workload situations, and performance results in the load test environment. Operational profile data is used to estimate the probability of occurrence of each workload situation in production (see Fig. 1).

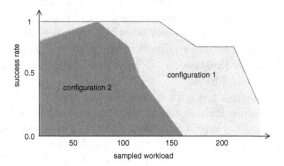

Fig. 2. Success rate per workload situation for different architecture deployment configurations of the test environment (adapted from [15]).

Scalability requirements are used to assess each architecture deployment configuration. The resulting quantitative assessment is a metric—the so-called success rate—with value between 0–1 that assesses the fitness of a certain architecture alternative to perform under a defined workload situation (see Fig. 2).

The so-called *domain-based metric* quantifies a configuration's ability to satisfy scalability requirements under a given operational profile, i.e., the set of workload situations with their relative frequency of occurrence.

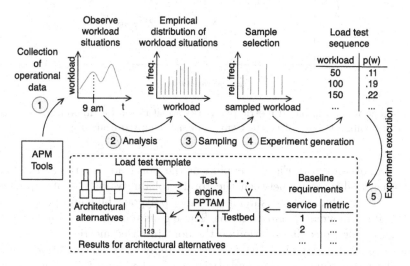

Fig. 3. Approach for computing the domain-based metric (adapted from [15]).

The approach for computing the domain-based metric, as illustrated in Fig. 3, consists of the following steps:

1. Step 1: *Collection of operational data*, i.e., data on normal system usage (e.g., HTTP requests) in a given time window are collected from Application Monitoring (APM) Tools,
2. Step 2: *Analysis of operational data*, i.e., the quantitative estimation of the probability of occurrence of a certain workload situation (e.g., number of concurrent users) based on the analysis of the operational data,
3. Step 3: *Sampling*, i.e., the selection of a subset of load tests to execute,
4. Step 4: *Experiment generation*, i.e., the automated generation of the load test cases for different deployment configurations under evaluation, and *baseline computation, quantitative definition of the scalability requirements*, i.e., the quantitative definition of the scalability requirements that consist of the expected pass/fail criteria for the load tests, e.g., based on a specified threshold of the system response time for the expected workload,
5. Step 5: *Experiment execution*, i.e., the execution of load test cases for the deployment configurations specified in the experiment generation step, and the computation of the domain-based metric.

The contribution to the domain-based metric of workload situations in a load test sequence can be displayed in plots. Such a plot depicts the degree to which a given system deployment configuration satisfies the fail/pass criterion.

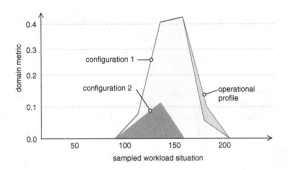

Fig. 4. Plots of domain-based metric per workload situation for different architecture deployment configurations of the test environment (adapted from [15]).

In the example shown in Fig. 4, the plots at the workload situations of the load test sequence show gaps between the total probability mass (outer polygon, orange) and the obtained measurements (inner polygons, blue and pink) for two architecture deployment configurations. These gaps represent the impact of the measured performance degradation on the domain-based metric.

To calculate the domain-based metric, we apply the following steps: we calculate the mean response time and variance of a low load for a microservice, as shown in Fig. 5a. We define an upper bound for the response time defined by the average response time before plus three standard deviations. In Fig. 5a, the area depicted in red depicts all those response times we consider above the upper bound, above the scalability requirement for the associated microservice.

The success rate is calculated for a given workload as shown in the gray crosses in Fig. 5b. Then, we can determine if — for that workload — the response time is below the set tolerance limit. If we now want to evaluate the scalability of the entire system, i.e., all services, at a given operating point (yellow line Fig. 5b), we evaluate each service and sum all relative call frequencies[1] of each service that responds within the set upper bound. In Fig. 5b, both services operate below their respective upper bound and in this case this leads to a success rate of 100%.

3   PPTAM Tool Overview

Figure 6 includes details on the tool ecosystem used to implement the proposed approach[2]. It comprises the following major components:

1. An analysis component that gathers the operational profile from a production system and computes the baseline probability of finding the system at a given state.

---

[1] The relative call frequency represents the proportion that a service contributes to accomplish the task of the system under study. If a service contributes 10% and fails, we consider the system to be 90% functional.

[2] PPTAM including a demo is publicly available at https://github.com/pptam.

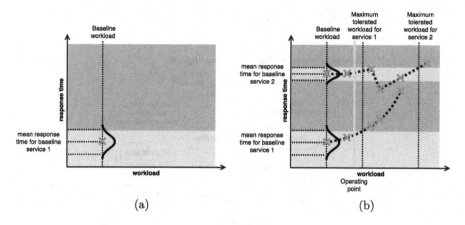

Fig. 5. Domain-based metric calculation steps 1 and 2 (5a) and 3 and 4 (5b)

2. An infrastructure that generates (driver) and executes (testbed) load test experiments with different architecture deployment configurations to collect system performance against a baseline.
3. A graphical user interface that calculates and visualizes the current performance metric in a report and on a smartphone user interface (dashboard).

Each of these components is operated by a series of tools that we developed or integrated. For gathering the operational profile, we utilize Application Performance Monitoring (APM) [16] tools, e.g., an open-source tool from the OpenAPM initiative[3]. These tools commonly utilize time-series databases, e.g., InfluxData[4], for storing the monitored operational data. Our tool (packaged as a Jupiter Notebook[5]) connects to an InfluxDB, retrieves the raw operational data, and generates the empirical distribution of the workload situations (best test masses) defined in the script. The infrastructure for load testing uses the open-source tool Locust[6] to automate the deployment of the defined experiments (building on container-based virtualization using Docker) for the defined workload situations and system configurations. Our load testing framework runs the experiments, collects the performance measures, and automates the analysis of the testing results. Load test specifications are either manually defined or extracted automatically (e.g., using ContinuITy [19]). Python scripts (packaged as a Jupyter Notebook application) are used to evaluate the performance of the test against a baseline, compute the performance for each test at each state of the system, generate the plots of total distribution mass and the previously obtained domain-based metric curves, and compute the sensitivity analysis and plots.

---

[3] https://openapm.io/.
[4] https://www.influxdata.com/.
[5] https://jupyter.org/.
[6] https://locust.io.

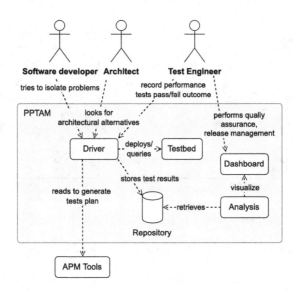

Fig. 6. Overview of the architecture (adapted from [4]).

4   Software Performance Anti-pattern Detection

Software Performance Anti-patterns (*SPAs*) have been extensively studied in the literature [1,14,18,20,22] as support for interpreting performance analysis results and providing feedback to software architects [8,9,12,13,21,23]. In our approach, we focus our attention on the usage of anti-patterns for the verification and validation of microservice systems. In the following, we report on our approaches developed for this scope and we argue on challenges ahead.

In [3] we have developed a multivariate approach for the classification of micro-service components. This classification approach was used to support computationally efficient risk assessment algorithms that leverage the introduced approach for automated scalability requirements derivation. We have also applied this approach for the characterization of SPAs. The application of the multivariate approach for micro-service classification was used to create algorithms for SPA detection that could be implemented in CI/CDD pipelines. We have evaluated this new methodology's effectiveness by using simulation and analytical modeling [3]. We have obtained good results for effectively detecting two SPAs: the Extensive Database Call and Continuous Violated Requirement SPA. The approach was used in a large complex telecom system at Ericsson. An SPA injection methodology was applied to the simulation model of the Ericsson system, and we were able to assess the precision and recall of our approach using a simulation environment to validate the modeling-based approach [2].

The proposed approach is reported in Fig. 7, the main operational steps are: (i) extraction of operational data; (ii) calculation of pass/fail criteria based on baseline requirements; (iii) matching multivariate analysis results to characterize and detect SPAs; (iv) simulation to assess modeling assumptions. This latest

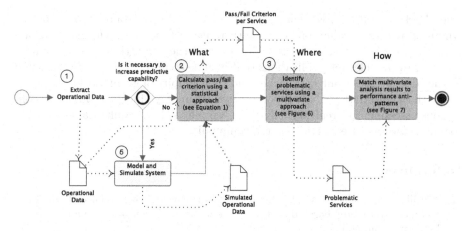

Fig. 7. Proposed approach for anti-pattern detection (adapted from [3])

step has been investigated in [2] where we collect the simulation results for the baseline case, i.e., with no injected SPAs, and the SPA injection experiments. Four SPAs were characterized: Expensive Database Call, Application Hiccups, Stifle, and Continuous Violated Requirements. The simulation results are shown in [2], and we can point out that the proposed approach is able to detect Expensive Database Call and Continuous Violated Requirement SPAs; the former anti-pattern has a significant impact on both the normalized distance and the slope measures, whereas the latter anti-pattern has a lower impact on the same measures. Our experience recommends the approach for SPA detection within CI/CDD pipelines to (i) detect performance degradation using normalized distance and slope, and (ii) detect a small number of SPAs that can be automatically classified with good precision and recall [2].

There exist further challenges that we are interested to investigate as part of our future research. First, the accuracy of the approach can be improved by using real systems and comparing monitored performance measurements with simulation-based results. Second, the integration of the approach into automated performance testing and analysis tools [5] is indeed valuable to encourage software architects in adopting our research to their daily practices.

5   Conclusion

In this paper, we summarized the tutorial carried out at the 16th European Conference on Software Architecture (ECSA 2022) in which we presented an overview of our approach and tooling infrastructure for continuous verification and validation of microservices systems, with special focus on the detection of performance issues such as scalability bottlenecks and software performance anti-patterns. The major contributions of our approach include: the definition of the domain-based metric and approach for scalability assessment of microservices using load tests; the implementation of the PPTAM open-source tooling infrastructure; and the evaluation of a multivariate approach for efficient software performance anti-pattern detection. For each of these contributions, the reader can refer to the relevant publications that include comprehensive discussions and further details about our approaches and their empirical evaluations.

With the ultimate goal of supporting performance engineers dealing with continuous assessment of real-world systems, we released our configurable PPTAM tooling infrastructure to the research community.

References

1. Arcelli, D., Cortellessa, V., Trubiani, C.: Experimenting the influence of numerical thresholds on model-based detection and refactoring of performance antipatterns. Electron. Commun. EASST. **59** (2014)
2. Avritzer, A., et al.: Scalability testing automation using multivariate characterization and detection of software performance antipatterns. J. Syst. Softw. **193** (2022)
3. Avritzer, A., et al.: A multivariate characterization and detection of software performance antipatterns. In: ICPE 2021: ACM/SPEC International Conference on Performance Engineering. ACM (2021)
4. Avritzer, A., et al.: Pptam$^\lambda$: What, where, and how of cross-domain scalability assessment. In: 18th IEEE International Conference on Software Architecture (ICSA). IEEE (2021)
5. Avritzer, A., et al.: Scalability assessment of microservice architecture deployment configurations: a domain-based approach leveraging operational profiles and load tests. J. Syst. Softw. **165** (2020)
6. Avritzer, A., Ferme, V., Janes, A., Russo, B., Schulz, H., van Hoorn, A.: A quantitative approach for the assessment of microservice architecture deployment alternatives by automated performance testing. In: Proceedings of the European Conference on Software Architecture (ECSA) (2018)
7. Avritzer, A., et al.: PPTAM: production and performance testing based application monitoring. In: Companion of the ACM/SPEC International Conference on Performance Engineering (ICPE) (2019)
8. Calinescu, R., Cortellessa, V., Stefanakos, I., Trubiani, C.: Analysis and Refactoring of Software Systems Using Performance Antipattern Profiles (2020). https://doi.org/10.1007/978-3-030-45234-6_18
9. Camilli, M., Russo, B.: Modeling performance of microservices systems with growth theory. Empir. Softw. Eng. **27**(2), 1–44 (2022). https://doi.org/10.1007/s10664-021-10088-0
10. Camilli, M., Colarusso, C., Russo, B., Zimeo, E.: Domain metric driven decomposition of data-intensive applications. In: 2020 IEEE International Symposium on Software Reliability Engineering Workshops (ISSREW), pp. 189–196 (2020). https://doi.org/10.1109/ISSREW51248.2020.00071
11. Camilli, M., Colarusso, C., Russo, B., Zimeo, E.: Actor-driven decomposition of microservices through multi-level scalability assessment. ACM Trans. Softw. Eng. Methodol. (2023, to appear)
12. Camilli, M., Guerriero, A., Janes, A., Russo, B., Russo, S.: Microservices integrated performance and reliability testing. In: Proceedings of the 3rd ACM/IEEE International Conference on Automation of Software Test. ACM (2022)

13. Camilli, M., Janes, A., Russo, B.: Automated test-based learning and verification of performance models for microservices systems. JSS **187** (2022)
14. Cortellessa, V., Di Marco, A., Eramo, R., Pierantonio, A., Trubiani, C.: Approaching the model-driven generation of feedback to remove software performance flaws. In: Euromicro Conference on Software Engineering and Advanced Applications (2009)
15. Cusick, J., Avritzer, A., Tse, A., Janes, A.: Automated Dependability Assessment in DevOps Environments. In: IEEE International Symposium on Software Reliability Engineering Workshops, ISSRE 2022 - Workshops, Charlotte, NC, USA, October 31–November 3, 2022. IEEE (2022)
16. Heger, C., van Hoorn, A., Mann, M., Okanovic, D.: Application performance management: state of the art and challenges for the future. In: Proceedings of the 2017 ACM/SPEC International Conference on Performance Engineering (ICPE) (2017)
17. Microsoft: Performance tuning a distributed application (2019). https://docs.microsoft.com/en-us/azure/architecture/performance/
18. Pinciroli, R., Smith, C.U., Trubiani, C.: QN-based modeling and analysis of software performance antipatterns for cyber-physical systems. In: Proceedings of the ACM/SPEC International Conference on Performance Engineering (2021)
19. Schulz, H., Okanovic, D., van Hoorn, A., Ferme, V., Pautasso, C.: Behavior-driven load testing using contextual knowledge-approach and experiences. In: Companion of the ACM/SPEC International Conference on Performance Engineering (ICPE) (2019)
20. Smith, C.U., Williams, L.G.: Software performance antipatterns for identifying and correcting performance problems. In: International Computer Measurement Group Conference (2012)
21. Jansen, A., Malavolta, I., Muccini, H., Ozkaya, I., Zimmermann, O. (eds.) ECSA 2020. LNCS, vol. 12292. Springer, Cham (2020). https://doi.org/10.1007/978-3-030-58923-3
22. Trubiani, C., Di Marco, A., Cortellessa, V., Mani, N., Petriu, D.: Exploring synergies between bottleneck analysis and performance antipatterns. In: Proceedings of the 5th ACM/SPEC International Conference on Performance Engineering (2014)
23. Trubiani, C., Ghabi, A., Egyed, A.: Exploiting traceability uncertainty between software architectural models and performance analysis results. In: Weyns, D., Mirandola, R., Crnkovic, I. (eds.) ECSA 2015. LNCS, vol. 9278, pp. 305–321. Springer, Cham (2015). https://doi.org/10.1007/978-3-319-23727-5_26

8th International Workshop on Automotive System/Software Architectures (WASA)

Assessing Security of Internal Vehicle Networks

Anas Alkoutli, Joakim Anderlind, Carl-Johan Björnson, Mathias Drage,
Morgan Thowsen, Antonia Welzel, and Miroslaw Staron[✉]

Chalmers | University of Gothenburg, Gothenburg, Sweden
miroslaw.staron@gu.se

Abstract. Automotive software grows exponentially in size. In premium vehicles, the size can reach over 100 million lines of code. One of the challenges in such a large software is how it is architecturally designed and whether this design leads to security vulnerabilities. In this paper, we report on a design science research study aimed at understanding the vulnerabilities of modern premium vehicles. We used machine learning to identify and reconstruct signals within the vehicle's communication networks. The results show that the distributed software architectures can have security vulnerabilities due to the high connectivity of modern vehicles; and that the security needs to be seen holistically – both when constructing the vehicle's software and when designing communication channels with cloud services. The paper proposed a number of measures that can help to address the identified vulnerabilities.

1 Introduction

Automotive software is one of the areas of software engineering which is growing exponentially [1]. The number of electronic control units has reached over 100 and the size of the software can be around 100 million lines of code. The number of architectural components has also grown and can be measured in hundreds, which causes software architects to use federated software architectures and centralized software architectures. These two styles can reduce the number of electronic control units, but they can also increase potential security vulnerabilities (due to increased communication).

Although the size of the automotive software grows, there have been reports about the challenges with keeping this large software secure [2,3] and reliable [4]. In fact, there even exists a taxonomy of security vulnerabilities targeted towards automotive software [5]. However, there are still open questions about whether an adversary (a hacker) would require a specific understanding of the details of the particular vehicle model targeted. It is also not clear whether the adversary needs vendor-specific equipment to make an intrusion.

While assessments of live vehicles have been carried out, they do not use the type of commodity hardware used by a hacker. And, while commodity hardware has been used for assessment in related work, it has exclusively been carried out on specific components extracted from a vehicle, thus not in a live setting.

T. Batista et al. (Eds.): ECSA 2022, LNCS 13928, pp. 151–164, 2023.
https://doi.org/10.1007/978-3-031-36889-9_12

This paper studies vulnerabilities found with commodity hardware[1] in a live setting and aims to discuss and propose software solutions to resolve discovered vulnerabilities.

The research questions are as follows:

1. How resilient are in-vehicle networks against unauthorized access and manipulation, conducted with cost-efficient hardware and without expert knowledge?

2. What software solutions could have prevented methods exercised in question 1?

To address these questions, we analyzed two vehicle models, by analyzing signals on their CAN and Ethernet networks. We found vulnerabilities that enable data extraction and manipulation. Based on our analysis of these vulnerabilities, we found that, for CAN, a counter-based solution could prevent many intrusions. In Ethernet, a list of recommendations is proposed, such as leveraging existing encryption models for application-level encryption, randomized Media Access Control (MAC) addresses, and the use of existing authentication models for the Local Area Network (LAN).

The remainder of the paper is structured as follows. Section 2 presents the most important related work to our study. Section 3 describes the design of the study, while Sect. 4 presents the results. Section 5 presents the proposals for the solutions and their validation with our industrial partner. Section 6 proposes how the findings of our study can impact the architectural design of modern vehicles. Finally, Sect. 7 summarizes the conclusions drawn from this study.

2　Related Work

In 2010, Koscher et al. [6] conducted a comprehensive experimental security analysis on two modern automobiles. Similarly to our study, their purpose was to assess the level of resilience a conventional automobile has against digital attacks. Their attack methodology consisted of packet sniffing in combination with targeted probing, fuzzing, and reverse engineering. As a result, they managed to manipulate every ECU that was tested and therefore achieved complete control over components such as door locks and brakes. Koscher et al.'s strategies included advanced hardware and techniques that require expert knowledge about the components and electrical systems in the vehicle. Our study on the other hand examines whether similar vulnerabilities are present in a production vehicle from 10 years later restricted to more commodity hardware and limited access to the test bed.

Another experimental security analysis, but in a simulated vehicle environment, was conducted by Buttigieg et al. [7]. Their objective was to analyze the resilience of the CAN protocol specifically. By conducting a Man-in-the-middle

---

[1] For ethical reasons and the safety of passengers, we do not provide any details about the used hardware or software. Details can be obtained upon request (and approval by the industrial partner) by contacting the authors.

attack with the use of commodity hardware, they managed to control the instrument cluster extracted from a BMW E90. Our study presents an alternative and less physically intrusive method for taking control over specific components by exploiting security issues in the CAN protocol. Furthermore, we present experimental results from an industrial automotive test bed that together with the results from Buttigieg et al. strengthen the need for security measures in the CAN protocol.

Lin and Sangiovanni-Vincentelli [8] proposed a software-only security mechanism for the CAN protocol to help prevent masquerade and replay attacks, which are also attack methods exercised in our study. Lin and Sangiovanni-Vincentelli focused on a security mechanism that keeps the bus utilization as low as possible to fit the CAN bus's limited bandwidth. Their solution consisted of three elements: ID tables, pair-wise secret keys between nodes, and message counters. The solution mechanism proposed by Lin and Sangiovanni-Vincentelli was used as a base for finding appropriate security solutions based on our experimental findings.

Kiravuo et al. [9] conducted a survey of vulnerabilities present in LAN Ethernet networks. The survey states that Ethernet's prevalence in computer networks is partly due to its ease of configuration and simplicity. However, these attributes also make Ethernet networks vulnerable. Kiravuo et al. lists known vulnerabilities of Ethernet networks and presents possible mitigation of these vulnerabilities. This paper verifies the existence of the vulnerabilities that were listed by Kiravuo et al. in automotive Ethernet networks.

Corbett et al. [10] discuss the impact of the vulnerabilities documented by Kiravuo et al. [9] on automotive Ethernet networks. Since the safety of the vehicle depends on accurate and timely readings from its sensors, the authors decided to focus on protecting the integrity of the network. Their paper compares the attributes of the Ethernet with other automotive network standards and presents a list of security challenges and opportunities that differentiate Ethernet from the alternatives. Corbett et al. conclude with a list of recommendations to protect the automotive Ethernet network from misuse, such as fingerprinting ECUs based on physical layer attributes. This paper provides alternative mitigation measures than presented by Corbett et al. based on our experimental evidence.

3 Study Design

The aim of this paper was to assess the security of the in-vehicle network in a vehicle with limited resources and without expert knowledge on the electrical system. Since we did not have any prior knowledge about the automotive software architecture and in-vehicle communication, it made it difficult to plan a single experiment that would give us the information needed to answer our research questions. Subsequently, we chose to follow the *Design Science Research* approach since it allowed us to progressively build knowledge about the system [11]. The approach is a flexible research method with the objective of gaining a better understanding of a problem through multiple iterations and finding possible solutions through the process of developing an artifact [12] and its measurement and assessment [13]. This makes it very suitable for a project with an exploratory nature such as this one. The test bed used during the project was only available on two separate occasions.

This limited access to the test bed resulted in the project being formed as two iterations, where each visit contributed to the evaluation of our artifact as well as new information for developing our approach to attacking the in-vehicle security in the next iteration.

3.1 Artefact

As mentioned above, the artifact in this project is made up of both the test harnesses, which consist of hardware and software, as well as our general approach to making the assessment of the in-vehicle security[2]. Our method for making the assessment of the in-vehicle network security consists of capturing signals and developed into injections by evaluating our results from the previous iteration.

We used a multi-meter to identify CAN bus wires among the kilometers of wires present in the test bed. While oscilloscopes are well suited for this task, a multi-meter is portable and emphasizes the uninitiated approach. For collecting data, the CANutils application CANdump was utilized which captures all traffic on the bus. The captured traffic is then saved to a log file which can be re-injected onto the network with the application CANplay. Manually interacting with the use case-specific component, while capturing the data traffic to a log file, may capture an executive frame or set of frames. In order to verify that executive frames were captured, a replay attack with the log file and CANplay was conducted. If the vehicle during the replay attack exhibited behavior corresponding to the manual interaction then executive frames had indeed been captured.

For each use case component, a 3–4 s interaction was captured. In addition, a 2-min log file was recorded without any manual interaction.

3.2 Evaluation of the Artefact

The artifact was evaluated after each iteration in order to improve it and in the end be able to address our research questions and make an assessment of the security in the in-vehicle networks as well as to propose solutions to the found vulnerabilities. The method used for the evaluation was testing, specifically functional (black box) testing on specific components in the in-vehicle network security. The use cases were chosen based on the expected complexity of extracting information, and more importantly their relevance to the vehicle's security by evaluating the consequent security issues from retrieving the information and manipulating the component.

---

[2] For ethical reasons, and the safety of passengers, we do not provide details about the equipment used to make intrusions.

3.3   Test Bed

The test bed provided by our partner in the automotive industry consisted of an entire vehicular electronic system with all electronic components included, as seen in Fig. 1. In other words, a stripped-down version of a real vehicle without mechanical parts such as chassis, engine, and wheels. This allowed for human interaction with the system which could be used for testing. The electronic system in the test rig was fully functional and it was possible to put it in active mode, which would mimic a started vehicle.

There were multiple reasons for the experiment to be conducted on a test bed instead of an actual production vehicle. For one, testing on an actual vehicle would be a costly process in terms of both resources and time. Moreover, whether the experiments are conducted on the test bed or a real vehicle does not affect the outcome, since both networks are the same and the physical accessibility is not considered in the assessment of the security. Lastly, trying to manipulate the network on a live vehicle may be dangerous as it is difficult to predict the vehicle's behavior through various manipulations.

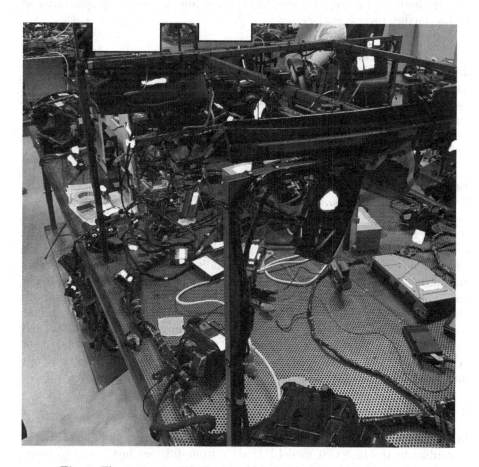

Fig. 1. The test unit with the in-vehicle network used in this study

3.4   Use Cases

In order to structure our investigations, we decided to define three use cases – two for the CAN network and one for the Ethernet network. These use cases simulated adversarial attacks on the vehicle network with the goal to understand the vehicle architecture and, eventually, be able to take control.

CAN: Headlights. Controlling the headlights shows that the network is not resilient against unauthorized access and manipulation. The possible states of the headlights are small, for example, off, low-beam and high-beam. This eased the search process for identifying corresponding CAN frames since the payload should only contain a small set of discrete values. Furthermore, headlights are an exterior component with easily accessible wiring making it a vulnerable entry point to the CAN bus. Control of the headlights is a proof of concept in the assessment of the CAN bus as a whole. This does not imply that the same vulnerabilities may be exploited for functions such as gas and brake. However, control of the headlights shows that the network does not provide a layer of security itself. Unauthorized manipulation was conducted by replay attacks as well as further reverse engineering.

CAN: Door Locks. Door locks are components that are expected to be secure due to the potential consequences of a vulnerability. While manipulation of head-lights is a proof of concept, control of the door locks would imply low resilience even in security-critical components. The outcome of this together with the afore-mentioned use case will provide enough insight for the thesis to reason about the *level* of the resilience of the CAN bus. Replay attacks were performed in order to assess the level of resilience.

Ethernet: Control of the Infotainment System. Due to the nature of the IP protocol [14], data sent by devices is encoded by multiple layers of network headers. The infotainment system in a vehicle is able to store different kinds of personal information through for example logs from connected mobile devices such as the contact list. Moreover, different vehicle functions are controlled via the infotainment system, such as the air-conditioning unit, settings of sensors and also the interface through which the user accesses the ADAS. An attack on the infotainment system would therefore be a serious threat regarding both safety and privacy. The specific features handled by the infotainment system that we focused on were the air-conditioning unit, cameras used in the ADAS and the media player. The attack we conducted to take control of the infotainment system was a Man-in-the-middle attack. This enabled data collection without interfering with the connection in this point-to-point network.

4   Results

In this section, we document the results of the data capturing and data analysis. According to the ISO/OSI model [15], data from different layers was collected from the in-vehicle networks. For CAN the data was captured from the data link layer, while for Ethernet data was obtained from both the transport layer in the form of UDP/TCP packets and the application layer in the form of JSON objects. An overview of the attacks and their outcome is shown in Table 1.

Table 1. The results of the conducted attacks for the use cases for both CAN and Ethernet. The green check mark indicates that the attack was successful, the red X indicates that the attack was unsuccessful, and the hyphen indicates that the attack was not performed.

Attacks on the in-vehicle networks		
Attack	Ethernet	CAN
	Infotainment	Headlights	Door locks
Sniffing	✓	✓	✓
Injection	X	✓	-
Replay	-	✓	X

4.1 CAN

The results related to CAN are organized in the following way: First, we present the results from establishing a connection to the CAN bus. Secondly, results associated with the specific use cases' are presented. Lastly, we provide recommendations on how to increase security based on the outcome of our experiments.

Establishing Connection. CAN bus wiring was identified by tracking cables from a headlight which only had two wires operating on the CAN standardized $2.5V$. With the cables identified and with the use of inexpensive cable tap products, the connection was established without interfering with or breaking the original one. A successful connection was made evident by attempting to sniff data with CANdump in which no data would be shown if there was a connection fault. This was due to CANdump being set up to not display frames not validated by the CAN frame checksum. A connection fault could be either the wires being set up wrong or a mismatch in bit rate between the CAN bus and capture device. The correct bit rate was found by testing the most common bit rates 125kbit/s and 500kbit/s. A connection to the internal CAN bus was established within the first hour of experimenting with the test bed without previous knowledge of the vehicle model. Therefore, CAN cables should be better protected from physical intrusion.

Use Case Headlights. Connected to the same CAN bus as the headlights, the hazard lights were turned on while capturing frames with CANdump. The log file was used in a replay attack while the hazard lights were turned off. This resulted in the test bed flashing the front hazard lights which implied a replay attack vulnerability. Since only the front hazard lights flashed, it led us to believe that a second CAN bus was present. This hypothesis was confirmed by conducting the same replay attack while connected to a CAN bus adjacent to the rear lights, which flashed the rear hazard lights but did not affect the front hazard lights. This is positive in terms of security since a malicious connection to a single CAN bus only compromises a subset of the vehicle's communication and functionality. However, a total mapping of which functionality is present on the different busses would be needed to assess the extent of this security measure.

The replay attack vulnerability in the headlights showed that it was possible to manipulate CAN-connected components through the network. This means that the in-vehicle network was compromised. While an arguably simple manipulation of the hazard lights is possible, the complex sequences needed for stealing the vehicle are expected to be substantially harder or even impossible.

The log file used in the successful replay attack of the front hazard lights, progressed as designed in our study using machine learning to find patterns in the CAN frames. The analysis was successful, resulting in a complete reverse engineering of the front direction indicators.

By iterative bitflips on the payload of the original frame and reinjection, a single hexadecimal character responsible for controlling the direction indicators was found. The result is visualized in the remaining rows of the figure.

This bitwise reverse engineering is made possible when the integrity of the frames is not protected with in-message checksums. The result is that it allows an uninitiated to reach a low-level understanding of the system. In our case, among the thousands CAN frames captured, we could determine that the fourth hexadecimal character in the frame with ID A25 was responsible for the direction indicators. The same complete procedure was successfully executed for flashing the high beams independently. To ensure that the success of our method was not model specific, flashing of headlights was performed on a second vehicle model with the same outcome.

With the obtained knowledge about the frame responsible for the direction indicators, more precise control of the headlights was achieved. The frame denoted "Off" was then injected repeatedly with the result that user interaction with front direction indicators was blocked. Blocking of user input was attempted with the original large log file with the result that functions corresponding to the other frames were affected and a bus overload ensued. A high-precision payload such as the "Off" frame enables an efficient DoS attack with no risk of bus overload.

The presence of a second bus led us to investigate whether a replay attack, affecting both rear and front hazard lights, was possible from the OBD-II port. The OBD-II port operated on the same bit rate as the internal busses. However, upon sniffing it was made evident that the OBD-II functioned differently as it was utilizing the extended CAN format made evident by the longer ID as seen in Fig. 2.

```
ID          PAYLOAD                          ID    PAYLOAD
21DAD0A0#00000F1120000000                    04C#000D0D0A0F2A0F10
21DAD120#100EDDE0012100DE                    04C#000D0D0A0F2A0F90
21DAD122#0010000005100101                    052#C7C0008005512290
21DAD122#0000000000020020                    077#000D0D0A0F2A0F10
21DAD12E#F121F0000515E20F                    077#000D0D0A0F2A0F90
21DAD0F0#0000100120000000                    091#000E0C67701F0256
21DAD12F#000000000DDF5002                    091#000E0C07701F0256
21DAD0A0#00000F1120000000                    333#000D0D0A0F2A0F10
21DAD0F0#0000100120000000                    333#000D0D0A0F2A0F90
21DAD02F#1000100000100021                    A25#000D0D0A0F2A0F10
21DAD110#00000F0000000000                    A25#000D0D0A0F2A0F90
21DAD11F#2DDE10100DD01AED                    AF5#000D0D0A0F2A0F10
21DAD120#0000000000000010|                   AF5#001D0D0A0F2A0F90
21DAD121#000020000DDF5002                    F21#000E0C67704F0236
21DAD0A0#00000F1120000000
```

Fig. 2. Extended CAN frames captured from OBD-II (left) compared to standard CAN frames captured from internal CAN bus (right). Notice the longer ID section of each frame.

Presuming that the two detected CAN busses both operated at above half capacity, it would be impossible for the sum of the two networks' traffic to fit the CAN bus interface exposed by the OBD-II port without a doubled bit rate. In fact, the internal CAN busses would have to operate at less than half of their capacity since the extended-CAN format itself increases the overhead. Since access to all ECUs is a prerequisite for diagnostics, it leads us to believe that either the OBD-II is filtered to fit the bandwidth limit or operates differently. Attempting a replay attack as conducted on the internal CAN bus yielded no results. This implies that none of the executive frames for hazard lights were captured. This could mean that the OBD-II port operates on a request basis, and all frames captured were response- or status messages, not executive frames. If no executive frames are sent while logging, then replay attacks are impossible to conduct. The reduced number of frames present on a request-based interface could enable the use of security in the form of authentication and counters since the bus load is low when idle.

Use Case Door Locks. Connected to the same CAN bus as the driver-side door panel, the door locks were toggled while frames were captured with CAN-dump. However, replay attacks showed no results on the door lock mechanism. Neither activation nor deactivation was possible. With no successful replay log, further data analysis was not possible. This implied that the network provided varying levels of resilience depending on the component, where critical functions were better protected. The strategy employed for high-precision reverse engineering on headlight functions was accounted for. In order for replay attacks to have no effect, old messages have to be invalidated. Prolific protection against replay attacks on the CAN bus is a counter mechanism, but other authentication methods may very well be present. Since no executive frames could be found, the existence of checksums is unknown.

4.2   Ethernet

Our results below relate to the use case "Control of the infotainment system". Finally, we propose recommendations for solutions that could have prevented the methods used for our findings.

Nature of Captured Traffic. By performing a Man-in-the-middle attack, we were able to log the traffic sent and received from the infotainment ECU, as well as log its connections to other components.

Analyzing the recorded network traffic in Wireshark, we could determine the use of multiple protocols, including TCP, UDP, DNS requests, and SOME/IP. We could also infer that the ECU is connected to some sort of network switch.

We were also able to determine that the majority of the recorded network communications followed patterns that were repeated at fixed intervals.

Identifying Components. It was possible to read the IP headers from all captured packages. Additionally, it was possible to read the headers in TCP and UDP packages. The source, destination IP addresses, and ports in these headers were used to analyze the flow of information between devices and the topology of the network. From the captured Ethernet frames we were also able to read the source and destination MAC addresses. These were cross-referenced. While not all addresses were registered with IEEE, the devices whose addresses were registered could be connected to known manufacturers.

By scanning the test bed's OBD-II port with the network scanner *Nmap*, we were able to extract information about which version of Android is running on an Android device on the network.

Charting the Network Topology. After understanding the nature of the captured data, we were able to draw a map of the identified devices in the network and reconstruct how these different parties communicate with each other. By listing the IP addresses from the recorded packets, a graph of the network topology could be constructed. The packet flow from the data recordings indicated two different sub-systems, both providing different functionality to the network since the intercepted packets showed no direct communication between these two sub-systems. The two sub-systems will be referred to as network 1 and network 2.

Network 1 is closely linked to vehicle telemetry. This was concluded as some intercepted packets contained clear-text telemetry information. We were able to validate this information based on the coordinates of the test bed. We concluded that network 2 shown is closely linked to the user interface for the infotainment system.

5   Solution Proposals

Based on the study, and the study of the literature on improving the security of software in general, we could propose a number of solutions to remedy the vulnerabilities found.

CAN: Recommendations. Security enhancements for the CAN communications bus are complex due to the limitations present such as bandwidth and timing. This theoretically blocks replay attacks since recordings will not contain any valid executive frames.

Counters on the CAN bus are used in the industry today. Practically, counters are of finite size, frames once valid and then invalidated are bound to be valid again in the future. The time until a frame is valid again depends on the size of the counter as well as the update frequency.

Due to the previously mentioned limitations of the CAN bus, we propose a low-frequency global counter with no checksum attached. This will render replay attacks non-deterministic which complicates reverse engineering. The frequency and size of the counter may be adapted to suit the computational limitations of the ECUs. Ideally, only a single ECU transmits the counter onto the bus at set intervals.

The proposed solution is a first barrier of defense and would not provide theoretical security.

Ethernet: MACsec. Our findings from the Ethernet network were possible due to the link layer being vulnerable to passive listening attacks. To mitigate this vulnerability a standard such as IEEE 802.1AE or the link layer network security standard MACsec can be implemented.

The reason for this choice is that MACsec protects the confidentiality of low-level network protocols such as ARP, which was instrumental in discovering the network topology.

Ethernet: Obfuscated MAC Addresses. Coupling a manufacturer to the MAC address on an otherwise unknown ECU could immensely accelerate the reverse engineering process. To hinder this, we recommend randomizing the MAC address so that this coupling cannot be made. This method is already in use in consumer devices such as smartphones, where for example IOS devices automatically generate a random MAC address every 24 h to prevent fingerprinting, where attackers gather information about the network by scanning it or analyzing its response after injecting packets [16]. Continuously regenerating MAC addresses would be unnecessary in this case and would only increase the complexity of the network. Instead generating new MAC addresses during the assembly process would be sufficient.

Ethernet: TLS. Finally, we propose Ethernet networks to utilize application-level encryption for non-critical services such as telemetry and infotainment systems. While MACsec protects the links between devices, if a malicious agent gains control of the switch or any of the devices in-between, then the guarantee of confidentiality is lost. Implementing end-to-end encryption between services with lax latency requirements guarantees stronger protection against reverse engineering and the loss of confidentiality of sensitive information. TLS could be a suitable candidate for such end-to-end encryption. TLS has been well-tested as the standard behind HTTPS, and the 1.3 release included many latency improvements [17]. However, further research is needed to find if TLS is actually suitable for automotive networks.

6   Impact on Architectural Design

The above suggestions are focused on the mechanisms that provide more secure communication in vehicles. However, these mechanisms require certain architectural changes in order to be effective.

First, these changes require an update of all communication component to include the security mechanisms. Some of them are rudimentary and do not require significant changes – e.g., including the counters in the CAN messages. However, certain others require a significant redesign – e.g., using TLS would require additional handling of keys and certificates.

The additional handling of keys and certificates requires mechanisms to update these keys and certificates during the vehicle lifecycle. Since the certificates' validity expires, then all components relying on them need to be updated – this update needs to be secure and online, as this process should not require a visit to a workshop. The secure distribution of keys and certificates requires more secure communication protocols (or maybe even components) between vehicles and the update database.

In addition, obfuscating MAC addresses, as an example, requires additional protocols and these protocols need to be maintained and configured. This poses significant challenges on the entire update process – e.g., keeping track of compatible certificate, keys, addresses even in the event of repairing a broken component on the aftermarket.

This means that increased security requires the ability to create architecture that stretches outside of the vehicle itself. We need to secure that the vehicles, its update databases and communication channels. We also need to include protocols to update components based on the updates of other components (e.g., when a certificate is compromised).

Therefore, security is not just a concern or an aspect of software development. It needs to be included in the architectural design from the beginning.

7   Conclusions

In this paper, we set off to understand and evaluate how resilient are in-vehicle networks against unauthorized access and manipulation, conducted with cost-efficient hardware and without expert knowledge. We found that it is, to some extent, possible to access the networks with privileged access and an understanding of the CAN technology. We have presented suggestions for software solutions that would have prevented our findings, for both CAN and Ethernet. For CAN we suggest the use of a reference counter to protect the integrity of CAN frames, while for Ethernet we suggest using multiple standards to protect the multiple layers of the OSI network stack.

Our further work includes a more in-depth analysis of how one could discover the entire architecture of the software system of the vehicle and how to prevent this.

Acknowledgment. The authors would like to thank our industrial partner for their ability to do the study and for their help and support. We would like to thank the engineers from the company for their dedication in helping us conduct the study.

References

1. Staron, M.: Automotive Software Architectures. Springer, Cham (2021). https://doi.org/10.1007/978-3-030-65939-4
2. Sagstetter, F., et al.: Security challenges in automotive hardware/software architecture design. In: 2013 Design, Automation & Test in Europe Conference & Exhibition (DATE), pp. 458–463. IEEE (2013)
3. Bayer, S., Enderle, T., Oka, D.-K., Wolf, M.: Automotive security testing—the digital crash test. In: Langheim, J. (ed.) Energy Consumption and Autonomous Driving. LNM, pp. 13–22. Springer, Cham (2016). https://doi.org/10.1007/978-3-319-19818-7_2
4. Rana, R., et al.: Evaluation of standard reliability growth models in the context of automotive software systems. In: Heidrich, J., Oivo, M., Jedlitschka, A., Baldassarre, M.T. (eds.) PROFES 2013. LNCS, vol. 7983, pp. 324–329. Springer, Heidelberg (2013). https://doi.org/10.1007/978-3-642-39259-7_26
5. Sommer, F., Dürrwang, J., Kriesten, R.: Survey and classification of automotive security attacks. Information **10**(4), 148 (2019)
6. Koscher, K., et al.: Experimental security analysis of a modern automobile. In: 2010 IEEE Symposium on Security and Privacy, July 2010. https://doi.org/10.1109/sp.2010.34
7. Buttigieg, R., Farrugia, M., Meli, C.: Security issues in controller area networks in automobiles. In: 2017 18th International Conference on Sciences and Techniques of Automatic Control and Computer Engineering (STA), pp. 93–98, 2017. https://doi.org/10.1109/STA.2017.8314877
8. Nowdehi, N., Lautenbach, A., Olovsson, T.: In-vehicle can message authentication: an evaluation based on industrial criteria. In: 2017 IEEE 86th Vehicular Technology Conference (VTC-Fall), pp. 1–7 (2017). https://doi.org/10.1109/VTCFall.2017.8288327
9. Kiravuo, T., Sarela, M., Manner, J.: A survey of ethernet LAN security. IEEE Commun. Surv. Tutor. **15**(3), 1477–1491 (2013). https://doi.org/10.1109/SURV.2012.121112.00190
10. Corbett, C., Schoch, E., Kargl, F., Preussner, F.: Automotive ethernet: Security opportunity or challenge? Sicherheit 2016 - Sicherheit, Schutz und Zuverlässigkeit (2016)

11. Staron, M.: Action Research in Software Engineering. Springer, Cham (2020). https://doi.org/10.1007/978-3-030-32610-4
12. Hevner, A., March, S., Park, J., Ram, S.: Design science in information systems research. Manag. Inf. Syst. Q. **28**(1), 75–105 (2004)
13. Staron, M., Meding, W.: Software Development Measurement Programs. Springer, Cham (2018). https://doi.org/10.1007/978-3-319-91836-5
14. INTERNET PROTOCOL. RFC 791, University of Southern California, September 1981. https://tools.ietf.org/html/rfc791.html
15. Popescu-Zeletin, R.: Implementing the ISO-OSI reference model. ACM SIGCOMM Comput. Commun. Rev. **13**(4), 56–66 (1983)
16. Use private wi-fi addresses in ios 14, ipados 14 and watchos 7. https://web.archive.org/web/20210424120018/support.apple.com/en-gb/HT211227
17. Differences between tls 1.2 and tls 1.3. https://web.archive.org/web/20190919000200/www.wolfssl.com/differences-between-tls-12-and-tls-13-9/

Methodical Approach for Centralization Evaluation of Modern Automotive E/E Architectures

Lucas Mauser[1]([✉]) [ID], Stefan Wagner[2] [ID], and Peter Ziegler[1]

[1] Daimler Truck AG, Fasanenweg 10, 70771 Leinfelden-Echterdingen, Germany
lucas.mauser@daimlertruck.com
[2] University of Stuttgart, Universitätsstraße 38, 70569 Stuttgart, Germany

Abstract. Centralization is considered as a key enabler to master the CPU-intensive features of the modern car. The development and architecture change towards the next generation car is influenced by ADAS, connectivity, infotainment and the consequential need for cyber-security. There is already a high number of papers describing future centralized E/E architectures and technical instruments for centralization. What is missing is a methodical approach to analyze an existing system and find its potential for centralization on the function level. This paper introduces an approach that serves a system designer or engineer to abstract functions and thus enables to shape a more centralized system architecture. The commonly known E/E architecture designs and the named instruments of current research are the basis for this abstraction. Based on the approach, new system architecture proposals can be set up to discuss and outweigh advantages and disadvantages of those. The approach is validated by applying it step by step to the inlet's derating function of a modern electric vehicle. A following discussion points out that many different factors affect the potential for centralization and centralization may not be the future of every function and system in general.

Keywords: function abstraction · centralization of E/E architectures · microservices · separation of computing and I/O · zone-oriented

1 Introduction

The domain-oriented E/E architecture is commonly known as state of the practice in established automotive manufacturers such as Daimler, Ford or Renault. Their verti-cal architectures are characterized by approximately five domain areas each con-taining a high number of specialized Electronic Control Units (ECUs) resulting in high-ly distributed functionalities [1]. Those vertical architectures miss flexibility and scalability to satisfy the modern trends in automotive where new players enter the market starting from the scratch and gaining design freedom [2]. Not only Advanced Driver Assistance Systems (ADAS) with their high computing power demand require a redesign of common E/E architectures. Also the connectivity of the modern car with its linkage to services of the world wide web, the TCP/IP protocols and communication bandwidth hungry infotainment systems are pushing the trend of centralization forward [3, 4]. Last but not least, the connectivity of the vehicle involves cyber-security requirements.

T. Batista et al. (Eds.): ECSA 2022, LNCS 13928, pp. 165–179, 2023.
https://doi.org/10.1007/978-3-031-36889-9_13

Under the high cost pressure of the automotive industry, decentral and well-established platforms are limited in their scalability and are no more able to handle the complexity. The comparison of a Tesla model Y, a VW ID.4 and a Ford Mach E regarding their number of ECUs and communication networks in Table 1 accentuates this statement where Volkswagen and Ford are still captured in their legacy platforms. Instead of a revolution, the established automotive OEMs are in an evolution.

Many Tier-1 suppliers are already serving the need for centralized High-Performance Computing (HPC) ECUs as masters of zone-oriented E/E architectures surrounded by their smart actuators and sensors. This principle separates computing power and I/O to centralize and bundle complex functions into one ECU making complexity manageable [5]. Another technical approach that the Tier-1 suppliers' solutions have in common is the service-oriented design and communication that allows to process the high amount of data that will further increase in the future [5–7].

The current trend of vertical integration within companies [8] supports the centralization of E/E architectures as know-how is increasing in the staff. In this elaboration, we point out technical and structural approaches to centralize E/E architectures based on related work. In a next step, those approaches are brought together into a methodical approach. Additionally, we discuss the limits of centralization critically. Before we deep-dive in approaches for centralization, the characteristics of domain- and zone-oriented E/E architectures are worked out to better classify those approaches.

Table 1. Comparison Tesla Model Y, VW ID.4 and Ford Mach E [9]

	ID.4	Model Y	Mach E
ECUs	52	26	51
CAN	7	10	8
CAN-FD	6	Some CAN buses FD capable	1
Ethernet	12	2	4
LIN	9 masters, 43 slaves	5 masters, 24 slaves	13 masters, 44 slaves
LVDS	3	10	3
Other	-	A2B, BroadR	A2B

2   Dominating E/E Architectures and Trends

2.1   Domain-Oriented E/E Architectures

On top of a domain-oriented E/E architecture is the so called domain controller which is a powerful master CPU responsible for controlling and monitoring a dedicated domain, for example, the powertrain domain. The domain controller bundles and consolidates functionality and thus meets the need of increasing complexity and increasing demands of computing power. Below the domain controller, specialized ECUs with less computing power than the domain controller handle function specific tasks that might require a certain hardware or a dedicated location. Those specialized ECUs are connected to its domain controller by typical communication networks like e.g. LIN for simple I/O actuator control and sensor monitoring but also CAN for highly interactive ECUs. To enable higher data rates, CAN-FD with up to 5 Mbit/s is commonly used which might be sufficient for domain-oriented E/E architectures with regards to the actual, centralization-driven development. Automotive Ethernet can enable even higher data rates but it is more seen as backbone communication path between two or more domains [1, 10]. Figure 1 shows an example of such a domain-oriented E/E architecture. Commonly there are four to five domains in a vehicle which got established. For example, at Mercedes-Benz these are Infotainment and Telematics, the Body and Comfort, ADAS and Powertrain. They represent also the main domains in literature [1, 10].

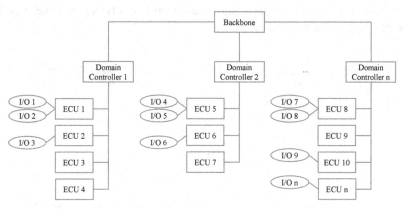

Fig. 1. Domain-oriented E/E architecture

2.2 Limitations and Challenges

The two domains ADAS and powertrain underline the limitation that a domain-oriented E/E architecture can have. Both domains need to work together closely to enable autonomous driving. There is much information to be exchanged over do-main borders by which the functionality suffers from a certain distribution and de-centralization [11]. With increasing implementation complexity and number of inter-faces, manageability and scalability decrease. At that moment an evaluation to rede-sign the E/E architecture in the direction of a cross-domain- or zone-oriented E/E architecture will be useful. This kind of architecture and its characteristics will be presented in the following.

2.3 Cross-Domain- and Zone-Oriented E/E Architectures

Cross-domain-oriented E/E architectures are one intermediate step towards zone-oriented E/E architectures. The cross-domain controller gets more powerful by accom-modating functions of different domains which for example have a lot of common inter-faces or common requirements for specialized software and hardware. By combining such synergies in one, a cross-domain controller can increase efficiency in implementation, performance, communication and further serving a better manage-ability and scalability of vehicle functions [1].

Centralizing one step further brings us to the zone-oriented E/E architecture whose development a lot of Tier-1 suppliers are already pushing forward as stated in the introduction. The zone-oriented E/E architecture is characterized by a central master as a powerful vehicle computer. It combines all the functionalities of the former do-main controllers by technical solutions as virtualization, containerization and further which will be investigated later in this elaboration [1, 11].

The rest of the vehicle is physically divided into zones that consist each of a zone controller as gateway to I/O hardware like for example actuators or sensors that cannot be centralized. The gateway zone controllers translate signals for and from the central computer. Direct signal lines and communication channel types must be chosen dependent on the hardware and the required bandwidth [1]. A typical zone-oriented E/E architectures is illustrated in Fig. 2.

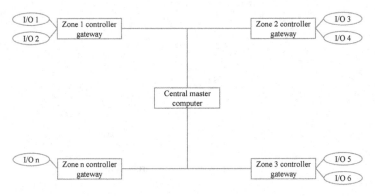

Fig. 2. Zone-oriented E/E architecture

2.4 Limitations and Challenges

While investigating advantages and disadvantages of centralization in literature, there were by the majority positive aspects of a centralization with focus on the cur-rent and future development of the vehicle's technologies. Two disadvantages are emphasized which need to be addressed by technical, methodical and design-specific solutions.

First, a centralized E/E architecture is characterized by a much higher number of wire length and cut leads which can be addressed by a smart design and distribution of the zones. Second, there is the more critical disadvantage of single point of failure which a centralized system constitutes. In case the central computer fails, the overall vehicle will fail. This must be already considered during design and development phase both in software and in hardware to satisfy the automotive industry's ASIL ratings [12].

There are many different technical approaches to enable the transformation to a zone-oriented E/E architecture and the resultant challenges. Those technical approaches will be presented in the next section and will be used to design methodical approaches for function abstraction and function centralization.

3   Technical Approaches for Centralization

Within this section, we will classify technical approaches to enable centralization from bottom to top of an ECU according to AUTOSAR's open and standardized software architecture. By this, one does not lose the relation to current architectures in vehicles. AUTOSAR's Classic platform representing established ECU architectures divides the ECU into its components from hardware towards application as can be seen in Fig. 3 [13]. The automotive system designers and function engineers focus on the application layer to develop their functional software. A virtual bus named runtime environment connects the application layer with the lower layer software parts that are modules standardized by AUTOSAR. By this, automotive system de-signers and function engineers can focus on their application software independent of the used hardware layer. AUTOSAR Classic is developed for real-time and time-critical applications. [13].

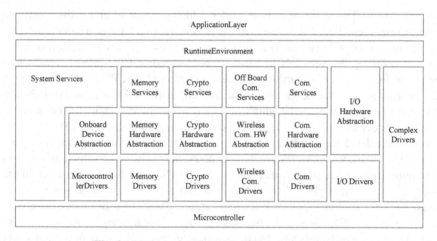

Fig. 3. R21–11 of AUTOSAR Classic following [13]

On the contrary, AUTOSAR's Adaptive platform is developed for service-oriented architectures and applications. It covers future vehicle ECU architectures based on for an example POSIX. By this, AUTOSAR Adaptive shall satisfy the requirements of the next generation car that is facing limitations as for an example the ones pointed out in Sect. 2.2. The layered software architecture of AUTOSAR Adaptive is dis-played in Fig. 4 [14]. The figure emphasizes the opportunities that AUTOSAR Adaptive enables by for an example the operating system interface layer or the virtual machine and container layer. More details about the characteristics will be discussed within this section.

In addition, we pay particular attention to the company's organization itself. The section will be closed by a cultural and a structural approach that can support automotive industry to realize the technical approaches. By this, automotive companies release potential to get closer to IT development and its toolchains to satisfy the needs of a software-driven vehicle architecture.

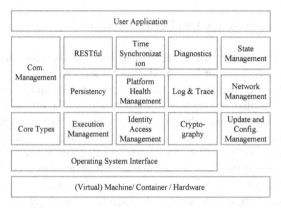

Fig. 4. R21–11 of AUTOSAR Adaptive following [14]

Centralized HPC ECUs need to consider a high amount of computing power to process the incidental data. Also the increase in demand over time of a software-driven vehicle must be considered due to further functionalities that may be flashed over the air (FOTA) during the vehicle's lifetime. To accommodate CPU-intensive tasks in a centralized ECU efficiently, hardware accelerators can reduce CPU load by overtaking specific tasks. A hardware accelerator is specialized hardware for dedicated tasks as it is for an example commonly used in graphics display of computers. Those can be switched on and off on demand and thus support the overall computing efficiency [3].

As vehicle development moves forward with an increasing number of functions and new CPU-intensive technologies, single-core processing is no more sufficient to satisfy the requirements. A continuous increase in the CPU's frequency is restricted due to power dissipation limits [15]. Thus multi-core and manycore processors are seen as key enablers for centralization of E/E architectures. Those type of processors enable parallelism of task allocation and by this increase the available computing power. Multi-core can also support the temporal freedom of interference which is an important safety factor with regards to virtualization and usage of different operating systems (real time versus server client) on the same CPU. At the same time complexity will increase and backward compatibility for legacy platforms needs to be considered. For this purpose, there are various software mechanisms and different approaches to reach a balanced load of the cores and avoid misallocation while following computation sequences. Those will not be further discussed here and can be investigated in [4, 15–17].

Coming one step closer on the ECU level to the application, the microcontroller abstraction layer (MCAL) as lowest layer of the Basic Software (BSW) comes into focus. It makes the upper software layers independent of the main processor and its on-chip peripherals like communication modules, memory, I/O and further. Operating systems interact with the hardware by the MCAL on an abstract level which al-lows programmers to code their SW device-independent. Thus, the MCAL increases SW portability to other ECUs which are closer to a potential central master ECU [4].

ADAS and infotainment systems process and handle a high amount of data so that classic time-driven operating systems like AUTOSAR Classic in embedded ECU development reach its limits. The younger, POSIX-based AUTOSAR Adaptive standard enables automotive developers to implement in an event-driven, client-server oriented way as the adaptive platform enables dynamically linkage of services and clients during runtime. Those characteristics make it possible for ECUs to handle the complexity and computational load of recent and future vehicle functionalities. Nevertheless, AUTOSAR Adaptive will not displace AUTOSAR Classic which will still be applied for hard real-time, time-critical applications with low computational load [3, 18, 19]. Both may need to coexist within the same CPU for their related functions and applications bringing us to a further key enabler for centralization, the virtualization. Virtualization enables to run multiple operating systems on the same hardware and in-creases by this the potential to centralize two ECUs with different requirements as for an example deterministic and non-deterministic behavior on one common hardware [1].

The parallel execution of multiple operating systems on the same CPU requires the implementation of a hypervisor. The hypervisor is also called virtual machine monitor (VMM) and isolates the hardware from the virtual machines (VM) and its operating systems. The hypervisor monitors the hardware needs of the related VMs and manages the hardware distribution based on the needs. We distinguish two types of hypervisors: type 1 and type 2. The type 1 hypervisor, also called bare metal hypervisor, is the direct interface towards the hardware acting as host operating system. It manages the resources retrieval of the guest operating systems running on it. The type 2 hypervisor runs on the already available host operating system as an application requesting resources for the guest operating systems via host. The type 2 hypervisor performs pure software virtualization. Also virtualization requires same as for multi-core processing methods and patterns to ensure freedom of interference, memory protection, safety according to ISO 26262 [20] or communication regulation over VM borders [1, 21].

Concluding with the impact of virtualization and operation systems on centralization of E/E architectures, middleware is reached on the way from ECU hardware to the application. It abstracts the application from the basis software, operating system and hardware. A middleware increases the flexibility of software components (SWCs) and enables that the software developer can fully focus on the function implementation without the need to consider lower layers. Smart middleware solutions will be the key enabler for the modern vehicle to access services of the IT domain and thus of the world wide web. By integration of a middleware, services can be properly trans-lated and interpreted by both sides. While AUTOSAR Classic's time-driven middle-ware is called Runtime Environment, AUTOSAR Adaptive uses a middleware called ARA which handles communication between server and clients [18, 19, 22].

In this context it gets clearer that smart middleware solutions are required to centralize and virtualize ECUs to ensure the connectivity of the software-driven vehicle.

This abstraction must also be supported by the application in form of SWCs that are designed flexible with defined interfaces. To reduce complexity and increase flex-ibility, the paradigm *divide and conquer* can support in designing applications out of decoupled microservices taking responsibility for smaller tasks. Microservices increase scalability and exchangeability of functions and software architectures. By orchestration, microservices can be reused for different applications [2].

Putting a microservice together with everything it needs to run like for an example system libraries, configuration, tools and runtimes, a container is created representing an independent unit of deployment. Containers and containerization in general support realization of DevOps' practice continuous integration / continuous deployment (CI/CD). Containers can be seen as a unifying technical approach to design applications already in the beginning independent of the future hardware or host on that it will run. It gives the application a better potential for relocatability on a central master ECU and to manage increasing complexity when keeping the principle of microservices [23].

While the presented technical approaches are already established in IT domain, automotive industry just started to introduce them with increasing digitalization in the automobile. Cultural and structural approaches can increase the potential to put all of the presented technical approaches into practice. Differences can be seen when comparing working methods and organizational structures of companies out of automotive industry with companies out of the IT domain. While in the automotive industry development according to the V model and vertical structures currently pre-vail, it is DevOps and horizontal structures in the IT domain.

DevOps, as the name indicates, combines development and operations by a number of various technical, methodical and cultural approaches. The goal is to fasten the development, the testing and the release process to improve software quality. By fusion of development and operations, feedback of operators and/or customers can directly feed into the development creating an endless loop which enables the principle continuous integration/continuous deployment (CI/CD). As the future vehicle will be more and more software-driven with the possibility to update single functions on demand, the automotive industry's working methods will evolve towards DevOps [2, 22, 24]. It is open if DevOps will replace the V model, if both will coexist or if a combination of both will be applied in future automotive development.

In addition, the organizational structures, especially the communication structures, impact the developed system's architecture as Conway's Law states [3]. Applied to E/E architecture in vehicles, it means the E/E architecture represents the communication structure of the company. As current E/E architectures of vehicles are still characterized by vertical orientation, the vertical organizational structures could be one of the root causes according to Conway's Law. In other words, communication and organizational structures must be centralized to push forward centralization of E/E architectures. [3].

Taking the previously discussed technical approaches into account, a system and its functions must be in a first run separated into its single components before a methodical approach for function centralization can be set up. The next section defines a concept of function separation. Based on this, a methodical concept is developed which applies the technical solutions on abstracted functions with the aim to evaluate centralization potential. This methodical approach will support system designers and function engineers in decisions about how to distribute functions within a system with focus on the presented current trends and challenges in automotive development.

4 Development of Methodical Approaches

4.1 Methodical Approach for Function Abstraction

While SW can be designed in a flexible way and thus be location-independent as presented, HW has stronger dependencies due to its tasks to, for example, actuate charge inlet locks or sense charge inlet temperatures. It is not for each I/O possible to root analog signal lines over longer distances directly to a central master ECU which will be part of the validation and discussion part. Thus a classic decentralized function can serve as an example to abstract it into its elementary components.

Each ECU or controller project starts with HW as a basis. Necessarily some computing power and control logic is required by CPUs and Microcontroller Units (MCUs). Those will be the home for operating systems which distribute tasks from SWCs to the hardware kernels and cores or monitor and operate I/O electric circuits. The circuits will be also handled as the element HW which operates as interface between I/O like actuators or sensors and the processing unit serving the evaluation and control logic. In a next step I/O can be connected to the processing ECU in a centralized or decentralized way [12]. Thus the abstraction approach needs to consider direct ana-log I/O signaling lines (centralized) and digital communication protocols like LIN and CAN, Ethernet or even wireless according to the IEE 802.11 standards (decentral-ized). Centralized I/O has the advantage to reduce the number of ECUs as no gate-ways are needed and the information will be directly processed from a more powerful and bigger centralized master ECU [12]. Nevertheless, it also implies disadvantages that will be listed in the discussion.

By this the four chosen elementary components HW, SW, I/O signaling line and I/O COM are already sufficient to abstract functions which enables to evaluate the function's potential for centralization. Figure 5 shows the generic illustration of the elementary components which will be used for the validation based on a temperature current derating function which is used in modern hybrid and electric vehicles.

4.2 Methodical Approach for Function Centralization

The methodical approach starts from a domain-oriented E/E architecture which is handled as state of the art. By centralizing as much as logic as possible in the domain controller, the domain controller evolves towards a central master computer as in best case only smart actuators and sensors will be left. In a next elaboration, a methodical concept can be developed to centralize the logic of the domains into cross-domains or into one central computer so that the domain controllers remain as simple translating zone gateway controllers.

Figure 6 shows the UML activity diagram which we created based on the technical solutions and the basic idea of centralization to be capable of manage current trends and challenges. The aim is to move forward in function centralization from a decentralized and distributed domain-oriented function architecture. The evaluation must be performed for each of the domain's function to accommodate as much as functionality within the domain ECU itself evolving to a central master computer.

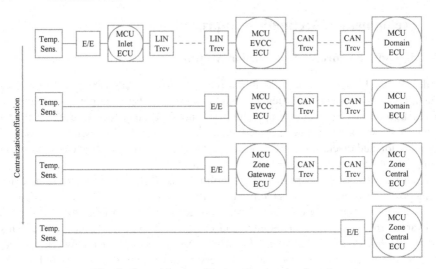

Fig. 5. Stepwise centralization of a derating function

4.3 Validation of Methodical Approach

To validate the methodical approach shown in the UML activity diagram, a temperature current derating function which is typical for hybrid and electric vehicles is used. Based on temperatures of sensors within the charging inlet, the charging current drawn by the vehicle will be regulated to prevent damage and injury. This function has an ASIL rating of B according to ISO 26262 [20]. The relevance of this information on the potential of centralization will be part of the discussion.

In a first step, the current function architecture must be abstracted according to the presented methodical approach for function abstraction in Sect. 4.1. Figure 5 shows on top the actual function architecture with its elementary hardware components, the corresponding circuits and the ECUs and MCUs which run the SWCs. Top down the function gets centralized until first its architecture equals the principle of a zone-oriented E/E architecture as described in Sect. 2.3 and second its architecture is centralized as much as possible. The technical approaches out of Sect. 3 and the UML activity diagram out of Sect. 4.2 are used therefore.

The main logic consists of two parts. Part one evaluates the temperature sensors by an electric circuit and provides the temperature values of the AC and the DC pins. This evaluation is mandatory as according to IEC 62196, it must be ensured that the maximum temperature at touchable, non-metallic parts shall not exceed 85 °C. Part two of the main logic processes the temperature values and calculates the potential current which can be drawn. The derating function can be seen as a quality performance function. The charging can be also performed with a continuous, maximum current. By this the threshold of 85 °C might be reached quickly and charging needs to be stopped even if the target state of charge of the vehicle is not reached yet. Thus the derating function shall regulate the current so that the charging process does not directly run in the threshold and needs to be stopped. Instead the charging shall be continued with a lower current to reach the optimal time span until the target state of charge is reached.

Part one of the main logic cannot be shifted freely due to its connection and reliance on the sensors and corresponding electric circuit. Whereas part two of the main logic can be designed as a kind of microservice according to Sect. 3. It has clear inputs like the temperature values and clear outputs meaning the actual maximum current based on its calculation. This fact makes the SWC or microservice *temperature current derating* flexible and independent of its location.

As can be seen on top of Fig. 5, the function *temperature current derating* is allocated to three different ECUs. Following the UML activity diagram, part two of the main logic above can be shifted in an ECU closer to the domain controller. In the first step this will be the ECU *EVCC*. The I/O of the sensors including their electric circuit is centralized by a direct analog signaling line from sensor towards *EVCC*. By this, the function itself does no more have the need for the ECU *Inlet*. It does only apply for this dedicated function so that the ECU *Inlet* cannot be removed in general. This is also the reason why the UML activity diagram must be executed for every function x of a domain. The function with the least potential for centralization limits the removal of components. The new architecture of the function is the second from the top of Fig. 5.

Going one step further with regards to a zone-oriented E/E architecture, the ECU *EVCC* will be converted into a simple zone gateway ECU by shifting part 2 of the main logic into the domain ECU which shall evolve to a central computer. The zone gateway ECU serves now as a simple smart sensor which monitors and translates for the domain controller. Below the zone gateway ECU, further sensors and actuators could be placed which will be monitored and processed for the domain controller. The new function architecture is displayed in the third row of Fig. 5. In the last step of the UML diagram, even the zone gateway ECU will be removed by centralizing once more the I/O directly to its domain controller. This leads to a shift of the electric circuit into the domain controller reducing also the number of communication lines. This most centralized function architecture is shown in the last row of Fig. 5. As a further centralization of the function *temperature current derating* is no more possible, a discussion on the advantages, disadvantages and challenges of the different variants will follow.

5   Discussion

The most obvious advantage of the fourth and most centralized function design is the reduction of components, electric circuits and communication channels. Development costs can be saved, busload and latency decrease, reliability increases and the scalability is less restricted in a software-driven central computer [12].

Applying the technical approaches of Sect. 3 on the central computer, functions can be handled as known from smartphones. New functions can be added and outdated functions can be updated continuously as it is done in IT domain principles like for an example CI/CD [22].

At the same time, the centralization reduces modularity and flexibility as a clear advantage of actual decentralized architectures. It impacts especially the HW design of the domain or central controller which by this may include components that are only needed in certain vehicle variants. In addition to that, centralized I/O also in-creases the wire lengths and number of cut leads (point-to-point wire connections) as sensors and actuators cannot be connected as close as possible to the nearest bus [12].

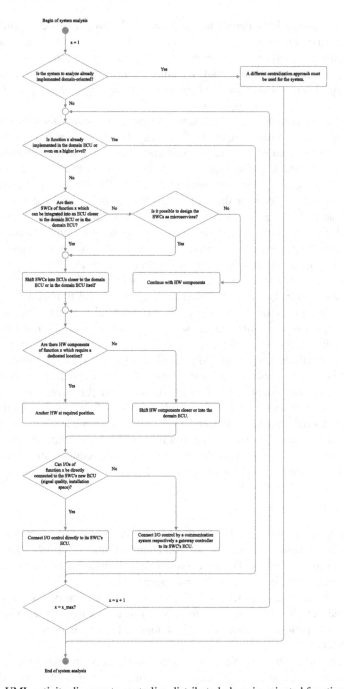

Fig. 6. UML activity diagram to centralize distributed, domain-oriented function designs

The longer the wire, the higher the impact of environmental influences and signal losses. In a vehicle, especially environmental impacts and EMC can result in loss of signal accuracy over longer distances. With a view to proper signal qualities and reliabilities to satisfy ASIL ratings and the ISO 26262 [20], twist and shield might be necessary which increases material, evaluation and certification costs. To eliminate those disadvantages, the zone-oriented E/E architecture with decentralized I/O connected by communication busses can be chosen. This function design with a zone gateway ECU equals the third design in Fig. 5.

Another risk of a fully centralized E/E architecture design is the single point of failure. The central computer in a vehicle needs to fulfill ASIL ratings up to ASIL D to avoid damage and injury. By this the central computer must show redundancy for power supply, communication and further. [20] It is a high challenge also on SW level which requires appropriate counter measures to ensure the timely achieving of the vehicle's or system's safe state.

6 Conclusion

Within this paper, we propose a methodical approach supporting system and function engineers in centralization of E/E architectures. Actual technical solutions out of research were collected, investigated and merged into an UML activity diagram by means of which different function designs can be worked out and centralized. Nevertheless, centralization cannot be seen as general panacea for each function of an E/E architecture. In general, it will improve manageability and reduce complexity of future technologies like ADAS or infotainment systems which are characterized by a high amount of code lines and data. Those might not be manageable otherwise in the near future. However, there are also disadvantages when centralizing functions which must be elaborated in detail especially when it refers to conventional functions and functions that do not require high computing power or high amounts of data.

In future work, a methodical approach that shifts the functions of the domain controllers into a central master computer and transforms domain controllers into zone gateway controllers can be worked out. Additionally, the future of the V model under the influence of DevOps needs to be revised. By designing integration concepts of DevOps into the V model, the impact on the flexibility and quality of the development process can be evaluated.

References

1. Bandur, V., Pantelic, V., Dawson, M., Schaap, A., Wasacz, B., Lawfor, M.: A domain-centralized automotive powertrain E/E architecture. In: SAE Technical Paper 2021-01-0786 (2021)
2. Schneider, T.: Achieving cloud scalability with microservices and DevOps in the connected car domain. In: CEUR Workshop Proceedings (2016)
3. Zerfowski, D., Lock, A.: Functional architecture and E/E-Architecture - A challenge for the automotive industry. In: 19. Internationales Stuttgarter Symposium, pp. 99–110. Springer, Vieweg (2019). https://doi.org/10.1007/978-3-658-25939-6_70

4. Bandur, V., Selim, G., Pantelic, V., Lawford, M.: Making the case for centralized automotive E/E architectures. IEEE Trans. Veh. Technol. 1230–1245 (2021)
5. Bauer, L.: Smart vehicle architecture - a sustainable approach to Builting the next generation of vehicles (2020)
6. GmbH, R.B.: Fahrzeugzentrische und zonenorientierte E/E-Architektur mit Fahrzeugcomputern. Robert Bosch GmbH. https://www.bosch-mobility-solutions.com/de/mobility-themen/ee-architektur/. Accessed 29 May 2022
7. Ziegenbein, D., Saidi, S., Hu, X., Steinhorst, S.: Future Automotive HW/SW Platform Design (Dagstuhl Seminar 19502). In Dagstuhl Reports, Dagstuhl (2020)
8. Benam, B.: Why Vertical Integration Made Tesla More Powerful," 24th October 2020. https://medium.com/@bhbenam/why-vertical-integration-made-tesla-more-powerful-8b33b6aee773. Accessed 29 May 2022
9. Munro, S., Koch, D., Bellestri, S., Waner, D.: Comparing Tesla, Ford, & VW's Electrical Architectures," 3IS Inc. (2021). https://www.youtube.com/watch?v=ZRkm6-bBk4U. Accessed 29 May 2022
10. Scheer, D., Glodd, O., Günther, H., Duhr, Y., Schmid, A.: STAR3 - Eine neue Generation der E/E-Architektur Sonderprojekte. ATZ/MTZ.**25**(1), 72–79 (2020).https://doi.org/10.1007/s41491-020-0056-5
11. Sommer, S., et al.: RACE: a centralized platform computer based architecture for automotive applications. In: 2013 IEEE International Electric Vehicle Conference (IEVC) (2013)
12. Kanajan, S., Pinello, C., Zeng, H., Sangiovanni-Vincentelli, A.: Exploring trade-off's between centralized versus decentralized automotive architectures using a virtual integration environment. In: Proceedings of the Design Automation & Test in Europe Conference, Munich (2006)
13. AUTOSAR (2021). https://www.autosar.org/standards/adaptive-platform/. Accessed 29 May 2022
14. AUTOSAR (2021). https://www.autosar.org/standards/classic-platform/. Accessed 29 May 2022
15. Claraz, D., Grimal, F., Leydier, T., Mader, R., Wirrer, G.: Introducing Multi-Core at Automotive Engine Systems. Research archive HAL (2019)
16. Macher, G., Höller, A., Armengaud, E., Kreiner, C.: Automotive embedded software: migration challenges to multi-core computing platforms. In: 2015 IEEE 13th International Conference on Industrial Informatics (INDIN), Cambridge (2015)
17. Michel, L., Flaemig, T., Claraz, D., Mader, R.: Shared SW development in multi-core automotive. Research archive HAL (2016)
18. Jesse, B., Weber, M., Helmling, M.: The Future with SOA, POSIX, TSN. Automobil-Elektronik, 11th December 2017
19. Menar, C., Goens, A., Lohstroh, M., Castrillon, J.: Achieving determinism in adaptive AUTOSAR. In: 2020 Design, Automation & Test in Europe Conference & Exhibition (DATE), Grenoble (2020)
20. ISO, Road vehicles - Functional safety - Part 2: Management of functional safety, ISO (2018)
21. Ruest, N.: ComputerWeekly.de, 25 August 2014. https://www.computerweekly.com/de/tipp/Vergleich-zwischen-Typ-1-und-Typ-2-Den-richtigen-Hypervisor-auswaehlen. Accessed 29 May 2022
22. Zerfowski, D., Antonov, S., Hammel, C.: Building the bridge between automotive SW engineering and DevOps approaches for automated driving SW development. In: Automatisiertes Fahren, 2021 Wiesbaden, pp. 41–49. Springer, Vieweg (2021)

23. Kugele, S., Hettler, D., Peter, J.: Data-centric communication and containerization for future automotive software architectures. In: 2018 IEEE International Conference on Software Architecture (ICSA), Seattle (2018)

24. Myklebust, T., Stålhane, T., Hanssen, G.: Agile safety case and DevOps for the automotive industry. In: Proceedings of the 30th European Safety and Reliability Conference and the 15th Probabilistic Safety Assessment and Management Conference (2020)

5th Context-Aware, Autonomous and Smart Architectures International Workshop (CASA)

MockSAS: Facilitating the Evaluation of Bandit Algorithms in Self-adaptive Systems

Elvin Alberts[1], Ilias Gerostathopoulos[1]([✉]), and Tomas Bures[2]

[1] Vrije Universiteit Amsterdam, Amsterdam, The Netherlands
{e.g.alberts,i.g.gerostathopoulos}@vu.nl
[2] Charles University in Prague, Prague, Czech Republic
bures@d3s.mff.cuni.cz

Abstract. To be able to optimize themselves at runtime even in situations not specifically designed for, self-adaptive systems (SAS) often employ online learning that takes the form of sequentially applying actions to learn their effect on system utility. Employing multi-armed bandit (MAB) policies is a promising approach for implementing online learning in SAS. A main problem when employing MAB policies in this setting is that it is difficult to evaluate and compare different policies on their effectiveness in optimizing system utility. This stems from the high number of runs that are necessary for a trustworthy evaluation of a policy under different contexts. The problem is amplified when several policies and several contexts are considered. It is however pivotal for wider adoption of MAB policies in online learning in SAS to facilitate such evaluation and comparison. Towards this end, we provide a Python package, MockSAS, and a grammar that allows for specifying and running mocks of SAS: profiles of SAS that capture the relations between the contexts, the actions, and the rewards. Using MockSAS can drastically reduce the time and resources of performing comparisons of MAB policies in SAS. We evaluate the applicability of MockSAS and its accuracy in obtaining results compared to using the real system in a self-adaptation exemplar.

Keywords: self-adaptive systems · multi-armed bandits · profiling

1 Introduction

Self-adaptive systems (SAS) are able to adapt to changes in their environment and internal state to ensure or optimize a number of adaptation goals related to e.g. application performance, resource consumption, and failure avoidance [12]. To make them capable to react to different situations at runtime, even to those unanticipated at design time, SAS can be equipped with an online learning loop that performs different adaptation actions, monitors their effect in terms of the overall utility of the system after each action is performed, and selects the actions that maximizes such utility [9,15].

T. Batista et al. (Eds.): ECSA 2022, LNCS 13928, pp. 183–198, 2023.
https://doi.org/10.1007/978-3-031-36889-9_14

One possible way to implement online learning in SAS is to rely on multi-armed bandit (MAB) policies [13]. Such policies are a class of reinforcement learning algorithms that can be used for sequential decision making between a set of options. An MAB policy can be used to select an action out of a number of discrete options (called *arms*) by balancing exploration – picking an arm to learn its utility (called *reward*) – and exploitation – picking the so-far best arm to maximize the cumulative utility. Since this process maps well to a SAS trying actions at runtime to observe their effect and optimize its performance, MAB policies are a natural candidate to consider for online learning in SAS. At the same time, different MAB policies – including ϵ-greedy, different variants of Upper Confidence Bound (UCB), and Explore-Then-Commit – exist and several have already been proposed for online learning in SAS [1,6,14,17]. Each policy, or policy variant/configuration, performs better compared to other policies in certain operation scenarios (e.g. high variance in reward, frequent changes in context) and worse in others.

The problem we have encountered when employing MAB policies for online learning is that it is difficult to evaluate the effectiveness of different policy types (e.g. greedy, stochastic, contextual) in optimizing the overall system utility, and, consequently, to compare them based on such effectiveness and select the best policy for a given SAS [1]. The main problem stems from the fact that the evaluation needs to consider the stochasticity of the environment (e.g. different situations that the SAS may reside in), of the SAS itself (e.g. different processing times due to resource overload), and of the MAB policies themselves (e.g. randomization inherent in the logic of certain policies). To back up any evaluation/comparison results in this complicated setting with statistical confidence, one therefore needs to perform a huge number of runs covering all the foreseeable system and environment states. For instance, in a typical case one would need to compare e.g. five different MAB policies over three system contexts by performing 30 runs, each of which consists of 100 rounds (where each round evaluates an action and may last for one minute). This yields $5 * 3 * 30 * 100 = 45,000$ mins or $31,25$ days of evaluation time (in real time when the runs are not parallelized). Clearly, this is both a time-consuming and resource-intensive process – while at the same time essential for the wider adoption of MAB policies in SAS.

To tackle the above problem, we propose to perform evaluations and comparisons of MAB policies on a *profile* of a SAS that captures the relations between the contexts, the actions, and the rewards. This profile acts similar to a mock object in unit testing: it helps isolating the behavior of the object under test (MAB policy) by simulating the behavior of the real object it depends on (SAS), when it is impractical to directly use the latter. To create such a profile, different metrics of the real system need to be measured under different contexts and actions and derive statistical distributions that can be used for generating rewards in each system state that corresponds to a (context, action) pair. However, it is important to note that this profiling needs to be done only once and can be reused for the evaluation of different MAB policies, saving time and resources. Additionally, it potentially allows non-measured contexts to be extrapolated and included in the profile should a complete recreation of the factors evaluating actions be not feasible.

The contribution of this paper is to describe a Python package, called Mock-SAS, and related grammar that we developed for (i) specifying profiles of SAS, and (ii) using them in a loop with a MAB policy for fast evaluations. In particular, we provide a first version of the process that allows for defining profiles of SAS using the MockSAS grammar, and demonstrate its applicability on a self-adaptation exemplar (Sect. 3). Finally, we evaluate the accuracy of the MAB policy comparison results obtained when using a profile versus the real SAS on the same self-adaptation exemplar (Sect. 4).

2   Background

2.1   Multi-armed Bandits

Multi-armed bandit (MAB) algorithms or *policies* are a class of reinforcement learning (RL) algorithms which deal with choosing between a set of K options called *arms* [13,18]. Formally, this setting corresponds to a Markov Decision Process with a single state and K actions, while compared to the general RL setting, actions in an MAB policy are assumed to not influence future states of the environment. In this setting, an MAB policy balances *exploration* with *exploitation*: it tries to explore arms to gain knowledge about them while at the same time using the best-known arm regularly to exploit the knowledge it has already gained.

In particular, each arm has an associated reward (or payoff) whose value at a time t is not known prior to selecting (*"pulling"*) it. Arms are selected sequentially and their rewards are gradually revealed; an MAB policy prescribes with arm should be selected at each round. MAB policies try to minimize the *regret* they incur, i.e. the loss in performance by using them compared to the optimal policy of playing the best arm at each round. Equivalently, they try to maximize the cumulative reward. Formally, given K arms and sequences of rewards $X_{i,1}, X_{i,2}, ...$ associated with each arm i, the regret R_n of a policy after n plays $I_1, ..., I_n$ is [5]

$$R_n = \max_{i=1,...,K} \sum_{t=1}^{n} X_{i,t} - \sum_{t=1}^{n} X_{I_t,t}$$

Different MAB policies can be categorized according to their assumptions on (i) their application horizon, (ii) the nature of the reward process, and (iii) the setting they are applied to. Depending on the application horizon, policies can be categorized as *anytime* and *fixed-horizon*. Depending on the assumed nature of the reward process, MAB policies are categorized into *stochastic*, *adversarial*, and *Markovian* [5]. Depending on their application setting, we distinguish between *contextual* (or associative) and *non-contextual* bandits.

Implementation. The MABs we use in this paper are implemented in a Python library[1] developed across our previous works [1,2]. Each MAB bandit is provided

---

[1] https://github.com/EGAlberts/MASCed_bandits.

with some abstract sense of a list of arms to choose between, the user decides whether these should be a strings, integers, or any other abstraction user-defined or not. The multi-armed bandit then uses its specific exploration-exploitation strategy to choose one of these arms. The expectation is that this choice of arm is used to execute some adaptation tactic in a self-adaptive system. The consequence of this execution is then provided as feedback to the MAB in the form of a reward. Based on this reward and the specific strategy the next arm is chosen. In Fig. 1 we have included the implementation of a simple MAB namely ϵ-greedy, which chooses between exploiting the arm with the highest average reward and exploring a random arm, based on threshold provided as a hyperparameter.

```
1  class egreedy(Bandit):
2
3    def get_next_arm(self, reward):
4      self.arm_reward_pairs[self.prev_chosen_arm][CUM_REWARD]+=reward
5
6      choice = np.random.random()
7      if(choice < self.epsilon):
8        next_arm = np.random.choice(self.arms)
9      else:
10       next_arm = max(self.arms, key=lambda arm: reward_average(arm))
11
12     self.prev_chosen_arm = next_arm
13     return next_arm
```

Fig. 1. ϵ-greedy bandit.

As can be seen on line 6 a random value is generated between 0 and 1, which then based on the ϵ value within [0,1] provided as a hyper-parameter either explores a random arm (line 8) or exploits the arm with highest average reward (line 10). That arm is then returned to be provided to the self-adaptive system on line 13.

2.2 Online Learning with MABs in Self-adaptive Systems

A SAS is typically composed of a managed system that is responsible for the business goals of the system and a managing system that is responsible for its adaptation goals (e.g. optimizing its performance). As depicted in Fig. 2, the managing system typically follows the well-known Monitor-Analyze-Plan-Execute over Knowledge (MAPE-K) loop [8]. The Monitor phase collects data regarding the managed system and its environment, Analyze decides based on the data whether an adaptation is needed, Plan identifies the best adaptation action to perform and prepares a plan for it, and Execute performs the adaptation action to change the managed system. In this setting, online learning with MAB policies can be part of the Plan phase: when a SAS is in a situation for which the best action is unknown, it launches an online learning cycle. In this cycle, an MAB policy is used to select an action (arm) that is applied to the managed system. The reward for an action is calculated by combining different monitored attributes of the managed system into a utility value. Based on the reward for an action, a next action is selected from the policy and applied. An online learning cycle ends by either having the policy converge to an action or reaching a maximum number of rounds.

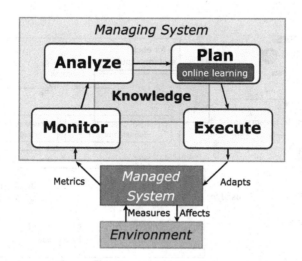

Fig. 2. MAPE-K with online learning within the Plan phase.

2.3 Running Example: SWIM

Simulator for Web Infrastructure and Management (SWIM) is a SEAMS arte- fact [16] representing the management of server infrastructure for a fictitious web location. The simulator allows real web traces to be replayed in simulated time, making it possible to adapt to hours of web traffic in a span of min- utes. The adaptation goals of SWIM are to minimize the average response time for requests while at the same time also minimize the infrastructure cost and maximize the profit made by serving advertisements within the served requests. To reach these goals, SWIM is equipped with two adaptation mechanisms: (i) changing the number of servers used to serve requests, and (ii) changing the dim- mer value that controls the percentage of responses that contain advertisements. SWIM's overall utility is based on the degree of satisfaction of its adaptation goals. An adaptation action – arm in MAB – sets the number of servers or the dimmer value. In our experiment in Sect. 4 we only focus on the first type of actions.

3 Approach

3.1 MockSAS Process

In order to facilitate the evaluation of MAB policies in online learning in SAS we have created MockSAS. Figure 3 illustrates the process of using MockSAS to profile a SAS – in particular its *managed system* part (Fig. 2) – as well as how the profile is used in evaluating MAB policies.

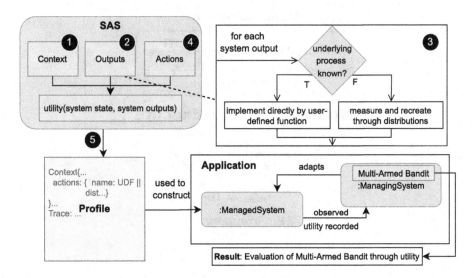

Fig. 3. Process for creating MockSAS profiles and evaluating MAB policies.

The required steps of the process for creating a profile are as follows:

1. Determine the system context(s) to be profiled. A profile consists of a series of contexts distinguished by features which when combined with the current system configuration constitute a system state. Contexts are operating scenarios of the system where the utility of one or more system states differs significantly. For instance, in SWIM a context feature is the number of requests received per second.
2. Identify which outputs influence the calculation of the reward. Outputs are the metrics we assume the managed system generates depending on its state.
3. Of the identified outputs, determine which require profiling and are thus *profiled outputs*. Some outputs may have an established relationship with context features which can be directly specified instead of profiled.
4. Identify the adaptation actions per context whose effects on the reward should be measured. A system may have more adaptation actions than are applicable to the chosen contexts.

```
 1 SixtyRequests{
 2   features: {
 3     rq_rate: uniform(54,66)
 4   }
 5   actions: {
 6     ThreeServers:    utilitySWIM(rq_rate, 1.0, normal(.064,.009), 13, 3)
 7     SixServers:      utilitySWIM(rq_rate, 1.0, normal(.039,.001), 13, 6)
 8     EightServers:    utilitySWIM(rq_rate, 1.0, normal(.039,.001), 13, 8)
 9     ElevenServers:   utilitySWIM(rq_rate, 1.0, normal(.039,.001), 13, 11)
10     ThirteenServers: utilitySWIM(rq_rate, 1.0, normal(.039,.002), 13, 13)
11   } }
12
13 EightyRequests{
14   features: {
15     rq_rate: uniform(72,88)
16   }
17   actions: {
18     ThreeServers:    utilitySWIM(rq_rate, 1.0, normal(1.68,1.44), 13, 3)
19     SixServers:      utilitySWIM(rq_rate, 1.0, normal(.041,.001), 13, 6)
20     EightServers:    utilitySWIM   (rq_rate, 1.0, normal(.039,.0004), 13, 8)
21     ElevenServers:   utilitySWIM(rq_rate, 1.0, normal(.039,.001), 13, 11)
22     ThirteenServers: utilitySWIM(rq_rate, 1.0, normal(.039,.001), 13, 13)
23   }
24 }
25 Trace: (SixtyRequests, 166) (EightyRequests,166)
```

Fig. 4. MockSAS profile of SWIM. Reserved keywords of our domain-specific language are shown in blue, names of contexts and actions in green, names of feature variables in red, and user-defined functions in violet (Color figure online).

5. For each action in each context, collect sufficient values of the profiled outputs to be able to identify their distribution.

The listing in Fig. 4 shows a profile of SWIM created using the implemented profile grammar included in MockSAS[2]. We will use this listing to describe each part of the process in greater detail.

Step 1: Determining the System Context(s) to be Profiled. We choose to discretize the operating environment a SAS faces into contexts. The implication is that each distinct context influences the rewards per action. The listing defines two contexts, SixtyRequests and EightyRequests. Contexts may or may not have measurable features which distinguish them. When these are present we specify them as features of the context such as in lines 2–4. These features in turn may play a role in the reward as will be covered in steps 2 and 3. To determine system contexts thus requires observing how a system's reward changes over time. For SWIM it is straight-forward to distinguish contexts by the arrival rate of requests. Taking the context SixtyRequests as an example, for realism the

[2] https://github.com/EGAlberts/MockSAS/blob/main/environmentgrammar.py.

request rate is a uniform distribution of 10% below and above the average of 60 request/s as defined on line 3. Within this range of requests/s the rewards achieved per action are similar enough to be grouped as one context. Line 25 shows the trace of contexts; this simply specifies how many 'rounds' (adaptation opportunities) each context is active for and in what order. The total number of rounds across all contexts in a MockSAS trace determines the overall duration of the trace.

Step 2: Identifying Outputs. A system may have numerous outputs that are continuously monitored. A subset of these outputs can be used to evaluate a system state's utility. The utility of the state resulting from an adaptation is its reward. For SWIM, a utility function was already defined and used in lines 6–10 and 18–22 to define the reward per action. Should the system to be profiled not have a utility function defined, one can do so based on its requirements and the goals that stem from it [10]. Depending on a system utility function, different outputs may parameterize it – those which do should be identified. The signature of the utility function used in our listing is `utilitySWIM(arrival_rate, dimmer, avg_response_time, max_servers, servers)`. The `arrival_rate` as covered is specified on line 3 of the listing. This is implemented through the user-defined function functionality of the grammar which allows any function written in Python to supply utility values. The `dimmer` and `servers` are both determined by the specific action, the former is held constant and represents optional content served in responses. The `response_time` is the latency in serving those responses. Lastly, `max_servers` represents the maximum servers a SWIM adaptation can result in using, in our case this is 13.

Step 3: Profiled and Non-profiled Outputs. There may be an established relationship between system outputs and the feature of a context. Further, some outputs may directly stem from the system state by way of the current configuration. If we look at line 6 of the listing, the second, penultimate, and last parameter of the utility function can be directly derived from the context features and the fact that the adaptation has three servers (value of the last parameter). In particular, 1.0 represents that the 'dimmer' value is kept constant, and 13 the maximum servers across adaptations. Similarly, the request rate can be used directly as it is a known context feature. Contrarily, the process behind response time is not precisely traceable for SWIM, so response time is a profiled output.

Step 4: Identify Actions. A system may have myriad potential adaptation actions. However, not every action is applicable to every situation. Simultaneously, the fewer actions there are, the more efficiently a MAB policy can perform. Thus it is in the interest of the user to minimize the number of adaptation actions by identifying those appropriate. For the listed profile, five adaptation actions, 3, 6, 8, 11 and 13 servers are identified for each context. This is as for the low end of the `SixtyRequests` context 3 servers can be sufficient, while up to 13 are required to deal with the high end of the `EightyRequests` context.

Step 5: Profile Actions per Context. Now that the desired contexts and actions have been identified, they can be profiled for the necessary profiled outputs. In the case of SWIM this means subjecting each number of servers to the `SixtyRequests` and `EightyRequests` context and measuring the response times outputted. This was done for a sufficient amount of time to accurately determine the mean and standard deviation of the response time. We specify this through a normal distribution in each action definition e.g. line 6 `normal(.064,.009)`. It should be noted that we did have prior knowledge the distribution would be Gaussian. We do not yet provide a general-purpose solution for profiled outputs of which the underlying distribution is not known prior although the grammar allows for specifying different distributions (e.g. normal, logistic, constant). These different distributions are provided as user-defined functions we have already defined to be reused.

3.2   Application

MockSAS is implemented as a Python package which consists of abstractions of MAPE-K's managed system, managing system and environment and a grammar within which to specify profiles. The grammar is developed using the Lark Python library [7]. The source code of MockSAS can be found in a GitHub repository[3]. MockSAS accepts defined profiles as input as we have seen in Fig. 4. A `ManagedSystem` abstraction is constructed with a given profile as its parameter. The instance of the `ManagedSystem` is assigned to an instance of the `ManagingSystem` to be managed by it. This `ManagingSystem` is itself constructed with an instance of a MAB policy, provided by the MASCed_bandits library[4] developed in our previous work [2]. After the necessary objects have been constructed, the operation loop of the MockSAS begins. All this is shown in the code snippet of Fig. 5.

In a typical execution the `ManagedSystem` initially observes its environment as specified by its profile (line 28–29, 32). Then, it notifies the `ManagingSystem`, which observes it, that an adaptation is required (line 37–42). As can be seen on line 38, the reward generators per action are grabbed (relying on the current state of features and variables) and then passed to the `ManagingSystem` on line 41. This essentially constitutes updating the runtime model of the `ManagedSystem`. The `ManagingSystem` queries the MAB policy for a new action (line 13), using the rewards it gathers for the previously chosen action i.e. the current *active* action (line 11). By using generators, the rewards as well as context features resulting from functions are only calculated on-demand making the implementation resource-efficient. The policy uses all the rewards received in its lifetime to advise which adaptation action/arm should be enacted next. For evaluation of the choices the policy has made, the reward is stored (line 16).

The described behaviour loops until the end of the trace specified in the profile, or in the case of an indefinite trace until the user interrupts it. That is why we need track of each iteration (line 18).

---

[3] https://github.com/EGAlberts/MockSAS.
[4] https://github.com/EGAlberts/MASCed_bandits/.

```
1  class ManagingSystem:
2    def __init__(self, policy_tuple, managed, actions):
3
4      self.policy = init_bandit(**policy_tuple)
5
6      for managed_system in managed:
7        managed_system.register_observer(self)
8
9    def notify(self, reward_generator_dict):
10     if(reward_generators):
11       reward = next(reward_generator_dict[self.current_action])
12
13       self.current_action = self.policy.get_next_arm(reward)
14       self.avg_reward = self.average_reward + ((1/self.round) \
15                         * (reward - self.avg_reward))
16       self.avg_rw_record.append(self.average_reward)
17
18       self.round+=1
19       return True
20
21     else: return False
22
23 class ManagedSystem:
24   def __init__(self, rew_generator, env_generator):
25     self._observers = []
26     self.observations = {}
27     self.generator = rew_generator
28     self.environment = self.Environment(env_generator)
29     self.environment.register_observer(self)
30
31   def get_observations(self):
32     return self.observations
33
34   def register_observer(self, observer):
35     self._observers.append(observer)
36
37   def notify_observers(self):
38     round_gens = next(self.generator)
39     acks = []
40     for obs in self._observers:
41       acks.append(obs.notify(round_gens))
42     return acks
```

Fig. 5. Managing System and Managed System abstractions.

4   Evaluation

4.1   Setup

We have designed one experiment in which MAB policies are evaluated and perform it using both the actual SWIM exemplar and our profile based on it as described in Fig. 4. In doing so we seek to answer how accurately the evaluation of the policies done through MockSAS matches that of the actual SWIM exemplar.

Setting. The experiment uses the trace as specified at the end of the profile in Fig. 4 as its setting. There are 166 rounds of a server load of around 60 request/s followed by another 166 of around 80 requests/s. This number of rounds provides ample opportunity for all the policies we evaluate to determine the optimal action (with the highest average reward). The range of response times per action within each context have been measured prior to the experiment and used to define the profile used for the MockSAS portion. This is reflected in the `normal(mean,stdev)` function seen throughout the reward specification for actions in the profile.

MAB Policies. For the experiments four different MAB policies are used; when considering different hyperparameter values in total 15 policies are run. We will now describe each policy and provide the rationale for its inclusion.

- ϵ-**greedy**: ϵ-greedy is a classical solution to the exploration-exploitation trade off. The policy serves as a baseline, with a fixed rate of exploration being specified through its *epsilon* hyperparameter e.g. with $\epsilon = 0.8$ has an 80% chance of exploring in a given round. At each round it either does this exploration, or exploits by choosing the arm/action with maximum average reward so far. As a baseline, it is useful in evaluating more complex policies against what is a naive and simple solution.
- **UCB-Tuned**: UCB, Upper Confidence Bound, and its tuned variant is a well-cited MAB policy known for its relatively high performance guarantees [3]. The policy constructs a confidence bound on the true mean of each arm, using the distance between the means per arm to ascertain with high certainty which arm provides an optimal reward. It balances exploiting the arm with the highest certainty of being optimal against exploring arms about which there is more uncertainty. Its ubiquity and expected performance motivate its inclusion in our experiment. UCB-Tuned does not require a hyperparameter.
- **EXP3**: EXP3 [4] is a policy similar to UCB, with the key difference being that it does not assume there to be a probability distribution generating the rewards. Instead, rewards are presumed to be chosen by an adversary. Rather than ascertaining confidence, EXP3 instead uses a exponentially weighted

distribution with weights provided by observed rewards per arm. At each round it samples this distribution to choose the next arm. As EXP3 makes fewer assumptions than UCB it is of interest especially in application to SAS (when considering a desire for general-purpose solutions). We use one hyperparameter which is based on the total number of rounds the policy expects to face.

- **Discounted UCB (DUCB)**: DUCB [11] is a variation on UCB to handle *non-stationary* environments. For our purposes, these are environments with multiple contexts which cause an abrupt change in the expected rewards per arm. The policy tackles this by discounting rewards as they age, biasing more recent observations. As the environment we specify for the experiment contains multiple contexts, it is of interest to evaluate DUCB's performance relative to policies designed for stationary environments (all the other policies in our experiment). The hyperparameter *gamma* of DUCB controls the degree of discounting of old rewards; the closer it comes to 1, the closer DUCB approximates UCB-Tuned. From our previous work [2] we know that small variations of *gamma* can have a large effect on the performance of DUCB.

We have implemented these policies among others in a Python library MASCed_bandits in our previous work [2]. We make use of this library for the experiment on both platforms.

SWIM Exemplar. As established through prior work [1,2], we use an extension developed to SWIM which allows Python libraries to act as an 'AdaptationManager'. Through this extension, each MAB policy is used to implement the Plan phase of the MAPE-K-based adaptation logic for the system. Using this adaptation logic, 30 runs with differing randomization seeds are done per policy. The results of these runs are averaged and compiled in Table 1. The 30 runs are chosen as a tradeoff of statistical significance and time feasibility. Although SWIM can make use of simulated time, conducting 30*15 runs of more than 300 rounds each (with 60 simulated seconds per run), 120 min of real time were necessary to complete the experiment.

MockSAS. We setup the experiment in MockSAS to recreate the conditions of the SWIM exemplar closely. A Python script simply loops through 30 different randomization seeds, similar to the SWIM case. Within each iteration, for each of the 15 policies a MockSAS object is instantiated, run for the duration of the trace, and its results are recorded. These results are averaged over the 30 runs and presented in Table 1. For the same number of runs as in SWIM, the experiment in MockSAS took 10 mins, only 8% of the time needed for SWIM.

Table 1. MockSAS vs SWIM experiment results.

MAB Policy	Hyper-parameter	SWIM Median Reward	MockSAS Median Reward	SWIM Position	MockSAS AVG Position	AVG Match
UCB-Tuned	-	0.75	0.76	1	1.27	80.00%
ϵ-greedy	$\epsilon = 0.2$	0.72	0.73	2	2.60	40.00%
DUCB	$\gamma = 0.997$	0.71	0.73	3	2.57	50.00%
	$\gamma = 0.995$	0.70	0.72	4	3.93	73.33%
ϵ-greedy	$\epsilon = 0.4$	0.68	0.69	5	5.53	46.67%
DUCB	$\gamma = 0.992$	0.67	0.69	6	5.67	53.33%
	$\gamma = 0.99$	0.65	0.68	7	7.20	50.00%
EXP3-FH	$h = 333$	0.65	0.66	8	8	23.33%
ϵ-greedy	$\epsilon = 0.6$	0.64	0.66	9	8.33	36.67%
	$\epsilon = 0.8$	0.60	0.62	10	11.90	3.33%
DUCB	$\gamma = 0.97$	0.60	0.63	11	9.90	3.33%
	$\gamma = 0.95$	0.58	0.62	12	11.63	56.67%
ϵ-greedy (Random)	$\epsilon = 1.0$	0.57	0.58	13	14.83	6.67%
DUCB	$\gamma = 0.92$	0.57	0.61	14	12.70	10.00%
	$\gamma = 0.89$	0.56	0.60	15	13.90	10.00%

4.2   Results

Table 1 compiles the results of the experiment on both platforms. The table is sorted by the median reward achieved by each policy on SWIM across the 30 runs, where the reward refers to the average reward achieved by the policy for a run irrespective of which choices were made. This entails that not only choosing the optimal action is emphasized (as a convergence measure would) but also how lucrative its non-optimal choices were. The 'MockSAS average position' refers to the position each policy had at the end of a run relative to one another. This indicates in what range of positions policies were evaluated. This can be contrasted with the position held statically after the 30 SWIM runs ('SWIM Position' column). If a policy mismatches SWIM yet has proximity in its average position that inconsistency is less significant. The average match percentages in the last column acts towards the same end. Whenever at the end of a run a policy's position was the same as in SWIM, this is considered a match. For instance, in 80.00% of runs (24 out of 30), UCB-Tuned is 'correctly' ranked by MockSAS at the same position as in SWIM (i.e. first).

The results show that when it comes to the top performing policy, UCB-Tuned, there is heavy agreement between MockSAS and SWIM. Similarly, DUCB's variants enjoy the same relatively high agreement. This can be explained by their being based on the original UCB. These are also the only two policies which enjoy determinism in their decision logic. This may go towards explaining their consistency with SWIM as they also have internal consistency i.e. the variance in their performance is generally smaller than that of non-deterministic policies. This argument is further supported by the fact that the policy which makes the most random choices, $\epsilon - greedy$ with a 1.0 (maximal) exploration factor matches the SWIM position the fewest times. These more random policies such as $\epsilon - greedy$ with a 0.8 have such volatile final positions even despite seeding that they appear to lower the match percentage of those policies near them in ranking such as DUCB with a γ of 0.97. It is likely that due to the small margins in median reward and the unpredictable positions of the more random policies the final positions of non-random policies mismatches the static target of SWIM positions more often than not. The margin in median reward between the lowest performing policies is generally quite small across both platforms, which also causes less consistency. The distributions which generate randomness in the reward could not be seeded and can account for the small margins seen. These margins can also unpredictably influence the internal rankings of each platform.

From the results we can conclude that for a majority of deterministic policies MockSAS accurately reflects evaluation by the real system SWIM. For the remaining deterministic policies their extreme proximity in median reward to non-deterministic policies obfuscates the matching in overall position. With the elimination of these from ranking even those deterministic policies with low matching to SWIM would be accurately ranked. For the random policies seeding has been used to try and have more comparable performance between the two platforms. This sees the less random of them reach even a match percentage of 40%, but there is still not much significant matching. It is clear that more work needs to be done to explore what causes this low percentage, with a potential solution being using a metric with less inter-dependency than final rankings of median rewards.

5   Conclusions and Further Work

In this paper we propose a process for creating profiles of SAS to facilitate the evaluation of online learning policies, specifically MAB policies. We demonstrate how one can profile a SAS through the running example of SWIM. To enable this process we implemented a Python package MockSAS, with an associated grammar to parse defined profiles. MockSAS simulates the interaction between the MAB policies and the managed system of SWIM and reports on their performance. We used this for our experiment where we measure how accurately the profile of SWIM in MockSAS evaluates MAB policies compared to the real system SWIM. Our results show that for deterministic policies the MockSAS profile can accurately reproduce the same ranking of policies as SWIM. While for non-deterministic policies, more has to be done to control the random process before its accuracy can be truly determined.

For future work, a general-purpose solution should be found for handling profiled outputs, even when the type of underlying distribution is unknown. As it stands, we make use of detailed knowledge of SWIM to recreate the response time but this cannot always be assumed to be possible. Besides this, we see a possibility of extending the use of MockSAS (or only its process) for other online learning solutions than MAB policies. Although it is implemented as such, there is no strong dependency in the MockSAS code on the use of MABs, rather any policy which suggests an adaptation action/arm could be used in its place. Further, we believe the concepts relied upon for the use of these policies in the profiles of MockSAS to hold generally across self-adaptive systems. This of course remains to be proven with the use of MockSAS to profile more systems.

References

1. Alberts, E., Gerostathopoulos, I.: Measuring convergence inertia: online learning in self-adaptive systems with context shifts. In: Margaria, T., Steffen, B. (eds.) Leveraging Applications of Formal Methods, Verification and Validation. Adaptation and Learning. pp. 231–248. Springer, Cham (2022). https://doi.org/10.1007/978-3-031-19759-8_15

2. Alberts, E.G.: Adapting with regret: using multi-armed bandits with self-adaptive systems. Master's thesis, University of Amsterdam (2022). https://scripties.uba.uva.nl/search?id=727497

3. Auer, P., Cesa-Bianchi, N., Fischer, P.: Finite-time Analysis of the multiarmed bandit problem. Mach. Learn. **47**(2), 235–256 (2002). https://doi.org/10.1023/A:1013689704352

4. Auer, P., Cesa-Bianchi, N., Freund, Y., Schapire, R.E.: The Nonstochastic multiarmed bandit problem. SIAM J. Comput. **32**(1), 48–77 (2002). https://doi.org/10.1137/S0097539701398375

5. Bubeck, S.: Regret analysis of stochastic and nonstochastic multi-armed bandit problems. Found. Trends Mach. Learn. **5**(1), 1–122 (2012). https://doi.org/10.1561/2200000024

6. Cabri, G., Capodieci, N.: Applying multi-armed bandit strategies to change of collaboration patterns at runtime. In: 2013 1st International Conference on Artificial Intelligence, Modelling and Simulation, pp. 151–156. IEEE, Kota Kinabalu, Malaysia (December 2013). https://doi.org/10.1109/AIMS.2013.31

7. Erezsh: Lark parser. https://github.com/lark-parser/lark (2022)

8. Kephart, J., Chess, D.: The vision of autonomic computing. Computer **36**(1), 41–50 (2003)

9. Kim, D., Park, S.: Reinforcement learning-based dynamic adaptation planning method for architecture-based self-managed software. In: 2009 ICSE Workshop on Software Engineering for Adaptive and Self-Managing Systems, pp. 76–85 (May 2009). https://doi.org/10.1109/SEAMS.2009.5069076, iSSN: 2157-2321

10. Kim, D., Park, S.: Reinforcement learning-based dynamic adaptation planning method for architecture-based self-managed software. In: 2009 ICSE Workshop on Software Engineering for Adaptive and Self-Managing Systems, pp. 76–85 (2009). https://doi.org/10.1109/SEAMS.2009.5069076

11. Kivinen, J., Szepesvári, C., Ukkonen, E., Zeugmann, T. (eds.): 22nd International Conference on Algorithmic Learning Theory: ALT 2011, Espoo, Finland, 5-7 October 2011. Proceedings, LNCS, vol. 6925. Springer, Heidelberg (2011). https://doi.org/10.1007/978-3-642-24412-4

12. Krupitzer, C., Roth, F.M., VanSyckel, S., Schiele, G., Becker, C.: A survey on engineering approaches for self-adaptive systems. Pervasive Mob. Comput. **17**, 184–206 (2015). https://doi.org/10.1016/j.pmcj.2014.09.009

13. Lattimore, T., Szepesvári, C.: Bandit Algorithms. Cambridge University Press, 1 edn. (July 2020). https://doi.org/10.1017/9781108571401, https://www.cambridge.org/core/product/identifier/9781108571401/type/book

14. Lewis, P.R., Esterle, L., Chandra, A., Rinner, B., Yao, X.: Learning to be different: heterogeneity and efficiency in distributed smart camera networks. In: 2013 IEEE 7th International Conference on Self-Adaptive and Self-Organizing Systems, pp. 209–218. IEEE, Philadelphia, PA, USA (Septebfer 2013). https://doi.org/10.1109/SASO.2013.20, http://ieeexplore.ieee.org/document/6676508/

15. Metzger, A., Quinton, C., Mann, Z.A., Baresi, L., Pohl, K.: Feature-model-guided online learning for self-adaptive systems. arXiv:1907.09158 [cs] 12571, 269–286 (2020). https://doi.org/10.1007/978-3-030-65310-1_20, arXiv: 1907.09158
16. Moreno, G.A., Schmerl, B., Garlan, D.: SWIM: an exemplar for evaluation and comparison of self-adaptation approaches for web applications. In: Proceedings of the 13th International Conference on Software Engineering for Adaptive and Self-Managing Systems, pp. 137–143. ACM, Gothenburg Sweden (May 2018). https://doi.org/10.1145/3194133.3194163
17. Porter, B., Rodrigues Filho, R.: Distributed emergent software: assembling, perceiving and learning systems at scale. In: 2019 IEEE 13th International Conference on Self-Adaptive and Self-Organizing Systems (SASO), pp. 127–136 (June 2019). https://doi.org/10.1109/SASO.2019.00024, iSSN: 1949-3681
18. Slivkins, A.: Introduction to multi-armed bandits. found. Trends Mach. Learn. **12**(1–2), 1–286 (2019). https://doi.org/10.1561/2200000068, publisher: Now Publishers Inc

Towards Uncertainty Reduction Tactics for Behavior Adaptation

Andreas Kreutz[1]([✉]), Gereon Weiss[1], and Mario Trapp[2]

[1] Fraunhofer-Institute for Cognitive Systems IKS, Munich, Germany
{andreas.kreutz,gereon.weiss}@iks.fraunhofer.de
[2] Technical University of Munich, Munich, Germany
mario.trapp@in.tum.de

Abstract. An autonomous system must continuously adapt its behavior to its context in order to fulfill its goals in dynamic environments. Obtaining information about the context, however, often leads to partial knowledge, only, with a high degree of uncertainty. Enabling the systems to actively reduce these uncertainties at run-time by performing additional actions, such as changing a mobile robot's position to improve the perception with additional perspectives, can increase the systems' performance. However, incorporating these techniques by adapting behavior plans is not trivial as the potential benefit of such so-called tactics highly depends on the specific context. In this paper, we present an analysis of the performance improvement that can theoretically be achieved with uncertainty reduction tactics. Furthermore, we describe a modeling methodology based on probabilistic data types that makes it possible to estimate the suitability of a tactic in a situation. This methodology is the first step towards enabling autonomous systems to use uncertainty reduction in practice and to plan behavior with more optimal performance.

Keywords: Self-adaptive systems · Uncertainty · Uncertainty reduction

1 Introduction

Robots and other autonomous systems have the potential to replace humans in many applications, leading to more efficient processes while relieving humans of performing tedious and repetitive tasks. Autonomous systems have already found successful application in static and well-defined environments [5]. However, so far they are unable to safely function with acceptable performance in dynamic and unpredictable environments [12]. For such environments, systems cannot be developed with predetermined, static behavior, as the real manifestation of the highly variable context remains unknown at design time. This creates the need to enable autonomous systems to adapt themselves and their behavior at run-time, when this information becomes available.

In turn, this requires that systems have an accurate representation of their context. This particularly means that models of the context need to reflect

T. Batista et al. (Eds.): ECSA 2022, LNCS 13928, pp. 199–214, 2023.
https://doi.org/10.1007/978-3-031-36889-9_15

the uncertainty associated with information [11]. Any approach for adapting the planned behavior is, thus, constrained by the confidence in the information contained in the context model and can only be approximately correct for the situation.

An alternative to observing and then passively reacting to uncertainties in the subsequent processing steps was proposed by Moreno et al. [17]. They suggest proactively reducing uncertainties using specific counter measures, which they call tactics. Such a tactic, for example, could entail a mobile robot changing its position to scan an object from a different perspective or counteracting a detrimental aspect of the environment, such as insufficient illumination of a scene, by switching to a sensor that is less susceptible to it. Moreno et al. demonstrate that executing a tactic can lead to more accurate knowledge and thus better adaptation decisions. They note, however, that there exists a trade-off between the cost of executing a tactic and its expected benefit. Additionally considering that such an approach increases the systems' complexity, this cost could easily jeopardize the overall benefit.

In this paper, we therefore conduct a theoretical analysis of this trade-off to investigate the potential benefits of equipping autonomous systems with tactics for uncertainty reduction. With our analysis we determine the key decision parameters that need to be determined at run-time to realise the achievable benefit. Furthermore, building upon our analysis results, we propose a modeling methodology based on probabilistic data types [2,6] for describing a system's uncertain knowledge of its context. We use the semantics defined for these types to estimate the decision parameters, enabling the system to determine whether a tactic is likely to succeed for a situation. For determining the efficacy of a tactic, we propose to rely on context information contained in the environment model and describe the first step towards realizing this with our methodology. Our evaluation of the approach with a use case from the robotics domain indicates that the theoretical benefit of uncertainty reduction is achievable in practice using the proposed modeling methodology.

The remainder of the paper is structured as follows: Sect. 2 presents related work on uncertainty mitigation. We analyze the potential benefit of uncertainty reduction in Sect. 3. Section 4 describes the proposed modeling methodology and Sect. 5 reports on our evaluation results. Section 6 concludes the paper.

2   Related Work

Mitigating uncertainty in autonomous and self-adaptive systems has gained much attention in the last years. A recent survey [7,15] confirms that researchers in the field consider uncertainty to be one of the main challenges in realizing self-adaptive systems. The effort of establishing a taxonomy of uncertainty has resulted in several publications [10,14,19,20]. With respect to this taxonomy, our contribution addresses uncertainties that emerge at run-time and are located in the environment of an autonomous system.

In order to create context awareness, the self-adaptive systems community uses models at run-time [4] that represent the knowledge required to enable systems to adapt themselves [8]. In the models community, uncertainty has also become a focal topic. Troya et al. [23] present a summary of the recent work. For their literature survey, they define six types of uncertainty, two of which are relevant for our work: measurement uncertainty and occurrence uncertainty. Measurement uncertainty refers to the impreciseness resulting from using sensors to measure physical quantities whereas occurrence uncertainty is the degree of belief about the actual existence of an entity. It results from the issue of detecting an object in the environment as well as correctly assigning a class in the model to it. As we are concerned with the proactive reduction of uncertainty, we only consider uncertainty that manifests due to a lack of knowledge, i.e. epistemic uncertainty. This means that we also regard measurement uncertainty – which is usually treated as aleatoric [3] – as having an epistemic component that can be reduced via appropriate tactics.

For the mitigation of uncertainty, also the self-adaptive systems community has proposed numerous approaches [9,13,16,21]. Solano et al. [21] describe multiple enhancements to goal-oriented requirements engineering to model how uncertainty affects the goals of a self-adaptive system. Uncertainty resulting from observing the environment – which is the focus of this paper – is addressed by modeling the dependency of adaptation tactics on the context and considering the influence of sensor noise on the environment model. The resulting uncertainty is mitigated by a sub-task *filter data*, however, Solano et al. do not provide details on how this sub-task can be accomplished.

Cámera et al. [9] describe an explicit treatment of uncertainty in the environment model. Their approach uses model checking of stochastic multiplayer games to reason about the optimal adaptation strategy in an uncertain context, induced by inaccuracy in sensing. Compared to the proposed solution of this paper, they do not consider uncertainty reducing actions and, as a result, can only plan strategies which are optimal for a given level of noise.

The logical next step, uncertainty reduction, was proposed by Moreno et al. [17]. They present three open research challenges: formally specifying the impact of tactics, creating a catalogue of tactics applicable to a wide variety of systems, and developing a decision procedure to evaluate the trade-off between cost and benefit of a tactic. In this paper, we extend their work by analyzing the key parameters that affect the benefit achievable with uncertainty reduction tactics. Furthermore, we describe a methodology for modeling uncertain knowledge, which builds on the results of our analysis and makes it possible to estimate these key parameters at run-time.

At this stage of our research, we assume that the cost of executing a tactic is a fixed value in order to focus on the decision-making process itself. In the future, existing work on the volatility of a tactic's cost, such as by Palmerino et al. [18], could be integrated into the proposed approach.

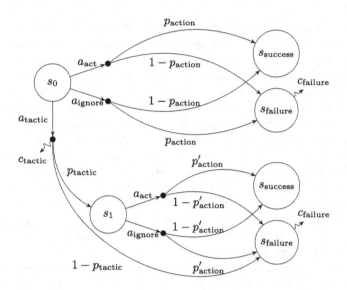

Fig. 1. Action planning as a parametric Markov decision process. The states s_{success} and s_{failure} are duplicated to improve readability.

3   Achievable Benefit of Uncertainty Reduction

As additional actions for reducing uncertainty lead to additional cost and increase the systems' complexity, we analyzed the potential benefit of such an approach. Following the idea of the analysis performed by Moreno et al. [17], we model the decision between acting as planned and reducing uncertainty as a Markov decision process (MDP). In contrast to Moreno's analysis, we generalize the problem and describe a parametric MDP in order to examine the qualitative impact of changing the parameter values on the system's utility. In the next subsections, we first describe the model that our analysis is based on and then present the results and our interpretation.

3.1   Preliminaries: A Markov Decision Process for Modeling Uncertainty Reduction

Figure 1 shows a parametric MDP modeling the decision-making problem. The decision-maker, i.e. the agent, needs to decide whether or not to act (a_{act} or a_{ignore}) in a situation. Which choice is more beneficial depends on the probability p_{action} that the action is admissible in the situation and the cost associated with making a wrong decision c_{failure}. Alternatively, the agent can execute an uncertainty reduction tactic (a_{tactic}) to first reduce uncertainty before deciding. This incurs a cost of c_{tactic}. As with the action, the probability p_{tactic} determines if the tactic is admissible, which results in a situation where the system's certainty of whether the action will succeed is p'_{action}. For this value it holds that

$$|p'_{\text{action}} - 0.5| \geq |p_{\text{action}} - 0.5|, \tag{1}$$

i.e. the distance from a state of complete uncertainty is not smaller for p'_{action} than for p_{action}. Thereby, p'_{action} corresponds to the information gain that is achievable with the tactic, including no gain whatsoever. Same as before, with a probability of $1 - p_{\text{tactic}}$ the tactic is not admissible and will fail. In this case, the agent also incurs the cost of a wrong decision c_{failure}. Without loss of generality, we set $c_{\text{failure}} = 1$ and $c_{\text{tactic}} \in [0, 1]$ to model relative costs. Thus, c_{tactic} becomes the cost of the tactic as a fraction of the cost of making a wrong decision.

Using this parametric MDP, an agent can derive the optimal decision-making policy for a situation [1]. This policy chooses the best action $a \in A$ for each state $s \in S$ according to the state-action cost function $Q^* : S \times A \rightarrow \mathbb{R}$. Given that we only consider the cost of failure c_{failure} and for executing a tactic c_{tactic}, and further assuming that $c_{\text{failure}} = 1$, this function is defined for the given MDP by

$$Q^*(s_0, a_{\text{act}}) = 1 - p_{\text{action}}, \tag{2}$$

$$Q^*(s_0, a_{\text{ignore}}) = p_{\text{action}}, \tag{3}$$

$$Q^*(s_0, a_{\text{tactic}}) = c_{\text{tactic}} + p_{\text{tactic}} \cdot \min\left\{(1 - p'_{\text{action}}), p'_{\text{action}}\right\} + (1 - p_{\text{tactic}}). \tag{4}$$

The expected cost that an agent using a greedy policy will incur, thus, is

$$\mathbb{E}\left[C \mid p_{\text{action}}, p_{\text{tactic}}, p'_{\text{action}}, c_{\text{tactic}}\right] = \min\left\{ \begin{array}{l} Q^*(s_0, a_{\text{act}}), \\ Q^*(s_0, a_{\text{ignore}}), \\ Q^*(s_0, a_{\text{tactic}}) \end{array} \right\}. \tag{5}$$

As a baseline for comparing the resulting strategies we use the expected cost of a system without uncertainty reduction, i.e.,

$$\mathbb{E}\left[C_{\text{baseline}} \mid p_{\text{action}}\right] = \min\left\{Q^*(s_0, a_{\text{act}}), Q^*(s_0, a_{\text{ignore}})\right\}. \tag{6}$$

To ensure that the strategy is beneficial for all situations, we calculate the mean expected costs over all values of $p_{\text{action}} \in [0, 1]$. The score of a strategy, thus, is

$$S(p_{\text{tactic}}, p'_{\text{action}}, c_{\text{tactic}}) = \frac{\int_0^1 \mathbb{E}\left[C \mid p_{\text{action}}, p_{\text{tactic}}, p'_{\text{action}}, c_{\text{tactic}}\right] dp_{\text{action}}}{\int_0^1 \mathbb{E}\left[C_{\text{baseline}} \mid p_{\text{action}}\right] dp_{\text{action}}}, \tag{7}$$

with $p_{\text{tactic}} \in [0, 1]$, $p'_{\text{action}} \in [0, 1]$, and $c_{\text{tactic}} \in [0, 1]$. $S(p_{\text{tactic}}, p'_{\text{action}}, c_{\text{tactic}})$ is the relative expected cost reduction when using uncertainty reduction.

3.2   Results and Interpretation

In order to determine the qualitative impact of parameter changes, we evaluate the score function over its input domain. The results are shown in Fig. 2. It is evident that the benefit of uncertainty reduction on decision-making increases with increasing p_{tactic}, decreasing c_{tactic}, and increasing $|p'_{\text{action}} - 0.5|$. It can also be observed that the parameter space where there is no improvement at all ($S(p_{\text{tactic}}, p'_{\text{action}}, c_{\text{tactic}}) = 1.0$) is very large. A substantial cost reduction is only possible if all three parameters are near their optimal value.

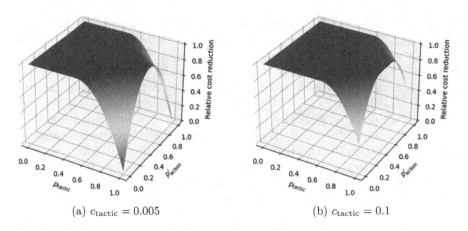

(a) $c_{\text{tactic}} = 0.005$ (b) $c_{\text{tactic}} = 0.1$

Fig. 2. Relative expected cost reduction for two values of c_{tactic}.

This means that systems making use of uncertainty reduction need to be carefully designed to ensure that the realized performance gain outweighs the added cost of developing a more complex system. Tactics should only be implemented for situations that the system is likely to encounter, as each additional tactic raises the complexity of the system, making it more expensive to develop. Furthermore, our analysis indicates that only uncertainty reduction tactics with a low cost relative to the cost of failure (c_{tactic}) are useful additions to the system. Inversely, this also means that uncertainty reduction is especially suitable when the cost of failure is very high, such as in safety-critical applications if, for example, we want to use information about the context to dynamically assure safety [22]. Then, even costly tactics will lead to an overall increased system utility.

The other parameters, p_{tactic} and p'_{action}, depend on the situation that the system currently faces. Thus, it must be able to determine these values at run-time in order to evaluate Q^* and decide which action or tactic minimizes its expected cost in the current situation. In the following, we present a modeling methodology that can support the system in this.

4   Concept for Behavior Planning with Uncertainty Reduction

In this section, we describe our approach for enabling the run-time decision of which tactic to execute when facing uncertainty, along with a running example. The models we introduce make it possible to represent uncertain knowledge of a system's environment, thus permitting the estimation of p_{tactic} and p'_{action}. We first present our chosen strategy for reflecting uncertainty in software models, which uses Unified Modeling Language (UML) class diagrams and uncertain Object Constraint Language (OCL) data types [2,6]. Using the operations defined for these types, we formulate constraints that need to be fulfilled so that a tactic is likely to succeed, resulting in an estimate for p_{tactic}. Additionally, we propose to use context information to derive the expected benefit of a tactic p'_{action}.

4.1   Running Example

To better explain the concepts described in this section, we introduce a mobile picking robot as an example for an autonomous system. The robot operates in a warehouse environment containing rectangular boxes, each with a barcode. It is equipped with a camera for detecting the presence of such boxes and measuring their attributes, as well as with a gripper to pick them up using an action *Pick*. The gripper can only handle boxes within a certain size range and, additionally, only boxes with a specific barcode should be picked up. Furthermore, the robot is capable of the tactics *Reposition* and *Turn on light* to reduce uncertainty affecting its perception. In the following we describe how the robot can use our methodology for planning adaptive behavior.

4.2   Uncertain Environment Representation

As described in Sect. 2, in the scope of this paper we focus on environment uncertainty, specifically measurement and occurrence uncertainty. Many proposals exist for representing these two uncertainty types in models [23], most of which are defined using either a new domain specific language or based on UML. Measurement uncertainty is most often described using probability theory, in accordance with international standards [3]. UML class diagrams and their extensions are well-established tools in software modeling. To remain compatible with established technologies, we use the extension of OCL primitive data types presented by Bertoa et al. [2] to represent measurement uncertainty and the proposal of Burgueño et al. [6] for including occurrence uncertainty in UML class diagrams.

Figure 3 shows how these extensions can be used to describe the environment of the picking robot: In addition to standard primitive data types, such as `String` and `Real`, uncertain types, such as `UString` and `UReal`, can be used to represent measurement uncertainty associated with attribute values. Classes that can be affected by occurrence uncertainty inherit from an added class `ProbableElement`, which has an attribute `confidence` expressing the occurrence probability of that class as a real value between 0 and 1.

Such a class diagram for modeling the environment of a system is developed at design time by domain experts. At run-time, the agent maintains an instance as an UML object diagram. Which classes are currently present in the environment, as well as their attributes' values and associated uncertainties, is determined by the system through various means of observation, such as sensor-based perception or communication with other agents. This forms the basis for the decision of which action or tactic to execute.

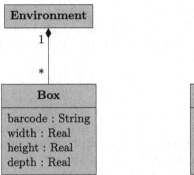
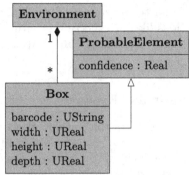

(a) A standard UML class diagram of the environment containing boxes.

(b) With uncertain data types, information obtained by stochastic perception can be modeled more accurately.

Fig. 3. Two UML class diagrams to model the environment of the mobile robot.

4.3   Admissibility of Actions and Tactics

As described in Sect. 3.1, the optimal decision policy of whether to act as planned or execute a tactic depends on the action's admissibility in the current situation. With the previously defined environment model, we can express this admissibility as a set of constraints on the attributes of classes. By evaluating these constraints at run-time, the agent can estimate the values of p_{action} and p_{tactic} (c.f. Fig. 1), which enables it to act more optimally.

A constraint $f = (x, a, o)$ consists of a condition x that is formulated referencing an attribute a of a class o in the environment model. x can be expressed using the operations defined for the uncertain OCL primitive data types [2] as well as the attribute a. Evaluating x yields an uncertain Boolean value, which is a tuple (b_x, c_x), where b_x is a Boolean value – *True* or *False* – and $c_x \in [0, 1]$ is the confidence in that value. For example, the admissibility of the action *Pick* of our running example can be expressed by two constraints $f_1 = (x_1, \texttt{width}, \texttt{Box})$ and $f_2 = (x_2, \texttt{barcode}, \texttt{Box})$ with respect to the class diagram in Fig. 3b. The two conditions x_1 and x_2 are defined in OCL as

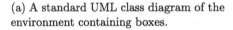

```
context Box: width ≥ 0.45 and width ≤ 0.55        // x₁
context Box: barcode.uEquals("1234")              // x₂
```

The conditions use the $\leq$- and $\geq$-operators to express the likelihood that two uncertain floating values compare less or equal, respectively greater or equal. The formal definitions of these operators and of the function .uEquals can be found in [2].

As indicated by their data type in Fig. 3b, the attributes referenced by the two conditions are affected by measurement uncertainty. To additionally include occurrence uncertainty into the evaluation, the confidence attribute of o also has to be considered when evaluating constraints, if o is a descendant

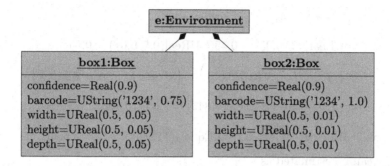

Fig. 4. An object diagram for the class diagram defined in Fig. 3b.

of `ProbableElement`. For this purpose, the attribute can be interpreted as the confidence value c_o of an uncertain Boolean value ($True, c_o$), which represents the likelihood that an object of the class o is present in the environment. This value needs to be taken into account when evaluating a constraint f.

We assume that an action is admissible, if all constraints $F = \{f_1, \ldots, f_n\}$ formulated for that action hold simultaneously. This is the case if all conditions $X = \{x : \forall(x, a, o) \in F\}$ are fulfilled and if an object of each of the unique classes $O = \{o : \forall(x, a, o) \in F\}$ referenced by the constraints F is present in the environment. The probability p that the action is admissible can, thus, be approximated as

$$p = \begin{cases} C, & \text{if } B = True, \\ 1 - C & \text{otherwise,} \end{cases} \quad \text{with } (B, C) = \bigwedge_{x \in X} x \bigwedge_{o \in O} (True, c_o). \quad (8)$$

This makes use of the $\wedge$-operator, which is defined by Bertoa et al. [2] as

$$\wedge : \text{UBoolean} \times \text{UBoolean} \to \text{UBoolean}$$
$$((b_1, c_1), (b_2, c_2)) \mapsto (b_1 \wedge b_2, c_1 \cdot c_2). \quad (9)$$

Example. The robot in our running example can only execute the action *Pick*, if both constraints $f_1 = (x_1, \texttt{width}, \texttt{Box})$ and $f_2 = (x_2, \texttt{barcode}, \texttt{Box})$ are fulfilled. Figure 4 depicts a run-time situation, where two boxes with different attributes and levels of uncertainty have been detected. Specifically, `Box.width` has been detected to be UReal(0.5, 0.05), which means that the actual width is normally distributed with mean 0.5 and standard deviation 0.05. `Box.barcode` has been detected as UString('1234', 0.75), meaning that the actual barcode is at most one change (insertion, deletion or substitution of a single character) away from '1234' (c.f. definitions of the data types by Bertoa et al. [2]. For the object box1, the conditions x_1 and x_2 therefore evaluate to

$$x_1 = \text{UReal}(0.5, 0.05) \geq 0.45 \wedge \text{UReal}(0.5, 0.01) \leq 0.55$$
$$= \left(True, \int_{0.45}^{\infty} \mathcal{N}(0.5, 0.05) \right) \wedge \left(True, \int_{-\infty}^{0.55} \mathcal{N}(0.5, 0.05) \right) \quad (10)$$
$$\approx (True, 0.841) \wedge (True, 0.841) \approx (True, 0.708),$$

$$x_2 = \text{UString}(\text{"1234"}, 0.75).\text{uEquals}(\text{"1234"}) = (True, 0.75), \quad (11)$$

and p_{pick} can be estimated as

$$x_1 \wedge x_2 \wedge (True, c_{\text{Box}}) = (True, 0.708) \wedge (True, 0.75) \wedge (True, 0.9)$$
$$= (True, 0.478), \quad (12)$$

resulting in $p_{\text{pick}} = 0.478$. For object box2, p_{pick} similarly evaluates to 0.9. This means that the action *Pick* is very likely to succeed for the object box2. For the object box1, the decision of whether to execute the action is less clear and the robot is likely to incur the cost of a wrong decision. This is where a suitable uncertainty reduction tactic can be beneficial.

4.4   Suitability of Tactics

In situations like the previous example, uncertainty reduction tactics can improve the expected utility of the agent by obtaining more accurate information before deciding on the appropriate course of action. As derived in Sect. 3, executing a tactic incurs a cost c_{tactic}, which needs to be weighed against the probability that the tactic is admissible p_{tactic} and its expected benefit p'_{action}. To evaluate p_{tactic}, the approach we described in Sect. 4.3 can be used by also formulating the constraints that are required for the success of the tactic. Estimating p'_{action} is a complex research challenge which in part still requires more work. In this section we present a solution for the first step: determining the fundamental suitability of a tactic to the problem that the system has encountered.

Two aspects are relevant for the expected benefit of a tactic: its suitability for solving the problem that the system is facing and how well the tactic will perform in the current situation. Using the previously introduced modeling methodology, the problem-specific part can directly be derived when calculating p_{action} from the constraints $(x, a, o) \in F$. Any condition x that evaluates to a value with low confidence indicates that the attribute a of the class o referenced by x is affected by too much uncertainty. Therefore, it is beneficial to execute a tactic which lowers the uncertainty in a to facilitate a decision with confidence. To leverage this, tactics are annotated at design time with the attributes for which they can reduce uncertainty at run-time.

Example. For the running example this means that the tactics *Reposition* and *Turn on light* are annotated as shown in Table 1a Based on Eq. 12, p_{pick} for box1

Table 1. Annotations of the two example tactics.

(a) Achievable attribute improvement.			(b) Achievable uncertainty mitigation.		
Tactic	Reposition	Turn on light	**Tactic**	Reposition	Turn on light
Improves attributes	Box.width, Box.barcode	Box.width, Box.barcode	**Counters uncertainty**	Occlusion by obstacles	Bad illumination

(c.f. Fig. 4) only evaluates to 0.478, which means that a suitable uncertainty reduction tactic with a high p'_{pick} could improve the picking robot's utility. The problem-specific part of p'_{pick} is that the tactic must obtain information which increases the confidence that the constraints $f \in F$ are fulfilled. In the case of the example, the conditions of both constraints $f1 = (x_1, a_1, o_1)$ and $f2 = (x_2, a_2, o_2)$ evaluate to values with low confidence, $x_1 = (True, 0.708)$ and $x_2 = (True, 0.75)$. A suitable tactic, therefore, needs to be able to improve the system's knowledge of either the `width` or the `barcode` attribute of <u>box1</u>. Thus, both tactics that the robot is capable of would be suitable for the problem.

4.5 Benefit of Tactics

With the suitable tactics for the problem known, the system must then decide which of them is likely to provide a significant benefit for the system's knowledge. Estimating this expected benefit is currently not yet possible with our approach. Thus, in this section we outline the extensions necessary to address this open issue.

We argue that the expected benefit of a tactic depends on its ability to mitigate the source of uncertainty that hinders the system to perceive its environment with the required certainty. To determine the source of uncertainty, the system must first deduce the means by which the information in its knowledge was originally obtained. Then, it can find out how this means of perception might be disturbed by the influences that are present in the current context.

This necessitates several extensions to our modeling methodology: First, the means of observation needs to be modeled for each attribute in the environment model and a set of possible sources of uncertainty for each of them needs to be defined. Additionally, a link needs to be created between context information in the environment model and the sources of uncertainty to determine which of them is currently hindering accurate perception. Finally, each of the tactics needs to be annotated with which sources of uncertainty it can counteract.

Example. The picking robot described in the running example obtains the attributes of boxes using the means of observation *vision-based perception*. This observation means is affected by uncertainty due to, among other reasons, *occlusion* of the observed object and *insufficient illumination* of the scene. To detect these issues at run-time, the class `Box` is extended with an attribute `occlusion_rate` and the environment itself with an attribute `luminance`. For

(a) A mobile picking robot equipped with a gripper and a camera sensor (red lines).

(b) Seven boxes of different sizes. Only the green ones can be picked by the robot.

Fig. 5. Experiment setup (Color figure online)

the sources of uncertainty *occlusion* or *insufficient illumination* to be active, threshold values for the occlusion rate and luminance are defined. The tactics *Reposition* and *Turn on light* are annotated with the source of uncertainty they can mitigate, c.f. Table 1b. With these extensions, the robot can now determine which source of uncertainty is currently active and if any of the tactics it is capable of can mitigate this source of uncertainty.

5   Evaluation

For an initial evaluation of our concept and a demonstration of the use of uncertainty reduction in practice, we have implemented a simulation of the use case introduced in Sect. 4.1 and described throughout this paper. Since estimating the benefit of tactics is not yet possible with the presented approach, the focus in this section is on the run-time evaluation of action admissibility (c.f. Sect. 4.3) and its influence on the robot's behavior, planned according to the MDP from Sect. 3.1.

5.1   Simulation Setup

The simulation of the robot and its environment is shown in Fig. 5a. In the experiment, the robot drives forwards in between two storage surfaces. The surface on its left contains boxes of different sizes. The goal of the robot is to pick up all boxes that it is able to and move them to the right storage surface using the action *Pick*. It aims to complete its task in the least amount of time possible, which is why executing tactics incurs an additional cost.

Figure 5b shows the experiment setup. The robot encounters seven boxes of different sizes and, for each one, needs to decide whether the box can be picked up or should be ignored. It can measure the size of a box it is next to using its camera sensor. This measurement is affected by uncertainty, which is quantified according to the Guide to the Expression of Uncertainty in Measurement [3] and depends on how far away from the box the measurement was obtained.

Table 2. Total costs without and with tactic (Mean ± SD of 10 runs).

	No tactic	c_{tactic}		
		0.05	0.1	0.25
Total costs	1.98 ± 1.07	0.41 ± 0.37	0.71 ± 0.54	1.58 ± 0.88

This means that the tactic *Reposition* allows the robot to make a more precise measurement by first driving closer towards the box before measuring. The additional execution time incurred by this tactic is modeled with the fixed cost c_{tactic}.

To decide whether to pick, ignore, or reduce uncertainty, the robot needs to estimate the remaining decision parameters p_{action}, p_{tactic}, and p'_{action} (c.f. Eqs. 2, 3, and 4) at run-time. The admissibility of the action p_{action} can be determined using the constraints of *Pick* described in Sect. 4.3. Similarly, constraints can be formulated for *Reposition* in order to estimate p_{tactic}. However to improve the clarity of the presentation we omit them here and instead set $p_{\text{tactic}} = 1.0$, which means we assume that the tactic is always admissible. As estimating the benefit of tactics is not yet entirely supported by our approach, we set $p'_{\text{action}} \in \{0.0, 1.0\}$. Executing the tactic *Reposition*, therefore, completely removes the uncertainty associated with the box width. As the decision parameters are thus all known at run-time, the robot can use the MDP described in Sect. 3.1 to plan its behavior.

While running the simulation, we keep track of the total cost that the robot accumulates due to incorrect decisions and the execution of tactics. We repeat the experiment for different values for c_{tactic} and, for each one, average the resulting total cost values over 10 runs to eliminate statistical outliers in the uncertainty quantification. As a baseline for comparison, we also measure the cost values accrued by the plain approach that does not make use of uncertainty reduction tactics.

5.2   Results and Discussion

The results of the experiment are shown in Table 2: The use of tactics in all cases reduces the total cost. With increasing c_{tactic}, the observed benefit decreases.

The experiment indicates that using tactics to adapt the robot's behavior has the potential for improving its picking performance, if the benefit of a tactic p'_{action} can be estimated as well as we have assumed for our initial experiment. We acknowledge that this simplified setup does not represent a realistic scenario, however, the results provide evidence that the theoretical benefits derived in Sect. 3 could be achieved, provided the complexity of more realistic environments can be managed. Methods for estimating p'_{action} – which we plan to develop in future work – therefore will need to be evaluated with more detailed use cases and additional experiments with more complex setups to ensure that the assumptions we have made in this paper are reasonable.

6   Conclusion

In this paper, we analyse uncertainty reduction using tactics by modeling the decision as a parametric decision problem. We show that the benefit this technique can bring greatly depends on the system's ability to estimate the likelihood that an action or a tactic will succeed and the expected benefit that a tactic will provide in a situation. Furthermore, we present a modeling methodology using UML class diagrams and uncertain datatypes which makes it possible to calculate the admissibility at run-time. While the estimation of the benefit of tactics is not yet entirely possible with our methodology, a preliminary evaluation already indicates that tactics can be beneficial for adapting the behavior of a mobile picking robot. In future work, we intend to investigate the missing extensions to our framework. Furthermore, we will evaluate the approach more rigorously using a more complex simulation scenario.

Acknowledgements. This work was funded by the Bavarian Ministry of Economic Affairs, Regional Development and Energy as part of the RoboDevOps project.

References

1. Bellman, R.: Dynamic programming. Science **153**(3731), 34–37 (1966). https://doi.org/10.1126/science.153.3731.34
2. Bertoa, M.F., Burgueño, L., Moreno, N., Vallecillo, A.: Incorporating measurement uncertainty into OCL/UML primitive datatypes. Softw. Syst. Model. **19**(5), 1163–1189 (2019). https://doi.org/10.1007/s10270-019-00741-0
3. BIPM, IEC, IFCC, ISO, IUPAC, IUPAP, OIML: Evaluation of Measurement Data - Guide to the Expression of Uncertainty in Measurement (GUM) (September 2008)
4. Blair, G., Bencomo, N., France, R.B.: Models@ run.time. Computer **42**(10), 22–27 (2009). https://doi.org/10.1109/MC.2009.326
5. Boscher, S., et al.: Symbiotic Autonomous Systems: White Paper III. Tech. rep, IEEE DigitalReality (November 2019)
6. Burgueño, L., Bertoa, M.F., Moreno, N., Vallecillo, A.: Expressing confidence in models and in model transformation elements. In: Proceedings of the 21th ACM/IEEE International Conference on Model Driven Engineering Languages and Systems, pp. 57–66. ACM, Copenhagen Denmark (Oct 2018). https://doi.org/10.1145/3239372.3239394
7. Calinescu, R., Mirandola, R., Perez-Palacin, D., Weyns, D.: Understanding uncertainty in self-adaptive systems. In: 2020 IEEE International Conference on Autonomic Computing and Self-Organizing Systems (ACSOS), pp. 242–251. IEEE, Washington, DC, USA (August 2020). https://doi.org/10.1109/ACSOS49614.2020.00047
8. Cheng, B.H.C., et al.: Using models at runtime to address assurance for self-adaptive systems. In: Bencomo, N., France, R., Cheng, B.H.C., Aßmann, U. (eds.) Models@run.time. LNCS, vol. 8378, pp. 101–136. Springer, Cham (2014). https://doi.org/10.1007/978-3-319-08915-7_4

9. Cámara, J., Peng, W., Garlan, D., Schmerl, B.: Reasoning about sensing uncertainty in decision-making for self-adaptation. In: Cerone, A., Roveri, M. (eds.) SEFM 2017. LNCS, vol. 10729, pp. 523–540. Springer, Cham (2018). https://doi.org/10.1007/978-3-319-74781-1_35

10. Esfahani, N., Malek, S.: Uncertainty in self-adaptive software systems. In: de Lemos, R., Giese, H., Müller, H.A., Shaw, M. (eds.) Software Engineering for Self-Adaptive Systems II. LNCS, vol. 7475, pp. 214–238. Springer, Heidelberg (2013). https://doi.org/10.1007/978-3-642-35813-5_9

11. Garlan, D.: Software engineering in an uncertain world. In: Proceedings of the FSE/SDP Workshop on Future of Software Engineering Research - FoSER 2010. p. 125. ACM Press, Santa Fe, New Mexico, USA (2010). https://doi.org/10.1145/1882362.1882389

12. Harel, D., Marron, A., Sifakis, J.: Autonomics: In search of a foundation for next-generation autonomous systems. Proc. Natl. Acad. Sci. **117**(30), 17491–17498 (2020). https://doi.org/10.1073/pnas.2003162117

13. Kinneer, C., Coker, Z., Wang, J., Garlan, D.: Managing uncertainty in self-adaptive systems with plan reuse and stochastic search. In: Proceedings of the 13th International Conference on Software Engineering for Adaptive and Self-Managing Systems, p. 11 (2018). https://doi.org/10.1145/3194133.3194145

14. Mahdavi-Hezavehi, S., Avgeriou, P., Weyns, D.: A classification framework of uncertainty in architecture-based self-adaptive systems with multiple quality requirements. In: Managing Trade-Offs in Adaptable Software Architecture, pp. 45–77. Elsevier (2017). https://doi.org/10.1016/B978-0-12-802855-1.00003-4

15. Mahdavi-Hezavehi, S., Weyns, D., Avgeriou, P., Calinescu, R., Mirandola, R., Perez-Palacin, D.: Uncertainty in self-adaptive systems: a research community perspective. ACM Trans. Autono. Adapt. Syst. **15**(4), 1–36 (2020). https://doi.org/10.1145/3487921

16. Moreno, G.A., Camara, J., Garlan, D., Schmerl, B.: Efficient decision-making under uncertainty for proactive self-adaptation. In: 2016 IEEE International Conference on Autonomic Computing (ICAC), pp. 147–156. IEEE, Wurzburg (July 2016). https://doi.org/10.1109/ICAC.2016.59

17. Moreno, G.A., Cámara, J., Garlan, D., Klein, M.: Uncertainty reduction in self-adaptive systems. In: Proceedings of the 13th International Conference on Software Engineering for Adaptive and Self-Managing Systems, pp. 51–57. ACM, Gothenburg Sweden (May 2018). https://doi.org/10.1145/3194133.3194144

18. Palmerino, J., Yu, Q., Desell, T., Krutz, D.: Improving the decision-making process of self-adaptive systems by accounting for tactic volatility. In: 2019 34th IEEE/ACM International Conference on Automated Software Engineering (ASE), pp. 949–961. IEEE, San Diego, CA, USA (November 2019). https://doi.org/10.1109/ASE.2019.00092

19. Perez-Palacin, D., Mirandola, R.: Uncertainties in the modeling of self-adaptive systems: a taxonomy and an example of availability evaluation. In: Proceedings of the 5th ACM/SPEC International Conference on Performance Engineering. pp. 3–14. ACM, Dublin Ireland (March 2014). https://doi.org/10.1145/2568088.2568095

20. Ramirez, A.J., Jensen, A.C., Cheng, B.H.C.: A taxonomy of uncertainty for dynamically adaptive systems. In: 2012 7th International Symposium on Software Engineering for Adaptive and Self-Managing Systems (SEAMS), pp. 99–108 (June 2012). https://doi.org/10.1109/SEAMS.2012.6224396

21. Solano, G.F., Caldas, R.D., Rodrigues, B.N., Vogel, T., Pelliccione, P.: Taming uncertainty in the assurance process of self-adaptive systems: a goal-oriented approach. In: Proceedings of the 2019 IEEE/ACM 14th International Symposium on Software Engineering for Adaptive and Self-Managing Systems SEAMS 2019. p. 11 (May 2019). https://doi.org/10.1109/SEAMS.2019.00020
22. Trapp, M., Schneider, D., Weiss, G.: Towards safety-awareness and dynamic safety management. In: 2018 14th European Dependable Computing Conference (EDCC), pp. 107–111. IEEE (2018). https://doi.org/10.1109/EDCC.2018.00027
23. Troya, J., Moreno, N., Bertoa, M.F., Vallecillo, A.: Uncertainty representation in software models: a survey. Softw. Syst. Model. **20**(4), 1183–1213 (2021). https://doi.org/10.1007/s10270-020-00842-1

Towards Characterization of Edge-Cloud Continuum

Danylo Khalyeyev, Tomas Bureš, and Petr Hnětynka[✉]

Charles University, Prague, Czech Republic
{khalyeyev,bures,hnetynka}@d3s.mff.cuni.cz

Abstract. Internet of Things and cloud computing are two technological paradigms that reached widespread adoption in recent years. These paradigms are complementary: IoT applications often rely on the computational resources of the cloud to process the data generated by IoT devices. The highly distributed nature of IoT applications and the giant amounts of data involved led to significant parts of computation being moved from the centralized cloud to the edge of the network. This gave rise to new hybrid paradigms, such as edge-cloud computing and fog computing. Recent advances in IoT hardware, combined with the continued increase in complexity and variability of the edge-cloud environment, led to an emergence of a new vision of edge-cloud continuum: the next step of integration between the IoT and the cloud, where software components can seamlessly move between the levels of computational hierarchy. However, as this concept is very new, there is still no established view of what exactly it entails. Several views on the future edge-cloud continuum have been proposed, each with its own set of requirements and expected characteristics. In order to move the discussion of this concept forward, these views need to be put into a coherent picture. In this paper, we provide a review and generalization of the existing literature on edge-cloud continuum, point out its expected features, and discuss the challenges that need to be addressed in order to bring about this envisioned environment for the next generation of smart distributed applications.

Keywords: edge computing · fog computing · Internet of Things · edge-cloud continuum

1 Introduction

Recent years saw rapid development in cloud technologies and a raise of the cloud computing paradigm to widespread adoption [1]. This trend is driven by the unique benefits offered by cloud computing, such as high availability and scalability of computational resources [26]. At the same time, the rise of cloud computing has been accompanied by another trend—increasing prevalence of smart end devices (Internet of Things and Cyber-Physical Systems) [15]. These two trends seem to push the IT ecosystem in opposing directions: while the cloud paradigm favors centralized services, the IoT and CPS paradigms allow

© The Author(s), under exclusive license to Springer Nature Switzerland AG 2023
T. Batista et al. (Eds.): ECSA 2022, LNCS 13928, pp. 215–230, 2023.
https://doi.org/10.1007/978-3-031-36889-9_16

for previously unseen levels of decentralization by bringing the "smart" properties into the devices that directly interact with the physical world. In order to fully utilize the benefits of vast computational capacities offered by the centralized cloud, and the benefits of ubiquitous availability and versatility of smart end devices, there is a need to provide a unifying paradigm that would connect this diverse ecosystem from the large data centers, through the intermediate computational, network, and storage nodes, all the way to the end devices [6].

Recognizing the need to address the challenges of increased prevalence, mobility, and network connectivity of end devices, there have been proposed multiple approaches to make cloud computing more distributed, such as edge computing [28], fog computing [11], transparent computing [40], etc. However, these approaches, while providing a remedy to the problems of geographic distribution and mobility, do not propose a coherent framework that could be used to reason about the applications that span multiple layers of this diverse ecosystem.

In this search for a unifying paradigm, there has been proposed the concept of Edge-Cloud continuum (ECC) [23] (also referred to as Mobile-Edge-Cloud Continuum [4] and Device-Edge-Cloud Continuum [36]). This concept envisions the cloud-to-end-device chain as a single unified space with flexible boundaries between levels, in which applications coexist in a highly distributed, yet highly interconnected and resource-rich environment.

Since this concept appeared only very recently, there is no common understanding of it, and there are several distinct views on it. Thus, in its current state, edge-cloud continuum is more of a vision than a coherent paradigm. Yet, given that this vision is aimed to provide an insight into the future of a potentially very impactful technology, there is a need in a more systematic and clear-cut understanding of edge-cloud continuum and related concepts.

In this paper, we (i) review the existing work on edge-cloud continuum and related concepts, (ii) provide a generalized overview of the expected properties and features of ECC based on that review, and (iii) put forward the questions that need to be answered in future research on the topic. With this contribution, we aim to advance the discussion on the future of IoT and edge computing towards a more well-founded vision.

The rest of the paper is structured as follows. Section 2 provides a brief overview of the developments in cloud computing and IoT that led to the emergence of the idea of ECC. Section 3 provides an overview of the literature related to ECC and adjacent topics. Section 4 distills the existing views on ECC into a common picture. Section 5 presents a list of open questions about ECC that need to be addressed in further research on the topic, and Sect. 6 concludes the paper.

2   Background

The idea of edge computing emerged several years ago as a response to the challenges posed by the rapid growth in usage of mobile devices, and the increasing reliance of mobile applications on cloud services [28]. The traditional centralized cloud systems could not guarantee a sufficiently low end-to-end latency to accommodate the needs of mobile device users, and as a response to that, the idea to move the computation closer to the users appeared. One of the most commonly adopted ways to do it is using edge servers, also known as cloudlets [29]. A cloudlet is a small server that is supposed to be located just one network hop away from the devices it serves. Thus, it is often assumed to be located near the closest gateway (base transceiver station, router, etc.), or no further than immediately above it (from the perspective of network topology). Using the cloudlet architecture helps to improve user experience not only by reducing the latency between a mobile device and a cloud service, but also by masking network outages to some degree, thus providing a more smooth user experience overall [28].

The idea of fog computing [11] is closely related to edge computing. While the term edge computing more often appears when talking about mobile devices [31], such as smartphones, fog computing is more often used in the context of Internet of Things [7].

There exists certain confusion in the literature around the terms edge computing and fog computing, as different authors see distinctions between these paradigms differently. Sometimes, fog computing is seen as a sub-case of edge computing, one of its multiple implementations [13]. Other authors consider fog computing as an architecture where the whole network is under the control of a single provider, while in the edge computing the network is more fragmented and shared between edge devices that are unaware of each other and have no information about the entire network [32]. Yet another view is that edge computing moves only the computation and the data storage closer to the end user, while fog computing is also related to moving other aspects, such as networking, control, and decision making [38]. Thus, the line between edge and fog computing is blurred and, especially in the context of edge-cloud continuum, it makes little sense to talk separately about edge and fog. Thus, in the rest of the text, we do not distinguish between these terms.

3   Existing Views on Edge-Cloud Continuum

The first mentions of edge-cloud continuum (ECC) appeared in 2017 [8], including under the names cloud continuum [9] and Device-Fog-Cloud continuum [19]. Since then, the term and its variations had appeared in hundreds of papers. In most of those papers, the term is mentioned only briefly, without an explanation or a reference. Here, we focus primarily on the works that attempt to define the term or to provide a more general overview of it. The notion of ECC is understood differently in different papers, and different authors focus on different properties. Thus, in this section, we provide a general overview of the features of ECC proposed in the existing literature and the requirements that ECC is expected to fulfill.

3.1   Main Elements of the Edge-Cloud Continuum

Being the result of a fusion of IoT and cloud, ECC includes all kinds of entities that can be found in IoT and cloud systems.

Generally, the entities within IoT can be categorized into five types [35]: end devices, gateways, applications, cloud, and administrative monitoring tools. This classification includes both hardware (end devices, gateways) and software (applications, administrative monitoring tools) entities. Applications there are understood as mobile OS applications, while software monitoring tools are primarily web-based tools. This classification features the cloud as a singular entity, without distinguishing the entities within it. This may be sufficient for modeling IoT applications from the perspective of the end devices, but not enough if we want to model a complete ECC ecosystem. In that case, we would need to distinguish components within the cloud, such as containers, virtual machines, and service endpoints.

The hardware within ECC is highly heterogeneous. It may come in all sizes, from giant data centers to the smallest single-purpose network-connected sensors and microcontrollers. Basically, any device with at least very basic computational capability and network connectivity can be a part of ECC. Software platforms running on that hardware are also very heterogeneous. In general, they can be categorized into [36]: device-specific firmware without an OS, real-time OS, language runtime, full OS (e.g. Linux), App OS (e.g. Android Wear), server OS (e.g. Linux + Node.js), and container OS (e.g. Linux + Docker).

Networks also play a large role in ECC, as all devices need to be somehow connected in order to be a part of the same continuum. Networks also consist of both hardware and software elements, since software-defined networking and network function virtualization are considered to be important enabling technologies of ECC [10,30].

The network technologies and standards used across ECC are also very diverse [6]. This variety is especially high among the wireless networking standards, ranging from the most common technologies like WiFi, Bluetooth, and NFC, to less widely known protocols, such as ZigBee, Z-Wave, MiWi, etc. This variety is partially due to a lack of standardization in this emerging industry (which is expected to improve soon, with new common standards supported by all major IoT platform companies being developed, such as Matter[1]). Another reason for this network heterogeneity is the fact that various applications in ECC have different requirements on the networks they run in, most often these are power consumption, latency, and throughput [6].

Edge-cloud is often discussed in the context of 5G [8] and the coming 6G technologies [24]. These technologies can provide much higher network throughput, but the area served by one base transceiver station is smaller than in the previous cellular networks [2]. For ECC this means that each cloudlet deployed in such a network would be able to serve the devices in a smaller geographical area. This means that in order to achieve the "near-zero" latency that 6G networks

---

[1] https://csa-iot.org/all-solutions/matter/.

are expected to provide to mobile users, more frequent service handovers will be required, thus the need for dynamic adaptation of workload placement will increase (see Sect. 3.2).

In order to categorize the spectrum of entities involved in ECC, it is usually divided into levels, forming a "computational hierarchy".

In general, almost all authors distinguish at least three levels of computational hierarchy in the edge-cloud continuum. The highest level, almost universally referred to as the cloud, is characterized by abundant, virtually endless resources, geographical remoteness from the end devices, and typically high latency. This level is ideal for placing workloads that do not require low response time but do require large amounts of computational resources. This level can be represented by large private data centers and/or rented sections of public clouds. The workloads running on this level come in the form of virtual machines or (increasingly commonly) containerized microservices.

The middle level is usually referred to as the edge or fog level. It is made of units that are often referred to as fog nodes, edge nodes, or cloudlets [29]. These nodes typically provide limited computational, storage, and network capacities that are used by the services serving the end devices in their immediate vicinity.

Some authors suggest that the future edge-cloud continuum would contain an intermediary level between the fog and the cloud [2]. This level would consist of groups of geographically adjacent cloudlets formed dynamically according to the task being currently solved. In many ways, such a dynamic, task-oriented grouping is similar to the concept of ensembles that exists in component systems [39]. A group like this does not have a central element and relies on dynamic coordination between cloudlets (or individual services running on those cloudlets).

Sometimes, the fog level is modeled as a sequence of N nested layers [6]. A higher layer is assumed to be composed of servers of larger computational capacity that serve smaller servers on a layer below it.

The last level is most commonly referred to as the device level. The terminology may be sometimes confusing since some authors refer to it as edge level [34] (in contrast to the fog level above), or fog level [17] (in contrast to the edge level above). This level contains a large variety of end devices, from the devices running full-fledged operating systems, such as smartphones or laptops, to robots running on real-time operating systems, to network-connected home appliances, to one-purpose smart sensors, such as temperature sensors or cameras. The important distinguishing property of the devices on this level is that they interface directly with people or the physical world. In contrast, all entities on the levels above provide services and resources that are used either by end devices or by people through interfaces available on end devices.

3.2   Workload Placement

It is envisioned that the placement of workloads in ECC is dynamic, and is determined by the current conditions in the ECC environment, and by the current needs of each application [2]. This means that the same software component may run on different hardware nodes, or even on different levels of computational hierarchy, depending on its current environment and resource requirements. There are many factors that can be taken into account when deciding where to place a workload. According to an industry survey, currently, the most influential factors that determine the preferred placement of a workload are security and cost [23], however, much more factors can be considered depending on a particular use case. These include platform reliability, application performance, end-to-end latency, government regulations, corporate regulations, software vendor requirements, etc.

Such a large number of potential factors influencing the placement of software components in the continuum, combined with the inherent unpredictability of edge-cloud environment leads to a need to establish mechanisms for adaptive workload placement, which would determine the exact venue of workload execution at runtime. In recent years, there has been a lot of research into QoS-oriented runtime adaptation in the edge-cloud environment [5,21,27], however, all that research has been focused on the methods of adaptation within one level of the continuum (either cloud or edge/fog). Yet, edge-cloud continuum, as it is envisioned, should be able to run the same software components on different levels of the continuum, depending on the current needs of individual applications and overall circumstances [23,34,36]. This means that the ECC environment has to be able to support fully liquid software [36].

The term liquid software refers to the kind of software that can move between multiple devices in a seamless manner [14]. In the context of ECC, this can mean two things: either seamless migration and handover of software components between the nodes of the same type (which has been already demonstrated [12]), or seamless migration between devices of different types (which is currently only an idea [36]). We will refer to software that can perform both kinds of migrations as *fully liquid software*.

Implementing fully liquid software has two major challenges. The first is that the migration between different devices has to be performed seamlessly, while continuing normal operation, without introducing any data inconsistencies or impairing user experience. The second challenge is that the same kind of software component has to be able to run on different kinds of devices (different hardware platforms, OS types, etc.). Currently, this is possible only by re-implementing the component for each platform individually, which significantly complicates application development and maintenance, and exacerbates the seamless migration problem.

So far, there is no working framework that would allow implementing fully liquid software in ECC, but some ideas have been suggested, such as using Function-as-a-Service principles to encapsulate common functions into cross-level executable tasks [18,33], and implementing isomorphic software [22]. The idea of isomorphic software is particularly interesting, since, if implemented, it would allow the same code to run on all levels of ECC, in exactly the same version. This idea requires an underlying platform that would be able to run not only in the cloud and edge/fog but also on IoT devices that are not operated by traditional OSs. The authors of the idea suggest that given the progress in IoT device hardware, eventually, they could run some form of lightweight containers that would encapsulate exactly the same code as the one running on the server side.

3.3   Artificial Intelligence in Edge-Cloud Continuum

One of the key characteristics of ECC is the presence of edge intelligence. The term edge intelligence refers to a practice of locating AI-enabled components, in particular ML models, in the edge and device levels of ECC. The main purpose of this is to provide smart on-the-spot analysis of the data generated by the end devices. The amount of these data may be so large that transferring them over the network all the way to the cloud might be quite expensive and lead to high network bandwidth consumption. At the same time, such network transfers may incur a high latency cost on the results of that analysis.

There are two primary computational processes involved in machine learning: training and inference. These processes can potentially be located at any level across the device-to-cloud hierarchy or even on a combination of levels. Various authors distinguish six [41] or seven [24] levels of ML placement within ECC. These levels include in-cloud training and inference, cloud training with cloud-edge co-inference, cloud-edge co-training and co-inference, in-edge training and inference, on-device training and inference, and intermediary options between these.

Apart from edge training and edge inference, edge intelligence also includes two other processes: edge caching and edge offloading [37]. *Edge caching* involves storing the data generated on devices with little storage and processing capability on more powerful nodes, such as vehicle-located cloudlets or edge servers. The stored data are then used as inputs to both training and inference processes. Apart from storing raw data (e.g. video feeds from cameras), edge caching is also used for storing the results of inference operations (e.g. results of object recognition on video streams). This is done in order to reduce the usage of computational resources on inference and to make those results available to edge devices that lack their own inferencing capability.

The term *edge offloading* refers to the practice of transferring the processes of edge training, edge inference, and edge caching to another hardware node, typically when additional computational resources are needed. Edge offloading is particularly important since it makes it possible to utilize the full spectrum of resources of ECC. Offloading may be done either to an upper level of computational hierarchy (device-to-edge or device-to-cloud offloading) or to another device on the same level (device-to-device offloading) [37]. Ideally, edge offloading should be implemented in a fully transparent way, in which case it can be considered to be a type of liquid software.

Figure 1 shows the relationship between the processes involved in edge intelligence and the devices that interact with it.

Edge intelligence, just like many other features of ECC, is in large part enabled by the recent progress in the end device hardware. In recent years, there has been a boom of new kinds of dedicated Edge AI application-specific integrated circuits designed specifically to run on the edge, such as vision processing

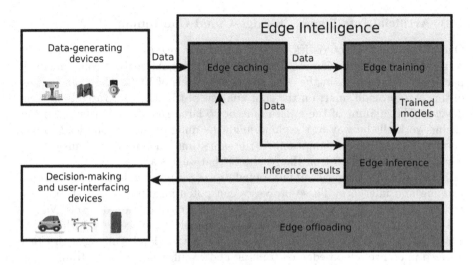

Fig. 1. The processes making up edge intelligence and the devices interfacing with it. Arrows represent data flow. Edge offloading underpins the other edge intelligence processes, providing them with additional computational resources when needed.

units (e.g., Intel Movidius VPUs[2]), tensor processing units (e.g., Google Edge TPU[3]), and neural processing units (e.g., Arm Ethos U55 Machine Learning Processor[4]).

Another reason for employing edge intelligence is privacy and security concerns [25]. When the data generated on edge is sufficiently sensitive, stakeholders might not be willing to share it with a third party, such as a cloud service provider. Edge analytics, in this case, becomes a good alternative to establishing a private on-premises cluster to deal with the sensitive part of the data only, as it cuts the cost and the complexity of the system significantly. Some edge AI hardware producers, such as Coral[5], highlight data privacy as one of the most important features of their solutions, along with the ability to work offline, in the areas where connectivity might be limited.

4   Common Properties

Based on the analysis of the existing literature related to ECC, we can make some conclusions about the properties it is expected to have. In this section, we synthesize the existing views on the edge-cloud continuum and distill their common properties. Below, we focus on each of these properties individually.

---

[2] https://www.intel.com/content/www/us/en/products/details/processors/movidius-vpu.html.
[3] https://cloud.google.com/edge-tpu.
[4] https://www.arm.com/products/silicon-ip-cpu/ethos/ethos-u55.
[5] https://www.coral.ai/.

Hierarchical Structure. The concept of edge-cloud continuum comes from the idea that there is a computational continuum of devices of various capabilities existing between the cloud, with its virtually endless resources, and the substantially resource-constrained end devices. In between these two extremes, there may exist a whole array of nodes of different capabilities. These include smaller servers that can serve a limited number of (typically closely located) clients, smartphones and other consumer devices that, while having limited resources, still can host multiple applications with open-ended functionality, and smart devices, such as wearables, smart home appliances, smart urban sensors, etc. that are often designed to carry out a limited number of simple tasks only. A three-tiered structure is often assumed (device-fog-cloud), but the actual topology may be more complex. The number of levels does not even have to be the same across the whole ECC, with different applications utilizing the computational continuum in different ways. The amount of memory, storage, network capacity, and computational power, as well as connectivity to other devices in the network, is higher on the higher levels of the hierarchy.

Thus, the hierarchical structure of ECC is, first of all, a fact about the hardware of the devices involved in the ECC environment. It is important to understand, though, that given the continued increase in hardware heterogeneity, some devices may not have a properly defined "place in the hierarchy". The important feature of this architecture is that a potentially resource-constrained device may rely on the resources available "higher up" the hierarchy when the need arises. Thus, the same device may theoretically be considered to be on different levels of the hierarchy with respect to different kinds of resources.

Cross-Level Situation-Aware Cooperation Between Components. The software written for ECC not only has to run in a highly heterogeneous environment, but also to be able to adapt to very variable and unpredictable conditions. The diverse ECC environment offers unparalleled opportunities for self-adaptation, but seizing these opportunities would require adopting less traditional software development paradigms.

In particular, this may mean developing software consisting of components with a substantial degree of autonomy. These components then might be able to form dynamic task-oriented groups (ensembles), either in the course of their regular operation or as a way to resolve some "critical situations". These groups can be formed either between the components of the same kind or between different kinds of components potentially spanning multiple levels of ECC.

Fully Liquid Software. Another mechanism that will make the ECC applications more adaptable and resilient towards unpredictable changes is software liquidity, which may be expressed as either ability of software components to migrate between the levels of the computational continuum, or their ability to offload certain functions and responsibilities to the higher levels of the continuum.

A software component that belongs to an ECC application may run on different levels of the computational continuum, depending on current circumstances, like network conditions, current workload, or resource availability. In order to ensure that, the component must be able to run in different environments (different hardware platforms, operating systems, etc.). In addition, seamless handovers during such migrations must be ensured.

Software liquidity may also refer to the ability of software components to migrate between nodes of the same type in different locations. This kind of migration might help to ensure low latency and reduce network usage (e.g., if it is done to follow client mobility), but is not enough to address resource constraints and environmental variability, for which a solution like isomorphic software is needed.

Edge Intelligence. Rapid development and proliferation of AI technologies, particularly deep learning, is another contemporary trend that accompanies the current shift towards edge computing. The convergence of these trends is likely to continue, as AI can potentially provide means of achieving some of the above-mentioned "smart environment" properties of ECC. In particular, dynamic situation-aware cooperation in ECC can be achieved by enhancing software components with properties of agents with cognitive capabilities, such as the ability to learn and proactively determine the course of action with respect to self-adaptation.

Additionally, the highly distributed architecture of ECC provides new opportunities for machine learning applications. The enormous amounts of data generated by end devices can be processed on the spot (by means of device-edge-cloud co-training and co-inference) without overloading the networks with excessive data transfers. Thus, we can expect to see larger usage of federated learning and device-edge-cloud co-training and co-inference.

4.1   Reference Example

Having discussed the trademark characteristics of ECC, we can now construct an example of an application that would demonstrate these characteristics and showcase the benefits that such an environment could provide. This example is centered around smart mobility, real-time urban situation awareness, and route planning. Figure 2 provides an illustration of the example.

In this example, an end user wants to find a route from its current location to a particular point within a city. The user is equipped with an internet-connected smartphone that has a route planning application installed. The application uses the cloud services located in a local edge data center in order to carry out the route computation. In order to get to its destination, the user may use one of the smart vehicles (SV) available through a car sharing application. Once the user enters an SV, the route and travel duration computation is offloaded to a cloudlet located in the vehicle itself. At this point, the user's smartphone does not use its own GPS to determine its location and does not make direct requests regarding its route to the cloud, instead relying on more accurate data provided by the SV.

While in the urban environment, the SV relies on the cloud services (running in the local edge nodes) that gather and process the data from millions of sensors, cameras, and other smart vehicles located throughout the city. Thus, in the urban

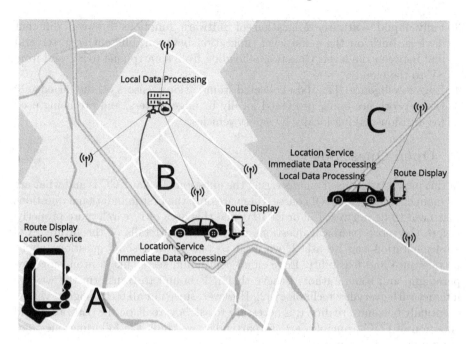

Fig. 2. Illustration of the reference example. Case A: a user device relies on its own location service. Case B: the location service component is offloaded to the car, while the car itself relies on local edge servers to process the data from sensors in the neighborhood. Case C: the car runs the local data processing on its own hardware.

environment, where major computational nodes are locally available, the SV directly processes only the data from its immediate environment. All the higher-level calculations regarding the route and traffic conditions that are based on the data from thousands of sources are offloaded to the local edge servers. Outside of the urban environment, where there are much fewer sources of information available and where the network connection is not as reliable, the SV performs those calculations on its local hardware.

The centralized parts of the route-planning application (such as authentication and personal data storage) are handled by the cloud services that may not be located anywhere close to the end user.

This example demonstrates all the properties of an integrated edge-cloud continuum:

1. Hierarchical organization. Devices of various sizes and computational capabilities (from smart sensors, through smartphones, smart cars, and edge servers, to data centers) are vertically integrated into one seamless ecosystem.
2. Cross-level cooperation. The components of the ecosystem cooperate with each other in a situation-aware way to deliver an experience of a single "smart space" to the end user. This allows a smartphone user to rely upon data generated by thousands of remotely located end devices (cameras, sensors, vehicles) in real time.

3. Fully liquid software. Migration of software functions between different devices, both on the same level (migration between different edge servers) and between the levels (function offloading from smartphone to SV and from SV to the cloud).
4. Edge intelligence. The data collected from various sensors on the far edge of the network are being processed locally by edge servers, and are being used for decision-making locally by smart vehicles.

5   Open Questions

In this paper, we focused on answering the question of what ECC is and what are its main characteristics. Of course, these are only the first foundational questions that need to be answered in order to define this area of research more properly. Before the more technical questions related to the details of the future ECC implementation can be asked, we need to put forward some questions about its relevance and feasibility. Edge-cloud continuum seems like a promising new paradigm, and some authors believe that it is bound to transform the way we interact with everyday technology [2]. However, since not all technological visions eventually become a reality, it is necessary to ask how realistic the realization and adoption of ECC principles are. In particular, we think the following questions are important to answer.

Q1: Will Hardware Capabilities be Sufficient, and How Soon? We have mentioned several times that one of the main drivers of edge computing that eventually led to the emergence of the vision of edge-cloud continuum was progress in IoT hardware. Some elements of this vision assume continued progress in that area. And while we probably can expect some further incremental quantitative improvements in hardware capabilities, it is not guaranteed that they will be sufficient to provide a platform for the implementation of some envisioned features of ECC. For instance, achieving fully isomorphic software [36] would require end devices to be able to host containerized applications, at least in some form. Whether this is possible in principle, especially for devices running real-time operating systems, is not yet clear.

Q2: To What Degree is it Possible to Achieve ECC Properties with Current Software Approaches? As it was mentioned before, achieving some of the envisioned properties of ECC would require advanced self-adaption at runtime. Currently, there exist some examples demonstrating architectural self-adaptation targeted at edge-cloud scenarios [5,21,27], and none of them demonstrate the properties of ECC. AI is sometimes suggested as a technology that would allow achieving architectural self-adaptation in such a complex environment [24]; however, it remains to be seen whether it is suitable for the task. There needs to be more research into AI-directed architectural self-adaptation in ECC, as well as into the self-adaptation mechanisms suitable for edge-cloud continuum in general.

Q3: Are There Sufficient Incentives to Adopt the ECC Paradigm in Industry, and How to Create Them? Even if this paradigm is technologically feasible and beneficial for the end users, its eventual adoption is dependent on the willingness of major players in the industry to move towards it. This question is especially complex in the case of ECC since its adoption requires cooperation between many different parties, such as infrastructure maintainers, mobile operators, cloud service providers, application developers, etc. All of these parties need to see a sufficient benefit in moving towards ECC in order for it to become a reality. Thus, a more comprehensive analysis of economic incentives behind adopting the principles of ECC is needed.

It must also be noted, that the name edge-cloud continuum itself might not survive the transition from theory to practice: in the future, the environment with the properties outlined in this paper may be referred to differently.

Q4: What are the Representative Examples? Perhaps one of the best ways to establish the relevance of the ECC paradigm would be to identify realistic real-world examples of applications that will be enabled by ECC that are not possible to implement within the existing paradigms. Yet, most examples used in the relevant literature today are too far from the state of the art to be considered realistic by the industry.

For instance, many ECC use case examples feature autonomous vehicles in urban environments [2]. However, it is quite possible that the timelines for the adoption of smart urban mobility are quite far away in the future. The technologies that are expected to enable the shift towards edge-cloud continuum either already exist or will arrive in the next couple of years, while smart urban mobility might be more than a decade away [16]. Thus, examples more relevant to the current day are required. Having such examples could significantly speed up the process of ECC adoption and make it more attractive to the industry. Some promising areas in which suitable examples could be found are natural disaster early warning [3], and emergency situation management [20].

6   Conclusion

In this paper, we have provided a review of the existing literature on edge-cloud continuum and the related concepts, trends, and paradigms. As a result of that review, we have provided a generalized look at the properties that define edge-cloud continuum according to the current state of the discussion. These properties are the presence of a hierarchy of devices with different computational capabilities, dynamic cross-level cooperation between application components, software liquidity, and ubiquitous edge intelligence. We have also raised some important questions that are important for understanding whether this technological vision can become a reality.

The vision of edge-cloud continuum aims to provide insight into how people will interact with smart technology in the near future. It presents a picture of a "smart space" in which people will have instantaneous access to a wealth of applications and devices, seamlessly interacting with each other and the physical world. There still are a lot of hurdles to overcome on the path toward ECC, and some of them are yet to be identified. In this work, we have put this vision into more concrete terms, highlighting its current limitations and the areas of future research.

Acknowledgment. This work has been partially supported by Charles University institutional funding SVV 260698/2023, partially by the Charles University Grant Agency project 408622, and partially by the European Research Council (ERC) under the European Union's Horizon 2020 research and innovation programme (grant agreement No. 810115).

References

1. Alam, T.: Cloud computing and its role in the information technology. IAIC Trans. Sustain. Digit. Innov. (ITSDI) **1**(2), 108–115 (2020). https://doi.org/10.34306/itsdi.v1i2.103
2. Arulraj, J., Chatterjee, A., Daglis, A., Dhekne, A., Ramachandran, U.: eCloud: a vision for the evolution of the edge-cloud continuum. Computer **54**(5), 24–33 (2021). https://doi.org/10.1109/MC.2021.3059737
3. Balouek-Thomert, D., Renart, E.G., Zamani, A.R., Simonet, A., Parashar, M.: Towards a computing continuum: enabling edge-to-cloud integration for data-driven workflows. Int. J. High Perform. Comput. Appl. **33**(6), 1159–1174 (2019). https://doi.org/10.1177/1094342019877383
4. Baresi, L., Mendonça, D.F., Garriga, M., Guinea, S., Quattrocchi, G.: A unified model for the mobile-edge-cloud continuum. ACM Trans. Internet Technol. **19**(2) (2019). https://doi.org/10.1145/3226644
5. Bellavista, P., Zanni, A., Solimando, M.: A migration-enhanced edge computing support for mobile devices in hostile environments. In: Proceedings of IWCMC 2017, Valencia, Spain), pp. 957–962. IEEE (2017). https://doi.org/10.1109/IWCMC.2017.7986415 <error l="305" c="Invalid <error l="303" c="Invalid command: paragraph not started." /> command: paragraph not started." />
6. Bittencourt, I., et al.: The internet of things, fog and cloud continuum: integration and challenges. Internet of Things **3–4**, 134–155 (2018). https://doi.org/10.1016/j.iot.2018.09.005
7. Bonomi, F., Milito, R., Zhu, J., Addepalli, S.: Fog computing and its role in the internet of things. In: Proceedings of MCC 2012, Helsinki, Finland. p. 13–16. ACM (2012). https://doi.org/10.1145/2342509.2342513
8. Carmo, M.S., Jardim, S., Neto, A.V., Aguiar, R., Corujo, D.: Towards fog-based slice-defined WLAN infrastructures to cope with future 5g use cases. In: Proceedings of NCA 2017, Cambridge, MA, USA (2017). https://doi.org/10.1109/NCA.2017.8171397
9. Carrega, A., Repetto, M.: A network-centric architecture for building the cloud continuum. In: Proceedings of ICNC 2017, Silicon Valley, CA, USA. pp. 701–705 (2017). https://doi.org/10.1109/ICCNC.2017.7876215
10. Dai, M., Su, Z., Li, R., Yu, S.: A software-defined-networking-enabled approach for edge-cloud computing in the internet of things. IEEE Netw. **35**(5), 66–73 (2021). https://doi.org/10.1109/MNET.101.2100052
11. Dastjerdi, A.V., Buyya, R.: Fog computing: Helping the internet of things realize its potential. Computer **49**(8), 112–116 (2016). https://doi.org/10.1109/MC.2016.245
12. Doan, T.V., Fan, Z., Nguyen, G.T., Salah, H., You, D., Fitzek, F.H.: Follow me, if you can: a framework for seamless migration in mobile edge cloud. In: Proceedings of IEEE INFOCOM 2020 Workshops, Toronto, ON, Canada, pp. 1178–1183. IEEE (2020). https://doi.org/10.1109/INFOCOMWKSHPS50562.2020.9162992

13. Dolui, K., Datta, S.K.: Comparison of edge computing implementations: fog computing, cloudlet and mobile edge computing. In: Proceedigns of GIoTS 2017, Geneva, Switzerland (2017). https://doi.org/10.1109/GIOTS.2017.8016213

14. Gallidabino, A., Pautasso, C., Mikkonen, T., Systa, K., Voutilainen, J.P., Taivalsaari, A.: Architecting liquid software. J. Web Eng. **16**(5–6), 433–470 (2017)

15. Greer, C., Burns, M., Wollman, D., Griffor, E., et al.: Cyber-physical systems and internet of things. Special Publication (NIST SP) - 1900–202 (2019). https://doi.org/10.6028/NIST.SP.1900-202

16. Jameel, F., Chang, Z., Huang, J., Ristaniemi, T.: Internet of autonomous vehicles: architecture, features, and socio-technological challenges. IEEE Wirel. Commun. **26**(4), 21–29 (2019). https://doi.org/10.1109/MWC.2019.1800522

17. Kar, B., Yahya, W., Lin, Y.D., Ali, A.: A survey on offloading in federated cloud-edge-fog systems with traditional optimization and machine learning. arXiv preprint arXiv:2202.10628 (2022). https://doi.org/10.48550/arXiv.2202.10628

18. Luckow, A., Rattan, K., Jha, S.: Pilot-edge: Distributed resource management along the edge-to-cloud continuum. In: Proceedings of IPDPSW 2021, Portland, OR, USA, pp. 874–878 (2021). https://doi.org/10.1109/IPDPSW52791.2021.00130

19. Martin, B.A., et al.:Openfog security requirements and approaches. In: Proceedings of IEEE Fog World Congress (FWC), Santa Clara, CA, USA (2017). https://doi.org/10.1109/FWC.2017.8368537

20. Masip-Bruin, X., et al.: Managing the cloud continuum: Lessons learnt from a real fog-to-cloud deployment. Sensors 21(9) (2021). DOIurl10.3390/s21092974, https://www.mdpi.com/1424-8220/21/9/2974

21. Mendonça, N.C., Jamshidi, P., Garlan, D., Pahl, C.: Developing self-adaptive microservice systems: challenges and directions. IEEE Softw. **38**(2), 70–79 (2019). https://doi.org/10.1109/MS.2019.2955937

22. Mikkonen, T., Pautasso, C., Taivalsaari, A.: Isomorphic internet of things architectures with web technologies. Computer **54**(7), 69–78 (2021). https://doi.org/10.1109/MC.2021.3074258

23. Milojicic, D.: The edge-to-cloud continuum. Computer **53**(11), 16-25 (2020). https://doi.org/10.1109/MC.2020.3007297

24. Peltonen, E., et al.: 6g white paper on edge intelligence. CoRR abs/2004.14850 (2020). 10.48550/arXiv. 2004.14850

25. Plastiras, G., Terzi, M., Kyrkou, C., Theocharidcs, T.: Edge intelligence: challenges and opportunities of near-sensor machine learning applications. In: Proceedings of ASAP 2018, Milan, Italy (2018). https://doi.org/10.1109/ASAP.2018.8445118

26. Rodríguez-Monroy, C., Arias, C., Núñez Guerrero, Y.: The new cloud computing paradigm: the way to IT seen as a utility. Latin American and Caribbean J. Eng. Educ. **6**, 24–31 (2012)

27. Rossi, F., Cardellini, V., Presti, F.L., Nardelli, M.: Geo-distributed efficient deployment of containers with kubernetes. Comput. Commun. **159**, 161–174 (2020). https://doi.org/10.1016/j.comcom.2020.04.061

28. Satyanarayanan, M.: The emergence of edge computing. Computer **50**(1), 30–39 (2017). https://doi.org/10.1109/MC.2017.9

29. Satyanarayanan, M., Bahl, P., Caceres, R., Davies, N.: The case for vm-based cloudlets in mobile computing. IEEE Pervasive Comput. **8**(4), 14–23 (2009). https://doi.org/10.1109/MPRV.2009.82

30. Shah, S.D.A., Gregory, M.A., Li, S.: Cloud-native network slicing using software defined networking based multi-access edge computing: A survey. IEEE Access **9**, 10903–10924 (2021). https://doi.org/10.1109/ACCESS.2021.3050155

31. Shahzadi, S., Iqbal, M., Dagiuklas, T., Qayyum, Z.U.: Multi-access edge computing: open issues, challenges and future perspectives. J. Cloud Comput. **6**(1), 1–13 (2017). https://doi.org/10.1186/s13677-017-0097-9

32. Singh, S.P., Nayyar, A., Kumar, R., Sharma, A.: Fog computing: from architecture to edge computing and big data processing. J. Supercomput. **75**(4), 2070–2105 (2018). https://doi.org/10.1007/s11227-018-2701-2

33. Spillner, J.: Self-balancing architectures based on liquid functions across computing continuums. In: Proceedings of UCC 20'21, Leicester, UK (2021). https://doi.org/10.1145/3492323.3495589

34. Taherizadeh, S., Stankovski, V., Grobelnik, M.: A capillary computing architecture for dynamic internet of things: orchestration of microservices from edge devices to fog and cloud providers. Sensors **18**(9), 2938 (2018). https://doi.org/10.3390/s18092938

35. Taivalsaari, A., Mikkonen, T.: A roadmap to the programmable world: software challenges in the IoT era. IEEE Softw. **34**(1), 72–80 (2017). https://doi.org/10.1109/MS.2017.26

36. Taivalsaari, A., Mikkonen, T., Pautasso, C.: Towards seamless IoT device-edge-cloud continuum. In: Proceedings of ICWE 2021 Workshops, Biarritz, France, pp. 82–98 (2022). https://doi.org/10.1007/978-3-030-92231-3_8

37. Xu, D., et al.: Edge intelligence: empowering intelligence to the edge of network. Proc. IEEE **109**(11), 1778–1837 (2021). https://doi.org/10.1109/JPROC.2021.3119950

38. Yousefpour, A., et al.: All one needs to know about fog computing and related edge computing paradigms: a complete survey. J. Syst. Architect. **98**, 289–330 (2019). https://doi.org/10.1016/j.sysarc.2019.02.009

39. Zambonelli, F., Bicocchi, N., Cabri, G., Leonardi, L., Puviani, M.: On self-adaptation, self-expression, and self-awareness in autonomic service component ensembles. In: Proceedings of SASOW 2011, Ann Arbor, MI, USA. pp. 108–113 (2011). https://doi.org/10.1109/SASOW.2011.24

40. Zhang, Y., Zhou, Y.: Transparent computing: a new paradigm for pervasive computing. In: Proceedings of UIC 2006, Wuhan, China (2006). https://doi.org/10.1007/11833529_1

41. Zhou, Z., Chen, X., Li, E., Zeng, L., Luo, K., Zhang, J.: Edge intelligence: paving the last mile of artificial intelligence with edge computing. Proc. IEEE **107**(8), 1738–1762 (2019). https://doi.org/10.1109/JPROC.2019.2918951

6th International Workshop on Formal Approaches for Advanced Computing Systems (FAACS)

Towards Online Testing Under Uncertainty Using Model-Based Reinforcement Learning

Matteo Camilli[1]([✉]), Raffaela Mirandola[1], Patrizia Scandurra[2],
and Catia Trubiani[3]

[1] Department of Electronics, Information and Bioengineering (DEIB),
Politecnico di Milano, Milan, Italy
{matteo.camilli,raffaela.mirandola}@polimi.it
[2] Department of Management, Information and Production Engineering (DIGIP),
Università degli Studi di Bergamo, Bergamo, Italy
patrizia.scandurra@unibg.it
[3] Gran Sasso Science Institute, L'Aquila, Italy
catia.trubiani@gssi.it

Abstract. Modern software operates in complex ecosystems and is exposed to multiple sources of uncertainty that emerge in different phases of the development lifecycle, such as early requirement analysis or late testing and in-field monitoring. This paper envisions a novel methodology to deal with uncertainty in online model-based testing. We make use of model-based reinforcement learning to gather runtime evidence, spot and quantify existing uncertainties of the system under test. Preliminary experiments show that our novel testing approach has the potential of overcoming the major weaknesses of existing online testing techniques tailored to uncertainty quantification.

Keywords: Model-based Testing · Markov Decision Processes · Uncertainty quantification · Bayesian Reinforcement Learning

1 Introduction

Model-based testing (MBT) relies on explicit architectural models encoding the behavior of interactions between components of a System Under Test (SUT). The main goal is to find observable differences between the intended behavior and runtime evidence [1]. However, modern software-intensive, autonomous and Cyber-Physical Systems (CPSs) are often exposed to multiple sources of uncertainty that can arise from complex execution environments [2,3]. For such systems, predictability is very hard to achieve at design-time. This leads in turn to partial, incomplete, and continuously evolving software architecture specifications [4].

Thus, engineers should follow systematic approaches to deal with uncertainty during the design stage to understand how it could affect the behavior of the

T. Batista et al. (Eds.): ECSA 2022, LNCS 13928, pp. 233–245, 2023.
https://doi.org/10.1007/978-3-031-36889-9_17

target system. Then, uncertainty should be quantified and mitigated by means of proper validation and verification activities.

To deal with these challenges, testing techniques have been tailored not only to detect failures, but also to actively learn the dynamics of the SUT as well as its surroundings to verify initial hypotheses [1]. In particular, endowing testing with techniques and practices able to model, quantify, and mitigate uncertainty turned out to be a promising approach [5]. Therefore, recent research directions propose enhanced MBT approaches with awareness of possible sources of uncertainty and ability to quantify them by actively querying the SUT through testing strategies [6]. In our previous work [7–9] we defined a modeling approach that gives the ability to include uncertain aspects in the specification of the system behavior. Uncertainty is explicitly modeled by means of probability distributions describing prior knowledge of possible outcomes. Uncertainty is then quantified accounting for evidence during testing. Namely, runtime observations feed a Bayesian inference process that incrementally refines the prior knowledge and delivers posterior probability distributions. Nevertheless, a number of issues remain. To the best of our knowledge, little effort has been devoted to study fine grained test generation strategies able to spot uncertainties as well as quantify them to verify system level requirements.

In this paper, we introduce our vision on MBT equipped with awareness on the trade-off between: (i) *exploration* to acquire more information and spot where the system behavior is affected by uncertainty; and (ii) *exploitation* of the external stimuli that have the highest expected payoff in terms of uncertainty quantification. Our novel proposal consists of leveraging on a Model-based Bayesian Reinforcement Learning (RL) [10] approach to testing. The RL conceptual framework plays a key role since it can be used to explore the state space in a controlled way and then elevate the focus of testing on specific locations of the specification, i.e., those locations that need more attention due to sensible changes with respect to the prior knowledge.

The rest of the paper is organized as follows. In Sect. 2 we introduce background concepts used in the rest of the paper. In Sect. 3, we introduce a running example in the domain of CPSs. In Sect. 4, we introduce our envisioned approach and we briefly discuss its theoretical foundation. In Sect. 5 we discuss our preliminary evaluation. In Sect. 6, we present related work and then we discuss our current research roadmap and challenges ahead in Sect. 7,

2   Background

In this section, we introduce background concepts used in the rest of the paper. In particular, we briefly describe Markov Decision Processes (Sect. 2.1), Bayesian inference (Sect. 2.2), and Reinforcement Learning (Sect. 2.3).

2.1   Markov Decision Processes and Rewards

Markov Decision Processes [11,12] (MDPs) represent a widely used formalism for modeling systems exhibiting both probabilistic and nondeterministic behavior. Formally, a MDP is defined as a tuple $\mathcal{M} = (S, s_0, A, \delta)$, where:

- S is a finite set of states ($s_0 \in S$ initial state);
- A is a finite alphabet of actions;
- $\delta : S \times A \to Dist(S)$ is a partial probabilistic transition function, where $Dist(S)$ is the set of all discrete probability distributions over the countable set S.

State transitions occur in two steps:

- a nondeterministic choice among the actions from state s: $A(s) = \{a \in A : \exists \delta(s,a)\}$;
- a stochastic choice of the successor state s', according to the probability distribution δ, such that $\delta(s,a)(s')$ represents the probability that a transition from s to s' occurs when a happens.

The function δ satisfies $\sum_{s'} \delta(s,a)(s') = 1$, for each source state s, action a and target state s'.

MDPs can be augmented with *rewards* to quantify a benefit (or loss) due to the sojourn in a specific state or to the occurrence of a certain state transition. A reward is a non-negative value assigned to states and/or transitions that can represent information such as average execution time, power consumption or usability. A reward structure associated with a MDP $\mathcal{M}$ is defined as a pair $r = (r_s, r_a)$ composed of a *state* reward function $r_s : S \to \mathbb{R}_{\geq 0}$ and an *action* reward function $r_a : S \times A \times S \to \mathbb{R}_{\geq 0}$ that assigns rewards to states and transitions, respectively. Given a reward structure, a common problem is to find a policy function π that specifies the action $\pi(s)$ chosen by a decision maker when state s holds. The best policy π^* maximizes some function of the cumulated rewards, typically the expected discounted sum over a potentially infinite path. Namely, given a reward structure r, π^* can be computed solving a *dynamic decision problem* [11]. The best policy π^* returns for each state s the action that allows the cumulated reward to be maximized.

2.2   Bayesian Inference

A very common goal in statistics is to learn about one (or more) uncertain parameter(s) θ describing some details of a stochastic phenomenon of interest. To learn about θ, we observe the phenomenon and collect a data sample $y = (y_1, y_2, ..., y_n)$ to compute the conditional density $f(y|\theta)$ of the observed data given θ, i.e., the *likelihood* function. The Bayesian inference approach consists of taking into account the hypothesis (or assumptions) about θ. This information is often available from external sources, such as expert information based on past experience or previous studies [13]. The hypothesis is given in probabilistic terms distribution $f(\theta)$, so called *prior*. The Bayes' theorem formulation given below defines how the prior and the likelihood can be combined to obtain the *posterior* distribution:

$$Posterior \propto Likelihood \cdot Prior \tag{1}$$

The *posterior* $f(\theta|y)$ describes the best knowledge of the true value of θ, given the data sample y. It can be used in turn to perform point and interval estimation of the uncertain parameters. The estimation yields the notion of *updated beliefs*. As described in [14], this is typically addressed by summarizing the distribution through the posterior *mean* and the smallest possible credible region of 0.95 probability, called *Highest Density Region* (HDR). This region is defined as the set of θ values, such that $\text{HDR}_\theta = \{\theta : f(\theta|y) \geq 0.95\}$. The HDR contains the values considered most likely a posteriori (i.e., credible values having the highest density). The magnitude of the region, denoted as $\|\text{HDR}_\theta\|$, is traditionally used in Bayesian statistics as a measure of the highest possible accuracy in the estimation [13]. Namely, it represents the confidence of the inference process, i.e., the smaller the magnitude, the higher the confidence.

2.3   Reinforcement Learning

Reinforcement learning [10] (RL) refers to a specific area of machine learning concerned with incremental learning software agents that can take actions in an environment to maximize the notion of cumulative reward. In its basic formulation, a RL agent interacts with its environment in discrete time steps. At each time step t, the agents chooses and executes an action a_t (from those available) from the current state s_t. At this point, the environment moves to a new state s_{t+1} and sends a reward r_{t+1} to the agent. Thus, the goal of the agent is to learn the policy π^* that maximizes the expected cumulative reward. It is worth noting that the agent cannot directly compute the best policy by solving a dynamic decision problem since the underlying MDP model of the environment as well as the reward structure is usually unknown (or partially known). Bayesian RL methods explicitly maintain a posterior over the model parameters and use this posterior to select actions. Actions can be selected to collect knowledge and achieve a better posterior (i.e., exploration), or use the collected knowledge to achieve maximal return in terms of cumulative reward (i.e., exploitation). We let the reader refer to [10] for a comprehensive descriptions of existing Bayesian RL algorithms.

3   A Running Example: The SafeHome System

The SafeHome is an existing benchmarking example in the domain of CPSs [15]. The system controls and configures alarms and related sensors that implement a number of security and safety features, such as intrusion detection. Figure 1 shows part of the SafeHome system using the UML state diagram notation.

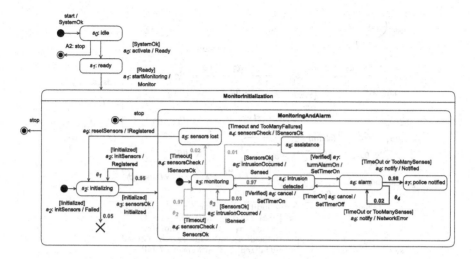

Fig. 1. The SafeHome system benchmark.

In the following we introduce a high level description of the behavior of the SafeHome by emphasizing its relevant characteristics for our problem domain.

After the setup phase, the system exhibits three main phases: *initializing*, *monitoring* and *alarm*, in charge of sensor initialization, detection, and alarm handling, respectively. As described in [15], sources of uncertainty affect the behavior of the SafeHome at different levels: *application*, level, due to events/data originating from software components running upon physical units; *infrastructure*, level, due to data transmission through networking and/or cloud infrastructure; and *integration*. level, due to interactions among physical units at either application or infrastructure levels. Uncertain behavior at different levels might lead to the invalidation of functional and non-functional requirements (e.g., reliability, performance). Some common scenarios in the SafeHome are discussed in the following.

Figure 2 shows the MDP model of the SafeHome mechanically obtained from the corresponding UML diagram. The model also illustrates a mapping from transitions to labels that follow the standard notation "[pre-condition] trigger/post-condition" and provides guidance to the interpretation of the MDP model. As an example, from state s_2 (during *monitor initialization*), the SafeHome system tries to initialize all the available sensors by executing the a_2 action, i.e., the trigger of *initSensors*. If the task succeeds, the sensors are correctly registered and the a_3 action can be executed (i.e., the pre-condition *initialized* holds) to proceed towards the *monitoring* and *alarm* phases.

To exemplify some of how sources of uncertainty may affect the system's behavior, let us consider the following scenario. When the system is in state s_3, it means that *monitoring* holds, sensors can send the a_5: *intrusionOccurred* trigger to the security system that makes the alarm ring via the effect of a_7: *turnAlarmOn* attached to the outgoing transition of the state s_4 *intrusionDetected*.

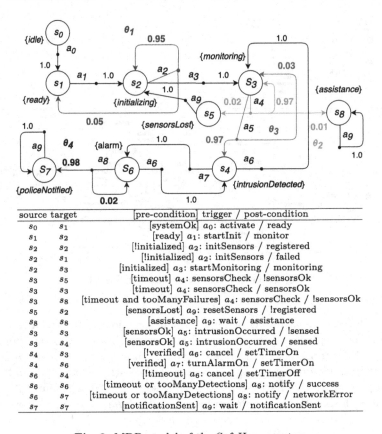

source	target	[pre-condition] trigger / post-condition
s_0	s_1	[systemOk] a_0: activate / ready
s_1	s_2	[ready] a_1: startInit / monitor
s_2	s_2	[!initialized] a_2: initSensors / registered
s_2	s_1	[!initialized] a_2: initSensors / failed
s_2	s_3	[initialized] a_3: startMonitoring / monitoring
s_3	s_5	[timeout] a_4: sensorsCheck / !sensorsOk
s_3	s_3	[timeout] a_4: sensorsCheck / sensorsOk
s_3	s_8	[timeout and tooManyFailures] a_4: sensorsCheck / !sensorsOk
s_5	s_2	[sensorsLost] a_9: resetSensors / !registered
s_8	s_8	[assistance] a_9: wait / assistance
s_3	s_3	[sensorsOk] a_5: intrusionOccurred / !sensed
s_3	s_4	[sensorsOk] a_5: intrusionOccurred / sensed
s_4	s_3	[!verified] a_6: cancel / setTimerOn
s_4	s_6	[verified] a_7: turnAlarmOn / setTimerOn
s_6	s_4	[!timeout] a_6: cancel / setTimerOff
s_6	s_6	[timeout or tooManyDetections] a_8: notify / success
s_6	s_7	[timeout or tooManyDetections] a_8: notify / networkError
s_7	s_7	[notificationSent] a_9: wait / notificationSent

Fig. 2. MDP model of the SafeHome system

Nevertheless, the intrusion detection capability is affected by uncertainty at the integration level. This capability is influenced by the interaction of sensors and their individual ability of correctly sensing the physical environment. Thus, the a_5 action leads to either state s_4 (i.e., the intrusion has been sensed) or state s_3 (i.e., the intrusion has not been sensed) with a substantial degree of uncertainty. This uncertain outcome is explicitly represented by uncertain probability values (i.e., 0.97 and 0.03, respectively), as shown in the arcs of the MDP model. Another example scenario is the notification event to third-party services (input a_8 from the state s_6). The communication might use an unreliable infrastructure that lead to uncertain throughput and latency, jeopardizing the possibility of observing deterministic outcomes out of a detection event.

We refer to a set of uncertain probability values associated with a state-action pair in the model as *uncertain region* and we denote it as θ_i. Note that the disjoint union of all θ_i is θ, i.e., the set of uncertain model parameters.

4   Envisioned Approach

Our online testing approach makes use of MDPs as system models. As antici-pated in Sect. 2, such a formalism represents a widely accepted and convenient way to specify both non-deterministic and stochastic facets of phenomena of interest. Figure 2 shows an extract of the MDP model mechanically obtained from the state diagram of the SafeHome system. By using our modeling frame-work [9], the tester represents partial knowledge (i.e., beliefs) as parameters attached to MDP transitions. Beliefs are described by means of *prior* probabil-ity density functions, or simply priors [13]. Specifically, each region θ_i is modeled through a categorical distribution, while the natural conjugate prior of the cate-gorical distribution is the Dirichlet distribution. As an example, Eq. 2 shows the prior of θ_2 as well as the degree of uncertainty expressed in terms of credible intervals computed through the Highest Density Region (HDR) of the distribu-tion (i.e., the smallest region for the confidence level 0.95):

$$f(\theta_2) = Dir(47, 2, 1), \ HDR[f(\theta_2)] = ([0.87, 0.99], [0.00, 0.09], [0.00, 0.05]) \quad (2)$$

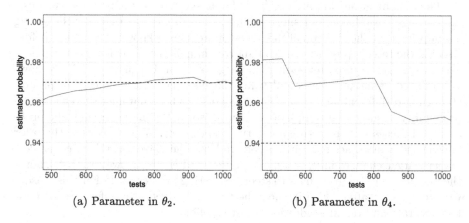

(a) Parameter in θ_2.   (b) Parameter in θ_4.

Fig. 3. Inference of uncertain model parameters.

Assuming we know the location of each region θ_i (e.g., the location of possible unreliable sensors in the SafeHome), dynamic programming [8] can be used to compute the best *exploration policies* that test the system. Essentially, for each target region we can identify the actions (i.e., external stimuli or inputs) that maximize the probability to reach the related model location.

In our previous work [8,9], we introduced a MBT approach that uses these best policies to drive the generation of test cases according to the degree of uncertainty expressed by the Dirichlet priors. Regions associated with less infor-mative priors (i.e., larger HDRs) are likely to receive more tests of the whole budget to collect evidence and increase the posterior knowledge computed by applying a *Bayesian* inference process [13].

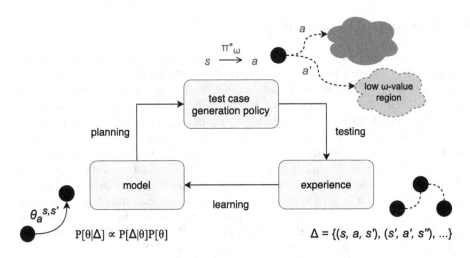

Fig. 4. Model-based RL approach to testing.

The aforementioned approach, henceforth referred to as *Dist* (Distance testing strategy [16]), has major shortcomings. Indeed, Dist works under the strong assumption that the location of the uncertain regions is known in advance, before running the testing process. Another shortcoming is that Dist ignores the posterior knowledge acquired by testing the target system. For instance, Fig. 3 shows the inferred value and the actual value (dashed line) of two uncertain parameters in two different model regions: θ_2 and θ_4. These parameters refer to the probability of successful completion of the sensor check procedure and the probability of successfully notifying an alarm, respectively. We can see that the prior knowledge is more accurate in Fig. 3a. Indeed, the Bayesian inference process detects larger changes in θ_4 compared to θ_2 (see Fig. 3b). However, Dist ignores the magnitude of these changes to steer the testing process itself. For this reason, we can see that after $1k$ tests (i.e., the testing budget), the inference for θ_4 is less accurate and requires additional testing effort.

To deal with these issues, we propose a novel technique that leverages on the theoretical framework of model-based Bayesian RL [10]. This choice is justified by the practical need of equipping the testing with the ability to spot locations of interest (through exploration) and then maximize the accuracy of the uncertainty quantification (through exploitation). As an example, in the SafeHome we might want to explore the state space of the system to spot the location of unreliable sensors whose ability to detect intrusion triggers is uncertain. At this point the acquired knowledge can be exploited to guide further testing towards the usage of these sensors in order to collect evidence and quantify the uncertain behavior.

Figure 4 shows the main elements and activities involved in this approach where the testing *agent* alternates planning and testing in a closed loop. The model here is a *Bayes-Adaptive* MDP [10], i.e., a formal model for planning scenarios where agents operate under uncertain information. Namely, we assume a

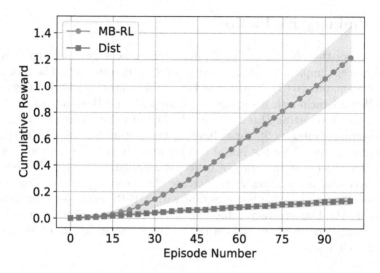

Fig. 5. Comparison of Model-based RL and Dist.

finite and known state-action domain (e.g., functional states of the SafeHome and possible inputs received for the surroundings), whereas the transition probability values follow an unknown/uncertain distribution θ_a^s for each pair (s, a) state-action (e.g., uncertain outcome out of an alarm sent to a third party service). Based on this formulation, we can learn the uncertain parameters by belief monitoring during the testing process. For each executed test, the belief $\theta_a^{s,s'}$ in terms of Prior probability is updated based on the *experience* (s, a, s') using Bayesian inference [13] to compute the posterior knowledge, as shown in Fig. 4. The testing agent provides external stimuli to the SUT, collects experience, and then feeds a Bayesian inference process that leverages runtime evidence to compute the posteriors knowledge of the uncertain model parameters.

The Model-based Bayesian RL approach [17] in Fig. 4 takes uncertainty of the learned θ_a^s explicitly into account. Here, the *Bayes-Adaptive* MDP provides a means to predict how the SUT will respond to external stimuli through a stochastic description of all possible next states and rewards. The Bayesian exploration policy π^* computed from the model solves the exploitation-exploration trade-off implicitly by considering how actions affect the state of the SUT, but also the agent's internal belief about the SUT itself.

In our approach we use Model-based Bayesian RL to perform test case generation driven by the learning process. The key idea is the definition of a quantitative *measure* ω for the expected learning magnitude and use this measure as reward to drive the planning process. Intuitively, the higher the level of uncertainty of θ_a^s, the higher the $\omega(s, a)$ value. Hence, the measure ω is a nonstationary function in $\mathbb{R}_{\geq 0}$ that changes along with the new collected experience. Such a measure of uncertainty can be formalized as the distance between the prior and the posterior knowledge. Thus, the planning agent can leverage the posterior model to plan with respect to ω that steers the testing process towards the model regions whose posterior is incompatible with the prior knowledge.

5   Preliminary Evaluation

Figure 5 shows the outcome of preliminary experiments we conducted with a proof-of-concept implementation of our novel testing approach. The plot shows the expected cumulative ω reward (and the credible interval) obtained by testing the SafeHome benchmark using our novel model-based Bayesian RL (MB-RL) approach and the existing *Dist* strategy [16]. Data has been collected by running the two testing strategies 25 times limiting the testing budget to 100 episodes (i.e., number of runs from the initial to a terminal state). We can see that MB-RL is better than Dist in terms of expected cumulative reward. Furthermore, the gap between the two strategies increases by increasing the testing budget. After 100 episodes, the cumulative reward with MB-RL is almost 5 times higher compared to the Dist strategy. This supports MB-RL as a promising technique to better exploit the budget by focusing on those uncertain model regions that yield larger changes.

6   Related Work

Taxonomies of potential sources of uncertainty in software systems are presented in [18,19]. An overview over the current state of the art can be found in [20], where the results of a systematic literature review are presented, highlighting uncertainty types, approaches, and application domains. A survey conducted in the community of self-adaptive systems to better understand the definition of uncertainty together with its possible souces and mitigation methods is presented in [21]. Recent research activities show increasing effort in delivering approaches and techniques that jointly consider testing and uncertainty quantification methods. Uncertainty sampling has been introduced in [22] to generate suitable test data. The so-called "Query Strategy Framework" is adopted to infer a behavioral model and then select those tests on which the behavior of the system is uncertain. This approach outperforms conventional and adaptive random testing at exposing faults. The uncertainty-wise UML-based modeling framework has been introduced in [23] with the aim of creating models that can be executed to test CPSs. A offline MBT approach that leverages on the uncertainty-wise modeling framework has been presented in [15]. The approach generates test cases in a cost-effective way by minimizing the number of tests but maintaining coverage of models. Further approaches dealing with uncertainty-related concerns for CPSs and self-adaptive systems have been recently instroduces [24,25]. This line of research investigates runtime verification techniques to mitigate the uncertainty related to the model selection process, that is, whenever one model is chosen over plausible alternatives to represent the understanding of a system and make predictions about future observations. Bernardi et al. [26] point out how the combination of different formal models can increase or decrease the overall uncertainty, and model-based performance analysis highlights the challenges related to the awareness of uncertainty. Arcaini et al. [27] develop a formal transformation from feature design models to queueing network performance models while transferring the system uncertainties. Aleti et al. [28] propose a machine learning technique, i.e., the so-called *polynomial chaos expansion*, to understand the impact of a variegate set of system uncertainties (e.g., workload, software/hardware requests, etc.) on software performance characteristics, and results demonstrate that uncertainty indeed has a large influence on software performance. The approach presented in [8,9] incorporates uncertainty mitigation into an online MBT framework, while different online testing strategies have been introduced in [16]. These strategies have major shortcomings since they ignore the information collected during testing to steer the testing process itself, as further explained in the next sections.

7 Conclusion and Future Work

Our ongoing research activity is expected to contribute the state-of-the-art by providing an online testing approach grounded on the theoretical framework of model-based Bayesian RL. The ultimate goal is to provide software engineers with an automated testing method able to quantify existing uncertainties while increasing the level of assurance of the target system. Preliminary experiments show that our Model-based Bayesian RL testing approach has the potential of overcoming the major weaknesses of existing online testing techniques tailored to uncertainty quantification [16]. We are currently investigating the major challenges associated with planning the optimal policy from distribution models that is known as a very expensive task [10]. Nonetheless, the common structure between learning and planning in RL suggests that many ideas and algorithms can be transferred between these two activities. RL algorithms can be substituted for the key update step of a planning method in order to reduce the cost of the planning process. Our roadmap includes the development and assessment of different model-based Bayesian RL testing strategies. We aim at applying such strategies to different case studies to systematically study the cost-effectiveness of our approach.

Acknowledgements. This work has been partially funded by MUR PRIN project 2017TWRCNB SEDUCE, and the PNRR MUR project VITALITY (ECS00000041) Spoke 2 ASTRA - Advanced Space Technologies and Research Alliance.

References

1. Aichernig, B.K., Mostowski, W., Mousavi, M.R., Tappler, M., Taromirad, M.: Model learning and model-based testing. In: Bennaceur, A., Hähnle, R., Meinke, K. (eds.) Machine Learning for Dynamic Software Analysis: Potentials and Limits. LNCS, vol. 11026, pp. 74–100. Springer, Cham (2018). https://doi.org/10.1007/978-3-319-96562-8_3
2. Perez-Palacin, D., Mirandola, R.: Uncertainties in the modeling of self-adaptive systems: a taxonomy and an example of availability evaluation. In: International Conference on Performance Engineering, pp. 3–14 (2014)

3. Trubiani, C., Apel, S.: PLUS: performance learning for uncertainty of software. In: International Conference on Software Engineering: NIER, pp. 77–80 (2019)

4. Garlan, D.: Software engineering in an uncertain world. In: International Workshop on Future of Software Engineering Research, pp. 125–128 (2010)

5. Zhang, M., Ali, S., Yue, T.: Uncertainty-wise test case generation and minimization for cyber-physical systems. J. Syst. Softw. **153**, 1–21 (2019). https://www.sciencedirect.com/science/article/pii/S0164121219300561

6. Menghi, C., Nejati, S., Briand, L., Parache, Y.I.: Approximation-refinement testing of compute-intensive cyber-physical models: an approach based on system identification. In: Proceedings of the International Conference on Software Engineering, pp. 372–384 (2020)

7. Camilli, M., Gargantini, A., Scandurra, P., Bellettini, C.: Towards inverse uncertainty quantification in software development (short paper). In: Cimatti, A., Sirjani, M. (eds.) SEFM 2017. LNCS, vol. 10469, pp. 375–381. Springer, Cham (2017). https://doi.org/10.1007/978-3-319-66197-1_24

8. Camilli, M., Bellettini, C., Gargantini, A., Scandurra, P.: Online model-based testing under uncertainty. In: International Symposium on Software Reliability Engineering, pp. 36–46 (2018)

9. Camilli, M., Gargantini, A., Scandurra, P.: Model-based hypothesis testing of uncertain software systems. Softw. Test. Verif. Reliab. **30**(2), e1730 (2020)

10. Ghavamzadeh, M., Mannor, S., Pineau, J., Tamar, A.: Bayesian reinforcement learning: a survey. Found. Trends Mach. Learn. **8**(5–6), 359–483 (2015). https://doi.org/10.1561/2200000049

11. Puterman, M.L.: Markov Decision Processes: Discrete Stochastic Dynamic Programming. Wiley, Hoboken (1994)

12. Forejt, V., Kwiatkowska, M., Norman, G., Parker, D.: Automated verification techniques for probabilistic systems. In: Bernardo, M., Issarny, V. (eds.) SFM 2011. LNCS, vol. 6659, pp. 53–113. Springer, Heidelberg (2011). https://doi.org/10.1007/978-3-642-21455-4_3

13. Robert, C.P.: The Bayesian Choice: From Decision-Theoretic Foundations to Computational Implementation, 2nd edn. Springer, New York (2007). https://doi.org/10.1007/0-387-71599-1

14. Insua, D., Ruggeri, F., Wiper, M.: Bayesian Analysis of Stochastic Process Models. Wiley Series in Probability and Statistics. Wiley, Hoboken (2012)

15. Zhang, M., Ali, S., Yue, T.: Uncertainty-wise test case generation and minimization for cyber-physical systems. J. Syst. Softw. **153**, 1–21 (2019). https://doi.org/10.1016/j.jss.2019.03.011

16. Camilli, M., Gargantini, A., Scandurra, P., Trubiani, C.: Uncertainty-aware exploration in model-based testing. In: 2021 14th IEEE Conference on Software Testing, Verification and Validation (ICST), pp. 71–81 (2021)

17. Vlassis, N., Ghavamzadeh, M., Mannor, S., Poupart, P.: Bayesian reinforcement learning. In: Wiering, M., van Otterlo, M. (eds.) Reinforcement Learning, pp. 359–386. Springer, Heidelberg (2012). https://doi.org/10.1007/978-3-642-27645-3_11

18. Ramirez, A.J., Jensen, A.C., Cheng, B.H.C.: A taxonomy of uncertainty for dynamically adaptive systems. In: International Symposium on Software Engineering for Adaptive and Self-Managing Systems, pp. 99–108 (2012)

19. Perez-Palacin, D., Mirandola, R.: Uncertainties in the modeling of self-adaptive systems: a taxonomy and an example of availability evaluation. In: Proceedings of the 5th ACM/SPEC International Conference on Performance Engineering, ICPE 2014, pp. 3–14. ACM, New York (2014). http://doi.acm.org/10.1145/2568088.2568095

20. Troya, J., Moreno, N., Bertoa, M.F., Vallecillo, A.: Uncertainty representation in software models: a survey. Softw. Syst. Model. **20**(4), 1183–1213 (2021). https://doi.org/10.1007/s10270-020-00842-1

21. Mahdavi-Hezavehi, S., Weyns, D., Avgeriou, P., Calinescu, R., Mirandola, R., Perez-Palacin, D.: Uncertainty in self-adaptive systems: a research community perspective. ACM Trans. Adapt. Auton. Syst. **15**(4), 1–36 (2021)

22. Walkinshaw, N., Fraser, G.: Uncertainty-driven black-box test data generation. In: 2017 IEEE International Conference on Software Testing, Verification and Validation (ICST), pp. 253–263 (2017)

23. Zhang, M., Ali, S., Yue, T., Norgren, R., Okariz, O.: Uncertainty-wise cyber-physical system test modeling. Softw. Syst. Model. **18**(2), 1379–1418 (2017). https://doi.org/10.1007/s10270-017-0609-6

24. Camilli, M., Mirandola, R., Scandurra, P.: Runtime equilibrium verification for resilient cyber-physical systems. In: IEEE International Conference on Autonomic Computing and Self-Organizing Systems (ACSOS) 2021, pp. 71–80 (2021)

25. Camilli, M., Mirandola, R., Scandurra, P.: Taming model uncertainty in self-adaptive systems using Bayesian model averaging. In: Proceedings of the 17th Symposium on Software Engineering for Adaptive and Self-Managing Systems, SEAMS 2022, pp. 25–35. Association for Computing Machinery, New York (2022). https://doi.org/10.1145/3524844.3528056

26. Bernardi, S., et al.: Living with uncertainty in model-based development. In: Heinrich, R., Durán, F., Talcott, C., Zschaler, S. (eds.) Composing Model-Based Analysis Tools, pp. 159–185. Springer, Cham (2021). https://doi.org/10.1007/978-3-030-81915-6_8

27. Arcaini, P., Inverso, O., Trubiani, C.: Automated model-based performance analysis of software product lines under uncertainty. Inf. Softw. Technol. **127**, 106371 (2020)

28. Aleti, A., Trubiani, C., van Hoorn, A., Jamshidi, P.: An efficient method for uncertainty propagation in robust software performance estimation. J. Syst. Softw. **138**, 222–235 (2018)

A Maude Formalization of Object Nets

Lorenzo Capra[1] and Michael Köhler-Bußmeier[2]

[1] Dipartimento di Informatica, Università degli Studi di Milano, Milan, Italy
capra@di.unimi.it
[2] University of Applied Science Hamburg, Hamburg, Germany
michael.koehler-bussmeier@haw-hamburg.de

Abstract. Self-adaptive systems gain growing attention by raising service quality and reducing development costs. But on the other hand, self-adaptation is a source of complexity that needs suitable methodologies/models/tools supporting the entire life cycle. A particularly challenging point is the dynamic reconfiguration of a system. This feature, typical of modern distributed systems, has led to the definition of specialized formalisms, e.g. the pi-calculus or Nets-within-Nets, which essentially build on top of the concept of a changing system structure. But even with syntactic sugar, these formalisms differ enough from the 'daily' programming languages. This work aims to bridge the gap between theory and practice by introducing an abstract machine for the base type of Nets-within-Nets. Our encoding is in the well-known `Maude` language, whose rewriting logic semantics ensures the mathematical soundness needed for analysis and an intuitive operational perspective.

Keywords: Dynamically-reconfigurable systems · `Maude` · Nets-within-nets

1 Introduction

Self-adaptive or self-organizing systems gain more and more attention trying to raise service quality at reduced development costs. On the other hand, self-adaptation is a source of complexity and therefore requires suitable models/methodologies/tools both at design time and run-time. In this context, formal methods can play an important role. [10,27] present a survey of formal methods for modelling/analysis of self-adaptive systems. Significant examples are [11], specifying MAPE-K templates for a family of self-adaptive systems, and [28], presenting an end-to-end approach for engineering self-adaptive systems during the life cycle of a feedback loop.

In this paper, we focus on the most challenging point of self-adaption, namely *dynamic reconfiguration* of system components. This feature is typical of modern distributed systems, more generally, and has led to the development of some specialized formalisms, e.g. the π-calculus or nets-within-nets, which essentially build on top of the concept of a changeable system structure. But even with extra

© The Author(s), under exclusive license to Springer Nature Switzerland AG 2023
T. Batista et al. (Eds.): ECSA 2022, LNCS 13928, pp. 246–261, 2023.
https://doi.org/10.1007/978-3-031-36889-9_18

syntactic sugar, these formalisms are different enough from 'daily' programming languages in which reconfiguration often boils down to add-delete operations.

This work aims to bridge the gap between theory and practice, by presenting an abstract machine for the Nets-within-Nets approach. Our formalization uses the well-known Maude language since specifications given in rewriting logic enjoy the mathematical soundness needed for analysis and provide developers with an intuitive operational perspective that has been used to specify adaptive systems before [2].

We first briefly introduce Nets-within-Nets and Maude (Sect. 2) and then present (Sect. 3) the Maude encoding of base object-nets in general. Section 4 describes the running example: An adaptable production line. We include some significant evidence of property verification and deal with scalability. Section 5 summarises the lessons learned so far and gives insights into current research.

2   Background

Petri Nets (PN). PN is a family of formalism known to be a reference/central model for concurrent/distributed systems. In our work, we refer to (*Turing-powerful*) Place-Transitions (PT) nets. A PT net is a kind of bipartite graph $N := (P, T, I, O, H)$, where: P and T are finite, disjoint sets whose elements are called *places* –state variables, drawn as circles– and *transitions* –events changing the current state, drawn as bars–, respectively; Letting $Bag[P]$ denote the set of multisets defined on P, $\{I, O, H\}$ are maps $T \to Bag[P]$ representing weighted input/output/inhibitor edges, respectively. The distributed state of a PT net, or *marking*, is $m \in Bag[P]$. PT nets have intuitive semantics (we use the component-wise operator extension to multiset): $t \in T$ *enabled* in m if and only if: $I(t) \leq m \land H(t) > m$ ('>' being restricted to the support of $H(t)$). If t is enabled in m it may *fire*, leading to $m' = m + O(t) - I(t)$.

A PT *system* is a pair $\langle N, m \rangle$: Its interleaving semantics is expressed by a T-labelled directed graph whose nodes are the markings reachable from m, and whose edges match direct state transitions.

Nets-within-Nets. In recent years we studied systems with a changeable layout in the *object-net* formalism [12,16], which follows the *Nets-within-Nets* paradigm proposed by Valk [26]. HORNETS [13] is an extension of object-nets with algebraic operators that allow one to modify net-tokens' structure through transition firing. It is a generalization of the approach of algebraic nets [24], where terms replace anonymous (black) tokens. Reflective Petri nets [7,8] are conceptually related to Nets-within-Nets, even though they build on meta-modelling.

Our Maude formalisation refers to the class of *elementary object-net systems* (EOS) [12], which are the two-level specialization of object-nets [12,16]. The EOS formalism makes a fair trade-off between expressivity and analysis complexity. For our theoretical studies, we also introduced *elementary* HORNETS [19], which have a two-level nesting structure, in analogy to EOS. It turns out that elementary HORNETS have greater complexity than EOS, though more expressive: On the one hand, we have shown in [15,17,18] that most problems (including reachability and liveness) for *safe* EOS are PSPACE-complete. Namely, safe EOS are no more complex than PT nets for these problems. On the other hand, we have shown in [14, 20] that for *safe, elementary* HORNETS "the reachability problem requires exponential space".

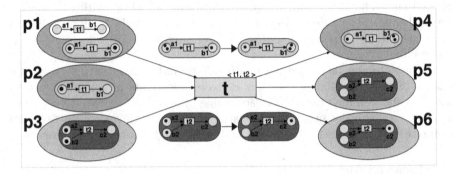

Fig. 1. An Elementary Object Net System (EOS)

EOS. With object-nets, we mean Petri nets where tokens (graphically denoting a PN marking) are nets again, i.e., we have a *nested* marking. An EOS consists of a *system-net* whose places may hold net-tokens of a certain type. In our encoding, the graph structure of both the system-net and net-tokens is a PT net. Net-tokens, however, do not allow any further nesting of nets, i.e., they represent *marked* PT nets. In the example given in Fig. 1 there are two different types of net-tokens, that we call net_1, net_2; Both the system-net and the net-tokens consist of a single transition connected to I/O places by weight-one edges.

EOS events are nested, accordingly. There may be three different kinds:

1. System-autonomous: A system-net transition (e.g., t) fires autonomously, which consistently moves the net-tokens from t's post-set (places p_i, $i : 1 \ldots 3$) to the post-set (p_j, $j : 4 \ldots 6$), without changing their marking.
2. Object autonomous: A net-token, e.g., that of type net_1 in the system-net place p_2, fires transition t_1 by "moving" a black token from a_1 to b_1. The net-token remains in place p_2.
3. Synchronisation (illustrated in Fig. 1): Whenever we add matching synchronization inscriptions, e.g., between the system-net transition t and the nested transitions t_1, t_2, then they must fire synchronously: The net-tokens move from the post-set to the post-set of t, consistently; at the same time, the black tokens inside nested nets move from the pre-set to the post-set of t_1, t_2.

Notice that there may be several *firing instances* for a system-net transition: If many net-tokens of a certain type are in transition's post-set, their *cumulative* marking is distributed on output places of the same type (possibly after a nested firing step, in the case of a synchronization). Each possible combination of adding/distributing net-token markings results in a separate instance. We give further details in Sect. 3.

Maude [9] is an expressive, purely declarative language with a rewriting logic semantics [3]. Statements are (conditional) *equations* (eq) and *rules* (rl). Both sides of a rule/equation are terms of a given *kind* that may contain variables. Rules and equations have simple rewriting semantics in which instances of the lefthand side are replaced by corresponding instances of the righthand side. Maude's expressivity is achieved through equational pattern matching modulo operator equational attributes; user-definable operator syntax/evaluation strategy; sub-typing and partiality; generic types; reflection.

A Maude *functional* module (fmod) contains only *equations* and is a functional program defining one or more operations through equations, used as simplification rules. A functional module (with all the imported modules) specifies an *equational theory* in membership equational logic [1]. Formally, such a theory is a pair $(\Sigma, E \cup A)$, where Σ is the signature, that is, the specification of all the (sub)sort, kind[1], and operator declarations; E is the set of (conditional) equations and membership axioms, and A is the set of operator equational attributes (assoc, comm,..). The model of $(\Sigma, E \cup A)$ is the *initial algebra* (denoted $T_{\Sigma/E \cup A}$), which is both junk- and confusion-free and mathematically corresponds to the quotient of the (ground) term-algebra. Under certain conditions on E and A, the final values (*canonical* forms) of all ground terms form an algebra isomorphic to the initial algebra, i.e., the denotational and operational semantics coincide.

A Maude *system module* (mod) contains *rewrite rules* and possibly equations. Rules represent local transitions in a concurrent system. Formally, a system module specifies a generalized *rewrite theory* [3], a four-tuple $\mathcal{R} = (\Sigma, E \cup A, \phi, R)$ where $(\Sigma, E \cup A)$ is a membership equational theory; ϕ specifies, for each operator in Σ, the frozen arguments; and R is a set of rewrite rules[2]. A rewrite theory specifies a concurrent system. $(\Sigma, E \cup A)$ defines the algebraic structure of the states. R and ϕ specify the system's concurrent transitions. The initial model of $\mathcal{R}$ associates to each kind k a labeled transition system (category) whose states are $T_{\Sigma/E \cup A, k}$, and whose transitions take the form: $[t] \xrightarrow{[\alpha]} [t']$, with $[t], [t'] \in T_{\Sigma/E \cup A, k}$, and $[\alpha]$ an equivalence class of rewrites. The *ground coherence* property ensures that a strategy in which terms are first reduced to the canonical form and then rewritten according to the rules is sound and complete.

3   MAUDE Implementation of EOS

In this section, we describe and briefly discuss the Maude formalization of EOS, which extends that of (rewritable) PT systems given in [4,6]. In our description, we use a few Maude code excerpts and refer to Fig. 1 as an example. The Maude sources are available at https://github.com/lgcapra/rewpt/tree/main/new/EOS.

The EOS formalization relies on three generic functional modules, BAG{X}, MAP+{X,Y}, SET+{X} (the last two extensions of built-in modules). These modules

---

[1] A *kind* is an equivalence class grouping sorts directly or indirectly related by subsort order; terms in a kind without a specific sort are *undefined* or *error* terms.

[2] Rules don't apply to frozen arguments.

may be arbitrarily nested thanks to a flexible mechanism of parameterized views (instantiating the type parameters of a generic module). Differently from other `Maude` formalisations of PNs [23,25], bags are not merely represented as free commutative monoids: A few operators provide abstraction: `_._`, `_+_`, `_[_]` `_-_`, `_<=_`, `_>'_`, set, `_*_`. The first two (*constructors*) appear in canonical forms. We intuitively represent a bag as an associative weighted sum, e.g., 3 . a + 1 . b. The module `MAP+` defines a map term as a "set" of entries juxtaposed using the associative `_;_` operator. Sub-sort `Entry` of `Map` has as a unique constructor `_|->_`. Module `MAP+` supplies a predicate verifying the uniqueness of map keys which is exploited in membership equations to implement consistency checks.

PT System Formalization. The `Maude` specification in [4], here summarized, supplies an efficient operational semantics for *dynamically reconfigurable* PT nets and represents the basis for EoS formalization. According to EoS definition, however, dynamic adaptation comes down to net-tokens manipulation. Reconfiguration at the system-net level is part of ongoing work.

Places/transitions are denoted by indexed/labelled terms, e.g., p(2,"net1"), t(1,"sys"). A transition's incidence matrix is a triplet (constructor [_,_,_] defined in module `IMATRIX`) of terms of sort `Bag{Place}` (defined in `BAGP`, an instance of `BAG{X}`)[3]. The modules `PT-NET` and `PT-SYS` hold the signature of a PT net/system. A net is a term of sort `Map{Tran,Imatrix}` (renamed `Net`), i.e., a semicolon-separated set of entries t(k,"lab")|-> [i,o,h],, each entry being a term in subsort `ImatrixT` of `Net`. A PT system is the empty juxtaposition (`__` : Net Bag{Place} -> [System]) of a `Net` term and a `Bag{Place}` term representing the net's marking. The use of a *kind* as the operator's range means that it defines a partial function: the reason is that the net sub-term must be a consistent, non-empty map. A *membership axiom* characterizes well-defined `System` terms. This approach, typical of membership equational logic, is a good trade-off between rewriting efficiency and code compactness.

The *system* module `PT-EMU` (listed below) specifies the operational semantics of PT systems by exploiting the effective algebraic representation of PT nets.

```
mod PT−EMU is
 pr PT−SYS.
 var T : Tran.
 vars I O H S : Bag{Place}.
 var N N' : Net.
 crl [firing] : N S => N S + O − I if T |−> [I,O,H] ; N' := N /\ I <= S /\ H >' S .
endm
```

The conditional rewrite rule `firing` intuitively encodes the PT firing rule. All the involved operators are bag operators. The matching equation (t := t') in rule's condition makes it very compact. The model-specific part consists of a system module importing `PT-EMU` and containing two zero-arity operators of range `Net` and `Bag{Place}`, respectively, describing a given PT system.

---

[3] They represent the input, output, inhibitor connections, respectively.

3.1 EOS Specification

The EOS specification extends and reflects in part that of reconfigurable PT systems: A few functional modules specify the EOS algebraic structure. A system module (EOS-EMU) specifies the EOS operation semantics. A couple of auxiliary modules (BAG-SPLIT, MAP-PROD) define some operators needed to mime the inner steps of transition firing, in particular, the computation of firing instances of a system-net transition and the consequent (possibly non-deterministic) distribution of net-tokens on its post-set. Finally, a specific system module instantiates a given EOS model. For the reader's convenience, we insert a few code excerpts and use Fig. 1 to illustrate the main concepts.

EOS *Net*. A term describing an EOS net (module EOS-NET) is the empty juxtaposition of three sub-terms of *sorts* Net, Map{String,Net} (renamed NeTypeS) and Map{Tran,Map{String,Bag{Tran}}} (renamed Syncmap). The resulting whole term is of *kind* [Sysnet] (because of possible inconsistencies among its components). The 2nd and 3rd sub-terms specify the types of net-tokens and the synchronization between system- and object-net transitions (for each object-net type), respectively. These sub-terms are equipped with ad-hoc operators and separately defined (modules NET-TYPES and SYNCHRO). A system-net transition may synchronize with multiple occurrences of object-net transitions.

The type of net-tokens a system-net place may hold is that associated with the place's label in NeTypeS sub-term. If there is no association, the system-net place may only hold "black-tokens". Instead, the three categories of events possible in a EOS meet the following conventions.

1. System-autonomous: system-net transitions not occurring in Syncmap.
2. Object autonomous: nested transitions for which the predicate
   op synchronized : Syncmap Tran -> Bool
   evaluates to false (this predicate checks that a given transition appears among the values -that are maps, in turn- of Syncmap sub-term).
3. Synchronisations: defined implicitly by exclusion.

A membership-axiom connotes well-formed EOS as terms of sort Sysnet (N:Net, Ty:NeTypeS, Sy:Syncmap are variables, the predicate coherent(Sy, Ty) checks that every nested transition occurring in Syncmap belongs to the corresponding net-type).

cmb N Ty Sy : Sysnet if welldef(N) and—then welldef(Ty) and—then
      not(repeatedKeys(Sy)) and—then coherent(Sy, Ty)

Using a uniform syntax (that of "enriched" PT nets) for the system-net and net-tokens is convenient in terms of description/algebraic manipulation and significantly enhances EOS expressivity. Furthermore, the adopted signature may be easily adapted to support an arbitrary nesting of nets.

EOS *System*. The EOS dynamics is mimed using a structured state representation, in which the basic generic types are reciprocally nested. A term of sort

Map{Place,Bag{Bag{Place}}} specifies an Eos marking as a map from system-net places to nested multisets of net-token places: a term of sort Bag{Place} indeed represents a marking of the net-token type associated to a certain system-net place, its multiplicity in the top multiset is the number of net-tokens in the system-net place with that marking. The nil ground term (representing the empty Bag{Place}) may also denote -without any ambiguity- anonymous tokens in untyped system-net places.

For example, the Eos marking in Fig. 1 is described by the term ("net1","net2" refer to the net-token types):

$$p(1,\text{``net1''}) |-> 1 . \text{nil} + 1 . (1 . p(1, \text{``a1''}) + 1 . p(2, \text{``b1''})) ; p(2,\text{``net1''}) |-> 1 .$$
$$1 . p(1, \text{``a1''}) ; p(3,\text{``net2''}) |-> 1 . (1 . p(1, \text{``a2''}) + 1 . p(2, \text{``b2''}))$$

A marked Eos is formally described by the empty juxtaposition of a Sysnet sub-term and a Map{Place,Bag{Bag{Place}}} sub-term (module EOSYS). Due to possible inconsistencies, the operator's arity is the kind [Eosystem]. As usual, we use a membership axiom to connote terms of sort Eosystem as those in which every system-net place is a key in the Eos marking sub-term. No check is done on net-token places, for the sake of efficiency and coherently with the fact that (in a mutable context) they may contain isolated places.

var S : Sysnet . var M : Map{Place,Bag{Bag{Place}}} .
cmb S M : Eosystem if not(repeatedKeys(M)) and—then places(net(S)) subset
    keySet(M).

Eos *Operational Semantics.* In accordance with the two-level structure of Eos, two firing rules are encoded as rewrite rules: One for system-net transitions (taking account of possible synchronizations), the other for autonomous, net-token transitions. As in any High-Level PN, a system-net transitions t may fire in different modes in a Eos marking m. An *instance* of t has the same algebraic representation as m, i.e., it is a Map{Place,Bag{Bag{Place}}} term whose map's keys are the t's post-set. In other words, an instance of t is a sub-multiset of m. Both Eos firing rules use the firing rule of PT systems. The system-net firing rule exploits two main operators (module EOSYS):

    op firingmap : Eosystem —> Map{Tran, Set{Map{Place,Bag{Bag{Place}}}}} .
    op firings : ImatrixT Map{Place, Bag{Bag{Place}}} Syncmap —> [Set{Map{
    Place, Bag{Bag{Place}}}}] .

firingmap computes the enabled firing instances for every system-net transition, taking account of synchronizations. It builds on a few auxiliary operators defined in generic modules BAG-SPLIT, MAP-PROD, in particular:

op split : Bag{X} Nat —> Set{Bag{X}}
op prod : Map{X,Set{Y}} —> [Set{Map{X,Y}}]

The former splits a bag into sub-bags of a given size, and the latter performs a kind of Cartesian product of maps having sets as values. In the event of synchronization, t's instances are filtered according to the enabling of synchronized nested transitions in the current marking.

The system module EOS-EMU formalizes the Eos operation semantics.

```
mod EOS-EMU is
  pr EOSYS .
  inc PT-EMU .
  var FM : Map{Tran, Set{Map{Place,Bag{Bag{Place}}}}} . *** whole firing map
  var TI : Entry{Tran, Set{Map{Place,Bag{Bag{Place}}}}} . *** transition instance
  var NeFS : NeSet{Map{Place,Bag{Bag{Place}}}} .
  var FS : Set{Map{Place,Bag{Bag{Place}}}} . *** output firing set
  vars I O M M' : Map{Place,Bag{Bag{Place}}} . *** firing instance/EOS marking
  vars N N' : Net . var T : Tran . var Ty : NeTypeS . var Sy : Syncmap .
  var Q : Imatrix . var S : String . vars J K : NzNat .
  vars B B' : Bag{Place} . var B2 : Bag{Bag{Place}} .
  rl [select] : I U NeFS => I . *** non-deterministic extraction of an instance
  crl [inst] : N Ty Sy M => N Ty Sy (M - I) + O if N' ; T |-> Q := N /\
      firingmap(N Ty Sy M)[T] => I /\ firings(T |-> Q, I, Sy) => O .
  crl [aut] : SN (p(J,S) |-> K . B + B2) => SN (p(J,S) |-> (K . B - 1 . B) + 1 . B' +
      B2) if N (S |-> (T |-> Q ; N') ; Ty) Sy := SN /\ not(synchronized(Sy, T)) /\
      (T |-> Q) B => (T |-> Q) B' .
endm
```

Rules inst and aut encode the firing of a system-net transition and of an autonomous nested transition, respectively. Rule inst relies in turn on select, which emulates the non-deterministic selection of an instance. We exploit the opportunity that conditional rewrite rules can have very general conditions involving matching equations, memberships and also *other rewrites*. Rule inst implements double non-determinism: for selecting an (enabled) instance of t, then for choosing one of the possible output markings generated by that instance. The rule uses the operators _+_, _-_ defined on Map{Place,Bag{Bag{Place}}} terms. In the event of synchronization, the operator firings embeds the changes to the markings of net-tokens. Rule aut exploits the synchronized predicate and the PT system firing rule encoded in module PT-EMU.

The firing of an instance of t may be non-deterministic, i.e., result in alternative multisets of net-tokens to distribute on t's post-set (Sect. 1). firings calculates this set for a system-net transition instance (the transition's incidence matrix and the synchronization map are the other arguments). It builds on:

```
op distribute : Bag{Place} Bag{Place} -> [Set{Map{Place,Bag{Bag{Place}}}}]
```

that distributes the (pre-calculated) cumulative marking obtained by an instance of t (1st arg) to t's post-set (2nd arg), assuming that the two arguments refer to system-net places of the same type. This operation is tricky and reduces to enumerating the partitions of a multiset. The intrinsic complexity of all these operations may be alleviated using the memo operator attribute.

As a concrete example of Maude formalization of Eos, we include the system module SIMPLE-EOS which specifies the Eos in Fig. 1, where we assume that only the system-net places $\{p_i\}$, $i : 1 \ldots 3$, are initially marked.

```
mod SIMPLE-EOS is
  inc EOS-EMU .
  ops net type1 type2 : -> Net .
  op netype : -> NeTypeS .
```

```
op m0 : −> Map{Place,Bag{Bag{Place}}} .
op eosnet : −> Sysnet .
op sync : −> Syncmap .
eq net = t(1,"sys") |−> [1 . p(1,"net1") + 1 . p(2,"net1")+ 1 . p(3,"net2"), 1 . p
    (4,"net1") + 1 . p(5,"net2")+ 1 . p(6,"net2"), nil] .
eq type1 = t(1, "") |−> [1 . p(1,"a1"), 1 . p(2,"b1"), nil] .
eq type2 = t(2,"") |−> [1 . p(1,"a2") + 1 . p(2,"b2"), 1 . p(3,"c2"), nil] .
eq netype = "net1" |−> type1 ; "net2" |−> type2 .
eq sync = t(1,"sys") |−> ("net1" |−> 1 . t(1,"") ; "net2" |−> 1 . t(2,"") ) .
eq eosnet = net netype sync .
eq m0 = p(1,"net1") |−> 1 . nil + 1 . (1 . p(1,"a1") + 1 . p(2,"b1")); p(2,"net1")
    |−> 1 . 1 . p(1,"a1") ; p(3,"net2") |−> 1 . (1 . p(1,"a2") + 1 . p(2,"b2")).
endm
```

We refer to the Eos with the term eosnet m0 using simple aliasing. By running the **reduce** inline command of the Maude interpreter

```
Maude> red firinginstances(eosnet m0, t(1, "sys"))
```

we get two enabled instances for the system-net transition t(1,"sys"), in accordance with the two net-tokens of type "net1" in place p(1,"net1") (Fig. 1).

The following command, instead, searches for reachable *final* (!) states.

```
Maude> search eosnet m0 =>! X:Eosystem .
```

The command has *four* matches which express the non-determinism of Eos transition firing: For each instance of t(1,"sys") there are indeed two possible output markings, as the ways to distribute the net-token "net2" on places p_5, p_6.

4   An Example: The Production Line

We consider a production plant with two production lines as an example. This scenario has been used as a case study for Rewritable PT Nets [4] in previous work. Here, we will model the scenario in terms of nets-within-nets.

We have raw material, two operations $t1$ and $t2$ working on pieces of this, and two *production lines* (i.e., robots), both being capable of performing $t1$ and $t2$. We assume that the two lines have different qualities for these operations, i.e., it is better to execute $t1$ in line 1 and $t2$ in line 2. This is the standard production plan. During the execution, one of the two lines may get faulty (a double failure has a negligible probability). The scenario is well suited for a Eos-model as we have two obvious levels: The production site and the production plans. The model is specified in the syntax of the RENEW tool [22].

The system level shown in Fig. 2 describes the two production lines, the execution life cycle of the production plan, and the dropout of lines. Place $p0$ in the system-net indicates normal operation. In this mode, transition $t0$ takes two tokens (i.e., the raw material) from place $p1$ and activates the normal production plan, i.e. it generates a net-token of type *plan* via the inscription *x:new plan*.

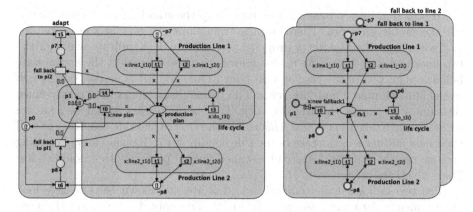

Fig. 2. The System Net modelling the Production Lines (color figure online)

The two production lines are shown as blocks. Their transitions are side-conditions to the place *production plan*. They synchronise via the channel inscriptions of the form *x:line1_t1()*. These channels have a counterpart in the net-tokens (e.g. the net *plan* – shown in Fig. 3 – has the corresponding inscription *line1_t1()*). Therefore, we have a synchronous firing of the transition in the production line and in the production plan.

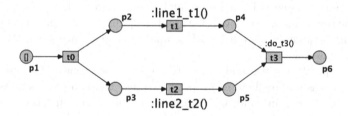

Fig. 3. The Object Net *plan* modelling the standard Production Plan

The net-tokens describe the different production plans: The production plan for normal operation is given as the net *plan* shown in Fig. 3, while we also have two fall back plans *fallback 1* and *2* for the case of dropouts. Specifically, the given production plan from Fig. 3 specifies a synchronisation via *line1_t1()* and via *line2_t2()*, so we will execute *t1* in line 1 and *t2* in line 2. When the production plan is finished we synchronise via *do_t3()* and delete the net-token, i.e. the plan. For simplicity, the scenario restarts via the transition *t4* which regenerates two raw materials again on place *p1*. This reset makes the main loop (the *life cycle* part) of the model live, allowing an infinite repetition of production.

Now, we will look at the adaption part and how the model preserves this liveness even in the case of dropouts. On the left part of Fig. 2 (the yellow nodes) we have the adaption part: Transitions *t5* and *t6* model the dropout of one production line. Whenever we have a drop the standard production plan is not executable anymore. Therefore, the transitions *fall back to production line 1/2* withdraws them. After a dropout, places $p7$ and $p8$ indicate which of the two lines is down. According to this information, we will select the appropriate fallback plan, i.e., in the case of a dropout in line one ($p7$ is marked) we switch to the fallback plan 2 and vice versa. The two fallback blocks have pretty much the same structure as the original block. The only difference is that we generate a different net-token via *x:new fallback1* in the case of the side condition $p8$ and via *x:new fallback2* in the case of the side condition $p7$. To avoid lots of crossing arcs we use the RENEW feature of so-called virtual places (with a double outer line), which are references to the original places.

The two fallback plans *fallback 1* and *2* are not shown here as they look almost identical to the basic plan in Fig. 2. The only difference are the used channels: The plan *fallback 1* works with the production line 1, which is expressed by using the channels *line1_t1()* and via *line1_t2()*. Analogously for *fallback 2*.

The Maude specification of the adaptable Production Line Eos is highly modular (at both system- and object-net levels). We got it by composing a few base sub-nets through the associative net-juxtaposition operator. We refer to https://github.com/lgcapra/rewpt/tree/main/new/EOS/PLINE-EOS. maude for the complete formalization.

4.1 Analysis of the Maude Representation

Below we report some evidence of formal verification with the only intent of showing the potential of our model. We also briefly discuss the model's scalability, by sketching a possible approach to face analysis complexity when the number of net-tokens doubles.

Since we specify adaptation in a way to preserve the liveness of the production process, we focus on this kind of property. We use the two basic analysis tools, namely the reduce command, which prints out the canonical form of a ground term, and the search state-space explorer (both available inline with the Maude's interpreter). A more advanced tool provided by the Maude system is an on-the-fly model-checker of LTL formulae. Using this tool we might for example verify that the Eos initial marking is a *home state*, i.e., it is reachable from any other reachable (Eos) marking.

As usual, we manage wordy terms using intuitive aliasing. For example, the net term describes the system-net component of the Eos, whereas the eosnet term includes the net-token description and synchronizations. Terms m0 and eosm0 denote the initial marking of the net (seen as a PT system) and of the Eos, respectively.

We can use the reduce command both to unfold these aliases and to perform a preliminary formal *validation*: If it assigns the final form *sort* Eosystem, it means that the initial term represents a well-defined Eos specification:

```
Maude> reduce in PLINE-EOS : eosnet eosm0 .
result Eosystem: (... unfolded term)
```

The next two searches operate on the PT-system we obtain from the system-net by replacing net-tokens with anonymous tokens. One of the advantages of Eos indeed is that we can separately consider and analyze the two net levels.

The first search verifies a state *invariant* which characterizes the production plan's life-cycle, in a configuration where place p_1 initially holds four tokens. The search has no matches (solutions) indeed, consistent with the fact that we are looking for a counter-example. It is worth noticing two things. An obvious implicit outcome of the command is that the PT system derived from the system-net is bounded because the state space turns out to be finite. The checked invariant is actually *structural*, i.e., it holds for any configuration with $2 * K$ tokens initially in place p_1 (K being the model's parameter). By the way, we cannot prove a parametric invariant using simple state-space exploration.

The second search, instead, checks the absence of final (dead) states. Again, the command has no matches.

```
Maude> search in pline-SYS : net m0 =>* X:System such that
    marking(X:System)[p(1,"")] + 2 * marking(X:System)[p(2,"
    plan")] + 2 * marking(X:System)[p(2,"fb1")] + 2 * marking
    (X:System)[p(2,"fb2")]  + 2 * marking(X:System)[p(6,"")]
    =/= 4 .

Maude> search in pline-SYS : net m0 =>! X:System .
```

Analogously, we can start searching from an Eosystem term specifying the whole Eos. For example, the following (unmatched) search is much more significant than the previous ones, because it formally verifies that the whole Eos (including nested nets) is deadlock-free (and implicitly, bounded). Both the state space and the execution time grow up.

```
Maude> search in pline-EOS : eosnet eosm0 =>! E:Eosystem .
```

Table 1 reports the performances of the last search, as the system's parameter varies on an Intel Core i7-6700 equipped with 32 GB of RAM.

Scalability. Model-checking techniques suffer from state space explosion, which may be alleviated by carrying out bounded searches (the search command has a number of options for that) or making some abstractions, as done in the first two searches (in which we anonymized net-tokens). For the complete analysis of an Eos, we need to struggle with scalability as state space may grow even worse than in ordinary PT systems. This happens, e.g., when considering non-safe Eos, in which system-net places may hold multiple occurrences of net-tokens.

A possible approach consists of canonizing net-tokens to capture symmetries in their behaviour. For that purpose, we have slightly adapted the canonization technique for rewritable PT systems defined in [5], fully integrated into Maude. According to this technique, a PT system is seen as a coloured graph and put into a "minimal" isomorphic form by incrementally permuting node indices. The canonization procedure first considers the marking (Bag{Place}) sub-term of a System term and then the Net sub-term. A simple adaptation working with

Table 1. Performance of `search` command as the model's parameter varies

K	# states	# rewrites	time (ms)
2	262	19 801	38
5	2 802	180 539	453
10	13 932	995 724	3 192
20	104 007	19 737 494	56 090
50	4 186 132	111 564 504	906 253

Table 2. Performance of `search` command – model with doubled plans

K	# states	time (ms)	# can. states	can. time (ms)
2	3856	640	411	40 457
5	46 856	9 567	4 989	530 560
10	678 768	100 439	69 517	6 240 063

nested markings allowed us to apply the same canonization technique (once integrated with firing rules) to `Eosystem` terms. Table 2 shows the effect of canonization on a variant of the running example (Sect. 4) in which there are two production plans and two fallback net-tokens. The system-net looks like Fig. 2 but for an extra synchronization transition. The significant gain in terms of space reduction is paid in execution times raising much more than proportionally. This is due to the fact that the canonization algorithm in [5], though general, works well for nets having an irregular structure (contrary to the net-tokens used here). Canonization overhead might be dramatically reduced

1. by exploiting modularity in model construction to automatically recognize groups of automorphic nodes by labels
2. by taking advantage of the fact that `Nets` in Eos are immutable.

Another important drawback of model-checking is that, in general, we cannot infer parametric outcomes, not depending on the initial state. Structural analysis, which considers the PT graph structure, is an effective alternative (complementary) to state-space inspection. We may use it to infer parametric outcomes, e.g., structural state-invariants (semiflows). Structural analysis of Eos looks promising because it may take advantage of the fact that the types of net-tokens flowing through the system-net's places are a finite set.

5   Summary and Outlook

In this paper we have defined a `Maude` representation of nets-within-nets, more concretely: Eos. We are going to give some insights into our project.

What are the Strengths of the Approach? The `Maude` formalization presented here is an extension of our previous work on the formalization of rewritable PT nets [4]. Therefore a lot of code could be reused, which is beneficial for the implementation's reliability and efficiency as well.

The formalisation preserves central design issues of EOS, namely, it supports a uniform view: The system-net and net-tokens have the same structure in `Maude`, which is essential as the same is true for EOS. This aspect is relevant when the architecture is extended to an unbounded nesting of net-tokens in a marking [16] or to HORNETS [13]. Standard `Maude` facilities for formal verification (e.g., state-space search and model-checking) may be used with no additional costs.

Additionally, the EOS firing rule is defined in a way that moving net-tokens around cannot be distinguished from moving ordinary tokens in PT nets. Therefore, we can easily define abstractions on the system's state (e.g. forgetting about the marking of net-tokens), which is essential when performing state space exploration efficiently.

Our approach naturally allows for model extensions. A natural one would be the usage of inhibitor arcs. While the extension from EOS to HORNETS is a rather large step, which involves several new constructs like net-algebra operators, the formalizing of HORNETS in `Maude` seems very simple. A basic net-algebra has been already defined, which allows us to introduce new types of net-tokens by composing existing ones. So, we may easily go one step forward, towards "rewritable" EOS, where the structure of both the system net and of net-tokens may change over time.

What was Complex? The most challenging aspect of the formalisation was the integration of the so-called *firing modes*. Roughly speaking the firing rule of a system-autonomous event in an EOS collects the tokens of all net-tokens coming from the system net places in the post-set. When the system net transition fires it distributes all these tokens on freshly generated net-tokens in the post-set. The firing rule allows any of these possible distributions – an aspect which requires some tricky handling of the binding in `Maude`.

Limitations. The current formalisation fulfils the requirement that it provides a link to the world of programming. But we have to admit that like in any algebraic specification, terms describing EOS may be wordy, structurally complex and (consequently) difficult to read and manage. An aliasing mechanism (used in a naive way) might greatly help a modeller. Also, syntactic sugar would sweeten the approach. Of course, an automated translation from a high-level (graphical) description of EOS to the corresponding `Maude` module would be highly desirable.

Ongoing Work. In this paper, we were mainly concerned with the `Maude` encoding of EOS. Our main motivation for this is to obtain a representation closer to the usual programming language world. But our aim is also to benefit from the advantages of a formal specification, i.e. the possibility to apply analysis techniques more easily. In the case of `Maude` the first idea is to apply state space-related techniques, like LTL model checking. We also like to integrate structural PN techniques for EOS [21].

For the analysis of EOS, we need to struggle with scalability issues as the state space of EOS is growing even worse than that of PT nets. Possible approaches to face scalability are the canonization of net-tokens (currently implemented in a non-optimized way), and the use of abstractions on markings to obtain condensed state spaces. The latter can be expressed quite easily in `Maude` by adding additional equations on markings. The former might be significantly improved and extended to the system-net as well.

References

1. Bouhoula, A., Jouannaud, J.P., Meseguer, J.: Specification and proof in membership equational logic. Theoret. Comput. Sci. **236**(1), 35–132 (2000). https://doi.org/10.1016/S0304-3975(99)00206-6
2. Bruni, R., Corradini, A., Gadducci, F., Lluch Lafuente, A., Vandin, A.: Modelling and analyzing adaptive self-assembly strategies with Maude. Sci. Comput. Program. **99**, 75–94 (2015). Selected Papers from the Ninth International Workshop on Rewriting Logic and its Applications (WRLA 2012)
3. Bruni, R., Meseguer, J.: Generalized rewrite theories. In: Baeten, J.C.M., Lenstra, J.K., Parrow, J., Woeginger, G.J. (eds.) Automata, Languages and Programming. pp. 252–266. Springer, Berlin (2003). https://doi.org/10.1007/3-540-45061-0_22
4. Capra, L.: A Maude implementation of rewritable Petri nets: a feasible model for dynamically reconfigurable systems. In: Gleirscher, M., Pol, J.v.d., Woodcock, J. (eds.) Proceedings of the First Workshop on Applicable Formal Methods, 2021. Electronic Proceedings in Theoretical Computer Science, vol. 349, pp. 31–49. Open Publishing Association (2021). https://doi.org/10.4204/EPTCS.349.3
5. Capra, L.: Canonization of reconfigurable pt nets in Maude. In: Lin, A.W., Zetzsche, G., Potapov, I. (eds.) Reachability Problems. pp. 160–177. Springer, Cham (2022). https://doi.org/10.1007/978-3-031-19135-0_11
6. Capra, L.: Rewriting logic and Petri nets: a natural model for reconfigurable distributed systems. In: Bapi, R., Kulkarni, S., Mohalik, S., Peri, S. (eds.) Distributed Computing and Intelligent Technology, pp. 140–156. Springer, Cham (2022). https://doi.org/10.1007/978-3-030-94876-4_9
7. Capra, L., Cazzola, W.: A Petri-net based reflective framework for the evolution of dynamic systems. Electr. Notes Theoret. Comput. Sci. **159**, 41–59 (2006). https://doi.org/10.1016/j.entcs.2005.12.061. In: Proceedings of the First IPM International Workshop on Foundations of Software Engineering (FSEN 2005)
8. Capra, L., Cazzola, W.: Self-evolving Petri nets. JUCS - J. Univ. Comput. Sci. **13**, 2002–2034 (2007). https://doi.org/10.3217/jucs-013-13-2002
9. Clavel, M., et al.: All About Maude - a High-Performance Logical Framework: How to Specify, Program, and Verify Systems in Rewriting Logic. LNCS, Springer, CHam (2007). https://doi.org/10.1007/978-3-540-71999-1
10. Hachicha, M., Halima, R.B., Kacem, A.H.: Formal verification approaches of self-adaptive systems: a survey. Procedia Comput. Sci. **159**, 1853–1862 (2019). https://doi.org/10.1016/j.procs.2019.09.357
11. Iglesia, D.G.D.L., Weyns, D.: MAPE-K formal templates to rigorously design behaviors for self-adaptive systems. ACM Trans. Auton. Adapt. Syst. **10**(3) (2015). https://doi.org/10.1145/2724719

12. Köhler, M., Rölke, H.: Properties of object petri nets. In: Cortadella, J., Reisig, W. (eds.) ICATPN 2004. LNCS, vol. 3099, pp. 278–297. Springer, Heidelberg (2004). https://doi.org/10.1007/978-3-540-27793-4_16

13. Köhler-Bußmeier, M.: Hornets: nets within nets combined with net algebra. In: Franceschinis, G., Wolf, K. (eds.) PETRI NETS 2009. LNCS, vol. 5606, pp. 243–262. Springer, Heidelberg (2009). https://doi.org/10.1007/978-3-642-02424-5_15

14. Köhler-Bußmeier, M.: On the complexity of the reachability problem for safe, elementary Hornets. Fundamenta Informaticae **129**, 101–116 (2014), dedicated to the Memory of Professor Manfred Kudlek

15. Köhler-Bußmeier, M.: A survey on decidability results for elementary object systems. Fund. Inform. **130**(1), 99–123 (2014)

16. Köhler-Bußmeier, M., Heitmann, F.: On the expressiveness of communication channels for object nets. Fund. Inform. **93**(1–3), 205–219 (2009)

17. Köhler-Bußmeier, M., Heitmann, F.: Safeness for object nets. Fund. Inform. **101**(1–2), 29–43 (2010)

18. Köhler-Bußmeier, M., Heitmann, F.: Liveness of safe object nets. Fund. Inform. **112**(1), 73–87 (2011)

19. Köhler-Bußmeier, M., Heitmann, F.: Complexity results for elementary hornets. In: Colom, J.-M., Desel, J. (eds.) PETRI NETS 2013. LNCS, vol. 7927, pp. 150–169. Springer, Heidelberg (2013). https://doi.org/10.1007/978-3-642-38697-8_9

20. Köhler-Bußmeier, M., Heitmann, F.: An upper bound for the reachability problem of safe, elementary hornets. Fund. Inform. **143**, 89–100 (2016)

21. Köhler-Bußmeier, M., Moldt, D.: Analysis of mobile agents using invariants of object nets. Electronic Communications of the EASST: Special Issue on Formal Modeling of Adaptive and Mobile Processes 12p (2009)

22. Kummer, Q., et al.: An extensible editor and simulation engine for petri nets: RENEW. In: Cortadella, J., Reisig, W. (eds.) ICATPN 2004. LNCS, vol. 3099, pp. 484–493. Springer, Heidelberg (2004). https://doi.org/10.1007/978-3-540-27793-4_29

23. Padberg, J., Schulz, A.: Model checking reconfigurable petri nets with maude. In: Echahed, R., Minas, M. (eds.) ICGT 2016. LNCS, vol. 9761, pp. 54–70. Springer, Cham (2016). https://doi.org/10.1007/978-3-319-40530-8_4

24. Reisig, W.: Petri nets and algebraic specifications. Theoret. Comput. Sci. **80**, 1–34 (1991)

25. Stehr, M.O., Meseguer, J., Ölveczky, P.C.: Rewriting Logic as a Unifying Framework for Petri Nets, pp. 250–303. Springer-Verlag, Berlin, Heidelberg (2001). https://doi.org/10.1007/3-540-45541-8_9

26. Valk, R.: Object Petri nets: Using the nets-within-nets paradigm. In: Desel, J., Reisig, W., Rozenberg, G. (eds.) Advanced Course on Petri Nets 2003. LNCS, vol. 3098, pp. 819–848. Springer,-Verlag (2003). https://doi.org/10.1007/b98282

27. Weyns, D., Iftikhar, M.U., de la Iglesia, D.G., Ahmad, T.: A survey of formal methods in self-adaptive systems. In: Proceedings of the Fifth International C* Conference on Computer Science and Software Engineering. pp. 67–79. C3S2E 2012, Association for Computing Machinery, New York, NY, USA (2012). DOIurl10.1145/2347583.2347592

28. Weyns, D., Iftikhar, U.M.: Activforms: a formally-founded model-based approach to engineer self-adaptive systems. ACM Trans. Softw. Eng. Methodol. (2022). https://doi.org/10.1145/3522585

3rd Workshop on Systems, Architectures, and Solutions for Industry 4.0 (SASI4)

Developing an AI-Enabled IIoT Platform - Lessons Learned from Early Use Case Validation

Holger Eichelberger[1]([✉]), Gregory Palmer[2], Svenja Reimer[3], Tat Trong Vu[2],
Hieu Do[2], Sofiane Laridi[2], Alexander Weber[1], Claudia Niederée[2],
and Thomas Hildebrandt[4]

[1] Software Systems Engineering, University of Hildesheim, Universitätsplatz 1,
31141 Hildesheim, Germany
eichelberger@sse.uni-hildesheim.de
[2] L3S, University of Hannover, Appelstraße 9a, 30617 Hannover, Germany
[3] IFW, University of Hannover, An der Universität 2, 30832 Garbsen, Germany
[4] PHOENIX CONTACT Deutschland GmbH, Flachsmarktstraße 8, 32825 Blomberg,
Germany

Abstract. For a broader adoption of AI in industrial production, adequate infrastructure capabilities and ecosystems are crucial. This includes easing the integration of AI with industrial devices, support for distributed deployment, monitoring, and consistent system configuration. IIoT platforms can play a major role here by providing a unified layer for the heterogeneous Industry 4.0/IIoT context.

However, existing IIoT platforms still lack required capabilities to flexibly integrate reusable AI services and relevant standards such as Asset Administration Shells or OPC UA in an open, ecosystem-based manner. This is exactly what our *next level Intelligent Industrial Production Ecosphere* (IIP-Ecosphere) platform addresses, employing a highly configurable low-code based approach.

In this paper, we introduce the design of this platform and discuss an early evaluation in terms of a demonstrator for AI-enabled visual quality inspection. This is complemented by insights and lessons learned during this early evaluation activity.

Keywords: IIoT · Industry 4.0 · Platform · Artificial Intelligence · Asset Administration Shells

1 Introduction

The field of artificial intelligence (AI) has made significant progress in recent years, in particular thanks to leveraging advances in the training of deep neural networks [20]. In numerous areas AI performance is comparable to human performance, e. g., for object detection and image classification tasks [26,33]. As a

Supported by the German Ministry of Economics and Climate Action (BMWK) under grant numbers 01MK20006A and 01MK20006D.

T. Batista et al. (Eds.): ECSA 2022, LNCS 13928, pp. 265–283, 2023.
https://doi.org/10.1007/978-3-031-36889-9_19

result AI-based methods are increasingly being applied in a large variety of application domains for supporting automated decision processes [35]. An economically highly relevant application domain for AI is industrial production [1,29]. Here AI-based methods can increase effectiveness, improve quality and reduce costs as well as energy consumption [28]. The most prominent example is AI-based condition monitoring, which intelligently reduces maintenance costs and down times [6]. Further promising application areas include AI-based quality control [21,27], job-shop scheduling [8,38] and smart assembly systems [22].

A number of tools and libraries exist for easing the development and training of AI models – further augmented by the availability of powerful pre-trained models [13]. However, other steps in the data science process for intelligent production are less well supported. This includes, for example, data acquisition (often not supported by the existing, long-lived and expensive legacy production systems) and the deployment of AI methods within close proximity of the target machines, i. e., on industrial edge devices.

Operating an AI solution in an industrial context requires many supporting capabilities, such as monitoring, resource management, data storage, integration with production and business processes, and configuration [34]. Although several Industrial Internet of Things (IIoT) platforms (also known as Industry 4.0 platforms) do exist, e.g., Siemens MindSphere[1], PTC ThingWorkx[2] or AWS IoT (Core)[3], they usually fall short in some of the aforementioned aspects. Furthermore, they lack in flexibility, openness, freedom of installation (cloud vs. on-premise) or timely support for relevant standards [32], which are crucial for the demand-driven development and the operation of evolving, long-lived production systems. Researching and developing concepts for a flexible, open, standard-enabled and yet vendor-neutral IIoT platform is one of the core aims of the IIP-Ecosphere project (next level Intelligent Industrial Production ecosphere)[4]. Our IIP-Ecosphere platform aims for a low-code approach combining model-based configuration, code-generation techniques with relevant industrial standards, e.g., OPC UA (Companion Specs) or the currently trending Asset Administration Shells (AAS) [17,30]. An AAS describes assets, e.g., products or tools, in a machine-readable and vendor-independent manner, thus, smoothing information exchange and enabling innovative cross-company processes.

Our platform is the first with a wide exploitation of AAS ranging from device interfaces over IIoT applications running on the platform to the platform as a whole. Besides the wide use of AAS, our platform provides tool-enabled configuration support on all levels. Thus, the platform enables easy integration of heterogeneous devices (via AAS) and flexible adaptation of platform instances and AI-based applications to diverse and changing customer-specific requirements and settings (via customization).

---

[1] https://siemens.mindsphere.io/de.
[2] https://www.ptc.com/de/products/thingworx.
[3] https://aws.amazon.com/de/iot-core/.
[4] https://www.iip-ecosphere.de/.

In this paper, we introduce the IIP-Ecosphere platform and an early validation with a use case on AI-enabled visual quality inspection. We presented our use case at the *Hannover Messe 2022*, one of the world's largest trade fairs exhibiting innovative technological developments in industry. This paper also identifies challenges imposed by such an application and lessons learned for the engineering of intelligent IIoT platforms and the development of AI-based IIoT applications. Our main contributions can be summarized as follows:

- a flexible, extensible and open AI-enabled IIoT platform heavily relying on low-code and AAS (Sect. 3).
- the validation of the platform with a first industrial AI-enabled use case on visual quality inspection of lot 1 personalized production (Sects. 4 and 5)
- important lessons learned for IIoT platform and application developers, developers of IIoT standards, and providers of AI technologies on IIoT container virtualization, the use of AI in production context, the use of AAS and platform development using low-code approaches (Sect. 6).

2   Related Work

In [32], we analyzed 21 industrial IIoT platforms. The platforms of highest industrial relevance were selected for this analysis from the large and evolving set of existing IIoT platforms - some sources mention more than 450 different software platforms and [19] found more than 1200 vendors. We focused on 16 topics that are relevant for AI application in production, including AI capabilities, edge support, configurability, cloud vs. on-premise installation, use of standards including AAS integration. While most of the platforms provide some AI capabilities, the support is currently rather diverse, ranging from advanced service integrations to plain Python AI frameworks. Except for one platform, which allows on-premise installation, all other reviewed platforms are cloud-based. Most of the analyzed platforms do not allow a deployment of own (AI) services on edge devices and recent standards such as OPC UA are rarely supported or, for AAS, not supported at all. As surveyed in [25] with 75 companies, only 50% utilize cloud, while only 30% operate a platform. For the platform users, complexity, unclear license and cost models limit or even prevent the adoption of an IIoT platform. On the scientific side, an ongoing SLR reveals that researched platforms usually focus on a narrow inclusion of standards (MQTT, OPC UA), very limited configuration approaches, or non-industrial edge devices such as Raspberry PI. Notable platform concepts are discussed for protocols in [31], edge usage [7,31], on-premise option, [12,24,31], configurability [12,24] or AI capabilities [7,12,31].

In contrast, we present an AI-enabled IIoT platform that addresses identified gaps and industry-relevant capabilities. In particular, our platform focuses on openness, standard support, interoperability, configurability, industrial edge devices and production-relevant AI capabilities. Furthermore, our platform is to our knowledge the first to rely on a deep integration of AAS, e.g., to represent (runtime) component information or to steer platform operations.

With respect to the AI-services, we evaluate our platform using SOTA convolutional neural networks (CNNs), which have enabled a significant number of recent breakthroughs in the fields of computer vision and image processing [15]. CNNs' strength is their ability to automatically learn feature representations from raw image data [3]. With ever more advanced architectures emerging, CNNs are increasingly being utilized within an Industry 4.0 context – from end-of-the-line visual inspection tasks [27] to predictive maintenance and fault detection [36]. In addition, while our current use case focuses on visual inspection, approaches where CNNs process encoded time-series data as images are increasingly being used in intelligent manufacturing [14,18,37].

3   IIoT Platform

The IIP-Ecosphere platform is a *virtual platform*, which can easily be added to existing production environments and augments existing functionality with AI capabilities, particularly through standardized protocols. During an intensive and interactive requirements collection for the platform [10], our industrial stakeholders expressed in particular three core demands, namely:

1. the use of AAS to facilitate interoperability between products, processes and platforms. While the standardization of formats for AAS is still in progress, the aim here is to explore the capabilities and limitations of AAS, while also considering more advanced uses, e.g., for software components. This early validation is also used to feed back requirements into the development of the AAS standard;
2. the vendor-independent deployment of AI and data processing components within close proximity of the machines. This involves exploiting heterogeneous industrial edge devices in an open manner. In our case, this is smoothly integrated with the overall AAS approach of the platform by equipping the edge devices with a (vendor-provided or own) AAS providing deployment control operations;
3. a loose integration of AI tools, in particular for the development of an AI approach and for AI training. In other words, the platform shall support a data scientist in the development of the solution while not limiting the freedom of choice regarding AI and data science tools.

In a nutshell, our platform interconnects distributed and diverse entities, usually equipped with individual processing capabilities and software installation, thus, forming a system-of-systems. The connected entities have different roles in the system, including: *data sources* (such as datastreams captured by sensors); *data processing services* (such as data transformers or AI algorithms); and *data sinks* (such as machines to be controlled, databases or dashboards). To ease the development of stream-based IIoT applications consisting of connected entities, the platform provides basic capabilities such as data transport, distributed service deployment, runtime monitoring, but also an open and extensible set of services, ranging from platform-supplied to user-defined or application-specific services. To unburden application developers from error-prone and partially complex integration tasks, we rely on a model-based approach that allows for the generation of integration glue code, deployable artifacts or (application-specific) containers representing deployment units for heterogeneous target devices.

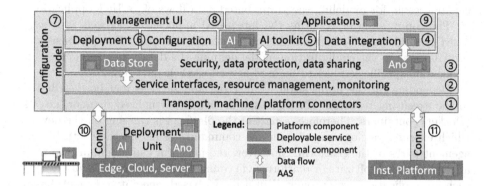

Fig. 1. Platform component overview.

Based on more than 150 top-level requirements collected in an intensive interactive process with industry partners [10], we designed a layered, service-oriented architecture for our platform. As we have to deal with a wide variety of service realizations including Java classes, Python scripts and even binary executables, we employ a rather open notion of the term *service*[5].

Figure 1 illustrates the main building blocks: The lowest layer ① focuses on the communication, i.e., the data *transport* among components (such as MQTT or AMQP), but also with machines or other platforms through pluggable *connectors* (e.g., OPC UA, MQTT, AAS).

The *services layer* ② defines the service management interfaces and realizes mechanisms for resource management and monitoring. Moreover, this component contains language-specific execution environments to ease the realization, integration and execution of individual services, e.g., for Java or Python.

The extensible *security services layer* ③ implements additional services provided by the platform, which enable security and data processing to be improved. Here, one example service is a generic anonymization and pseudonymization service that can safeguard the processing of data about persons.

The components in the next layer realizes an advanced set of extensible, reusable services. For the data processing, these are a semantic *data integration* ④ of multiple data sources as well as production-specific AI methods in terms of an *AI toolkit* ⑤. Besides an integration of open source components such as Python packages, the platform can also integrate commercial components, e.g., the RapidMiner Real Time Scoring Agent (RTSA)[6], a generic execution environment for AI workflows.

---

[5] In more details, for us a service is a function with defined input- and output data/management interfaces, which can process data either in synchronous or asynchronous fashion, and can optionally be distributable.

[6] https://docs.rapidminer.com/9.4/scoring-agent/deploy-rts/.

In the same layer, two core components of the platform are located, the mechanisms for consistent configuration and control of the heterogeneous service deployment to execution resources ⑥. The configuration component is based on a cross-cutting configuration model ⑦, which integrates classical software product line concepts [23] like optionalities, alternatives and constraints with topological capabilities [9] for modeling the graph-based data flows of an IIoT application.

The top-most layer contains the integrated applications as well as a *web-based user interface* ⑧ for managing the platform. An *application* ⑨ consists of contributions to the configuration model defining the data types and generic or application-specific services to be used as well as their data flows.

Depending on the application, connectors and services can be distributed to the executing resources ⑩, e.g., edge devices in virtualized manner, i.e., as (Docker) containers. Therefore, a part of the platform is running on the device, which executes deployment and service commands issued by the central management parts of the platform. Moreover, the platform can communicate with already installed software or platforms via connectors ⑪. Many tasks of creating such an application are automated in a model-based, generative fashion based on the configuration model. Examples are the generation of interfaces and basic implementations of application-specific services, the adaptation of generic services to application-specific data formats by glue code, the generation of machine connectors based on low-code specifications in the configuration model, or integration and packaging of an IIoT application.

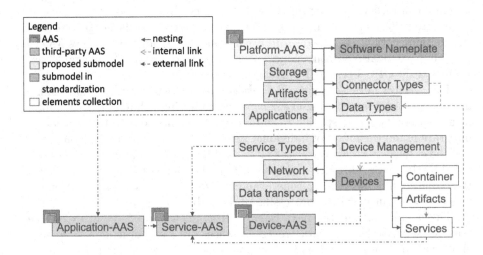

Fig. 2. Overview of the IIP-Ecosphere platform AAS.

As mentioned above, the platform supports actual standards in the IIoT domain and, in particular, the currently evolving AAS. Based on a standardized description format, an asset administration shell is composed from an identifier and a set of submodels, each describing different aspects of the respective asset. In turn, a submodel consists of typed properties, operations, semantic identifiers and (nested) collections of these elements. Typically, AAS are used for the digital representation of devices and products enabling an easy, cross-organizational exchange of relevant asset information[7]. Obviously, consistent, cross-organizational identification of assets plays a crucial role here. This is where further AAS infrastructure components such as AAS registries come into play. In our platform, we follow a more far-reaching approach: We utilize AAS to describe software components including their API and their runtime properties, the platform as a whole and links to external AAS, e.g., for employed devices (see Fig. 2 for an overview). From the use of a uniform standard format across different types of "assets" within the platform we expect a better integration of software- and hardware components as well as a higher degree of interoperability among platforms and their ecosystems, e.g., for communication and service exchange.

In more detail, as indicated in Fig. 2, we represent (third-party) components such as services, applications or devices/machines as an AAS, e.g., through a (pragmatic use of) the standardized nameplate for industrial devices [2]. Note, that the representation of software components and specific aspects of an IIoT platform requires dedicated submodel formats (see "proposed submodels" in Fig. 2), which could be standardized in future.

The platform also maintains an encompassing AAS for itself. This consists of 11 submodels, which references the AAS of platform-supplied and third-party components and provides additional elements, e.g., runtime monitoring properties [4] or management operations, that we use for distributed control, e.g., to deploy containers or to start applications and services.

For the development of the open source IIP-Ecosphere platform[8], we build upon and integrate at the time of writing 23 open source components, in particular from the Eclipse IoT ecosystem such as BaSyx[9] for the realization of AAS. All integrated components (including BaSyx) are treated as optionalities or alternatives [23] and utilized in the platform only through platform interfaces and code adapting the component to the respective interface. On the one hand, this facilitates openness and systematic variability, e.g., of the platform transport protocol. On the other hand, an interface-based integration eases coping with unexpected external changes of components, as in most situations only the implementation of the interface must be adjusted accordingly.

4   Demonstrator Use-Case Description

For a first validation of our platform we have selected a use case consisting of a simple AI-based quality inspection for individualized products. The use case

---

[7] This is also what they are originally designed for. In this context, a typical submodel is the "product nameplate", which describes the product with optional figure, the classification of the product, the vendor including address, contact information, etc.

[8] https://github.com/iip-ecosphere.

[9] https://www.eclipse.org/basyx/.

utilizes industrial components such as a cobot and an industrial edge device for realistic validation results. Therefore, despite being of small scale, the use case is tailored to investigate the following questions:

Q1 What are the practical challenges when bringing AI-based quality inspection close to the machines, i.e., onto an edge device? And which of the platform features are especially useful for this task?
Q2 How can AAS be exploited in support of quality inspection in lot-size-one (individualized) production settings?
Q3 How well does the platform support integrating IIoT technologies (AI, cobot, edge, etc.) and developing the respective IIoT application?
Q4 What are the typical interdisciplinary issues and needs that emerge when developing AI-based IIoT applications? Often, interdisciplinarity is seen as a special challenge when realizing, e.g., data analysis [16] or cyber-physical systems [11].

As products we are using small aluminum cars, which are produced for this purpose. The cars vary w. r. t. product properties such as wheel color or engravings. Accompanying production, AAS capturing those properties are generated and made available to the platform via an AAS registry. Quality inspection is performed based on three position images taken of the car models using a 5 axis cobot arm with a mounted camera. AI models trained for this purpose are used for quality control and deployed onto the edge for this purpose. Based on the AI results, the quality is measured along two axis: a) conformance with production specification (as given by the product's AAS) and b) quality of production (existence of scratches).

5   Demonstrator Realization

The demonstrator use case has been successfully implemented. In the following, we provide insights into the employed hardware, the interaction of the components/services, the role of our platform and describe the AI service.

The IIoT hardware of the demonstrator consists of a Universal Robots UR5e cobot[10] equipped with a Robotiq wrist cam[11] as well as a Phoenix Contact AXC F 3152, a combined Programmable Logic Controller (PLC) and edge device[12] with an Intel Atom processor, 2 GB RAM, and 32 GB SD-based hard drive. In addition, a usual PC plays the role of the central IT running our platform and a tablet is used to present the application user interface.

The software side consists of four main components, the `Cam source` as image input, the `Python AI`, the `Action Decider` controlling the overall process and the `App AAS` as data sink. Furthermore, two connectors, the `OPC UA connector` and the `AAS connector` integrate the hardware as well as the external car AAS.

---

[10] https://www.universal-robots.com/de/produkte/ur5-roboter/.
[11] https://www.universal-robots.com/plus/products/robotiq/robotiq-wrist-camera/.
[12] https://www.phoenixcontact.com/de-de/produkte/steuerung-axc-f-3152-1069208.

As illustrated in Fig. 3, those components together form the demonstrator application[13]. We briefly describe the design of the components and their interactions in terms of a normal execution sequence[14].

The quality inspection process is initiated by pressing a physical button connected to the AXC ①, which reflects the button status on its OPC UA server. A customized OPC UA connector provided by our platform observes the change and informs the `Action Decider`. Alternatively, the user can press a UI button on the tablet. The UI is based on an application AAS provided by the `App AAS` service, which provides processing results as well as operations, such as starting the inspection process.

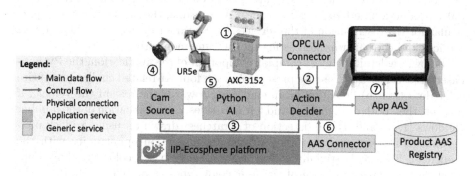

Fig. 3. Demonstrator components and data flows.

The `Action Decider` ② initiates a movement of the robot arm to one of the three visual scanning positions (QR position, left or right car side) and requests the `Cam Source` ③ to take a picture from the wrist cam ④. In the QR position, the `Cam Source` performs a QR-code detection and augments the input data by the QR payload. Pictures are subsequently taken for the left and right car side. Each picture is streamed to the `Python AI`, which aims to detect the product properties ⑤. The AI results including the actual picture form the input to the `Action Decider`. Based on the QR payload, the `Action Decider` obtains the product AAS ⑥ and compares the information detected by the AI and the configured information.

The comparison results as well as trace information on all intermediary steps are handed over to the `App AAS` ⑦, which is presented by the Angular-based application UI on the tablet. The UI application is entirely based on AAS. It enables following the entire quality inspection process, visually browsing backward and forward on demand. Furthermore, is confronts in an illustrative way the picture of the product according to the specification with a picture of the

---

[13] The source code of the demonstrator will be published with the platform release (See Footnote 8).

[14] A video showing our setup is available at: https://youtu.be/36Xtw1L2XkQ.

product as it is seen by the AI. This has proven to be very useful for the demonstration of the use case on the trade fair. Moreover, it allows the inspection of all underlying services running on the platform through their individual AAS.

With respect to the platform, the application as depicted in Fig. 3 is modeled as data flow in the platform configuration model. The application instantiation process created application-specific interfaces of the three application-specific services (Cam Source, Python AI, Action Decider), customized generic connectors and services (OPC UA connector, AAS connector and App AAS) for their use in the application, generated glue code for the distributed stream-based service execution and performed the Maven-based integration and packaging of the application. In summary, the application (except for the application UI) consists of about 8.2 KLOC, whereby 51% are generated and 49% are manually written (30% production and 19% testing code). At runtime, the platform cares in particular for the distribution of the services to the target devices, the execution of services and container as well as for the runtime monitoring.

Below, we detail the most complex component of the application, the Python-based AI service. Our use-case presents us with four AI-related challenges: a) tire color detection; b) detection of an engraving towards the rear of the vehicle, if present, then both on right rear and left rear sides; c) classification of the number windows [1, 3]; and d) the detection of scratches (drawn on using a black non-permanent marker pen, also allowing for an interaction opportunity with the audience). Task a) is trivially solved using a range based color threshold approach, where ranges for each of the four color types (red, green, yellow, black) are found upon converting our training images into HSV color-space. For the remaining tasks we utilized deep CNNs. We find that each problem benefits from a custom preprocessing step, prior to feeding the image into the model. Furthermore, given the limited capacity of the edge device, we train a distinct model for each task that can be loaded when required, instead of training one big model for all three tasks. Given the small size of our dataset (consisting of 200 images), common dataset augmentation techniques (e. g., random flipping, rotation and zooming in/out) are utilized to avoid overfitting our models. We describe each model and respective preprocessing steps in detail below. Hyperparameters that are consistent across our models include: an Adam optimizer; a learning rate of 1e−4; $\beta_1 = 0.9$; $\beta_2 = 0.999$; $\epsilon = 1e−07$; 1000 training epochs; a batch size of 20; Relu activation layers; and a training/test ratio of 9:1. All models reach ∼99% and ∼95% accuracy on the training and testing datasets respectively.

Scratches Detection: For preprocessing we first apply the same color range based thresholding approach to eliminate colors within the range of the car's color (see Fig. 4). The CNN for this task consists of separable convolutional layers [15], representing a light weight alternative to normal convolutional layers without significantly impacting performance. Separable convolutional layers are therefore well suited for edge devices with limited capacity w. r. t. memory. The model is trained using a binary cross entropy loss function (sigmoid).

Engraving Detection: For this task we used OpenCV's edge detection to find a mask that can highlight the engraving (see Fig. 5 for examples). The rest of the process is the same as for the scratch detection outlined above.

Windows Detection: This task is more challenging than the others, as windows can be confused with "scratches" (see Fig. 6). To overcome this challenge we utilize a model that receives two inputs: 1) a mask that highlights both the car windows and the scratches; and 2) the mask from the first task (scratches detection). Feeding in both masks allows the model to learn to recognise anomalies. A categorical cross entropy loss function (softmax) is used for training the model, since we have three different window configurations.

Fig. 4. Result of applying our preprocessing prior to scratch detection.

Fig. 5. Two examples of before/after preprocessing for detecting the engraving.

(a) Original Image   (b) Mask 1   (c) Mask 2

Fig. 6. Window detection task example, where a window is drawn onto the vehicle. Both mask from Sub-Figs. 6b and 6c are fed into the model, the first highlighting both windows and scratches, while Mask 2 emphasises the scratch.

To gain first insights into the performance of executing the AI on the employed hardware, we pragmatically measure the inference time per image in the target setup. Per image, the `Python AI` consumes 0.4–0.5 s on the PC and 3–5 s on the edge device. A performance drop is not surprising here, as the edge is a resource-constrained device, which dedicates parts of its CPU and memory to hard realtime processes. Moreover, the hard drive is SD-based, which may limit file transfer, e.g., when reading AI models. However, the measurements of both devices exceed by far the required production machine pace of 8 ms [10]. Thus, further optimizations are needed, e.g., by employing a GPU or TPU co-processor (a TPU module is available for the AXC F 3152) or programming level optimizations, e.g., to avoid re-loading models in a streaming setup.

6   Lessons Learned

We implemented our use case and successfully demonstrated it and the under-lying platform at Hannover Messe 2022 – a large international industrial trade fair. In addition, in realizing the use case we collected a number of experiences and encountered a diverse set of unexpected issues.

In this section, we discuss the most relevant experiences and issues as lessons learned. The lessons learned address different target audiences: IIoT Platform Developers (TA1), Developers of AI-based IIoT Applications (TA2), Developers of standards and infrastructure for IIoT (TA3), and providers of AI Technologies (TA4) as well as researchers in the respective areas. For every lesson learned we mark the main target audience(s), although the lessons learned might also be relevant for other groups. The lessons LL1 to LL7 have been compiled in a way to capture reusable knowledge for the respective target audiences beyond IIP-Ecosphere. In more detail, we consider the reusable knowledge captured in LL2, LL3, LL5 and LL7 of special value for the respective target audiences.

Within the lessons, we revisit also the questions Q1–Q4 from Sect. 4.

LL1 - IIoT Integration [TA2, TA3]: Incorporating the cobot, the edge, the camera as well as the IT components and the AI models into an IIoT application (and make them interact "smoothly") was well supported by the platform. This is especially due to integrated protocols, generated connectors as well as data flows (Q3). However, it also proved to be much more challenging than expected. A major reason for this is that several technological borders have to be bridged, where each of those technologies comes with their own paradigms, languages, and (only partially documented) limitations. We especially experienced this, when incorporating the cobot (edge - cobot interaction) and the camera (edge - camera interaction).

For the *edge-cobot communication*, several integration paths have been explored. This included ProfiNet, direct wiring and a software solution based on the robot operating system ROS[15]. Although ProfiNet is a standardized net-work protocol and the Phoenix Contact PLCnext programming environment

---

[15] https://www.ros.org/.

provides a function brick for the integration of UR cobots, the establishment of a reliable bi-directional communication between edge and cobot was hindered by a lack of sufficient documentation. Alternatively, direct wiring of digital in- and outputs between edge and cobot is a feasible approach, but limited in flexi- bility due to the number of supported wires and difficult in realization, as here low-level signal details must be considered for the programming. In the end a ROS-based solution was selected due to its easier integration with the platform.

From the *integration of the camera with the edge* we learned that the capacity of the involved devices might depend upon the way they are connected - and not all devices support all types of connections. For the case of the camera, for example, some functionalities such as explicitly controlling the focal length, lighting, or image preprocessing - although supported when connected via USB - are not accessible via other communication paths. Since the employed edge does not support USB, it had to be connected indirectly via a Web Server and networking limiting the available functionalities.

In summary, we learned that integrating IIoT devices requires cross-domain expertise (Q4), e.g., in our case from the automation domain, the robot manu- facturer and the application/software side. Here, more plug-and-play opportuni- ties or agreed protocols such as OPC UA are desirable. However, this seems to require further standardization efforts as the actual OPC companion specifica- tion for robots only allows for reading the robot state rather than taking control over a robot.

LL2 - Container Virtualization on Constrained Resources [TA4, TA1]: To support heterogeneous devices, the platform encourages the virtualization of the distributed service execution through container technology. However, build- ing a container for an edge device requires a careful software selection, consid- eration of processor capacities, memory and disk spaces as well as subsequent optimization of the container (Q1). For achieving the container-based AI deploy- ment on the employed edge, for example, several iterations were required. The initially used TensorFlow is shipped as a monolithic 2 GB Python package. How- ever, installing all required components results in a container with a 4.2 GB disk footprint, which can easily exceed the capacity of the employed edge device. Fur- thermore, TensorFlow did not support the Atom processor of the edge device. We therefore switched to TensorFlow light, which requires an upfront conversion of the AI model and, in effect, leads to a container size of about 2.6 GB. An alternative is to utilize tailored compilations for such devices, if available. Here, better modularization of such libraries, e.g., an inference-only TensorFlow as well as official, easy-accessible builds of native software for different processor ver- sions would be desirable. However, inference only models are at a disadvantage within non-stationary domains that require online learning.

LL3 - AI in Production Context [TA2]: Our experience regarding AI for production is twofold. On the one hand, it is important to carefully assess whether complex AI methods really bring benefits over algorithmic methods, e.g., a threshold-based method for wheel color detection. This is in particular important when deploying AI to resource constrained devices. On the other hand, AI tasks in an industrial production context, are in many cases more complex than expected from theory, because the physical environment of the AI application may have a strong influence, e.g., light, heat, vibration. In our case, AI needed to be tuned due to light reflection on polished aluminium and changing lighting conditions in different settings (lab, trade fair ground). Furthermore, careful data preprocessing also proved to be very effective already in our relatively controlled environment.

LL4 - Service Testing Sandbox [TA1]: Besides platform components, it is essential to test application-specific services and components. Setting up such tests is a complex task, depending on the frameworks, techniques and conventions employed by the platform. We experienced this when integrating the Python-based AI service as it implicitly involves different programming languages as well as the underlying stream processing environment, in our case Spring Cloud Stream (SCS)[16]. In other words, such a test requires setting up a SCS-based service test, which calls the managing Java stream component and, through the Python service environment, the actual Python service code. Moreover, it is desirable to enable testing for application developers, who do not (yet) have deep knowledge about platform internals (Q4). To ease testing for platform users and based on the integration experiences that we made, we plan to generate a test basis for each application service, which transparently sets up the SCS environment and also feeds the service with test data in a uniform manner.

LL5 - Asset Administration Shells [TA3]: The exploitation of AAS in the context of lot size 1 production has proven very useful (Q2). AAS provide a manageable means to capture, update and check individualized production information across individual processes (in our case production and quality control) and across unit and organizational borders in an interoperable way[17]. However, it has also shown that accompanying tools and infrastructure are crucial to make the use of AAS feasible (see also the discussion of BaSyx below). This is especially true, when AAS instances are required for individual products (not only for machines). In this case, an AAS editor, such as the frequently mentioned AASX package explorer[18], may be helpful for AAS templates, but it is of little use for creating instances, as it is meant for supporting manual rather than for mass creation of AAS instances. Here, the automatic generation of AAS instances has proven to be a viable and effective way to create individual AAS based on production data. This is also very much in line with the low-code approach of our platform, which heavily relies on generated software artifacts (e.g., service code). With respect to the further use of AAS, e.g., for the description of software components, our experience was promising. APIs of distributed components such as services can be described in terms of AAS, made available through a registry and queried/called irrespective of their physical origin, e.g., an edge device attached

---

[16] https://spring.io/projects/spring-cloud-stream.

[17] In the future, AAS formats that are currently in standardization will probably further facilitate interoperability.

[18] https://github.com/admin-shell/aasx-package-explorer.

to a machine. However, the application of the platform has also shown that large numbers of ASS as well as the use of AAS for runtime properties requires special attention with respect to efficiency and performance [4].

LL6 - BaSyx Experience [TA3]: Overall, our experience with BaSyx was mostly positive, as it allows to effectively realize complex, distributed AAS-based applications or our platform AAS. However, it also became obvious that BaSyx is still in development and lacks some stability. For example, adding many elements (more than 1000 in a few seconds) to a submodel or removing such elements (e.g., by parallel processes) caused excessive CPU consumption. In our case, we mitigated these problems by aggressive filtering to focus on relevant information. Moreover, a more fine-grained modularization of BaSyx for application on resource-constrained devices would be desirable (although not causing issues on the same scale as, e.g., TensorFlow).

LL7 - Platform Benefits [TA1]: Although the consideration of benefits refers to the IIP-Ecosphere Platform, we believe a lot can be learned for the development and evolution of other IIoT platforms. Overall, using the IIP-Ecosphere platform allowed us to build the demonstrator in relatively short time (within four weeks from first conception, including planning, discussions, workarounds and bug fixing). To a large degree, we attribute this to the low-code model-based approach, which implies guidelines and structuring principles. For example, as an initial model of the application must exist before services can be implemented, the involved parties are motivated to agree on an application design first strengthening their joint vision and understanding (Q4). From a technical and an organizational perspective, the service interfaces that we derived next, led to a clear separation of interests but also to ownerships, which contributes to Q3 (here into AI, UI, robot control and supporting services). Moreover, the platform approach also gives structural guidance, e.g., on the organization of code artifacts for different programming languages so that packaged application artifacts can be deployed and executed by the platform. Further, the code generation helped us speeding up the development. In particular, the complete generation of OPC UA and AAS connectors from the model saved considerable amount of time. As already mentioned in Sect. 4, more than half of the application code was generated, relying on frameworks that were already tested and integrated into the platform. Further, the code generation even enabled us to quickly realize changes to the processing in an agile and consistent manner. Although the standardization of AAS is currently in progress, the existing AAS modeling concepts are already beneficial in data exchange as they lead to a uniform representation of data structures that are helpful, e.g., when realizing an application UI. A further benefit is that a platform provides an environment to realize services more easily, even without knowing details on machine connectors, data transport, monitoring or deployment. Here, an adequate abstraction of a functional unit, e.g., a service, allows to deploy and to distribute, e.g., AI, in a flexible and easy manner, e.g., to edge devices (Q1).

As a more **general lesson** learned (also mainly for TA1), it is definitely worth while to validate complex software systems such as a platform with realistic use cases, since it also brings improvements for the platform itself. Although our platform is subject to regression tests on different levels of granularity, the demonstrator involved several unexpected situations. For example, some of the control flow communication paths in the demonstrator that failed without (observable) reason. An initial workaround for the demonstrator finally led to a general revision of the code generation for these paths in the platform. Another example are services that need longer for their startup than expected by the tests, such as a Python script utilizing TensorFlow-light AI models. As the service startup was assigned to the wrong service lifecycle phase, these services were accidentally started multiple times by the service framework due to time-outs. Correcting the assignment for all services helped to further stabilize the platform.

7 Future Work and Conclusion

In this paper, we provided an overview of our IIoT platform approach – the open source IIP-Ecosphere platform – and introduced its architecture. Although supported through more than 20 integrated open source components, the design and development of such a platform is a technical challenge in itself. In addition, it is important to validate and evaluate the approach with industrial devices and use cases. As a first step in this direction, we presented an AI-based visual quality inspection, which combines industrial devices (edge, cobot), recent and upcoming standards (OPC UA, AAS) with actual AI methods. From the realization of the demonstrator, we derived and discussed lessons learned, which pinpoint actual problems but also indicate positive experiences that can be helpful for other work in the field.

As future work, we plan to investigate some of the open problems from our lessons learned discussion and further applications, e.g., selection and optimization of AI for resource-constrained devices, federated AI models [5] architecture in a federated multi-device setup, automated container building for Industry 4.0 applications, AAS-based plug-and-play for industrial edge devices during onboarding into an IIoT platform or AAS efficiency/scalability. Besides these topics, we will improve and stabilize the realization of our platform, which already raised various industrial interests outside the consortium, as a basis for deeper evaluations and further demonstrators.

References

1. Angelopoulos, A., et al.: Tackling faults in the industry 4.0 era-a survey of machine-learning solutions and key aspects. Sensors **20**(1), 109 (2019)
2. Bader, S., Bedenbecker, H., Billmann, M., et al.: Generic Frame for Technical Data for Industrial Equipment in Manufacturing (Version 1.1) (2020). https://www.zvei.org/fileadmin/user_upload/Presse_und_Medien/Publikationen/2020/Dezember/Submodel_Templates_of_the_Asset_Administration_Shell/201117_I40_ZVEI_SG2_Submodel_Spec_ZVEI_Technical_Data_Version_1_1.pdf

3. Bansod, G., Khandekar, S., Khurana, S.: Analysis of convolution neural network architectures and their applications in industry 4.0. In: Metaheuristic Algorithms in Industry 4.0, pp. 139–162. CRC Press (2021)
4. Casado, M.G., Eichelberger, H.: Industry 4.0 resource monitoring - experiences with micrometer and asset administration shells. In: CEUR-WS Proceedings of Symposium on Software Performance 2021 (SSP 2021) (2021)
5. Chang, Y., Laridi, S., Ren, Z., Palmer, G., Schuller, B.W., Fisichella, M.: Robust federated learning against adversarial attacks for speech emotion recognition. arXiv preprint arXiv:2203.04696 (2022)
6. Chen, J., Lim, C.P., Tan, K.H., Govindan, K., Kumar, A.: Artificial intelligence-based human-centric decision support framework: an application to predictive maintenance in asset management under pandemic environments. Ann. Oper. Res. 1–24 (2021). https://doi.org/10.1007/s10479-021-04373-w
7. Chen, S., Li, Q., Zhang, H., Zhu, F., Xiong, G., Tang, Y.: An IoT edge computing system architecture and its application. In: International Conference on Networking, Sensing and Control (ICNSC), pp. 1–7 (2020)
8. Denkena, B., Dittrich, M.A., Fohlmeister, S., Kemp, D., Palmer, G.: Scalable cooperative multi-agent-reinforcement-learning for order-controlled on schedule manufacturing in flexible manufacturing systems. In: Simulation in Produktion und Logistik 2021, Erlangen, 15–17 September 2021, p. 305 (2021)
9. Eichelberger, H., Qin, C., Sizonenko, R., Schmid, K.: Using IVML to model the topology of big data processing pipelines. In: International Systems and Software Product Line Conference, pp. 204–208 (2016)
10. Eichelberger, H., Stichweh, H., Sauer, C.: Requirements for an AI-enabled Industry 4.0 platform - integrating industrial and scientific views. In: International Conference on Advances and Trends in Software Engineering, pp. 7–14 (2022)
11. Feichtinger, K., et al.: Industry voices on software engineering challenges in cyber-physical production systems engineering. In: 2022 IEEE 27th International Conference on Emerging Technologies and Factory Automation (ETFA), Stuttgart, Germany, pp. 1–8. IEEE Press (2022). https://doi.org/10.1109/ETFA52439.2022.9921568
12. Foukalas, F.: Cognitive IoT platform for fog computing industrial applications. Comput. Electr. Eng. **87**, 106770 (2020)
13. Han, X., et al.: Pre-trained models: past, present and future. AI Open **2**, 225–250 (2021)
14. Hoang, D.T., Kang, H.J.: Rolling element bearing fault diagnosis using convolutional neural network and vibration image. Cogn. Syst. Res. **53**, 42–50 (2019). Advanced Intelligent Computing
15. Howard, A.G., et al.: MobileNets: efficient convolutional neural networks for mobile vision applications. arXiv preprint arXiv:1704.04861 (2017)
16. Hummel, O., Eichelberger, H., Giloj, A., Werle, D., Schmid, K.: A collection of software engineering challenges for big data system development. In: Euromicro Conference on Software Engineering and Advanced Applications, pp. 362–369 (2018)
17. Kannoth, S., et al.: Enabling SMEs to industry 4.0 using the BaSyx middleware: a case study. In: Biffl, S., Navarro, E., Löwe, W., Sirjani, M., Mirandola, R., Weyns, D. (eds.) ECSA 2021. LNCS, vol. 12857, pp. 277–294. Springer, Cham (2021). https://doi.org/10.1007/978-3-030-86044-8_19
18. Kiangala, K.S., Wang, Z.: An effective predictive maintenance framework for conveyor motors using dual time-series imaging and convolutional neural network in an industry 4.0 environment. IEEE Access **8**, 121033–121049 (2020)

19. Krause, T., Strauß, O., Scheffler, G., Kett, H., Lehmann, K., Renner, T.: IT-Plattformen für das Internet der Dinge (IoT) (2017)
20. LeCun, Y., Bengio, Y., Hinton, G.: Deep learning. Nature **521**(7553), 436–444 (2015)
21. Lee, S.M., Lee, D., Kim, Y.S.: The quality management ecosystem for predictive maintenance in the Industry 4.0 era. Int. J. Qual. Innov. **5**(1), 1–11 (2019). https://doi.org/10.1186/s40887-019-0029-5
22. Lin, C.H., Wang, K.J., Tadesse, A.A., Woldegiorgis, B.H.: Human-robot collaboration empowered by hidden semi-Markov model for operator behaviour prediction in a smart assembly system. J. Manuf. Syst. **62**, 317–333 (2022)
23. van der Linden, F., Schmid, K., Rommes, E.: Software Product Lines in Action - The Best Industrial Practice in Product Line Engineering. Springer, Heidelberg (2007). https://doi.org/10.1007/978-3-540-71437-8
24. Lins, T., Oliveira, R.A.R., Correia, L.H.A., Silva, J.S.: Industry 4.0 retrofitting. In: Brazilian Symposium on Computing Systems Engineering (SBESC), pp. 8–15 (2018)
25. Niederée, C., Eichelberger, H., Schmees, H.D., Broos, A., Schreiber, P.: KI in der Produktion - Quo vadis? (2021). https://doi.org/10.5281/zenodo.6334521
26. Pal, S.K., Pramanik, A., Maiti, J., Mitra, P.: Deep learning in multi-object detection and tracking: state of the art. Appl. Intell. **51**(9), 6400–6429 (2021). https://doi.org/10.1007/s10489-021-02293-7
27. Palmer, G., Schnieders, B., Savani, R., Tuyls, K., Fossel, J., Flore, H.: The automated inspection of opaque liquid vaccines. In: ECAI 2020, pp. 1898–1905 (2020)
28. Patalas-Maliszewska, J., Pajkak, I., Skrzeszewska, M.: AI-based decision-making model for the development of a manufacturing company in the context of industry 4.0. In: International Conference on Fuzzy Systems (FUZZ-IEEE), pp. 1–7 (2020)
29. Peres, R.S., Jia, X., Lee, J., Sun, K., Colombo, A.W., Barata, J.: Industrial artificial intelligence in industry 4.0 - systematic review, challenges and outlook. IEEE Access **8**, 220121–220139 (2020)
30. Platform Industrie 4.0: Details of the Asset Administration Shell. https://industrialdigitaltwin.org/wp-content/uploads/2021/09/07_details_of_the_asset_administration_shell_part1_v3_en_2020.pdf
31. Raileanu, S., Borangiu, T., Morariu, O., Iacob, I.: Edge computing in industrial IoT framework for cloud-based manufacturing control. In: International Conference on System Theory, Control and Computing (ICSTCC), pp. 261–266 (2018)
32. Sauer, C., Eichelberger, H., Ahmadian, A.S., Dewes, A., Jürjens, J.: Current Industrie 4.0 Platforms - An Overview (2021). https://zenodo.org/record/4485756
33. Schnieders, B., Luo, S., Palmer, G., Tuyls, K.: Fully convolutional one-shot object segmentation for industrial robotics. In: International Conference on Autonomous Agents and MultiAgent Systems, pp. 1161–1169 (2019)
34. Sculley, D., et al.: Hidden technical debt in machine learning systems. In: Advances in Neural Information Processing Systems, vol. 28, pp. 2503–2511 (2015)
35. Shinde, P.P., Shah, S.: A review of machine learning and deep learning applications. In: International Conference on Computing Communication Control and Automation (ICCUBEA), pp. 1–6 (2018)
36. Silva, W., Capretz, M.: Assets predictive maintenance using convolutional neural networks. In: International Conference on Software Engineering, Artificial Intelligence, Networking and Parallel/Distributed Computing (SNPD), pp. 59–66 (2019)

37. Wang, H., Li, S., Song, L., Cui, L.: A novel convolutional neural network based fault recognition method via image fusion of multi-vibration-signals. Comput. Ind. **105**, 182–190 (2019)
38. Zhuang, C., Liu, J., Xiong, H.: Digital twin-based smart production management and control framework for the complex product assembly shop-floor. Int. J. Adv. Manuf. Technol. **96**, 1149–1163 (2018). https://doi.org/10.1007/s00170-018-1617-6

DevOps in Robotics: Challenges and Practices

Alexandre Sawczuk da Silva[1]([✉]), Andreas Kreutz[1], Gereon Weiss[1], Johannes Rothe[2], and Christoph Ihrke[2]

[1] Fraunhofer Institute for Cognitive Systems IKS, Munich, Germany
{alexandre.sawczuk.da.silva,andreas.kreutz,
gereon.weiss}@iks.fraunhofer.de
[2] Magazino GmbH, Munich, Germany
{rothe,ihrke}@magazino.eu

Abstract. DevOps, which refers to a set of practices for streamlining the development and operations of software companies, is becoming increasingly popular as businesses strive to adopt a loosely coupled architecture that supports frequent software delivery. As a result, DevOps is also gaining traction in other domains and involved architectures, including robotics, though research in this area is still lacking. To address this gap, this paper investigates how to adapt key DevOps principles from the domain of software engineering to the domain of robotics. In order to demonstrate the feasibility of this in practice, an industrial robotics case study is conducted. The results indicate that the adoption of these principles is also beneficial for robotic software architectures, though general DevOps approaches may require some adaptation to match the existing infrastructure.

Keywords: DevOps · Robotics · Case study · Metrics

1 Introduction

As technology companies adapt to remain competitive in a rapidly changing market, the principle of frequent delivery becomes increasingly important [22]. The core idea behind this practice is to regularly provide new features to users, which keeps customers engaged and reduces the risks typically associated with larger releases [16]. However, working in this agile manner requires not only team commitment, but also a flexible architecture along with processes and tools that help automate and streamline the development and release life cycle. This, in turn, introduces the need for the principles encompassed by DevOps [21]. DevOps can be defined as a set of practices that connect development and operation activities, supporting continuous integration, robust testing, and automated deployment. These practices are complementary to the concept of a

This work was funded by the Bavarian Ministry of Economic Affairs, Regional Development and Energy as part of the RoboDevOps project.

loosely coupled architecture, which allows teams to independently and efficiently develop, test, and deploy the components of a system [21].

The current literature on the subject shows that DevOps is mainly utilized in the context of software development [10]. Its principles can theoretically be employed in closely related areas, including Cyber-Physical Systems (CPS) and robotics [18,23], though these works do not present practical case studies for this in the area of robotics. Naturally, the implementation of DevOps concepts faces different obstacles that are particular to the industry they are applied to. For instance, adopting DevOps in the domain of CPS can be difficult due to siloed teams and a lack of access to customer data [13]. Likewise, the implementation of DevOps in a robotics context is challenging due to difficulties in test automation and quality assurance [1]. These challenges reveal the need for research that investigates practical ways of adapting and employing DevOps concepts to areas other than software development. Unfortunately, peer-reviewed literature on the subject is still scant and leaves practitioners with open questions.

To address this gap from the robotics perspective, the goal of this paper is twofold: first, it discusses DevOps practices employed in the software domain and how they could be adapted for a robotics context; second, it presents a case study where we adopt these practices to improve the product development process of a robotics company. To achieve this goal, the main contributions of this work are the following:

- Identification of DevOps practices used in software development that are applicable in a robotics context.
- Feasibility study of adopting DevOps strategies to industrial robotics and their application to real-world development environments.
- Findings and results gathered during the DevOps adoption process to a Cyber-Physical Systems domain.

The remainder of this paper is structured as follows. Section 2 discusses related work in this area. Section 3 presents common DevOps practices and discusses their suitability for robotics. Section 4 introduces the target domain of industrial robotics. Section 5 describes the adoption of these practices to the robotics domain by an example use case. Section 6 further analyzes the case study and presents results of the current adoption status. Section 7 concludes the paper.

2   Related Work

There are currently few peer-reviewed publications on DevOps applied to robotics, so publications in complementary areas were also considered in our literature review. We structure related work in the following by the three main clusters: DevOps in robotics and CPS, robotics testing, and performance metrics.

2.1   DevOps in Robotics and Cyber-Physical Systems

The work in [18] investigates the mapping of DevOps practices from the software engineering domain to the robotics development process. It defines a list of DevOps practices that are recurrent in a software context and maps them to the corresponding robotic development life cycle step. Then, it interviews experts to determine the applicability and effectiveness of this mapping. In [23], authors determine that it is possible to apply DevOps to CPS development, despite its specific use of architectures and automation technologies. In [13], authors identify the key challenges in adopting DevOps in the domain of CPS, including teams that are not always cross-functional and the difficulty to configure test environments in a representative way.

Research Gap: While these works argue that it is possible to use DevOps in areas other than software development, they do not supply concrete usage examples of DevOps principles for these areas (e.g., for robotics architectures). To address this, the present work includes a case study where DevOps principles are selected and adopted for real-world industrial robotics development.

2.2   Robotics Testing

Testing is a particularly important topic within DevOps [8]. The work in [8] investigates practitioners' definitions of testing in the context of DevOps, revealing that perspectives are not always consistent but generally advocate for early involvement of testers and for the use of test automation technology. In [1], authors interview robotics practitioners to understand how simulation is used as part of their testing strategies. Results show that current simulators do not easily provide ways of automating tests, and that at times, setting up the simulator is more time consuming than directly using the hardware for testing. In [2], further testing practices and challenges are discussed, such as determining whether the chosen test cases are representative of the real-life scenarios faced by robots. The work in [12] proposes a high-level methodology for testing robots. Specifically, it presents five levels of testing based on different combinations of behavior and environment. The five levels are ordered by complexity, which maximizes the safety of tests. In [25], practices for supporting continuous testing in DevOps are discussed, emphasizing the importance of test automation, process formalization, and quality gates to ensure that standards are met.

Research Gap: While these works provide some guidance regarding testing strategies for DevOps in robotics, they do not give a clear starting point or adoption strategies for these principles. To address this, the present work selects fundamental practices and investigates their implementation.

2.3   Performance Metrics

Metrics are fundamental for successful DevOps approaches [20]. The work in [20] discusses four key metrics for measuring an organization's level of DevOps adoption, centered around deployment frequency and code quality. Specifically, it seeks to determine a way in which these metrics can be automatically measured. In [7], metrics for measuring the effectiveness of the testing process are introduced, focusing on the cost of detecting and fixing defects. The work in [6] proposes integration testing metrics in the domain of robotics, based on the interaction between different ROS components. The core idea is to generate a call graph that shows ROS nodes and their possible communication channels. Then, tests for the different application requirements are conducted, and the coverage percentage for elements in the call graph can be calculated. The work in [17] discusses the idea of using a quality gate to determine whether a software release should move forward after testing. The core concept is to connect the operations and development steps in the product life cycle, leading to an increasingly accurate reliability profile over time. The quality gate is implemented as a reliability threshold (i.e., how often failures are expected to happen) based on monitoring data from the production environment.

Research Gap: While the metrics discussed in these works could generally be applied to DevOps in robotics, they were designed with the software domain in mind and used accordingly. The present work investigates the transfer and application of key DevOps metrics to the domain of robotics.

3   DevOps Practices for Robotics

Even though DevOps practices are theoretically applicable to a range of domains, they have been originally conceived for the software industry [9]. Because of that, they rely upon underlying concepts that are not always directly transferable to other areas. With robotics, the main stumbling block for DevOps is that processes must cater not only to the software architecture used for controlling the robots, but also to the hardware itself. This results in a significantly different way of developing, testing, and deploying the product, which requires DevOps elements to be adapted accordingly. With the help of industrial practitioners, we identified the following three areas demanding particular attention, as they pose foundational steps in the adoption of DevOps: (1) calculating metrics provides measurable evidence that the DevOps practices adopted are indeed beneficial [20]; (2) documenting the test pipeline is the first step in moving towards a continuous testing/deployment platform, which is the backbone of DevOps [25]; (3) identifying a representative and efficient-to-execute set of tests improves quality standards without slowing down the development process [15]. Each of these areas is discussed in more detail in the following subsections.

3.1   DevOps Metrics

The tracking of metrics is crucial to DevOps, as it provides quantitative evidence of the benefits yielded by adopting other practices [20]. In general, these metrics assess high-level characteristics of the process, so in principle it should be possible to transfer them into the robotics domain without many modifications. In software engineering, four metrics have been identified to reflect the performance of software delivery [20]: *lead time for change*, which refers to the amount of time from when code is committed to when it is available in production; *deployment frequency*, which refers to the number of times code is deployed production over a given time period; *time to restore service*, which refers to the amount of time required to recover from an incident in production (e.g., a service outage); *change failure rate*, which refers to the percentage of changes released in production that required some form of remediation (e.g., a hot fix or a rollback). In general, the goal of these metrics is to measure the team's development speed, rhythm, responsiveness, and quality. As shown in Table 1, most of these metrics are compatible with the robotics product life cycle. The *time to restore service* metric is domain-specific, so it may not always be applicable to robotics (e.g. in the case of multiple robots working in a distributed fashion). Therefore, this metric can be replaced with other domain-specific alternatives that reflect product stability (an example of this is discussed in Table 2).

Table 1. Mapping of DevOps metrics from the software to the robotics domain.

Original metric	Description	Does it work for robotics?
Lead time for change	The time it takes for code to go from committed to production. **Goal:** To measure the team's speed when executing changes	**Yes.** This metric could be generalized as the time required for a product feature to go from implementation to release
Deployment frequency	How often code is moved to production. **Goal:** To measure the team's overall development rhythm	**Yes.** This metric depicts how often a feature is rolled out/deployed onto the systems
Time to restore service	How quickly the service can be back up after an incident. **Goal:** To measure how responsive the team is to unforeseen circumstances	**Maybe.** This is a domain-specific stability metric, so other alternatives may be used instead.
Change failure rate	Percentage of changes that required remediation. **Goal:** To measure the quality of the team's process	**Yes.** As long as issues can be mapped to specific changes, this metric is applicable to robotics

3.2   Test Pipeline

DevOps advocates the idea of testing early, testing often, and testing automatically as much as possible [3]. In a software development context, this is facilitated by continuous integration (CI) and continuous deployment (CD) platforms, which carry out automated tests whenever new system features are added and before they are deployed to production [3]. These testing steps should form a pipeline that is triggered whenever a code change happens, giving developers immediate feedback on whether this modification causes any failures. In robotics, however, this is only part of the required testing. In addition, hardware components and their interaction with software modules must also be extensively validated, and this is challenging to automate [1]. Consequently, the test pipeline is complex and may not be entirely formalized, especially when also considering integration, simulation, field, and release testing. Given this variety of tools, it can be challenging to represent all pipeline steps. The first step to address this complexity in robotics then becomes the creation of a clear overview of the complete test pipeline. This reveals potential bottlenecks and steps that could be automated next. Additionally, it uncovers testing phases that would benefit from the addition of quality gates, i.e., formal validation checkpoints to ensure that the product is ready for the next testing phase. In order to introduce these gates, it is necessary to identify and use metrics that provide a quantifiable confidence measure of testing activities. Once these checkpoints are in place, it becomes easier to determine whether to proceed to later testing phases, which can be more time consuming.

3.3   Scenario Coverage

The testing conducted as part of DevOps must strike a balance between quality and execution time [15]. To ensure major software faults are already revealed during testing, the tests must sufficiently cover a representative sample of scenarios that the system will encounter in operation. At the same time, testing should not become a bottleneck for development. In robotics, and in particular in the subdomain of autonomous mobile robots, it is difficult to create a representative scenario sample with a reasonably small size for testing. This is because the operations environment that the tests need to replicate is the real world, which makes the scenarios faced by the systems highly complex and heterogeneous. In fact, there can often be a degree of uncertainty about what the system might encounter in operation, further complicating the issue of creating tests to verify that the system behaves correctly in these situations. This, in conjunction with the previously mentioned constraints on execution time, means that it is crucial to carefully select a meaningful subset of tests to be conducted regularly. To adapt this practice to the domain of robotics, the most relevant parts of the environment that are subject to high variability need to be identified. Additionally, the dimensions describing how variability can manifest for these sources of variability need to be catalogued. Then, as the next step, a testing strategy can be developed to address a range of scenarios where variability in the environment could lead to unintended behavior.

4   Autonomous Mobile Robots for Intralogistics

This work is carried out in the domain of production and development of autonomous robots for intralogistics operations. The focus of this domain is on designing robots that can operate alongside humans, assisting with tasks such as picking and placing products within a warehouse environment [4]. In this scenario, the robots on the warehouse floor are sent orders from a centralized management system, and they fulfill these orders by locating, grasping, and moving the corresponding boxes to a packaging area for further processing. The objective is to fulfill orders as fast as possible, while simultaneously keeping a low failure rate. The development of perception-guided autonomous robots as commercial products is an upcoming area, so there are still no well-established best practices [4].

In this setting, robust engineering and validation standards are needed. The system architecture, for instance, is designed to be as modular as possible, which helps to simplify the development and testing of components. With testing, in particular, this modular approach allows each package to be validated according to its specification. Then, integration test suites ensure that the interactions between packages function as expected. Finally, it is also necessary to test how the full robotic system interacts with the real world. This is accomplished through simulations for specific system characteristics, a physics-based simulation, and later through physical testing. Interestingly, a portion of the latter can be accomplished in operation [19], relying on techniques that include canary deployment (where updates are only released to a subset of operating robots, which minimizes the effect of any remaining issues) and blue-green deployment (where a new release runs in parallel with the old one for runtime validation, before making the final switch).

In addition to the use of a modular architecture and the establishment of a testing workflow, the development and usage of metrics for the DevOps and testing processes are needed. These are crucial to assess how streamlined the development process has become and whether the overall DevOps process needs to be adjusted. In the case of testing, metrics can quantify how thorough the current test suite is and reveal any areas of the system in which potential problems may be found. However, creating representative metrics for the robotics DevOps process is complex, since it is necessary to account for the different configurations and environments in which the system operates. Specifically, the items tackled by robots are placed in shelves following a logistics strategy known as *chaotic storage*, which consists of putting items wherever there is room. This allows for the available storage space to be used as efficiently as possible. However, it also means that items can have an almost infinite number of different configurations. In addition to the location of items, each robot has a unique set of calibration and description parameters (set according to hardware features depending on the product version), while a subset of a robot fleet could have different feature toggles. All of these factors contribute to making testing and the use of metrics incredibly challenging. Thus, we introduce our approach and methods for adopting DevOps to robotics in the next section. Within the scope of this paper, we mainly address DevOps for a robotics software architecture.

5   Case Study

To ascertain that DevOps practices can indeed be transferred from the software to the robotics domain, a case study was conducted as a collaborative project between Magazino (a company that produces autonomous robots for intralogistics) and Fraunhofer IKS (an applied research institute) [11]. The primary goal was to further improve the DevOps process of the company, with the additional outcome of providing further insight into DevOps for robotics in general. Together, the team worked on incorporating DevOps practices into the company's product life cycle. Note that stability metrics and automated testing were already in use by the company at the beginning of the case study, while the other DevOps practices discussed below were introduced as part of it. The following subsections provide more detail on this endeavor.

5.1   DevOps Metrics

As previously discussed, most of the DevOps metrics used in the software domain can be employed for robotics without extensive adaptation, and this was indeed found to be the case. The previous discussion also highlights the need to employ domain-specific metrics for monitoring system stability and reliability. For this case study, these domain-specific metrics correspond to metrics already regularly measured within the company, as shown in Table 2. These metrics have proven to capture the customer satisfaction with robotics systems in logistics processes. As a next step, Magazino is planning to set up alerting based on service-level objectives [5] in order to guarantee a consistently high level of reliability.

Table 2. Domain-specific reliability metrics used at Magazino.

Stability metric	Description
Availability	Amount of time the robots are effectively operating during the time they are utilized
Latency	Amount of time it takes to finish a request
Throughput	Amount of requests that are successfully executed by the robots in a certain amount of time
Utilization	Amount of time the robots are utilized during the total switched on time
Errors	The number of interventions as a fraction of the total requests
Aborts	The number of aborted requests as a fraction of the total requests

Aside from the domain-specific stability metrics discussed above, the other DevOps metrics have not been tracked yet in our application case. As part of this case study, the tracking has been extended to include the deployment frequency, lead time for change, and change failure rate. The calculation of the *deployment frequency* metric is accomplished by retrieving information from the package version watcher, which tracks the current version being run by each robot whenever its software is restarted. The process begins by selecting a given time frame (e.g., the last 100 days) from which data will be retrieved. Based on this time frame, version data entries are retrieved for each robot. This initial set of entries contains new deployments (i.e., when the version has changed since the previous restart) and simple restarts (i.e., when the version has not changed), so it is filtered to exclude the latter category. Finally, the deployment frequency is calculated as the average number of deployments per time frame per robot in the fleet. Note that in our implementation the version updates are tracked by package, so a program modification spanning multiple packages will be counted as multiple new deployments.

The calculation of the *lead time for change* metric is also accomplished using the new deployment entries recorded by the package version watcher. Once again, the data is retrieved for a given time frame, and only new deployment entries are considered. First, the timestamp of each new deployment is collected, along with the name of the repository the package was installed from and the corresponding commit tag. Then, based on the repository name and commit tag, it is possible to query the repository in order to recover the timestamp for the commit. Finally, the difference between the deployment date and the commit date is calculated for each new deployment, and the average of all of these differences is reported as the lead time for change. Note that in our implementation only new deployments whose package names can be matched to a repository are counted in this metric. Additionally, external packages and nested repositories are excluded from this calculation.

The *change failure rate* metric is calculated using the information contained in release snapshots, which are records of the specific version for each package included in a given release. First, the snapshots of the previous and of the current releases are compared, to determine how many package versions have changed between then and now. The number of updated packages corresponds the total number of changes introduced in the current release. Then, any further package changes that happen within the lifespan of the current release (i.e., hot fixes) are counted, as these likely correspond to corrections to failed changes introduced by the current release. Finally, the number of hot fixes is divided by the total number of changes in the current release, yielding the change failure rate. Note that in our implementation this calculation only includes internal packages.

To ensure the wide adoption of these metrics throughout the development, the plan is to create a centralized dashboard in which they can be viewed. Inspired by the architecture discussed in [20], a robust metrics collection system can be developed around two components: a collector, which retrieves the required data from various sources for computing the metrics, and an aggregator, which performs the calculations and updates the metrics dashboard.

5.2   Test Pipeline

To formalize the testing pipeline and introduce additional quality controls where necessary, we derived an overview of the existing testing processes of the case study, summarized in Fig. 1. The testing pipeline consists of three phases executed throughout the product life cycle. The first phase is the *development phase*, in which manual and automated testing of hardware components is carried out during the development of new features. Additionally, unit tests are run for different software components, and system logs are collected and replayed as necessary. Finally, automated simulations are conducted before more extensive testing with hardware. The second phase is the *release freeze*, where no additional software commits (aside from bug fixes) or hardware changes occur. Instead, the focus is on testing the new features on the hardware, executing scenarios that verify the robots' navigation and grasping capabilities. This phase also includes regression testing, to ensure that previously released features still perform as intended, and performance testing, to ensure that robots can handle different task loads. The third phase refers to *testing in live operation*, which validates the peculiarities of each customer's process and environment setup, as well as tests for verifying new functionality in operation. This phase uses staged rollouts, which means robots are gradually upgraded and closely monitored during this process. This limits the impact of updates until they are fully rolled out.

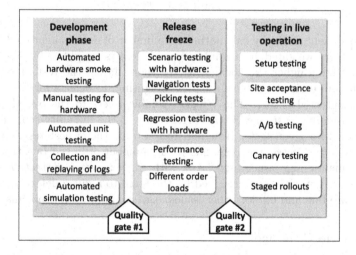

Fig. 1. Overview of testing activities conducted at Magazino.

One of the development team's key concerns is ensuring that tests always reach a certain level of quality, thus, providing some assurance that new features are ready to proceed to the next step in the product life cycle. A natural solution to this is the introduction of *quality gates*, which require tests to meet specific thresholds before they can be approved. As illustrated in Fig. 1, the team opted for the introduction of two quality gates, first between the development and release freeze phases, and second between release freeze and testing in production. For the first gate, the objective is to prevent unnecessary hardware testing – which can be costly – before the software is mature enough. Meanwhile, the objective of the second gate is to ensure features are stable enough before being released to customers.

For the first gate, the chosen quality measures comprise: (1) code coverage levels, which are provided by the automation server; (2) the percentage of successfully executed simulation tests, which are run using multiple simulators. For the second gate, the chosen measures comprise: (1) a performance score for navigation tasks, to establish that the robot can traverse the environment as expected; (2) the presence of outliers in job phase duration, which ensures that robots can complete tasks within an acceptable amount of time (when compared to older releases); (3) a regression coefficient for grasping tests, which acts as a warning for the state of the software as it passes the gate (i.e., if it steadily rises, then that indicates that the pipeline up to that point has flaws). The regression coefficient is calculated using defects uncovered through testing, as follows:

$$r_{weighted} = \sum_{i=1}^{\#tests} \frac{1}{\#tests} \times test\_weight(i) \times$$
$$\sum_{j=1}^{\#defects(i)} (defect\_weight(j)) \tag{1}$$

The coefficient works by calculating the number of defects identified by each test, with tests weighted by complexity and defects weighted by severity. In this context, the higher the coefficient, the more flawed the test pipeline. For the calculation, easier tests have a higher weighting, as defects for these should have been detected earlier. The $\#tests$ variable refers to the overall number of tests considered, $test\_weight(i)$ corresponds to the difficulty score assigned by the team to a given test i (ranging from 1.0 for the easiest tests to 0.1 for the hardest), $\#defects(i)$ corresponds to the number of linked bug tickets and comments mentioning issues associated with a given test i, $defect\_weight(j)$ corresponds to severity score assigned by the team to a given defect j (with 1.0 for a software bug and 0.5 for other issues, e.g., configuration problems).

5.3   Scenario Coverage

To improve scenario coverage of testing in a structured way, the sources and dimensions of variability that affect the system need to be understood. In the scope of the case study, a framework for supporting this process was developed. The framework aims at discovering variability in the environment by identifying uncertain knowledge about the operating conditions of a robot. The notion of uncertainty has intensively been studied in many research fields [14,24], resulting in several taxonomies for uncertainty. Aside from separating uncertainties into distinct classes, we have found that such a framework can also be useful for identifying uncertain aspects of a system that have previously been overlooked. Therefore, we have adapted the classification framework by Mahdavi-Hezavehi et al. [14] to put the focus on uncertainties that affect robots. We differentiate uncertainties according to the four dimensions shown in Table 3. In their work, Mahdavi-Hezavehi et al. furthermore collect a number of sources of uncertainty for each value of the location dimension from the literature (c.f. Table 4). Using the abstract framework and these more practical examples directly supports reasoning about uncertainty at design time and, thus, the variability the system will encounter at run-time.

Table 3. Dimensions of uncertainty.

Dimension	Value
Location in the system	Environment
	Models
	Functions and their effects
	Goals
	Available resources
Nature of uncertainty	Epistemic
	Aleatory
Level/spectrum of uncertainty	No uncertainty
	Lack of knowledge
	Lack of awareness
	Lack of ability to gain awareness
Emerging time	Requirements definition
	Design time
	Run-time

6 Preliminary Results and Discussion

The application of DevOps in the aforementioned case study is a continuous process, so the results discussed in this section are taken at the current stage of adoption. This enables an overall analysis of trends.

For the DevOps metrics, initial *deployment frequency, lead time for change,* and *change failure rate* values were calculated using recent development data. These results can be compared to the benchmark presented in [21]. It categorizes software DevOps practitioners as low, medium, high, and elite performers for each DevOps metrics according to their velocity and stability. The performer groups were identified by statistically analyzing data collected from over 32,000 professionals [21], and Table 5 reproduces the general criteria that applies to

Table 4. Sources of uncertainty.

Location	Sources of uncertainty
Environment	Execution context, Human-in-the-loop, Multiple ownership
Model	Abstraction, Incompleteness, Model drift, Different sources of information, Complex models
Functions	Sensing, Effecting, Automatic learning, Decentralization, Changes in functions, Fault localization and identification
Goals	Goal dependencies, Future goal changes, Future new goals, Goal specification, Outdated goals
Resources	New resources, Changing resources

the different categories for the *deployment frequency, lead time for change,* and *change failure rate* metrics. Based on this classification, initial results would place the development team of the examined case study as medium performers regarding *lead time for change,* high performers regarding *deployment frequency,* and non-elite performers regarding *change failure rate.* However, this benchmark was developed by taking into account data from teams in a range of industries, meaning that it does not specifically reflect DevOps trends in the robotics domain. As robotics companies must also account for the development and integration of hardware, it is likely that their overall velocity is naturally different than that of a company exclusively focused on software architectures. Thus, while this classification provides a general indication of the current DevOps maturity level within this case study, further investigation is necessary to better understand the accuracy of this representation.

Table 5. Categorization of DevOps practitioners according to metrics (reproduced from [21]). Magazino's classification is highlighted in gray for each metric.

DevOps metric	Elite	High	Medium	Low
Lead time for change	Less than one hour	Between one day and one week	Between one month and six months	More than six months
Deployment frequency	On-demand (multiple deploys per day)	Between once per week and once per month	Between once per month and once every six months	Fewer than once per six months
Change failure rate	0%-15%	16%-30%		

For the test pipeline, the adoption of the regression coefficient provided a useful early indicator of the number of regressions that can be expected during the release life cycle. However, long-term monitoring is necessary to ascertain how accurate this forecasting is.

For the scenario coverage, the use of the previously described framework helped with the identification of a large number of uncertainties, which were limited to three clusters within the scope of this work: inventory items, interaction with humans, and environment. This provided a better understanding of the variability the robots face in terms of the appearance and physical attributes of inventory items, how humans interact with the robots, and what different warehouse environments look like. Then, quality assurance engineers and developers jointly compiled a testing strategy that leverages simulators to generate a varied range of scenarios. By including them into the testing pipeline, the scenario coverage of testing could be greatly increased. This would lead to high-quality software that is less susceptible to corner-case scenarios which, by chance, might manifest in production.

Most importantly, these results provide evidence that DevOps practices can indeed be successfully adapted to the robotics domain. Some aspects of this process, such as the calculation of metrics, test pipeline setup, and test suite design, need to be modified to match a different development and operational infrastructure, but the core advantages provided by DevOps are still visible. The adoption of these practices can also be the catalyst to other important changes, such as increased communication among different teams and the gradual convergence towards a software architecture that supports greater independence between system components. Ultimately, these improvements would pave the way for the development of Industry 4.0 systems on the shop floor.

7   Conclusion

This paper discussed the adoption of DevOps principles, which are complementary to the concept of a loosely coupled architecture, to the robotics domain. While it should theoretically be possible to adapt these practices from the software engineering domain to robotics, the transfer of DevOps principles to real-world robotics is still an open challenge. The present work addressed this gap, investigating how to adapt key DevOps practices to the new domain and conducting a case study of their application to the life cycle of a robotics company. Results show that DevOps practices are also beneficial in a robotics context, though, some adaptation in the team's processes is required. A promising future research direction in this area would be to track the DevOps practices of a robotics development team over a longer period of time, which would give insight into the extended impact of adopting these principles. Another research direction is to investigate a direct robotics adaptation to the *time to restore service* metric, using the time required to develop and roll out bug fixes in its calculation.

References

1. Afzal, A., Katz, D.S., Le Goues, C., Timperley, C.S.: Simulation for robotics test automation: developer perspectives. In: 2021 14th IEEE Conference on Software Testing, Verification and Validation (ICST), pp. 263–274. IEEE (2021)
2. Afzal, A., Le Goues, C., Hilton, M., Timperley, C.S.: A study on challenges of testing robotic systems. In: 2020 IEEE 13th International Conference on Software Testing, Validation and Verification (ICST), pp. 96–107. IEEE (2020)
3. Agrawal, P., Rawat, N.: DevOps, a new approach to cloud development & testing. In: 2019 International Conference on Issues and Challenges in Intelligent Computing Techniques (ICICT), vol. 1, pp. 1–4. IEEE (2019)
4. Bartels, G., Beetz, M.: Perception-guided mobile manipulation robots for automation of warehouse logistics. KI-Künstliche Intelligenz **33**(2), 189–192 (2019). https://doi.org/10.1007/s13218-019-00585-2
5. Beyer, B., Jones, C., Petoff, J., Murphy, N.R.: Site Reliability Engineering: How Google Runs Production Systems. O'Reilly Media, Inc. (2016)
6. Brito, M.A.S., Souza, S.R.S., Souza, P.S.L.: Integration testing for robotic systems. Softw. Qual. J. **30**, 3–35 (2020). https://doi.org/10.1007/s11219-020-09535-w
7. Cherkashin, A., Medvedeva, M., Spasov, K.: Evaluation of the software testing process effectiveness based on calculated metrics. In: AIP Conference Proceedings, vol. 2343, p. 040014. AIP Publishing LLC (2021)
8. Doležel, M.: Defining TestOps: collaborative behaviors and technology-driven workflows seen as enablers of effective software testing in DevOps. In: Paasivaara, M., Kruchten, P. (eds.) XP 2020. LNBIP, vol. 396, pp. 253–261. Springer, Cham (2020). https://doi.org/10.1007/978-3-030-58858-8_26
9. Erich, F.M., Amrit, C., Daneva, M.: A qualitative study of DevOps usage in practice. J. Softw. Evol. Process **29**(6), e1885 (2017)
10. Jabbari, R., bin Ali, N., Petersen, K., Tanveer, B.: What is DevOps? A systematic mapping study on definitions and practices. In: Proceedings of the Scientific Workshop Proceedings of XP2016, pp. 1–11 (2016)
11. Kreutz, A., Weiss, G., Rothe, J., Tenorth, M.: DevOps for developing cyberphysical systems. White paper, Fraunhofer Institute for Cognitive Systems IKS, Magazino GmbH, April 2021
12. Laval, J., Fabresse, L., Bouraqadi, N.: A methodology for testing mobile autonomous robots. In: 2013 IEEE/RSJ International Conference on Intelligent Robots and Systems, pp. 1842–1847. IEEE (2013)
13. Lwakatare, L.E., et al.: Towards DevOps in the embedded systems domain: why is it so hard? In: 2016 49th Hawaii International Conference on System Sciences (HICSS), pp. 5437–5446. IEEE (2016)
14. Mahdavi-Hezavehi, S., Avgeriou, P., Weyns, D.: A classification framework of uncertainty in architecture-based self-adaptive systems with multiple quality requirements. In: Managing Trade-Offs in Adaptable Software Architectures, pp. 45–77. Elsevier (2017). https://doi.org/10.1016/B978-0-12-802855-1.00003-4
15. Marijan, D., Liaaen, M., Sen, S.: DevOps improvements for reduced cycle times with integrated test optimizations for continuous integration. In: 2018 IEEE 42nd Annual Computer Software and Applications Conference (COMPSAC), vol. 1, pp. 22–27. IEEE (2018)
16. Meso, P., Jain, R.: Agile software development: adaptive systems principles and best practices. Inf. Syst. Manag. **23**(3), 19–30 (2006)

17. Pietrantuono, R., Bertolino, A., De Angelis, G., Miranda, B., Russo, S.: Towards continuous software reliability testing in DevOps. In: 2019 IEEE/ACM 14th International Workshop on Automation of Software Test (AST), pp. 21–27. IEEE (2019)
18. Ronanki, K.C.: Robotic software development using DevOps. Master's thesis, Faculty of Computing, Blekinge Institute of Technology (2021)
19. Rudrabhatla, C.K.: Comparison of zero downtime based deployment techniques in public cloud infrastructure. In: 2020 Fourth International Conference on I-SMAC (IoT in Social, Mobile, Analytics and Cloud) (I-SMAC), pp. 1082–1086. IEEE (2020)
20. Sallin, M., Kropp, M., Anslow, C., Quilty, J.W., Meier, A.: Measuring software delivery performance using the four key metrics of DevOps. In: Gregory, P., Lassenius, C., Wang, X., Kruchten, P. (eds.) XP 2021. LNBIP, vol. 419, pp. 103–119. Springer, Cham (2021). https://doi.org/10.1007/978-3-030-78098-2_7
21. Smith, D., Villalba, D., Irvine, M., Stanke, D., Harvey, N.: Accelerate: state of DevOps. Technical report, DORA (2021)
22. Stoica, M., Mircea, M., Ghilic-Micu, B.: Software development: agile vs. traditional. Informatica Economica **17**(4), 64–76 (2013)
23. Wijaya, P.E., Rosyadi, I., Taryana, A.: An attempt to adopt DevOps on embedded system development: empirical evidence. In: Journal of Physics: Conference Series, vol. 1367, p. 012078. IOP Publishing (2019)
24. Zhang, M., Selic, B., Ali, S., Yue, T., Okariz, O., Norgren, R.: Understanding uncertainty in cyber-physical systems: a conceptual model. In: Wąsowski, A., Lönn, H. (eds.) ECMFA 2016. LNCS, vol. 9764, pp. 247–264. Springer, Cham (2016). https://doi.org/10.1007/978-3-319-42061-5_16
25. Zimmerer, P.: Strategy for continuous testing in iDevOps. In: Proceedings of the 40th International Conference on Software Engineering: Companion Proceedings, pp. 532–533 (2018)

Enabling IoT Connectivity and Interoperability by Using Automated Gateways

Jasminka Matevska$^{(\boxtimes)}$ and Marvin Soldin

City University of Applied Sciences, Flughafenallee 10, 28199 Bremen, Germany
jasminka.matevska@hs-bremen.de, marvin.soldin@outlook.de

Abstract. As an essential part of the Industry 4.0 strategy, the Internet of Things is developing to "Internet of Everything". The number of interconnected devices and the amount of data produced increases constantly. Various devices are communicating using various protocols, exchanging data using various data formats and connecting to various software applications. In an IoT-Architecture, a gateway is a fundamental component needed for enabling device interoperability. While a great deal of research has already been done on IoT in cloud computing, fog computing, and edge computing, there is still no intensive activity in the field of gateways in particular. Even the basic gateways can act as a proxy between low-end IoT devices and data centres, automated gateways can provide significantly higher functionality to solve the problems of diversity of protocols, data formats and the custom needs of various devices including used applications. This paper presents a concept of an automated gateway dealing with the problems of protocol conversion, device management, middleware abstraction, resource management and traffic optimisation. The gateway is designed as a modular plug-and-play architecture and was evaluated for MQTT, ZigBee, WebSocket and Amazon WebServices. The architecture can be extended by including additional modules to support further protocols and services. Finally, the gateway defines its protocol and translates incoming messages into an optional uniform format, which can be used by the client to enable more complex message flows. Thus, it provides a solid foundation for further development towards standardization of communication interfaces and interoperability of IoT devices.

Keywords: Industry 4.0 · Internet of Things · IoT Architecture · Interoperability · Connectivity · Automated Gateway · Communication Protocols

1 Introduction

In recent years, many smart devices have been connected to the Internet to record and process data for various purposes. For example, the applications smart health, smart city and smart home are most common. However, also various private applications fall into this field. In general, this concept can be described as the Internet of Things (IoT) [7].

With the growing number of devices, especially in the scope of the Industry 4.0 digitisation of the production, this environment is becoming more and more important. Nowadays, almost everything is networked, so the amount of data being produced is constantly increasing. In 2025, it is predicted that the total number of IoT devices will be approximately 75.44 billion [1]. Furthermore, in the industrial IoT context (IIoT) various industrial and production processes require an efficient and reliable capture, transmission and processing of device data. The devices, including sensors and actuators, rely on a gateway to aggregate the data transmitted by heterogeneous devices using various communication protocols. The gateway usually forwards the data from one to another destination using different processing and storage platforms like cloud computing. Thus, a gateway is a decisive part of the Internet of Things. As per IoT architecture, a gateway is a device that acts as a connection point between IoT devices and their applications. It is an essential aspect of an IoT system since most IoT devices cannot establish a direct connection to the cloud [4].

While a great deal of research has already been done on IoT in cloud computing, fog computing, and edge computing, little seems to have happened in the field of gateways in particular [4]. Therefore, there are still many problems to be solved in this field. One of the obstacles to IoT development is the lack of standardization of communications, especially considering the heterogeneity of protocols for communication with the devices and the high variability of these devices. It is common for sensor manufacturers to use closed standard protocols or different messaging protocols that prevent or hinder their use by third-party applications. This situation leads to the so-called interoperability crisis in IoT [8]. Furthermore, the protocols heterogeneity causes problems and the device management itself. Each device must be configured in order to connect to the cloud. This involves configuration on the device side and the cloud side. Unfortunately, current gateways operate either passively or semi-automatically. This means that the user has to add new devices manually [19]. Unfortunately, these are not the only challenges a gateway has to deal with. Another problem that emerges from this challenge is that IoT gateways need to forward a large amount of data in a short time, which requires IoT gateways to have the ability to handle concurrent mass data. If more devices are added, the gateway may be overloaded and no longer be able to process the amount of data [20].

A concept that can be called automatic gateway is required to solve these problems by minimizing manual intervention. In this paper we present a modular extensible architecture of an automated gateway as a possibility to deal with these problems thus pawing the way for further development towards a standardized solution. The initial prototype of the gateway was developed in the context of the master's thesis [23] and is a subject of ongoing research work in the IoT Systems Lab at the Bremen City University of Applied Sciences.

This paper is structured as follows. First we present the state of the art and define the terms (e.g. gateways types and characteristics) used. The following two sections identify the challenges of solving the open issues and summarize the related work. In the Sect. 4 we propose a modular extensible architecture and a corresponding prototype addressing the identified challenges. In the Sect. 5 we show that such an approach is feasible at principle. Additionally, the Sect. 6 compares our proposed solution with already existing ones from the economic sector. Finally, in the Sect. 7 we conclude the achievement and point to necessary and possible future work.

2   State of the Art

In the Internet of Things, a gateway acts as an intermediary between several different sensors and cloud platforms. These gateways aim to solve the heterogeneity created by different devices and protocols at the sensor level and to forward the resulting data to the cloud [4].

2.1   Types of Gateways

IoT Gateway can be fundamentally divided into the basic gateway and the smart gateway. While basic gateways only act as a proxy between low-end IoT devices and data centres, smart gateways include significantly more functionality. In contrast, a smart gateway handles data efficiently by preprocessing, filtering, analyzing, and delivering only the related or necessary data to the data centre. Furthermore, these intermediate devices are designed to handle harsh environmental conditions to recover from failure while solving the communication gap in minimal time. A smart gateway can be divided into three subtypes based on its functionalities: passive, semi-automated and automated gateways [4]. Sometimes gateways are designed to act smart by discovering IoT devices, registering them to the network, or removing them for better performance. When using passive gateways, these functionalities are performed manually. The user is adding or removing devices by himself/herself while using a specific setup manual/guide. However, these gateways are not customizable and flexible [4].

On the other hand, a semi-automated gateway manages a link between newly added devices and automatically creates connections to new devices. These gateways support a pluggable configuration architecture, which means they can be plugged in based on the requirement of the network device. As a result, these gateways are more flexible than passive gateways and perform better in real-time applications. As a next level, there is a fully-automated gateway, that is self-configurable and self-manageable. There is no human intervention, and the devices can be added and removed automatically. Furthermore, these gateways can operate efficiently in a heterogeneous network and communicate over many different protocols such as Wireless Fidelity (Wi-Fi), Message Queueing Telemetry Transport (MQTT), Constrained Application Protocol (CoAP), Bluetooth, ZigBee or Ethernet and many more. Work has been done in this specific field, but it is still in the growing phase, and researchers focus on making gateways smart enough to provide better performance and Quality of Service (QoS) [4].

According to [4], the criteria a gateway shall fulfill in order to be considered an automated gateway are highlighted as follows.

- *Protocol conversion*: The gateway should contain an approach to solve the so-called interoperability crisis in the IoT area. Therefore, the gateway should be able to support several protocols. The incoming messages should then be transformed into another protocol explicitly selected for the cloud communication.
- *Device management*: Device management should be as automatic as possible, i.e. devices that connect to the gateway should be automatically registered and integrated into the communication with the cloud.
- *Middleware abstraction*: As already described, the gateway is to mediate between intelligent devices and IoT middleware/cloud applications. It is possible to connect to different cloud providers available on the market with such a function.
- *Resource management*: The gateway should work as reliably as possible and react automatically to overloads. This means that the available resources are monitored and automatically distributed. Therefore, the gateway should be able to recognise high-priority applications. The goal of operability is crucial here because the gateway should always be accessible for remote maintenance.
- *Traffic optimization*: There are some promising possibilities to gain performance using streaming optimisation techniques, such as segmenting data into queues, performing packet prioritisation on specific queues, and queuing compression and deduplication for transmission.

2.2   Open Issues and Challenges

The paper "A systematic literature review on IoT gateways" [4] was used for initial analysis on this topic. Based on 2347 articles from the last then years, i.e., from 2011 till July 2021, 75% of the research was conducted in the field of passive gateways, while 18% was on semi-automated and only 7% on fully-automated gateways. For this reason, there are still various problems to be solved. Some of the open issues and research challenges are summarized as follows.

- *Heterogeneity*: IoT applications deal with many heterogeneous smart devices to gather data in different formats and sizes. The gateway is a bridge between all the connecting devices and should handle heterogeneous data among different protocols. While several models and architectures have been proposed to solve this problem, there is still no standardized solution.
- *Scalability*: Gateways should handle the increasing amount of IoT devices without deteriorating the services applied to them. With growing technology, smart devices are also exponentially increasing, leading to issues regarding scalability. For this reason, it is an open issue to distribute the computing resources smartly so that failures do not occur.
- *QoS*: While dealing with a large amount of data and services, the gateway should also provide a quality of service while dealing with real-time data.

Many parameters were individually considered, like reliability, latency, energy efficiency, scalability, but parameters like throughput, roundtrip delay and jitter were overlooked. Furthermore, the simultaneous parameters should also be considered for improving QoS at gateways in IoT.

- *Security and Privacy*: Since gateways are one of the significant data entry points to the network, it is more vulnerable to threats and malicious activities. There was already some work focused on network security, but algorithms and architectures can also opt for more secure gateways and IoT architecture.
- *Intelligence*: Gateways should be smart enough to deal with intelligent data offloading. It is still an open problem how much data should be offloaded, in which case, for how much processing.
- *Robustness*: Based on the previous work, no concepts of recovery of the gateway, fault tolerance, and self-healing were found. Thus, no work has been invested in these topics yet.

Based on these existing problems and research gaps, several exciting research directions have been identified. While much work has already been done to deal with heterogeneity, scalability and interoperability problems individually, there is still a need for a standardized solution to solve these problems simultaneously. Additionally, QoS parameters can also be measured simultaneously to improve IoT systems' performance. Furthermore, machine learning and deep learning techniques are exciting topics because they could be used in combination with traditional security algorithms to deal with privacy and security concerns in IoT gateways. However, working on fully automated gateways is particularly important. Gateways must make spontaneous decisions based on user behavioural patterns and complex situations. Therefore, working more with intelligent and smart gateway can be an exciting challenge. Nevertheless, this aspect is not the only important; in the future, there is a need for self-healing and fault-tolerant gateways to deal with the colossal amount of data. In dealing with Big Data, gateways should be reliable, fault-tolerant, self-manageable and self-healed [4].

3   Related Work

The open problems and challenges discussed in the previous section are treated by different research and development approaches. Some of them are partly covering the aspects related to the presented approach and thus presented as follows.

In [6] a Semantic Gateway as a Service (SGS) was presented that enables the translation of message protocols such as the Extensible Messaging and Presence Protocol (XMPP), CoAP and MQTT via a multi-protocol proxy architecture. The SGS also provides intelligent solution by integrating Semantic Web technologies with existing sensor and service standards. The SGS is also integrated with semantic service such as SemSOS [15] to further elevate interoperability at service level.

Another gateway was presented in [18]. The proposed result is similar to the client/server model of the Hypertext Transfer Protocol (HTTP) and uses CoAP for device-to-device (D2D) communication. An operation is equivalent to that of HTTP and is sent by a client to request action on a resource identified by a Uniform Resource Identifier (URI) on a server. The server then sends a response with a response code. The gateway was especially designed to be suitable for in-home-scale environments. Additionally to this, future work is planned to extend the gateway to large-scale and energy-aware mobile environments.

The last gateway examined in [14], introduces configurable smart gateway system which can be flexibly configured to adapt to different application requirements. It can also reduce the development cycle, difficulty, costs, and more easily and quickly be applied to new applications. To achieve this goal, the gateway uses its own message structure in combination with a pluggable design, whose modules with different communication protocols can be customized and plugged in according to different networks. The proposed result packages data on the gateway in its data format to overcome different data problems.

Additionally to design aspects of the system, packet scheduling is an essential function in most networks systems. In [5] this topic was further investigated. This work proposes an approach to include a classifier, which analyzes the messages received by the gateway and separates them into queues. The messages were divided into High Priority (HP) and Best Effort (BE). A modified version of the Hierarchical Token Bucket (HTB) algorithm was used, which aimed to achieve fair treatment of the requests. The experimental evaluation showed that high priority messages achieved a 24% reduction in latency without discards or losses of packages in this queue.

Summarized, the discussed approaches concentrate on one or few dedicated aspects in contrast to the integrated concept presented in this paper.

4   Design and Implementation of the Proposed Automatic Gateway

The design of the proposed gateway [23] is presented in more detail in the following sections. Only the chosen subset of problems and their solutions are considered in more detail. The Open Service Gateway Initiative (OSGi) [2] was used for the development, since this framework supports the implementation of component-based, service-oriented applications in Java [25]. For this reason, Java version 11 was also used for the first prototype. In addition, the software was developed specifically for the Raspberry Pi 3B+ as an evaluation system.

4.1   Overall Architecture

For reference, the overall architecture used to evaluate the prototype is shown in the following Fig. 1. However, the Raspberry Pi device (gateway) is particularly important for this article, as this is the target component to be developed. It runs an Apache Karaf [9] server (OSGi implementation), which also allows OSGi

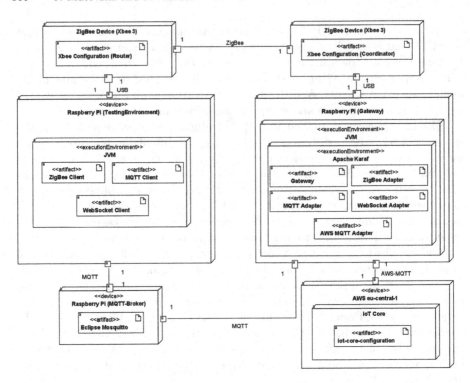

Fig. 1. Deployment diagram of the evaluation system.

compatible software bundles to be installed at runtime. The following chapters will further explain the most important functionalities of the actual gateway. In addition, the test instruments are displayed. These include Digi XBee SMT Module (Xbee 3) [16], as well as Eclipse Mosquitto [10] and AWS IoT Core [17]. There are also lightweight test clients for each protocol used to simulate loads on the gateway.

The actual functionalities of the gateway are encapsulated in their own service domain. Various interfaces are defined for the gateway to communicate with the existing adapters (Fig. 2). These interfaces are then bundled via another interface, which adapters can use via OSGi. The adapters can finally access these functionalities through a predefined interface, as shown in Fig. 3. Since the responsibilities in the gateway are separated, additional functionalities can be implemented without changing the old ones.

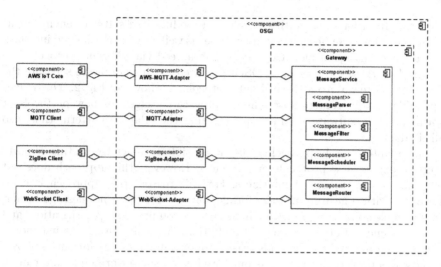

Fig. 2. OSGi container with provided software modules.

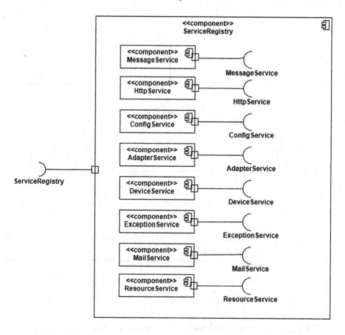

Fig. 3. Service Registry with predefined interfaces.

4.2   Protocol Conversion

Protocol conversion is one of the biggest problems in IoT, as there is no standardised interface for communication due to heterogeneity. Therefore, many manufacturers use their standards or fall back on one of the many freely available standards. In order to solve this problem, a modularised software environment is required, which can be changed at runtime, as well as a clearly defined interface so that the exchange of messages can be guaranteed via different protocols.

Based on these requirements, OSGi was used as an example to separate the logic of the gateway from the utilised protocols, as shown in Fig. 2. This makes it possible to add, configure or remove software packages for new protocols at runtime. These software modules are utilizing the adapter pattern, thus also called adapters.

The adapter-based approach makes it possible to react to existing requirements to embed new protocols or interfaces. However, this approach does not yet enable a cross-protocol interfaces. For this reason, this approach is complemented with a custom message format for IoT devices. The message format should enable supporting functionalities such as compression, prioritisation, and end-to-end encryption of messages. In addition, direct device addressing should be supported in any case. For this reason, an example message format as shown in Fig. 4 was implemented. This is only used as a proof-of-principle and can be exchanged with another message format, if necessary.

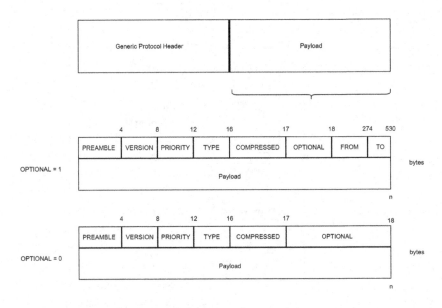

Fig. 4. Customized message format of the gateway.

The message format as described in Table 1 can be used by clients, but it is not mandatory. If this is not the case, messages are interpreted as legacy and reformatted by the gateway to simply send them to a defined end consumer. This only works if the used protocol can supply enough metadata to transform this message into the uniform format. This metadata includes data such as IP addresses or names to uniquely identify the devices. As said, this format is optional and does not have to be adopted, so the solution is supported by a wide variety of devices. However, it is not possible to use advanced functionalities of the gateway without this format.

Table 1. Message format description

TYPE	Description
PREAMBLE	This field defines a fixed value, which is used as identification. If this value is set, then communication is in the specified format. If not, then the client is considered as legacy
VERSION	This field defines the protocol version for further changes or upgrades
PRIORITY	This field defines the message's priority, currently supported are 0 = BEST_EFFORT and 1 = HIGH_PRIORITY
TYPE	This field defines the type of this message
COMPRESSED	This field indicates if this message is compressed with gzip
OPTIONAL	This field defines if the FROM and TO header is available, this option is specifically for low bandwidth protocols like ZigBee
FROM	This field defines the device id where the message comes from
TO	This field defines the device id where the message goes to
PAYLOAD	This field includes the message's payload, which format does not matter

These two exemplary approaches show a way to solve the problem of protocol conversion. However, the data format used so far is still a rudimentary and not fully developed version. Therefore, further work has to be invested in this topic to create a possible general IoT standard message format for a comprehensive solution.

4.3   Device Management

Device management is a topic that increases in complexity with growing depth. For this reason, the proposed approach only provides a fundamental problem solution.

In the proposed approach, each gateway manages a database of all connected devices and thus can detect whether devices have already been registered or not. When an unregistered device connects to the gateway, a registration process is automatically performed. To include other consumer systems, the gateway propagate this registration requests to other software modules responsible for protocols or end-systems like Amazon Web Services.

This simple solution shows the functional feasibility of the approach and allows devices to be registered in the cloud without much effort, since the adapter is managing the registration. This means that there is less need for configuration in the cloud itself. However, this approach is not covering a precise security mechanism yet. This shall be extended in the future work, because providing a suitable security mechanism is essential for the professional usage of this feature. In addition, further possibilities of configuration on the device side were not considered in this prototype. In order to enable this feature, this concept can be extended with user-predefined device configurations for specific device types. This can be done by extending the already existing message format. The last step would be to extend this concept to include a device discovery so that devices can be included in the communication without much effort.

4.4 Middleware Abstraction

Middleware abstraction is an additional problem besides the already existing heterogeneity of protocols. Nowadays, there are many cloud providers, and in some case, even several applications are used simultaneously. Moreover, these cloud providers always differ in their interfaces and partly include a vendor lock-in, so no consistent communication is possible.

Therefore, this paper proposes to supplement the already used adapter approach to solve this problem. The adapter allows the protocols and the cloud-specific interfaces to be translated. Of course, this presupposes that these can be covered by the message format and the internal communication of the gateway.

This simple approach is able to demonstrate what an accurate middleware abstraction can look like. Furthermore, due to the modular approach, extending the already presented solution does not require high effort.

4.5 Resource Management

In order for resource management to be automated, several parameters must be monitored. For this reason, the following metrics are measured in an interval.

- CPU utilisation of the system
- CPU utilisation of the process
- Heap memory usage
- Non-heap memory usage
- Throughput of messages

Based on the related work concentrating on this aspect, this is only a part of the metrics, but it can be measured without much effort and is providing enough initial information for estimation of the feasibility of our concept as an integrated solution. In addition, these measurements are used to prioritize messages and adjust QoS levels. Adjusting QoS levels is only possible by utilizing the unified message format, which is used to define such messages. This allowing, for example, to lower or raise the intervals of messages of clients. As a consequence, devices that do not implement this format can not be managed.

At principle, there are still various possibilities for expansion. For example, mechanisms could be built to increase the prioritisation of processes. For example, individual protocols could be prioritised if the load on the respective interface increases. For a network of individual gateways, these could even exchange information to distribute loads. These are only two examples, but the potential in this environment is still large.

4.6   Traffic Optimization

Traffic optimization is a very complex topic. There are many different approaches to increase throughput, and they all need to be evaluated and assessed for this use case. In this approach only simple methods were used to improve the system behaviour as a part of the solution integrating the different aspects.

For this purpose, the incoming messages are segmented into two queues. Then, the messages are placed in this queues based on priorities. The exact algorithm used is a simple version of Weighted-Fair-Queuing (WFQ) with fixed weights. In addition to scheduling, compression of messages was introduced. This is important for protocols like ZigBee, as the rate of data transfer is only about 250 kbps [24].

Of course, as a future work, different algorithms need to be investigated and compared in order to determine the best suited ones. The prototype allows an exchange of the algorithm through adaptation of the configuration. This is possible without any problems due to the modular design.

5   Experimental Results

To test the system, we set up several measurement targets. The main objective of the measurements was to answer the following questions:

1. How much delay is caused by the system design, and can the system communicate in near real-time?
2. How many messages can the gateway handle simultaneously, and what impact does a high message count have on the gateway?
3. What impact the prioritisation of messages has on response time?
4. How long does the gateway run without errors, or more precisely, what are the mean time to failure (MTTF) and mean time between failures (MTBF)?

For this reason, loads were simulated on the MQTT and WebSocket protocols. Unfortunately, this was not possible for ZigBee since this protocol does not allow high data transfer rates and, therefore, only consumes low resources. In each measurement, the message had a size of 579 bytes in total and the measurement duration was one hour.

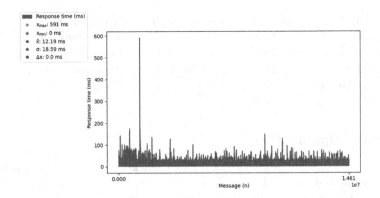

Fig. 5. Response time of MQTT with an average load of 4000 messages per second.

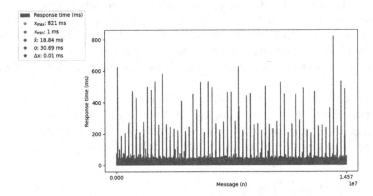

Fig. 6. Response time of WebSocket with an average load of 4000 messages per second.

The measurements as summarized in the Table 2 have shown that a message load of 4000 messages per second can be considered acceptable, independent of the protocol. In the Fig. 5 and Fig. 6 the evaluated measurement data for the response time of 4000 messages per second are illustrated in more detail. While even 8000 messages were still within the realm of possibility for WebSocket, this does not apply to MQTT. Nevertheless, the response time increased to almost 100 ms for WebSocket as well. Measurements with more messages per second could not be performed because the connections were constantly interrupted. In addition to the measured values, prioritising messages improved the response time approximately 242%. For this, the response times between two clients with 2000 messages per second were compared. One of the two had a high priority and the other a normal priority. As a complement to the performance measurements, the runtime behaviour was monitored over two months. No critical errors occurred, therefore it can be assumed that the presented design runs considerably reliable. For productive use, extended time periods shall be considered.

Table 2. Average measured values of the evaluation

Messages/s	CPU system	CPU process	Heap memory	Non Heap memory	Response Time	Test successful
Baseline						
–	0.6%	0.35%	49.48 MB	56.23 MB	–	✓
MQTT						
1000	18%	18%	40.18 MB	61.94 MB	5.25 ms	✓
2000	27%	27%	76.05 MB	52.93 MB	5.9 ms	✓
4000	54%	54%	55.75 MB	52.95 MB	12.19 ms	✓
8000	43%	42%	168.92 MB	53 MB	212.36463 s	–
WebSocket						
1000	10%	8%	46.37 MB	55.08 MB	14.74 ms	✓
2000	17%	13%	47.43 MB	55.24 MB	15.67 ms	✓
4000	24%	19%	46.2 MB	55.08 MB	18.84 ms	✓
8000	43%	34%	45.48 MB	55.19 MB	91.82 ms	✓

6 Comparison to Existing Frameworks

As an assessment of the added value, our proposed approach was compared with existing solutions from the economic sector. For this purpose, various open source projects were examined for protocol conversion, device management, middleware abstraction, resource management and traffic optimisation. The frameworks examined include Eclipse Kura, EdgeX Foundry, OpenHAB and Things-Board IoT Gateway.

Eclipse Kura is an extensible open-source IoT Edge Framework based on Java/OSGi. Kura offers API access to the hardware interfaces of IoT Gateways (serial ports, GPS, Watchdog, GPIO or I2C). It features ready-to-use field protocols (including Modbus or OPC-UA), an application container, and a web-based visual data flow programming to acquire data from the field, process it at the edge, and publish it to leading IoT Cloud Platforms through MQTT connectivity. While Eclipse Kura already partially solves the protocol conversion for devices, only MQTT is offered on the cloud side. In addition, only one device is created in the cloud, the gateway itself. However, the gateway can still call all endpoints and thus modify the data of other devices, but it cannot automatically register devices due to the implementation. There is no middleware abstraction either, as only the cloud platforms such as Eurotech Everyware Cloud, Amazon AWS IoT Core, Azure IoT Hub, Eclipse Kapua and Eclipse Hono are supported. At the moment, nothing can be found in the documentation about resource management [12].

EdgeX Foundry is a highly flexible, scalable and vendor-neutral open-source framework hosted by the Linux Foundation that facilitates the development of data collection, analytics and cloud connector services. The applications act as cloud-to-edge middleware with a plug-and-play distributed microservice architecture. EdgeX Foundry was designed to provide broad industry support. For this reason, not only many device protocols are supported, but also different protocols on the cloud side. Furthermore, EdgeX Foundry's architecture enables middleware abstraction, so nobody depends on specific cloud providers. Also, the application supports resource management mechanisms by measuring parameters such as round trip time to achieve the lowest possible latency. In addition, EdgeX can identify which data needs to be sent to the cloud and processed cost-effectively on edge. However, there seem to be no prioritization options for individual packets. In device management, nevertheless, there is static and automatic device discovery, so devices no longer need to be added manually [13].

The open Home Automation Bus (openHAB) is an open-source home automation software based on Java and OSGi. It is deployed on-premise and connects to devices and services from different vendors. As of 2019, openHAB already included around 300 bindings available as OSGi modules. While openHAB is a home automation software, that does not mean it cannot be used for IoT purposes. For example, support for different device protocols and services has been implemented, yet integrating different cloud applications is missing. In fact, openHAB only focuses on the openHAB Cloud. There seems to be no concrete resource management or traffic optimization mechanism either. Nevertheless, the application has a device discovery function so that devices can be added automatically [11].

The ThingsBoard IoT Gateway is an open-source solution to integrate devices with ThingsBoard. However, the IoT Gateway is built on top of Python and is different from similar projects that leverage OSGi technology. The gateway supports custom connectors to connect to new devices or servers and custom converters for processing data from devices. The ThingsBoard IoT Gateway also solves the protocol translation on the device side, yet it also lacks different cloud protocols. This fact leads to inevitably having to work with the ThingsBoard solution. Furthermore, there is no indication of resource management or a traffic optimization mechanism. However, the gateway can create devices automatically, so there is no need to create them manually [3].

Comparing the summarized solutions with the one, developed within the proposed approach, we can notify that the developed solution offers significantly more modularity. The architecture design makes it possible to install different protocols and services at runtime. However, the most important processes such as scheduling are still controlled by the gateway. For this reason, aspects such as protocol conversion and middleware abstraction are fully implemented in the proposed design. Only EdgeX Foundry offers this modularity to the same extent. The device management of the proposed solution is not yet mature enough to be able to compare it with the other solutions, but enables including additional features such as the automatic change of QoS levels. Regarding resource management and traffic optimisation, the proposed solution and EdgeX Foundry are the only applications that implement these to a certain extent. However, it must be mentioned that in this area EdgeX Foundry implements other functionalities than our proposed gateway, so a comparison of these aspects is difficult. However, it should be noted that the proposed solution, in contrast to EdgeX Foundry, already includes prioritisation mechanisms. In summary, it can be stated that the developed solution is only a prototype and does not yet implement all the designed aspects into detail. Therefore, a comparison to other productive solutions cannot be done at this early stage of development. Nevertheless, it shows the first steps towards an integrated solution, which is obviously not the aim of the existing solutions.

7 Conclusion and Future Work

Internet of Things as an essential part of the Industry 4.0 strategy is a fast-growing area and is thus becoming increasingly important. Unfortunately, strong growth is also associated with many different problems. While a great deal of research has already been done on the topic of IoT in the fields of cloud computing, fog computing, and edge computing, little seems to have happened in the field of the gateways in particular.

A concept that can be called automatic gateway is required to solve these problems and minimize the manual intervention in order to recognize, add or remove devices and establish the communication link. In this paper we proposed an integrated modular and extensible concept for enabling of an automatic protocol conversion, device management, middleware abstraction, resource management and traffic optimisation. In order to demonstrate the feasibility of the proposed approach, we implemented an initial prototype of the automatic gateway and evaluated the performance of this gateway for a Raspberry Pi 3B+. The measurements have shown that a load of 28.96 kbs (4000 messages/s with 579 bytes per message) up to 57.9 kbs (8000 messages/s with 579 bytes per message) can be considered acceptable. The prioritization of messages improved the response time by approximately 242% in this approach. In addition to the performance measurements the gateway was able to run over two months without critical errors. Therefore this approach can be considered feasible and reliable.

The proposed gateway provides a modular solution to solve the mentioned problems. The gateway can be easily extended to support additional protocols and consumers. Device management is also automated, reducing a significant administrative burden. Also, some aspects are supported to increase the scalability and robustness of the system. Nevertheless, the approach has to be considered as an initial feasibility study. In contrast to the approaches presented as related work, that are concentrating on one main aspect, our concept aims at providing an integrated extensible solution on conceptual and architectural level for the main problems addressed.

The proposed solution does not yet completely implement the individual subset of problems for the variety of protocols, data formats, devices and storage. In this context additional trade-offs considering feasibility vs. effort for each aspect have to be performed in order to determine the reasonable limits of such an integrated generic solution for a practical and productive use. The possibility of integrating the compared existing solutions will also be analysed and considered for further development. Additionally, the prototype needs to be further optimised to improve performance (to utilise the whole bandwidth of the Raspberry Pi 3B+). Therefore, existing traffic optimization approaches have to be considered and evaluated. Furthermore, the problem of security has to be addressed as a next step, since it is necessary for productive use.

Besides addressing different functionality aspects, an extension of the gateway in the context of the OPC/UA infrastructure under consideration of the UA Companion Specifications [22] is planned as a future work. In this context both the client/server approach and the enhancement to publish/subscribe [21] will be analysed.

Finally, the initial evaluation of the existing solution shall be improved and all planned extensions need to be evaluated in a comprehensive way.

References

1. Alam, T.: A reliable communication framework and its use in Internet of Things (IoT). CSEIT1835111, pp. 450–456. Received 10 May 2018
2. OSGi Alliance: OSGi Core, Release 8, October 2020. https://docs.osgi.org/specification/. Accessed 21 June 2022
3. ThingsBoard Authors: ThingsBoard IoT Gateway documentation, August 2022. https://thingsboard.io/docs/iot-gateway/. Accessed 08 Apr 2022
4. Beniwal, G., Singhrova, A.: A systematic literature review on IoT gateways. J. King Saud Univ.-Comput. Inf. Sci. **34**(10), 9541–9563 (2021). https://doi.org/10.1016/j.jksuci.2021.11.007
5. de Caldas Filho, F.L., Rocha, R.L., Abbas, C.J., Martins, L.M.E., Canedo, E.D., de Sousa, R.T.: QoS scheduling algorithm for a fog IoT gateway. In: 2019 Workshop on Communication Networks and Power Systems (WCNPS), pp. 1–6. IEEE (2019). https://doi.org/10.1109/WCNPS.2019.8896311
6. Desai, P., Sheth, A., Anantharam, P.: Semantic gateway as a service architecture for IoT interoperability. In: 2015 IEEE International Conference on Mobile Services, pp. 313–319. IEEE (2015). https://doi.org/10.1109/MobServ.2015.51
7. Fan, Q., Ansari, N.: Towards workload balancing in fog computing empowered IoT. IEEE Trans. Netw. Sci. Eng. **7**(1), 253–262 (2018). https://doi.org/10.1109/TNSE.2018.2852762
8. Filho, F.L.C., Martins, L.M.E., Araújo, I.P., de Mendonça, F.L., da Costa, J.P.C., de Sousa Júnior, R.T.: Design and evaluation of a semantic gateway prototype for IoT networks. In: Companion Proceedings of the10th International Conference on Utility and Cloud Computing, pp. 195–201 (2017). https://doi.org/10.1145/3147234.3148091
9. The Apache Software Foundation: Apache Karaf container 4.x - documentation, August 2022. https://karaf.apache.org/manual/latest/. Accessed 08 Apr 2022
10. Eclipse Foundation: Eclipse Mosquitto^{TM}, August 2022. https://mosquitto.org/. Accessed 08 Apr 2022
11. openHAB Foundation: openHab documentation, August 2022. https://www.openhab.org/docs/. Accessed 08 Apr 2022
12. Eclipse Foundation: The extensible open source Java/OSGi IoT Edge Framework, August 2022. https://www.eclipse.org/kura/. Accessed 08 Apr 2022
13. EdgeX Foundry: Edgex foundry documentation, August 2022. https://docs.edgexfoundry.org/2.1/. Accessed 08 Apr 2022
14. Guoqiang, S., Yanming, C., Chao, Z., Yanxu, Z.: Design and implementation of a smart IoT gateway. In: 2013 IEEE International Conference on Green Computing and Communications and IEEE Internet of Things and IEEE Cyber, Physical and Social Computing, pp. 720–723. IEEE (2013). https://doi.org/10.1109/GreenCom-iThings-CPSCom.2013.130

15. Henson, C.A., Pschorr, J.K., Sheth, A.P., Thirunarayan, K.: SemSOS: semantic sensor observation service. In: 2009 International Symposium on Collaborative Technologies and Systems, pp. 44–53 (2009). https://doi.org/10.1109/CTS.2009.5067461

16. Digi International Inc.: DigiXBee® 3 ZigBee®, August 2022. https://www.digi.com/resources/documentation/digidocs/pdfs/90001539.pdf. Accessed 08 Apr 2022

17. Amazon Web Services IoT Core: AWS IoT Core- Developer Guide, August 2022. https://docs.aws.amazon.com/iot/latest/developerguide/what-is-aws-iot.html. Accessed 08 Apr 2022

18. Kang, B., Choo, H.: An experimental study of a reliable IoT gateway. ICT Express 4(3), 130–133 (2018). https://doi.org/10.1016/j.icte.2017.04.002. https://www.sciencedirect.com/science/article/pii/S2405959516301485

19. Kang, B., Kim, D., Choo, H.: Internet of everything: a large-scale autonomic IoT gateway. IEEE Trans. Multi-Scale Comput. Syst. 3(3), 206–214 (2017). https://doi.org/10.1109/TMSCS.2017.2705683

20. Min, D., Xiao, Z., Sheng, B., Quanyong, H., Xuwei, P.: Design and implementation of heterogeneous IOT gateway based on dynamic priority scheduling algorithm. Trans. Inst. Meas. Control. 36(7), 924–931 (2014). https://doi.org/10.1177/0142331214527600

21. OPC-Foundation: OPC UA is enhanced for Publish-Subscribe (Pub/Sub) (2016). https://opcconnect.opcfoundation.org/2016/03/opc-ua-is-enhanced-for-publish-subscribe-pubsub/. Accessed 21 June 2022

22. OPC-Foundation: OPC Unified Architecture (U/A) Specification (2017–2022). https://opcfoundation.org/developer-tools/specifications-unified-architecture. Accessed 21 June 2022

23. Soldin, M.: Design and implementation of an automated gateway prototype for the Internet of Things. Master's thesis, City University of Applied Sciences, Bremen, Germany, June 2022

24. Somani, N.A., Patel, Y.: ZigBee: a low power wireless technology for industrial applications. Int. J. Control Theory Comput. Model. (IJCTCM) 2(3), 27–33 (2012). https://doi.org/10.5121/ijctcm.2012.2303

25. Tavares, A.L., Valente, M.T.: A gentle introduction to OSGi. ACM SIGSOFT Softw. Eng. Notes 33(5), 1–5 (2008)

2nd International Workshop on Designing and Measuring Security in Software Architectures (DeMeSSA)

A Methodological Approach to Verify Architecture Resiliency

Joanna C. S. Santos[1]([✉]), Selma Suloglu[2], Néstor Cataño[3],
and Mehdi Mirakhorli[3]([✉])

[1] University of Notre Dame, Notre Dame, IN 46556, USA
`joannacss@nd.edu`
[2] Atilim University, Ankara, Turkey
`selma.suloglu@atilim.edu.tr`
[3] Rochester Institute of Technology, Rochester, NY 14623, USA
`{nxccics,mxmvse}@rit.edu`

Abstract. Architecture-first approach to address software resiliency is becoming the mainstream development method for mission-critical and software-intensive systems. In such approach, resiliency is built into the system from the ground up, starting with a robust software architecture design. As a result, a flaw in the design of a resilient architecture affects the system's ability to anticipate, withstand, recover from, and adapt to adverse conditions, stresses, attacks, or compromises on cyber-resources. In this paper, we present an architecture-centric reasoning and verification methodology for detecting design weaknesses in resilient systems. Our goal is to assist software architects in building sound architectural models of their systems. We showcase our approach with the aid of an Autonomous Robot modeled in AADL, in which we use our methodology to uncover three architectural weaknesses in the adoption of three architectural tactics.

Keywords: Cyber resiliency · Architecture Analysis and Design Language · AADL · Architecture Tactics

1 Introduction

Cyber-resiliency refers to a system's ability to anticipate potential compromises, to continue operating even under attacks (*to withstand*), to restore its operation in the face of attacks (*to recover*), and to adapt its behavior to minimize any compromises (*to evolve*) [5]. Achieving cyber-resiliency goals, therefore, involves designing a software system that addresses multiple quality attributes, such as performance, security, safety, or evolvability. Under these circumstances, the architecture-first development method [7] is becoming the mainstream approach for addressing cyber resiliency concerns in mission-critical and software-intensive systems [10,14]. Since the system's architecture design plays a crucial role in the software development process, weaknesses in the software system's architecture can have a greater impact on the system's ability to anticipate, withstand, recover from, and adapt to adverse conditions, stresses, attacks, or compromises on cyber resources [19].

T. Batista et al. (Eds.): ECSA 2022, LNCS 13928, pp. 321–336, 2023.
https://doi.org/10.1007/978-3-031-36889-9_22

Despite the importance of the architecture-first approach to enhance and ensure the resiliency of mission-critical systems, current research in the field focuses on the verification of requirements, functional or non-functional (e.g., safety, or security) of the system [1,16,31], and neglects an in-depth analysis of architectural weaknesses in the system's design. Some existing approaches for creating architectural models comply with domain-specific requirements (e.g., avionics) [6,20,27,31], or with the creation of reusable modeling components [16,17]. However, cyber-resiliency involves multiple quality attributes (availability, safety, security, etc.) and can be applied to multiple systems domains. Finally, the current state of practice requires systems engineers to have an in-depth understanding of potential mistakes associated with the design of resilient systems and use qualitative techniques to evaluate the design [22]. For instance, the Architecture Trade-off Analysis Method (ATAM) [22] has been widely used in mission and safety critical applications as a qualitative approach to risk and trade-off analysis of an architecture with respect to a set of clearly articulated quality scenarios. However, such approaches are not able to detect specific design weaknesses in complex applications with several components and interdependencies.

In this paper, we describe **an architecture-centric reasoning and verification methodology** for detecting design weaknesses in resilient systems. It is a model-driven methodology for aiding software architects to systematically analyze and formally verify the resiliency aspects of their architectural designs. It shifts the architecture evaluation from a primarily qualitative and subjective approach to an approach that is empowered by formal verification.

Our methodology encompasses four phases. ① The architecture is modelled using the Architecture Analysis and Design Language (AADL) [12]. ② The architecture model is enriched with *annotations* that map AADL components to elements in resiliency *tactics* and *patterns*. These annotations add semantics of resiliency tactics and patterns to AADL models, allowing reasoning about flaws associated to a resilient design. ③ A risk assessment is performed to identify *weaknesses* that may violate the properties of resiliency tactics in the system. In this phase, these weaknesses are specified in terms of *conceptual models* and a set of *formal rules*. These rules are written using the *Resolute* [13] language, which is application-independent and can be reused to analyze another system modeled in AADL. ④ Finally, these rules are checked against the annotated model to verify whether the current architecture design is flawed (i.e., it contains architectural weaknesses). We showcase our methodology in the context of an Autonomous Robot, for which we model its system architecture using the Architectural Analysis & Design Language (AADL) [12]. We use Resolute to specify three common architectural weaknesses to expose flaws in the Autonomous Robot's design.

The contributions of this paper are three-fold. (*i*) a novel methodology for the verification of architectural resiliency properties of AADL models. (*ii*) An approach to specify common architectural weaknesses as conceptual models which are converted into reusable rules written in an assurance case language (Resolute), which can be used to detect design weaknesses in various architectures. We use the *Resolute* [13] language for pragmatic reasons. This language was initially developed to model assurance cases, however, we adopt it because of its power to conduct reachability analysis of AADL models which can be leveraged to detect various design weaknesses. (*iii*) A case study demonstrating the feasibility and practicality of using our methodology to detect common architectural weaknesses in complex AADL models.

Paper Organization. Section 2 introduces concepts for our paper to be understood by a broader audience. Section 3 describes our model-driven methodology. Section 4 illustrates the methodology in the context of an autonomous robot. Section 5 discusses related work, whereas Sect. 6 concludes this paper.

2   Background

This section explains key concepts that are used throughout the paper.

2.1   Architectural Tactics

Software architects typically use a rich set of proven architectural *tactics* to design cyber-resilient systems [2]. They provide reusable solutions for addressing resiliency concerns, even when the system is under attack. They are grouped under five main categories: *detect, resist* (withstand), *react to, recover from,* and *prevent* cyber events [2,5,18]. Tactics play an important role in shaping the high-level design of software since they describe reusable techniques and concrete solutions for satisfying a wide range of quality concerns [2,15], including resiliency.

The Software Engineering Institute (SEI) at Carnegie Mellon University (CMU) released a comprehensive catalog of tactics for different quality attributes such as availability, security, and reliability [2]. This catalog is collected from existing literature. Besides, there is an extensive body of work about the importance of architectural tactics and their role in software quality [2,26].

There are many kinds of resiliency tactics. For example, a system with high reliability requirements might implement the *heartbeat* tactic [2,26] to monitor the availability of a critical component, or the voting tactic [26] to increase fault tolerance through integrating and processing information from a set of redundant components. Architectural tactics are pervasive in resilient and fault-tolerant systems [2,25].

2.2   Common Architectural Weaknesses

Although tactics provide well-formed strategies for a system to satisfy a specific quality concern, e.g., resist cyberattacks, if they are not carefully adopted in a system, they can result in *architectural weaknesses* (also referred in the literature as "design flaws") [19,28]. There is a fundamental difference between *architectural weaknesses* and *bugs*. While the latter are more code-level, such as buffer overflows caused by miscalculations, the former are at a higher level and much more subtle and sophisticated [19].

For instance, a system may adopt the *Authenticate Actors* tactic, but the authentication enforcement is performed in the client-side instead of the server-side [28]. In this example, a client/server product performs authentication within the client code, but not in the server code, allowing the authentication feature to be bypassed via a modified client which omits the authentication check. This design decision creates a weakness in the security architecture, which can be successfully exploited by an intruder with reverse-engineering skills. There are numerous examples of architectural weaknesses [19,21,28,33] that needs to be mitigated at the design time.

2.3   Architecture Modeling and AADL

The Architecture Analysis and Design Language (AADL) [12] is a modeling language which allows an architecture-centric, and model-based development approach throughout the system lifecycle. AADL models cover both *static* and *dynamic* system structure in terms of *components* and their *interactions*. As shown in Fig. 1, components are categorized as either *application system* components or *execution platform* components. Components include a set of *features*, *properties*, and *flows*.

Application system components interact with each other via *features* (one or more ports or data accesses). Features that are either data and/or event ports can be an input (*in*), output (*out*) or input/output (*in/out*) port. The interaction between components in an execution platform is provided by a *Bus* component type, which is the counterpart of a feature in the application system components.

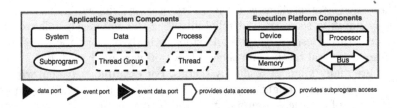

Fig. 1. AADL graphical notation

AADL also allows components to be annotated with *properties*, which define the characteristics of a component. These properties can be used to perform various analysis, such as model checking. AADL provides six predefined *property sets* but AADL models can also be extended with user-defined property sets.

2.4   Architecture Reasoning on AADL Using Resolute

Given that an AADL model provide a formalized presentation of the architecture, we can leverage its semantics to perform reasoning. For this purpose, *Resolute* [13] is a language and a tool to assure the system's architecture specified in

AADL meet its expectations, which are represented as a set of rules expressed in a declarative fashion. These rules are written in terms of *assurance cases*, each of which presents *claims* about the system and supporting *evidence* for them. These claims describe a quality attribute about the system (e.g., safety cases, security cases, etc.). The evidence for the claim is automatically extracted from the model based on the written rules.

For instance, one can claim that the system logs all security-relevant operations (i.e., it adopts the *Maintain Audit Trails* tactic [2]). As shown in Listing 1.1, this can be done by first defining a top-level claim (line 5) that describes using a first-order predicate how this claim can be proved. This check is implemented by querying the AADL model to verify that the system has (i) at least one Audit Manager, which is a component that tracks each transaction alongside with identifying information (line 7); and (ii) at least one Action Target, which is a component that perform security-critical operations (line 8). This top-level claim invokes a subclaim (all_action_targets_report_operations(s)[1] in line 9) to check whether all Action Targets do send their critical operation information to the Audit Manager for it to be logged.

```
1   annex resolute {**
2     has_role(s: aadl, role: string) :
3       bool = (has_property (s, Props::Role)) and member(role, property(s,
            Props::Role))
4
5     maintain_audit_trails(s: system) <=
6       ** "The system " s " logs security-relevant operations" **
7       exists(comp: component) . has_role(comp, "AuditManager") and
8       exists(comp: component) . has_role(comp, "ActionTarget") andthen
9       all_action_targets_report_operations(s)
10
11      -- more subclaims (...)
12  **};
```

Listing 1.1. Claims in Resolute

3   Architecture-Centric Verification Methodology

As shown in Fig. 2, the architecture-centric reasoning and verification methodology presented in this paper has four phases: ① An *architecture modeling* phase in which the software architect models the architectural design using AADL. ② A *common architectural weakness modeling and specification* phase in which the software architect selects a potential architectural flaw for inspection, draws a conceptual graph of the flaw, and converts it into a set of *reusable rules*, which are written in Resolute [13]. They describe the way the system should withstand to overcome the flaw. ③ A *model annotation* phase in which elements in the architectural model are tagged with *roles* and *properties*. A role describes a component's functionality, whereas a property defines the characteristics of a component. ④ An *architecture verification* phase, in which the architectural elements (components) tagged during the third phase are

---

[1] Due to space constraints, we do not show the definitions for all sub-claims.

checked against the Resolute rules encoded during the second one. The Resolute tool checks for (the absence of) weaknesses automatically.

These four phases are performed repeatedly until the software architecture achieves the intended level of resiliency. In what follows, we detail each phase.

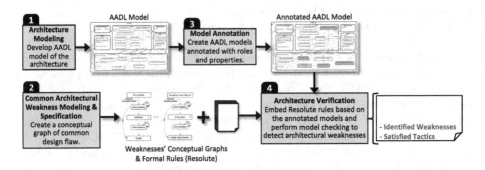

Fig. 2. The architecture-centric reasoning and verification methodology

3.1   Architecture Modeling

In this phase, the software architect uses AADL to describe system components, their interactions, as well as functional and non-functional properties of the software system. The software architect can use *property sets* and the *annexes* in AADL to specify behavioral details of the design, define the system's components (e.g., threads, subprograms, etc.) or the execution platform components (e.g., device, memory, etc.). For medium to large scale systems, these models are often non-trivial and may have several elements and interdependencies.

3.2   Common Architectural Weakness Modeling and Specification

In the second phase, the architect performs an assessment of *potential weaknesses*, which are captured in **Weaknesses Models** and **Specifications**.

Modeling Common Architectural Weaknesses. A *weakness model* can be used as a guideline for manual or automated inspection of a system's architecture. A weakness model is essentially a *reusable conceptual graph* centered around a specific *architectural tactic* and includes the following elements:

- A set of **architectural roles**, which represent the functionality assumed by an architectural element. These roles are modeled as **nodes** in the conceptual graph.
- A set of **properties** that are used to model how the system incorrectly behaves in the occurrence of a cyber-event. They correspond to the data flow and the control flow between the conceptual roles in a Weakness Model.

Unlike a data flow, a control flow is a flow that only occur if a condition is true. These data and control flow are **_directed edges_** in the conceptual graph. Edges have an attribute that specifies the *data type* flowing between the nodes. This attribute could be either *generic*, which means that its data type is not specified or matches all data types, or *typed*, which indicates its actual concrete data type.

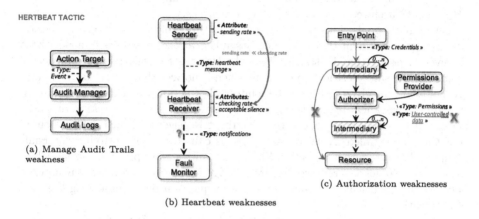

(a) Manage Audit Trails weakness

(b) Heartbeat weaknesses

(c) Authorization weaknesses

Fig. 3. Conceptual graphs

Capturing architectural weaknesses as conceptual graphs makes the Weakness Model **_language-agnostic_** and **_reusable_**. They can be used to guide the process of detecting architectural weaknesses in systems designs using different modeling languages such as AADL, SysML (Systems Modeling Language), among others. Although the modeling of weaknesses via conceptual graphs can be skipped, it helps the later development of weaknesses specifications, as it demonstrates how the flaw can happen.

Weakness Model Examples. Figure 3 contains examples of conceptual graphs for three weaknesses. Conditional flows, that is, data that only flows if a condition holds, are modeled as dashed arrows whereas data flows are modeled as full arrows in these conceptual graphs. Edges have an attribute that specifies the *data type* flowing between the nodes. This attribute could be either *generic*, which means that its data type is not specified or matches all data types, or *typed*, which indicates the actual data type. For instance, in Fig. 3c the Entry Point's returned data is of *credential* type and the data flowing from the Permissions Provider to the Authorizer node is of *user-controlled data* type (which is the root cause of the authorization bypass).

For instance, Fig. 3a depicts a weakness related to the "Manage Audit Trails" tactic [2], which can be adopted to log activities in the system for achieving non-repudiation goals and help with system recovery. In this tactic, Action Target components, that perform critical operations, report to the Audit Manager any critical operation being performed alongside with who made that request (i.e., the actor) such that the manager can record that operation in Audit Logs. The conceptual graph in Fig. 3a shows a weakness when the system does not record important activities within their logs because an Action Target is not sending these logs to the Audit Manager to be recorded. This is represented by a question mark that denotes a missing expected interaction between the components.

Figure 3b shows a conceptual model for two weaknesses associated with the "Heartbeat" architectural tactic [2,23], which is used for addressing reliability and availability goals. This tactic encompasses three roles: a safety-critical Heartbeat Sender component that periodically sends *heartbeat messages* to a Heartbeat Receiver to notify that it is still alive. The Heartbeat Receiver is able to detect failures in the safety-critical component when it notices that heartbeat messages are not being received. The Fault Monitor takes action upon detected failures. A potential weakness to this tactic occurs when the *heartbeat checking rate* outpaces the *sending rate* because the Heartbeat Receiver will mistakenly assume that the sender failed. A second weakness is caused by not notifying the Fault Monitor when a failure is detected. Figure 3b shows a conceptual graph modeling these two weaknesses (represented by an edge indicating the rates mismatches between the Sender and Receiver as well as a question mark indicating the lack of notification).

Figure 3c shows two weaknesses when adopting the "Authorize Actors" tactic [2,28]. This tactic enforces actors to hold certain privileges to access any resource that might require them. This Weakness Model has six distinct roles: the system's Entry Point (which is fed with user's inputs), multiple Intermediary nodes (any component transferring data), the Authenticator (used to check the user's identity), the Authorizer (which verifies the actor's permissions against the permissions given by the Permissions Provider), and the Resource node which is accessible to the user. These two weaknesses result in authorization bypasses. A path from an Entrypoint to a Resource without going through the Authorizer component (depicted with a red edge) is the root cause of the first bypass. Relying on user-controlled data to perform the authorization checks is the root cause of the second bypass. This second bypass is highlighted with a font colored in red for the data type provided to the Permissions Provider.

Specifying Common Architectural Weaknesses Formally. Conceptual graphs are good at depicting the information flow between architectural components. However, we need to use a language that allows us to conduct a reachability analysis across the system's components. This is realized as a set of rules in the Resolute language that describe how the system can withstand flaws (weaknesses). This reachability analysis is conducted with the Resolute tool. Creating the Resolute rules for specifying architectural weaknesses involves three activities [29]: **(1)** Writing a ***custom AADL property set*** [12] that declares roles, attributes, and data types; **(2)** Developing ***computation functions*** for checking/querying properties in the AADL model; and **(3)** Writing ***claims*** specifying the system behavior under certain conditions [13].

Weakness Specification Example. Figure 4a presents an example of *property set* definition in Resolute. It introduces role types such as `Resource`, `Entrypoint`, `Authorizer`, etc. The specification states that components such as "thread", "subprogram", "process", among others, can hold that type. These roles and role types can be used by software architects to define custom *computation functions* with the aid of annexes, as shown in Fig. 4b. The `has_role(s)` computation function returns true if the *s* AADL component contains the given role. The `get_all(role)` computation function returns all the AADL components with a specific role.

```
property set Props is
  RoleType: type enumeration
    (Resource, Entrypoint, Authorizer, ...);
  Role: list of Props::RoleType
    applies to (thread, subprogram, process, system, ...);
  DataType: enumeration (Credential, HeartbeatMessage, ...)
    applies to (data, data port, event data port, ...);
  (...)
end Props;
```

(a) Custom property set

```
annex resolute {**
  has_role(s: aadl, role: string):
    bool = has_property(s, Props::role) and
      member(role, property(s, Props::Role))
  get_all(role: string):
    {component} = {y for (x: component)
      (y: x) | has_role(x,role)}
  (...)
**};
```

(b) Examples of Computation functions

Fig. 4. Specification Rules for an Architectural Weakness

Once a set of computations is declared, the architect proceeds to develop structured Resolute *claims* that describe the architecture formally. For instance, for the conceptual graph in Fig. 3b, one can write structured claims as shown in Fig. 5, namely, (i) the system has the three required roles for the tactic (Sender, Receiver and Monitor), (ii) the safety-critical components send *heartbeat messages* to the receivers, (iii) the receivers periodically check whether the safety-critical component(s) are still functioning, (iv) the receivers notify the fault monitor upon a failure detection. Due to space constraints, we only show some high-level claims for enforcing the aforementioned properties.

```
check_heartbeat(s: system) <=
  ** "The system " s " adopts Heartbeat tactic"
  " to detect faults in critical components" **
  system_has_role(s,"HeartbeatReceiver") and
  system_has_role(s,"HeartbeatSender") and
  system_has_role(s,"FaultMonitor") and
  critical_components_sends_heartbeat(s) andthen
  receivers_checks_periodically(s) andthen
  receivers_notifies_monitors(s)
```

```
system_has_role(s: system, role: string) <=
  ** "The system " s " has a " role " component" **
  exists(comp: component) . has_role(comp, role)

critical_components_sends_heartbeat(s: system) <=
  ** " All the senders periodically send a heartbeat" **
  forall (sender : get_all("HeartbeatSender")) .
    exists(receiver : get_all("HeartbeatSender")).
    sends_heartbeat(sender, receiver) and
    property(sender, Props::SendingRate) =
    property(receiver, Props::CheckingRate)
```

Fig. 5. High-level claims for the Heartbeat tactic

3.3 Architectural Model Annotation

In this third phase, the architectural model is annotated with metadata about resiliency tactics. The metadata created in this phase is crucial to indicate which components implement resiliency tactics, and express the expected characteristics and behavior of the system. To perform these annotations, the architects first add an import statement into the system's AADL file to import the previously developed files that contain the custom property set, claims and computations. Then, the elements in the AADL model are annotated with an *architectural role* of components, their *attributes* and *data types*. Figure 6a shows an example of an architectural model of an Attitude and Orbit Control System (AOCS) [8], in which the TCP component is annotated with the Authorizer role to indicate that it is in charge of checking the privileges of actors interacting with the system whereas the ACF component is the target Resource (i.e., the component that needs to be protected against unauthorized access) [29].

```
package AOCS
public
with Props;
process implementation AOCSprocessing.impl
  subcomponents
    ACF: thread AttitudeControlFunction
      {Props::Role => (Resource);};
    TCP: thread TelecommandProcessing
      {Props::Role => (Authenticator);};
    (...)
end AOCSprocessing.impl;
end AOCS;
```

(a) An annotated AADL model

```
package AOCS
public
with Props;
with ResoluteRules;
system implementation AOCS.Impl
  subcomponents
    main: process AOCSprocessing.impl;
    (...)
    annex resolute {**
      prove(check_heartbeat(this))
    **};
end AOCS.Impl;
end AOCS;
```

(b) Inserting Resolute rules into an AADL model

Fig. 6. AADL Model Annotation and Rules Embedding Examples

3.4 Architecture Verification

During the final phase, the Resolute rules are added to the top-level implementation of the system. This is done by invoking the resolute claims using the prove keyword. For instance, Fig. 6b shows the inclusion of the Resolute rules to the top-level system implementation by using prove(check_heartbeat(this). When Resolute executes, it will verify the claims over the current system implementation (i.e., AOCS.Impl).

These claims can be checked using the Resolute plug-in installed on the Open Source AADL Tool Environment (OSATE) [11]. This plugin will then conduct a soundness proof over the entire system. Therefore, the proof is replicated (valid) for very instance of the component's implementation.

4   Case Example

We illustrate our approach with the aid of an autonomous robot based on the resources provided by the NASA Lunar Robot [24]. The robot's primary mission is to autonomously traverse the lunar surface, collect sample data related to comets, dust, and celestial objects, record temperatures, perform scientific experiments, and send results back to the earth-based Mission Control Center.

– **Phase 1: Modeling the Robot Architecture.** The Robot, whose architecture is shown in Fig. 7, has the capability of operating in two modes: *manual*

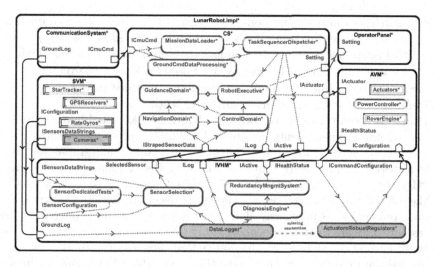

Fig. 7. High-Level Architecture Model of the Lunar Robot in AADL (Color figure online)

(remotely controlled by a ground control station) and *autonomous* (by following a pre-established flight plan). Its architecture is structured around a *Control System* (CS), an *Integrated Vehicle Health Management* (IVHM) system, the *Sensors Virtual Machine* (SVM), an *Actuators Virtual Machine* (AVM), a *Communication System*, and an *Operator Panel*. The *Communication System* implements the communication protocol to receive commands sent from the ground station and forwarding those to the *Control System* (CS). Data from the sensors is first passed through the IVHM component for correctness checking and is then forwarded to the CS. The CS uses the data to make decisions and to process high-level commands sent by the ground station. It then sends lower level commands to the actuators. The *Integrated Vehicle Health Management* (IVHM) is responsible for monitoring the health of the Lunar Robot, and when necessary, performing dynamic reconfigurations to maintain functionality. The Lunar Robot receives inputs from cameras, GPS receivers, rate gyros, and star trackers, and issues command to mechanical devices such as the power controller, wheels, and scientific instruments.

Resiliency Requirements & Adopted Tactics: To achieve resiliency, the lunar robot's design adopts the following tactics:

- **Heartbeat Tactic:** the sensors within the "SVM" component periodically heartbeat messages to the "Sensors Selection" component, which acts as both a Heartbeat Receiver and a Fault Monitor.
- **Authorize Actors:** the "Communication System" checks the identity and privileges of the Mission Control Center (MCC) before exchanging data and accepting commands from it.
- **Maintain Audit Trails:** Whenever the robot is in manual mode, but receives no commands from the MCC for an extended period of time, it

switches to autonomous mode and returns to the geographical coordinates of the last *point of known contact* (which is recorded in data logs). Given this requirement, the system adopts the *Maintain Audit Trails* tactic [2] for maintaining logs that can later be used for system recovery.

For this case example, we limit our discussion to three tactics, however, in medium to large scale systems, a variety of tactics are adopted.

- **Phase 2: Architectural Weaknesses Modeling & Specification.** Subsequently, the architect identifies potential weaknesses while adopting the aforementioned tactics. First, the architect creates conceptual graphs for these weaknesses, as previously shown in Fig. 3 for the "Maintain Audit Trails", "Heartbeat", and "Authorize Actors" tactics. Given these conceptual graphs, the software architect creates a property set declaring tactics' role types, and data properties, as previously shown in Fig. 4a. Using this property set file, resolute rules are written to formally verify that these weaknesses do not occur in the current design (e.g., Fig. 5). Notice that these models and specifications are written in such a way that make them ***reusable***. As a result, architects could re-use these models and specifications to verify the same weaknesses in other designs that also adopt these tactics, reducing the efforts in creating these artifacts from scratch.

- **Phase 3: Model Annotation.** Once weaknesses' models and specifications are created, architects manually tag the Lunar Robot's architecture with roles and properties, as shown in Fig. 8. This figure does not contain all the AADL model, but just the elements that have annotations.

- **Phase 4: Architecture Verification**

  The architect inserts the developed resolute rules (highlighted in blue in Fig. 8). Through performing a reasoning on top of this augmented model (containing analysis rules and annotations), the technique detects the following weaknesses (whose locations were colored in red in Fig. 7):

  Weakness #1: an *Omission of Security-relevant Information* because the *Data Logger* is not tracking information from the actuators. It is caused by a connection missing from the *Data Logger* to the *ActuatorsRobustRegulators*. Figure 9 shows the output of the resolute tool indicating this problem (notice the failed claim that all Action Targets are reporting critical operations to the Audit Manager).

  Weakness #2: a *Mismatch between Send and Receive Periods* which is caused by the *Cameras* sending heartbeat messages every 20 s whereas the checking rate of the "Sensor Selection" (Heartbeat receiver) is 10 s, as indicated in the *SendingRate* value colored in red in Fig. 8.

  Weakness #3: an *Authorization bypass* because the "Operator Panel" component, which is also an entrypoint to the system, directly communicates with the "Control System" (CS) without authorization (connection highlighted in red in Fig. 7).

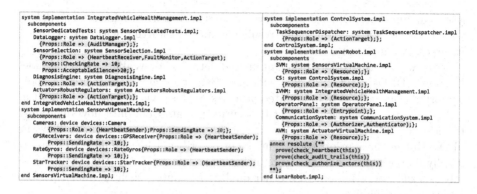

Fig. 8. Lunar Robot's AADL model annotated with roles (Color figure online)

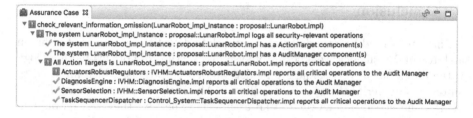

Fig. 9. Resolute output

5 Related Work

There are several streams of research on analyzing and verifying architectural models by translating AADL models into model checkers [6,20]. One major difference between these works and our work is the property notation used for specifying behavior; the prior work uses subsets of the AADL behavioral annex to focus on low level implementations issues. In contrast, we focus on design flows. Johnsen et al. [20] presents a technique for verifying the completeness and consistency of AADL specifications.

Furthermore, there have been various works which use ADDL along with a declarative formalism provided by languages such as AGREE, to verify the satisfaction of software requirements in the model [1]. However, these approaches will not address model checking of components and interdependencies among them, as well as specific resiliency properties. In contrast, we rely on Resolute that enables reachability analysis required to examine the dependencies between components and elements in AADL to detect various bypasses of mitigation techniques. For instance, the SPEEDS [1] approach uses a model-based engineering methodology supported by formal analyses. However, it focuses on verification of software requirements. It requires that the architectural description of the system (AADL models) to be annotated with assume-guarantee style contracts on components that implement software requirements.

Ellison et al. [9] proposes an enhancement for the AADL to incorporate security concerns based on Microsoft STRIDE framework. Similar to our work, they discuss a custom property set which is used to annotate and analyze the system architecture. Our work, however, differs in that we provide a *methodology* whereby we provide a continuous resiliency analysis starting with the system's architecture instead of a threat model.

Prior works also explored the automated detection of weaknesses in dataflow diagrams (DFDs) [3,30,32]. For example, Berger et al. [4] presented a tool-supported approach to help architectural risk analysis via threat modeling; the tool is used to automatically identify security threats from data flow diagrams. Tuma et al. [32] described the use of reusable queries to find security flaws in DFDs. Unlike these prior works, our paper describes a *methodology* to systematically find weaknesses in the system that affects its resiliency, that include not only security concerns, but also other quality attributes, such as safety, performance, and availability.

6   Conclusion

We have presented a methodological approach to detect the existence of common architectural resiliency weaknesses of systems. At the core of this methodology is the development of weaknesses models and specifications, which are used to automatically verify the system's resiliency. Although the construction of these models and specifications rely on an architects expertise, they can be built in such a way that can be reused across AADL models for different systems.

Our long-term goal is to provide software architects with mechanisms and tools to develop *certified* software (and hardware) all the way down from architectural design to implementations details. This preliminary work is the first part of our envisaged work. As future work, we plan to automate the verification process with the OSATE IDE [11] and Resolute tools [13]. We plan to conduct systematic literature reviews to create a complete catalog of resiliency tactics, write a comprehensive set of assurance cases for each tactic, and automate the process of design and checking of resiliency claims through the realization of an Osate plug-in. We will also conduct empirical evaluations on the effectiveness of the approach in detecting architectural weaknesses.

Acknowledgement. This work is partially supported by Defense Advanced Research Projects Agency (DARPA) under award number: 006376-002.

References

1. SPEculative and Exporatory Design in System engineering. http://www.speeds. eu.com/
2. Bass, L., Clements, P., Kazman, R.: Software Architecture in Practice, 3rd edn. Addison-Wesley Professional (2012)
3. Berger, B.J., Sohr, K., Koschke, R.: Extracting and analyzing the implemented security architecture of business applications. In: 17th European Conference on Software Maintenance and Reengineering (CSMR), pp. 285–294. IEEE (2013). https://doi.org/10.1109/CSMR.2013.37

4. Berger, B.J., Sohr, K., Koschke, R.: Automatically extracting threats from extended data flow diagrams. In: Caballero, J., Bodden, E., Athanasopoulos, E. (eds.) ESSoS 2016. LNCS, vol. 9639, pp. 56–71. Springer, Cham (2016). https://doi.org/10.1007/978-3-319-30806-7_4

5. Bodeau, D., Graubart, R.: Cyber resiliency design principles. MITRE (2017)

6. Bodeveix, J.P., Filali, M., Garnacho, M., Spadotti, R., Yang, Z.: Towards a verified transformation from AADL to the formal component-based language FIACRE. Sci. Comput. Program. **106**, 30–53 (2015)

7. Booch, G.: The economics of architecture-first. IEEE Softw. **24**(5), 18–20 (2007). https://doi.org/10.1109/MS.2007.146

8. Cechticky, V., Montalto, G., Pasetti, A., Salerno, N.: The AOCS framework. European Space Agency-Publications-ESA SP **516**, 535–540 (2003)

9. Ellison, R., Householder, A., Hudak, J., Kazman, R., Woody, C.: Extending AADL for security design assurance of cyber-physical systems. Technical report, CMU/SEI-2015-TR-014, Software Engineering Institute, Carnegie Mellon University, Pittsburgh, PA (2015). http://resources.sei.cmu.edu/library/asset-view.cfm?AssetID=449510

10. Feiler, P.H., Gluch, D., McGregor, J.D.: An architecture-led safety analysis method. In: 8th European Congress on Embedded Real Time Software and Systems (ERTS 2016) (2016)

11. Feiler, P.H., Gluch, D.P.: Model-Based Engineering with AADL: An Introduction to the SAE Architecture Analysis & Design Language. Addison-Wesley (2012)

12. Feiler, P.H., Gluch, D.P., Hudak, J.J.: The architecture analysis & design language (AADL): an introduction. Technical report, SEI (2006). https://doi.org/10.1184/R1/6584909.v1

13. Gacek, A., Backes, J., Cofer, D., Slind, K., Whalen, M.: Resolute: an assurance case language for architecture models. In: Proceedings of the 2014 ACM SIGAda Annual Conference on High Integrity Language Technology, pp. 19–28. ACM, New York (2014)

14. Goldman, H.G.: Building secure, resilient architectures for cyber mission assurance. Technical report, The MITRE Corporation (2010)

15. Hanmer, R.: Patterns for Fault Tolerant Software. Wiley Series in Software Design Patterns (2007)

16. Heyman, T., Scandariato, R., Joosen, W.: Reusable formal models for secure software architectures. In: 2012 Joint Working IEEE/IFIP Conference on Software Architecture (WICSA) and European Conference on Software Architecture (ECSA), pp. 41–50. IEEE (2012)

17. Hugues, J.: AADLib: a library of reusable AADL models. Technical report, SAE Technical Paper (2013)

18. Hukerikar, S., Engelmann, C.: Resilience design patterns: a structured approach to resilience at extreme scale. arXiv preprint arXiv:1708.07422 (2017)

19. IEEE Center for Secure Design: Avoiding the top 10 software security design flaws (2015). https://ieeecs-media.computer.org/media/technical-activities/CYBSI/docs/Top-10-Flaws.pdf. Accessed 10 June 2016

20. Johnsen, A., Lundqvist, K., Pettersson, P., Jaradat, O.: Automated verification of AADL-specifications using UPPAAL. In: Proceedings of the 2012 IEEE 14th International Symposium on High-Assurance Systems Engineering, HASE 2012, USA, pp. 130–138. IEEE Computer Society (2012)

21. Kazman, R., et al.: A case study in locating the architectural roots of technical debt. In: 2015 IEEE/ACM 37th IEEE International Conference on Software Engineering, vol. 2, pp. 179–188 (2015)

22. Kazman, R., Klein, M., Clements, P.: ATAM: a method for architecture evaluation. Software Engineering Institute (2000)
23. Kim, S., Kim, D.K., Lu, L., Park, S.Y.: A tactic-based approach to embodying non-functional requirements into software architectures. In: 2008 12th International IEEE Enterprise Distributed Object Computing Conference, pp. 139–148 (2008)
24. Mirakhorli, M., Cleland-Huang, J.: Using tactic traceability information models to reduce the risk of architectural degradation during system maintenance. In: Proceedings of the 2011 27th IEEE International Conference on Software Maintenance, ICSM 2011, Washington, DC, USA, pp. 123–132. IEEE Computer Society (2011)
25. Mirakhorli, M., Cleland-Huang, J.: Detecting, tracing, and monitoring architectural tactics in code. IEEE Trans. Softw. Eng. **42**(3), 205–220 (2015)
26. Mirakhorli, M., Shin, Y., Cleland-Huang, J., Cinar, M.: A tactic-centric approach for automating traceability of quality concerns. In: Proceedings of the 34th International Conference on Software Engineering, ICSE 2012. IEEE Press (2012)
27. Munoz, M.: Space systems modeling using the architecture analysis & design language (AADL). In: 2013 IEEE International Symposium on Software Reliability Engineering Workshops (ISSREW), pp. 97–98. IEEE (2013)
28. Santos, J.C.S., Tarrit, K., Mirakhorli, M.: A catalog of security architecture weaknesses. In: 2017 IEEE International Conference on Software Architecture Workshops (ICSAW), pp. 220–223, April 2017
29. Santos, J.C.S., Suloglu, S., Ye, J., Mirakhorli, M.: Towards an automated approach for detecting architectural weaknesses in critical systems, pp. 250–253. Association for Computing Machinery, New York (2020). https://doi.org/10.1145/3387940.3392222
30. Sion, L., Tuma, K., Scandariato, R., Yskout, K., Joosen, W.: Towards automated security design flaw detection. In: 2019 34th IEEE/ACM International Conference on Automated Software Engineering Workshop (ASEW). IEEE (2019)
31. Stewart, D., Whalen, M.W., Cofer, D., Heimdahl, M.P.E.: Architectural modeling and analysis for safety engineering. In: Bozzano, M., Papadopoulos, Y. (eds.) IMBSA 2017. LNCS, vol. 10437, pp. 97–111. Springer, Cham (2017). https://doi.org/10.1007/978-3-319-64119-5_7
32. Tuma, K., Sion, L., Scandariato, R., Yskout, K.: Automating the early detection of security design flaws. In: Proceedings of the 23rd ACM/IEEE International Conference on Model Driven Engineering Languages and Systems, pp. 332–342 (2020)
33. Vanciu, R., Abi-Antoun, M.: Finding architectural flaws in Android apps is easy. In: Proceedings of the 2013 Companion Publication for Conference on Systems, Programming, & Applications: Software for Humanity, SPLASH 2013, pp. 21–22 (2013)

Microservices Security: Bad vs. Good Practices

Francisco Ponce[1,2](✉) [iD], Jacopo Soldani[3] [iD], Hernán Astudillo[1] [iD],
and Antonio Brogi[3] [iD]

[1] Universidad Técnica Federico Santa María, Valparaíso, Chile
`francisco.ponceme@usm.cl, hernan@inf.utfsm.cl`
[2] Instituto de Tecnología para la Innovación en Salud y Bienestar,
Facultad de Ingeniería, Universidad Andrés Bello, Valparaíso, Chile
[3] University of Pisa, Pisa, Italy
`{jacopo.soldani,antonio.brogi}@unipi.it`

Abstract. The microservice architectural style is widespread in enterprise IT, making the securing of microservices a crucial issue. Many bad practices in securing microservices have been identified by researchers and practitioners, along with security good practices that, if adopted, allow to avoid the corresponding security issues. However, this knowledge is scattered across multiple pieces of white and grey literature, making its consulting complex and time consuming. We present here the results of a multivocal literature review that analyzes 44 primary studies discussing bad and good practices for microservice security. We were able to identify four bad and six good practices, and to associate each bad practice with specific bad smell(s) that signal it and with good practice(s) that avoid incurring in it. The resulting mapping between bad and good practices for microservice security can help practitioners and researchers to explore the systematic securing of microservice-based applications.

Keywords: microservices · security · bad practices · good practices

1 Introduction

Securing microservices has become crucial, due to their widespread use in enterprise IT nowadays [52]. However, the information on the state-of-the-art and state-of-practice on securing microservices is scattered among a vast amount of white and grey literature. This makes accessing the body of knowledge on the topic complex and time consuming, both for researchers aiming to propose novel research directions and/or solutions for securing microservice-based applications, and for practitioners daily working with microservices and needing to secure them.

With the perspective of helping researchers and practitioners, we first reviewed the white and grey literature on securing microservices to elicit known security smells, defined as possible symptoms of a bad, though unintentional, decisions while designing/developing microservices, which may impact on their security [41]. We also elicited the refactorings allowing to mitigate the effects of security smells [41]. To further help researchers and practitioners, this paper aims at complementing our former review [41] by eliciting what are not just "symptoms", but actually bad practices for securing microservices together with the security issues they may cause, as well as the good practices that, if adopted, enable avoiding to incur in such security issues. We indeed aim to answer the following two research questions:

(RQ1) What are the known bad practices when securing microservices?
(RQ2) What are the good practices known to avoid incurring in the security issues caused by the aforementioned bad practices?

To answer to our research questions, we report on what is being said by researchers and practitioners about bad/good practices for securing microservices, to provide a sort of "snapshot" of the state-of-the-art and state-of-practice on the topic. In particular, we present a taxonomy including four bad practices for securing microservices, and mapping such bad practices to six good practices that, if adopted, avoid incurring in the corresponding security issues. We then separately discuss each bad practice, by illustrating the bad smell(s) signaling it and the security issues it may cause. For each bad practice, we also describe the good practices known to enable avoiding its corresponding security issues.

The results of our study can help both practitioners and researchers interested in securing microservices. By complementing the results of our former review [41], a systematic presentation of bad and good practices for microservices security can indeed help practitioners to better understand what to avoid when securing microservice-based applications, as well as which good practices should be adopted to avoid it. In addition, the results in this paper, together with those in our former review [41], constitute a body of knowledge that can be used by researchers for developing new techniques and solutions, experimenting research implications, or delineating novel research directions.

The rest of this paper is organized as follows. Section 2 illustrates design of our multivocal literature review, whose resulting bad/good practices are then presented and discussed in Sect. 3. Section 4 discusses the potential threats to the validity of our study. Finally, Sect. 5 and 6 discuss related work and draw some concluding remarks, respectively.

2   Research Design

We hereafter illustrate how we selected the primary studies from which to extract bad/good practices for microservices security (Sect. 2.1), as well as the analysis process we enacted to elicit such bad/good practices from the selected primary studies (Sect. 2.2).[1]

---

[1] To encourage repeating our review process, a replication package (containing the sheets we used to run our review) has been released at https://docs.google.com/spreadsheets/d/1fY4lq3cdFjWCf7ZqaT5itnR7rw5vse-e/edit.

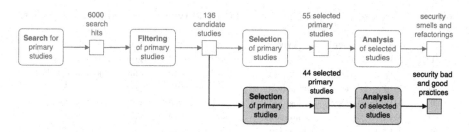

Fig. 1. Literature review process.

2.1   Literature Selection

Our aim is to complement the analysis of microservices' security smells and refactoring in our previous work [41], by eliciting the known bad/good practices for microservices security. We already elicited the 136 white/grey primary studies providing the state-of-the-art/state-of-practice in microservices security in [41], by following the guidelines for conducting systematic literature reviews in [21], combined with those in [12] for systematically reviewing grey literature. We hence started from such 136 candidate studies, as shown in Fig. 1. Still following the guidelines in [12,21], we applied different selection criteria to align with our research questions RQ1 and RQ2, namely to elicit the bad and good practices in microservices security.

(i_1) A study is to be selected if it discusses at least one *bad practice* for microservices security.

(i_2) A study is to be selected if it discusses at least one *good practice* to avoid incurring in bad practices for microservices security.

The first two authors of this paper applied the criteria i_1 and i_2 to the 136 candidate primary studies, by independently coding such studies as to be included/excluded. The Krippendorf $K\alpha$ coefficient [22] was then used to measure the inter-rater agreement on inclusion/exclusion of candidate primary studies. The measured, initial agreement was 87.5%, hence already significantly higher than the typical reference score of 80%. The missing 12.5% was caused by 17 mismatches, which were resolved by triangulation. Firstly, the last two authors of this paper independently coded the corresponding 17 primary studies. Then, a joint discussion –involving all authors– decided whether to include each of these 17 primary studies, based on the four independent codings. This yielded 44 primary studies, shown in Table 1.

Table 1 also indicates the year of publication, "colour" (viz., *white* vs. *grey* literature), and type of the selected primary studies. Notably, 39 out of the 44 selected primary studies are grey literature, confirming an observation of previous reviews [41,52], namely that grey literature constitutes the main source of information when analysing state-of-the-art/practice on microservices.

Table 1. Reference, year of publication, colour, and type of selected primary studies.

Ref.	Year	Colour	Type	Ref.	Year	Colour	Type
[1]	2019	grey	blog post	[31]	2020	grey	blog post
[3]	2017	grey	blog post	[32]	2019	white	journal article
[5]	2019	grey	blog post	[34]	2015	grey	book
[6]	2018	grey	blog post	[35]	2020	grey	blog post
[8]	2019	grey	whitepaper	[37]	2019	grey	video
[9]	2017	grey	blog post	[39]	2019	grey	video
[10]	2019	grey	video	[42]	2020	grey	blog post
[11]	2016	white	journal article	[43]	2020	grey	blog post
[13]	2018	grey	blog post	[45]	2019	grey	blog post
[14]	2016	grey	book	[46]	2017	grey	blog post
[16]	2018	grey	book chapter	[48]	2019	grey	video
[17]	2017	grey	book	[49]	2020	grey	blog post
[18]	2017	grey	video	[50]	2020	grey	book
[19]	2020	grey	blog post	[51]	2019	grey	blog post
[20]	2020	grey	blog post	[53]	2019	grey	blog post
[23]	2018	grey	blog post	[56]	2018	white	conference paper
[24]	2015	grey	blog post	[57]	2017	grey	blog post
[25]	2019	grey	blog post	[58]	2019	grey	blog post
[27]	2020	white	conference paper	[59]	2019	grey	blog post
[28]	2017	grey	blog post	[62]	2016	grey	book
[29]	2017	grey	blog post	[63]	2018	white	conference paper
[30]	2018	grey	book	[64]	2017	grey	book

2.2 Literature Analysis

We analysed the selected primary studies to elicit bad practices for microservice security, as well as the good practices to avoid the corresponding security issues. The analysis was enacted by adopting thematic coding [2] and Krippendorf $K\alpha$-based inter-rater reliability assessment [22]. The first two authors annotated and labelled the selected primary studies to elicit bad/good practices for microservice security. The annotation and labelling were executed in parallel over two complementary partitions of the selected primary studies, with the aim of reducing potential observer biases. The coders were then switched to evaluate the inter-rater agreement on the two emerging lists of bad and good practices for microservice security. The inter-rater agreement was again measured by exploiting the $K\alpha$ coefficient [22] to determine the agreement between the first two authors (who independently coded their partitions) on the emerging lists of bad and good practices for microservice security. The measured agreement amounted to 89.9%, again obtaining a value significantly higher than 80%, which is typically taken as reference score for inter-rater agreement [22].

A final triangulation step was then performed to further reduce potential biases. The last two authors cross-checked the coding performed by the first two authors, with no prior information on the coding itself. Their cross-checks were then discussed by organizing three feedback sessions: in the first two sessions, the feedback by the last two authors was separately discussed with the first two authors. Then, the independent codings and feedbacks were discussed in a plenary sessions involving all authors. This concluded our analysis process, which resulted in the taxonomy of bad and good practices shown in Fig. 2.

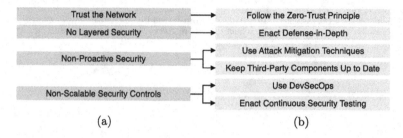

(a)   (b)

Fig. 2. (a) Bad and (b) good practices for microservice security.

3   Bad vs. Good Practices for Microservices Security

The identified bad/good practices for microservices security are displayed in Fig. 2, and their appearance in the selected primary studies is reported in Table 2. To align with our research questions RQ1 and RQ2, we hereafter describe each identified bad practice, together with the good practices known to enable avoiding its corresponding security issues. We also map the identified bad practices to the security smells discussed in [41] that may signal them.

3.1   Trust the Network vs. Zero-Trust Principle

Bad Practice. The authors of 13 selected primary studies identify TRUST THE NETWORK as a common bad practice when developing microservices. TRUST THE NETWORK is an approach that assumes that network communication between microservices is reliable and secure. This model employs a centralized security strategy, where all traffic is granted access by default, and security is upheld through network firewalls and other external security measures [11,14]. In a microservices-based application, services are frequently added, removed, and updated, making it challenging to sustain a centralized security approach that can adapt to these fluctuations. This is essentially because the TRUST THE NETWORK approach does not take into account such a dynamic and distributed nature of microservices-based applications.

TRUST THE NETWORK indeed means designing microservices by blindly trusting other software components, with the latter even being microservices or integration components used within the microservice-based application under consideration, nor their possible addition, removal, or updates. For instance, a microservice-based application may be designed without enforcing security in service-to-service communications among its internal microservices, by just relying on network-level security to secure such communications. Another common mistake is to trust integration components by their mere identity, when such

Table 2. Coverage of the identified bad/good practices for microservices security in the selected primary studies.

	TRUST THE NETWORK	NO LAYERED SECURITY	NON-PROACTIVE SECURITY			NON-SCALABLE SECURITY CONTROLS
	FOLLOW THE ZERO-TRUST PRINCIPLE	ENACT DEFENSE-IN-DEPTH	USE ATTACK MITIGATION TECHNIQUES	KEEP THIRD-PARTY COMPONENTS UP TO DATE	USE DEVSECOPS	ENACT CONTINUOUS SECURITY TESTING
[1]			✓			
[3]			✓			
[5]		✓	✓			
[6]		✓				
[8]			✓			
[9]			✓			
[10]		✓				
[11]	✓					
[13]			✓		✓	
[14]	✓	✓			✓	
[16]						✓
[17]			✓	✓		
[18]		✓	✓			
[19]		✓				
[20]		✓			✓	
[23]		✓			✓	✓
[24]	✓	✓				
[25]				✓		✓
[27]		✓				
[28]					✓	
[29]	✓		✓			
[30]	✓					
[31]	✓					
[32]			✓			✓
[34]	✓	✓	✓			
[35]		✓				✓
[37]	✓					
[39]	✓					
[42]					✓	✓
[43]			✓	✓	✓	
[45]		✓				✓
[46]			✓			✓
[48]	✓					
[49]	✓					
[50]	✓	✓				
[51]			✓			
[53]		✓				
[56]		✓				
[57]		✓				
[58]		✓	✓		✓	✓
[59]		✓			✓	✓
[62]		✓				
[63]	✓	✓				
[64]			✓			

components are used to let microservices interoperate within the system (e.g., message brokers) or with external clients (e.g., API Gateway). When these or similar situations happens, the involved communication channels create potential attack vectors that can be exploited by an intruder to violate the communicating microservices [31,50].

Related Security Smells. Blindly trusting software components and relying only on network-level security may result in introducing the following smells from [41]: NON-SECURED SERVICE-TO-SERVICE COMMUNICATIONS, UNAUTHENTICATED TRAFFIC and INSUFFICIENT ACCESS CONTROL. When any of such smells occurs in a microservice-based application, the latter's confidentiality, integrity, and authenticity may get compromised [41].

Good Practice. All the authors of the primary studies discussing the TRUST THE NETWORK bad practice agree on saying that, to avoid incurring in the security issues it may cause, application architects should FOLLOW THE ZERO-TRUST PRINCIPLE to design the security of a microservice-based application. The zero-trust principle consists of assuming that the network is always hostile and untrusted, by never taking anything for granted. Each request must be authenticated and authorized at each node before being accepted for further processing [50]. Even if a request originates from a microservice at the same network-level, development teams should never assume that they can trust the source microservice and they should verify it based on what the credentials are [39]. In other words, since microservices communicate with each other over the network, an application's microservices should be treated in the very same way as external third-party applications [37]. To achieve this and realize the zero-trust principle, the authors of the primary studies discussing the FOLLOW THE ZERO-TRUST PRINCIPLE good practice share the following recommendations:

- Use Mutual TLS [47] to secure microservices communication, as this protects the application from man-in-the-middle, eavesdropping, and tampering attacks.
- Use OpenID Connect [36] to verify the user identity at each microservice, as well as to obtain basic profile information about the end-user.
- Use OAuth 2.0 [15] to enforce access control at each level, hence enabling each microservice to have its own fine-grained access controls.
- Use network segmentation to divide the network into smaller segments and isolate some components, as this helps reducing the attack surface for an application.

3.2   No Layered Security Vs. Defense-in-Depth

Bad Practice. The authors of 21 of the selected primary studies discuss the NO LAYERED SECURITY bad practice. NO LAYERED SECURITY means designing a microservice-based application by relying only on perimeter defense, and/or by implementing a single security solution or practice [59]. Securing the perimeter or adopting a single security solution is not going to be enough, because microservices communicate with each other over the network and in disparate manners. Also, one such approach does not consider the dynamic and distributed nature of microservices architectures, where services are continuously added, removed, and updated, e.g., possibly getting exposed after some update. Therefore, microservices-based applications call for a more robust and dynamic defense involving multiple layers of security controls, both at the perimeter and at the level of each microservice/software component forming an application [63].

Related Security Smells. Relying on perimeter defense and/or implementing a single security solution may result in introducing the following smells from [41]: INSUFFICIENT ACCESS CONTROL, NON-SECURED SERVICE-TO-SERVICE COMMUNICATIONS, UNAUTHENTICATED TRAFFIC, UNNECESSARY PRIVILEGES TO MICROSERVICES and NON-ENCRYPTED DATA EXPOSURE. When any of such smells occurs in a microservice-based application, the latter's confidentiality, integrity, and authenticity may get compromised [41].

Good Practice. The authors of the primary studies discussing NO LAYERED SECURITY agree on saying that application architects should ENACT DEFENSE-IN-DEPTH when designing the security of microservice-based application, as this would enable avoiding the security issues due to the NO LAYERED SECURITY bad practice. Defense-in-depth is a strategy in which several layers of security controls are introduced to protect an application from different types of threats. In a microservices-based application, this might involve implementing security controls at the network, host, and application levels. Critical microservices/components should be protected with multiple security layers, so that a potential attacker who has exploited one of the microservices of an application may not be able to do so to other microservices or layers [20]. This security strategy helps slowing down attacks when one security mechanism fails, or a security vulnerability is identified. One of the advantages of the microservice architecture is that it allows the diversification of security layers that can be designed and implemented [35]. A layered security strategy helps designing the application in such a way that each layer handles different types of attacks and repels an attacker at the outermost layer [50]. These layers depend on the criticality of the application and its microservices, but the general recommendations from the authors of the primary studies discussing the ENACT DEFENSE-IN-DEPTH good practice are the following:

- Secure all microservices behind a firewall to ensure that only the allowed traffic arrives to the application.
- Use an API Gateway for enforcing security on all requests incoming to an application, including authentication, authorization, throttling, and message content validation for known security threats [50].
- Use Mutual TLS [47], OAuth 2.0 [15], and OpenID Connect [36] (as also recommended in Sect. 3.1) to secure service interactions.
- Follow the *Least Privilege Principle*, by allowing each service to *only* access the resources it needs to deliver its businesses [5,17].
- Encrypt all sensitive data and decrypt it only when needed [17,50].

– Validate all input passed to the microservices to ensure it is in the correct format and does not contain malicious content.
– Use logging and monitoring tools to collect information about the activity of microservices, and to detect and respond to security incidents.

3.3   Non-proactive vs. Proactive Security Measures

Bad Practice. Preventing exploits by intruders is only one part of securing a microservices-based application. Proactive detection and reaction are another essential part [44]. Though it is impossible to protect an application against all types of attacks, microservices must be provided with detection and prevention capabilities against, e.g., credential-stuffing and credential abuse attacks as well as the capability to detect malicious botnets [8]. This is highlighted by the authors of 16 of the selected primary studies, who identify NON-PROACTIVE SECURITY as a bad practice while designing microservice-based applications. Such a bad practice would indeed lead to not including security mechanisms that allow to proactively detect and react to potential or actual attacks. The lack of such proactive security measures can expose microservices-based applications to vulnerabilities, e.g., distributed denial-of-service attacks, with attacker attempting to (and possibly succeeding in) making an application unavailable to its users.

Related Security Smells. Without proactive detection and reaction to security issues, we may introduce the following smells from [41]: INSUFFICIENT ACCESS CONTROL, UNNECESSARY PRIVILEGES TO MICROSERVICES, OWN CRYPTO CODE, NON-ENCRYPTED DATA EXPOSURE, UNAUTHENTICATED TRAFFIC. When any of such smells occurs in a microservice-based application, the latter's confidentiality, integrity, and authenticity may get compromised [41].

Good Practices. The most discussed good practice to avoid the security issues due to NON-PROACTIVE SECURITY is USE ATTACK MITIGATION TECHNIQUES, which is discussed in 15 out of the 16 primary studies dealing with NON-PROACTIVE SECURITY. Attack mitigation techniques include all mechanisms and practices that are implemented to prevent security breaches and protect the application and its data from malicious attacks [17,18]. Concrete examples of attack mitigation techniques for microservices-based applications are web application firewalls [58] and rate limiting [51].

– A web application firewall is an application firewall for HTTP applications applying protection rules to HTTP conversations [17]. A web application firewall can also monitor the volume of cache misses to proactively detect that, e.g., an API gateway is constantly performing middle-tier service calls due to cache misses, which would suggest that the cache is potentially suffering a malicious attack [3]. Web application firewalls can hence be used to provide instant protection against SQL injection, cross-site scripting, illegal resource access, remote code execution, remote file inclusion, and other OWASP Top-10 threats [60].

– Application architects should also introduce rate-limiting API calls to mitigate distributed denial-of-service (DDoS) attacks and protecting the backend
application that process the API calls [51]. Rate limiting consists of counting
how many requests a server is accepting in a period and rejecting new ones
when a certain limit is reached [43].

Another good practice to avoid the security issues due to NON-PROACTIVE
SECURITY is KEEP THIRD-PARTY COMPONENTS UP TO DATE, even if less
discussed than the former. KEEP THIRD-PARTY COMPONENTS UP TO DATE
means that application administrators should ensure to include all the latest
security patches for the third-party components use in an application [17,44]. A
scanning software can be used on the source code repository to identify vulnerable dependencies (e.g., as done by GitHub bots), and this type of scan should
be enacted at any phase of the deployment pipeline.

The actual implementation of proactive security measures for microservices-
based applications (such as those described above) must be tailored to the specific technology stack and requirements of the application and its maintaining organization. It is crucial to recognize that maintaining the security of a
microservice-based application is a continual process, and therefore, the security
measures must be consistently evaluated and updated to remain efficient [43].

3.4 Non-scalable vs. Scalable Security Controls

Bad Practice. Microservices-based applications are typically designed and
developed by adopting continuous DevOps practices. While dealing with
microservices, there can indeed be quite frequent changes resulting in new
releases [52]. Continuous integration/continuous deployment (CI/CD) pipelines
are typically enacted to distribute microservice-based applications and to keep
them updated in production. CI/CD pipelines are themselves a source of possible
security issues, so they need fully automated, scalable security controls [20]. Suppose that, e.g., certain development team plan to upgrade a microservice-based
application by changing or adding functionalities to some of its microservices.
Without automation, they would be required to scan the added code and its
integration with the existing code for vulnerabilities and weaknesses before they
could deploy it [46]. This would go in contrast with the automation needs of
CI/CD pipelines, hence resulting in what the authors of the selected primary
studies consider the NON-SCALABLE SECURITY CONTROLS bad practice.

Related Security Smells. The lack of integration of security measures/testing
in CI/CD pipeplines may result in introducing the following smells from
[41], especially if considering that microservice-based applications are continuously updated: PUBLICLY ACCESSIBLE MICROSERVICES, UNNECESSARY PRIVI-
LEGES TO MICROSERVICES, OWN CRYPTO CODE, NON-SECURED SERVICE-TO-
SERVICE COMMUNICATIONS, UNAUTHENTICATED TRAFFIC. When any of such
smells occurs in a microservice-based application, the latter's confidentiality,
integrity, and authenticity may get compromised [41].

Good Practices. USE DEVSECOPS and ENACT CONTINUOUS SECURITY TESTING are the two good practices identified to avoid the security issues due to NON-SCALABLE SECURITY CONTROLS, both being highlighted in 9 out of the 15 primary studies discussing the NON-SCALABLE SECURITY CONTROLS bad practice. USE DEVSECOPS helps in integrating security processes, principles, good practices, and tools early in the development lifecycle, thereby encouraging collaboration among security experts and business analysts, architects, and development and operations teams, thus making everyone accountable and responsible for building secured systems [23]. On the other hand, automation is the key to integrating quality protection in a way that ensures quick feedback on the impact of new changes. Therefore, ENACT AUTOMATED SECURITY TESTING helps realizing the speed and flexibility needed in CI/CD pipelines, and it also ensures a faster recovery [59]. By incorporating automated security testing into the continuous integration and continuous delivery (CI/CD) pipeline, vulnerabilities can be identified and rectified at every stage of the development process. This approach enable application developers to proactively and early address any identified security issue, possibly before they can be really exploited by attackers in a production environment [43,58]. Automated security testing can create and update baselines before every release with OWASP Top 10 [60] and advanced libraries that are informed by discovered abnormalities across clients. Through automation, DevOps teams can meet their responsibility to facilitate fast releases and quicker code fixes [59].

4 Threats to Validity

Following the taxonomy in [61], we examine four kinds of threats to the validity of our study (viz., *external, construct, internal,* and *conclusions*).

Threats to External Validity. The *external* validity of our study may be threatened since the selected primary studies were taken from a large extent of online sources, which may be only partly applicable to the broader, more generic area of practices on microservices. To strenghten the external validity of our study, we run three feedback sessions among the authors of this study during the analysis of the selected primary studies, also with the goal of fine-tuning the taxonomy organizing the emerging lists of bad/good practices for microservices security (Fig. 2). We also carefully applied our selection criteria as follows: instead of checking whether a bad/good practice in our taxonomy was explicitly mentioned in a study, we rather checked whether a primary study was discussing security issues due to some bad practices, and whether it was discussing how to avoid such issues, even just by means of examples, which we later linked to and organized into the identified good practices. Finally, we prepared a replication package providing access to the sheets that we produced during our study, to encourage repeating it and ease the understanding of the data that we produced. All what above was aimed at making our results and observations more explicit, replicable, and applicable in practice.

Threats to Construct and Internal Validity. The *construct* and *internal* validity instead concern the method employed to study and analyse data, including the types of potentially involved biases [61]. To mitigate the potential threats to the construct and internal validity of our study, we selected and classified the primary studies by relying on validated techniques, namely theme coding, inter-rater reliability assessment, and triangulation (Sect. 2). These are known to limit potential biases [52], like observer and interpretation biases, hence allowing us to strenghten the validity of our analysis of the data that we collected.

Threats to Conclusions Validity. The aforementioned inter-rater reliability assessment also helped in mitigating the potential threats to the *conclusions* validity of our study, which concerns the degree to which our conclusions were reasonably based on the available data [61]. In addition to that, all authors of this paper independently drawn the observations and conclusions discussed in this paper, which were then discussed and double-checked against the selected primary studies in joint discussion session.

5   Related Work

Multiple secondary studies have been conducted on microservices, also aimed at classifying known issues and good practices. For instance, Carrasco *et al.* [7], Neri *et al.* [33], and Taibi *et al.* [54,55] report on bad smells, refactorings, and architectural patterns for microservices, aimed at supporting developers in identifying them and improving their microservice-based applications. They however focus on aspects other than securing microservices, and our study is hence intended to complement their results (and those of similar studies) along that direction.

As for microservice security, only a few secondary studies have been conducted. Berardi *et al.* [4] analyses the available white literature on microservices security, to identify the research communities where this is most discussed, the known security attacks, and the countermeasures to enact to secure microservice-based applications from such attacks. Hence, [4] differs from our study in the objectives: we indeed aim to elicit bad and good practices for microservices security, by considering the state-of-the-art and state-of-practice on the topic, taken from white and grey literature, respectively.

In this perspective, Pereira-Vale *et al.* [38] and Mao *et al.* [26] are closer to our study, as they consider both white and grey literature. Pereira-Vale *et al.* [38] report on existing mechanisms to secure microservice-based applications, while also identifying those most used. Mao *et al.* [26] instead reviews currently existing DevSecOps mechanisms, including those adopted to secure microservices. Pereira-Vale *et al.* [38] and Mao *et al.* [26] hence differ from ours because they focus on which existing mechanisms can be used to secure microservices, whereas we focus on distilling bad/good practices that should not/should be adopted to secure them. It is anyhow worth noting that our results and those by Pereira-Vale *et al.* [38] and Mao *et al.* [26] complement each other. For instance, the security mechanisms reviewed by Pereira-Vale *et al.* [38] and Mao *et al.* [26] can be used to implement the good practices that we identified.

To summarise, to the best of our knowledge, there is currently no study classifying the bad practices potentially causing security issues in microservice-based applications, nor the good practices that, if adopted, avoid incurring in such security issues. Our study is aimed to precisely cover this gap, by providing a systematic review of the known bad/good practices for microservice security.

6 Conclusions

In this paper, we provide a "snapshot" of the bad and good practices for securing microservices, by means of a multivocal review reporting on what is being said by researchers and practitioners on the topic. Our study complements our former review of security smells and refactorings [41], as well as existing studies on known issues and solutions for microservices [7,33,54], by covering the aspect of bad/good practices for microservices security. This can help practitioners, who can exploit the elicited bad/good practices in their daily work with microservices. Also, and together with our former review [41], it provides a first body of knowledge that can be exploited by researchers as a starting point to study new techniques/solutions for securing microservices, or to delineate novel directions for future research on the topic.

For future work, we plan to measure the actual impact on microservices' security and other quality properties of both the identified security bad/good practices and the smells/refactorings from our former review [41], e.g., with empirical studies involving practitioners. We then plan to exploit our results to develop a support for identifying suitable trade-offs when securing microservices, as we sketched in [40]. In that work, we indeed illustrate how trade-off analysis can be used to reason on whether to apply some changes to resolve security issues in microservice-based applications, based on the impacts of both the changes and the security issues on different quality attributes, as well as on the adherence of an application to microservices' key design principles.

Acknowledgements. This work was partially supported by *ANID PIA/APOYO AFB180002* (CCTVal), *Instituto de tecnología para la innovación en salud y bienestar, facultad de ingeniería* (Universidad Andrés Bello, Chile), and by the project *hOlistic Sustainable Management of distributed softWARE systems* (OSMWARE, UNIPI PRA_2022_64), funded by the University of Pisa, Italy.

References

1. Abasi, F.: Securing modern API- and microservices-based apps by design. IBM Developer (2019). https://ibm.co/3y8XS0n
2. Basit, T.: Manual or electronic? The role of coding in qualitative data analysis. Educ. Res. **45**(2), 143–154 (2003). https://doi.org/10.1080/0013188032000133548
3. Behrens, S., Payne, B.: Starting the avalanche: Application DDoS in microservice architectures. The Netflix Tech Blog (2017). https://bit.ly/3N80u2H
4. Berardi, D., Giallorenzo, S., Mauro, J., Melis, A., Montesi, F., Prandini, M.: Microservice security: a systematic literature review. PeerJ Comput. Sci. **8**, e779 (2022). https://doi.org/10.7717/peerj-cs.779

5. Boersma, E.: Top 10 security traps to avoid when migrating from a monolith to microservices. Sqreen (2019). https://bit.ly/3QBqlD1
6. Budko, R.: Five things you need to know about API security. The New Stack (2018). https://bit.ly/3NdfRXA
7. Carrasco, A., Bladel, B.v., Demeyer, S.: Migrating towards microservices: migration and architecture smells. In: Proceedings of the 2nd International Workshop on Refactoring. IWoR 2018, p. 1–6. ACM (2018). https://doi.org/10.1145/3242163.3242164
8. Chandramouli, R.: Security strategies for microservices-based application systems. NIST SP 800-204 (2019). https://doi.org/10.6028/NIST.SP.800-204
9. da Silva, R.: Best practices to protect your microservices architecture. Medium (2019). https://bit.ly/3HUrxO9x
10. Edureka: microservices security: best practices to secure microservicess (2019). https://youtu.be/wpA0N7kHaDo
11. Esposito, C., Castiglione, A., Choo, K.: Challenges in delivering software in the cloud as microservices. IEEE Cloud Comput. 3(5), 10–14 (2016). https://doi.org/10.1109/MCC.2016.105
12. Garousi, V., Felderer, M., Mantyla, M.V.: Guidelines for including grey literature and conducting multivocal literature reviews in software engineering. Inf. Softw. Technol. 106, 101–121 (2019). https://doi.org/10.1016/j.infsof.2018.09.006
13. Gupta, N.: Security strategies for DevOps, APIs, containers and microservices. Imperva (2018). https://bit.ly/3y8lBO5
14. Hofmann, M., Schnabel, E., Stanley, K.: Microservices Best Practices for Java. IBM Redbooks, New York (2016)
15. IETF OAuth Working Group: Open Authorization (OAuth), version 2.0 (2012). https://oauth.net/2/
16. Indrasiri, K., Siriwardena, P.: Microservices security fundamentals. In: Microservices for the Enterprise, pp. 313–345. Apress, Berkeley, CA (2018). https://doi.org/10.1007/978-1-4842-3858-5_11
17. Jackson, N.: Building Microservices with Go. Packt Publishing, Birmingham (2017)
18. Jain, C.: Top 10 security best practices to secure your microservices. AppSecUSA 2017, OWASP (2018). https://youtu.be/VtUQINsYXDM
19. Kamaruzzaman, M.: Microservice architecture and its 10 most important design patterns. Towards Data Science (2020). https://bit.ly/3n5Lsjo
20. Kanjilal, J.: 4 fundamental microservices security best practices. SearchAppArchitecture (2020). https://bit.ly/39DloJc
21. Kitchenham, B., Charters, S.: Guidelines for performing systematic literature reviews in software engineering. Technical Report EBSE-2007-01 (2007)
22. Krippendorff, K.: Content Analysis: An Introduction to its Methodology, 2nd edn. Sage Publications, Thousand Oaks (2004)
23. Krishnamurthy, T.: Transition to microservice architecture - challenges. BeingTechie (2018). https://bit.ly/3N9SiPB
24. Lea, G.: Microservices security: all the questions you should be asking (2015). https://bit.ly/3HEGbbQ
25. Lemos, R.: App security in the microservices age: 4 best practices. TechBeacon (2019). https://bit.ly/3HIu9i0
26. Mao, R., et al.: Preliminary findings about DevSecOps from grey literature. In: 2020 IEEE 20th International Conference on Software Quality, Reliability and Security (QRS), pp. 450–457. IEEE (2020). https://doi.org/10.1109/QRS51102.2020.00064

27. Mateus-Coelho, N., Cruz-Cunha, M., Ferreira, L.G.: Security in microservices architectures. In: CENTERIS/ProjMAN/HCist, Procedia Computer Science, pp. 1–12. Elsevier (2020). https://doi.org/10.1016/j.procs.2021.01.320

28. Matteson, S.: 10 tips for securing microservice architecture. TechRepublic (2017). https://tek.io/3xL16pa

29. Matteson, S.: How to establish strong microservices security using SSL, TLS, and API gateways. TechRepublic (2017). https://tek.io/3nnr9hH

30. McLarty, M., Wilson, R., Morrison, S.: Securing Microservices APIs. O'Reilly, Springfield (2018)

31. Mody, V.: From zero to zero trust. Teleport (2020). https://bit.ly/3N8PVwl

32. Nehme, A., Jesus, V., Mahbub, K., Abdallah, A.: Securing microservices. IT Prof. **21**(1), 42–49 (2019). https://doi.org/10.1109/MITP.2018.2876987

33. Neri, D., Soldani, J., Zimmermann, O., Brogi, A.: Design principles, architectural smells and refactorings for microservices: a multivocal review. SICS Softw.-Intensiv. Cyber-Phys. Syst. **35**(1), 3–15 (2020). https://doi.org/10.1007/s00450-019-00407-8

34. Newman, S.: Building Microservices. O'Reilly, Springfield (2015)

35. O'Neill, L.: Microservice security - what you need to know. CrashTest Security (2020). https://bit.ly/3tPXUaK

36. OpenID: Openid connect (2014). https://openid.net/connect/

37. Parecki, A.: OAuth: When things go wrong. Okta Developer (2019). https://www.youtube.com/watch?v=H6MxsFMAoP8

38. Pereira-Vale, A., Fernandez, E.B., Monge, R., Astudillo, H., Márquez, G.: Security in microservice-based systems: a multivocal literature review. Comput. Secur. **103**, 102200 (2021). https://doi.org/10.1016/j.cose.2021.102200

39. Poddar, N.: Simplifying microservices security with a service mesh. Cloud Native Computing Foundation, Webinar (2019). https://youtu.be/Ai8HlkI7Mm4

40. Ponce, F., Soldani, J., Astudillo, H., Brogi, A.: Should microservice security smells stay or be refactored? towards a trade-off analysis. In: Gerostathopoulos, I., Lewis, G., Batista, T., Bureš, T. (eds.) Software Architecture. ECSA 2022. Lecture Notes in Computer Science, vol. 13444, pp. 131–139. Springer International Publishing, Cham (2022). https://doi.org/10.1007/978-3-031-16697-6_9

41. Ponce, F., Soldani, J., Astudillo, H., Brogi, A.: Smells and refactorings for microservices security: a multivocal literature review. J. Syst. Softw. **192**, 111393 (2022). https://doi.org/10.1016/j.jss.2022.111393

42. Radware: microservice architectures challenge traditional security practices (2020). https://bit.ly/3n4N393

43. Raible, M.: 11 patterns to secure microservice architectures. DZone (2020). https://bit.ly/3tPQoNf

44. Raible, M.: Security patterns for microservice architectures. Okta Developer (2020). https://bit.ly/3tLMc0D

45. Sahni, V.: Best practices for building a microservice architecture. Vinay Sahni (2019). https://bit.ly/2UTHLNS

46. Sass, R.: Security in the world of microservices. ITProPortal (2017). https://bit.ly/3HIbFhe

47. Siriwardena, P.: Mutual authentication with TLS, pp. 47–58. Apress (2014). https://doi.org/10.1007/978-1-4302-6817-8_4

48. Siriwardena, P.: Microservices security landscape. WSO2 Integration Summit 2019 (2019). https://youtu.be/6jGePTpbgtI

49. Siriwardena, P.: Challenges of securing microservices. Medium (2020). https://bit.ly/3tRyF7T

50. Siriwardena, P., Dias, N.: Microservices security in action. Manning (2020)
51. Smith, T.: How to secure APIs. DZone (2019). https://bit.ly/3QyusQh
52. Soldani, J., Tamburri, D.A., Van Den Heuvel, W.J.: The pains and gains of microservices: a systematic grey literature review. J. Syst. Softw. **146**, 215–232 (2018). https://doi.org/10.1016/j.jss.2018.09.082
53. SumoLogic: improving security in your microservices architecture (2019). https://bit.ly/3zSSXls
54. Taibi, D., Lenarduzzi, V.: On the definition of microservice bad smells. IEEE Softw. **35**(3), 56–62 (2018). https://doi.org/10.1109/MS.2018.2141031
55. Taibi, D., Lenarduzzi, V., Pahl, C.: Architectural patterns for microservices: a systematic mapping study. In: Proceedings of the 8th International Conference on Cloud Computing and Services Science - Volume 1: CLOSER, pp. 221–232. SciTePress (2018). https://doi.org/10.5220/0006798302210232
56. Torkura, K.A., Sukmana, M.I., Kayem, A.V., Cheng, F., Meinel, C.: A cyber risk based moving target defense mechanism for microservice architectures. In: 2018 IEEE ISPA/IUCC/BDCloud/SocialCom/SustainCom, pp. 932–939. IEEE (2018). https://doi.org/10.1109/BDCloud.2018.00137
57. Troisi, M.: 8 best practices for microservices app sec. TechBeacon (2017). https://bit.ly/3HDgDvZ
58. Wallarm: A CISO's guide to cloud application security (2019). https://bit.ly/3QAQKB6
59. Wallarm: moving to microservices with security in mind (2019). https://bit.ly/3HItMnC
60. Wichers, D., Williams, J.: Owasp top-10 2017. OWASP Foundation (2017)
61. Wohlin, C., Runeson, P., Höst, M., Ohlsson, M.C., Regnell, B., Wesslén, A.: Experimentation in Software Engineering: An Introduction. Kluwer Academic Publishers, Alphen aan den Rijn (2000)
62. Wolff, E.: Microservices: Flexible Software Architecture. O'Reilly, Springfield (2016)
63. Yarygina, T., Bagge, A.: Overcoming security challenges in microservice architectures. In: 2018 IEEE Symposium on Service-Oriented System Engineering (SOSE), pp. 11–20. IEEE (2018). https://doi.org/10.1109/SOSE.2018.00011
64. Ziade, T.: Python Microservices Development. Packt Publishing, Birmingham (2017)

2nd International Workshop on Software Architecture and Machine Learning (SAML)

Multi-metric Approach for Decomposition of Microservice-Based Data Science Workflows

Christoph Schröer[1]([⊠])(iD), Sven Wittfoth[2], and Jorge Marx Gómez[1]

[1] University of Oldenburg, Oldenburg, Germany
christoph.schroeer@uni-oldenburg.de
[2] Volkswagen AG, Wolfsburg, Germany

Abstract. To support fast development cycles in data science, microservice architectures are becoming increasingly important. However, while the design and identification of microservices in transaction-oriented applications are already widely studied, software architects lack support for data science workflows. The identification of microservices for data science workflows differs due to high volume and velocity characteristics.

With this work, we aim to present a multi-metric approach for decomposition of microservice-based data science workflows. First, we select different metrics and evaluate their impact on workflow execution under different workload and data conditions. Within the approach, we provide a software architecture that enables microservice architectures to be deployed concurrently in cloud environments considering microservice design patterns such as orchestration of choreography. This architecture can be used to run real-world experiments, aggregate logs and analyze them in an automated way with respect to our chosen metrics. We evaluated our approach using a real-world data science workflow for automated startup assessments.

Our work has both practical, theoretical and economic implications. Practically, it can support software architects and data scientists in architecting microservices. In this context, it also has implications for MLOps, as microservices can be used to train and deploy ML models. Theoretically, our software architecture can be used for other research comparing microservice architectures. Economically, we also achieve business impact by looking at the cost of microservice architectures based on service activation time.

Keywords: Data Science Workflow · Microservice Architecture · Microservice Decomposition · Data Science Use Case

1 Introduction

Deploying machine learning models and data science workflows into production has gained importance and is often summarized under the term MLOps. This is accompanied by choosing an appropriate architecture that ensures fast, automated and continuous deployment cycles [19]. As data science becomes more important for automating business processes or supporting data-driven decision-making processes, MLOps is also gaining importance.

Microservice architectures consist of isolated, independently deployable componentes. This characteristic combined with automated CI/CD pipelines can support fast development cycles. Therefore, this architectural style is also increasingly important for data science. However, while the design and identification of microservices in transaction-oriented applications are already widely studied [5,16], support lacks for software architects for data science workflows here.

Technically, data science is also about the automated analysis of data. Integrating big data into data science, data could be characterized by volume, velocity, variety and sometimes also by value and veracity [14]. While value and veracity are mainly domain-specific characteristics, the volume, velocity and variety have the main impact on architectural decisions. Since microservices are technology agnostic, the variety of data could be supported by integrating suitable data storage technologies in each microservice. Regarding identifying microservices, we focus mainly on volume and velocity in this paper. These have impact on the architecture decisions, when huge amount of data have to be exchanged between microservices frequently. Furthermore, we consider long-running processing tasks such as the preparation of data and the training of ML models.

The question is to what extent software architects could be supported in choosing an appropriate microservice architecture for data science workflows. This question is divided into two sub-questions: (1) What metrics can be used to identify microservices in data science workflows? (2) To what extent can these metrics be combined to derive appropriate microservice architecture?

Our approach explicitly combines design and runtime metrics to derive and compare microservice architectures. For this purpose, we use a real-world use case from the enterprise context and evaluate this approach with several experiments. This work aims to present a multi-metric approach for decomposition of microservice-based data science workflows. Thus, a microservice architecture can be derived from domain-modeled data science workflows.

In the next section, we place this paper into the current state of research. In the third chapter, we present our approach and the selected metrics. In Sect. 4, the approach is demonstrated using a concrete use case. In Sect. 5, the results of design and runtime metrics are discussed. In addition, the contributions, implications, limitations and outlook are summarized and explained.

2 Related Work

In addition to the relevant literature on microservice architectures in general, this paper primarily addresses the areas of process models for the design of microservice architectures, the identification of microservices using design metrics and the consideration of runtime evaluations in microservice architectures.

Metrics to identify microservices have already been covered in the literature. First, good overviews by means of conducted literature reviews of current methods exist [6,8,16]. Second, concrete approaches investigate cohesion metrics [9,11] or coupling criteria [13] addressing the main characteristics of high cohesion and low coupling of microservices. Consideration of multiple, even competing, metrics such as coupling, cohesion and network overload with respect to different microservice architectures have also been addressed during migrations [1,7].

The runtime behavior of microservice architectures has already been widely researched. First, microservices can improve the runtime of transaction-oriented applications compared to monolithic applications [10]. Second, runtime metrics such as the Domain Metric could detect scalability requirements for microservices design [4]. Third, the design of microservices depends on various expected workloads [12]. Also, microservice architectures can be researched for workflow-based systems like how the performance of workflows can be modeled to achieve optimal scheduling and deployment of the involved microservices and thus to reduce workflow times [3]. However, cohesion metrics are lacking here.

In contrast, this paper is about combining existing design and runtime metrics that are relevant for data science workflows. Either it is assumed in current literature that microservices have already been designed [3] or microservice identification ends after the design phase [9]. Therefore, it is essential to derive microservice architectures using multiple metrics for design and runtime behavior and, most importantly, to determine the impact of design metrics on runtime behavior. While this is already being investigated for transaction-oriented applications with certain metrics [1], approaches for microservice-oriented data science workflows are lacking.

3   Multi-metric Approach for Decomposition of Microservice-based Data Science Workflows

We adapt the process model for identifying microservice architectures (see [17]) and extend it for application to data science workflows. Accordingly, we assume here not only candidates of a single architecture, but of several architecture candidates after the design phase. These architecture candidates are then explicitly compared and evaluated using runtime metrics. The adapted process model can be found in Fig. 1.

Furthermore, we instantiate the process model with concrete expressions of the individual process steps. Thus, we define the functions of the data science workflow as an atomar unit (1), relate them using an adjacency matrix (2) and annotate these relationships with cohesion metrics (3). Cohesion metrics serve as distance functions for downstream clustering (4) to identify microservice candidates. The challenge in clustering is to choose the number of clusters. Therefore, multiple microservice architectures can also be extracted with different cluster counts or microservices. Thus, we derive several architecture alternatives, which we further evaluate using runtime evaluation (6). This also requires implementing the microservice architectures (5). We apply selected metrics relevant to data science workflows in steps (3) and (6). However, we will also show to what extent additional metrics can extend the process model.

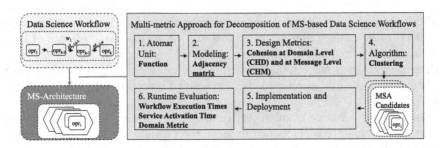

Fig. 1. Multi-metric approach for extracting microservice architecture for data science workflows.

3.1 Atomar Unit, Modeling and Identification

We define a processing function *opr* within a data science workflow $WF = \{opr_1, ..., opr_k\}$ as an atomar unit. The problem to be solved is an optimal assignment of functions to microservices. To extract suitable microservice architectures during the design phase, we apply cohesion metrics combined with hierarchical clustering to identify microservices. It is worth mentioning here that other metrics and algorithms can also be used. We extend the clustering approach of [2] and [11] by computing all possibilities for finding an appropriate cluster number and evaluate them using the combined metric CHA_i according to Eq. 1.

$$CHA_i = \frac{CHM_i + CHD_i}{2} \tag{1}$$

Here, CHM_i denotes the cohesion at message level and CHD_i denotes the cohesion at domain level of an architecture i [2,11]. These are composed of the respective cohesion metrics of the microservices and their associated functions. CHM_i considers the similarity $f_{msg}(opr_k, opr_m)$ between two operations based on the input and output parameter names. CHD_i considers the similarity $f_{dom}(opr_k, opr_m)$ between two operations based on the function names. If a microservice consists of only one function, cohesion is assumed to be 0, unlike [11]. By doing so, we integrate a penalty so that a microservice would not consist of only a single function.

The quality of the cohesion metrics is also strongly dependent on the choice of function and parameter names. Some standardization approaches exist in the literature about how names of data analytics APIs could be structured [20], e.g. using common verbs `retrieve_data`, `filter_data`, `sample_data`, `aggregate_data`. Also, specific entities can be added to the operation names, e.g. `retrieve_company_data`, `filter_company_data` or `retrieve_organization_data`. Showing, the influence of f_{dom} on the decomposition, e.g. based on the entity or based on the verbs, both the pair `retrieve_company_data`, `filter_company_data` and the pair `retrieve_company_data`, `retrieve_organization_data` result in the same cohesion value in this case.

Functions are assigned to clusters or microservices by hierarchical clustering. The distance function d in Eq. 2 between functions combines both f_{dom} and f_{msg}.

High cohesion means high domain similarity, which is seen as low distance. Cluster counts from a minimum of 1 to a maximum of the number of functions in the workflow.

$$d(opr_k, opr_m) = 1 - \frac{(f_{msg}(opr_k, opr_m) + f_{dom}(opr_k, opr_m))}{2} \quad \forall opr_k, opr_m \in WF \quad (2)$$

3.2 Implementation

Once several microservice architectures have been derived, it is necessary to implement them in preparation for the runtime evaluation. A high-level architecture for implementation can be found in Fig. 2. Here we differ between the workflow scheduling and the functions of the workflow being scheduled. In our microservice architecture, workflow functions are deployed in microservices and the order of execution is implemented in the workflow.

Workflows and their scheduling can be implemented with various tools such as Apache Airflow[1], a custom implementation of a workflow microservice, or with Jmeter[2] specifically for load testing. On the one hand, the data science workflow can be implemented using the microservice design patterns orchestration or choreography [15] and infrastructure components such as application load balancers or message queues. Depending on the use case, application load balancers can be used for synchronous communication and message queues for asynchronous communication. The latter is interesting, for example, for longer-running tasks within data science workflows. Furthermore, multiple microservice architectures need to be deployed. Here, a monolith-first approach is suitable (see [18]), in which all workflow functions are implemented. These functions are then deployed in multiple instances of the same service. Routing capabilities can then be used to assign the calls from the workflow to the conceptually corresponding microservices. Considering cloud environment, standardization approaches of cloud providers[3] or of open source communities[4] could support the automated deployment of infrastructure components, microservice architectures and there links between.

3.3 Runtime Evaluation Metrics

To evaluate the microservice architecture candidates, we will use the metrics Average Change of Workflow Execution Times $\overline{\Delta WET}(\alpha)$, Change of Total Service Activation Time $\Delta WSA(\alpha)$ and Domain Metric $DM(\alpha)$. For this purpose, the architectures will be evaluated under different workload conditions such as

---

[1] https://airflow.apache.org/ (Last accessed 03 August 2022).
[2] https://jmeter.apache.org/ (Last accessed 03 August 2022).
[3] https://aws.amazon.com/cloudformation/ (Last accessed 03 August 2022).
[4] https://www.oasis-open.org/committees/tosca/ (Last accessed 03 August 2022).

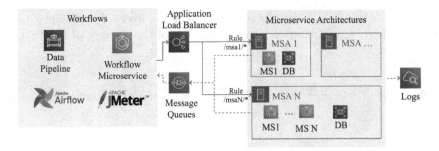

Fig. 2. High Level Reference Architecture for evaluating several microservice architectures at runtime.

volume and velocity workloads. Based on this evaluation, a further assessment can be made as to which architecture is best suited in terms of design and runtime metrics.

For the runtime evaluation, we define the following variables:

- The deployment of a microservice architecture MSA_i is denoted by α_i. The set of all deployed architectures is denoted by A. The distinction between conceptual microservice architecture MSA_i and a deployed architecture α_i is made because α_i is additionally provided with environment information such as configured resources.
- A workload configuration λ_t describes an experimental setting, including how many workflows are started in parallel or how much data volume is processed, a set of workload configurations is specified with Λ.
- Workflows can be started with certain parameters, e.g. with certain data filters for data selection. A workflow configuration is specified with e_u, a set of workflow configurations with E. If a workflow configuration exists only for certain workload conditions, this is specified with E_λ.

Average Change of Workflow Execution Times. The workflow execution time WET describes the sum of all execution times of the involved processing functions per workflow execution, see Eq. 3. To compare microservice architectures with each other, the average changes of this time per workflow execution compared to a baseline workload λ_0 are calculated (see Eq. 4). For comparison between architectures considering all workloads, we will add the probability $p(\lambda)$ that a certain workload occurs, see Eq. 6.

$$WET(e, \lambda, \alpha) = \sum_{\text{all } opr_k \in WF} ET_k(e, \lambda, \alpha) \tag{3}$$

$$\Delta WET(e, \lambda, \alpha) = \frac{WET(e, \lambda, \alpha) - WET(e, \lambda_0, \alpha)}{WET(e, \lambda_0, \alpha)} \tag{4}$$

$$\overline{\Delta WET}(\lambda, \alpha) = \frac{\sum_{\text{all } e_u \in E_\lambda} \Delta WET(e_u, \lambda, \alpha)}{|E_\lambda|} \tag{5}$$

$$\overline{\Delta WET}(\alpha) = \sum_{\text{all } \lambda_t \in \Lambda} p\left(\lambda_t\right) \overline{\Delta WET}(\lambda_t, \alpha) \tag{6}$$

Change of Total Service Activation Time. The workflow service activation time WSA describes how long individual services are involved in an experiment (see Eq. 7 and Eq. 8). We measure the end and beginning timestamps TSE and TSB by each service to calculate the service activation time SA. For comparisons between architectures, the changes of WSA to a baseline architecture α_0 are considered in Eq. 9. For comparison between architectures considering all workloads, we add the probability $p(\lambda)$ that a certain workload occurs, see Eq. 10.

$$SA_j(\lambda, \alpha) = \begin{array}{l} max\left(TSE_{jk}\left(e_u, \lambda, \alpha\right) \; : \forall k \text{ in } O_{ij}, \; \forall e_u \text{ in } E_\lambda\right) \\ - \, min\left(TSB_{jk}(e_u, \lambda, \alpha) \; : \forall k \text{ in } O_{ij}, \; \forall e_u \text{ in } E_\lambda\right) \end{array} \tag{7}$$

$$WSA(\lambda, \alpha) = \sum_{\text{all } j \in S_i} SA_j(\lambda, \alpha) \tag{8}$$

$$\Delta WSA(\lambda, \alpha) = \frac{WSA(\lambda, \alpha) - WSA(\lambda, \alpha_0)}{WSA(\lambda, \alpha_0)} \tag{9}$$

$$\Delta WSA(\alpha) = \sum_{\text{all } \lambda_t \in \Lambda} p\left(\lambda_t\right) \Delta WSA(\lambda_t, \alpha) \tag{10}$$

The service activation time also serves as a proxy for the costs of an architecture. This time can be combined with a pricing model since resources are often charged by time in cloud environments.

Domain Metric. The domain metric DM can be used to compare microservice architectures about scaling requirements [4]. For this purpose, thresholds Γ are defined. Therefore an operation could be marked as a failure if it would take too long under certain architecture or workload conditions. This threshold is calculated based on the average execution times μ of the operation with a baseline architecture α_0 and workload λ_0 (Eq. 11). An essential term of the domain metric is the success ratio $\hat{s}$ in Eq. 12. The Dirac function δ is used to count whether a function execution can be marked as success under workload and architecture conditions and this is multiplied by the frequency ν of function execution. In Eq. 13, the domain metric is formulated, which incorporates the probability of occurrence of a workload.

$$\mu_{ET_k}(\lambda, \alpha) > \Gamma_k\left(\lambda_0, \alpha_0\right), with \; \Gamma_k\left(\lambda_0, \alpha_0\right) = \mu_{ET_k}\left(\lambda_0, \alpha_0\right) + 3 \cdot \sigma_{ET_k}\left(\bar{\lambda}, \alpha_0\right) \tag{11}$$

$$\hat{s}\left(\lambda, \alpha\right) = \sum_{\text{all } opr_k \in WF} \nu_k \delta\left(opr_k, \lambda, \alpha\right) \tag{12}$$

$$DM(\alpha) = \sum_{\text{all } \lambda_t \in \Lambda} p\left(\lambda_t\right) \hat{s}\left(\lambda_t, \alpha\right) \tag{13}$$

4 Evaluation by Real-World Use Case

The multi-metric approach for decomposition of microservice-based data science workflows is now applied to a use case from corporate context. This chapter describes the use case, the derivation of the microservice architecture candidates, the implementation and execution of the runtime evaluation and the configuration of the experiments.

4.1 Use Case and Data Science Workflow

The use case is developed in the corporate foresight department of an automotive manufacturer. The use case aims to evaluate startups in an automated way using intelligent data selection, processing and a novel combination of algorithms, mainly of process mining and classification models. This assessment is then incorporated into subsequent decision support processes. To achieve this, a data science workflow was designed. This is to be implemented in a microservice architecture. The use case consists of several processing functions. The relevant functions are listed in Table 1.

For data selection phase, data is used from a external corporate database. For data preparation phase, several data filter and preprocessing techniques like cleansing and transformation are applied. Also, the application of process mining and their conformance checks are conducted during the data preparation phase since they are used for downstream tasks. For the modeling phase, classification models based on data of prior phase are trained and the best is selected. The best model can then be used for startup assessments.

We classify this use case in data science since the essential criteria for volume and velocity are fulfilled here. Regarding volume, a large amount of company data is selected for training or inference. Regarding velocity, high change of data requires continuous training as well as high founding activities require frequent inference. Consideration of training workflows, including continuous training, as well as inference of models can also be significantly characterized for data science. Here, a microservice architecture could support scaling requirements for training as well as reusability of functionalities for both training and inference.

4.2 Cohesion Metric Results

Figure 3 shows the cohesion for each microservice architecture. Microservice architecture 1 with one microservice achieves a CHA of more than 0.2. Microservice architecture 5 has the maximum (0.615), followed by 4 (0.614). The main difference between these architectures is the decomposition of train_company_classification (opr_{12}) into a separate microservices in MSA_5. In MSA_4, the select_companies and train_company_classification are in a single microservice. We also see that the penalty works when each operation is in its own microservice (see MSA_{25}).

Table 1. Selection of functions of the use case for training a machine learning model for start-up evaluation.

Id	Service Method	API Path	Sync/Async	Workflow Position
opr_1	select_companies	/company/select	Sync	1
opr_2	filter_companies	/company/filter	Sync	2
...	...	...		...
opr_6	select_keydevs	/keydevs/select	Sync	6
...	...	...		...
opr_9	obtain_processmodels	/obtain_processmodels	Sync	9
opr_{10}	check_conformance	/check_conformance	Async	10
opr_{11}	transform	/classification/transform	Sync	11
opr_{12}	train_ company_classification	/train/companies	Sync	12
...	...	...		...
opr_{25}	predict_company_class	/predict_company_class	Sync	

4.3 Runtime Evaluation and Experimental Setup

Due to the approximate cohesion equality of these microservice architectures, it is difficult to decide. Therefore, an evaluation at runtime is necessary. For this purpose, not all microservice architectures are evaluated, but MSA_1, MSA_4, MSA_5, MSA_6 with 1, 4, 5 and 6 microservices, respectively. The microservice architectures 4–6 reaches the highest cohesion. Microservice architecture 1 is monolithic and is used as a comparison.

The architecture from Fig. 2 is adapted for the implementation. Microservices provide a REST API that is used to access the functions. Table 1 also lists the communication methods. Almost all functions are called synchronously, except for one long-running task opr_{10} that is started via REST but returns the response asynchronously via message queues.

The scheduling of the workflow is implemented in Jmeter, since this can also be used for the load tests simultaneously. In Jmeter, we also configure a total of 6 workload configurations that are to take volume and velocity into account. The workload configurations are taken from practice. Initial data selections implement different data volumes (e.g., enterprise data that meet certain filter criteria). A total of 12 data selections are defined as less volume and 12 for high volume correspondingly. Since we configure 12 workflow data selections per volume area, we can execute them sequentially or multiple times in parallel. This results in the following workload configurations in total:

- Less Volume with Low Velocity (1 parallel), Medium Velocity (4 parallel), High Velocity (12 parallel), denoted as LV-1, LV-4, LV-12 respectively
- High Volume with Low Velocity (1 parallel), Medium Velocity (4 parallel), High Velocity (12 parallel), denoted as HV-1, HV-4, HV-12 respectively.

Jmeter is run on an EC2 instance. The microservices are packaged as Docker images and deployed on ECS Fargate instances, each with same resource configuration (4 CPU, 30Gb RAM). Each microservice is deployed as one single instance. Each microservice architecture has its own application load balancer and message queues. We explicitly exclude horizontal scaling to have fewer influencing factors and to focus on the design of the architectures. However, the domain metric can identify bottlenecks for scaling potentials.

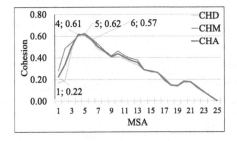

Fig. 3. Cohesion metrics of the microservice architectures by the cluster count.

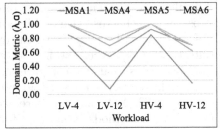

Fig. 4. Average Change of Workflow Execution Times compared to λ_0.

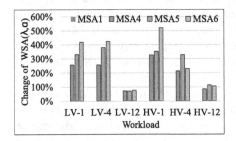

Fig. 5. Changes of Total Service Activation Time compared to MSA_1.

Fig. 6. Results of the domain metric.

4.4 Runtime Results

This section presents the results of the measured and calculated runtime metrics.

Average Change of Workflow Execution Times. The runtime evaluation of Average Change of Workflow Execution Times is shown in Fig. 4. The baseline workload λ_0 is Less Volume - Low Velocity (1 parallel) or High Volume - Low Velocity (1 parallel) in the respective architectures. The workloads Less Volume and High Volume are considered separately, since different data selections are used here that would not be directly comparable with each other.

The results show that higher workflow execution times are always to be expected. The MSA_6 achieves minor increases in the less volume area. In contrast, for the workload High Volume - High Velocity (12 parallel), the MSA_4 achieves the smallest increases and thus the best value.

Change of Total Service Activation Time. The results for Change of Total Service Activation Time are shown in Fig. 5. Here, the architecture MSA_1 is used as the baseline. Since multiple microservices are involved and deployed in the MSA_4, MSA_5 and MSA_6 architectures, higher service activation times are expected here in total overall workload configurations. MSA_4 achieves the smallest increases in almost all workload configurations (except for High Volume - Medium Velocity (4 parallel)) compared to the service activation times of MSA_1.

Domain Metric. The results of the DM evaluation can be seen in the Fig. 6. Baseline architecture and workload are MSA_1 and Less Volume - Low Velocity (1 parallel) and High Volume - Low Velocity (1 parallel), respectively. The higher the domain metric, the better, as the average execution times of the functions in the respective architectures are within the threshold. Here we see, on the one hand, that MSA_1 always performs worst. Especially with High Velocity, there are high scaling requirements. The MSA_6 always performs best here. Scaling requirement means, that start of new instances could be recommended.

5   Discussion and Architecture Recommendations

This section discusses how the determined metrics can support the selection of suitable microservice architectures. In Table 2, the design and runtime metrics are listed. Those values with which an architecture alternative performed best in the respective metric are marked in bold. Here, for the runtime metrics, equally distributed workloads are assumed to have $p(\lambda_t) = \frac{1}{|\Lambda|} \forall \lambda_t \in \Lambda$. Each microservice architecture achieves the best value in one metric. For the metrics CHA and DM, the maxima are the best values achieved by MSA_4 and MSA_6, respectively. For the metrics $\overline{\Delta WET}$ and ΔWSA, the minima are the best values, which MSA_5 and MSA_1 achieve, respectively.

Table 2. Overview of the resulted metrics with equally distributed workloads.

	MSA_1	MSA_4	MSA_5	MSA_6
Cohesion	0.2239	0.6148	**0.6151**	0.5681
Average Changes of Workflow Execution Time	162.95%	**115.93%**	127.64%	127.76%
Changes of Service Activation Time	**0.00%**	201.94%	262.72%	295.95%
Domain Metric	0.6282	0.8333	0.8846	**0.9103**

This is where the necessary trade-off decisions become apparent. Higher service activation times can be justified if this results in lower workflow execution times. To better reflect these trade-off decisions, the metrics are combined into a combined metric and given a weighting factor (see Eq. 14). Since the metrics are scaled differently, the metrics m are standardized to $\hat{m}$ and $\overline{\Delta WET(\alpha)}$ and $\Delta WSA(\alpha))$ are multiplied by -1 to define higher values as better values uniformly. Thus, the choice of an appropriate architecture alternative depends on the expected workload as well as the preference of individual metrics.

$$Com(\alpha) = \sum_{\text{all } m \in \{CHA, DM(\alpha), -1 \cdot \overline{\Delta WET(\alpha)}, -1 \cdot \Delta WSA(\alpha))\}} \omega(m) \cdot \hat{m} \qquad (14)$$

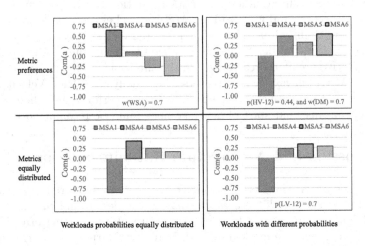

Fig. 7. Combined metric by different metric weights and workload probabilities.

Figure 7 shows an example of the influence of the choice of workload probabilities and metric preferences concerning the architecture choice. For example, by equal workload probabilities and metric preferences, the MSA_4 architecture is recommended. With a strong preference to ΔWSA as a proxy for cost, the

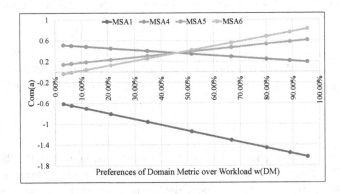

Fig. 8. Influence of different preferences of domain metric on combined metric.

MSA_1 architecture is recommended, which consists of only a single microservice. For these two examples, the selection seems very clear. However, if there is a preference for the domain metric and the workload HV-12 is more likely to be expected, the difference between MSA_4 and MSA_6 is not as clear.

To further investigate the influence of the choice of preferences, we vary the preference for the domain metric as an example. The preferences of the other metrics remain equally distributed. Figure 8 shows the result at what weight the choice of architecture changes. This should be kept in mind, especially when the combined metric of the individual architectures does not differ too much.

6   Implications and Conclusion

In conclusion, we have shown how our presented approach can be applied using a real-world use case to evaluate architecture alternatives with multiple metrics. Identifying microservices is a challenging task. With our approach, we bring together design and runtime metrics for designing microservice-oriented data science workflows.

In summary, we contribute (1) an abstract process model, the multi-metric approach for decomposition of microservice-based data science workflows, for deriving and evaluating microservice architectures of data science workflows. We also instantiate this abstract procedure model with selected metrics and algorithms relevant to data science workflows. Since the starting point is functions, the approach can be applied to arbitrary data science workflows. Also, we have configured workloads to include the Volume and Velocity characteristics. (2) Second, we contribute a software architecture that allows microservice architectures to be deployed concurrently in cloud environments and considers microservice design patterns orchestration and choreography. This architecture can be used to run real-world experiments, aggregate logs and analyze them in an automated fashion with respect to our selected metrics.

Our work has both practical, theoretical and economic implications. Practically, it can support software architects and data scientists in architecting microservices. In this context, it also has implications for MLOps, as microservices can be used to train and deploy ML models. Theoretically, our software architecture can be used for other research comparing microservice architectures. Economically, we also achieve business impact by looking at the cost of microservice architectures based on service activation time.

However, we also see some limitations. For one, we have only used a few workload configurations. We will conduct more experiments here in future work. Currently, we cannot make any recommendations for the weights of the metrics and workloads, so this currently depends on manual preferences of the software architects. The quality of the cohesion metrics is also strongly dependent on the choice of function and parameter names.

So that microservice architectures do not always have to be implemented for deriving them, part of future research will be to be able to describe and test the runtime behavior by simulations. In this way, architectures can be derived from data science workflows as early as the design phase of the architecture.

Acknowledgements. The results, opinions and conclusions expressed in this thesis are not necessarily those of Volkswagen Aktiengesellschaft.

References

1. Assunção, W.K.G., Colanzi, T.E., Carvalho, L., Pereira, J.A., Garcia, A., de Lima, M.J., Lucena, C.: A multi-criteria strategy for redesigning legacy features as microservices: an industrial case study. In: 2021 IEEE International Conference on Software Analysis, Evolution and Reengineering (SANER), pp. 377–387 (2021)
2. Athanasopoulos, D., Zarras, A.V., Miskos, G., Issarny, V., Vassiliadis, P.: Cohesion-driven decomposition of service interfaces without access to source code. IEEE Trans. Serv. Comput. 8(4), 550–562 (2015)
3. Bao, L., Wu, C., Bu, X., Ren, N., Shen, M.: Performance modeling and work-flow scheduling of microservice-based applications in clouds. IEEE Trans. Parallel Distrib. Syst. **30**(9), 2114–2129 (2019)
4. Camilli, M., Colarusso, C., Russo, B., Zimeo, E.: Domain metric driven decomposition of data-intensive applications. In; 2020 IEEE International Symposium on Software Reliability Engineering Workshops (ISSREW), pp. 189–196 (2020)
5. Capuano, R., Muccini, H.: A systematic literature review on migration to microservices: a quality attributes perspective. In: IEEE 19th International Conference on Software Architecture Companion (ICSA-C), vol. 19, pp. 120–123 (2022)
6. Cojocaru, M., Uta, A., Oprescu, A.: Attributes assessing the quality of microservices automatically decomposed from monolithic applications. In: 2019 18th International Symposium on Parallel and Distributed Computing (ISPDC), pp. 84–93 (2019)
7. Daoud, M., El Mezouari, A., Faci, N., Benslimane, D., Maamar, Z., El Fazziki, A.: A multi-model based microservices identification approach. J. Syst. Archit. **118**, 102200 (2021)
8. Fritzsch, J., Bogner, J., Zimmermann, A., Wagner, S.: From monolith to microservices: a classification of refactoring approaches. In: Bruel, J.M., Mazzara, M., Meyer, B. (eds.) Software Engineering Aspects of Continuous Development and New Paradigms of Software Production and Deployment, vol. 11350. Springer International Publishing, Cham (2019)
9. Gysel, M., Kölbener, L., Giersche, W., Zimmermann, O.: Service cutter: a systematic approach to service decomposition. In: Aiello, M., Johnsen, E.B., Dustdar, S., Georgievski, I. (eds.) ESOCC 2016. LNCS, vol. 9846, pp. 185–200. Springer, Cham (2016). https://doi.org/10.1007/978-3-319-44482-6_12
10. Hasselbring, W.: Microservices for scalability: keynote talk abstract. In: ICPE 2016: Proceedings of the 7th ACM/SPEC on International Conference on Performance Engineering, pp. 133–134 (2016)
11. Jin, W., Liu, T., Cai, Y., Kazman, R., Mo, R., Zheng, Q.: Service candidate identification from monolithic systems based on execution traces. IEEE Trans. Softw. Eng. **47**, 987–1007 (2019)
12. Klock, S., van der Werf, J.M.E.M., Guelen, J.P., Jansen, S.: Workload-based clustering of coherent feature sets in microservice architectures. In: 2017 IEEE International Conference on Software Architecture (ICSA), pp. 11–20 (2017)
13. Li, S., et al.: A dataflow-driven approach to identifying microservices from monolithic applications. J. Syst. Softw. **157**, 1–16 (2019). http://www.sciencedirect.com/science/article/pii/S0164121219301475

14. Provost, F., Fawcett, T.: Data science and its relationship to big data and data-driven decision making. Big Data **1**(1), 51–59 (2013)
15. Richardson, C.: Microservice Patterns: With Examples in Java. Manning, Shelter Island (2019)
16. Schröer, C., Kruse, F., Marx Gómez, J.: A qualitative literature review on microservices identification approaches. In: Dustdar, S. (ed.) SummerSOC 2020. CCIS, vol. 1310, pp. 151–168. Springer, Cham (2020). https://doi.org/10.1007/978-3-030-64846-6_9
17. Schröer, C., Wittfoth, S., Marx Gómez, J.: A process model for microservices design and identification. In: 2021 IEEE International Conference on Software Architecture Companion (ICSA-C), pp. 38–45 (2021)
18. Shimoda, A., Sunada, T.: Priority order determination method for extracting services stepwise from monolithic system. In: 2018 7th International Congress on Advanced Applied Informatics (IIAI-AAI), pp. 805–810 (2018)
19. Tamburri, D.A.: Sustainable MLOps: trends and challenges. In: 2020 22nd International Symposium on Symbolic and Numeric Algorithms for Scientific Computing (SYNASC), vol. 22, pp. 17–23 (2020)
20. Zhang, Y., Zhu, L., Xu, X., Chen, S., Tran, A.B.: Data service API design for data analytics. In: Ferreira, J.E., Spanoudakis, G., Ma, Y., Zhang, L.-J. (eds.) SCC 2018. LNCS, vol. 10969, pp. 87–102. Springer, Cham (2018). https://doi.org/10.1007/978-3-319-94376-3_6

Introducing Estimators—Abstraction for Easy ML Employment in Self-adaptive Architectures

Milad Abdullah, Michal Töpfer, Tomáš Bureš, Petr Hnětynka[✉],
Martin Kruliš, and František Plášil

Charles University, Prague, Czech Republic
{abdullah,topfer,bures,hnetynka,krulis,plasil}@d3s.mff.cuni.cz

Abstract. Machine learning (ML) has shown its potential in extending the ability of self-adaptive systems to deal with unknowns. To date, there have been several approaches to applying ML in different stages of the adaptation loop. However, the systematic inclusion of ML in the architecture of self-adaptive applications is still an objective that has not been very elaborated yet. In this paper, we show one approach to address this by introducing the concept of estimators in an architecture of a self-adaptive system. The estimator serves to provide predictions on future and currently unobservable values via ML. As a proof of concept, we show how estimators are employed in ML-DEECo—a dedicated ML-enabled component model for adaptive component architectures. It is based on our DEECo component model, which features autonomic components and dynamic component coalitions (ensembles). It makes it possible to specify ML-based adaptation already at the level of the component-based application architecture (i.e., at the model level) without having to explicitly deal with the intricacies of the adaptation loop. As part of the evaluation, we provide an open-source implementation of ML-DEECo run-time framework in Python.

Keywords: Self-adaptive · components · ensembles · machine learning

1 Introduction

In recent years, we have seen different applications of machine learning (ML) techniques in the area of adaptive systems [22,29,33,37]. These approaches integrate ML in the adaptation loop to perform regression over sensor indications (to make a future estimate of a value or to estimate a currently unobservable value) [29], to classify potential system actions (e.g., to prune the space of possible adaptations [36]), and to decide which action is likely to have the best effect [35].

Though these approaches systematically introduce ML in the adaptation loop, they are still lacking (at least partially) in the ability to provide more application-friendly abstractions and tools that would allow the architects to focus on the

T. Batista et al. (Eds.): ECSA 2022, LNCS 13928, pp. 370–385, 2023.
https://doi.org/10.1007/978-3-031-36889-9_25

application business logic rather than on the intricacies of integrating ML into the adaptation loop. We address this problem by introducing first-class ML concepts—*estimators*—serving to perform estimates on future and currently unobservable values in self-adaptive SW architectures. As a proof of concept, we show how estimators, relying on supervised learning, are employed in ML-DEECo—an extension to our DEECo component model [8] for designing component- and ensemble-based SW architectures (*CEB* architectures further on).

Similar to DEECo, ML-DEECo exploits the concept of autonomic component ensembles—self-adapting coalitions of components, which has proved to be a solid foundation for modeling dynamic architectures of cooperating autonomous agents. This has been demonstrated by a number of well-received papers [8,9, 11,12,27,28] in our community (e.g., at SEAMS, ECSA, ICSA) as well as in the community of coordination languages and attribute-based communication [3,4, 18,26]. As such, we exploit the concept of component ensembles in our work without justifying their benefits.

In ML-DEECo components, the architect declares *synthesized fields*, each yielding a predicted future or currently unobservable value. These synthesized fields, the value of which is determined by estimators, can be used in components and ensembles when deciding upon adaptation.

In a component, the architect declaratively binds the synthesized fields to other components' fields from which the training dataset is to be obtained. Based on such a declarative specification, ML-DEECo automatically takes care of training dataset collection at runtime, model training (and retraining), and inference. As a result, ML-DEECo requires the architect to have just a basic knowledge of ML and significantly reduces the effort to introduce ML in adaptation decisions.

The research presented in the paper falls under the umbrella of design research [34]. From this perspective, we focus on the following research questions:

Q1 How to incorporate ML in CEB architectures to support their self-adaptation?

Q2 How to design the ML models and semantics without having to recurringly write data collection and/or ML procedures?

Q3 How to map these concepts to a widely-used programming language?

Following the guidelines in [34], we evaluate the paper by demonstrating the proposed concepts related to estimators on a simplified case study coming from a recently finished EU project. Through a series of simulations, we further show how the inclusion of ML in CEB architectures improves the adaptation accuracy of a system. Last but not least, the open-source ML-DEECo run-time framework in Python and the replication package for the experiments have been made available online [2] so that the presented evaluation may be publicly verified.

The structure of the paper is as follows. Section 2 describes the running example and recalls the basics of DEECo. Section 3 describes and illustrates our solution, namely estimators and their application in ML-DEECo. The discussion and evaluation are provided in Sect. 4. Section 5 is devoted to related work, and Sect. 6 concludes the paper.

2   Running Example and Background

The running example we use in the paper comes from our recently finished ECSEL JU project AFarCloud[1] that focused on smart farming. It is a simple yet quite realistic scenario about protecting fields of crops against birds by drones.

The protection is performed by several autonomic drones that patrol the fields. By their presence (and the noise they create), the drones scare the flocks away to areas that do not need any protection; the exact number of drones required depends on the particular field size. The drones are powered by a battery and must be periodically recharged at a charger which can serve only a limited number of drones simultaneously.

There are two specific situations when the drones need to cooperate and adapt their behavior. First, based on the position and size of the particular flock, a sufficient number of drones need to be chosen and spread out over the fields to scare away as many of the birds as possible. Second, the drones need to move to a charger before they run out of battery while utilization of each charger has to be optimized. Obviously, the positions of flocks and the attributes of drones (i.e., position, battery charge level, mode) constitute the input to adaptation. The output of the adaptation is a new assignment of drones to the fields and chargers.

2.1   Modeling Self-adaptive Systems via Components and Ensembles

For modeling such an adaptive system, we use the abstractions of the DEECo ensemble-based component model [10]. All the entities in the system (drones, chargers, flocks of birds) are modeled as components that are described by their component type. In general, there are multiple instances (simply "components" in the paper) for each of the component types (i.e., multiple drones, flocks, etc.). Every component has a state represented as a set of data fields. The components that cannot be controlled directly (e.g., flocks of birds) are "beyond control components". In these components, the state is only observed via sensing or inferred but never directly modified.

An ensemble instance ("ensemble" for short) groups selected components together (e.g., assigns drones to a charger). A component can be in (be a "member" of) multiple ensembles at the same time.

The instantiation of ensembles happens dynamically at regular intervals at run-time to achieve adaptation of the system with respect to the current state of components. For example, if the battery charge of a drone component drops below a dangerous level, the drone will be assigned to a charger via a dedicated ensemble. There is one such ensemble per charger, grouping the components that are to be charged by the respective charger. The selection of such components is based on their distance to the charger and its availability. Naturally, there is mutual exclusion between these ensembles so that a particular drone can be assigned only to one charger.

---

[1]   https://www.ecsel.eu/projects/afarcloud.

There are different options for how to define the semantics of ensemble formation to handle a trade-off between expressiveness and scalability in particular. Thus, in our previous work [8,10], we experimented with different ideas. There are also other approaches to ensembles by different research groups [1,5,6,25,30]. For instance, the formation of ensembles can be perceived as a constraint optimization problem [10], but this makes their optimal formation an NP-complete problem. In this paper, we follow an approach scalable to thousands of components in which ensembles are formed eagerly based on their priorities. This has polynomial complexity w.r.t. to the number of ensembles and components.

Formally, an ensemble type definition consists of the following: (i) the `priority` that provides the order in which the ensembles are evaluated; (ii) the action to be performed on components selected in the ensemble (e.g., in the case of `DroneChargingAssignment` (Listing 2), the action sets a particular attribute of the components in the ensemble to refer to the selected charger); (iii) the set of roles that determine which components are to be included in the ensemble (i.e., become members of the ensemble). An ensemble may have multiple roles, which corresponds to the fact that components may have different responsibilities in the ensemble. A role has single or multiple cardinality determining whether single or multiple component instances can be assigned there. A role may have a selector (which determines if a component may be selected for the role) and a utility function ordering the potential components if there are more potential components than the role's cardinality limits.

For example, a `DroneChargingAssignment` (Listing 2) has two roles—one with cardinality 1 containing the charger component that the ensemble corresponds to, and another one with cardinality n for drones that are assigned to the charger.

3 Estimators

In this section, we present our approach to adding ML to CEB architectures. The key idea is that we do so by introducing the concept of the *estimator*. Typically, an estimator acts as a synthesized field of a component and provides predictions about a given quantity in decisions upon a state change of the component. Moreover, we allow the use of estimators in the conditions governing ensemble formation.

In principle, an estimator is realized by a neural network (supervised ML), the structure of which depends on the prediction goal of the estimator and its role in the CEB architecture as described in the taxonomy explained below. The estimator is functionally established by training the neural network. This requires a dataset that contains samples consisting of a vector of inputs and the expected output. Naturally, only valid samples are to be added to the dataset (i.e., the samples from the situations when the system is in an irrelevant state are to be disregarded). All this is determined declaratively in the architecture specification and supported (including the dataset collection, training, and estimator application) by the run-time framework we provide along with the paper [2].

3.1   Estimators in CEB Architectures

To give our approach a reasonable level of generality, we designed a taxonomy that reflects important concepts in CEB architectures and estimators (but otherwise is application-independent). This taxonomy is shown in Fig. 1 and its dimensions are described below.

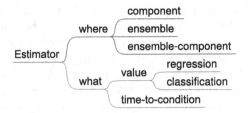

Fig. 1. Taxonomy of estimators

Where The "where" dimension describes with which abstractions an estimator is associated. Pursuing a CEB architecture with components and ensembles as first-class concepts, it is possible to associate an estimator with (i) a component, (ii) an ensemble, and (iii) an ensemble-component pair.

In the case of a component, the estimator is parameterized by the values of component fields. For instance, the field `position` of a `Drone` component (Listing 1) would be used as the input to the estimator that predicts the energy needed to get to the selected charger.

In the case of an ensemble, the estimator is parameterized by the values of its member component fields. For instance, the `DroneChargingAssignment` ensemble could have an estimator that predicts the number of drones waiting for a charger slot available at a specific time point in the future.

In the case of an ensemble-component pair, the estimator is dynamically associated with a component that is a potential member of a given ensemble. The estimator is parameterized by both the values of the ensemble's member components fields and the fields of the potential member. The difference from the previous case (of associating the estimator with the whole ensemble) is that the estimator is specific to the particular component. An example here is the estimator that predicts how long it would take a particular component to get a slot in the charger when it becomes part of the respective `DroneChargingAssignment` ensemble (Listing 2).

What The "what" dimension determines what is being predicted by an estimator. Trivially, one option is to predict a future value (as it is typically done in supervised learning).

In this case, the currently available observations are used to predict some value that can be observed only at some future point (typically after a specific amount of time steps). For example, we can use the current battery level and the mode of the drone to predict battery charge level after n time steps in the future, as shown in Listing 1.

Based on the type of predicted value, the prediction is usually based on regression or classification. We follow this distinction and distinguish between classification and regression in the estimators if a value is to be predicted. The choice of a particular estimator's task influences the structure of the neural network used for the prediction. Specifically, the choice determines the activation function of the last layer of the neural network and the loss function used for training.

Another option in the "what" dimension, especially handy for proactive control in self-adaptive systems, is predicting how long it will take until some condition becomes true. We call this option *time-to-condition* prediction. This is done by specifying a condition over specific future values of component fields. For example, it is possible to ask how long it will take until the battery charge level reaches a certain threshold or how long it will take until a `drone` component is assigned a slot in the charger (Listing 2).

3.2 Employing Estimators

In this section, we show how to integrate estimators into ML-DECCo, focusing on their "lifecycle" in particular.

First, we illustrate the key concepts on the fragment of the `Drone` component type specification (Listing 1) written in a simple specification language. A more complete specification, including meta-models, is a part of the replication package that comes with the paper [2]. Here a `Drone` component has three basic fields: `position`, `battery` (the current battery charge level), and `mode` (the mode of its currently activity). In addition, the component has a synthesized field—the estimator `futureBatery`, serving to predict battery charge level after given time steps. The `if` statement on the line illustrates the use of `futureBatery`; here, it yields an estimate of future battery charge level in the 50th future time step.

```
1  component type Drone
2    field position: Position
3    field battery: ChargeLevel
4    field mode: Enum
5              { IDLE, TERMINATED, MOVING_TO_CHARGER, CHARGING,...}
6    field regression estimator futureBattery:
7      input battery
8      input mode
9      output battery in T+<1,200>
10     guard mode != TERMINATED
11   # other code ...
12   # examples of estimator's employment:
13   if futureBattery(50) < 0.3 then ...
```
Listing 1. A fragment of Drone component type specification

The specification items `input`, `output`, and `guard` relate to the training datasets (each containing samples consisting of a vector of inputs and the expected outputs). The validity of the training data is controlled by the restriction imposed by the predicates in `guard` items.

For instance, a training dataset of `futureBattery` will consist of a sequence of triples $< \mathtt{battery}, \mathtt{mode}, \mathtt{battery\_in\_n} >$, where n is a time step in the range 1..200. The triples are collected only if `mode != TERMINATED` is continuously holding.

Listing 2 shows the `DroneChargingAssignment` ensemble type, an instance of which groups and coordinates the drones waiting for the charger associated with it. It has a role `charger` (of cardinality 1) and a role `drone` (for the grouped drones) of cardinality 0 to n. The `Drone` role has a time-to-condition estimator `waitingTime` assigned to it to predict the waiting time of the considered `drone` needed to be accepted for charging (i.e., its mode is set to `ACCEPTED_FOR_CHARGING`). In the membership condition of `Drone`, `waitingTime` is applied for each drone considered to be selected for charging. Moreover, the need for charging of such a `drone` is determined by the use of its `futureBattery` estimator, which predicts the battery charge level after the time steps determined by `waitingTime` are elapsed.

```
1  ensemble type DroneChargingAssignment
2    role charger: Charger
3    role multiple drone: Drone
4      with time−to−condition estimator waitingTime:
5        input distance(drone.position)
6        input drone.battery
7        input drone.mode
8        condition drone.mode == ACCEPTED_FOR_CHARGING
9        guard drone.mode != TERMINATED
10     cardinality <0, n>
11     membership drone.futureBattery(waitingTime) < 0.3
12     utility ...
13     priority ...
14     # other code here ...
15     action assignToCharger(drone)
16       ...
```

Listing 2. A fragment of DroneChargingAssignment ensemble type specification

Again, the specification items `input`, `output`, `guard`, and `condition` relate to the training datasets. Here, a training dataset of `waitingTime` will consist of a sequence of quadruples $< distance, batery, mode, timeToWait >$, where `timeToWait` is evaluated once the condition `mode == ACCEPTED_FOR_CHARGING` holds. Again the sequence is added to the dataset only if the condition `mode != TERMINATED` has continuously held. Note that there is no explicit `output` specification, since here the output is defined implicitly by the semantics of time-to-condition definition. Also, for simplicity, we assume that on the beginning of its functionality, the ensemble is without a training set; in the bootstrapping process of its training, the estimator yields a user-defined, application-dependent default estimates (not visible in Listing 2).

3.3 Mapping to Python

As a proof of concept, we developed an open-source Python-based framework that realizes the approach described in Sects. 3.1 and 3.2. The framework features API for defining components, ensembles, and estimators—thus providing an internal domain-specific language for the design of ensemble-based component systems that employ ML. The implementation and details about the framework are available in the replication package [2].

4   Discussion and Evaluation

In this paper, we designed a component model that provides abstractions for self-adaptive systems of autonomous components that employ ML (specifically predictions based on supervised learning). Our goal was to provide an architectural specification that makes it possible to include ML declaratively in the architectural model, thus freeing the developer from having to code data collection and training loops. To evaluate our approach, we present the following evidence (structured in three subsections below) that speaks in favor of the feasibility of the approach. We conclude the section by explicitly discussing the threats to validity.

4.1   Exemplar

We provide a model and implementation of the running example that features different variants of predictions and thus shows that a non-trivial problem can be successfully modeled using our approach. The implementation of the example is in Python and illustrates that estimators can be in a rather seamless way integrated into a specification of components and ensembles.

We do not quantify whether and how our approach saves the time of the developer. An important reason for not doing so in the paper is that we are not aware of any other component model focusing on adapting groups of autonomic components that would provide ML abstractions. As such, we are missing a non-trivial baseline for comparison.

A trivial baseline is to compare an implementation of the same use-case developed only with some basic libraries like TensorFlow and PyTorch. In this case, we can claim that we save the effort of the developer—roughly equivalent to the design effort of the ML-DEECo runtime framework that we make available along with the paper (as part of addressing research question Q3). However, we believe this comparison is trivial and does not constitute an evaluation worth elaborating in detail in the paper. In this context, we refer the reader to the replication package [2] which contains the code of the runtime framework.

4.2   Implementation of ML-DEECo Runtime Framework

We provide an open-source implementation of the ML-DEECo runtime framework, which allows the building ML-enabled self-adaptive architectures of distributed components with ensembles.

An important point to address here is the generality of the approach. We explicitly scope it to the estimators that are constructed using supervised ML. Thus the considered estimators can be constructed only for quantities that are observable at some later point in the future.

Within this scope, our approach and the supporting runtime framework have been designed independently of the use-case we demonstrate in Sects. 2 and 3. Nevertheless, the framework reflects the taxonomy of estimators in Sect. 3.1, which covers associating the estimators with all first-class concepts in the component model (i.e., component, ensemble, and ensemble-component pair). Also, following the primary distinction in supervised ML, we support both regression and classification. Given the fact we deal with systems evolving over time, we also include the predictions about time (in the form of the time-to-condition predictions). We believe this provides enough generality, irrespective of the target domain.

4.3   Simulation of the Use-Case and Evaluation of Machine-Learning Potential

We provide experimental results from running the use-case implementation within a simulator associated with the ML-DEECo runtime framework. On the one hand, this shows the complete end-to-end setup; on the other hand, it demonstrates one instance of how an application of ML has the potential to improve a self-adaptive system. All the code and the results (including a detailed description of the setup and the simulation) are a part of the replication package [2]. In this section, we highlight the main points.

To perform experiments, we developed a simulator that simulates the behavior of the flocks of birds and the movement and charging of drones on a map capturing fields and charger locations.

We have two implementations of drones: baseline and ML-based. In the baseline implementation, drones are called to the charger if the battery level drops below a threshold that is computed as a linear function of the distance to the closest charger (including a safety margin). In the ML-based implementation, there is additionally an estimator which predicts the time a drone is going to wait for an available charger. This waiting time cannot be easily estimated without ML because it depends on variable charging time (which non-linearly depends on the number of simultaneously charged drones and potentially other factors). The estimator used is the same as the one on line in Listing 2. In the baseline, the `waitingTime` is set to 0.

In the experiments, we compare the baseline and the ML-based implementation with respect to two metrics that reflect the overall success of the system: (a) the number of survived drones at the end of the simulation (i.e., how many drones did not run out of battery while waiting for the charger), (b) the extent of damaged crops over the simulation (measured by the total cumulative time the flocks of birds spent feasting on the fields without being scared away by a drone).

We simulated the scenario with different starting parameters (i.e., number of drones, number of flocks of birds, number of chargers, etc.—all are detailed in the replication package). Each simulation was repeated 5 times with the same parameter settings, and the results per a set of parameters were averaged. Figure 2 shows the number of survived drones for the two variants of the implementation with a different starting number of drones (higher is better). Figure 3 shows the comparison for the total amount of damaged crops with different flock sizes (lower is better). We can see that the ML-based approach consistently outperforms the baseline.

These measurements serve as an illustration of our approach and do not aim to provide a generic way to employ ML in self-adaptation. Nevertheless, it is worth emphasizing that: (a) Applying our approach requires just a basic knowledge of ML, in particular about neural network structure (at least that the learning capacity of the network depends on the size of the layers, more capacity means a greater chance for overfitting, and the more layers, the more complicated the training), and about the difference between classification and regression. (b) Assuming a basic tutorial is provided, the application of our approach requires, in our view, much less effort and ML knowledge than is the case with generic ML frameworks like TensorFlow and PyTorch. Specifically, there is a significant difference in that data collection and training data set preparation happens automatically at the run time of application and training and evaluation over the collected data as well.

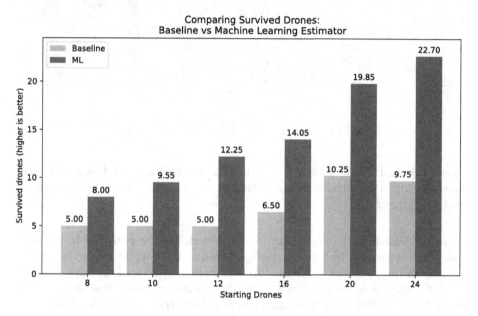

Fig. 2. Survived drones: baseline vs. ML-based estimators

4.4   Limitations and Threats to Validity

Given the limited scope of the paper, we are aware of several limitations and threats to the validity of our evaluation. We list the most important ones below. We organize them based on the schema in [32], where the validity classes are defined as follows: (i) construct validity, (ii) internal validity, (iii) external validity, and (iv) reliability.

Construct Validity. We construct our validation on the assumption that by providing the data collection and ML, the ML-DEECo framework saves design and coding effort in the need of predictions identified in Sect. 3.1. This could potentially be false, though we did our best to make the meta-model and the

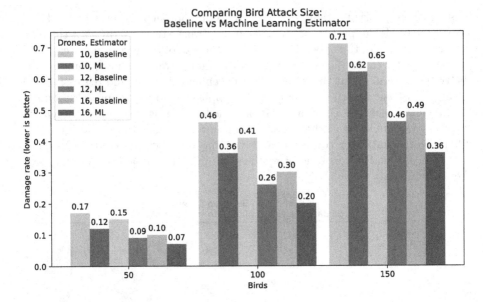

Fig. 3. Crops damage: baseline vs. ML-base estimators

corresponding Python API easy to use. Also, we provide several examples that show that different estimators can indeed be easily deployed just by a couple of lines in Python.

Internal Validity. To show that the framework has the potential to improve self-adaptive systems by introducing ML-based estimation, we made the experiment described in Sect. 4.3. We use two metrics as a measure of the improvement: the total amount of damaged crops and the number of drones that did not run out of battery till the end of the simulation. A potential threat here is that there is a hidden unknown factor that has a significant influence on the results. We mitigated this threat by the following: (1) We used exactly the same component and ensemble definitions for both the baseline and the ML-based architecture; the only difference was the value of `waitingTime`, which was set to 0 in the baseline and to the value of the estimator in the ML-based solution. (2) We conducted several experiments in which we varied individual parameters of the simulation and observed the effect on these metrics to ensure that we did not see any unexpected or random effects.

External Validity. We attempted to ensure our solution is general by basing it on the taxonomy of predictions (Sect. 4.3), which is independent of our running example and built as a combination of generally accepted abstractions. However, the use case we show and the simulation we did cannot by themselves guarantee generalizability. They serve rather as proof of feasibility. To show the full generalizability of our results, we would have to apply our approach to larger case studies. This is beyond the scope of this paper and constitutes future work.

Reliability. Though coming from an EU project with multiple partners, the implementation of the use-case we employed for the demonstration was created on our own, including the baseline and the ML-based solution. Being fully aware that this limits the significance of the results on one hand, we would like to emphasize on the other hand that the key difference between the baseline and the ML-based solution is only in the use of the estimator. Nevertheless, this still makes our results only an indicator of the potential improvement and feasibility. They do not permit quantification of the expected improvement in other applications.

5   Related Work

As set in Sect. 1, we have focused on creating a component model which is suitable for the development of adaptive systems and which allows for the direct specification of ML parameters on the level of an application architecture. Related approaches are thus those that incorporate ML to adaptive systems and those that define an explicit component model for developing adaptive systems. It turns out there are no existing solutions that would integrate ML and component models for adaptive systems. Thus in the rest of the section, we focus on partial approaches in either of the directions.

ML in Adaptive Systems: Incorporating machine-learning techniques to self-adaptive systems has been studied for already some time. In the systematic literature review [33], the authors analyze the usage of ML techniques in self-adaptive systems for the past 20 years, and there is a clear increasing trend in employing these techniques. Most commonly, ML techniques are used directly for adaptation. Another systematic literature review [22] also confirms the same trend and also documents the main focus on the usage of ML techniques in adaptation. Typically, these approaches use neural-network to predict future actions or optimize adaptation processes, etc. Still, contrary to our approach, these ML techniques are "hidden" within the implementation and "hard-coded". As the most recent and related to our approach, we list the following.

In [36], ML (based on neural networks) is used during the analysis and planning phases (of the MAPE-K loop) to reduce a large space of possible adaptations. A similar approach [35] (by a similar set of authors) combines ML with cost-benefit analysis (i.e., choosing adaptations with the best cost). Similarly, in [23], the reduction of adaptation space via ML is discussed and a theorem defining a theoretical bound on the impact of applying an ML method was defined.

In [21], a formal framework for the coevolution of an adaptive system and its tests is designed. ML is applied to restrict an adaptation space to achieve a meaningful system after adaptation. The paper [14] describes an approach combining ML with probabilistic model checking in order to select the best possible adaptation while refusing unfeasible ones in order to allow for faster convergence towards optimal decisions. In [31], the authors use online reinforcement learning to address design-time uncertainty and automate the development of self-adaptation logic. In particular, they propose an approach that removes the necessity of manual fine-tuning and other manual activities during the usage of reinforcement learning. SARDE [24] is a framework for continuous self-adaptive resource demand estimation. SARDE uses ML internally to select the best estimation approach from a set of available alternatives and to optimize the selected approaches to minimize estimation errors. The approach in [29] employs ML on the boundary of monitoring and analysis phases of the MAPE-K loop. Machine learning is used to forecast future values and thus allow for progressive adaptation.

The common trait of all these approaches is that they use ML internally to achieve some specific task. They do not provide general (application-independent) architectural abstractions (a) to equip a self-adaptive system with ML capabilities and (b) to allow the self-adaptive architecture to directly use the results of the ML (in our case, the estimators trained by supervised learning) in the specification of applications adaptation logic.

Component Models for Adaptive Systems: In the area of component models for adaptive systems, we can see a maturation of traditional static component models [15,16] and approaches based thereupon. This happened roughly in the span of 2010–2017. This coincides with the merger of the International Symposium on Component-Based Software Engineering (CBSE), which was the primary target for introducing new component models, into ICSA in 2017. Since 2017, there have been hardly any papers at ICSA featuring new component abstractions. The momentum around component abstractions continued at least partly in the community of collective adaptive systems, where it gave rise to the concept of component ensembles as a generalization of component connectors to address dynamically evolving adaptive systems.

The foundation in the ensemble-based component systems has been laid by SCEL (Service Component Ensemble Language) [30]. SCEL gives mathematical structures and describes the semantics of communication. However, its abstractions have been materialized in a Java-based runtime framework [1]. Another closely related approach is the Helena [25] ensemble framework.

Not exactly an ensemble-based but very similar to them approach is in the *AbC* calculus [5] (further formalized in [3] and with several case studies), which allows for defining systems via attribute-based communication between components. It has been implemented in Java as the Ab^aCuS framework [6]. As in our approach, components are defined as classes, and processes (that perform communication via component attributes similarly to ensembles) are also classes. Another implementation of *AbC* is ABEL [17], which is a DSL developed in the Erlang language.

DReAM [19] is a framework for dynamic reconfigurable architectures. It defines an architecture description language that is based on interaction logic and allows for describing dynamic coordination among components. Its mapping to Java, similarly to our approach, maps components and coordination to classes.

The propositional interaction logic in DReAM is based on the BIP component model [7], which focuses on the formal description of component behavior. In [13], a combination of UML components and BIP is proposed. The approach focuses on the description and verification of component behavior and communication. DR-BIP [20] is an extension of BIP, which adds support for dynamic reconfiguration.

The common trait of all these approaches is that they focus on semantics, but as of yet, they do not introduce any ML. This sets them apart from our approach, which combines the ensembles with ML.

6   Conclusion

In this paper, we have introduced the concept of the estimator in component-based architecture of self-adaptive systems. We have shown it in the ML-DEECo component model for architecting self-adaptive systems via ensembles of autonomic components. The novelty of ML-DEECo is that it integrates estimators as architectural abstractions that are directly used in the specification of components and ensembles without forcing the architect to deal with the intricacies of ML in the adaptation loop. In summary, our solution covers the identification of abstractions (addressing research question Q1), explanation of their semantics (addressing Q2), and realization in Python (addressing Q3). The Python implementation of the ML-DEECo runtime framework is available as open-source as part of our replication package [2]. The replication package provides a more detailed description of the framework and examples. In future work, we would like to extend the abstractions to cover other ML approaches—unsupervised learning and, most importantly, reinforcement learning. We also plan a larger use-case to evaluate our approach at a more complex scale.

Acknowledgment. This work has been partially supported by the Czech Science Foundation project 20-24814J, partially by Charles University institutional funding SVV 260698/2023, and partially by the Charles University Grant Agency project 269723.

References

1. jRESP: Java Runtime Environment for SCEL Programs. https://jresp.sourceforge.net/. Accessed 30 Mar 2023
2. Replication package. https://github.com/smartarch/ML-DEECo-replication-package
3. Abd Alrahman, Y., De Nicola, R., Loreti, M.: Programming interactions in collective adaptive systems by relying on attribute-based communication. Sci. Comput. Program. **192**, 102428 (2020)
4. Aguzzi, G., Casadei, R., Maltoni, N., Pianini, D., Viroli, M.: SCAFI-WEB: a web-based application for field-based coordination programming. In: Damiani, F., Dardha, O. (eds.) COORDINATION 2021. LNCS, vol. 12717, pp. 285–299. Springer, Cham (2021). https://doi.org/10.1007/978-3-030-78142-2_18

5. Abd Alrahman, Y., De Nicola, R., Loreti, M.: On the power of attribute-based communication. In: Albert, E., Lanese, I. (eds.) FORTE 2016. LNCS, vol. 9688, pp. 1–18. Springer, Cham (2016). https://doi.org/10.1007/978-3-319-39570-8_1

6. Abd Alrahman, Y., De Nicola, R., Loreti, M.: Programming of CAS systems by relying on attribute-based communication. In: Margaria, T., Steffen, B. (eds.) ISoLA 2016. LNCS, vol. 9952, pp. 539–553. Springer, Cham (2016). https://doi.org/10.1007/978-3-319-47166-2_38

7. Bliudze, S., Sifakis, J.: The algebra of connectors-structuring interaction in BIP. IEEE Trans. Comput. **57**(10) (2008)

8. Bures, T., Gerostathopoulos, I., Hnetynka, P., Keznikl, J., Kit, M., Plasil, F.: DEECO: an ensemble-based component system. In: Proceedings of CBSE 2013, Vancouver, Canada (2013)

9. Bures, T., Gerostathopoulos, I., Hnetynka, P., Keznikl, J., Kit, M., Plasil, F.: Gossiping components for cyber-physical systems. In: Avgeriou, P., Zdun, U. (eds.) ECSA 2014. LNCS, vol. 8627, pp. 250–266. Springer, Cham (2014). https://doi.org/10.1007/978-3-319-09970-5_23

10. Bures, T., et al.: A language and framework for dynamic component ensembles in smart systems. Int. J. Softw. Tools Technol. Transfer **22**(4), 497–509 (2020)

11. Bures, T., Hnetynka, P., Kofron, J., Al Ali, R., Skoda, D.: Statistical approach to architecture modes in smart cyber physical systems. In: Proceedings of WICSA 2016, Venice, Italy (2016)

12. Bures, T., Plasil, F., Kit, M., Tuma, P., Hoch, N.: Software abstractions for component interaction in the internet of things. Computer **49**(12), 50–59 (2016)

13. Chehida, S., Baouya, A., Bensalem, S.: Component-based approach combining UML and BIP for rigorous system design. In: Salaün, G., Wijs, A. (eds.) FACS 2021. LNCS, vol. 13077, pp. 27–43. Springer, Cham (2021). https://doi.org/10.1007/978-3-030-90636-8_2

14. Cámara, J., Muccini, H., Vaidhyanathan, K.: Quantitative verification-aided machine learning: a tandem approach for architecting self-adaptive IoT systems. In: Proceedings of ICSA 2021, Salvador, Brazil (2020)

15. Crnkovic, I., Larsson, M. (eds.): Building Reliable Component-Based Software Systems. Artech House, Boston (2002)

16. Crnkovic, I., Sentilles, S., Vulgarakis, A., Chaudron, M.: A classification framework for software component models. IEEE Trans. Softw. Eng. **37**(5), 593–615 (2011)

17. De Nicola, R., Duong, T., Loreti, M.: ABEL - a domain specific framework for programming with attribute-based communication. In: Riis Nielson, H., Tuosto, E. (eds.) COORDINATION 2019. LNCS, vol. 11533, pp. 111–128. Springer, Cham (2019). https://doi.org/10.1007/978-3-030-22397-7_7

18. De Nicola, R., Duong, T., Loreti, M.: Provably correct implementation of the AbC calculus. Sci. Comput. Program. **202**, 102567 (2021)

19. De Nicola, R., Maggi, A., Sifakis, J.: The DReAM framework for dynamic reconfigurable architecture modelling: theory and applications. Int. J. Softw. Tools Technol. Transfer **22**(4), 437–455 (2020)

20. El Ballouli, R., Bensalem, S., Bozga, M., Sifakis, J.: Programming dynamic reconfigurable systems. Int. J. Softw. Tools Technol. Transfer **23**(5), 701–719 (2021). https://doi.org/10.1007/s10009-020-00596-7

21. Gabor, T., et al.: The scenario coevolution paradigm: adaptive quality assurance for adaptive systems. Int. J. Softw. Tools Technol. Transfer **22**(4), 457–476 (2020). https://doi.org/10.1007/s10009-020-00560-5

22. Gheibi, O., Weyns, D., Quin, F.: Applying machine learning in self-adaptive systems: a systematic literature review. ACM Trans. Auton. Adapt. Syst. **15**(3), 1–37 (2021)
23. Gheibi, O., Weyns, D., Quin, F.: On the impact of applying machine learning in the decision-making of self-adaptive systems. In: Proceedings of SEAMS 2021, Madrid, Spain (2021)
24. Grohmann, J., et al.: SARDE: a framework for continuous and self-adaptive resource demand estimation. ACM Trans. Auton. Adapt. Syst. **15**(2), 1–31 (2021)
25. Hennicker, R., Klarl, A.: Foundations for ensemble modeling – the HELENA approach. In: Iida, S., Meseguer, J., Ogata, K. (eds.) Specification, Algebra, and Software. LNCS, vol. 8373, pp. 359–381. Springer, Heidelberg (2014). https://doi.org/10.1007/978-3-642-54624-2_18
26. Hennicker, R., Wirsing, M.: A dynamic logic for systems with predicate-based communication. In: Margaria, T., Steffen, B. (eds.) ISoLA 2020. LNCS, vol. 12477, pp. 224–242. Springer, Cham (2020). https://doi.org/10.1007/978-3-030-61470-6_14
27. Hnetynka, P., Bures, T., Gerostathopoulos, I., Pacovsky, J.: Using component ensembles for modeling autonomic component collaboration in smart farming. In: Proceedings of SEAMS 2020, Seoul, Korea (2020)
28. Krijt, F., Jiracek, Z., Bures, T., Hnetynka, P., Gerostathopoulos, I.: Intelligent ensembles - a declarative group description language and java framework. In: Proceedings of SEAMS 2017, Buenos Aires, Argentina (2017)
29. Muccini, H., Vaidhyanathan, K.: A machine learning-driven approach for proactive decision making in adaptive architectures. In: Companion Proceedings of ICSA 2019, Hamburg, Germany (2019)
30. De Nicola, R., et al.: The SCEL language: design, implementation, verification. In: Wirsing, M., Hölzl, M., Koch, N., Mayer, P. (eds.) Software Engineering for Collective Autonomic Systems. LNCS, vol. 8998, pp. 3–71. Springer, Cham (2015). https://doi.org/10.1007/978-3-319-16310-9_1
31. Palm, A., Metzger, A., Pohl, K.: Online reinforcement learning for self-adaptive information systems. In: Dustdar, S., Yu, E., Salinesi, C., Rieu, D., Pant, V. (eds.) CAiSE 2020. LNCS, vol. 12127, pp. 169–184. Springer, Cham (2020). https://doi.org/10.1007/978-3-030-49435-3_11
32. Runeson, P., Höst, M.: Guidelines for conducting and reporting case study research in software engineering. Empirical Softw. Eng. **14**(2), 131–164 (2009)
33. Saputri, T.R.D., Lee, S.W.: The application of machine learning in self-adaptive systems: a systematic literature review. IEEE Access **8**, 205948–205967 (2020)
34. Shaw, M.: Writing good software engineering research papers. In: Proceedings of ICSE 2003, Portland, OR, USA (2003)
35. Van Der Donckt, J., Weyns, D., Iftikhar, M.U., Buttar, S.S.: Effective decision making in self-adaptive systems using cost-benefit analysis at runtime and online learning of adaptation spaces. In: Damiani, E., Spanoudakis, G., Maciaszek, L.A. (eds.) ENASE 2018. CCIS, vol. 1023, pp. 373–403. Springer, Cham (2019). https://doi.org/10.1007/978-3-030-22559-9_17
36. Van Der Donckt, J., Weyns, D., Quin, F., Van Der Donckt, J., Michiels, S.: Applying deep learning to reduce large adaptation spaces of self-adaptive systems with multiple types of goals. In: Proceedings of SEAMS 2020, Seoul, South Korea (2020)
37. Weyns, D., et al.: towards better adaptive systems by combining MAPE, control theory, and machine learning. In: Proceedings of SEAMS 2021, Madrid, Spain (2021)

Generalization of Machine-Learning Adaptation in Ensemble-Based Self-adaptive Systems

Jan Pacovský, Petr Hnětynka$^{(\boxtimes)}$, and Martin Kruliš

Charles University, Prague, Czech Republic
{pacovsky,hnetynka,krulis}@d3s.mff.cuni.cz

Abstract. Smart self-adaptive systems are nowadays commonly employed almost in any application domain. Within them, groups of robots, autonomous vehicles, drones, and similar automatons dynamically cooperate to achieve a common goal. An approach to model such dynamic cooperation is via autonomic component ensembles, which are dynamically formed groups of components. Forming ensembles is described via a set of constraints (e.g., form an ensemble of three drones closest to a target that have sufficient battery level to reach the target and stay there). Evaluating these constraints by traditional means (such as a SAT solver) is computationally demanding and does not scale for large systems. This paper proposes an approach for solving ensemble formations based on machine learning which may be relatively faster. The method trains the model on a small instance of the system governed by a computationally demanding algorithm and then adapts it for large instances thanks to the generalization properties of the machine learning model.

Keywords: Self-adaptive Systems · Ensembles · Machine-learning

1   Introduction

Smart self-adaptive systems are nowadays commonly employed almost in any application domain. These systems are usually composed of a large number of components that cooperate to achieve a common goal. The cooperation among components defines the behavior of a whole system and is typically expressed via a set of application-specific collaboration rules.

As a particular example, we can consider a smart farming application where drones monitor fields. A given number of drones is required for sufficient monitoring of a particular field while the rest of the drone fleet is re-charging or kept on standby. The rules (i.e., constraints) for such an application would assign several drones to each field. Additionally, the selection of particular drones would consider the battery level of the drone, its distance from the field, and similar parameters. Therefore, the optimal operation of the system is achieved by finding a solution where all constraints are satisfied. As the system continuously

T. Batista et al. (Eds.): ECSA 2022, LNCS 13928, pp. 386–401, 2023.
https://doi.org/10.1007/978-3-031-36889-9_26

changes (e.g., the battery is depleted or the weather is changing), the evaluation of constraint satisfaction needs to be performed continuously.

To model the architecture of self-adaptive systems, we employ the concept of autonomous component *ensembles* [4]. An ensemble is a dynamically established group of collaborating components. Members of an ensemble are determined by a set of constraints—the hard constraints that have to be always satisfied and the soft ones intended for optimizations. This assignment of components to an ensemble we call *ensemble resolution*. Unfortunately, the resolution has exponential complexity, so it is quite time-demanding even with the contemporary state-of-the-art constraint solvers. To make matters worse, the resolution must be executed continuously to reflect changes in the modeled system.

In our previous work [3], we started experimenting with how to describe the ensemble resolution as a classification problem (instead of the constraint satisfaction problem) and solve it via machine learning methods. The initial results are quite promising, and we have been able to train classifiers to achieve even marginally a better solution than with the original one using a constraint solver. Nevertheless, an essential downside of the approach is that the underlying neural networks need to be specifically prepared for a particular number of components in the system, and also they need to be trained for the particular system configuration. In this paper, we present a method that overcomes this issue. It allows for the preparation of underlying neural networks for a limited system configuration and training them on small data sets (e.g., for six drones over three fields) and *generalizing* the results for any configuration of the system.

The structure of the paper is as follows. Section 2 provides a more detailed description of the running example and its architecture modeled via ensembles. Section 3 describes the principles of the proposed method, and its technical details are in Sect. 4. Section 5 evaluates the method on multiple configurations. Section 6 discusses related work, and Sect. 7 concludes the paper.

2   Running Example

As a running example (already partially introduced in the previous section), we are using a simple yet realistic use case taken from our recently successfully finished ECSEL JU project AFarCloud[1]. In the use case, there is a farm containing several fields where crops need to be protected from flocks of birds. A fleet of drones is used to scare the flocks away from the fields (to other farm areas that are not "birds-sensitive"). When a dangerous flock is detected, a sufficient number of drones form a group (to scare the birds effectively) and fly to protect the particular field. The drones can fly only for a limited amount of time, and then their battery needs to be recharged. At a single time, the charger can charge only a limited number of drones. For effective functioning, the system thus needs to balance between the number of drones flying and scaring the birds and the number of drones at the charger (too few scaring drones and the bird consume

---

[1] https://www.ecsel.eu/projects/afarcloud.

all the crop or too many drones scaring and the charger would not be able to charge them and the drones terminate).

As mentioned in the previous section, we model the architecture of self-adaptive systems via ensembles. All the entities in the system are modeled as components, while interactions among the components are modeled via ensembles that are dynamically established groups of components. In the running example, there are four components: Drone, Charger, Field, and Bird. Listing 1 shows a fragment of the Drone component type definition in a simple specification language. The components are modeled by the component type that contains a set of data fields holding the component state. Each component type can be instantiated multiple times. The Field and Bird components cannot be directly controlled, and their state is observed only.

```
1  component type Drone
2      field position: Position
3      field battery: ChargeLevel
4      field mode: Enum {
5          IDLE, TERMINATED, MOVING_TO_CHARGER, CHARGING ....
6      }
7      # ... other definitions here
```

Listing 1. A fragment of a component type specification

Within our simulator, fields are composed of pieces; each piece has two units of the crop, i.e., food for birds. A bird eats one unit of food per step. If a bird is not scared away by a drone, it randomly decides whether to eat, move to another piece, or move to another field. The drone battery discharges faster when the drone is flying or protecting the field than when it is idle.

There are three ensembles in the example: FieldProtectionEnsemble grouping drones to protect a particular field, DroneChargingPreAssignment grouping drones to the closest charger, and AcceptedDronesAssignment grouping drones in-need-to-be-charged with the charger and they can fly to the charger. Listing 2 shows a fragment of the DroneChargingPreAssignment ensemble specification.

```
1  ensemble type DroneChargingPreAssignment
2      role charger: Charger
3      role multiple drone: Drone
4          cardinality <0, n>
5          membership min(drone −> distance(charger.location, drone.location))
6          utility ...
7      # other code here ...
8      action assignCharger(drone)
9          ...
```

Listing 2. A fragment of an ensemble type specification

Like the definition of components, ensembles are also defined as types and can be instantiated multiple times (e.g., FieldProtectionEnsemble instantiated for each field). Each ensemble can have several *roles* in order to group components of a particular responsibility in the ensemble. A role has (i) a membership condition specifying if a component may be selected for the role (i.e., hard constraints), (ii) cardinality (i.e., how many components may be selected), (iii) a utility function for optimizations of component selection in the case the membership condition is satisfied by more components than required (i.e., soft constraints), and (iv) priority (importance of the role resulting in an order the role is resolved during ensemble resolution).

Finally, actions must be executed on components selected in the roles.

3   ANN-Driven Ensembles

In the described approach, a self-adaptive system is controlled through ensembles, which directly affect the behavior of enclosed components. We propose an ensemble resolution method based on artificial neural network (ANN) results. The neural network was trained on simulation data of the same scenario where ensemble resolution was implemented by a SAT solver. The neural network can extract and generalize the knowledge provided by the solver and compute its results much faster. However, it introduces instability as well as uncertainty into the system since the trained parameters of the ANN model cannot be easily interpreted or explicitly understood.

In order to moderate the imperfections raised by the neural network, we have implemented post-processing steps intended to ensure some level of control. We have also implemented two composition algorithms to resolve the ensembles based on the data from the neural network. The overall schema of the ensemble construction process is depicted in Fig. 1.

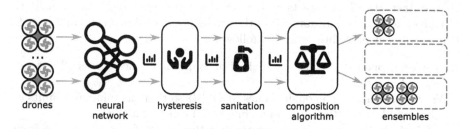

drones   neural   hysteresis   sanitation   composition   ensembles
                network   algorithm

Fig. 1. Ensemble composition pipeline

The neural network is evaluated for every drone independently (as each drone provides different inputs) and yields a discrete probability distribution that basically defines the drone's *preferences* to which ensemble it wants to be incorporated. The post-processing steps (sanitation and hysteresis) modify these distributions by adjusting the values of the individual preferences. The distributions of all drones are gathered as an input for the selected composition algorithm, which resolves ensembles (i.e., selects drones for them).

The method also applies to different scenarios; however, the neural network must be constructed and trained for a particular scenario with a fixed set of ensembles. Similarly, a domain expert must tailor the sanitation rules for a particular simulation. Although there are some ways to generalize these steps further, it is beyond the scope of this paper as we merely provide a proof-of-concept here.

3.1 Composition Algorithms

A composition algorithm constructs the ensembles based on the distribution of preferences calculated for every drone by the neural network. We have experimented with several approaches, and the best one seems to be a greedy algorithm with simple heuristics. In the evaluation section, we demonstrate that the greedy algorithm produces ensembles that are pretty close to the optimum from the perspective of the preferences.

The composition algorithm requires that there is always at least one suitable ensemble where a drone can be placed (i.e., a fallback ensemble which does not have a maximal limit). In our case, it is designated as an *idle* ensemble, where the drones have no particular function and merely patrol the fields until they are needed, or their battery needs to be recharged. Regarding ensemble roles (see Sect. 2), let us emphasize that the required number of drones of some ensembles may not always be satisfied since the number of drones may decrease over time if some drones run out of batteries. Hence, the composition algorithm treats the minimal limit only as a soft constraint.

There are two ways to approach the greedy selection—**drone-first** or **ensemble-first** depending on whether we iterate over the drones or the ensembles when looking for the best match.

Drone-first algorithm starts with a set of not-yet-selected drones (which are still alive) D. In each iteration, one of the drones is assigned to an ensemble $e \in E$. The assignment procedure works as follows:

1. Select a drone $d \in D$ with the highest absolute preference across all not-yet-selected drones.
2. Verify that there are enough drones in $D \backslash \{d\}$ so that the minimum limits of all ensembles (i.e., their corresponding roles) can be satisfied.
3. While drone d is not assigned, iterate over the vector of preferences of d from highest to lowest and for each ensemble e:
   (a) If the maximal limit of drones in e is not reached and verification in step (2) succeeded, assign d to e and continue with another drone.
   (b) If the minimal limit of drones in e is not fulfilled, assign d to e and continue with another drone.

Let us emphasize that a drone can always be placed into an ensemble since there is always the idle (fallback) ensemble. Furthermore, verification (2) along with condition (3b) ensures that all minimal limits are satisfied if it is technically possible.

Ensemble-first algorithm is suited for situations when it is more important to satisfy the ensembles based on their priorities. In our case, the charging ensembles would have the highest priority, while the idle (fallback) ensemble would have the lowest priority. The algorithm also starts with a set of not-yet-selected (alive) drones D and iterates over the ensemble instances E in the order of their priorities (highest priority first). For each ensemble $e \in E$, the algorithm performs the following steps:

1. A set of drone candidates C is constructed by a for-loop $x = 1 \ldots |E|$:
    (a) Select $S \subset D$ drones with e as their x-th choice according to their preferences.
    (b) $C \leftarrow C \cup S$
    (c) Break the for-loop if $|C| \geq$ minimal limit of e
2. If $|C|$ is greater than the maximal limit of e, crop the C to the maximal limit by removing drones with the lowest absolute preferences for ensemble e.
3. Assign all drones from C to e
4. $D \leftarrow D \backslash C$

The remaining drones are assigned to the idle ensemble. We also need to emphasize that the minimum limits of ensembles are more likely not to be satisfied by this algorithm (in contrast with the drone-first algorithm) as it may easily happen that more-than-needed drones are assigned to an ensemble with a higher priority, and there will be not enough drones left for ensembles with lower priorities.

3.2   ANN Post-processing

The primary purpose of the post-processing step that adjusts the distributions of drones' preferences is to mitigate possible negative aspects of the neural network, such as possible underfitting, overfitting, or simply the uncertainty caused by the fact that the ANN model is a black box. The post-processing is handled by two independent steps, which may also be skipped (as we demonstrate in the experimental section).

Hysteresis helps to increase the stability of the system by adding momentum to the decisions inferred from the neural network. We compute the hysteresis for each drone separately. For each drone, the algorithm keeps a history H of the last n drone-to-ensemble assignments. The assignment of a drone ($\overline{h_i} \in H$) is a one-hot encoded categorical vector with 1 in the position of the selected ensemble.

(i) First, the hysteresis evaluates a momentum $\overline{m}$, which is a vector of moments of one drone, where each of the elements corresponds to an ensemble. The momentum vector is calculated as follows $\overline{m} = (\sum_{i=0}^{n} r^{n-i} \cdot \overline{h_i})/r$, where the rate r is constant between 0 and 1 and $\overline{h_i} \in H$, the multiplication and division are element-wise, and the order of the elements is from oldest to newest.

(ii) Next, the hysteresis strength is determined by applying a clipping function on normalized $\overline{m}$ that constrains all the element values into the range of $[0, r]$. It does this in the following steps: (a) It finds the largest value M in the vector $\overline{m}$. (b) It normalizes the vector to the interval $[0, 1]$ by applying the following transformation: $\overline{m}' = \overline{m}/\min(1, M)$, where the division is done element-wise. (c) It applies a clipping function to the vector $\overline{m}'$ to constrain the values to the range $[0, r]$. This is done using the following function: $clip(L, U, x) = max[U, min(L, x)]$, where L and U denote the lower and upper bounds, respectively.

(iii) Finally, the momentum strength is merged with the ANN output $\overline{o}$: $\overline{o} = (\overline{m}' + \overline{o}_{ANN})$, and clipped to ensure that the preferences stay within the allowed $[0, 1]$ range.

Sanitation purpose is twofold—it corrects obvious mispredictions and performs additional class smoothing. The sanitation is performed after the hysteresis, so it may correct wrong decisions even if they are propelled by higher momentum. The class smoothing gently influences the decisions to a safer or better option.

We have implemented seven sanitation rules:

- Probability of the protection ensembles for a drone that does not have enough battery is set to zero.
- Probability of the protection ensemble corresponding to a field that is not occupied by birds at the moment is lowered by 0.3.
- Probability of the charging ensemble is adjusted by adding a result of a smoothing S-shaped function $-4 * (b - 0.55)^3$ (where b is the battery level). The probability is also decreased resp. increased when thresholds are overstepped in low resp. high battery situations by additional two rules.
- Probability of charging ensemble is lowered for a drone that has just traveled from the charger to its current location.
- Probability of idle ensemble is lowered for a charged drone.

To give greater priority to possible values that the neural network disregarded over forbidden values, we add a small ε to all probabilities that were not zeroed.

4   Technical Details

The main contribution of this paper is the process of knowledge generalization that allows us to learn our model on a small problem instance that could be solved by SAT and then use this model on larger instances and in an adaptive manner.

The problem that the SAT was solving was a single map with a single configuration of 4 drones, 5 flocks of birds, 5 fields, and 3 chargers that could charge only one drone at a time. The solver has supplied us with the optimal behavior for each drone in this particular scenario; however, the generalization properties of the ANNs actually extracted a more general knowledge that does not depend on the exact parameters of the scenario.

There are several technical details that are quite important for the generalization and training process, so we cover them in the following.

4.1   Data Transformation

One level of generalization is achieved by removing the explicit numbers and positions of various elements, except the number of fields that we have fixed to 5 for the sake of simplicity. Furthermore, the energy consumption rates and drone speeds were normalized by a distance measure that takes these variables into account.

Limiting the Drone Visibility Range. We modify the raw distances between points by limiting the sensing range of the drones. Objects beyond a certain limit are treated as infinitely far. Distances that are greater than the limit are set to a value of one, while the remaining distances are calculated as a fraction of the limit. In our case, we set this limit to 0.25 of the `max_fly_distance`. Which is computed as the maximum distance that a fully charged drone could travel with maximum speed before its battery runs out.

Removing Absolute Positions. The absolute positions are replaced with normalized, relative coordinates. The ANN does not take drone coordinated (x, y) as an input, but it is given normalized distances to the nearest m-fields and n-chargers:

$$x, y \Rightarrow [0, 1]^{m+n}$$

Additionally, the identity of fields resp. chargers are removed since they are re-ordered by the distance in their respective groups. This approach makes the problem invariant to transformations in which the elements are shifted by a constant amount.

Train and Evaluate One Drone at a Time. We split a single simulation step into multiple training steps—one for each of the drones, which results in a simpler and more stable training process. However, the neural network cannot capture any cooperative behavior among the drones. The network needs to be evaluated for each drone in each simulation step, which we perform simultaneously by setting the batch size to the number of drones.

Generalized Inputs. Since we compute each drone independently, we may replace the global environment data of the simulations with more useful statistics which are explicitly computed for each drone. However, we need to ensure that these statistics convey all the information needed for decision-making. The following statistics are computed and provided as input for the ANN:

- Normalized distances to the two closest flocks and drones.
- Percentage of free charger spaces.
- Minimum, mean, and maximum battery levels for drones that are currently charging and for those that are currently not (excluding terminated drones).

– For each field, we provide a percentage of drones and birds that are:
  • in the field,
  • closest to the particular field,
  • in one of four circles with an increasing radius centered in the middle of the particular field,
– Lastly, for each field, we provide two flags indicating
  • presence of birds and absence of drones (unprotected field under attack),
  • and presence of drones and absence of birds (unnecessary protection of the field).

4.2 Neural Network Architecture

We have experimented with multiple neural network architectures. In this particular scenario, small dense networks work very well, so the selected architecture comprises two fully-connected layers of 256 nodes wrapped in batch-normalization layers as depicted in Fig. 2. The network was trained for 50 epochs on the data of 10 million simulation steps with applied a categorical class smoothing of 0.1. We use a large batch size of 1800 and the Adam optimizer with cosine decay with an initial learning rate of 0.01. For the final result, we used an ensemble of three best-scoring models of the same architecture. This ensemble achieved an accuracy of 0.977.

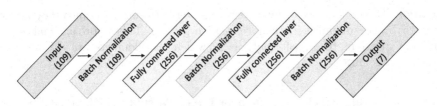

Fig. 2. Architecture of the used network. The input size is 109, and the output size is 7. As input, the network takes generalized and summary data from the simulation. Output labels correspond to one-hot-encoded ensembles that they represent.

During our experiments, we observed an interesting phenomenon—a deeper network achieved slightly better training accuracy, but it actually performed worse than a simpler network when incorporated into the whole ensemble resolution pipeline.

This behavior was traced back to the decision strength of the deep network, which was highly confident in its output and resulted in a preference vector with only a few non-zero values. This decision strength hindered the post-processing steps, especially the ensemble composition algorithm.

5 Evaluation

The evaluation uses two primary metrics—the **survival rate** and the **damage rate**. The survival rate is the ratio of the drones that kept their battery level above zero (i.e., how many drones remain operational) until the end of the simulation (higher is better). The damage rate is the ratio of units of food the birds consumed during the entire simulation divided by the total amount of food (lower is better). These two metrics are correlated since a lower survival rate typically affects the ability of the remaining drones to protect the fields.

The measurements evaluate the two proposed greedy algorithms (**drone first** and **ensemble first**) and compare them to three other algorithms:

- **Baseline**—an algorithm based on a few straightforward static rules, such as to fly to the nearest charger if the battery drops below a specified threshold or to fly to the nearest unprotected field otherwise.
- **Baseline + sanitation**—augments the baseline algorithm with the same sanitation rules employed before the greedy algorithms.
- **Plain neural network**—uses the same neural network as the proposed greedy algorithms, but the output is used directly (the drone is assigned to the ensemble corresponding to the class with the highest value).

The experiments were conducted on various map configurations to cover all sorts of corner cases; however, we have filtered only the most relevant results. In particular, we have eliminated uninteresting situations such as when there are not enough chargers (so most of the drones run out of batteries early in the simulation) or when the number of chargers and drones is saturated to keep all the fields protected at all times (even when simple baseline rules are employed). Furthermore, each experiment was repeated multiple times with 10 different random seeds. The presented results are averages of these runs.

The results, as well as the experimental code, are available in our replication package[2].

5.1   Aggregated Results

Figure 3 presents the aggregated results from one selected representative map using different numbers of drones. The map contains 26 locations on the fields that may need protection from the birds (i.e., where a drone needs to fly to scare the birds off) and 3 chargers, each with capacity given according to this function: $\lceil (d \cdot 1.3 \cdot e)/(ch \cdot r + ch \cdot 1.3 \cdot e) \rceil$, where d drone count, ch charger count, r charging rate and e is the energy consumption of a moving drone.

The first observation is that the proposed greedy algorithms significantly outperform the baselines and the plain neural network once the number of drones exceeds the minimum threshold. If the number of drones is too low, there are simply not enough drones to protect the fields, and the actual adaptation strategy is irrelevant.

In more detail, the plain neural network exhibits comparable performance to the baseline. However, the sanitation rules themselves have demonstrated that they can improve not only the neural network results but also the static baseline.

---

[2] https://github.com/pacovsky/ML-SAS-gaddapt-replication-package.git.

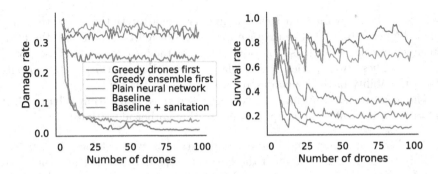

Fig. 3. Comparison of the presented methods on a single map

In the survival rate graph, significant oscillations can be detected on all measured algorithms. It is caused by the discrete nature of the equation that computes the capacity of the chargers, which naturally affects the length of the queues of drones that require charging.

5.2   Covering Various Configurations

Our experiments covered a wide range of parameter space to verify the proposed methods thoroughly. We have selected several representatives of the simulation instances for illustration (Fig. 4). Each instance is denoted by main configuration parameters: the size of the map (**S**mall, **M**edium, and **L**arge), number of chargers, drones, and flocks of birds. The black bars in the graph represent the standard deviation of the samples.

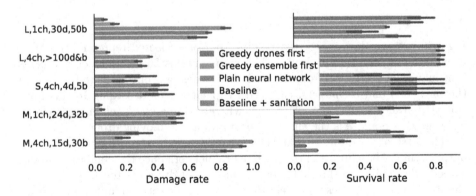

Fig. 4. Selected instances of the simulation configurations

We have observed that the proposed greedy methods yield better results in the damage rate metrics and almost always better results in the survival rate metrics. The two proposed greedy algorithms profiled themselves differently. The drone-first approach seems to perform better when the number of drones is higher, while the ensemble-first works better in more extreme cases when there are not enough drones to sufficiently protect the fields. This is due to the field preferences that hint in the latter case, where is a more significant need. With more drones, the ensemble-first methods tend to cover better priority fields but ignore the remaining, which allows the birds to cause damage on the not-so-protected fields, while the drone-first covers the fields more fairly. This leads to a longer response time within the field but shortens the response to other fields.

5.3   Detailed Evaluation of Individual Parts

The ensemble resolution pipeline comprises a neural network, hysteresis, sanitation, and the composition algorithm. In this section, we evaluate the individual contributions of each step. Figure 5 presents non-averaged results from the proposed methods as well as variations of composition methods that do not use sanitation or hysteresis. The x, y axes represent survival and damage rates, respectively, so the optimum is in the bottom right corner. The data points depicted by large markers refer to the complete methods; the small markers are the variations. Circular markers correspond to the whole pipeline, crosses represent a pipeline that has only the hysteresis (no sanitation), squares refer to a sanitation-only pipeline (no hysteresis), and plus-signs denote a pipeline with only a neural network and composition algorithm (sanitation and hysteresis steps are omitted).

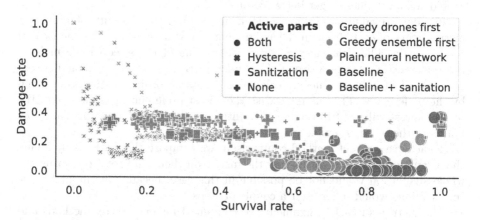

Fig. 5. Non-averaged results of all simulation runs and pipeline variations (Color figure online)

Let us first discuss the influence of the composition algorithm alone. We can compare the relative positions of the plain neural network (green plus-signs) and the positions of both greedy methods (the small blue and orange plus-signs).

The relative positions reveal an improvement in both axes, mainly in the survival rate.

The *sanitation* alone (small green squares) provides only a small improvement when applied on a plain neural network. However, the rules themselves are likely to be designed well as they improve the baseline, and in combination with the composition algorithm, we can see even more significant improvements as well.

The *hysteresis* alone is responsible for the worst results in the plot (all the crosses in the top left region). This result is expected since we use a strong momentum, and it takes a while to overcome the last decisions, which may be unfortunate when the decision is bad. This leads to a delay that often prevents a drone from starting charging in time before running out of batteries. The addition of the composition algorithms (although they exhibit an improvement over the Plain neural network) does not fully mitigate this effect.

The combination of *sanitation* and *hysteresis* has just a negligible effect on the improvement of the plain neural network. However, combining with composition algorithms, we achieved the best results when all parts were present.

5.4   Composition Method Quality

In this subsection, we compare our greedy composition methods with an *optimal method* that always chooses the best assignment possible, according to a given metric. The objective is to establish the distance between the optimum and the results provided by the greedy algorithms so we can determine whether it could be worth it to replace greedy algorithms with more complex and more time-demanding ones to get better results.

In order to evaluate the whole assignment, we sum up the results of individual metric scores of each drone in the assignment. We will be using *value* metric and *order* metric. The *value* metric returns the value of the selected ensemble in the preference vector of a drone. The *order* metric works in a similar manner, but instead of actual values, it calculates points according to the order given by the preferences. The ensemble with the lowest preference gets one point, the second-lowest will get two points, etc., until the highest preference gets as many points as there are ensembles.

To achieve a direct method comparison, we compare the methods by giving them sample inputs and evaluating the metric on their outputs. Comparing the whole simulation would not be possible in this case, because the input for the compositions would differ after a couple of steps.

The metrics of each assignment are computed for our greedy methods and the optimal algorithm. The proportion of cases in which our method was optimal according to a given metric is presented in Table 1.

The measurements showed that both greedy algorithms mostly produced ensemble assignment that was the same as for the optimal method. At most 12.1% of cases yielded a sub-optimal result; additionally, even in these cases, the results were not far from optimum. In Table 2 we analyzed only the results that were sub-optimal, and divided them with the metrics values of the optimal method. This shows the distance to optimum in normalized metric space.

Table 1. The comparison of our greedy methods against the optimal method. The proportion of cases in which our method was optimal according to a given metric.

	Greedy methods	Metrics	
		order	*value*
Percentage of cases that	ensemble first	88.61	88.28
a method chose the optimum	drone first	90.12	87.91

Table 2. The comparison of our greedy methods against the optimal method. Proportion of the metric value reached, in comparison to the values of the optimum case, when it was not in an optimal case.

	Greedy methods	Metrics	
		order	*value*
Closeness to the optimal	ensemble first	90.95	74.91
metric value (in %)	drone first	95.93	83.62

The results provide sufficient justification for implementing the greedy methods instead of using some approximation or an NP-complete algorithm. It is worth mentioning that we experimented with alternative algorithms; most notably, we have found that our problem is reducible to a variant of the Minimum-cost flow problem with cost and capacity limits (both min and max) for the edges. However, the implementation cost far exceeds any potential improvements, especially in light of the aforementioned results.

6   Related Work

Employing machine learning (ML) techniques in self-adaptive systems and their architectures is not a new approach, as is proven by several systematic literature reviews (SLR).

SLR in [13] shows that the interest in ML in self-adaptive systems has been steadily growing in the last two decades. Also, it shows that these systems primarily use ML techniques in the adaptation phase of the MAPE (Monitor-Analyze-Plan-Execute) loop. Another SLR in [8] confirms the same trend and the same point of ML employment.

In a more detailed look, ML is commonly applied to reduce a state-space that needs to be analyzed; either alone [15], or in combination with other techniques (e.g., with cost-based analysis [14], with the coevolution of a system and its test [7], with probabilistic model checking [5]), or with an analysis for the overall impact of application [9]. Compared to those approaches, our one is similar but goes in the opposite direction—i.e., we do not reduce the state space, but from a small one, we are generalizing behavior for a large one. Thus also, approaches using ML for predictions are closely related—for example, the approach in [11] but here, ML techniques are used to forecast values of QoS parameters and thus for proactive selection of adaptation strategies.

If we take a look at the area of ensemble-based systems (for whose the basis has been laid in the SCEL language [12]), there exist multiple implementations of them (e.g., jRESP [1], Helena [10]) or systems that are not precisely ensemble-based but share the same features (e.g., frameworks with attribute-based communication [2,6]) but not of them employ any ML techniques yet.

7 Conclusion

We have shown that a properly trained neural network can easily integrate into the self-adaptation process if its outputs are post-processed and correctly used to resolve ensembles. For this purpose, we introduced two simple yet effective greedy algorithms that can take drone preferences predicted by the ANN and use them to assign drones to the ensembles. Furthermore, we have developed post-processing methods to sanitize the ANN outputs to mitigate the most serious issues raised by the instability and unpredictability inherent to neural-network models.

We have demonstrated the viability of this approach by conducting a large number of experiments using different configurations of the simulation. The empirical data demonstrate that the ANN-controlled self-adaptation produces significantly better simulation results than the baselines created by simple static rules. Furthermore, the data suggest the method should scale well with the number of drones and the size of the fields.

We plan to experiment with the neural networks and other machine learning models further so that the training process does not have to be tailored to a specific simulation scenario and the knowledge from multiple similar self-adaptive systems can be generalized and applied across the systems (i.e., simulations). We are also planning to extend the training process to involve reinforcement learning, which should remove the need for the training data sources like the pre-fabricated data generated from a simulation governed by SAT-solver.

Acknowledgment. This work has been partially supported by the Czech Science Foundation project 20-24814J, and partially by Charles University institutional funding SVV 260698/2023.

References

1. jRESP: Java Runtime Environment for SCEL Programs. http://jresp.sourceforge.net/. Accessed 02 Jan 2023
2. Alrahman, Y.A., De Nicola, R., Loreti, M.: Programming interactions in collective adaptive systems by relying on attribute-based communication. Sci. Comput. Program. **192**, 102428 (2020). https://doi.org/10.1016/j.scico.2020.102428
3. Bureš, T., Gerostathopoulos, I., Hnětynka, P., Pacovský, J.: Forming ensembles at runtime: a machine learning approach. In: Margaria, T., Steffen, B. (eds.) ISoLA 2020. LNCS, vol. 12477, pp. 440–456. Springer, Cham (2020). https://doi.org/10.1007/978-3-030-61470-6_26

4. Bures, T., et al.: A language and framework for dynamic component ensembles in smart systems. Int. J. Softw. Tools Technol. Transfer **22**(4), 497–509 (2020). https://doi.org/10.1007/s10009-020-00558-z

5. Cámara, J., Muccini, H., Vaidhyanathan, K.: Quantitative verification-aided machine learning: a tandem approach for architecting self-adaptive IoT systems. In: Proceedings of ICSA 2021, Salvador, Brazil, pp. 11–22. IEEE, March 2020. https://doi.org/10.1109/ICSA47634.2020.00010

6. De Nicola, R., Duong, T., Loreti, M.: ABEL - a domain specific framework for programming with attribute-based communication. In: Riis Nielson, H., Tuosto, E. (eds.) COORDINATION 2019. LNCS, vol. 11533, pp. 111–128. Springer, Cham (2019). https://doi.org/10.1007/978-3-030-22397-7_7

7. Gabor, T., et al.: The scenario coevolution paradigm: adaptive quality assurance for adaptive systems. Int. J. Softw. Tools Technol. Transfer **22**(4), 457–476 (2020). https://doi.org/10.1007/s10009-020-00560-5

8. Gheibi, O., Weyns, D., Quin, F.: Applying machine learning in self-adaptive systems: a systematic literature review. ACM Trans. Auton. Adapt. Syst. **15**(3), 9:1–9:37 (2021). https://doi.org/10.1145/3469440

9. Gheibi, O., Weyns, D., Quin, F.: On the impact of applying machine learning in the decision-making of self-adaptive systems. In: Proceedings of SEAMS 2021, Madrid, Spain, pp. 104–110. IEEE, May 2021. https://doi.org/10.1109/SEAMS51251.2021.00023

10. Bjørner, D.: Domain endurants. In: Iida, S., Meseguer, J., Ogata, K. (eds.) Specification, Algebra, and Software. LNCS, vol. 8373, pp. 1–34. Springer, Heidelberg (2014). https://doi.org/10.1007/978-3-642-54624-2_1

11. Muccini, H., Vaidhyanathan, K.: A machine learning-driven approach for proactive decision making in adaptive architectures. In: Companion Proceedings of ICSA 2019, Hamburg, Germany, pp. 242–245 (2019). https://doi.org/10.1109/ICSA-C.2019.00050

12. De Nicola, R., et al.: The SCEL language: design, implementation, verification. In: Wirsing, M., Hölzl, M., Koch, N., Mayer, P. (eds.) Software Engineering for Collective Autonomic Systems. LNCS, vol. 8998, pp. 3–71. Springer, Cham (2015). https://doi.org/10.1007/978-3-319-16310-9_1

13. Saputri, T.R.D., Lee, S.W.: The application of machine learning in self-adaptive systems: a systematic literature review. IEEE Access **8**, 205948–205967 (2020). https://doi.org/10.1109/ACCESS.2020.3036037

14. Van Der Donckt, J., Weyns, D., Iftikhar, M.U., Buttar, S.S.: Effective decision making in self-adaptive systems using cost-benefit analysis at runtime and online learning of adaptation spaces. In: Damiani, E., Spanoudakis, G., Maciaszek, L.A. (eds.) ENASE 2018. CCIS, vol. 1023, pp. 373–403. Springer, Cham (2019). https://doi.org/10.1007/978-3-030-22559-9_17

15. Van Der Donckt, J., Weyns, D., Quin, F., Van Der Donckt, J., Michiels, S.: Applying deep learning to reduce large adaptation spaces of self-adaptive systems with multiple types of goals. In: Proceedings of SEAMS 2020, Seoul, South Korea, pp. 20–30. ACM (2020). https://doi.org/10.1145/3387939.3391605

Finding Reusable Machine Learning Components to Build Programming Language Processing Pipelines

Patrick Flynn[1,2], Tristan Vanderbruggen[1], Chunhua Liao[1], Pei-Hung Lin[1(✉)], Murali Emani[3], and Xipeng Shen[4]

[1] Lawrence Livermore National Laboratory, Livermore, CA 94550, USA
lin32@llnl.gov
[2] University of North Carolina at Charlotte, Charlotte, NC 28223, USA
[3] Argonne National Laboratory, Lemont, IL 60439, USA
[4] North Carolina State University, Raleigh, NC 27695, USA

Abstract. Programming Language Processing (PLP) using machine learning has made vast improvements in the past few years. Increasingly more people are interested in exploring this promising field. However, it is challenging for new researchers and developers to find the right components to construct their own machine learning pipelines, given the diverse PLP tasks to be solved, the large number of datasets and models being released, and the set of complex compilers or tools involved. To improve the findability, accessibility, interoperability and reusability (FAIRness) of machine learning components, we collect and analyze a set of representative papers in the domain of machine learning-based PLP. We then identify and characterize key concepts including PLP tasks, model architectures and supportive tools. Finally, we show some example use cases of leveraging the reusable components to construct machine learning pipelines to solve a set of PLP tasks.

Keywords: reusable datasets · reusable machine learning · programming language processing · interoperable pipelines

1 Introduction

In the past decade, machine learning (ML) has made tremendous progress in solving natural language processing (NLP) tasks. This was due to a variety of factors, including the advent of Transformer models, the availability of high quality datasets, and the development of more powerful computing systems. In

This work was performed in part under the auspices of the U.S. Department of Energy by Lawrence Livermore National Laboratory under Contract DE-AC52-07NA27344. It is based upon work supported by the U.S. Department of Energy, Office of Science, Advanced Scientific Computing Program (ASCR SC-21) under Award Number DE-SC0021293. This work used resources of the Argonne Leadership Computing Facility (ALCF), which is a DOE Office of Science User Facility supported under Contract DE-AC02-06CH1135. LLNL-CONF-837414.

T. Batista et al. (Eds.): ECSA 2022, LNCS 13928, pp. 402–417, 2023.
https://doi.org/10.1007/978-3-031-36889-9_27

particular, large-scale pretrained models, such as BERT [14, 29] and GPT-3 [7], have been a strong driver of innovation in the domain of NLP.

Similarly, programming language processing (PLP) tasks are benefiting from the availability of pretrained models and high quality datasets. The past few years saw a vast improvement in the ability of ML to perform a large number of tasks, such as code generation [31], clone detection [31], source-to-source translation [30], defect correction [6], code documentation [21] and so on. There is an increasing interest in the science community to either directly reuse or expand the ML models for PLP, in order to address software engineering challenges.

However, the rapid development of ML for PLP also brings challenges for researchers and developers who are interested in this promising field. First of all, a large number of different ML models and datasets are published each year. It is difficult for people, especially newcomers, to identify representative ones to get started. Secondly, different model architectures are used to solve different types of PLP tasks, ranging from program understanding to code generation. It is a daunting job for people to pick the right architectures for a given task. Third, machine learning workflows are typically split into a set of independent, reusable, modular components that can be pipelined together to create ML models. Mastering these components requires a significant amount of time and effort. Finally, in many cases, the trend is to add compiler analysis into the inputs of traditional NLP models in order to improve the quality of ML models for PLP. The use of compiler tools make the entire ML pipelines more complex, resulting in more constraints to its applicability to a given task.

To improve the findability, accessibility, interoperability and reusability (FAIRness) of machine learning components, we search through the literature to find representative papers in the domain of machine learning-based programming language processing. The goal of this paper is to facilitate the reuse of components of ML pipelines so researchers or developers can easily create customized ML pipelines to solve a given task.

We highlight the contributions of this paper as follows.

- We identify and characterize key components of the ML pipeline for PLP, including representative tasks, popular ML models, datasets, and tools.
- We extend the taxonomy for PLP tasks, adding code-to-analysis and semantic-matching categories of tasks.
- We propose a taxonomy of tokenization tools used in PLP based on compiler engineering terminology.
- We demonstrate how the identified components can be composed to form different pipelines to solve given tasks.

2 Selected Publications

Our search for relevant papers used the following method. We first selected a few recent high-impact publications (i.e., BERT [14, 29]) as our initial seed publications. These were either well-known in the research community or discovered by searching for specific keywords (mostly cross-product of "ML", "AI" with "source code", "code analysis", "code understanding") using Google Scholar. From these seed publications, we followed both older referenced publications and more recent publications citing them, especially looking for (1) the model architectures that inspired the publication, (2) their experiments (downstream tasks and datasets) and (3) which models they compared against. To narrow down the scope further, only representative publications with compelling artifacts, including released models, supportive tools and sufficient documentation, are selected. We still evaluated a few publications associated with some models that are only available through an API, such as AlphaCode [31] and OpenAI's CodeX [10]. We stopped the search, when no further related papers were to be collected, to build a cohesive picture of the PLP domain presented in this paper.

Out of the surveyed publications, CodeXGLUE [33] is the most significant. It is a benchmark dataset for code understanding and generation. It aggregates both datasets and baseline models in the PLP community. These models are based on CodeBERT [16] and CodeGPT [33], variations of BERT [14] and GPT [39] trained on code.

We selected SynCoBERT [45] and ProGraML [12] to be our reference models as together they cover most of the features to form our taxonomies. SynCoBERT is an extension to CodeBERT and CuBERT [27]. It considers source code, natural language text, and the corresponding AST to enable multi-modal pretraining for code representation. It also presents an evaluation with common code-to-code, code-to-text, and text-to-code tasks. ProGraML applies graph neural networks to graph representations of LLVM IR. Most importantly, ProGraML is used to solve five traditional compiler analysis tasks, including control- and data-flow, function boundaries, instruction types, and the type and order of operands over complex programs.

3   Taxonomies

A set of standard taxonomies are indispensable to enable findable, accessible, interoperable and reusable components in the domain of Programming Language Processing (PLP) using machine learning (ML). We extend CodeXGLUE's classification of PLP tasks, organize relevant model architectures, and propose a taxonomy of tokenization tools/methods.

3.1   PLP Tasks

The surveyed publications used a variety of downstream PLP tasks to evaluate the capability of their models. Most of these tasks fall clearly under one of the four categories introduced by CodeXGLUE: Code-to-Code, Code-to-Text, Text-to-Code, and Text-to-Text. Clearly, these categories are defined in terms of the input and output modalities.

However, the authors of CodeXGLUE only considered *code* and *text*, which are sequences of programming language and natural language tokens. It means that tasks where the output is a scalar value (classification and regression tasks) cannot be easily categorized. For example, defect detection aims at classifying code samples between correct and defective, it is a classification task. Clone detection and code search aim at predicting semantic matching between two sequences. ProGraML and its predecessor NCC use tasks that target scalar values: OpenCL device mapping, OpenCL thread coarsening factor, and algorithm classification.

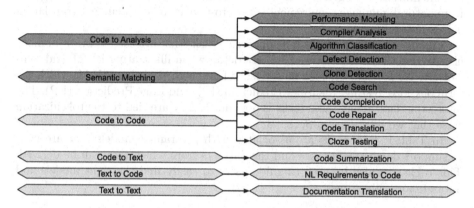

Fig. 1. Our taxonomy of tasks based on CodeXGLUE's categorization

Given the limitation of CodeXGLUE's task categorization, we propose to add two new categories of PLP tasks: code-to-analysis and semantic-matching. This is illustrated in Fig. 1.

The *Code-to-Analysis* category groups tasks taking code as input and generating results that are neither text nor code. We create four subcategories in this category: 1) Performance modeling either predicts a runtime metric of the code or a configuration that optimizes the said metric. 2) Compiler analysis includes traditional static compiler analysis tasks, particularly the reachability, dominator trees, and liveness analysis from ProGraML. 3) Algorithm detection is similar to clone detection, but we narrowly define it as detecting the use of a finite set of algorithms in a code. 4) Defect detection may use previous code commits with information about resolved vulnerabilities to predict detects in new code.

Semantic-matching includes both clone detection [42] and code search [21] tasks. The current state-of-the-art approaches use deep-learning to formulate search problems as the evaluation of the semantic similarity between a "query" and each element of a set of "candidates". The result of this formulation are models that take a pair of code-code (used by clone detection) or text-code (used by code search) sequences as inputs and predict a similarity score for the pair.

The Code-to-Code, Code-to-Text, Text-to-Code, and Text-to-Text categories are the same as described in CodeXGlue. The *Code-to-Code* category includes code completion, code repair, code translation, and cloze testing (occlusion test or "filling the blank" colloquially). Code completion aims to predict the next code token or the next section of code. Code repairs aims at reproducing a code without an existing defect. These defects are found by mining git repositories for very simple commits with descriptive messages of the issue being fixed. Code translation aims to convert a body of text from one programming language to another. Code-to-text includes code summarization, which aims to produce documentation for a given piece of code. Text-to-code includes generating code from natural language requirements. Text-to-text includes document translation across natural languages.

Finally, we must mention self-supervised tasks that are used to pretrain models. We describe a few of these in more detail when illustrating BERT and SynCoBert. We particularly look into Masked Language Modeling (MLM) which is a form of Cloze Testing, Identifier Prediction (IP), and Edge Prediction (EP). The interesting fact about these tasks is how much they are tied to the tokenization tools that we introduce in Sect. 3.3.

In Table 1, PLP tasks are associated with pretrained models that are used to support downstream tasks and the datasets from which they can be derived. This table can also be used to guide users to easily find the right models and datasets for a given task.

Table 1. Association between PLP tasks and publications (focused on either model or dataset. Only explicit associations are marked in this table since some models and datasets may be adapted to serve other tasks.)

Tasks	Models												Datasets																					
	PrograML[12]	SynCoBERT[45]	PLABART[2]	CodeT5[47]	Code-MVP[46]	TreeBERT[24]	ContraCode[23]	GraphCodeBERT[17]	CoTexT[37]	CodeBERT[16]	CodeGPT[33]	MICSAS[33]	CodeSearchNet[21]	DeepTune OpenCL[13]	POJ-104[35]	BigCloneBench[42]	Defects4J[25]	Devign[50]	DeepDataFlow[12]	DeepTyper[18]	PY150[40]	Github Java Corpus[4]	Tufano's dataset[43]	Nguyen's dataset[36]	CodeTrans[11]	AdvTest[21]	CONCODE[22]	CosQA[20]	CoNaLa[48]	DeepCom[19]	Python8000[38]	Google Code Jam[1]	CodeContests[31]	CodeXGlue[33]
Performance Modeling	✓													✓																				
Algorithm Classification	✓														✓			✓																
Defect Detection	✓	✓	✓	✓				✓									✓	✓	✓															✓
Compiler Analyses	✓																						✓	✓										
Code Completion						✓			✓												✓	✓												✓
Code Repair			✓				✓	✓															✓											✓
Code Translation	✓	✓	✓					✓																✓	✓				✓				✓	✓
Cloze Testing										✓		✓	✓																					✓
Text-to-Code Generation		✓	✓						✓	✓		✓															✓	✓						✓
Code Summarization		✓	✓			✓	✓		✓	✓		✓																		✓				✓
Document Translation																																		✓
Code Search	✓			✓			✓		✓				✓													✓								✓
Clone Detection	✓	✓	✓	✓			✓	✓		✓					✓	✓																	✓	✓

3.2 Model Architectures

We have seen that models can be trained to solve a number of different tasks. In this section, we categorize the various neural architectures used to solve PLP tasks. Being aware of the various architectures and how they can be composed is essential to leveraging the pretrained models. Indeed, often the input-output of the pretraining does not match the task that we wish to specialize it for. In this case, parts of the pretrained model are discarded and new components are trained from scratch. This leads to some confusion, as a given *model* is often used to refer to either its neural architecture or a trained instance of the said architecture.

We present a coarse taxonomy of the different architecture we have encountered, as shown in Fig. 2. Our taxonomy aims to be accessible to non-expert in machine learning. In comparison, fine-grained taxonomies could be confusing to users with too much low-level details. They may not be able to accommodate fast evolving machine learning technologies. It is based on the modality on which the architecture operates. This categorization is common for a general purpose presentation of Neural Networks. We redirect the reader toward [26,41] and [9] for taxonomies of NLP models and graph models, respectively.

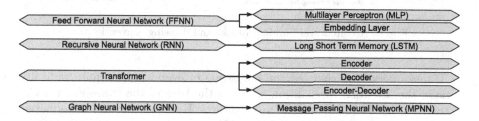

Fig. 2. Taxonomy of architectures based on the modality they operate on.

Figure 3 illustrates some common building blocks of various architectures. The top left diagram shows conventions for shapes and coloring. The figure also includes the most basic RNN (a), Message Passing Neural Network (c) and the coarse-grained details of the Transformer (d) to illustrate the fundamental difference between these architectures. While RNN must propagate information from the first token to the last, Transformers see all the input tokens and the decoder sees all the previous output tokens (and the encoded inputs). A full Transformer (b) is presented to illustrate BERT and SynCoBERT in Sect. 4.1. The Transformer is modeled with four blocks: token and positional embeddings, encoder-stack, decoder-stack, and finally embedding reversal.

Feed Forward Neural Networks (FFNN) operate on tensors. Their neurons' connections form a DAG. Common FFNNs are the multilayer perceptron (MLP) or a simple embedding layer. FFNNs are the building blocks of deep-learning. Recursive Neural Networks (RNN) operate on sequences (of tensors). RNNs have an initial state (tensor) that is updated for each element of the input sequence. After each update, an output can be produced while the final state can be used for sequence understanding. Long Short Term Memory (LSTM) is an advanced RNN architecture.

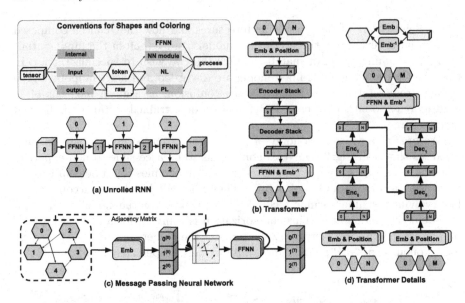

Fig. 3. Architectural building blocks and drawing conventions.

Transformers have changed the landscape of deep-learning quite radically. Initially the attention mechanism, which is the base of the transformer architecture, was used as part of RNN architectures. However, since its introduction in the aptly named "Attention is All You Need" paper in 2017 [44], Transformers have replaced RNNs for language modeling tasks. Transformers have also shown the ability to outperform convolutional neural networks (CNN) for image processing [8,15] and text-to-image [49].

The Transformer architecture uses attention, a deep-learning mechanism, whereas the dot-product of keys and queries measures the *attention* that should be given to a value. The nature of the attention mechanism makes transformers a set-to-set architecture. However, by simply adding a positional embedding to each token's embedding, Transformers act as sequence-to-sequence architectures.

In our taxonomy, we highlighted three sorts of transformers: Encoder, Decoder and Encoder-Decoder. In the original Transformers [44], both an encoder stack and a decoder stack are used to produce the output as depicted in Fig. 3d. However, the architecture can be split as shown in Fig. 3b. Following this realization, both encoder-only and decoder-only transformers have been devised. Bidirectional Encoder Representations from Transformers (BERT) [14], and Generative Pretrained Transformer (GPT) [39] are respective examples of the Encoder and the Decoder architecture. This separation between encoder and decoder components is common in ML. We illustrate in Fig. 4 how this paradigm applies to the processing of sequence of tokens.

Graph Neural Networks (GNN) generalize convolutional neural networks (CNN) from the grid of an image to the unstructured mesh defined by a graph. We focused on Message Passing Neural Networks (MPNN), a recent implemen-

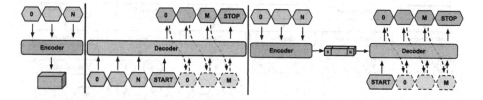

Fig. 4. Left-to-right: a) an encoder produces a tensor from a sequence of tokens, b) a decoder-based model sees an input sequence and autoregressively generates the output sequence, and c) an encoder-decoder uses the tensor from the encoder to parameterize an autoregressive decoder. (See color legend in Fig. 3)

tation of the paradigm which offers a lot of flexibility while having good computational performance (by exploiting the sparsity of the adjacency matrix).

Finally, Mixture-of-Expert (MoE) models are increasingly being used to scale large language models efficiently. The modern approach to MoE consists of sparsely activated models which minimizes resource utilization. For example [28] implemented the MoE-based model to scale a 700 million-parameter dense model from 1.8 billion parameters with eight experts to 10 billion parameters using 64 experts, with no impact on the model convergence. The building blocks within the core transformer model are still the same and it has little influence on reusability.

3.3   Tokenization Tools

One of the significant changes in the past few years is the integration of compiler-based analysis results in PLP to enrich the representation of code. In this section, we categorize the tokenization tools used in PLP as they are different from the traditional NL Tokenization tools (such as NLTK, spaCy, TextBlob, and WordPiece) (Fig. 5).

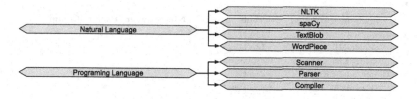

Fig. 5. Our taxonomy of tools.

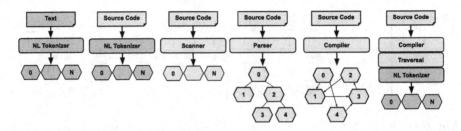

Fig. 6. Tokenization building block for the pipeline (See color legend in Fig. 3)

We organize Programming Language Tokenization tools based on three traditional stages in compiler frontends: lexical analysis, syntactic analysis, and semantic analysis (or elaboration). The names *scanner* and *parser* are typically used for the first two, while the more general term *compiler* is used for the last one. Although *compiler* generally refers to all three of these tools together, we use it here because it includes both semantic analysis and other advanced analyses that are compiler-specific, while differentiating from the *scanner* and *parser*. A *scanner* turns an input into a list of tokens whereas a *parser* converts the list of tokens, generated by a *scanner*, into a data structure, like a tree, according to the grammatical rules. This categorization differentiates the tools based on the output modalities: a sequence of tokens for *scanners*, a tree of tokens for *parsers*, and a graph of tokens for *compilers*. We illustrate the different scenarios in Fig. 6. We found that in many cases the right most construct is used to leverage compiler tools. In this case, the tree or graph is traversed using a predetermined *traversal*. The resulting sequence of tokens is then joined and tokenized using a NL tokenizer. We discuss in Sect. 4.1 how self-supervised pretraining tasks are constructed using additional information from the PL tokenizers.

In Table 2, we summarize the tokenizers used by several of the publications that we surveyed.

Table 2. Models & Tools with input types

Model	Tools	NL	Scanner	Parser	Compiler
NCC	LLVM				✓
PrograML	LLVM				✓
CodeBERT	WordPiece	✓			
GraphCodeBERT	tree-sitter	✓		✓	
SynCoBERT	tree-sitter	✓		✓	
PLABART	Custom	✓	✓		
TreeBERT	tree-sitter	✓		✓	
ContraCode	BabelJS (compiler)			✓	✓
CoTexT	Custom	✓	✓		
CodeT5	tree-sitter	✓	✓	✓	
Code-MVP	tree-sitter, Scalpel, Custom	✓	✓	✓	✓
MICSAS	Custom		✓	✓	

4 PLP Pipelines

In this section, we demonstrate how to assemble a PLP pipeline. It is built by composing model architectures to produce the targets specified by tasks given the tokens generated by tokenization tools. The pipeline models how raw representations flow through different components. Given the prohibitive cost of training large scale models, pretrained models can be the only way to solve complex downstream tasks. We look at two representative pretraining pipelines, and then model how it can be used to solve our downstream tasks.

4.1 Pretraining Pipelines

Figure 7 illustrates the pretraining pipeline of BERT [14]. On the left, we show a high-level view of the pipeline. It takes two sentences as inputs which are tokenized using WordPiece, prefixed with the classification token, and separated using a separator token. These tokens are encoded, and positional and segment embeddings are added. A transformer encoder stack is used to produce bidirectional embeddings of each token. The embedding of the classification token, referred to as "classification head", is used to predict whether sentence A directly precedes sentence B. All other embeddings are trained using the Masked Language Model (MLM) self-supervised tasks which we illustrate in the right part of Fig. 7.

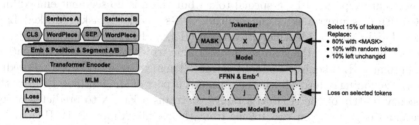

Fig. 7. Self-supervised pretraining pipeline of BERT. (See color legend in Fig. 3)

CodeBERT [16] uses the same pipeline with pairs of text and code instead of sentences. The classification head is made to predict whether the text and code are related. They used CodeSearchNet [21] to provide matching pairs of text and code.

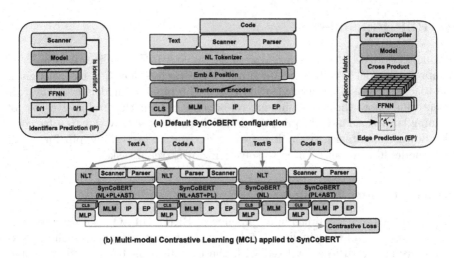

Fig. 8. SynCoBERT pretraining pipeline (See color legend in Fig. 3)

SynCoBERT [45] is a BERT-like PLP model which demonstrates a complex PLP pipeline, as shown in Fig. 8. During pretraining, SynCoBERT inputs can be text and/or code. The code is processed into scanned tokens and AST tokens (resulting from a pre-order depth-first traversal of the tree). The final text tokens, code tokens, and AST tokens are produced using a NL tokenizer. The different sequences are separated by a special token but there is no segment embedding. SynCoBERT is pretrained using multiple self-supervised tasks: Masked Language Model (MLM), Identifier Prediction (IP), and Edge Prediction (EP). IP uses information from the scanner to determine which of the tokens are part of an identifier (NL tokenizer can split words). Then, it trains a FFNN to predict from the encoding of a token whether or not it is part of an identifier. EP uses the adjacency matrix of the AST as a target. It trains a FFNN to predict whether there is an edge between two tokens from their embeddings. Both IP and EP aims at making the encoder understand the syntax of code and AST, and add that information into the embedding. Finally, SynCoBERT uses multi-modal contrastive learning (MCL) to train a multi-layer perceptron (MLP) on the classification head. This approach helps the encoder to produce a representation that distinguishes and correlates the different inputs.

4.2   Pipeline Specialization

We will now devise how we could leverage the pretrained CodeBERT or Syn-CoBert to solve our downstream tasks. The two example downstream tasks are: (1) code similarity analysis on a dataset of OpenMP codes, and (2) listing the fully qualified names of all declarations given a piece of C++ code.

The first task is to analyze the codes from DataRaceBench [32], a benchmark suite of both correct and defective OpenMP codes. This benchmark is designed to systematically and quantitatively evaluate the effectiveness of data race detection tools. We want to use ML to identify redundant source code and identify potential gaps in coverage of typical code patterns. This is a specialized code similarity analysis task.

For this task, we will use zero-shot or few-shot learning pipeline which has become practical with the advent of large scale pretrained models. In Fig. 9a, the pipeline applies pretrained BERT-like models to each of the samples and collects the embedding on the classification head. It then uses the same models to embed relevant text (we consider mining the publication for relevant sentences). After that, the pipeline applies clustering techniques based on cosine distance to analyze the dataset. The expectation here is to find sentences clustered alongside the code providing descriptions of the clusters. In the few-shot variation, we would first fine-tune the encoder on this dataset. This will not be as applicable for CodeBERT pretraining pipeline as the classification head requires paired inputs of text and code to be trained. For SynCoBERT, we could fine tune with paired code-code by only using (PL-AST) vs (AST-PL) in the MCL task. We are not sure how this code-only fine tuning would affect the quality of the text embeddings used for the reference sentences.

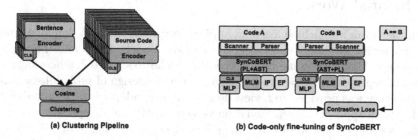

(a) Clustering Pipeline   (b) Code-only fine-tuning of SynCoBERT

Fig. 9. This figure illustrates the zero-shot approach to information discovery in a dataset of codes. To the left, we illustrate how a pretrained model can be used to produce embedding of codes and relevant sentences. These embeddings are then compared with pairwise cosine and clustered using conventional techniques. To the right, we illustrate how we could fine-tune SynCoBERT in the absence of text-code pairs. (See color legend in Fig. 3)

The second task is to list all declarations in C++ code (fully-qualified). This is the simplest task we could devise for a lexical analyzer (parser). For this task, we are using automatically generated C++ source codes. Targets are produced by the code generator (Fig. 10).

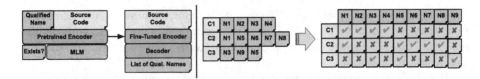

Fig. 10. On the left, we train an encoder to predict whether a qualified name refers to a declaration in a given code. Then this encoder is attached to a decoder to form a full transformer which we train to generate the full list of declarations. On the right, we illustrate how a batch of inputs (code and list of qualified names) can easily be used to form contrastive pairs to train the encoder. (See color legend in Fig. 3)

The first step of the pipeline for this task looks at fine-tuning a pretrained encoder to predict whether a qualified-name has a matching declaration in a code. There is a large number of paired inputs for this task. So we can easily create negative pairs to train the classification head of any classifier contrastively. The second step uses this fine-tuned encoder and trains a decoder to produce the full list of qualified names from C++ code.

5   Related Work

With the boom in machine learning applied to various research domains, many research activities survey and categorize the ML models, tasks, and the applied techniques. Allamanis *et al.* discuss how the similarities and differences between natural languages and program languages drive the design of probabilistic models. A survey was provided to review how researchers adapted these probabilistic models to an application areas and discusses crosscutting and application-specific challenges and opportunities [3]. Maas introduced a taxonomy of ML for systems that aims to provide guidance, based on the proposed decision diagram, if machine learning should be applied to a particular system problem [34]. A decision diagram is designed to provide recommendations to practitioners and researchers to choose the most suitable machine learning strategies. Ashouri *et al.* survey and classify recent research activities in compiler optimization, for optimization selection and phase ordering, with machine learning approaches [5]. Kalyan *et al.* summarize core concepts of transformer-based pretrained language models (T-PTLMs) and present taxonomy of T-PTLMs with brief overview of various benchmarks [26]. Sarker presents a deep learning taxonomy to cover techniques from major categories including supervised or discriminative learning, unsupervised or generative learning and hybrid learning [41]. Chami *et al.* present a taxonomy in graph representation learning (GRL) [9] to include GRL from network embedding, graph regularization and graph neural networks.

Different from the cited research works, this paper surveys and creates a set of taxonomies for multiple components in machine learning to represent the PLP tasks, ML model architectures and the tokenization tools associated with the ML models. In addition, this work demonstrates how to reference the taxonomies to assemble specialized PLP pipelines for new downstream machine learning tasks.

6   Conclusion

In this paper, we have selected a set of representative papers in the domain of programming language processing (PLP) using machine learning. We have identified and categorized common PLP tasks and the associated reusable components so newcomers can easily find the right models and datasets for a given task. Using two example tasks, we have shown that the discovered components can be easily reused to construct customized machine learning pipelines to solve the given tasks.

We started to implement the pipelines we have described above to learn more about DataRaceBench and construct challenging PLP problems. We will also encode the information into a formal knowledge representation such as ontology to enable automated pipeline adaptation using workflow synthesis techniques.

References

1. Google code jam. https://codingcompetitions.withgoogle.com/codejam
2. Ahmad, W., Chakraborty, S., Ray, B., Chang, K.W.: Unified pre-training for program understanding and generation. In: Proceedings of the 2021 Conference of the North American Chapter of the Association for Computational Linguistics: Human Language Technologies, pp. 2655–2668. Association for Computational Linguistics, June 2021
3. Allamanis, M., Barr, E.T., Devanbu, P., Sutton, C.: A survey of machine learning for big code and naturalness. ACM Comput. Surv. (CSUR) **51**(4), 81 (2018)
4. Allamanis, M., Sutton, C.: Mining source code repositories at massive scale using language modeling. In: The 10th Working Conference on Mining Software Repositories, pp. 207–216. IEEE (2013)
5. Ashouri, A.H., Killian, W., Cavazos, J., Palermo, G., Silvano, C.: A survey on compiler autotuning using machine learning. ACM Comput. Surv. **51**(5), 1–42 (2018)
6. Božič, J., Tabernik, D., Skočaj, D.: Mixed supervision for surface-defect detection: from weakly to fully supervised learning. Comput. Ind. **129**, 103459 (2021)
7. Brown, T., et al.: Language models are few-shot learners. In: Advances in Neural Information Processing Systems, vol. 33, pp. 1877–1901 (2020)
8. Carion, N., Massa, F., Synnaeve, G., Usunier, N., Kirillov, A., Zagoruyko, S.: End-to-end object detection with transformers. In: Vedaldi, A., Bischof, H., Brox, T., Frahm, J.-M. (eds.) ECCV 2020. LNCS, vol. 12346, pp. 213–229. Springer, Cham (2020). https://doi.org/10.1007/978-3-030-58452-8_13
9. Chami, I., Abu-El-Haija, S., Perozzi, B., Ré, C., Murphy, K.: Machine learning on graphs: a model and comprehensive taxonomy (2020)
10. Chen, M., et al.: Evaluating large language models trained on code. arXiv preprint arXiv:2107.03374 (2021)
11. Chen, X., Liu, C., Song, D.: Tree-to-tree neural networks for program translation. In: Proceedings of the 32nd International Conference on Neural Information Processing Systems, NIPS 2018, Red Hook, NY, USA, pp. 2552–2562. Curran Associates Inc. (2018)
12. Cummins, C., Fisches, Z., Ben-Nun, T., Hoefler, T., O'Boyle, M., Leather, H.: ProGraML: a graph-based program representation for data flow analysis and compiler optimizations. In: Thirty-Eighth International Conference on Machine Learning (ICML) (2021)

13. Cummins, C., Petoumenos, P., Wang, Z., Leather, H.: End-to-end deep learning of optimization heuristics. In: PACT. ACM (2017)
14. Devlin, J., Chang, M.W., Lee, K., Toutanova, K.: BERT: pre-training of deep bidirectional transformers for language understanding. arXiv preprint arXiv:1810.04805 (2018)
15. Dosovitskiy, A., et al.: An image is worth 16 × 16 words: transformers for image recognition at scale (2020)
16. Feng, Z., et al.: CodeBERT: a pre-trained model for programming and natural languages. arXiv preprint arXiv:2002.08155 (2020)
17. Guo, D., et al.: GraphCodeBERT: pre-training code representations with data flow (2020)
18. Hellendoorn, V.J., Bird, C., Barr, E.T., Allamanis, M.: Deep learning type inference. In: Proceedings of the 2018 26th ACM Joint Meeting on European Software Engineering Conference and Symposium on the Foundations of Software Engineering, ESEC/FSE 2018, pp. 152–162. Association for Computing Machinery, New York (2018)
19. Hu, X., Li, G., Xia, X., Lo, D., Jin, Z.: Deep code comment generation with hybrid lexical and syntactical information. Empir. Softw. Eng. **25**(3), 2179–2217 (2019). https://doi.org/10.1007/s10664-019-09730-9
20. Huang, J., et al.: CoSQA: 20,000+ web queries for code search and question answering (2021)
21. Husain, H., Wu, H.H., Gazit, T., Allamanis, M., Brockschmidt, M.: CodeSearchNet challenge: evaluating the state of semantic code search (2019)
22. Iyer, S., Konstas, I., Cheung, A., Zettlemoyer, L.: Mapping language to code in programmatic context (2018)
23. Jain, P., Jain, A., Zhang, T., Abbeel, P., Gonzalez, J.E., Stoica, I.: Contrastive code representation learning. arXiv preprint arXiv:2007.04973 (2020)
24. Jiang, X., Zheng, Z., Lyu, C., Li, L., Lyu, L.: TreeBERT: a tree-based pre-trained model for programming language. In: de Campos, C., Maathuis, M.H. (eds.) Proceedings of the Thirty-Seventh Conference on Uncertainty in Artificial Intelligence. Proceedings of Machine Learning Research, vol. 161, pp. 54–63. PMLR, 27–30 July 2021
25. Just, R., Jalali, D., Ernst, M.D.: Defects4J: a database of existing faults to enable controlled testing studies for Java programs. In: Proceedings of the 2014 International Symposium on Software Testing and Analysis, ISSTA 2014, pp. 437–440. Association for Computing Machinery, New York (2014)
26. Kalyan, K.S., Rajasekharan, A., Sangeetha, S.: AMMUS: a survey of transformer-based pretrained models in natural language processing (2021)
27. Kanade, A., Maniatis, P., Balakrishnan, G., Shi, K.: Learning and evaluating contextual embedding of source code (2020)
28. Kim, Y.J., et al.: Scalable and efficient MoE training for multitask multilingual models, September 2021
29. Koroteev, M.: BERT: a review of applications in natural language processing and understanding. arXiv preprint arXiv:2103.11943 (2021)
30. Lachaux, M.A., Roziere, B., Chanussot, L., Lample, G.: Unsupervised translation of programming languages (2020)
31. Li, Y., et al.: Competition-level code generation with AlphaCode. arXiv preprint arXiv:2203.07814 (2022)
32. Liao, C., Lin, P.H., Asplund, J., Schordan, M., Karlin, I.: DataRaceBench: a benchmark suite for systematic evaluation of data race detection tools. In: Proceedings

of the International Conference for High Performance Computing, Networking, Storage and Analysis, pp. 1–14 (2017)

33. Lu, S., et al.: CodeXGLUE: a machine learning benchmark dataset for code understanding and generation. CoRR abs/2102.04664 (2021)

34. Maas, M.: A taxonomy of ML for systems problems. IEEE Micro **40**(5), 8–16 (2020)

35. Mou, L., Li, G., Zhang, L., Wang, T., Jin, Z.: Convolutional neural networks over tree structures for programming language processing. In: Proceedings of the Thirtieth AAAI Conference on Artificial Intelligence, pp. 1287–1293 (2016)

36. Nguyen, A.T., Nguyen, T.T., Nguyen, T.N.: Divide-and-conquer approach for multi-phase statistical migration for source code (t). In: 2015 30th IEEE/ACM International Conference on Automated Software Engineering (ASE), pp. 585–596 (2015)

37. Phan, L., et al.: CoTexT: multi-task learning with code-text transformer. arXiv preprint arXiv:2105.08645 (2021)

38. Puri, R., et al.: CodeNet: a large-scale AI for code dataset for learning a diversity of coding tasks (2021)

39. Radford, A., Narasimhan, K., Salimans, T., Sutskever, I., et al.: Improving language understanding by generative pre-training (2018)

40. Raychev, V., Bielik, P., Vechev, M.: Probabilistic model for code with decision trees. SIGPLAN Not. **51**(10), 731–747 (2016)

41. Sarker, I.H.: Deep learning: a comprehensive overview on techniques, taxonomy, applications and research directions. SN Comput. Sci. **2**(6), 1–20 (2021). https://doi.org/10.1007/s42979-021-00815-110.1007/s42979-021-00815-1

42. Svajlenko, J., Islam, J.F., Keivanloo, I., Roy, C.K., Mia, M.M.: Towards a big data curated benchmark of inter-project code clones. In: 2014 IEEE International Conference on Software Maintenance and Evolution, pp. 476–480 (2014)

43. Tufano, M., Watson, C., Bavota, G., Penta, M.D., White, M., Poshyvanyk, D.: An empirical study on learning bug-fixing patches in the wild via neural machine translation. ACM Trans. Softw. Eng. Methodol. **28**(4), 1–29 (2019)

44. Vaswani, A., et al.: Attention is all you need. In: Advances in Neural Information Processing Systems, vol. 30 (2017)

45. Wang, X., et al.: SynCoBERT: syntax-guided multi-modal contrastive pre-training for code representation (2021)

46. Wang, X., et al.: CODE-MVP: learning to represent source code from multiple views with contrastive pre-training (2022)

47. Wang, Y., Wang, W., Joty, S., Hoi, S.C.: Code T5: identifier-aware unified pre-trained encoder-decoder models for code understanding and generation. In: Proceedings of the 2021 Conference on Empirical Methods in Natural Language Processing, Punta Cana, Dominican Republic, pp. 8696–8708. Association for Computational Linguistics, November 2021. https://doi.org/10.18653/v1/2021.emnlp-main.685

48. Yin, P., Deng, B., Chen, E., Vasilescu, B., Neubig, G.: Learning to mine aligned code and natural language pairs from stack overflow. In: International Conference on Mining Software Repositories, MSR, pp. 476–486. ACM (2018)

49. Yu, J., et al.: Scaling autoregressive models for content-rich text-to-image generation (2022)

50. Zhou, Y., Liu, S., Siow, J., Du, X., Liu, Y.: Devign: effective vulnerability identification by learning comprehensive program semantics via graph neural networks (2019)

9th Workshop on Software Architecture Erosion and Architectural Consistency (SAEroCon)

Optimized Machine Learning Input for Evolutionary Source Code to Architecture Mapping

Tobias Olsson$^{(\boxtimes)}$ (ID), Morgan Ericsson(ID), and Anna Wingkvist(ID)

Department of Computer Science and Media Technology, Linnaeus University,
Kalmar/Växjö, Sweden
{tobias.olsson,morgan.ericsson,anna.wingkvist}@lnu.se

Abstract. Automatically mapping source code to architectural modules is an interesting and difficult problem. Mapping can be considered a classification problem, and machine learning approaches have been used to automatically generate mappings. Feature engineering is an essential element of machine learning. We study which source code features are important for an algorithm to function effectively. Additionally, we examine stemming and data cleaning. We systematically evaluate various combinations of features on five datasets created from JabRef, TeamMates, ProM, and two Hadoop subsystems. The systems are open-source with well-established mappings. We find that no single set of features consistently provides the highest performance, and even the subsystems of Hadoop have varied optimal feature combinations. Stemming provided minimal benefit, and cleaning the data is not worth the effort, as it also provided minimal benefit.

Keywords: Orphan Adoption · Software Architecture · Clustering

1 Introduction

Mapping the source code entities of a system to the corresponding architectural modules is an interesting but challenging problem [1]. Challenges arise from the fact that the file structure of the source code only sometimes corresponds to the modular structure of the architecture. Architectural modules are not always designed using a low coupling principle. The source code evolves and is partially changed to reflect this evolution. Still, the source code semantics, for example, variable names, are only sometimes updated [8,11]. Machine learning can use important information from an initial mapping or architectural documentation [7,14,15]. When a mapping is completed and verified, the result is an essential input to, for example, static architecture conformance checking using reflexion modeling. Mapping techniques can also potentially be used in automatic software architecture reconstruction and to find source code entities that are not conformant (similar) to other source code entities in the same module [11].

However, machine learning techniques depend on high-quality data and good values for the hyperparameters to perform well [7]. Finding such data and values

T. Batista et al. (Eds.): ECSA 2022, LNCS 13928, pp. 421–435, 2023.
https://doi.org/10.1007/978-3-031-36889-9_28

is a difficult problem; for example, it has been shown that including a challenging subset of source code in the training data causes a performance decrease if the training data are small [11].

In many cases, the research on automatic mapping focused on creating a complete mapping from a small set of training data [6,7,14,15]. However, from a practical standpoint, such a comprehensive mapping only needs to be done once for a system. Then, the mapping is applied evolutionary. Optimally, the mapping effort starts when the first source code file is added to the system and is done incrementally during development. Most of the time, it is likely that a large set of previously mapped and verified entities already exists to learn from, and only a small set of entities to map or remap remains. Tiny commits that touch 1 to 5 files represent 80% of all commits, and only 1% of the commits touch more than 125 files [9].

We investigate whether different features affect the performance of a machine learning technique for mapping or if using all the features without any additional processing performs well enough. We also investigate whether removing hard-to-map source code entities from the training data improves performance. If we find positive differences, this suggests an opportunity to use a large initial set to optimize the input data of the machine learning technique. One of the cases that we investigate is two subsystems from the same system. Subsequently, it is interesting to compare whether the same information is valued or whether different subsystems require different features.

This paper is an invited extension of the work we presented in 2022 at the 9th Workshop on Software Architecture Erosion and Architectural Consistency (SAEroCon), co-located with the 16th European Conference on Software Architecture (ECSA 2022). For the extension, we have added two new systems (Team-Mates and ProM, see Table 1) to the evaluation and in effect extended the work by over 60% more data points analyzed.

2   Automated Mapping and Critera for Mapping

An automated mapping algorithm aims to map each entity to the correct module without human assistance. For example, classes in the implementation that deal with the application's business rules should be mapped to the module Logic. Figure 1 shows an example of a mapping situation where the automatic mapper can use the information in the source code file to be mapped and the already existing mappings to make a decision.

We rely on *orphan adoption* [16] to map source code entities (files, classes, etc.) to modules automatically. An unmapped entity is considered an orphan that should be adopted by one of the modules, e.g., *StringChange* in Fig. 1. Tzerpos and Holt identify four features that can affect the mapping. *Name*, naming standards can reveal which module is suitable. *Structure*, dependencies between an orphan and already mapped entities can be used as a mapping feature. *Style*, modules are often created using different design principles (e.g., high cohesion or not). *Semantics*, the source code itself can be analyzed to determine its purpose

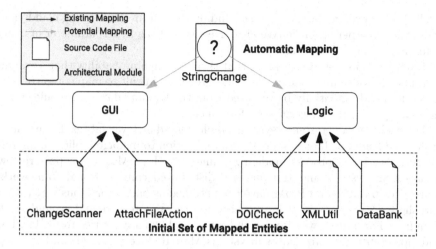

Fig. 1. An example mapping showing the initial sets of the *GUI* and *Logic* modules of JabRef 3.7. A new orphan *StringChange* is about to be mapped. Image reworked from [14].

and its similarity to the purpose of the modules. For machine learning, these features are used to train the model and infer new entities' mappings.

Previous research has focused on constructing attraction functions that use features individually to find an attraction between an entity and a module [3,6]. Our attraction function, *NBAttract*, combines ideas from previous research and considers the *structure*, *naming*, and *semantic* features in combination [10]. The approach is similar to that of Bittencourt et al., but we use a Naive Bayes classifier to determine similarity to other entities. To include the *structure* feature, *NBAttract* uses a novel approach, Concrete Dependency Abstraction (CDA), to encode dependencies as text [10]. NBAttract has outperformed other methods [14]. Therefore, we only use NBAttract in the remainder of this work. One general advantage of multinominal Naive Bayes is its ability to work well with limited training data. This is important when trying to map a new system fully but less so when doing an evolutionary mapping. In evolutionary mapping, it could be more important to have high-quality data for Naive Bayes to work well.

We have previously studied hard cases in mapping and found that there appears to exist a set of entities that are difficult to map [11]. Such entities could contain ambiguous information that would make a machine learning technique perform worse. If so, removing such entities is beneficial. One complicating factor is that such entities often belong to modules with few mapped entities, and further removing entities from small modules would likely not be helpful.

3   Method

We hypothesize that NBAttract should not always use all available features as training data. Some features (naming, structure, and semantics) are potentially not helpful or even ambiguous, and excluding these from the learning could yield better mapping performance. We also investigate if the hyperparameter of using stemming or not is beneficial.

From a previous study, we know that there is a high probability that a system contains a set of source code entities that are very difficult to map correctly [11]. This set should potentially be removed from the training data as it could introduce ambiguities that lower the performance.

We study four open-source systems implemented in Java; Jabref, TeamMates, ProM, and Hadoop. Jabref is a desktop application to manage bibliographic references, ProM is a process modeling framework, TeamMates is a peer review management system, and Hadoop is a distributed computational framework. Jabref, TeamMates, and ProM have been studied as part of previous SAEroCon workshops. A system expert has constructed the architecture and ground-truth mappings. For Jabref, we also use the set of problematic entities from [11]. For Hadoop, we use the two main subsystems Map/Reduce (Mapred) and Hadoop Distributed File System (DFS). We also removed many of the utility modules and modules with less than three source code files mapped to them to avoid having many small modules, which is known to be problematic. The Hadoop architecture and mapping have been the product of research studies in finding ground-truth systems for software architecture reconstruction techniques. We rely on their advice in this research regarding the subsystems and mappings [8]. The architecture is the product of a structured approach to architecture reconstruction, and senior Hadoop developers validated the recovered architecture.

Table 1 presents the versions and sizes of the systems in lines of code, number of files, and number of architectural modules.

Table 1. Subject Systems

Name	Version	#Lines	#Files	#Modules
Jabref	v3.7	59 235	1 017	6
Mapred	0.19.0	22 879	183	15
DFS	0.19.0	17 841	63	9
TeamMates	0.19.0	102 072	779	12
ProM	6.9	9 947	261	4

We have implemented a tool to evaluate different mapping approaches, including reporting detailed mapping results [13]. We use this tool to create a new data set over the mapping results for the various features, both individually and in combinations, including the use of stemming (or not) and excluding problematic entities from the training data for Jabref.

We run *NBAttract* with the following settings. The initial set of mapped entities is of random composition. The size of the initial set is at least 80% of the entities in the system. We extract package- and filenames from the source code entities for the name feature and identifier names for attributes and variables from the entities for the semantic feature. We apply the CDA technique for the structural features and extract the abstract dependencies for each source code entity. The name and semantic features are tokenized based on camel-case. The characters – and _, and tokens shorter than three characters are removed. We use a binary token frequency (present or not) and 0.9 as the threshold for automatic classification, as these are used in an earlier study [14]. We leave the use of stemming of the semantic features as a hyperparameter to be investigated.

We initially construct an experiment that investigates the performance of all individual features (name, structure, semantics, and semantics with stemming). Finally, we compare these to using all combinations of features, with the limitation of applying stemming or not considering the best results from the individual feature comparisons. Thus, we get four combinations: all features, name and semantics, name and structure, and structure and semantics.

To examine the removal of problematic entities from the learning data, we rely on the results of an earlier study in which we have information about such entities for one of the systems [11]. We use the same experiment as previously discussed, except that problematic entities that belong to large modules are excluded from the training data.

We run the experiments for at least 10 000 iterations to cover the random composition of the initial set to the greatest extent and collect performance information. We measure the precision, recall, and F1-scores for performance comparisons. The data will form a distribution for each experiment. We use visualizations to compare these along with median differences and statistical testing to determine the statistical validity of the difference and the effect size. More specifically, we test whether the feature or combination of features with the highest F1-score differs significantly from using all features for each data set. For JabRef, we also test if the mean F1-scores of the cleaned versus non-cleaned feature pairs are significantly different.

4 Results and Statistical Analysis

We performed the experiment and collected performance data for each system. We first ran the experiments using single features of information, including with stemming of the semantic information. Figure 2 shows the precision, recall and F1-score distributions of each mapping feature and data set. We note that for both the Jabref and Cleaned Jabref data sets, the name features have the highest precision, and the structure features have the highest recall. Cleaning the data seems to have a slight positive effect on the structure features overall and the name features precision. Stemming does not have a positive impact on Jabref or the cleaned Jabref data sets. For Mapred, the name features again have the highest precision, but recall is relatively poor. For Mapred, the best recall is found in using semantic information. Semantic features also have the highest F1-score. Stemming does not provide any benefit in the Mapred data set. For DFS, the name feature has the highest precision but the lowest recall. The structure feature has the highest recall and F1-score, and stemming provides a positive benefit for the semantic feature. The same pattern as in Jabref is repeated in TeamMates and ProM, the name feature has the best precision, and the structure feature has the best recall. Stemming does not provide a benefit in TeamMates and a slight benefit in ProM. Overall, ProM is structured very well, with a simple mapping reflected by the name feature's high performance.

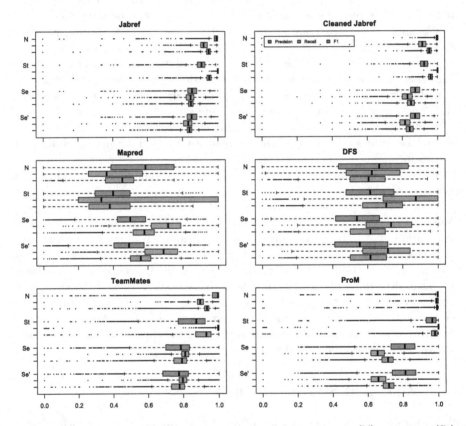

Fig. 2. The precision, recall and F1-scores for each feature; name (N), structure (St), semantics (Se) and semantics with stemming (Se').

Next, we present the results of the combined data set experiments. Stemming provided a positive benefit in the DFS and ProM data sets, so these data sets will use stemming for the semantic feature combinations. Figure 3 shows the precision, recall, and F1-score distributions for each mapping feature combination and data set. For Jabref, using all features is beneficial; this combination has the highest precision, recall, and F1-score. Combining the semantic and structure features also has a high recall but at the cost of lower precision.

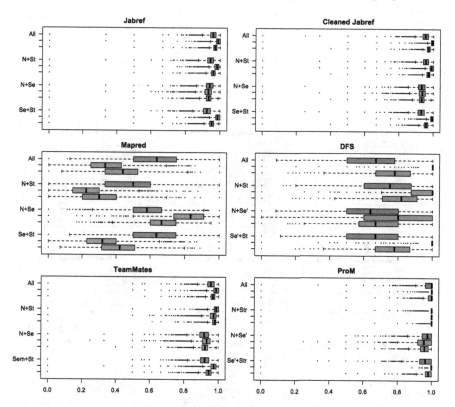

Fig. 3. Precision, recall, and F1-scores for each feature where name (N), structure (St), semantics (Se), and semantics with stemming (Se') are combined.

For Jabref with cleaned learning data, the name and structure features are even closer to the performance of using all features. However, the data from cleaning the training data look quite similar to the original data.

Using all features in Mapred gives the highest precision but a low recall. Instead, the name and semantic features are the best combinations with the third highest precision and the best recall and F1-scores.

In DFS, the best precision and F1-scores are achieved using a combination of name and structure features. The recall is high in all combinations that involve the structure features (all, name and structure, and semantic and structure).

We note that the Mapred and DFS data sets provide a greater challenge to the automatic mapper with considerably lower performance than the others.

TeamMates and ProM show the same pattern; using name and structure features in combination performs better, followed by using all features in combination.

We now compare the mean scores for each data set to find the best data sources. Note that we now combine the cleaned Jabref data set with Jabref in the same diagrams, as this would let us know if cleaning the learning data

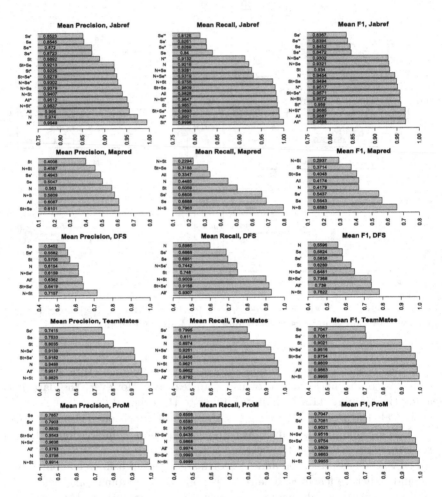

Fig. 4. Sorted mean precision, recall, and F1-scores for each feature and combination of features. The * and ' denote the cleaned dataset and use of stemming, respectively.

provides any benefit (cf. Fig. 4). The name features offer high precision, especially in the cleaned data set, but at the expense of lower recall. Using all features provides the highest F1-score, and cleaning the data does not seem favorable. Our general hypothesis is that using all features is not always beneficial. We construct hypotheses for testing based on using all features against the best combination of features. For Jabref, the best combination of features (except for using all the features) is name in combination with structure for the cleaned data set. Therefore, our first hypothesis uses these characteristics (cf. Eq. 1). For the Mapred data set, using the name and semantic features has the highest mean F1-score (cf. Fig. 4), so we construct the second hypothesis using these features. For the DFS data set, the name and structure features have the highest mean F1-score (cf. Fig. 4), and thus we construct the third hypothesis using those features. Finally, the fourth hypothesis considers whether using cleaned data is better than not using cleaned data for Jabref. Equations 1 to 4 summarize our hypotheses (the null hypotheses have been omitted to save space).

$$H1 : F1(\text{Jabref}_{\text{All}}) > F1(\text{Jabref}_{\text{name+structure*}}) \tag{1}$$

$$H2 : F1(\text{Mapred}_{\text{name+semantics}}) > F1(\text{Mapred}_{\text{All}}) \tag{2}$$

$$H3 : F1(\text{DFS}_{\text{name+structure}}) > F1(\text{DFS}_{\text{All}}) \tag{3}$$

$$H4 : F1(\text{Jabref*}) > F1(\text{Jabref}) \tag{4}$$

$$H5 : F1(\text{TeamMates}_{\text{name+structure}}) > F1(\text{TeamMates}_{\text{All}}) \tag{5}$$

$$H6 : F1(\text{ProM}_{\text{name+structure}}) > F1(\text{ProM}_{\text{All}}) \tag{6}$$

Finally, we test the hypothesis using a signed Wilcoxon rank sum test and present the median differences as an indication of the effect size. The effect size is the most crucial factor, as the sample size is considerably large; even minimal effects will be statistically significant.

Table 2. Results of statistical testing

Hypothesis	p	Z	r	Median diff
H1	<0.001	3.857	0.027	0.000
H2	<0.001	96.979	0.657	0.229
H3	<0.001	19.846	0.128	0.040
H4	<0.001	32.491	0.080	0.006
H5	<0.001	34.568	0.227	0.009
H6	<0.001	41.999	0.292	0.000

The conclusion of the statistical tests points to refuting the null hypothesis in all cases (see Table 2). However, in H1 and H6, the effect size is minimal. Using all features versus the name and structure features will not make any difference.

In H2, we observe a clear advantage of not using all features, with a rather large median difference. H3 and H5 show a minor but not negligible benefit of using the name and structure features compared to using all features. Finally, H4 indicates that the effect of purging the training data has a very low effect and will probably not be worth the effort needed. In summary, we find support for our overall hypothesis that NBAttract should not always use the entire set of available features. We also do not find strong support for using stemming or removing hard-to-main entities from the training data.

5   Related Work

There is recent and older work on orphan adoption [2–7,11,15,16] that evaluate and compare the performance of different approaches. In many cases, the same or overlapping systems are used. We highlight the conclusions of previous work regarding differences in what sources or combinations of data are used.

The naming of features, structure, style, and interface minimization are used in an algorithm evaluated in three case studies [16]. The algorithm does not use a machine learning approach but relies on system-specific parameters (e.g., name patterns). The algorithm also follows a hard-coded structure, first checking if a name pattern applies. If not, the structural stage is used, etc. The semantic stage is a manual tagging of source code entities as utility or not. Finally, interface minimization is only evaluated if the entity has a previous mapping. While this is not a machine learning approach, the basic features used are sound and are used in many other approaches with variations. This is the only work that mentioned remapping an entity due to system evolution.

Bibi et al. [2] compared the structural features part of the algorithm proposed by Tzerpos and Holt [16] with supervised machine learning approaches: Bayesian classification, k-nearest-neighbor, and neural networks. Their evaluation uses two versions of six open-source software systems. They find that dependencies between entities within the same module are essential to avoid misclassifications, especially when there are few dependencies between entities in different modules.

CountAttract and MQAttract are two attraction functions used in orphan adoption that have been evaluated in four case studies [5,6]. The focus is on evaluating the influence of two configuration parameters and comparing the performance of the attraction functions. Both attraction functions use the Structural features by using the dependencies in both the implementation and the intended architecture. A modular design based on the high-cohesion low-coupling style is assumed, and mapping would become problematic for modules designed to use a different style. There is no learning involved in the original attraction functions. Instead, they rely on weighting factors for the different types of dependencies. In a system with a rich set of dependencies, e.g., an object-oriented system, these become very hard for a human to set. We have previously shown that dependencies need to be weighted for the CountAttract function to perform well and that different systems often have different weightings. Such weights can be computed automatically using, e.g., a genetic algorithm from a large enough initial set [12].

Bittencourt et al. [3] introduce two attraction functions that rely on semantic information in the source code to calculate attractions based on cosine similarity (IRAttract) and latent semantic indexing (LSIAttract). They make a quantitative comparison between their attraction functions and CountAttract and MQAttract in an evolutionary setting. They find that a combination of attraction functions (e.g., if CountAttract fails, then try IRAttract) performs best. CountAttract usually misplaces entities on module borders, while IRAttract and LSIAttract perform better on entities on module borders and mapping entities in libraries but perform less well if modules share vocabulary but are not related. This work shows some merit to the hypothesis that different systems need different features.

Olsson et al. [14] presents an evaluation of NBAttract over several open-source systems with known source code mappings. In general, all features are used to minimize the need for user input. However, all systems are evaluated with or without using the Structural feature implemented using the CDA approach. All systems benefited from adding CDA terms to the training data across different sizes of the initial set.

Sinkala and Herold [15] introduce InMap that, instead of learning from an initial set, uses available architectural documentation [15]. This in itself is novel, as it adds another feature usable in mapping. InMap suggests mappings to the end-user, who can choose to accept the suggested mapping (or not). It is an iterative approach, where a number of mappings are presented and the accepted mappings are used to improve the suggested mappings further. The suggested mappings are produced with the help of information retrieval information similar to Bittencourt et al. [3] with the addition of a descriptive text for each architectural module. Entities are treated as a database of documents, and InMap uses Lucene to search this database using module information as a query. As InMap is highly interactive, it will also use negative evidence to some extent, i.e., a rejected mapping suggestion will not be suggested again. The results suggest that using only the module names as a search feature often results in high precision at the expense of recall. This is likely due to the fact that module names often reflect package names to some degree. Adding more and more module information in the query tends to lower precision but increase the recall, e.g., source code comments improve recall but lower precision in the mapping suggestions. InMap does not use the structural feature for mapping.

Florean et al. [7] compare and test different machine learning text classification techniques and different variations of features extracted from the source code, as well as two different pre-processing alternatives [8]. The features extracted are package declarations, import declarations, class declarations, public methods, and comments. The pre-processing steps tested are splitting compound words, e.g., camel-case notation and stemming. They evaluate three machine learning classifiers: Naive Bayes, Support Vector Machines, and Logistic Regression. One key difference compared to our study is that the evaluation is geared towards relatively small training sets. They find that all classifiers perform best on average using package and class-declaration data. This is attributed to the fact that all subject systems are fairly well structured in this regard. They find that alignment with package structure (or not) is likely a key variable. Without such an alignment, different classifiers likely benefit from different combinations of features.

6 Discussion and Validity

We find variations in the best features depending on the data set. Using all the data was not beneficial for Mapred, DFS, TeamMates, and ProM. Mapred was best mapped using a combination of naming and semantic features. DFS, TeamMates, and ProM were best mapped using a combination of name and structure features. Jabref, on the other hand, benefited the most by using all features. However, the difference between using the name and structure feature combination was minimal. The Naming features seem to offer relatively high precision but often lack recall. Stemming was valuable in DFS and ProM but not in the other data sets. In all five cases, the effect of stemming is low. This is in line with the results from Florean et al. [7], where the pre-processing alternatives did not significantly impact the standard deviation of the results.

Our results indicate that using individualized features and hyperparameters for each data set can achieve better mapping performance. As Mapred and DFS are both subsystems of Hadoop, it might even be the case that individualization is needed for every module. Different algorithms could even be used for different modules. As indicated by Florean et al. [7], there are differences in the performance of classifiers depending on the features used.

Such individualization is likely difficult for a human user to understand and set correctly for optimal results. However, in the case of evolutionary mapping, there is the possibility of using the large initial set to automatically learn what works well and transfer this knowledge when mapping new files and changes. The basic approach would be to run several mapping experiments on the initial set (in which the mappings are known) and find what features and hyperparameters work best. This could be done using standard hyperparameter optimization techniques, such as grid search, genetic algorithms, or ensemble learning. For constructing a completely new mapping from scratch, the best approach would be first to use all features, and then, if results are poor, try different combinations of name and other features.

The genetic algorithm approach would be attractive, as the best generation could be saved as an intermediate result and then used as the starting generation as the initial set grows during evolution. Ensemble learning is also attractive, as it is a standard way of combining several different machine learning models into one. The downside of all these approaches is the time needed; it is improbable to do such optimization on-the-fly. It would take several hours or even days to execute the required experiments. However, such optimization could be done offline after significant changes have been made to the initial set and would likely be relatively stable in large systems that do not undergo revolutionary changes to the architecture.

The performance of the Hadoop subsystems is generally not that good, especially compared to the other systems based on an intended architecture mapping [14]. Hadoop represents a reverse-engineered recovered architecture and is thus formed by the actual implementation, i.e., the implemented architecture. It could be the case that automatic mapping approaches generally do not work as well on these types of architecture or that some new feature is needed for efficient training. This could, for example, be source code comments or more advanced semantic topic model features.

Another explanation is that the intended architectures tend to be based on experiences from previous systems, and thus the modules and mappings could be dominated by generic and domain principles. The application-specific principles used could be discovered during implementation. They may not be captured well enough in the intended architecture, especially if the intended architecture is not changed to reflect this new knowledge. As the process suggested for the recovery of architectures implies that the application-specific principles override the lower-level principles, this could explain possible differences.

This study is limited to systems implemented in Java, a strongly-typed object-oriented language. This likely affects the types of dependencies that the structural features can use. In languages with less rich dependency types, the value of the structural features will probably be lower. There is also a tradition of dividing the application into packages in Java, which often align well with modular architectures. The generally good precision of the name features reflects this, but there are notable differences between the systems studied. For example, in Jabref the implementation aligns much better with the modular architecture than in Hadoop.

7   Conclusion and Future Work

Using a known semi-automatic machine learning technique, we investigated using different features to map the source code to architectural modules. The technique NBAttract uses Naive Bayes to calculate an attraction. We consider an evolutionary mapping scenario where there already exists a large initial set of data that can be used for training the model. The features are based on file names, structural information (dependencies), and semantic information (identifier names in the source code). We use these features individually and in all combinations to determine the best features for mapping. In addition, we investigate whether stemming is beneficial for the semantic features and if cleaning the data from known hard-to-map source code files is beneficial. We use six data sets based on four open-source systems, Jabref, TeamMates, ProM, and Hadoop. For Jabref, we have previously detected the hard-to-map source code files, so we have one original data set and one with clean data where the hard-to-map files are not included in the training data. For Hadoop, we investigate two subsystems; Mapred and DFS. We know the ground-truth mappings for all systems based on system experts' work. The evaluation was carried out using our mapping tool and we performed more than 10 000 mapping experiments to cover a wide range of randomly composed initial sets.

To conclude, there is no silver bullet regarding optimal features or pre-processing. The systems studied need different feature combinations to produce the best F1-scores of precision and recall. This is especially interesting in the case of Hadoop and could further indicate that even different modules (not only sub-systems) could need different features to produce more optimal results. Cleaning the training data showed little benefit, and stemming was only slightly beneficial in two cases. A machine learning approach could benefit from having individual features, hyperparameters, or techniques for each system or module for optimal results. Setting such parameters manually is not an easy task. However, in the case of evolutionary mapping, these could possibly be learned from a large initial set, an apparent future direction of our research in this area.

References

1. Ali, N., Baker, S., O'Crowley, R., Herold, S., Buckley, J.: Architecture consistency: state of the practice, challenges and requirements. Empir. Softw. Eng. **23**(1), 1–35 (2017)
2. Bibi, M., Maqbool, O., Kanwal, J.: Supervised learning for orphan adoption problem in software architecture recovery. Malays. J. Comput. Sci. **29**(4), 287–313 (2016)
3. Bittencourt, R.A., Jansen de Souza Santos, G., Guerrero, D.D.S., Murphy, G.C.: Improving automated mapping in reflexion models using information retrieval techniques. In: IEEE Working Conference on Reverse Engineering (WCRE), pp. 163–172 (2010)
4. Chen, F., Zhang, L., Lian, X.: An improved mapping method for automated consistency check between software architecture and source code. In: IEEE 20th International Conference on Software Quality, Reliability and Security (QRS), pp. 60–71 (2020)
5. Christl, A., Koschke, R., Storey, M.A.: Equipping the reflexion method with automated clustering. In: IEEE Working Conference on Reverse Engineering (WCRE), pp. 98–108 (2005)
6. Christl, A., Koschke, R., Storey, M.A.: Automated clustering to support the reflexion method. Inf. Softw. Technol. **49**(3), 255–274 (2007)
7. Florean, A., Jalal, L., Sinkala, Z.T., Herold, S.: A comparison of machine learning-based text classifiers for mapping source code to architectural modules. In: 15th European Conference on Software Architecture (ECSA) (2021)
8. Garcia, J., Krka, I., Mattmann, C., Medvidovic, N.: Obtaining ground-truth software architectures. In: 35th International Conference on Software Engineering (ICSE), pp. 901–910 (2013)
9. Hattori, L.P., Lanza, M.: On the nature of commits. In: 2008 23rd IEEE/ACM International Conference on Automated Software Engineering-Workshops, pp. 63–71. IEEE (2008)
10. Olsson, T., Ericsson, M., Wingkvist, A.: Semi-automatic mapping of source code using Naive Bayes. In: 13th European Conference on Software Architecture, vol. 2, pp. 209–216 (2019)
11. Olsson, T., Ericsson, M., Wingkvist, A.: Hard cases in source code to architecture mapping using Naive Bayes. In: 15th European Conference on Software Architecture (ECSA), pp. 13–17 (2021)

12. Olsson, T., Ericsson, M., Wingkvist, A.: Optimized dependency weights in source code clustering. In: Biffl, S., Navarro, E., Löwe, W., Sirjani, M., Mirandola, R., Weyns, D. (eds.) ECSA 2021. LNCS, vol. 12857, pp. 223–239. Springer, Cham (2021). https://doi.org/10.1007/978-3-030-86044-8_16

13. Olsson, T., Ericsson, M., Wingkvist, A.: s4rdm3x: a tool suite to explore code to architecture mapping techniques. J. Open Source Softw. **6**(58), 2791 (2021)

14. Olsson, T., Ericsson, M., Wingkvist, A.: To automatically map source code entities to architectural modules with naive bayes. J. Syst. Softw. **183**, 111095 (2022)

15. Sinkala, Z.T., Herold, S.: Inmap: automated interactive code-to-architecture mapping recommendations. In: IEEE 18th International Conference on Software Architecture (ICSA), pp. 173–183 (2021)

16. Tzerpos, V., Holt, R.C.: The orphan adoption problem in architecture maintenance. In: IEEE Working Conference on Reverse Engineering (WCRE), pp. 76–82 (1997)

2nd International Workshop on Mining Software Repositories for Software Architecture (MSR4SA)

A Taxonomy for Design Decisions in Software Architecture Documentation

Jan Keim[✉][iD], Tobias Hey[iD], Bjarne Sauer, and Anne Koziolek[iD]

KASTEL - Institute of Information Security and Dependability, Karlsruhe Institute
of Technology (KIT), Karlsruhe, Germany
{jan.keim,hey,koziolek}@kit.edu, bjarne.sauer@t-online.de

Abstract. A software system is the result of all design decisions that
were made during development and maintenance. Documentation, such
as software architecture documentation, captures a variety of different
design decisions. Classifying the kinds of design decisions facilitates various downstream tasks by enabling more targeted analyses. In this paper,
we propose a taxonomy for design decisions in software architecture
documentation to primarily support consistency checking. Existing taxonomies about design decisions have different purposes and do not fit well
because they are too coarse. We take an iterative approach, starting with
an initial taxonomy based on literature and considerations regarding consistency checking. Then, we mine open-source repositories to extract 17
software architecture documentations that we use to refine the taxonomy.
We evaluate the resulting taxonomy with regard to purpose, structure,
and application. Additionally, we explore the automatic identification
and classification of design decisions in software architecture documentation according to the taxonomy. We apply different machine learning
techniques, such as Logistic Regression, Decision Trees, Random Forests,
and BERT to the 17 software architecture documentations. The evaluation yields a F_1-score of up to 92.1% for identifying design decisions
and a F_1-score of up to 55.2% for the classification of the kind of design
decision.

Keywords: Design Decisions · Software Architecture ·
Documentation · Decision-Making · Software Design · Mining Software
Repositories

1 Introduction

During software development, a lot of design decisions about the system are
made. The architecture as well as the software system itself are the result of
all design decisions. The successful development and maintenance of a software
system, therefore, relies on everyone involved in the development understanding
the design decisions. With documentation, design decisions can be captured and
made easily available to, e.g., help new team members or to recapture past

T. Batista et al. (Eds.): ECSA 2022, LNCS 13928, pp. 439–454, 2023.
https://doi.org/10.1007/978-3-031-36889-9_29

decisions. As a result, the success of a software system also relies on the quality of its documentation (cf. Parnas [22]).

There are different kinds of architectural design decisions (ADDs) in a system and in software architecture documentation (SAD). For example, there are existence decisions about, e.g., components like "The Logic component handles the business logic." Other examples include decisions about the development process like "The system is fully written in Java" or decisions about design rules like "There should be no dependencies between microservices."

Taxonomies and ontologies help to structure a body of knowledge, provide a better understanding of interrelationships, and improve decision-making processes [29]. Taxonomies for ADDs, for example, can enable focused discussions about certain ADDs and can raise awareness of the different kinds of ADDs. There are already existing taxonomies and ontologies to classify ADDs. For example, there are Kruchten's ontology of design decisions [18], the architectural design decision model introduced by Jansen and Bosch [12], and the architectural design decision rationale framework by Falessi et al. [7]. Taxonomies always serve specific purposes and are designed for certain scopes. Existing taxonomies are rather broad. However, some purposes can benefit from fine-grained classes.

One example for such a purpose are consistency analyses. Various researchers already pointed out the importance of consistency checking in software architecture artifacts: Based on two surveys with industrial practitioners, Wohlrab et al. [30] conclude that there are various kinds of inconsistencies in software architecture artifacts that need to be addressed. Moreover, Keim et al. [15] as well as Lytra and Zdun [20] argue in favor of consistency analyses and inconsistency management to avoid missing or losing crucial information about the software system and underlying design decisions. Knowing the kind of ADDs allows analyzing consistency more targeted using different analyses. For example, analyses that check an ADD that prohibits dependencies between microservices need to identify dependencies and check for compliance. In contrast, to examine the existence of some component, other analyses have to investigate existing components and find said component.

Kruchten's ontology (cf. [18]) distinguishes three kinds of existence decisions: structural and behavioral decisions as well as ban or non-existence. For targeted consistency checking, this level of detail is insufficient. The same problem applies to alternatives like the model by Jansen and Bosch [12] or the framework by Falessi et al. [7]. Therefore, there is the need of a more fine-grained taxonomy to serve the purpose of consistency checking.

In this paper, we present a taxonomy of design decisions in SAD to enable in-depth analysis of ADDs. This taxonomy is intended for analyzing inconsistency, but might as well be helpful for other use cases that can make use of more fine-grained classifications, e.g., traceability link recovery or the generation of specific test cases. To construct the taxonomy, we create an initial taxonomy that is based on literature and theoretical considerations for consistency analyses. We then adapt and refine the taxonomy using SADs that we mined from 17 open-source repositories. The resulting taxonomy is both argumentatively and empirically evaluated. For the empirical evaluation, we perform a small user study. We additionally explore the automatic identification and classification of ADDs in informal textual SADs according to the proposed taxonomy. For this, we employ different machine learning techniques such as Logistic Regression (LR), Decision Trees (DTs), Random Forests (RFs), and the language model Bidirectional Encoder Representations from Transformers (BERT) [6].

The data to our research is published online [14]. This data contains the documentation texts and a classification of contained ADDs. Moreover, we provide the source code of our automated classification and the evaluation results.

The remainder of the paper is structured as follows: We present foundations and related work in Sect. 2 before we outline our procedure for creating the taxonomy in Sect. 3. The resulting taxonomy is presented in Sect. 4, and we evaluate and discuss this taxonomy in Sect. 5. We explore automated classification of design decisions in SAD and analyze the results on our dataset in Sect. 6. In Sect. 7, we argue about threats to validity before we finally conclude this paper in Sect. 8.

2 Foundations and Related Work

We divide research with particular high relevance to our work into foundations of taxonomy building and classification schemata/taxonomies for design decisions and automatic analysis of design decisions.

2.1 Foundations for Taxonomy Building

Ralph [23] recommends the following steps for generating a taxonomy: Choosing a strategy, selecting a site, collect data, analyze data, conceptually evaluate the taxonomy, writing-up and peer review. He recommends secondary studies, grounded theory, and interpretive case studies as possible strategies. Data collection and analyses are often conducted iteratively to let preliminary findings drive further insights.

Bedford [3] introduces the following principles that a taxonomy should fulfill: *consistency, affinity, differentiation, exclusiveness, ascertainability, currency,* and *exhaustiveness. Consistency* means that the rules for creating, changing, and retiring categories should be consistent. *Affinity* is the principle that states that each category definition should be based on its parent category and that categories in a lower hierarchy should have an increased intention. Moreover, when creating sub-categories, there should be at least two (*differentiation*). However, there does not need to be a differentiation on all levels. All categories should be *exclusive* so that two or more categories do not overlap, and each category has a clear scope and clear boundaries. Names should be immediately clear and understandable (*ascertainability*) and they should reflect the language of the domain (*currency*). Finally, categories should be *exhaustive* in a way that they cover the whole domain.

2.2 Classification Schemata for Design Decisions

There are several approaches to define a classification schema or taxonomy for design decisions. Kruchten [18] proposes an ontology of architectural design decisions that distinguishes between existence, property, and executive design decisions. Existence design decisions are further divided into structural, behavioral, and ban decisions. The former two are related to the creation or interaction of elements, whereas the latter state that a certain element will not appear in the design or implementation. Kruchten regards positively stated property decisions as design rules or guidelines, and calls negatively stated decisions constraints. In general, property decisions state traits or qualities of the system. According to Kruchten, executive decisions are driven by either the business environment, affect the development process, the people, or the organization, and extend the choices of technologies and tools.

In an expert survey, Miesbauer and Weinreich [21] noticed that developers often face existence decisions, whereas executive decisions are only present in a quarter of decisions. Property decisions even only constitute 10% of the cases. Additionally, they identify four levels of design decisions: implementation, architecture, project, and business.

Jansen and Bosch [12] regard software architecture as a composition of design decisions over time. They propose *Archium* that explicitly models the relations between design decisions and software architecture during the whole development process. The software architecture is then described as a set of design decisions, deltas, and design fragments.

Falessi et al. [7] present a framework that associates design decisions with their goals and available alternatives. The goal is to improve the maintenance of systems by improving the comprehensibility of design decisions.

Based on Kruchten's ontology and Falessi et al.'s use cases, Zimmermann et al. [31] structure the decision-making process according to the three steps: decision identification, decision making, and decision enforcement. They group similar design decisions under a shared topic. Then, each topic is assigned to one of the three levels of abstraction: conceptual, technology, and asset level.

In a survey on architectural design decision models and tools, Shahin et al. [26] identified decisions, constraints, solutions, and rationales as key elements of all nine considered models. The models mostly differ in the used terminology.

As our goal is to enable and improve tasks like consistency checking for software architecture documentation, existing work does not fit to our purposes. The approaches are often too coarse, or the abstraction level does not fit. In this work, we will explain why this is the case and present a more fine-grained taxonomy that solves this issue.

2.3 Automatic Analysis of Design Decisions

Approaches that automatically identify or analyze design decisions have the benefit that they reduce or even omit the costly manual effort needed to recover design decisions using a domain expert.

Bhat et al. [4] extract design decisions from issue trackers, using a machine learning-based approach. Based on the classification schema of Kruchten [18], they train a classifier on 1500 issues that is able to detect existence decisions and their subclasses, structural, behavioral, and ban decisions. By using Support Vector Machines (SVMs), they are able to detect existence decisions with an accuracy of 91.29% and classify them into the subclasses with 82.79% accuracy.

Li et al. [19] also use machine learning to extract design decisions, but focus on mailing lists. Their SVM-based classifier is able to detect whether a sentence in an e-mail contains a design decision with a F_1-score of 75.9%. By using an ensemble learning method and feature selection, Fu et al. [8] are able to improve the results achieved in a multi-class classification of decisions into the five classes design, requirement, management, construction, and testing decision. The ensemble of Naïve Bayes (NB), LR, and SVM with 50% features selected achieves the best result with a weighted F_1-score of 72.7%.

3 Research Design

Our process of creating the taxonomy is oriented towards the guidelines by Ralph [23]. We perform an iterative classification with 17 documentations from open-source projects. We use the insights after applying our taxonomy to identify shortcomings and adapt the taxonomy. This way, we try to also ensure Bedford's principles (cf. [3]).

We first develop an initial taxonomy that is based on literature, majorly on Kruchten's ontology [18]. We adopt the major classes (*Existence*, *Property*, and *Executive* decisions) and add additional insights from related work, e.g., by Jansen and Bosch [12], Bhat et al. [4], and Miesbauer and Weinreich [21]. For example, existence decisions are the most common kind of decisions [21] and, therefore, should be subdivided. Considering the rules for manual classification by Bhat et al. [4], there are two kinds of structural decisions: decisions about the structure within the system and decisions about third-party systems and external dependencies like libraries and plug-ins. We also consult literature and specifications about software architecture and software design (e.g., [5,9,24,27, 28]). Lastly, we make adaptations based on own considerations about needs for stated application areas. For example, we disagree with Kruchten for having *bans* only as a subclass of existence decisions as bans can appear in other categories such as executive decisions as well. As a result, we view bans as negatively formulated decisions and, as such, as a property of each kind of decision.

Next, we iteratively apply the taxonomy on a number of SADs and adapt the taxonomy based on shortcomings and problems during classification. After each iteration, we adapt the taxonomy. We first perform a pre-study (first iteration) with one case study and then use three case studies per iteration. This allows us to identify necessary adaptations early while minimizing the risk of overfitting. We end the whole iterative process when the taxonomy is stable, i.e., the taxonomy does not need to be updated in two consecutive iterations (six SADs).

For this process, we need a number of SADs. Therefore, we mine English SADs from open-source projects. We identify these by querying GitHub for

Table 1. The 17 case studies used for developing and evaluating the taxonomy. #Lines shows the number of lines in each documentation file (without empty lines). Links to the projects and the used documents can be found in our supplementary material [14].

Project	Domain	#Lines	Project	Domain	#Lines
CoronaWarnApp	Healthcare	369	SCons	Software Dev	79
Teammates	Teaching	252	OnionRouting	Networking	51
Beets	Media	125	Spacewalk	Operating System	38
ROD	Data Mgmt	119	Calipso	Web Dev	30
ZenGarden	Media	109	MunkeyIssues	Software Dev	23
MyTardis	Data Mgmt	100	BIBINT	Science	22
SpringXD	Data Mgmt	95	OpenRefine	Data Mgmt	21
QMiner	Data Analysis	92	tagm8vault	Media	16
IOSched	Event Mgmt	81			

"architecture" and randomly selecting 50 projects. We then manually filter those based on the following criteria: We select English documentation with acceptable text quality, different SAD size, and various domains. Overall, we use 17 case studies with different sizes and domains that are listed in Table 1 and that can be found in our dataset [14].

Finally, we evaluate the taxonomy both argumentatively and empirically and experiment with automatic classification based on the taxonomy.

4   Taxonomy of Design Decisions

Using the process described in Sect. 3, we gained valuable insights into design decisions in SADs. These insights play a crucial role in the final design of the taxonomy and, as such, also serve as reasoning for some classes. Generally, existing structures were often too general and broad, thus needed further distinction. For example, we further subdivide structural decisions, decisions about functionality, and technological executive design decisions.

After following the process described in Sect. 3, the final taxonomy is composed of the following classes that are also displayed in Fig. 1 and Fig. 2. The root of the taxonomy captures the existence of a design decision. Design decisions are then split into three main categories: existence decisions, property decisions, and executive decisions. These three categories originate from Kruchten's ontology [18], and we agree on his categorization. However, there is a major difference in how we see decisions about *Bans*, as we already stated in Sect. 3. While Kruchten sees bans as a subclass of existence decisions, we see a ban as a negatively formulated design decision and a ban can exist in other sub-categories such as executive decisions as well. For example, there can be a design decision that states that a certain component (e.g., *cache*) should not exist but also that a certain tool or process should not be employed (e.g., for legal reasons). As a consequence, there is no category that indicates bans in our taxonomy. We regard it as an attribute of a design decision that indicates inclusion or exclusion of something. The same applies to delayed decisions, i.e., decisions that are made but postponed to a later point in time.

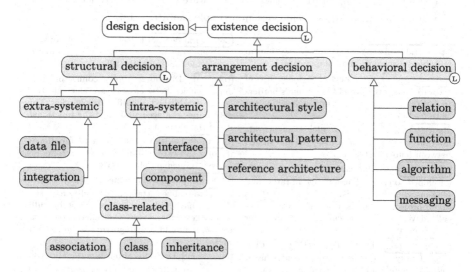

Fig. 1. Sub-categories of existence decisions with leaves highlighted in green and intermediate categories in orange. Categories derived from literature are labeled with Ⓛ (Color figure online).

The taxonomy subdivides existence decisions into structural decisions, arrangement decisions, and behavioral decisions. These three sub-categories are again further refined, as it is visible in Fig. 1. An important distinction that we make is between intra- and extra-systemic structural decisions. Coming from our insights, we define *systemic* as parts of the executable system that are developed for this particular system. Therefore, *extra-systemic* means everything that comes from external sources in regard to this system like libraries or external plug-ins. This definition helps us to draw a sharp line between external parts and parts that are developed especially as part of the system, which is especially useful for consistency analyses. External parts are often modelled in a fashion that uses, e.g., external calls. This clearly needs different checks than internal parts that are explicitly modelled.

Aside from existence decisions, there are property decisions and executive decisions. Figure 2 shows the sub-categorization of property decisions and executive decisions. In Table 2 and Table 3, we define the different categories and sub-categories and describe them in more detail.

5 Evaluation

In this chapter, we evaluate our taxonomy with respect to its suitability and different properties that we derive from the principles by Bedford [3] and the

Table 2. Existence decision and its sub-categories

existence decision: State whether some software element or artifact will be present in the system's design or implementation [18].

structural decision: Break down a system in reusable subsystems and components.

extra-systemic: Decisions that make use of software elements beyond the system's borders to add them to the system under development or to feed in data.

data file: Non-executable files that provide information that can be transferred and shared between (sub-) systems.

integration: In this category fall externally developed software elements like libraries and plug-ins, but also reused components from other projects/systems that are not specifically developed for the current system under development.

intra-systemic: Decisions affecting the division of a system in subsystems and smaller units developed for this particular system.

interface: Provide "a declaration of a set of public features and obligations that together constitute a coherent service" [5]. Interfaces within a software system serve to bundle functionality together.

component: A unit of composition with contractually specified interfaces and explicit context dependencies [28]. We additionally recognize packages as such compositions . This category comprises decisions about components that are developed for the system under development, not imported components (cf. *integration*).

class-related: Deal with the development of software systems along classes of objects. Even if class-related decisions may not be architectural in general, many architecture documentations contain them, so we include them in our taxonomy.

class: A set of objects with consistent properties and functionality [5]. One can make decisions about its existence, structure and naming.

association: A set of links that are tuple[s] of values that refer to typed objects [5].

inheritance: Through *inheritance*, a child class adopts properties of its parent class. Design decisions in this category include the existence and design of inheritance hierarchies and the determination of (abstract) parent and child classes.

behavioral decision: Relate to how software elements are connected and how they interact to provide functionality [18].

relation: Decisions about connectors and dependencies between software elements that can be established, modified or excluded. This determines the accessibility of the functionality of the elements.

function: Decisions about specific functionality of a software system. These *functions* are usually implemented as methods.

algorithm: Refer to a named sequence of operations to realize certain functionality for a specific problem. The procedures must be sufficiently general and state the general goal. Otherwise, it should be categorized as *function* or *messaging*.

messaging: Decisions about functionality concerning communication between software elements through method calls, sending messages, and data packages (cf. [11]). With messaging, the sender usually invokes some behavior at the receiver.

arrangement decision: Decisions for an *arrangement* of software elements in a known manner and under consideration of related principles. Decisions in this category will affect both structure and behavior of the system.

architectural style: Provide solution principles for architectural problems that are independent of the given application and should be used throughout the whole architecture [25]. Examples are Layered Architecture or Client-Server Architecture.

architectural pattern: A proven, reusable solution to a recurring problem. The scope is broader (concerning components) compared to design patterns (concerning code base parts) [24]. In relation to architectural styles, architectural patterns are more specific to a certain problem. Examples for architectural patterns are Model-View-Controller and Domain Model.

reference architecture: Defines a set of architectural design decisions for a specific application domain [24]. The AUTOSAR architecture for the automotive domain can be seen as an example.

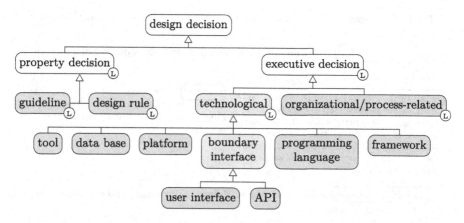

Fig. 2. Sub-categories of property decisions and executive decisions with leaves high-lighted in green and intermediate categories in orange. Categories derived from literature are labeled with ⓛ (Color figure online).

guidelines by Ralph [23] (cf. Sect. 2). We argue about the suitability for the intended purpose in Sect. 5.1. In Sect. 5.2, we consider the structure of the taxonomy and argue about the consistency, currency, affinity, differentiation, and exhaustiveness. Moreover, we look into the usability, application, and handling of the taxonomy, especially the exclusiveness and ascertainability in Sect. 5.3.

5.1   Evaluating the Purpose

The main purpose of the ontology is enabling consistency checking using documentation on one side and, e.g., formal architectural models or code on the other side. Consistency analyses need to treat certain kinds of design decisions differently. To enable that, the taxonomy needs clear differentiation and non-overlapping classes (exclusiveness, cf. Sects. 5.2 and 5.3). Moreover, the classes need to capture concepts and kinds of design decisions that need different treatment. This is obvious for classes belonging to different upper categories. For instance, structural decisions can be checked for consistency using a structural view on the architecture, while executive decisions cannot be checked this way. This also holds true for classes that fall under a certain sub-category. For example, components need to be treated differently from interfaces or associations, as all these have different attributes and involved elements. Treating named algorithms needs external knowledge to capture all involved parts. For messaging, there are different software elements involved and, therefore, the consistency check explicitly needs to check for these. We argue that similar argumentation can be done for all classes and categories. Overall, we conclude that the purpose for this taxonomy is clear and that the taxonomy fits to this purpose. However, we still need to collect further evidence by creating applications that use the taxonomy in future work.

Table 3. Property decision and executive decision and their sub-categories

---

property decision: State an enduring, overarching trait of quality of a system [18].

---

design rule: A rule, positively or negatively stated, expresses some trait or quality the system design must strictly fulfill. This is a combination of Kruchten's classes *design rules* and *constraint* [18]. This does not include observable quality attributes such as performance or reliability.

guideline: Recommended practices that improve the system's quality. They are less strict than design rules and usually not enforced.

---

executive decision executive decision: Relate to environmental aspects of the development process [18].

---

technological: State the choice for or against numerous technologies that enable and support software development.

tool: Developer *tools* can utilize and automate the development process.

data base: Decisions referring to storing data in *data bases* as well as decisions on query languages (e.g., SQL) and data base technologies (e.g., MongoDB).

platform: Decisions that refer to an environment of software and hardware components that allow development, deployment, and execution.

programming language: An agreed *programming language* for a system or components leads to syntactical and semantic rules for writing code.

framework: Abstractions that allow the development of extensive applications. A framework can either be an architecture framework (cf. [1]) or a software framework like a web framework (e.g., Django).

boundary interface: Interfaces that are located on the system's boundary and enable the connection from and to other systems and technologies.

API: *Application programming interfaces* provide external functions that can be used in another software system. If a design decision is not about the functionality of communications but about used protocols like HTTP and TCP, we also classify it into this class.

user interface: Located between the (human) user and the technical system, and allows the user to enter commands. There are different kinds of user interfaces like graphical user interfaces (GUIs) or command line interfaces (CLIs).

organizational/process-related: Sum up all decisions concerned with the development process, the methodological procedure, and the project organization.

5.2 Evaluating the Structure

The proposed taxonomy is based on related work and refines the ontology proposed by Kruchten [18]. As Kruchten's proposal is widely used in the community, especially as a foundation for approaches that automatically classify design decisions, our taxonomy can be regarded as consistent with existing work. Our taxonomy only breaks with the structure of Kruchten's ontology at one instance: We regard inclusive/exclusive wording as an attribute of each design decision instead of explicitly modelling ban decisions as a sub-category of existence decisions. With this decision, our taxonomy allows modelling excluding statements on different occasions and at a more fine-grained level. For example, we can model excluding executive decisions. Such excluding executive decisions occurred in our case studies and, therefore, we argue that our taxonomy is more exhaustive. Besides Kruchten's proposed classes, we also regarded Bhat et al.'s rules [4] for manual identification of design decisions while refining the taxonomy.

We reflect the language of the domain by using well-known and widely accepted names and terms within the software architecture domain (currency). We further ensure that there is an affinity of each subclass to its superclasses by iteratively adding new subclasses to existing classes in a top-down fashion. The proposed taxonomy also fulfills the differentiation principle, as each further refined class has at least two subclasses. Concerning the taxonomy's exhaustiveness, we cannot eliminate the possibility that other case studies may include decisions that would require different subclasses. However, as our superclasses stem from Kruchten's ontology and these classes were sufficient to classify each occurring design decision in various related work (cf. [4,21]), our taxonomy is at least as exhaustive as related work.

Additionally, our iterative approach follows the methodology of the National Information Standards Organization [2] and produced no further subclasses even for heterogeneous documentations (length and domain).

5.3 Evaluating the Application

We base our evaluation for the applicability and reliability on the guidelines by Kaplan et al. [13]. We let two software engineers (doctoral researchers) independently classify the design decisions in the case studies Calipso, Spacewalk, and SpringXD with only the information on the taxonomy provided in Sect. 4 at hand. We calculate Krippendorff's α (Kα) [17] to measure the inter-annotator agreement. The annotators achieved an overall Kα of 0.771 across the three studies. If the results are calculated per project, we achieve an average Kα of 0.841. The discrepancy stems from the documentation of SpringXD seemingly being more difficult. The documentation of SpringXD is far longer than the other two and contains several parts that were no actual architecture documentation. Thus, we state that the difficulty and uniformity of different users applying the taxonomy depends on the quality of the documentation. Still, the Kα values indicate a reasonable agreement that clearly exceed the lower bound of 0.66 and come close or exceed the commonly accepted threshold of 0.8 (cf. Krippendorff [16]). These results are promising regarding that the taxonomy comprises 24 leaf classes. As the annotators were also able to identify a fitting class for each decision, we are confident to state that the taxonomy can be applied in cases where a refined classification of design decisions is beneficial.

6   Exploratory Automated Application

To be able to efficiently utilize design decisions in SAD in other approaches they have to be automatically identified and classified. The ability to automatically identify the design decisions and their subclasses also heavily affects the taxonomy's applicability. To measure this, we employed different established supervised machine learning-based approaches to classify sentences in SADs according

Table 4. Distribution of design decisions in our dataset [14]

Taxonomy class						Primary	Secondary	Total
existence	structural	extra			integration	38	7	45
					data file	17	6	23
		intra			component	132	23	155
					interface	19	0	19
			class-r.		class	77	26	103
					association	65	12	77
					inheritance	19	3	22
	arrang.				architectural style	26	14	40
					architectural pattern	21	3	24
					reference architecture	4	2	6
	behavioral				function	271	43	314
					relation	56	14	70
					algorithm	48	6	54
					messaging	37	11	48
property					design rule	73	0	73
					guideline	8	2	10
executive	technological				organizational/process-related	9	1	10
					platform	72	15	87
					programming language	39	19	58
					framework	32	13	45
					data base	40	14	54
					tool	5	2	7
		boundary i.			API	51	12	63
					user interface	31	10	41
identified design decisions (in 1622 lines)						1190	258	1448
lines without a design decision								432

Table 5. Classification results of classifying if a line contains a design decision (binary), the kind of the most prevalent design decision (multi-class, weighted average) and the kinds of a design decision (multi-label, weighted average). Weighted average can produce F_1-scores not in between precision (P) and recall (R).

	$LR_{trigram}$			DT_{BoW}			RF_{bigram}			BERT		
	P	R	F_1	P	R	F_1	P	R	F_1	P	R	F_1
binary	0.877	0.894	0.885	0.850	0.852	0.851	0.831	0.970	0.895	0.901	0.942	**0.921**
multi-class	0.452	0.451	0.427	0.314	0.322	0.304	0.346	0.353	0.269	0.575	0.559	**0.552**
multi-label	0.578	0.326	0.396	0.453	0.394	0.406	0.482	0.090	0.145	0.679	0.427	**0.500**

to our taxonomy. To train the classifiers, we use the dataset that resulted from our taxonomy building process. The dataset consists of the 1622 lines of the 17 case studies (cf. Table 1). Table 4 gives an overview on the distribution of classes in the dataset. We labeled only the most prevalent primary and also the most obvious secondary decision per line.

To train the classifiers, we experimented with the preprocessing steps stop word removal, lemmatization, transformation to lowercase, and their combinations. For preprocessing, only lemmatization and lowercasing shows positive effects on the results. Likewise, we experimented with bag-of-words (BoW), term frequency-inverse document frequency (tf-idf), and bi- or trigrams as vector representations for the preprocessed lines. Based on the vector representations, we use Logistic Regression (LR), Decision Trees (DTs), and Random Forests (RFs) as ML techniques. This aligns with approaches in literature (e.g., [4,19]). For the sake of brevity we only report the best combinations here. Additionally, we use BERT [6] as a language model-based approach. For BERT, we use the same setup that performed well for our approach for classifying requirements. For details, see Hey et al. [10]. We fine-tune a classifier based on the *bert-base-uncased* model with 16 epochs, a batch size of 8, and use lowercasing.

To train and test the models on the dataset, we perform a random 5-fold cross validation with three repetitions. For multi-class and multi-label classification we report the weighted F_1-score as it takes the imbalanced dataset into account. Table 5 shows the results for three different classification tasks. For binary classification into design or no design decision, the best performing configuration is the BERT-based classifier achieving 92.1% F_1-score. As the input differs from existing work, we cannot directly compare the results. However, our results are similar to the results by Bhat et al. [4] for identifying design decisions in issue trackers. Our results are also better than the results by Li et al. [19] for identifying design decisions in mailing lists.

Based on these promising results, we apply the multi-class classification to lines containing a design decision. Here, BERT outperforms the best other approaches by over 12.5% points. Given the number of classes and the limited dataset, the result of 55.2% weighted F_1-score is promising. As the abstraction levels of the leaves deviate, the performance of a single multi-class classifier might be limited. In the future, we plan to apply hierarchical approaches.

To be able to identify multiple decisions in one line, a multi-label classification is needed. For BERT, we use a multi-label implementation. For the other approaches, we train One-vs-Rest classifiers for each label. Performance decreases slightly in this more difficult setting, but results are still close to our best results for non-multi-label classification. Again, BERT outperforms the other approaches with a weighted F_1-score of 50%. In this setting, the decision tree classifier performs far better and even outperforms the logistic regression.

7 Threats to Validity

To discuss threats to validity, we follow the guidelines by Runeson and Höst [25].

Construct Validity—We applied commonly used experimental designs and common metrics for classification tasks. However, there might be a certain bias in the selection of the use cases. We ensured construct validity by using projects from different domains and with different characteristics like size or architecture styles and patterns.

Internal Validity—We used the same case studies for the taxonomy creation and automated classification. This way, we create a fitting classification schema but assume representative documentations. Additionally, we only labeled the most prevalent direct decisions and the most obvious implicit decisions. In rare cases, there are more decisions and, thus, there is potential bias in the selection.

External Validity—In our evaluation, we examined 17 publicly available case studies from different domains. We aimed for a representative selection, but we risk that not all facets and aspects of design decisions are covered. All classes are represented, but some classes only have small representation (cf. Table 4). This is caused by the nature of some kind of design decisions to be mentioned only once per documentation (e.g., reference architecture) compared to those occurring more often (e.g., decisions about components).

Reliability—For our experiments on automated classification, we manually created a gold standard. We tried to minimize bias from single researchers by discussing the taxonomy in detail and how to decide on the most prevalent design decision. Moreover, we discussed certain classifications.

8 Conclusion

SAD captures design decisions about the architecture and executive decisions and makes these decisions easily available. In SADs, there are different kinds of design decisions that cover aspects about the structure, execution, or certain properties and guidelines of the system.

In this paper, we argued in favor of a taxonomy about design decisions in SADs with the main purpose to enable and improve consistency analyses. For this, we propose a taxonomy that is based on literature and an iterative process of applying and improving the taxonomy on 17 open-source SADs. This taxonomy consists of 24 leaf-classes, where the new fine-grained classes are designed to support consistency analyses.

We evaluated the taxonomy by arguing for its validity and fitness for its purpose. We argue why our taxonomy and its construction follow the principles by Bedford [3] and the guidelines by Ralph [23]. Moreover, we performed an empirical study with two subjects classifying design decisions achieving a good inter-annotator agreement ($K\alpha = 0.771$).

Lastly, we explored different widely used approaches to automatically identify and classify design decisions in SADs. The results are promising and show that we can identify design decisions with a F_1-score of up to 92.1%. We can also classify into the leaf-classes of our taxonomy with a F_1-score of up to 55.2%. We publish our data and source code online [14].

In the future, we want to obtain feedback from open source architects about the taxonomy and classification. We also plan to further explore the usage of this taxonomy with applications that use classification for inconsistency detection. This way, we can also collect more evidence about the applicability, usability, and suitability. Moreover, we want to identify and fine-tune further approaches for the automatic classification to get reliable results.

References

1. ISO/IEC/IEEE Systems and software engineering - Architecture description. ISO/IEC/IEEE 42010:2011(E) (2011). https://doi.org/10.1109/IEEESTD.2011. 6129467
2. ANSI/NISO: Guidelines for the Construction, Format, and Management of Monolingual Controlled Vocabularies. Standard, NISO (2005). https://www.niso.org/publications/ansiniso-z3919-2005-r2010
3. Bedford, D.: Evaluating classification schema and classification decisions. Bull. Am. Soc. Inf. Sci. Technol. **39**(2), 13–21 (2013). https://doi.org/10.1002/bult.2013. 1720390206
4. Bhat, M., Shumaiev, K., Biesdorf, A., Hohenstein, U., Matthes, F.: Automatic extraction of design decisions from issue management systems: a machine learning based approach. In: Lopes, A., de Lemos, R. (eds.) ECSA 2017. LNCS, vol. 10475, pp. 138–154. Springer, Cham (2017). https://doi.org/10.1007/978-3-319-65831-5_10
5. Cook, S., et al.: Unified modeling language (UML) version 2.5.1. Standard, Object Management Group (OMG) (2017). https://www.omg.org/spec/UML/2.5.1
6. Devlin, J., Chang, M.W., Lee, K., Toutanova, K.: BERT: pre-training of deep bidirectional transformers for language understanding. In: Proceedings of the 2019 NAACL, pp. 4171–4186. ACL (2019). https://doi.org/10.18653/v1/N19-1423
7. Falessi, D., Becker, M., Cantone, G.: Design decision rationale: experiences and steps ahead towards systematic use. SIGSOFT Softw. Eng. Notes **31**(5), 2-es (2006). https://doi.org/10.1145/1163514.1178642
8. Fu, L., Liang, P., Li, X., Yang, C.: A machine learning based ensemble method for automatic multiclass classification of decisions. In: Evaluation and Assessment in Software Engineering, EASE 2021, pp. 40–49. Association for Computing Machinery, New York (2021). https://doi.org/10.1145/3463274.3463325
9. Golden, B.: A unified formalism for complex systems architecture. Ph.D. thesis, Ecole Polytechnique X (2013)
10. Hey, T., Keim, J., Koziolek, A., Tichy, W.F.: NoRBERT: transfer learning for requirements classification. In: IEEE 28th RE, pp. 169–179 (2020). https://doi.org/10.1007/978-3-319-65831-5_10
11. Hoare, C.A.R.: Communicating sequential processes. Commun. ACM **21**(8), 666–677 (1978). https://doi.org/10.1145/359576.359585
12. Jansen, A., Bosch, J.: Software architecture as a set of architectural design decisions. In: 5th Working IEEE/IFIP Conference on Software Architecture (WICSA 2005), pp. 109–120 (2005). https://doi.org/10.1109/WICSA.2005.61
13. Kaplan, A., et al.: Introducing an evaluation method for taxonomies. In: EASE 2022: Evaluation and Assessment in Software Engineering. ACM (2022)
14. Keim, J., Hey, T., Sauer, B., Koziolek, A.: Supplementary Material of "A Taxonomy for Design Decisions in Software Architecture Documentation" (2022). https://doi.org/10.5281/zenodo.6956851

15. Keim, J., Koziolek, A.: Towards consistency checking between software architecture and informal documentation. In: 2019 ICSA, pp. 250–253 (2019)
16. Krippendorff, K.: Reliability in content analysis: some common misconceptions and recommendations. Hum. Commun. Res. **30**(3), 411–433 (2004)
17. Krippendorff, K.: Content Analysis: An Introduction to Its Methodology. SAGE Publications, Thousand Oaks (2018)
18. Kruchten, P.: An ontology of architectural design decisions in software-intensive systems. In: 2nd Groningen Workshop on Software Variability, pp. 54–61 (2004)
19. Li, X., Liang, P., Li, Z.: Automatic identification of decisions from the hibernate developer mailing list. In: Proceedings of EASE 2020, pp. 51–60. ACM (2020)
20. Lytra, I., Zdun, U.: Inconsistency management between architectural decisions and designs using constraints and model fixes. In: 23rd Australian Software Engineering Conference (2014). https://doi.org/10.1109/ASWEC.2014.33
21. Miesbauer, C., Weinreich, R.: Classification of design decisions – an expert survey in practice. In: Drira, K. (ed.) ECSA 2013. LNCS, vol. 7957, pp. 130–145. Springer, Heidelberg (2013). https://doi.org/10.1007/978-3-642-39031-9_12
22. Parnas, D.L.: Precise documentation: the key to better software. In: Nanz, S. (ed.) The Future of Software Engineering, pp. 125–148. Springer, Heidelberg (2011). https://doi.org/10.1007/978-3-642-15187-3_8
23. Ralph, P.: Toward methodological guidelines for process theories and taxonomies in software engineering. IEEE Trans. Software Eng. **45**(7), 712–735 (2019). https://doi.org/10.1109/TSE.2018.2796554
24. Reussner, R.H., Becker, S., Happe, J., Heinrich, R., Koziolek, A.: Modeling and Simulating Software Architectures: The Palladio Approach. MIT Press, Cambridge (2016)
25. Runeson, P., Höst, M.: Guidelines for conducting and reporting case study research in software engineering. Empir. Software Eng. **14**(2), 131 (2008)
26. Shahin, M., Liang, P., Khayyambashi, M.R.: Architectural design decision: Existing models and tools. In: 2009 Joint WICSA & ECSA, pp. 293–296 (2009)
27. Sullivan, K.J., Griswold, W.G., Cai, Y., Hallen, B.: The structure and value of modularity in software design. SIGSOFT SE Notes **26**(5), 99–108 (2001)
28. Szyperski, C., Gruntz, D., Murer, S.: Component Software: Beyond Object-Oriented Programming. Pearson Education, London (2002)
29. Vegas, S., Juristo, N., Basili, V.R.: Maturing software engineering knowledge through classifications: a case study on unit testing techniques. IEEE Trans. Softw. Eng. **35**(4), 551–565 (2009). https://doi.org/10.1109/TSE.2009.13
30. Wohlrab, R., Eliasson, U., Pelliccione, P., Heldal, R.: Improving the consistency and usefulness of architecture descriptions: guidelines for architects. In: 2019 ICSA, pp. 151–160 (2019). https://doi.org/10.1109/ICSA.2019.00024
31. Zimmermann, O., Gschwind, T., Küster, J., Leymann, F., Schuster, N.: Reusable architectural decision models for enterprise application development. In: Overhage, S., Szyperski, C.A., Reussner, R., Stafford, J.A. (eds.) QoSA 2007. LNCS, vol. 4880, pp. 15–32. Springer, Heidelberg (2007). https://doi.org/10.1007/978-3-540-77619-2_2

Establishing a Benchmark Dataset for Traceability Link Recovery Between Software Architecture Documentation and Models

Dominik Fuchß$^{(\boxtimes)}$ ⓘ, Sophie Corallo ⓘ, Jan Keim ⓘ, Janek Speit,
and Anne Koziolek ⓘ

KASTEL - Institute of Information Security and Dependability, Karlsruhe Institute
of Technology, Karlsruhe, Germany
{dominik.fuchss,sophie.corallo,jan.keim,koziolek}@kit.edu

Abstract. In research, evaluation plays a key role to assess the performance of an approach. When evaluating approaches, there is a wide range of possible types of studies that can be used, each with different properties. Benchmarks have the benefit that they establish clearly defined standards and baselines. However, when creating new benchmarks, researchers face various problems regarding the identification of potential data, its mining, as well as the creation of baselines. As a result, some research domains do not have any benchmarks at all. This is the case for traceability link recovery between software architecture documentation and software architecture models. In this paper, we create and describe an open-source benchmark dataset for this research domain. With this benchmark, we define a baseline with a simple approach based on information retrieval techniques. This way, we provide other researchers a way to evaluate and compare their approaches.

Keywords: Software Architecture Documentation · Natural Language Processing · Traceability link recovery · Mining Software Repositories

1 Introduction

Benchmarks for evaluation bring numerous benefits (cf. Sim et al. [17]). These benefits include, among others, clearly defined standards and expectations, an increased awareness on related work as well as more frequent collaborations within a domain. However, a recent study by Konersmann et al. [9] shows that between 2017 and 2021 only 2.6% of the 153 full technical papers at the conference-series European Conference on Software Architecture (ECSA) and International Conference on Software Architecture (ICSA) used benchmarks for evaluation. Instead, the most used evaluation strategies are case studies and technical experiments (57%). In order to counteract, the authors propose to mine the public available case studies from the papers to create benchmarks. According to von Kistowski et al. [7], studies can result in such a benchmark.

T. Batista et al. (Eds.): ECSA 2022, LNCS 13928, pp. 455–464, 2023.
https://doi.org/10.1007/978-3-031-36889-9_30

456   D. Fuchß et al.

For this purpose, Konersmann et al. [9] provide an overview of different papers
that made their case studies publicly available.

Mining existing case studies and example systems to build datasets is a great
opportunity for the software engineering domain. The main difficulty is to find
such case studies that are reliable and comparable to a specific problem domain.
However, it might be hard to find these comparable and exchangeable data.
In our case, we look into the well-established research area of traceability link
recovery (TLR). TLR approaches create trace links between two or more existing
artifacts. These links are particularly helpful for maintenance but help for the
overall understanding of a system and how different artifacts and views are connected. However, there are different kinds of artifacts that are traced. Common
artifacts are requirement documents, code documents, and issues, but may also
include documentation (e.g., textual software architecture documentation) and
models. Consequently, many approaches focus on links between requirements
and code [1,3,14,18,19], test cases [12], and architecture [11]. Our main focus
is recovering trace links between textual software architecture documentation
(SAD) and software architecture models (SAM) (cf. [6]). Whenever we mention
SAD in the following, we refer to natural language text. SAMs are machine-
readable models with an explicit meta-model.

To the best of our knowledge, there is no other work, yet, dealing with links
between architecture documentation and models. To allow replicability and to
promote comparability, we create a benchmark for traceability link recovery
between SAD and SAM. For this, we mine public software repositories, transform
the extracted data in unified formats, and label them. The resulting dataset is
publicly available [5]. Further, we present a baseline approach to show how the
dataset can be used in an evaluation and to provide reference values.

The rest of the paper is structured as follows: We first present the creation
of the benchmark dataset (Sect. 2). Following that, we describe its contents in
detail (Sect. 3). Lastly, we discuss challenges and opportunities we encountered
during creation in Sect. 4.

2   Creating a Benchmark Dataset

Before we created the benchmark dataset, we searched for used datasets in the
TLR community. Thereby we found the *CoEST*[1] repository. It currently consists
of 15 projects with gold standards for TLR between requirements and source
code. However, *CoEST* is not applicable for our work: On the one hand, *CoEST*
does not consider architectural descriptions. Further, several projects contain
languages other than English. On the other hand, the dataset does not include
any architectural models. Although it is possible to synthesize single artifacts by
transforming from the other existing artifacts, creating all artifacts synthetically
is undesirable. As a result, we can state that we are not aware of a dataset that
provides the needed information for TLR between SAD and SAM.

---

[1] http://sarec.nd.edu/coest/datasets.html.

We started to mine open-source software projects for documentations and models to create an initial dataset. In order to find relevant data for our approach, we searched for open-source projects that already contain SADs. We contacted the authors of [2] and retrieved a list of open-source projects that have some architecture documentation from them. In addition, we looked at the repositories of the *Lindholmen dataset* [4]. Even so, we did not find projects with an extensive SAD and a presentation of the architecture (as figure, diagram, or something similar). The lack of architecture documentation in open-source projects is common for small projects. Architecture documents are more often created and maintained in large, successful projects [2].

Since we want the dataset to be heterogeneous, we searched for case studies and example systems of other SAM-based approaches and chose five projects for our initial benchmark dataset:

MediaStore[2] is a "model application built after the iTunes Store". Its architecture was used for exemplary performance analyses on SAMs.

TEAMMATES[3] is an open-source "online tool for managing peer evaluations and other feedback paths of your students". TEAMMATES is used as a case study in several SAD-based approaches (cf. [6,15]).

BigBlueButton[4] is a non-scientific application that provides a web conferencing system with the focus on creating a "global teaching platform".

TeaStore[5] is a scientific application [8] that is used as a "micro-service reference test application". Like MediaStore, it is used for evaluations of architecture performance analyses.

JabRef[6] is a tool to manage citations and references in bibliographies. It has features to collect, organize, cite, and share research work.

In order to get more information about the projects used for the benchmark, Table 1 provides a short characterization of them. The table summarizes the main languages (w.r.t. their lines of code), the number of forks, and the amount of contributors. For the MediaStore project, we could not count the number of forks or contributors since it is not published on GitHub.

For each project, we created SAMs for the projects based on either existing models or with the help of the documentation of the projects. We extracted plain-text version from their SADs and created a sentence-wise gold standard for TLR between the SAD and the SAM. More details about the creation of the gold standard and the other artifacts follow in Sect. 3.

---

[2] http://sdq.kastel.kit.edu/wiki/Media_Store.
[3] http://github.com/TEAMMATES.
[4] http://bigbluebutton.org.
[5] http://github.com/DescartesResearch/TeaStore.
[6] http://github.com/JabRef/jabref.

The resulting benchmark dataset is described in detail in Sect. 3 and can be found in our public repository [5]. By making the dataset publicly available, we give other researchers the possibility to replicate our results and compare the results of their approaches.

Table 1. Characteristics of the projects in the benchmark.

Project	Languages (kLOC)[a]	Forks	Contributors
MediaStore	Java(4)	N/A	N/A
TEAMMATES	Java(91), TypeScript(54)	$\approx 2.6k$	≈ 500
BigBlueButton	JavaScript(69), JSX(47), Scala(22), Java(21)	$\approx 5.8k$	≈ 180
TeaStore	Java(12)	$\approx 0.1k$	≈ 15
JabRef	Java(157)	$\approx 2.0k$	≈ 490

[a] rounded kLOC for programming languages with most LOC (calculated via `cloc`)

3   A Benchmark Dataset for TLR Between SAD and SAM

As described in Sect. 2, traceability link recovery benchmarks are very specific regarding their (different) inputs, outputs, and gold standards. Nevertheless, the format of the data should be easily applicable for others. In this section, we provide a closer look on the parts of our dataset and describe our considerations.

3.1   Software Architecture Documentations

Software architecture documentations are one of two input artifacts in our TLR approach. For the benchmark, we obtained the texts of each project by searching their repositories for documentation and looking on their websites for their SAD. Since texts are usually read in and pre-processed with natural language processing tools, we removed tables and figures from the descriptions to provide processable plain text. We additionally cleaned up the texts so that, for example, special characters like curly brackets or captions were removed. For reproduction, we documented all changes made to the texts in the repository. We created for each project a text file containing all sentences of their documentations. In order to simplify the definition of a gold standard for linking sentences and model elements, each line of the file contains exactly one sentence.

In Table 2, we provide insights about the resulting SADs of the projects used for the benchmark dataset, i.e., the number of words and sentences for each SAD. Currently, the shortest SAD of the benchmark consists of 13 sentences (JabRef). The largest includes 198 sentences (TEAMMATES).

3.2   Software Architectural Models

There are different ways to represent software architecture models. MediaStore and TeaStore are systems that we considered for the initial dataset. Since they

Table 2. Information about the SADs of the projects in the benchmark.

Project	Words	Sentences
Mediastore	572	37
TeaStore	661	43
TEAMMATES	2509	198
BigBlueButton	1190	85
JabRef	237	13

have already been modeled with the Palladio Component Model (PCM) [13], PCM is our main candidate. Moreover, we chose PCM as meta model because it can cover different views of software architecture (e.g., components and deployment). Thereby, we want to ensure that the benchmark can easily extended. The repository view contains the minimum information to describe the components of a software system. This is enough to run all currently existing approaches. Therefore, when adding further cases to the benchmark that do not provide SAMs as PCM, we only provide the repository view describing the components. If the PCM model of a project already contained more views (e.g., allocation model), we also provide these in our benchmark repository. In general, we plan to add further views to provide more than just the component information of a system. Additionally, we also plan to expand to more model types than just PCM models. In order to increase the benchmark's compatibility with existing approaches, we created UML component models[7] that match the PCM models.

Concluding this section, we summarize information about the different architecture models of the benchmark's projects in Table 3. Since current approaches for TLR between SAD and SAM focus on components, we provide the number of component and number of interfaces of the models of our benchmark. The number of components per project range from 6 to 14 components. Due to the focus on components, the model of JabRef does not contain interfaces.

Table 3. Information about the SAMs of the projects in the benchmark.

Project	Components	Interfaces
Mediastore	14	9
TeaStore	11	8
TEAMMATES	8	8
BigBlueButton	12	12
JabRef	6	–

---

[7] http://www.eclipse.org/papyrus/.

3.3   Gold Standard

Besides the input data (SADs and SAMs), the core artifact of our dataset is the manually created gold standard for TLR between SAD and SAM. For each project, the gold standard is available as CSV file. It defines the expected trace links between the sentences of the software architecture documentation and the architectural model elements.

The first project that has been added to our benchmark was TEAMMATES. Its trace links base on a small user study performed as part of a master's thesis [16]. For the other projects, the gold standards have been created separately. To do so, for each project a gold standard has been manually created by one of the authors. Afterwards, the gold standards were analyzed by another author. In the case of different traceability links, the differences were discussed and resolved together. Finally, the gold standard is stored as a CSV file.

To give an example, we consider the eleventh sentence of *MediaStore's* SAD: "The UserManagement component answers the requests for registration and authentication." The repository model of MediaStore contains, among other elements, *Basic Components* that represent components of the system. Since the example sentence mentions the component *UserManagement*, the gold standard contains a link that connects the eleventh sentence referenced by the sentence number (starting at 1) and the component referenced by its unique identifier.

In order to provide more insights about the different projects of the benchmark, we provide numbers for each gold standard in Table 4. We provide the number of trace links, the number of components that have at least one trace link, and the number of sentences that have at least one trace link. Regarding components, we observe that not all components are part of a trace link. Only the SAD of TEAMMATES mentions all components of the model. Additionally, we observe that the share of sentences that contain trace links varies noticeably depending on the project (20% for TEAMMATES and up to 77% for JabRef).

Table 4. Information about the gold standards of the projects in the benchmark.

Project	Trace Links	Components with TL	Sentences with TL
Mediastore	29	10	28
TeaStore	27	6	23
TEAMMATES	50	8	39
BigBlueButton	52	11	41
JabRef	18	5	10

3.4   Simple Tracelink Discovery (STD)

Together with our dataset, we provide Simple Tracelink Discovery (STD)[8], a baseline approach for TLR between SAD and SAM. We provide this approach to provide a simple baseline. Additionally, the approach provides an example on how to use the benchmark and, thus, works as guidance for other researchers.

The main idea of STD is to provide a lower bound. In TLR, it is often assumed that same elements in different artifacts have same names. Thus, a simple base line is to create trace links only when the name of a model element, like a component, is directly mentioned in the text. Therefore, STD matches n-grams of model element names with n-grams of the words within the documentation text. As a result, the precision is usually high while the recall suffers due to the strict assumption. To relax this restriction, there is the option to employ normalized Levenshtein Distance (cf. [10]) to assess name equality, based on a defined threshold. Table 5 displays the evaluation results of STD for the benchmark.

Table 5. Evaluation results for the baseline approach STD on the benchmark.

Project	Precision	Recall	F1-Score
Mediastore	1.00	0.62	0.77
TeaStore	0.94	0.57	0.71
TEAMMATES	0.89	0.57	0.70
BigBlueButton	0.88	0.44	0.59
JabRef	0.87	0.42	0.57

The approach is intended for recovering links between SAD and SAM. Due to its simplicity, it can be easily adapted for other types of artifacts. However, the approach does not perform well if the names of model elements do not appear in both artifacts. For example, if artifacts have a vastly different level of abstraction (e.g., between requirements and code), this baseline approach will most likely perform much worse.

4   Discussion

In this paper, we first discussed the benefits and need for benchmark datasets. Benchmarks enable clear evaluations, comparisons, and provide room for collaborations [17]. Therefore, benchmarks should be established in more research areas. However, lots of research areas are very specific, tailored to particular input and special outputs, and have only small communities. In any of these cases, it is hard to create a dataset or benchmark for the evaluation of an approach. Not only the mining of software repositories and the creation of benchmarks is a difficult problem, but also the identification of potentially usable data. Therefore,

---

[8] http://github.com/ArDoCo/SimpleTracelinkDiscovery.

we suggested to extract such data from case studies or examples from other scientific publications relying on the same or very similar inputs. With this data, a dataset with a gold standard can be created.

We followed this idea to create a benchmark dataset with software architectures, texts of software architecture documentation, a gold standard for traceability link recovery, as well as a baseline approach. We also showed the applicability of this process by means of a baseline approach for this traceability link recovery problem.

There are some threats to the validity for the process and our resulting benchmark dataset. First, there may be a threat to validity due to the selected projects. These projects are selected based on literature. All projects have different size and have different architecture styles and patterns. The projects are also from different domains, although they are web-based applications. Additionally, we also assumed similar abstraction levels for SADs and SAMs, which might introduce some bias. Lastly, we created the gold standards ourselves and, thus, might have introduced some bias. We used commonly used techniques like mediation sessions for creating these gold standards, but we cannot rule out that there can still be a certain amount of bias.

In future work, we plan to extend the benchmark dataset with more details for already existing projects. This includes other types of models, more detailed models etc. Moreover, we plan to add more projects to better ensure generalizability of the results when applying the benchmark.

Acknowledgments. This work was supported by funding from the topic Engineering Secure Systems of the Helmholtz Association (HGF) and by KASTEL Security Research Labs. This publication is based on the research project SofDCar, which is funded by the German Federal Ministry for Economic Affairs and Climate Action.

References

1. Borg, M., Runeson, P., Ardö, A.: Recovering from a decade: a systematic mapping of information retrieval approaches to software traceability. Empir. Softw. Eng. **19**(6), 1565–1616 (2013). https://doi.org/10.1007/s10664-013-9255-y
2. Ding, W., Liang, P., Tang, A., Van Vliet, H., Shahin, M.: How do open source communities document software architecture: an exploratory survey. In: 2014 19th International Conference on Engineering of Complex Computer Systems, pp. 136–145 (2014). https://doi.org/10.1109/ICECCS.2014.26
3. Guo, J., Cheng, J., Cleland-Huang, J.: Semantically enhanced software traceability using deep learning techniques. In: Proceedings of the 39th International Conference on Software Engineering, ICSE 2017, pp. 3–14. IEEE Press (2017). https://doi.org/10.1109/ICSE.2017.9
4. Hebig, R., Quang, T.H., Chaudron, M.R.V., Robles, G., Fernandez, M.A.: The quest for open source projects that use UML: mining github. In: Proceedings of the ACM/IEEE 19th International Conference on Model Driven Engineering Languages and Systems, MODELS 2016, pp. 173–183. Association for Computing Machinery, New York (2016). https://doi.org/10.1145/2976767.2976778

5. Keim, J., Fuchß, D., Corallo, S.: Architecture Documentation Consistency Benchmark (2022). https://doi.org/10.5281/zenodo.6966831, https://github.com/ArDoCo/Benchmark

6. Keim, J., Schulz, S., Fuchß, D., Kocher, C., Speit, J., Koziolek, A.: Trace link recovery for software architecture documentation. In: Biffl, S., Navarro, E., Löwe, W., Sirjani, M., Mirandola, R., Weyns, D. (eds.) ECSA 2021. LNCS, vol. 12857, pp. 101–116. Springer, Cham (2021). https://doi.org/10.1007/978-3-030-86044-8_7

7. v. Kistowski, J., Arnold, J.A., Huppler, K., Lange, K.D., Henning, J.L., Cao, P.: How to build a benchmark. In: Proceedings of the 6th ACM/SPEC International Conference on Performance Engineering, ICPE 2015, pp. 333–336. Association for Computing Machinery, New York (2015). https://doi.org/10.1145/2668930.2688819

8. von Kistowski, J., Eismann, S., Schmitt, N., Bauer, A., Grohmann, J., Kounev, S.: TeaStore: a micro-service reference application for benchmarking, modeling and resource management research. In: Proceedings of the 26th IEEE International Symposium on the Modelling, Analysis, and Simulation of Computer and Telecommunication Systems. MASCOTS 2018, September 2018. https://doi.org/10.1109/MASCOTS.2018.00030

9. Konersmann, M., et al.: Evaluation methods and replicability of software architecture research objects. In: 2022 IEEE 19th International Conference on Software Architecture (ICSA), pp. 157–168 (2022). https://doi.org/10.1109/ICSA53651.2022.00023

10. Levenshtein, V.I., et al.: Binary codes capable of correcting deletions, insertions, and reversals. In: Soviet physics doklady, vol. 10, pp. 707–710. Soviet Union (1966)

11. Molenaar, S., Spijkman, T., Dalpiaz, F., Brinkkemper, S.: Explicit alignment of requirements and architecture in agile development. In: Madhavji, N., Pasquale, L., Ferrari, A., Gnesi, S. (eds.) REFSQ 2020. LNCS, vol. 12045, pp. 169–185. Springer, Cham (2020). https://doi.org/10.1007/978-3-030-44429-7_13

12. Rempel, P., Mäder, P.: Estimating the implementation risk of requirements in agile software development projects with traceability metrics. In: Fricker, S.A., Schneider, K. (eds.) REFSQ 2015. LNCS, vol. 9013, pp. 81–97. Springer, Cham (2015). https://doi.org/10.1007/978-3-319-16101-3_6

13. Reussner, R., et al.: The palladio component model. Technical Report 14, Karlsruher Institut für Technologie (KIT) (2011). https://doi.org/10.5445/IR/1000022503

14. Rodriguez, D.V., Carver, D.L.: Multi-objective information retrieval-based NSGA-II optimization for requirements traceability recovery. In: 2020 IEEE International Conference on Electro Information Technology (EIT), pp. 271–280 (2020). https://doi.org/10.1109/EIT48999.2020.9208233, ISSN: 2154-0373

15. Schröder, S., Riebisch, M.: An ontology-based approach for documenting and validating architecture rules. In: Proceedings of the 12th European Conference on Software Architecture: Companion Proceedings, ECSA 2018, Association for Computing Machinery, New York (2018). https://doi.org/10.1145/3241403.3241457

16. Schulz, S.: Linking software architecture documentation and models. Master's thesis, Karlsruher Institut für Technologie (KIT) (2020). https://doi.org/10.5445/IR/1000126194

17. Sim, S.E., Easterbrook, S., Holt, R.C.: Using benchmarking to advance research: a challenge to software engineering. In: Proceedings of the 25th International Conference on Software Engineering, ICSE 2003, pp. 74–83. IEEE Computer Society, USA (2003)

18. Wang, W., Niu, N., Liu, H., Niu, Z.: Enhancing automated requirements traceability by resolving polysemy. In: 2018 IEEE 26th International Requirements Engineering Conference, pp. 40–51 (2018). https://doi.org/10.1109/RE.2018.00-53
19. Zhang, Y., Wan, C., Jin, B.: An empirical study on recovering requirement-to-code links. In: 2016 17th IEEE/ACIS International Conference on Software Engineering, Artificial Intelligence, Networking and Parallel/Distributed Computing (SNPD), pp. 121–126 (2016). https://doi.org/10.1109/SNPD.2016.7515889

1st International Workshop on Digital Twin Architecture (TwinArch)

Engineering of Trust Analysis-Driven Digital Twins for a Medical Device

Marcello M. Bersani[1], Chiara Braghin[2], Angelo Gargantini[3], Raffaela Mirandola[1],

Elvinia Riccobene[2], and Patrizia Scandurra[3(⊠)]

[1] Politecnico di Milano, Milano, Italy
[2] Università degli Studi di Milano, Milano, Italy
[3] Università degli Studi di Bergamo, Bergamo, Italy
patrizia.scandurra@unibg.it

Abstract. The DT paradigm has emerged as a suitable way to cope with the complexity of analyzing, controlling, and adapting complex systems in diverse domains. For medical systems, however, the DT paradigm is not fully exploited mainly due to the complexity of dealing with uncertain human behavior, and of preventing sensitive information leakage (e.g., patient personal medical profiles).

We present the first results of a long-term recently launched research aiming at engineering a DT for a medical device endowed with trust analyses techniques able to deal with human and environmental uncertainty, and security protection.

As a proof of concept, we apply our DT vision to the case study of a mechanical ventilator developed for Covid 19 patient care. The long-term aim is engineering a new generation of lung ventilators where the use of a DT can prevent unreliability and untrustworthiness of a system where interactions, both physical (machine-patient) and operational (machine-medical staff), are characterized by the presence of uncertainty and vulnerabilities.

Keywords: Digital Twin · Medical Cyber-physical Systems · Trust analysis · formal methods

1 Introduction

A Digital Twin (DT) is a machine-processable high-fidelity virtual representation of a physical system, called Physical Twin (PT), to which it is coupled through a continuous, bidirectional flow of data (e.g., monitored data and results of predictive/prescriptive analysis). The DT paradigm has emerged as a suitable way to cope with the complexity of analyzing, designing, implementing, controlling, and adapting complex systems belonging to diverse domains such as cyber-physical, business, and societal systems (e.g., [17,24,33]). In particular, one of the field in which the concept of DT has been largely used is manufacturing, where a categorical literature review [24] has set the stage for a consolidated definition of DT.

The healthcare sector is also keen to implement these technological solutions to enhance medical care and patient treatment. DTs can provide informed and relevant responses in real time, support decisions and assess risks for the patients through simulation and analysis of up-to-date models that represent physical agents and machinery pieces, and also be adopted for medical staff training. To this aim, serious steps

T. Batista et al. (Eds.): ECSA 2022, LNCS 13928, pp. 467–482, 2023.
https://doi.org/10.1007/978-3-031-36889-9_31

have been taken in creating DTs of patients as well as DTs of medical devices [4, 22], with potential multiple benefits for doctors such as discovering undeveloped illnesses, experimenting with treatments, and improving preparation for surgeries. However, there are several barriers to the adoption of DTs. Besides technological and methodological aspects, hindrances can be the complexity of modeling human behaviors, human physiology, and operational workflows, of dealing with uncertainty, and of preventing sensitive information leakage (e.g., patient personal medical profiles). In general, the DT full exploitation also heavily depends on the trust that stakeholders have in DTs and the insights they provide. The actual corpus of study mainly focuses on security and privacy [18] and overlooks many of the aspects that are of particular interest to the system's stakeholders. Indeed, a stakeholder will hardly rely on a DT that guarantees acceptable levels of security and privacy but fails to meet required performance, dependability, or safety levels, or that does not even reflect the mirrored medical cyber-physical system (hereafter indicated as MPT for medical physical twin), as it will likely provide out-of-time or wrong feedback.

In this paper, we present the first results of a recently launched long-term research aiming at engineering a DT for a medical device that makes use of formal methods and analysis techniques. In particular, we here contribute with a reference architecture model for DT trust assurance. We concretely show how DT components of this architecture model are built and connected by embedding formal models and quality analysis techniques for their use at runtime [5, 34] within DT engineering platforms emerging on the market. These last are to be intended as runtime implementation platforms and currently are mainly data-oriented since only offer data analytic services. A very preliminary version of our DT trust assurance vision was presented as a poster at the ICSA conference 2022 [6]. Here, we make a step ahead and present a reference architecture model that concretely realizes our vision by complementing current DT engineering platforms with formal modeling and analysis techniques for behavior-oriented analysis. Specifically, with this architecture we envision a solution aiming at: (i) taming the complexity in modeling the heterogeneity of the DT components that must be developed, deployed, and evolve together with their physical counterparts; (ii) increasing the level of trust in the results and prescriptions coming from a DT, despite uncertainties due to modeling approximations and incomplete or imprecise data collected in the field. We also concretely show the potential applicability of the proposed architecture model through a running example, namely the Mechanical Ventilator Milano (MVM) [3]. Such a system has been developed during the Covid 19 pandemic to answer the high request of mechanical lung ventilators. MVM is a low-cost and fast-to-develop medical system that has been successfully designed, certified, and is currently built and delivered (especially to emerging countries). Applying our vision of DT to the MVM enables the design and development of complex medical scenarios that take place in physical environments in which human agents (e.g., patients and medical staff) interact with a new generation of lung ventilators and the interactions, both physical (machine-patient) and operational (machine-medical staff) are characterized by the presence of uncertainty.

In the proposed architecture model, trust assurance is realized through model-based quality assessment techniques, allowing both *if-what* and *what-if* analyses. The first one is executed on the DT and allows for detecting violations of the quality and security

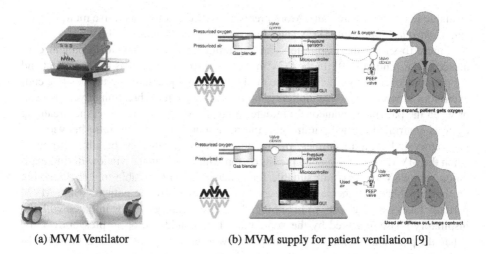

(a) MVM Ventilator   (b) MVM supply for patient ventilation [9]

Fig. 1. Mechanical Ventilator Milano

requirements that may compromise the quality of the patient's interaction with the system. Hence, changes to the digital models are evaluated and possibly reflected into the MPT (e.g. the analysis over the ventilator model may show that it is not able to detect a high inspiratory pressure in a particular patient state; hence a modification of the model and possibly of the MPT is mandated). What-if analysis, on the other hand, applied on DT detects forthcoming criticalities and might suggest requirements evolution (e.g. the ventilator waveform analysis detects patient-ventilator asynchronies which require a change in the ventilator settings - like the trigger sensitivity). The proposed techniques can be opportunely combined by introducing methods that allow for the composition of analysis, and the combination of analysis results within a DT [32]. A major benefit in using composed model-based analysis is the ability to carry experiments that would be costly on a real system.

This paper is organized as follows. Section 2 describes the running example in the domain of medical cyber-physical systems. Section 3 presents our view of a Digital Twin, while Sect. 4 illustrates fragments of the formal models adopted for the running example. Section 5 shows an example of compositional reliability analysis trough a reliability model for the overall DT system, and also examples of analysis from a security perspective. Finally, Sect. 6 concludes the work.

2   Running Example: MVM Case Study

MVM (Mechanical Ventilator Milano) [3] is an electro-mechanical ventilator (see Fig. 1a), which is intended to provide ventilation support for patients that are in intensive therapy and that require mechanical ventilation. MVM works in pressure-mode, i.e., the respiratory time cycle of the patient is controlled by the pressure, and, therefore, this ventilator requires a source of compressed oxygen and medical air that are readily available in intensive care units. More precisely, MVM has two operative modes: *Pressure Controlled Ventilation* (PCV) and *Pressure Support Ventilation* (PSV).

Figure 1b shows the inspiration and expiration breathing flows of a patient connected to the ventilator [9]. In the PCV mode, the respiratory cycle is kept constant and the pressure level changes between the target inspiratory pressure and the positive end-expiratory pressure. New inspiration is initiated either after a breathing cycle is over, or when the patient spontaneously initiates a breath. In the former case, the breathing cycle is controlled by two parameters: the respiratory rate and the ratio between the inspiratory and expiratory times. In the latter case, a spontaneous breath is triggered when the MVM detects a sudden pressure drop within the trigger window during expiration. The PSV mode is not suitable for patients that are not able to start breathing on their own because the respiratory cycle is controlled by the patient, while MVM partially takes over the work of breathing. A new respiratory cycle is initiated with the inspiratory phase, detected by the ventilator when a sudden drop in pressure occurs. When the patient's inspiratory flow drops below a set fraction of the peak flow, MVM stops the pressure support, thus allowing exhalation. If a new inspiratory phase is not detected within a certain amount of time (apnea lag), MVM will automatically switch to the PCV mode because it is assumed that the patient is not able to breathe alone.

To give an idea of the complexity of the entire MVM, its detailed behavior is described in the requirements documents which count altogether about 1000 requirements, each being a brief sentence. One document describes the behavior of the overall system, while 15 requirements documents describe the detailed behavior of software components. The controller itself has its own requirement document which consists of 31 pages and 157 requirements.

3   Our View of a Digital Twin

We take an ensemble modeling approach in which DT analysis tasks are carried out with multiple multi-paradigm models. Specifically, we propose a two-layer architecture: the *Physical Twin*, and the *Digital twin*.

The *Digital twin* layer realizes a *twin model graph* (see Fig. 2) made of digital models of real-world entities of interest (things, places, devices, processes and people) connected via relationships. This layer is further split into two sub-layers: the *DT runtime models* and the *DT engineering technology*. In the following we describe these two sub-layers and detail how trust assurance could be realized according to this reference framework. Some concrete examples of runtime models and types of analysis for the MVM running example are instead given in Sect. 4 and 5.

3.1   DT Runtime Models

This is the highest layer of digital models and trust analysis. Digital models are analysis/analytical models used as *living models* at runtime [5,34]. The composition of model formalisms and property formalisms enables a global DT analysis for trust, considering both the heterogeneity of the evolving models and the uncertainties both at physical and digital level. DT analysis questions can be managed at the level of the models and data

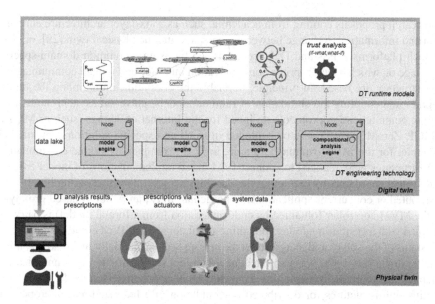

Fig. 2. DT engineering: a twin model graph contextualized for the ventilator case study. Dashed lines show the correspondences between system elements and digital entities.

involved, by defining and applying appropriate composition/decomposition relational operators (e.g., merge, union, focus, restriction, etc.). These operators are grounded on the semantic domains of the composed formalisms and their associated analysis techniques and engines [20].

3.2 DT Engineering Technology

This is the layer where the development, deployment, and interconnection of the DT-PT components occurs. It is also responsible for the execution and interconnection among runtime models to develop the basis of the twin model graph and accomplish the function of trust analysis. A DT engineering platform may be used as development infrastructure for such a scope. Such a technology would allow us to create a comprehensive digital representation of the individual PT entities/environments and types of relationships, but also to embed conventional model execution and analysis tools for enabling the use of formal/analytical models at runtime, and connect such models to each other. The DT engineering platform also facilitates us in exploring the data and the models in the DT graph (through a visual tool, or via API calls, or CLI commands) to view, query, and manage the models, their relationships and analysis results.

A central concept of the DT engineering platform is how to connect the runtime data to the model graph (PT-DT *system data*), and how to connect the models (and therefore the model engines) of the graph to each other. The DT engineering platforms currently available range from solutions coming from industry, such as Azure Digital Twins[1],

---

[1] https://azure.microsoft.com/en-us/services/digital-twins/.

to research proposals coming from academia, such as a six-layer architecture enabling data and information exchange between cyberspace and the physical twin [29], or [23]. In such platforms, CPSs and DTs are integrated by using a common domain-specific language on which an appropriate communication interface and related communication infrastructure are based. In principle, to enable the communication among the model engines and coupling the simulation of runtime models, universal asynchronous messaging communication protocols designed for the Internet of Things (such as MQTT, AMQP, ZeroMQ, etc.) could be exploited in small and specific solution contexts. For example, for the MVM running example, in [7,8] examples of simple co-simulation infrastructures were realized to connect JVM-based implementations of model engines and system simulators by exploiting the ZeroMQ asynchronous messaging library[2] for distributed or concurrent applications. In particular, in [7] an Arduino-based prototype of the MVM controller (obtained by code generation from a formal model) is pairwise coupled with a custom-made Java breathing simulator so the MVM could communicate the status of the valves and therefore set the pressure of the ventilator and read breathing events; first a serial port was exploited, and then in a second version a communication channel was realized by exploiting ZeroMQ. More appropriate standards and related runtime infrastructures for distributed co-simulation in a federated and interoperable simulation environment – such as the IEEE 1516 High Level Architecture (HLA) and the Functional Mockup Interface (FMI) [2] – are also being adopted [21].

Another important concept for engineering a DT is the *twinning rate* [36], namely, how often the synchronization between the PT and the DT (in both directions), and therefore the trust analysis, should take place. Usually, in near real-time scenarios, the twins are always aligned, but there could be phases in which the data within the DT could be outdated w.r.t. the PT. Regarding the trust analysis, different analysis rates could be adopted, also depending on the type of analysis conducted. Analysis could be, for example, triggered on request, or executed periodically from time to time or according to a specific plan, or triggered as a consequence of critical or adverse events (such as death of patients, latency in the medical intervention, etc.), or even continuously in an underground mode with a certain time granularity.

3.3 Trust Assurance

Trust assurance is realized through quality properties techniques allowing both if-what and what-if analyses. Specifically, if-what analysis exploits runtime QoS analysis techniques (such as analytical and simulation approaches [1], runtime verification [12], security and safety enforcement [16], and reactive adaptation [35]) to detect violations of the quality properties that may lead to evaluate changes to the digital models and possibly to the MPT. What-if analysis is mainly conducted from the adoption of forecasting methods: statistical techniques and machine learning algorithms, combined with proactive adaptation [35] to supply predictions of the evolution of the DT-MPT in the near future and the re-alignment of MPT w.r.t. DT (e.g. the runtime monitoring of the ventilator can detect critical situations like insufficient tidal inspiratory volume - computed

---

[2] https://zeromq.org/.

by integration of the measured air flow - and signal it with an alarm for the medical staff).

Applying our vision of DT to the MVM enables the design and development of complex medical scenarios that take place in physical environments in which human agents of various kinds, such as patients and medical staff, interact with a new generation of lung ventilators; the interactions, both physical (machine-patient) and operational (machine-medical staff ruled by medical procedures), are characterized by the presence of uncertainty. In such scenarios trust, prediction, and adjustment play a central role. Based on our framework, a DT for a medical scenario, such as a pneumology ward using a system like MVM for the therapy of patients, can help clinicians evaluate and improve the care. Enhanced analysis and monitoring capabilities help the medical staff identify possible situations that may lead to a decrease in the quality of the service provided to patients caused, for example, by delays in the provision of treatment, by unsuitable instrument settings or potential failures of the devices. The outcomes of the analysis can therefore be useful to initiate a maintenance phase for instruments or procedures, and also support the design and testing of new medical procedures and more powerful and safer ventilators before their use with actual patients.

4   DT Runtime Models

This section presents examples of analysis models used as living models at runtime within the DT.

Model of the Lung. There exist many models for the human lungs, and most of them exploit the analogy with electrical circuits, where the voltage is the pressure and the current intensity is the air flow. By means of these models of increasing complexity, researchers aim to capture different aspects of human breathing cycle, like the capacity (often called compliance) of the lungs, the capacity and resistance of other parts of the human body (trachea or other parts), and other patient features (including the capability of spontaneous breath).

Three models of human lung are shown in Fig. 3. Figure 3a reports a model, taken from [13], in which a simple non-sophisticated electric circuit show the input from the ventilator, several parts of the human lung, and their contributions in terms of compliance and resistance. By short-circuiting at the junction of R1 and R2, the diagram represents the conditions pertaining when the patient breathes spontaneously.

Simple lung models can be extended as shown in Fig. 3b, that reports a model presented in [15]. These models con be used for generating synthetic data sets for machine learning and for educational use.

The simplest possible model of lungs is shown in Fig. 3c and briefly illustrated in the following. The *capacity* or compliance (C) describes the elastic property of the respiratory system, and is usually expressed in ml/cmH2O. In patients with a normal lung undergoing mechanical ventilation, C is 50–60 ml/cmH2O. Decreased compliance may occur, for example, in the case of acute respiratory distress syndrome (ARDS). Monitoring and continuously estimating compliance in patients can provide information about the volume of the aerated lung.

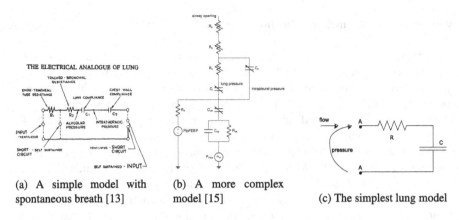

(a) A simple model with spontaneous breath [13]

(b) A more complex model [15]

(c) The simplest lung model

Fig. 3. Lung models of different complexity

The *resistance* (R) describes the opposition to a gas flow entering the respiratory system during inspiration, and can be calculated as the ratio between the pressure driving a given flow and the resulting flow rate. The dimension of resistance is usually cmH2O/(l/s). Estimating R is of extreme importance because it allows the doctors to choose the right inspiratory pressure and the right time cycle.

Model of the Doctor. When designing a complex digital twin that includes human agents, the designer must take into account different sources of uncertainty caused by the autonomous action of humans. Human action is subject to numerous influences, mostly stemming from free will, prior experience and physiological factors (e.g. the fatigue, focus, etc.). These components can cause the expected human behavior to deviate from a known operational workflow. Moreover, human action can be subject to error. Even if the intention of a trained operator is to act with respect to a known plan, the action realized by the operator may not be implemented through the actions prescribed by the plan or may not fulfill some of the desired qualitative properties. As shown in [25,26], it is possible to model the workflow of actions, certain physiological factors and human errors by means of Stochastic Hybrid Automata (SHA). A stochastic hybrid automaton is defined by a finite number of locations, modeling different operational states of the operator, and a number of continuous-time real variables, the evolution of which is described in each location by means of appropriate differential equations expressed with respect to real time (called *flow conditions*). Intuitively, when the automaton remains in a location for a certain time t, each time-dependent variable evolves as a function of t, and possibly other parameters. Real variables model physical quantities with complex temporal dynamics as a function of the current operational state. In [25,26], an individual's muscle fatigue is modeled by states of fatigue and recover, each characterized by several exponential-type equations. In a SHA, the transition between one operational state and another occurs through the execution of an edge that connects the two locations. The execution of an edge corresponds to the occurrence of an event in the system. In SHAs, edges can be stochastic as they are associated with

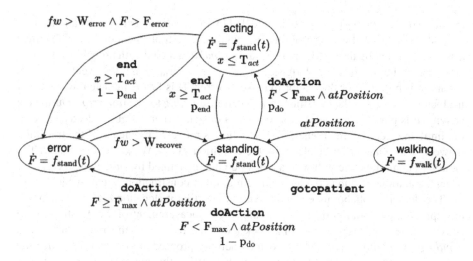

Fig. 4. SHA modeling a doctor collaborating with the ventilator.

a probabilistic weight and labeled with conditions expressed by variables in the SHA. When an edge is executed, the associated condition is true at the time of execution.

Figure 4 shows a simple example of a SHA modeling four operational states of a doctor working in a ward. The SHA has three locations called *standing*, *walking* and *acting* representing, respectively, the actions of standing, walking in the ward and operation through the ventilator. The *error* location models any potentially harmful situation that occurs during the activity with the ventilator, e.g., because of a wrong command issued with the dashboard. In each location, fatigue is the physiological quantity of interest, which is modeled by a variable F whose derivative is bound to a specific equation; in standing, acting and error, fatigue decreases (equation f_{stand}) while in walking, fatigue increases (equation f_{walk}). Some of the transitions are labeled with the actions *gotopatient*, *doAction* and *end* which represent the customary events in a workflow of a doctor. The initial state of the automaton is *standing*, as it represents the doctor waiting for the start of the medical procedure or the occurrence of an alarm, which occurs when action *gotopatient* is taken.

A medical procedure or an alarm implies an initial walking phase of the doctor leaving the office to join the patient in the ward. To keep the model simple, the walking phase is devoid of deviations caused by human free will but, in general, uncertainty can also characterize this phase. When the doctor is again standing because the patient has been reached (transition between walking and standing labeled with predicate *atPosition*), the diagnostic activity can begin; this fact is modeled by the event *doAction*. The action being modeled is a collaborative action that the doctor performs with the ventilator, and it represents the start event that occurs when the doctor issues a command from the ventilator's dashboard. Upon the occurrence of this event, the doctor can start the activity (location *acting*) if his fatigue is below a limit value F_{max}, but even in this condition, the doctor may decide to delay the activity due to free will. The actual initiation of the diagnostic activity is modeled by the transition between location *standing* and *acting* labeled with probability p_{do}; while the postponement of the collaborative action is modeled by the self-loop on location *standing* labeled with probability $1 - p_{do}$. However, if the doctor is too fatigued, i.e. when $F \geq F_{max}$, and the event *doAction* occurs, it is possible for the doctor to make an error. This fact is modeled by means of the location *error* and the transition from location *standing* to location *error*. During the activity, it is possible for the doctor to make a mistake when fatigue exceeds a threshold limit and free will intervenes. This situation is modeled by means of the transition between *acting* and *error* labeled with the condition $fw > W_{error} \wedge F > F_{error}$. The variable fw models free will with a real value that is defined by simulating a coin toss when the automaton enters the location acting (other constructions are possible).

The doctor's collaborative activity with the ventilator (location *acting*), has in this example a fixed duration of T_{act} time units. The measurement of the duration of the activity in the model is by means of a clock x which is reset when the transition between *standing* and *acting* occurs. If the doctor's activity proceeds to the end, i.e. when the activity has lasted T_{act} units of time, the doctor notifies the end of the action. This fact is modeled by the event *end*. Even in this situation, due to free will, the interaction with the dashboard can be wrong. The end of the activity without error is modeled by the transition between location *acting* and *standing*, labeled with probability p_{end}; the occurrence of an error is modeled by the transition between location *acting* and *error*, labelled with probability $1 - p_{end}$. After the occurrence of an error, the free will of the doctor governs the return to a nominal operating phase and the reestablishment of a non-emergency working condition. This fact is modeled by the transition between *error* and *standing*, labeled with the condition $fw > W_{recover}$. Again, the value of fw is calculated while the automaton is in the *error* state and the return to *standing* occurs when the value of the human's free will is greater than a predetermined threshold value.

Models of the MVM Controller. For modeling the behaviour of the MVM components, we used the Abstract State Machines (ASMs) formal method [10,11], which is an extension of Finite State Machines (FSMs) where unstructured control states are replaced by states with arbitrarily complex data. ASM *states* are mathematical structures, i.e., domains of objects with functions and predicates defined on them. A *run* of an ASM model is a finite or infinite sequence s_0, s_1, ...s_{i-1},s_i ... of states of the machine, where s_0 is an initial state and the *transition* from state s_i to the next state s_{i+1} is obtained by firing the set of all ASM *transition rules* invoked by a unique *main* rule, which is the starting point of a computation step. The *update* rule, as assignment of the form $f(t_1, \ldots, t_n) := v$, is the basic unit of rules construction, being f a n-ary function, t_i terms, and v the new value of $f(t_1, \ldots, t_n)$ in the next state. By a limited but powerful set of *rule constructors*, function updates can be combined to express other forms of machine actions as, for example, guarded actions (if-then) and simultaneous parallel actions (par). ASMs are endowed with a set of tools, ASMETA [1], which provides the user with modeling notations and different analysis (V&V) techniques. In particular, a runtime simulation engine, AsmetaS@run.time [30], has been developed within ASMETA as extension of the offline simulator AsmetaS [19] to handle an ASM as a living model [5,34] to run in tandem with a real software system.

```
main rule r_Main =
par
if state = STARTUP then r_startup[] endif
if state = SELFTEST then r_selftest[] endif
if state = VENTILATIONOFF then r_ventilationoff[] endif
if state = PCV_STATE then r_runPCV[] endif
if state = PSV_STATE then r_runPSV[] endif
endpar
```

Code 1: MVM Controller main rule

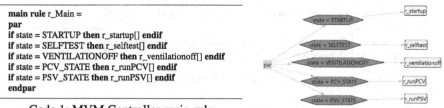

Fig. 5. RDT for the MVM controller

Fig. 6. MVM state diagram

MVM model. The *Controller* is the core component of the MVM device. Its model has been developed in ASMs through a sequence of model refinements: (1) The first model describes the transition between the main operation phases: startup, self-test, ventilation off, PCV, and PSV modes. (2) The second model introduces the modeling of inspiration and expiration in both PCV and PSV, (3) while the third model adds further MVM operation features (as the expiratory/inspiratory pauses, the recruitment manoeuvrer, and the apnea). (4) The last refinement step introduces (in both PCV and PSV) the transition between expiration and inspiration in case of pressure drop, and the transition between inspiration and expiration in case the pressure exceeds a threshold.

The ASM model shown in Code 6 refers to the more abstract level and specifies the controller's operation phases: the main rule specifies the transitions among the MVM states by setting the value of the **state** variable (initialized at the **STARTUP** value). Depending on the **state** value, the corresponding rule (not reported here) is executed.

Figure 5 provides a tree-based graphical representation of the model structure by using an equivalent visual representation for ASMs. This will be exploited for developing a model for reliability evaluation (see Sect. 5).

The semantic visualization of the model, and in particular of the main rule, is shown in Fig. 6. It represents the MVM operation in terms of a control state machine: the value of the variable **state** is used as state mode to determine machine states.

Models interaction. Having multiple models allows applying analysis techniques to the whole systems, like the simulation of critical scenarios and the proper answer of the overall system.

For example, consider the **scenario** of *alarm handling due to a low value of breathing flow when MVM is ventilating the patient* (both in PCV or in PSV mode). The data flow among the lung, MVM controller and doctor models is captured by the communication diagram in Fig. 7. The implementation of this scenario, and, therefore, the model co-simulation and the concrete way in which data are exchanged among the models, depends on the specific runtime infrastructure adopted, as described in Sect. 3.

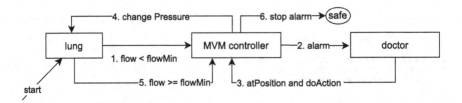

Fig. 7. *Low flow alarm handling* Scenario

1. The model of lung (see Fig. 3c) reveals that the current value of breathing flow is below a minimum threshold (see condition *flow < flowMin* in Fig. 7) and alerts the ventilator.
2. The model of the controller (see Code 1) reveals the unsafe situation and raises an alarm to alert the doctor (rules `r_runPCV` and `r_runPSV` – not shown here – are responsible, each for the relative ventilation mode, for checking this unsafe breathing condition and raising the suitable alarm).
3. The doctor (see the model in Fig. 4) is at the position, he/she is not fatigued and free wills to do the right action; the transition from `standing` to `acting` is performed and the doctor, by the GUI of the MVM, `does the action` of increasing the value of the pressure flow delivered the patent.
4. The increased pressure value is used by the controller model to change the pressure delivered to the patient (rules `r_runPCV` and `r_runPSV` are responsible, in their respective ventilation mode, for performing the pressure change);
5. The model of the lung communicates to the ventilator a flow value above the minimum level (the condition *flow ≥ flowMin* holds).
6. Finally, the controller stops the alarm (rules `r_runPCV` and `r_runPSV` are responsible, in the respective ventilation modes they manage, to stop the alarms).

5   DT Trust Analysis

As described in Sect. 3, the *DT runtime analysis models* layer includes the definition of models and related quality-based if-what and what-if analysis techniques, which will empower this level with the ability to carry experiments that would be costly on a real system. Here we focus on if-what analysis type and provide some examples on how conventional formal analysis techniques can be used for the analysis of a safe interaction between humans and the system. If-what analysis is executed on the DT and allows for detecting violations of the quality and security requirements that may compromise the quality of the patient's interaction with the system. Hence, changes to the digital models are evaluated and possibly reflected into the MPT.

From a *reliability perspective*, for example, we take into account the DT models we have described so far: (i) lung, (ii) doctor and (iii) MVM. From a reliability point of view, the DT can be computationally represented as a set of components, each representing, from an high-level point of view, one of the three models (i)-(iii), connected as in Fig. 8, using a reliability block diagram (RBD) notation [31]. The rationale behind

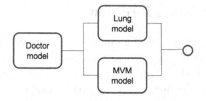

Fig. 8. Reliability block diagram for the MVM DT

this RBD is that the overall system works when the doctor is working and when at least one between the lung and the MVM components is working. Adopting standard analysis techniques [31], the overall reliability can be computed as:

$$R_{DT} = R_D \cdot (1 - (1 - R_L) \cdot (1 - R_{MVM}))$$

where R_{DT} denotes the overall reliability, R_D is the reliability of the doctor that is computed solving the model in Fig. 4 with the UPPAAL tool [14] to obtain its failure probability through stochastic model checking. Specifically, this amounts to determine the probability of the automaton reaching the error state. R_L represents the reliability of the lung, that it can be evaluated by the estimated values of C and R (see Fig. 3c) using a table that helps classifing the condition of the patient as obstructive disease, restrictive conditions, acute situation, or healthy. To each condition, it can be assigned a number in the interval [0,1], where 0 denotes a non functioning lung and 1 a perfect functioning one. Finally, R_{MVM} is the reliability of the ASM modeling the MVM controller. This is computed by exploiting the approach proposed in [28] that considers the internal structure of an ASM and computes its reliability inductively along the call tree of the ASM rules and the structure of the rule bodies.

From a *security perspective*, the analysis on the DT must guarantee that all interactions with the MVM are correct and satisfy the security requirements, even under a cybersecurity attack. In this case, two different analysis scenarios should be considered: (i) a wrong (either intended or unintended) behavior by an authorized user of the system; (ii) an attack by an external actor. The first scenario can be modeled by extending the model of the doctor with new locations and new actions, such as the doctor saving a patient's medical profile on a USB pen drive or selecting the wrong button in the MVM GUI. The second scenario exploits the ASM model of the MVM and the possibility to express distributed *multiple* agents with Abstract State Machines, who can interact synchronously or asynchronously with the other agents. The idea is to model both the doctor and the malicious user as an agent, and to verify by means of model checking if the security requirements expressed in temporal logic are satisfied. The approach is similar to the one taken for security protocol verification [27], with the attacker trying to exploit the system vulnerabilities to perform an attack, such as using the USB port to upload unauthorized firmware, connecting via wireless communication capabilities and trying to impersonate the doctor, or changing MVM settings using the touchscreen.

6   Conclusion and Future Directions

We presented the first results in investigating the extent to which it is possible to engineer a DT for a medical device endowed with trust analysis. We envisioned a framework that makes use of a twin model graph for trust analysis that exploits well-known formal analysis techniques. We, in particular, focused on if-what trust analysis and illustrated with the help of the MVM case study a couple of composition analysis examples.

As future work, we plan to explore different research lines. We intend to investigate the DT engineering technology level by experimenting with different existing platforms. Concerning the DT runtime models, we plan to include different model notations and to devise ad-hoc compositional analysis techniques. For trust analysis, we plan to investigate on what-if analysis techniques, and on how to concretely integrate such analysis models and techniques in a systematic way within a DT engineering framework.

Acknowledgment. This work was partially supported by project SERICS (PE00000014) under the NRRP MUR program funded by the EU - NextGenerationEU.

References

1. ASMETA (ASM mETAmodeling) toolset, https://asmeta.github.io/
2. Functional Mock-up Interface, https://fmi-standard.org/
3. Abba, A., et al.: The novel Mechanical Ventilator Milano for the COVID-19 pandemic. Physics of Fluids 33(3), 037122 (mar 2021). https://doi.org/10.1063/5.0044445
4. Ahmed, H., Devoto, L.: The potential of a digital twin in surgery. Surgical Innovation 28, 509-/510 (12 2020). https://doi.org/10.1177/1553350620975896
5. Bencomo, N., Götz, S., Song, H.: Models@run.time: a guided tour of the state of the art and research challenges. Software & Systems Modeling **18**(5), 3049–3082 (2019). https://doi.org/10.1007/s10270-018-00712-x
6. Bersani, M.M., et al.: Towards trust-preserving continuous co-evolution of digital twins. In: 2022 IEEE 19th International Conference on Software Architecture Companion (ICSA-C). pp. 96–99 (2022). https://doi.org/10.1109/ICSA-C54293.2022.00024
7. Bombarda, A., Bonfanti, S., Gargantini, A., Riccobene, E.: Developing a prototype of a mechanical ventilator controller from requirements to code with ASMETA. In: Proceedings First Workshop on Applicable Formal Methods, AppFM@FM 2021, virtual, 23rd November 2021. EPTCS, vol. 349, pp. 13–29 (2021). https://doi.org/10.4204/EPTCS.349.2
8. Bonfanti, S., Riccobene, E., Scandurra, P.: A component framework for the runtime enforcement of safety properties. Journal of Systems and Software **198**, 111605 (2023). https://doi.org/10.1016/j.jss.2022.111605
9. Bonivento, W., Gargantini, A., Krücken, R., Razeto, A.: The Mechanical Ventilator Milano. Nuclear Physics News **31**(3), 30–33 (2021). https://doi.org/10.1080/10619127.2021.1915047
10. Börger, E., Raschke, A.: Modeling Companion for Software Practitioners. Springer, Berlin, Heidelberg (2018). https://doi.org/10.1007/978-3-662-56641-1
11. Börger, E., Stärk, R.: Abstract State Machines: A Method for High-Level System Design and Analysis. Springer Verlag (2003)
12. Camilli, M., Mirandola, R., Scandurra, P.: Runtime equilibrium verification for resilient cyber-physical systems. In: IEEE International Conference on Autonomic Computing and Self-Organizing Systems, ACSOS 2021, Washington, DC, USA, September 27 - Oct. 1, 2021. pp. 71–80. IEEE (2021). https://doi.org/10.1109/ACSOS52086.2021.00025

13. Campbell, D., Brown, J.: The Electrical Analogue of Lung. British Journal of Anaesthesia 35(11), 684–692 (nov 1963). https://doi.org/10.1093/bja/35.11.684

14. David, A., Larsen, K.G., Legay, A., Mikučionis, M., Poulsen, D.B.: UPPAAL SMC tutorial. International Journal on Software Tools for Technology Transfer 17(4), 397–415 (2015). https://doi.org/10.1007/s10009-014-0361-y

15. van Diepen, A., et al.: A Model-Based Approach to Synthetic Data Set Generation for Patient-Ventilator Waveforms for Machine Learning and Educational Use. Journal of Clinical Monitoring and Computing (2022). https://doi.org/10.1007/s10877-022-00822-4

16. Falcone, Y., Mariani, L., Rollet, A., Saha, S.: Runtime failure prevention and reaction. In: Bartocci, E., Falcone, Y. (eds.) Lectures on Runtime Verification - Introductory and Advanced Topics, LNCS, vol. 10457, pp. 103–134. Springer (2018). https://doi.org/10.1007/978-3-319-75632-5_4

17. Fitzgerald, J., Larsen, P.G., Margaria, T., Woodcock, J.: Engineering of digital twins for cyber-physical systems. In: ISoLA 2020. p. 49–53. Springer-Verlag, Berlin, Heidelberg (2020). https://doi.org/10.1007/978-3-030-83723-5_4

18. Fuller, A., Fan, Z., Day, C., Barlow, C.: Digital twin: Enabling technologies, challenges and open research. IEEE Access **8**, 108952–108971 (2020). https://doi.org/10.1109/ACCESS.2020.2998358

19. Gargantini, A., Riccobene, E., Scandurra, P.: A Metamodel-based Language and a Simulation Engine for Abstract State Machines. J. UCS 14(12) (2008). https://doi.org/10.3217/jucs-014-12-1949

20. Heinrich, R., Durán, F., Talcott, C.L., Zschaler, S. (eds.): Composing Model-Based Analysis Tools. Springer (2021). https://doi.org/10.4230/DagRep.9.11.97

21. Huiskamp, W., van den Berg, T.: Federated Simulations, pp. 109–137. Springer International Publishing, Cham (2016). https://doi.org/10.1007/978-3-319-51043-9_6

22. Jimenez, J.I., Jahankhani, H., Kendzierskyj, S.: Health Care in the Cyberspace: Medical Cyber-Physical System and Digital Twin Challenges, pp. 79–92. Springer International Publishing, Cham (2020). DOI: https://doi.org/10.1007/978-3-030-18732-3_6

23. Kirchhof, J.C., Michael, J., Rumpe, B., Varga, S., Wortmann, A.: Model-Driven Digital Twin Construction: Synthesizing the Integration of Cyber-Physical Systems with Their Information Systems. In: Proceedings of the 23rd ACM/IEEE International Conference on Model Driven Engineering Languages and Systems. p. 90–101. MODELS '20, Association for Computing Machinery, New York, NY, USA (2020). https://doi.org/10.1145/3365438.3410941

24. Kritzinger, W., Karner, M., Traar, G., Henjes, J., Sihn, W.: Digital twin in manufacturing: A categorical literature review and classification. IFAC-PapersOnLine **51**(11), 1016–1022 (2018). https://doi.org/10.1016/j.ifacol.2018.08.474, 16th IFAC Symposium on Information Control Problems in Manufacturing INCOM 2018

25. Lestingi, L., Askarpour, M., Bersani, M.M., Rossi, M.: Formal Verification of Human-Robot Interaction in Healthcare Scenarios. In: de Boer, F., Cerone, A. (eds.) Software Engineering and Formal Methods. pp. 303–324. Springer International Publishing, Cham (2020). https://doi.org/10.1007/978-3-030-58768-0_17

26. Lestingi, L., Sbrolli, C., Scarmozzino, P., Romeo, G., Bersani, M.M., Rossi, M.: Formal modeling and verification of multi-robot interactive scenarios in service settings. In: 2022 IEEE/ACM 10th International Conference on Formal Methods in Software Engineering (FormaliSE). pp. 80–90 (2022). https://doi.org/10.1145/3524482.3527653

27. Lilli, M., Braghin, C., Riccobene, E.: Formal Proof of a Vulnerability in Z-Wave IoT Protocol. In: Proc. of Int. Conf. on Security and Cryptography - SECRYPT, pp. 198–209 (2021). https://doi.org/10.5220/0010553301980209

28. Mirandola, R., Potena, P., Riccobene, E., Scandurra, P.: A reliability model for service component architectures. J. Syst. Softw. **89**, 109–127 (2014). https://doi.org/10.1016/j.jss.2013.11.002

29. Redelinghuys, A.J.H., Basson, A.H., Kruger, K.: A six-layer architecture for the digital twin: a manufacturing case study implementation. Journal of Intelligent Manufacturing **31**(6), 1383–1402 (2019). https://doi.org/10.1007/s10845-019-01516-6

30. Riccobene, E., Scandurra, P.: Model-based simulation at runtime with abstract state machines. In: Communications in Computer and Information Science, pp. 395–410. Springer International Publishing (2020). https://doi.org/10.1007/978-3-030-59155-7_29

31. Signoret, J.P., Leroy, A.: Reliability Block Diagrams (RBDs), pp. 195–208. Springer International Publishing, Cham (2021). https://doi.org/10.1007/978-3-030-64708-7_15

32. Talcott, C., et al.: Composition of Languages, Models, and Analyses, pp. 45–70. Springer International Publishing, Cham (2021). https://doi.org/10.1007/978-3-030-81915-6<_4

33. Tao, F., Zhang, H., Liu, A., Nee, A.Y.C.: Digital twin in industry: State-of-the-art. IEEE Transactions on Industrial Informatics **15**(4), 2405–2415 (2019). https://doi.org/10.1109/TII.2018.2873186

34. Van Tendeloo, Y., Van Mierlo, S., Vangheluwe, H.: A Multi-Paradigm Modelling approach to live modelling. Software & Systems Modeling **18**(5), 2821–2842 (2018). https://doi.org/10.1007/s10270-018-0700-7

35. Weyns, D.: Software engineering of self-adaptive systems. In: Cha, S., Taylor, R.N., Kang, K.C. (eds.) Handbook of Software Engineering, pp. 399–443. Springer (2019). https://doi.org/10.1007/978-3-642-02161-9_1

36. Yue, T., Arcaini, P., Ali, S.: Understanding digital twins for cyber-physical systems: A conceptual model. In: Margaria, T., Steffen, B. (eds.) ISoLA 2020. Lecture Notes in Computer Science, vol. 12479, pp. 54–71. Springer (2020). https://doi.org/10.1007/978-3-030-83723-5_5

Using I4.0 Digital Twins in Agriculture

Rodrigo Falcão(✉)(iD), Raghad Matar(iD), and Bernd Rauch(iD)

Fraunhofer IESE, Kaiserslautern, Germany
{rodrigo.falcao,raghad.matar,bernd.rauch}@iese.fraunhofer.de

Abstract. Agriculture is a huge domain where an enormous landscape of systems interact to support agricultural processes, which are becoming increasingly digital. From the perspective of agricultural service providers, a prominent challenge is interoperability. In the Fraunhofer lighthouse project Cognitive Agriculture (COGNAC), we investigated how the usage of Industry 4.0 digital twins (I4.0 DTs) can help overcome this challenge. This paper contributes architecture drivers and a solution concept using I4.0 DTs in the agricultural domain. Furthermore, we discuss the opportunities and limitations offered by I4.0 DTs for the agricultural domain.

Keywords: Interoperability · Digital field twin · Digital transformation

1 Introduction

Digital transformation, i.e., the conception of innovative and digital business models, is taking place and disrupting many major sectors of the economy. We have observed several traditional industries such as transportation, banking, hotel business, and entertainment, that have been impacted by the rise of software companies that approach not simply their products or their processes, but their fundamental businesses digitally [25]. Agriculture, as a major sector of the economy, is already a software-intensive industry where several players cooperate in huge and complex value chains. At the technical level, the digital transformation in agriculture requires digitally available data from the environment, farms, machines, and processes to enable software-supported products and services to work smoothly [31].

However, regarding digital systems, the agricultural domain is rather fragmented [22]: There are various systems, with various data formats, complying with various different standards within its multiple subdomains. Therefore, enabling interoperability in agriculture is challenging [31]. Data is typically distributed in exclusive data storage of suppliers' digital ecosystems. On top of that, there is no or only little semantic interoperability – meaning the ability of applications to exchange data with a shared meaning –, which leads to huge efforts in communication and orchestration for delivering complex end-to-end solutions for farmers [6].

Nowadays, farmers are dealing with several systems to accomplish their goals in all production steps across seasons. Mostly, such systems belong to their own digital

---

This work has been developed in the context of the Fraunhofer lighthouse project "Cognitive Agriculture (COGNAC)".

ecosystems: Machine manufacturers, for example, usually offer cloud-based solutions to channel data collected from the machinery of their respective fleet, which results in distributed data storages if farmers own machines from different manufacturers. In other cases, systems only cover data from their respective business processes and offer no data exchange across farm systems. As a consequence, farmers often face a situation where they have to use different systems with exclusive data vaults and no or only limited connectivity between those systems (see Fig. 1).

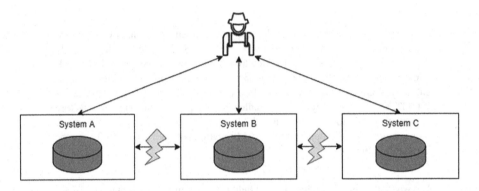

Fig. 1. Different IT-systems with exclusive data storage and no or limited connectivity.

The situation becomes even more challenging for farmers as well as service providers when various digital ecosystems emerge but lack proper ways to exchange data among them. As a consequence, farmers struggle with having their agronomic data distributed among different systems and ecosystems. On the other side, service providers of digital services need to integrate different data sources into their respective service environments in order to offer innovative services for farmers. Therefore, not only farmers but all stakeholders still yearn for a frictionless, yet secure, experience.

In recent years, the idea of digital twins (DTs) in agriculture has been explored (e.g., [28,31]). The concept of DTs was coined by Michael Grieves in 2003, referring to virtual representations of physical products with two-way communication between them [11]. Initially introduced in the context of product lifecycle management, the concept has evolved, and nowadays DTs refer to the digital representation of any real entity, be it physical (e.g., machines) or not (e.g., services or processes) [20,21]. However, there is still ambiguity about when a system can be identified as a DT due to the many definitions of DTs in different domains [28].

When it comes to their usage in the agricultural domain, existing research on DTs has not put emphasis on how or whether they could be used to address the interoperability challenge. DTs have been used to tackle interoperability challenges in another domain, though: In Industry 4.0 (I4.0), the notion of DTs has been realized through one of its core components: the *asset administration shell* (AAS) [2,13,17]. The term was coined in 2015 [27] in the context of the German research project Platform Industry 4.0[1]. Although the term "digital twin" was not used in the project, over time the conver-

---
[1]   https://www.plattform-i40.de.

gence of the terms "asset administration shell" and "digital twin" has become evident [32]. In fact, AASs have materialized DTs in the context of I4.0, as declared in [24]: "The Asset Administration Shell helps implementing digital twins for I4.0 and creating interoperability across the solutions of different suppliers.".

Since AASs have been used to enable interoperability in I4.0, in this paper we investigate to which extent the same concept could be applied to the agricultural domain, focusing on interoperability. We first present two architecture drivers for interoperability from the agricultural service providers' point of view. Then we describe three architectural decisions, which in combination form our solution concept based on I4.0 DTs. Finally, we discuss the opportunities and limitations we encountered during our investigation.

The remainder of this paper is structured as follows: Sect. 2 introduces general concepts of the COGNAC project and I4.0 DTs; Sect. 3 presents related work; Sect. 4 presents the architecture drivers and a solution concept for I4.0 DTs in the agricultural domain; in Sect. 5 we discuss our solution; and Sect. 6 concludes the paper.

2   Background

In the Fraunhofer lighthouse project "Cognitive Agriculture" (COGNAC)[2], eight Fraunhofer Institutes have conducted joint research in the area of Smart Farming since 2018. Exploring applied solutions in field automation, novel sensing, smart services, and digital data spaces, the project's core focus has been on the digital transformation of farming processes in the context of evolving digital ecosystems. In this context, different systems, services, and actors interact and collaborate in agricultural processes, building a common *agricultural data space (ADS)* [18]. By analyzing the requirements, we identified interoperability as one of the major challenges in the domain. In our research of suitable solution concepts, we found DTs as a potential approach for coping with interoperability in a digitalized farming setting. In recent years, much research has been conducted on the utilization of DTs for agricultural assets (see Sect. 3); however, the challenges emerging from interoperability in smart farming have not been covered explicitly. In COGNAC, we drew inspiration from I4.0 and are exploring the use of DTs to realize interoperability between digital services and systems.

The usage of DTs in industry automation has been observed prominently in the context of I4.0 [4]. One example is RAMI 4.0 – the Reference Architectural Model Industry 4.0 [12], which focuses on digitalization and interoperability in manufacturing [13]. RAMI 4.0 prescribes a layered architecture framework that simultaneously organizes the vocabulary of I4.0 and breaks down the domain complexity into smaller pieces. At the lowest level of the reference architecture, the layer "asset" corresponds to the physical entities (such as machines); right above it, the layer "integration" implements the glue to support the next layer, "communication", which provides access to information. Further layers are "information', "functional", and "business".

---

[2] https://cognitive-agriculture.de.

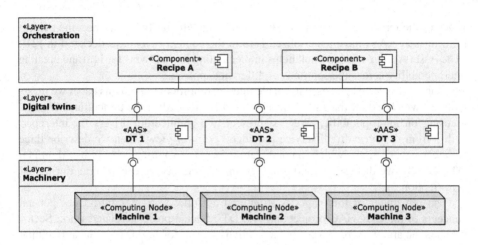

Fig. 2. Functional view of an illustrative implementation of DTs in a factory.

DTs are a perfect fit for the realization of the integration layer, and reference implementations are already available. One example is the research project BaSys 4.0[3], which defines a middleware for production systems in the context of I4.0 and puts a strong focus on the implementation of DTs for the production pipeline, where interoperability is an essential quality attribute for high automation levels in processes that take place in a heterogeneous environment. For example, consider a certain production process where different devices cooperate to manufacture lots of a certain item. These devices may come from different producers, use different data formats, and understand different communication protocols. BaSys 4.0 prescribes the implementation of standardized DTs for these devices – the *asset administration shells* –, allowing them to be orchestrated on a higher level of abstraction to enable flexible production lines. This could lead to "lot size one" production being virtually as cost-effective as massive production.

Figure 2 provides a high-level functional view on the usage of I4.0 DTs in a fictional factory, from the factory's perspective. At the bottom layer (Machinery), the physical machines that belong to the factory and are located on the shop floor are represented as computing nodes – in this case, the factory has three machines. In the middle layer (Digital Twins), asset administration shell components implemented in the factory realize digital representations of the machines. Their properties and functions are expressed in terms of *submodels*, as I4.0 calls them. These submodels may or may not be provided by the machine manufacturer – in the former case, it would be good to use them to promote standardization and streamline interoperability; in the latter case, the factory models them as desired. Finally, at the top layer (Orchestration), the DTs are orchestrated into *recipes*, which describe how the different machines should cooperate to implement certain industrial processes.

This model supports interoperability in different ways. First, asset administration shells have a standardized data structure, so at the technical level, all DTs implemented through asset administration shells are interoperable. Moreover, they work as

[3] http://basys40.de.

adapters to convert vendor-specific APIs into a standardized representation of information, which enables syntactic interoperability. Finally, semantic interoperability is supported through references to external type definitions, which should be accessible in order to become part of the domain's shared vocabulary. Such an architecture makes it easy to modify industrial processes by creating new recipes or adjusting existing ones at the orchestration level, despite the potential technical diversity in the factory's machine park, because orchestration happens through the asset administration shells. Furthermore, machines can be replaced at the machinery layer with no impact on the orchestration layer, whereas only minor impact is expected in the digital twin layer if the new machines provide submodels that comply with an established standard for the functionality they offer. In this example, DTs are created to represent devices (i.e., machines in a factory). From a conceptual perspective, however, there could also be DTs of products (e.g., items being produced in the factory), processes (i.e., the processes can be designed, changed, combined, executed, and monitored digitally), or services (systems that support the processes).

3 Related Work

To analyze the degree of DT adoption in agriculture, Pylianidis et al. [28] conducted a literature review investigating scientific and gray literature studies published between 2017 and 2020. The authors identified 28 use cases from different agriculture subdomains, which illustrated multiple benefits of using DTs. The results show that the majority of the identified DTs represent agricultural fields, farms, landscapes, and buildings, and are mostly concerned with monitoring and optimization operations. As for the maturity level, most of the identified DTs are only concepts or prototypes. Moreover, the authors conducted a survey of case studies on the usage of DTs in other disciplines and identified 68 use cases as a result. The results show a delay in the exploration of DTs in agriculture compared to other domains and suggest that the exploration of DTs in agriculture is relatively limited compared with other disciplines. Furthermore, the results reveal that DTs in other disciples provide a wider range of benefits and services. The authors argue that the superficial description of DT applications in the literature has hindered the realization of their benefits and thus slowed their adoption in agriculture. Additionally, inspired by DTs' characteristics and use cases from other domains, the authors suggest a roadmap for the possible future adoption of DTs in agriculture.

Nasirahmadi et al. [23] conducted another literature review investigating the state-of-the-art of DTs concepts and technologies in various agricultural fields and discussed the challenges and future needs regarding their implementation in agriculture. According to the authors, digital twins in agriculture have been exploited very little in research so far.

In another study, Verdouw et al. [31] analyzed how leveraging DTs for farm management can improve productivity and increase sustainability in smart farming. Combining the highlighted aspects of DTs in both Internet of Things (IoT) and ProductLife

Cycle (PLC) literature, the authors propose a definition of DTs, summarize their main characteristics, and suggest a typology for DTs based on their role in the asset life cycle. Furthermore, the authors propose a conceptual framework for designing and implementing DTs in smart farming for farm management activities, including planning, monitoring, controlling, and optimizing farm operations. The introduced framework supports the whole lifecycle of physical farm objects and the implementation of the main characteristics of the six DT types in the proposed typology. The authors validated the proposed framework using five smart farming use cases.

Chaux et al. [7] suggest a DT architecture for optimizing the productivity of Controlled Environment Agriculture (CEA) systems by achieving better yield and higher quality of crops with fewer resources. The proposed framework utilizes two simulation softwares as DTs and uses them as test beds for assessing crop treatment and climate control strategies. Furthermore, it has an intelligence layer that generates multiple alternative strategies and selects the optimal one. The authors validated the suggested architecture by building a prototype of an automated greenhouse and performing latency tests to certify the success of the bidirectional communication of the DT architecture. According to the authors, more effort should be invested before the proposed architecture can be used in production.

Moshrefzadeh et al. [22] introduced the notion of Distributed DTs of agricultural landscapes to optimize data integration and thus support diverse stakeholders in establishing a common understanding of the landscape and its objects, and to achieve coordinated decision-making. The concept is part of the Smart Rural Area Data Infrastructure – SRADI, a multidisciplinary information infrastructure developed to handle multiple stakeholders, applications, and distributed information resources [9]. Its core component is the *Catalog*, a metadata registry for distributed landscape resources, such as projects, software, and raw data from landscape objects. The metadata model covers the varied types of information resources related to agricultural landscapes and supports different data formats and privacy levels. Furthermore, the catalog establishes semantic relations between the distributed pieces of information. To achieve interoperability, communication and data modeling are based on open standards. To demonstrate the concept, the authors developed a data infrastructure for the Agricultural Research Center of the Technical University of Munich to support its 30 chair members and organize their cooperation when conducting research on the same land parcels. However, in their proposed solution, the authors achieve interoperability on the level of the metadata and not the data itself.

The usage of DTs for inter-organizational data exchange is rarely discussed in the literature. In their work [13], Haße et al. developed a Shared DT (SDT) architecture to facilitate sovereign and multilateral data sharing across different organizations. The authors leveraged the AAS of the Plattform Industrie 4.0 to achieve multilateral interoperability, and the International Data Space (IDS) concepts [15] to ensure data sovereignty. The authors validated the concept using one use case in logistics networks.

To the best of our knowledge, no study in the literature investigates the usage of I4.0 DTs for achieving interoperability on the data exchange level among the different actors in the agricultural domain.

4   Using I4.0 DTs in the Agricultural Domain

We used the GQM template [5] to frame the goal of our research as follows: "Analyze Industry 4.0 Digital Twins for the purpose of evaluation with respect to interoperability from the point of the view of agricultural service providers in the context of the project COGNAC". To achieve the goal, we had to know the architecture drivers – i.e., the architecture-relevant requirements – related to interoperability in the agricultural domain. Then we explored the solution space, but constrained ourselves to the use of I4.0 DTs, as our goal is to check their adequacy for addressing the interoperability challenge in the agriculture domain.

For eliciting the architecture drivers and designing solutions, we used the software architecture evaluation approach of Knodel and Naab [19]. Each architecture driver was defined in terms of quantified environments, stimuli, and responses, whereas for each design solution, the decisions were characterized with opportunities, assumptions, cons/risks, and trade-offs. We assessed drivers and solutions through reviews.

4.1   Architecture Drivers

Architecture drivers are a particular type of requirements that focus on what matters most for architecture purposes: business goals, constraints, key functional requirements, and quality requirements [19]. Regarding quality requirements, architecture drivers can be expressed as *architecture scenarios*. As defined by Rozanski and Woods, an architecture scenario is "a crisp, concise description of a situation that the system is likely to face, along with a definition of the response required of the system" [29]. Architecture scenarios, also referred to as "quality attribute scenarios" [3], ensure that the quality requirement is expressed in a concrete and measurable way.

From our experience with COGNAC and a feasibility study about data management and Farm Management Information Systems (FMISs) [14], we derived two typical interoperability scenarios in agriculture. In this domain, interoperability relates to software-based systems exchanging data to perform certain agricultural processes (e.g., fertilization, weed control, etc.), which are usually implemented by service providers.

The first scenario (AD.IOP.1) Takes Place within the Boundaries of Service Providers. From the point of view of the farmer, who is the end user, they use only one service, provided by one service provider, to perform a certain agricultural process of interest. On their part, service providers often use several systems to implement such agricultural processes, but these systems are not necessarily developed or operated by the service providers, but also by other companies. For example, a service provider who harvests fields may own and use machinery (and corresponding services) built by different manufacturers. Table 1 summarizes AD.IOP.1. Consider, for example, a service provider that offers a weed control service. For the sake of simplification, let's assume that internally, the service provider uses only two systems to implement the weed control process: the "main" service (Sys_1), which plans the work and sends instructions to the second system, and a field robot (Sys_2), which performs the actual field work and sends the data back to the main service, which in turn generates the work record for the farmer. Consider now that the service provider wants to expand their machine park by acquiring more field robots, but this time from another manufacturer (Sys_3). They

Table 1. AD.IOP.1: Intra-company data exchange.

	Description	Quantification
Environment	· Service provider SP_1 uses two systems, Sys_1 and Sys_2, to perform a certain agricultural process P, which is controlled via software. · Sys_1 and Sys_2 are able to exchange data	n/a
Stimulus	· The service provider replaces Sys_2 with Sys_3, which is maintained by a third-party company	n/a
Response	· Sys_1 and Sys_3 are able to exchange data	· No modification at design time is required for the implementation of the process P

Table 2. AD.IOP.2: Cross-company data exchange.

	Description	Quantification
Environment	· Service S_1 needs field data to provide its service.	· S_1 needs one-time access to field data
Stimulus	· S_1 requests field data from the new FMIS	n/a
Response	· S_1 receives and can understand the field data from the new FMIS	· No modification at design time is required in S_1 to be able to interoperate with the new FMIS

will therefore have two models of field robots in their machine park, built by different manufacturers, and may use one or another model to execute a farm job, depending on their availability. Sys_1 should be able to exchange data with Sys_3 (the new field robot) without the need of any design-time change in the implementation of the process.

The Second Scenario Refers to Cross-Company Data Exchange. In this scenario, the farmer is aware of the fact that they are using more than one system and explicitly authorizes the data exchange. Examples are FMISs and fertilization recommendation services. A farmer F_1 may use $FMIS_1$, provided by service provider SP_1, and the fertilization recommendation service FRS_1 to get recommendations. FRS_1 requires field data to provide the recommendation, so it should somehow get the data from $FMIS_1$. Next year, the farmer may decide to change either their FMIS or their fertilization recommendation service (or both). In such a situation, they still want their service providers to be able to exchange data as before. Table 2 summarizes AD.IOP.2. In this scenario, a service provider operates the service S_1, which is already established in the market. In order to provide its service, S_1 needs one-time access to read certain field data, which in turn is managed by the farmer through their FMIS. S_1 is already capable of getting field data from the lead FMISs on the market; however, a new FMIS now enters the market and starts to gain popularity among farmers. One of these early adopters of the new FMIS wants to use S_1. Assuming that all accesses have already been granted, S_1 should be able to retrieve the required field data from the new FMIS without the need for any design-time modification.

4.2   Solution Concept

Concerning the intra-company interoperability issue, we envision the *service provider* in agriculture as analog to the *factory* in I4.0. In a factory (company), several machines (production means) are orchestrated to perform industrial activities (process), which results in the manufacturing of industrial goods (product). Conversely, in the agricultural domain, service providers (company) use several systems (production means) to perform agriculture-related activities (processes). However, the results are not necessarily tangible: The process may act directly on the field and have an impact on its status – for example, after a certain agriculture process, a field may be fertilized, protected, or harvested, among other possibilities. It would also be possible to think of the crop or the yield as the product that is impacted by the agricultural process, even though such impact is not necessarily perceived immediately (e.g., a fertilized field will influence the growth of the plants, but this can only be observed afterwards). On the other hand, there are agricultural process that do not produce tangible (i.e., physical) results at all, for example recommendation processes, which are quite common in the agricultural domain.

The first design decision (DD.1) is *the Usage of AASs as Representatives of All Software Systems that are to Interoperate in the ADS*. This decision can be traced directly to the architecture solution blueprint for I4.0 applications introduced by Antonino et al. [1], who make a case for the "use of Digital Twins as digital representatives of the different physical and logical entities involved in the production process". In our case, we are talking about *logical entities*: the systems. Each AAS will therefore work as an Adapter (structural architectural pattern described by Gamma et al. [10]) between the software system and those who want to interoperate with it. Opportunities, assumptions, risks, and trade-offs are presented in Table 3.

Table 3. DD1: Implementation of AASs as representatives of all systems in the ADS.

Opportunities/pros	AASs provide standardized interfaces and data structure constructs, so from a technical point of view, all systems will expose their properties and functionalities in the same way, making it easier for clients to communicate with them
Assumptions	The constructs available to create the submodels (and therefore to design the AASs) are generic enough to express the variety of properties and functions in the agricultural domain
Cons/Risks	The usage of generic constructs to describe the submodels might result in sub-optimal data structures
Trade-offs	The overhead required at design time to implement the *digital twin layer* (see Fig. 3). Furthermore, some impact may be noted at runtime from the required data transformations

Table 4. DD2: Implementation of AASs as representatives of fields.

Opportunities/pros	Digital field twins represent a single source of truth for field-related data, making data available in a standardized, up-to-date, and non-redundant way. All services can get field data from one place
Assumptions	The digital fields twins are hosted in a infrastructure that is reachable through the Internet, and both hosts and digital field twins are uniquely identified
Cons/Risks	In case a digital field twin is unavailable, all inter-company interoperability that depends on the corresponding field data is affected
Trade-offs	Additional (dedicated) infrastructure, along with the associated costs for implementation, operation, and maintenance, is required to deploy digital field twins

Table 5. DD3: Use of a mediator to process field-related data exchange requests.

Opportunities/pros	Systems that are interested in field data do not have to comply with a given specific interface provided by the digital field twin. New field data can be incorporated into the twin through generic commands
Assumptions	All participants agree on the usage of an open shared vocabulary, providing the data with semantics
Cons/Risks	There is a risk that the usage of generic constructs will make the usage of the mediator complex, depending on the data involved
Trade-offs	The complexity of the interaction between systems is replaced by the complexity of the mediator itself (as foreseen in [10]). Furthermore, the overhead caused by data transformations and the need for multiple calls to transfer complex data can impact performance

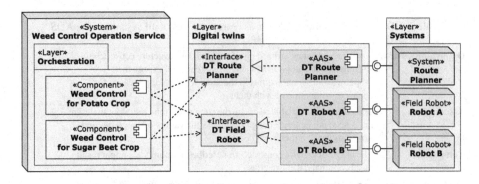

Fig. 3. Functional view of the usage of DT by a weed control company.

Figure 3 illustrates a functional view of the implementation of DTs in an automated weed control company for both potato and sugar beet crops. Consider that the service provider has a main Weed Control Operation System, which is used by their employees to plan and carry out the jobs. Let's assume that internally, the company uses two additional systems (production means) to support their work: field robots, which are programmed to do the actual job on the field and collect data about it, and a route planner, which calculates the optimal route for the field robots. In the orchestration layer, the service provider can program two *recipes* that implement the weed control processes; i.e., they describe how to perform weed control on a potato crop and on a sugar beet crop. These recipes would rely on DTs of the *production means*: the route planner system and the field robot. In the example, two field robots are available. Their respective DTs should implement the same interface (see DTs layer) that is used in the orchestration layer. Finally, in the systems layer, each individual system exposes its specific interfaces, which are used directly in the implementation details of their respective DTs.

The service provider is in the best position to define how the data must flow among participants in the ecosystem, so they should implement the recipes for performing different types of jobs (one recipe for each crop type). If there is then a business need to change the process (maybe to allow working on a third crop type), a new recipe is created at the orchestration level. Conversely, if there is a need to replace Robot A with Robot B, the recipe remains untouched, since both robots, potentially from different manufacturers, are accessed through the standardized DT layer.

When it comes to inter-company interoperability, our experience not only in the project COGNAC but also in multiple industry projects has revealed the prominent role of field-related data in the agricultural domain. Service providers need field data, which is typically stored in more than one FMIS used by farmers, in order to provide their services. Field data has different dimensions, including geographic (e.g., field boundaries and terrain slope), environmental (e.g. weather – past, current, and forecast), agronomic (e.g., soil nutrient levels and plant health status). Having digital representations of the systems involved would not suffice to enable adequate interoperability regarding field-related data because the data is scattered across several FMISs, which jeopardizes data qualities such as completeness, currentness, consistency, and availability [16]. This led us to **the second design decision (DD.2): *the use of AASs to implement digital representatives of fields*** – referred to as *digital field twins*. When providing a service, the service provider should acquire the needed field data from the digital field twin; if the corresponding services generate field-related data, the data should also be sent to and stored in the digital field twin. To realize this, we introduce the concept of TwinHub, a vendor-neutral digital platform that hosts a farmer's digital field twins. Table 4 characterizes this design decision.

The implementation of digital field twins, as described to this point, has an additional assumption that has not been made explicit in Table 4. Systems that need field data can benefit from the digital field twin only if they know its interface in advance, whereas such an interface should statically reflect how the digital field twin exposes a representation of its data model. However, this may or may not be a valid assumption. If the client knows the interface provided by the digital field twin and complies with it, syntactic interoperability – where two systems can exchange data because there is a known data structure [30] – can be achieved. The digital field twin could be accessed from a recipe in the orchestration layer of a certain system and the field data would be available to support the process described in the corresponding recipe.

Conversely, if the data structure of the digital field twin cannot be known (or even defined) at design time, we need something else to enable interoperability, which takes us to **our third design decision (DD.3):** *the use of a mediator to process data exchange requests between digital field twins and other digital twins*. The mediator is a self-contained service that must know the reflexive syntax of AASs in order to be able to call any AAS. This solution combines characteristics of the architectural patterns *Mediator* and *Command* [10]: It centralizes the control of communication between several parties and exposes an API to receive data exchange requests (e.g., "get *field boundaries* and *crop type* from *digital field twin A* and send it to *digital twin B*"). Such an interface should be called by the system that wants to exchange data. Table 5 summarizes the characteristics of this decision, and Fig. 4 illustrates both DD.2 and DD.3. All participant systems use a reference vocabulary and request field-related data exchanges through the Mediator, which in turn accesses the digital field twin and the corresponding DTs of each participant system.

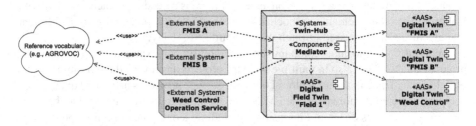

Fig. 4. Functional view of the use of digital field twins (DD.2) and a mediator (DD.3).

5   Discussion

We have investigated the usage of I4.0 DTs in agriculture, which may raise the question of whether DTs are a good idea for this domain in the first place. The increasing interest in the topic that can be observed in recent years has indicated so. DTs have generally been perceived as an enabler for interoperability [26]. In the agricultural domain, their importance has grown as well, although it has not yet reached maturity. Agricultural DTs are directly or indirectly concerned with living systems, which distinguishes them from DTs in other domains [28]. Their physical twins can be as small as a single plant or animal or as large as a whole farm. There is still disagreement on essential aspects, such as to which extent real-time data synchronization between DTs and real entities is needed [31] or not [28]. Moreover, with respect to technical aspects of the realization of DTs in agriculture, the results are usually presented at the conceptual level through illustrative use cases; i.e., they do not explain how interoperability can be achieved technically. In the current state of digital farming, the few implementations of DTs are limited to single-system contexts and there is no overall concept for collaboratively utilizing DTs across system boundaries.

This is where, from our point of view, I4.0 DTs can offer their maturity to support the agricultural domain. In I4.0, stakeholders have agreed upon a reference model and have developed not only reference architectures but also reference implementations for DTs (e.g., [8]). Following the idea of having DTs to represent the production means, we looked at systems that contribute to agricultural processes as production means, which led us to decide to create DTs for these systems. Since DTs are usually thought of as digital representatives of *physical* entities, we considered the creation of *DTs for systems* counter-intuitive at first though. On the other hand, the idea of having *digital field twins* was mostly straightforward. The field is a central entity in the context of a farm and field data plays a central role in all agricultural processes. Furthermore, fields are physical entities. Still, we should remember that the DT definition comprises a closed loop between the real and the digital entity (i.e., changes in the real entity are reflected in the DT, and vice-versa).

It seems to be clear that when the value of a soil nutrient such as nitrogen changes in the real field, this information can be captured by sensors and reflected in the digital field twin. However, how could it be possible to increase, for instance, the nitrogen level in the digital field twin and have it reflected in the real entity? One solution could be to have the digital field twin trigger an agricultural process (e.g., fertilization) that would, in turn, raise the nitrogen level. Note, however, that it would be an update that is far from real time: While the new nitrogen level would be set in the digital twin instantly, several days would be needed to cause the planned impact on the real counterpart. Furthermore, due to the inherent uncertainty of the natural environment and the complexity of such operations, it may happen that the agricultural process will not cause *precisely* the planned impact. Therefore, we consider it essential for digital twins in the agricultural domain to provide technical constructs to explicitly handle status differences between the real and the digital entities. For example, when the nitrogen level of a field is increased in a digital field twin, the new value should be recorded in the digital twin as an *intent*; after the fertilization process is finished, the new values of the nitrogen level should be captured by sensors on the field and sent back to the digital twin.

Apart from technical aspects, one of the main drivers of DT development in I4.0 is the market players' demand for interoperability and standardization. In agriculture, however, the digital ecosystem is still lacking a common interest in comprehensive interoperability as some market players are reluctant to collaborate with others and try to gain market shares within their own digital ecosystems. The implementation of the proposed utilization of I4.0 DTs would require domain-wide agreement on a common technological framework, which poses a major challenge for its success. The technical solution approach could initially be implemented by smaller parts of the domain and be expanded later. There are also open organizational questions, such as who would implement and operate data hubs offering digital field twin interfaces (such as the TwinHub).

Among the limitations we identified during our investigation is the need for better support for cross-twin operations. I4.0 seems to work on the assumption that all DTs that are needed to support a certain process are known and can therefore be discovered directly and integrated into a recipe. However, for digital field twins, it seems to be necessary to first search for and filter sets of twins. As far as we know, such higher-level operations are not supported yet. Another limitation is that it is not possible to access properties via their semantic definitions (even though it is possible to add semantic annotations to the properties).

Threats to Validity. Threats to validity of this work include the usage of reviews, which are limited methods [19], to assess drivers and solutions. It is also worth noting that our analysis may be biased by the characteristics of Eclipse BaSyx 1.0 [8], a specific AAS implementation, which we used in the early development stages of our prototypes.

6   Conclusion

Interoperability is a huge challenge for digital transformation in the agricultural domain. Given the increasing interest in DTs in agriculture and the fact that DTs have been used to address interoperability in I4.0, in the project COGNAC we investigated how they could help to improve the current situation. In this paper, we described two architecture drivers for interoperability in the agricultural domain and presented a solution concept using I4.0 DTs. To the best of our knowledge, no previous study in the literature has examined the usage of I4.0 DTs for achieving interoperability on the data exchange level among the different actors in the agricultural domain. From a technical point of view, we believe that smart farming can move towards concrete solutions by benefiting from the progress already made by I4.0 DTs as it has been tested in a domain that is more mature in the implementation of the concept and therefore can provide off-the-shelf components to realize DTs at code level.

As future work, we will further develop our current prototype to increase the level of confidence in the solution, focusing on digital field twins, which have a more obvious impact on inter-company interoperability.

References

1. Antonino, P.O., Schnicke, F., Zhang, Z., Kuhn, T.: Blueprints for architecture drivers and architecture solutions for industry 4.0 shopfloor applications. In: ECSA 2019 - Volume 2, pp. 261–268 (2019)
2. Bächle, K., Gregorzik, S.: Digital twins in industrial applications-requirements to a comprehensive data model. J. Inno., 1–14 (2019)
3. Bass, L., Clements, P., Kazman, R.: Software Architecture in Practice. Addison-Wesley Professional, Boston (2003)
4. Bauer, T., Antonino, P.O., Kuhn, T.: Towards architecting digital twin-pervaded systems. In: SESoS 2019 and WDES 2019, pp. 66–69. IEEE (2019)
5. Caldiera, V.R.B.G., Rombach, H.D.: The goal question metric approach. Encycl. Softw. Eng., 528–532 (1994)
6. Calvet, E., Falcão, R., Thom, L.H.: Business process model for interoperability improvement in the agricultural domain using digital twins. In: PACIS 2022. AIS (2022)
7. Chaux, J.D., Sanchez-Londono, D., Barbieri, G.: A digital twin architecture to optimize productivity within controlled environment agriculture. Appl. Sci. **11**(19), 8875 (2021)

8. Eclipse: Eclipse BaSyx. bit.ly/3XcoUO8 (2022). Accessed 07 June 2022
9. Gackstetter, D., Moshrefzadeh, M., Machl, T., Kolbe, T.H.: Smart rural areas data infrastructure (sradi)-an information logistics framework for digital agriculture based on open standards. 41. GIL-Jahrestagung, Informations-und Kommunikationstechnologie in kritischen Zeiten (2021)
10. Gamma, E., Helm, R., Johnson, R., Johnson, R.E., Vlissides, J., et al.: Elements of reusable object-oriented software. Des. Patterns. Pearson Deutschland GmbH (1995)
11. Grieves, M.: Digital twin: manufacturing excellence through virtual factory replication. White paper **1**, 1–7 (2014)
12. Hankel, M., Rexroth, B.: The reference architectural model industrie 4.0 (rami 4.0). ZVEI **2**(2), 4–9 (2015)
13. Haße, H., van der Valk, H., Weißenberg, N., Otto, B.: Shared digital twins: data sovereignty in logistics networks. In: Data Science and Innovation in Supply Chain Management: How Data Transforms the Value Chain. HICL, vol. 29, pp. 763–795. epubli GmbH, Berlin (2020)
14. Herlitzius, T., et al.: Betriebliches datenmanagement und fmis (2022)
15. IDS Association: IDS Reference Architecture (2019). https://internationaldataspaces.org/wp-content/uploads/IDS-Reference-Architecture-Model-3.0-2019.pdf. Accessed 27 June 2022
16. ISO/IEC 25024:2015. Systems and software engineering - Systems and software Quality Requirements and Evaluation (SQuaRE) - Measurement of data quality. Standard, ISO (2015)
17. Jacoby, M., Volz, F., Weißenbacher, C., Stojanovic, L., Usländer, T.: An approach for industrie 4.0-compliant and data-sovereign digital twins. at-Automatisierungstechnik **69**(12), 1051–1061 (2021)
18. Kalmar, R., Rauch, B., Dörr, J., Liggesmeyer, P.: Agricultural data space. Des. Data Spaces, 279 (2022)
19. Knodel, J., Naab, M.: Pragmatic Evaluation of Software Architectures, vol. 1. Springer, Cham (2016). https://doi.org/10.1007/978-3-319-34177-4
20. Kuhn, T.: Digitaler Zwilling. Informatik-Spektrum **40**(5), 440–444 (2017)
21. Malakuti, S., et al.: Digital twins for industrial applications: definition. In: An Industrial Internet Consortium Whitepaper, Business Values, Design Aspects, Standards and Use Cases (2020)
22. Moshrefzadeh, M., Machl, T., Gackstetter, D., Donaubauer, A., Kolbe, T.H.: Towards a distributed digital twin of the agricultural landscape. JoDLA **5**, 173–186 (2020)
23. Nasirahmadi, A., Hensel, O.: Toward the next generation of digitalization in agriculture based on digital twin paradigm. Sensors **22**(2), 498 (2022)
24. Neidig, J., Orzelski, A., Pollmeier, S.: Asset Administration Shell – Reading Guide (2022). https://www.plattform-i40.de/IP/Redaktion/DE/Downloads/Publikation/AAS-ReadingGuide_202201.html. Accessed 02 June 2022
25. Parker, G.G., Van Alstyne, M.W., Choudary, S.P.: Platform Revolution: How Networked Markets are Transforming the Economy and How to Make them Work for You. WW Norton & Company, New York (2016)
26. Piroumian, V.: Digital twins: Universal interoperability for the digital age. Computer **54**(1), 61–69 (2021)
27. Platform Industrie 4.0: Umsetzungsstrategie Industrie 4.0: Ergebnisbericht der Plattform Industrie 4.0 (2015). http://bit.ly/3vPHaBd. Accessed 02 June 2022
28. Pylianidis, C., Osinga, S., Athanasiadis, I.N.: Introducing digital twins to agriculture. Comput. Electron. Agric. **184**, 105942 (2021)
29. Rozanski, N., Woods, E.: Software Systems Architecture: Working with Stakeholders Using Viewpoints and Perspectives. Addison-Wesley, Boston (2012)

30. Valle, P.H.D., Garcés, L., Nakagawa, E.Y.: A typology of architectural strategies for interoperability. In: SBCARS 2019, pp. 3–12 (2019)
31. Verdouw, C., Tekinerdogan, B., Beulens, A., Wolfert, S.: Digital twins in smart farming. Agric. Syst. **189**, 103046 (2021)
32. Wagner, C., et al.: The role of the industry 4.0 asset administration shell and the digital twin during the life cycle of a plant. In: ETFA 2017, pp. 1–8. IEEE (2017)

Author Index